THE GOLDEN AGE OF

Chinese Archaeology

CELEBRATED DISCOVERIES
FROM THE
PEOPLE'S REPUBLIC OF CHINA

THE GOLDEN AGE OF

Chinese Archaeology

CELEBRATED DISCOVERIES
FROM THE
PEOPLE'S REPUBLIC OF CHINA

Edited by
Xiaoneng Yang

National Gallery of Art,
Washington

The Nelson-Atkins Museum
of Art, Kansas City

Yale University Press,
New Haven and London

The exhibition is sponsored by Eastman Kodak Company

Additional support for this exhibition is provided by The Henry Luce Foundation.

The catalogue is supported by a grant from the E. Rhodes and Leona B. Carpenter Foundation.

The exhibition is supported by an indemnity from the Federal Council on the Arts and the Humanities.

EXHIBITION DATES:

National Gallery of Art, Washington
19 September 1999 – 2 January 2000

The Museum of Fine Arts, Houston
13 February – 7 May 2000

Asian Art Museum of San Francisco
17 June – 11 September 2000

The exhibition is organized by the National Gallery of Art, Washington, and The Nelson-Atkins Museum of Art, Kansas City, in cooperation with the State Administration of Cultural Heritage and Art Exhibitions China, The People's Republic of China.

Front cover: cat. 152, detail
Back cover: cat. 175, detail
Title page: cat. 151, detail
Opposite: cat. 132, detail
Page 14: cat. 117, detail
Page 47: cat. 151, detail
Pages 48 – 49: cat. 24, detail
Pages 136 – 137: cat. 69, detail
Pages 264 – 265: cat. 110, detail
Pages 360 – 361: cat. 143, detail
Pages 514 – 515: cat. 159, detail

This book has been produced by the Editors Office, National Gallery of Art, Washington.
Editor-in-chief, Frances P. Smyth
Senior editor, Mary Yakush
Editor, Charles Dibble
Indexed by Andrew Christenson
Designed by Chris Vogel
with production assistance from Margaret Bauer, Susan Rabin, Nancy van Meter, and Jennifer Wahlberg

Typeset by Duke Typography in Charlotte Book.
Printed on Biberest by Snoeck, Ducaju & Zoon, Ghent, Belgium.

The clothbound edition is published by Yale University Press, London and New Haven.

Library of Congress
Cataloging-in-Publication Data
The Golden Age of Chinese
Archaeology / edited by
Xiaoneng Yang.
p. cm.
Includes bibliographical references and index.
ISBN 0-300-08132-4 (hard)
ISBN 0-89468-245-8 (soft)
1. China — Antiquities Exhibitions.
2. Antiquities, Prehistoric — China Exhibitions. 3. China — Civilization Exhibitions. 4. Prehistoric peoples— China Exhibitions. I. Yang, Xiaoneng.

DS715.G65 1999   99-16620
931'.0074'753 — dc21   CIP

cat. 26

cat. 67

cat. 121

cat. 170

July 29, 1999

It is of great significance to inaugurate the exhibition entitled *The Golden Age of Chinese Archaeology: Celebrated Discoveries from The People's Republic of China* at the National Gallery in Washington, D.C. on the occasion of the fiftieth anniversary of the founding of The People's Republic of China. On behalf of the Chinese government, the Chinese people, and in my own name, I would like to extend my sincere greetings to the American people, and my best wishes for the success of this exhibition.

China is a great nation with a long history of 5000 years. The Chinese people, diligent and intelligent, once created a glorious ancient civilization and made indelible contributions to the progress of human civilization. I am sure that this exhibition shall enhance the American peoples' knowledge of China from historical and cultural perspectives, strengthen mutual understanding and friendship, and promote the cultural exchange between our two nations as well as the development of Sino-US relations.

I wish a complete success to *The Golden Age of Chinese Archaeology: Celebrated Discoveries from The People's Republic of China* exhibition.

Jiang Zemin
President,
The People's Republic of China

THE WHITE HOUSE

WASHINGTON

June 24, 1999

I am delighted to extend warm greetings to all those attending the National Gallery of Art's new exhibition, *The Golden Age of Chinese Archaeology: Celebrated Discoveries from The People's Republic of China.*

Twenty-five years ago, the government of China presented to the American people the first major exhibition of Chinese archaeological treasures unearthed since the 1949 founding of The People's Republic of China. That epochal cultural exchange, *Archaeological Finds of The People's Republic of China,* opened at the National Gallery of Art in 1974 and vastly enhanced our knowledge and understanding of China's art and culture.

The works exhibited in 1974 were selected to represent many of the most significant discoveries made in the first quarter-century of the PRC. Working with their Chinese counterparts, the organizers of that exhibition were the National Gallery of Art in Washington and The Nelson-Atkins Museum in Kansas City. It is appropriate, therefore, that these two institutions have once again joined forces, this time with colleagues at the State Administration of Cultural Heritage and Art Exhibitions China, Beijing, to organize this latest superb exhibition, one that will bring to the American public some of the remarkable archaeological discoveries made in China over the past 25 years.

Hillary and I remember with great pleasure our 1998 trip to China, where we had the opportunity to see some of these archaeological finds in their native land. We are grateful to the organizers of this exhibit and to the Chinese government for sharing these treasures with the American people.

Bill Clinton

Foreword

Several times in the past five decades, the West's attention has been riveted by news of astonishing archaeological finds in China. Such discoveries as that of the Bronze Age Erlitou culture are among the many achievements of a five-decade-long effort to encourage and support archaeological projects throughout the Republic, not only through "rescue" archaeology but also through analytical and scientific means. The world's understanding of ancient Chinese history has been vastly expanded as a result, leading to our description of the second half of the twentieth century, and the present exhibition, as *The Golden Age of Chinese Archaeology*. Each work of art exhibited here will help the visitor along the path that leads toward understanding the profundity and grandeur of Chinese civilization. Each work exhibited is precious, embodying the history of Chinese art and science, and each was painstakingly recovered through the often arduous archaeological process.

In 1982, the Standing Committee of the People's Congress passed a "Cultural Relics Preservation Law of The People's Republic of China," further strengthening an already firm national commitment to archaeology. While governmental support has allowed the discipline to grow, its successes are owed in no small measure to the determination and hard work of Chinese archaeologists, aided by colleagues from the West, and especially from the United States. In the 1920s the Rockefeller Foundation supported a large-scale systematic excavation at Zhoukoudian, where Chinese and Western scholars worked side-by-side. Since then, close collaborative investigations have continued, for example, at Mogaoku and Longmen Grottos, with the support of the Getty Conservation Institute, the Dunhuang Research Institute, and the Cultural Relics Department of Luoyang. Many American universities and research institutions participate in archaeological surveys, investigations, and excavations across China: the Palaeolithic site at Nihewang Basin; the Neolithic sites in Xianrendong, Wangnian, Jiangxi province, and in western China; the Lower Xiajiadian culture site in Inner Mongolia province; Shandong province's Rizhao sites; and the salt industry sites in the Chengdu Plain and its adjacent areas.

President Jiang Zemin, in a speech at Harvard University in November 1997, said, "Mutual understanding is the premise of developing a friendly relationship between countries.... In order to understand China, there can be many different points of view. The present China is the extension of the historical China, which is a country with five thousand years of history and civilization. We should comprehend and discern China from the perspectives of its history and cultural heritage." *The Golden Age of Chinese Archaeology*, with its exquisite works from 5000 BCE to the tenth century CE, provides an excellent opportunity for our American friends to study Chinese history and culture. Through these ancient works we hope that you will become acquainted not only with a brilliant culture, but come to understand better China's historical struggles, its longing for peace, and its strength.

The country and its people are brimming over with confidence as they assume new, proactive roles in archaeology as well as in world society. With great good will and enthusiasm,

China offers this important exhibition to the United States at the dawn of the new millennium. I wholeheartedly applaud all those who made the exhibition a success.

Zhang Wenbin
Director General, State Administration of Cultural Heritage
The People's Republic of China

Foreword

Wenwu, the modern Chinese word for "antiquities" or, in the classical Chinese language, "objects of accomplishment," embodies profound meanings. *Wenwu* refers not merely to excellence of artistry, but also to moral refinement and cultural literacy. In traditional China, *wenwu* often served as material standards marking distinctions of rank. As such, they made manifest the social order of Chinese civilization and defined its identity. Over thousands of years, collectors coveted ancient objects not merely for their physical beauty but as tokens of an enduring intellectual and emotional connection with the sages of antiquity.

Modern archaeology, or *kaogu,* was introduced to China in the 1920s. Since then, it has put a new face on the notion of *wenwu.* Excavations under carefully controlled conditions have made it possible to reconstruct in far greater detail than ever before the cultural meaning of ancient works of art in their own times. No longer isolated "objects of accomplishment," *wenwu* have become constituent parts of a panorama of Chinese history, complementing, expanding, and at times correcting the textual record. By identifying, in several Neolithic cultures in northern and central China, features that are recognizably "Chinese," archaeology can now reliably trace the cultural ancestry of the historical dynasties to remote prehistoric times, to periods that, in fact, antedate the time spans traditionally accepted. Archaeology has also shown that Chinese civilization did not develop from a single root or in a linear fashion, but that different parts of China had their own distinctive cultural traditions, which gradually merged over the course of millennia.

The astonishing works of art exhibited here are good indicators for the rich diversity of the earliest times, and for the way in which increasingly uniform cultural standards were imposed over the centuries. The present exhibition expands upon a foundation laid in 1974 – 1975, when our two institutions collaborated on *The Exhibition of Archaeological Finds from The People's Republic of China.* Dating from prehistoric times to the tenth century, many of the exhibited works have never been seen in the United States, and some were discovered only in 1997. An exhibition such as this requires many resources, but above all it is the immense and sustained effort made by generations of Chinese archaeologists, across more than five decades, that enables us to present this great exhibition to the American people. Their work has resulted in nothing less than the rewriting of the history of Chinese civilization. We look forward to great archaeological discoveries still to come.

A large debt of gratitude is owed to the State Administration of Cultural Heritage, headed by Mr. Zhang Wenbin, without whose cooperation and goodwill our joint project might never have been realized. We thank the many museums and archaeological institutions throughout the Republic who lent to this exhibition, and our colleagues at Art Exhibitions China for their extensive efforts on our behalf. We are grateful to Ambassador Li Zhaoxing for his support. Xiaoneng Yang, curator of Chinese art at The Nelson-Atkins Museum of Art, chose the works and provided the vision that makes it possible for Westerners to place these often surprising works of art within the continuum of Chinese civilization. In this task he was aided by scholars from several continents, whose illuminating texts are published here. We wish to thank Eastman Kodak for its generosity in making this exhibition possible, and in particular, George M. Fisher, chairman and chief executive officer, for his vision and understanding of the importance of cultural exchange between China and the United States. The Henry Luce Foundation provided essential funds in the planning stages of our project, and we are grateful to vice president Terrill E. Lautz for his support. The E. Rhodes and Leona B. Carpenter Foundation, whose vice president Paul Day responded enthusiastically to our request for support for the exhibition catalogue, deserves our hearty thanks. We thank the Federal Council on the Arts and the Humanities for the indemnity granted to this exhibition. The Asian Cultural Council, New York, and the Metropolitan Center for Far Eastern Studies, Kyoto, also supported research in China.

Finally, to the Chinese people, who have shared so many of their most ancient and revered cultural properties, we are profoundly grateful. The citizens of both our nations are sure to enjoy new heights of mutual appreciation and understanding as the result.

Earl A. Powell III
Director, National Gallery of Art

Marc F. Wilson
Director, The Nelson-Atkins Museum of Art

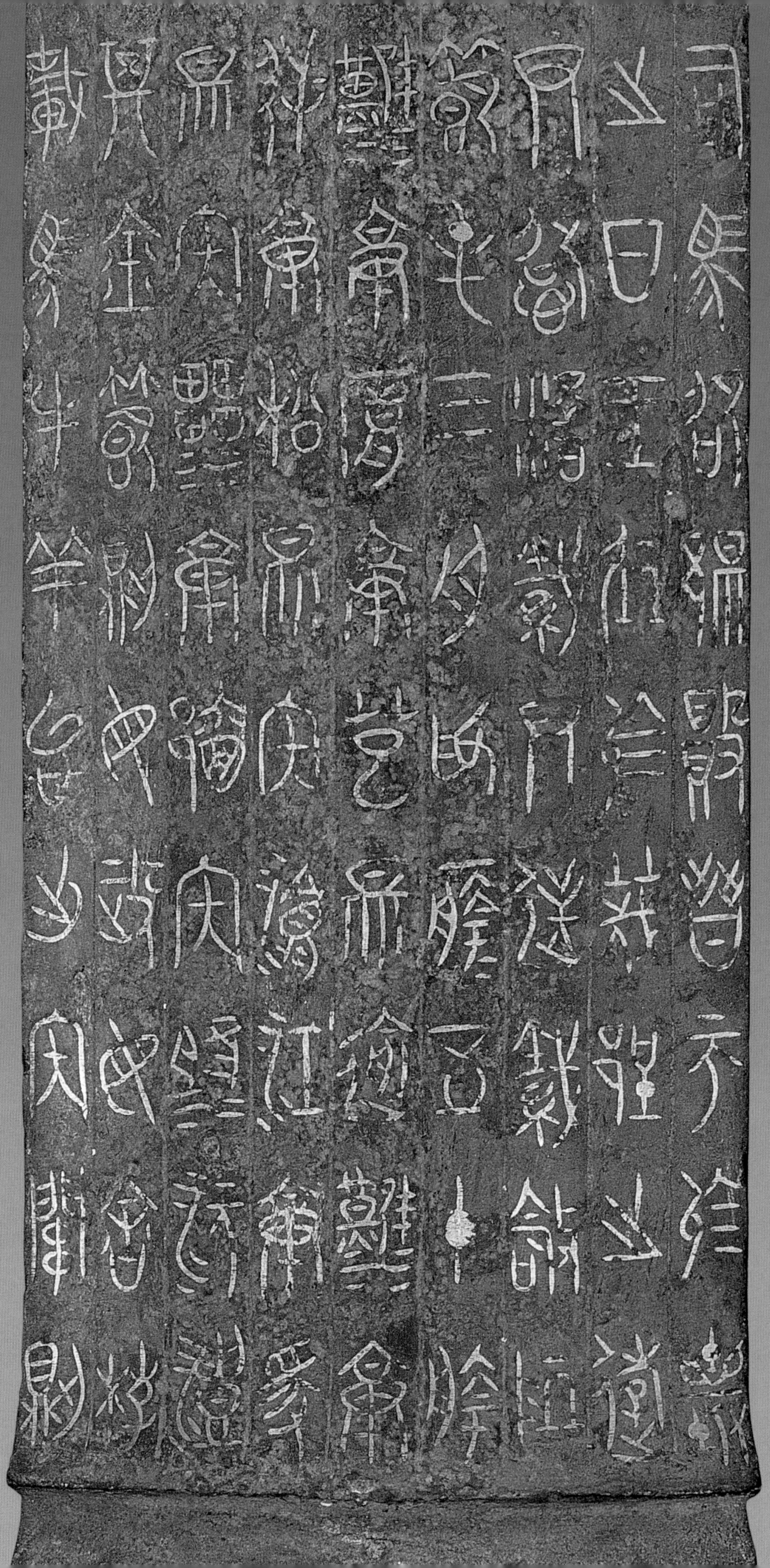

Lenders to the Exhibition

Chunhua County Cultural Relics Museum, Chunhua, Shaanxi Province

Famen Monastery Museum, Fufeng, Shaanxi Province

Gansu Provincial Bureau of Cultural Heritage, Lanzhou, Gansu Province

Gansu Provincial Museum, Lanzhou, Gansu Province

Guangdong Provincial Bureau of Culture, Guangzhou, Guangdong Province

Hebei Provincial Bureau of Cultural Heritage, Shijiazhuang, Hebei Province

Hebei Provincial Cultural Relics Institute, Shijiazhuang, Hebei Province

Hebei Provincial Museum, Shijiazhuang, Hebei Province

Henan Museum, Zhengzhou, Henan Province

Henan Provincial Bureau of Cultural Heritage, Zhengzhou, Henan Province

Hubei Provincial Bureau of Cultural Heritage, Wuhan, Hubei Province

Hubei Provincial Museum, Wuhan, Hubei Province

The Institute of Archaeology, Chinese Academy of Social Sciences, Beijing

Jiangxi Provincial Bureau of Cultural Heritage, Nanchang, Jiangxi Province

Jiangxi Provincial Museum, Nanchang, Jiangxi Province

Jingzhou Prefecture Museum, Jingzhou, Hubei Province

Liaoning Provincial Bureau of Cultural Heritage, Shenyang, Liaoning Province

Liaoning Provincial Institute of Archaeology, Shenyang, Liaoning Province

Liaoning Provincial Museum, Shenyang, Liaoning Province

Lintong County Museum, Lintong, Shaanxi Province

The Museum of the Western Han Tomb of the Nanyue King, Guangzhou, Guangdong Province

The National Museum of Chinese History, Beijing

Qin Terra-cotta Museum, Lintong, Shaanxi Province

Qingzhou Municipal Museum, Qingzhou, Shandong Province

Sanxingdui Museum, Sanxingdui, Guanghan, Sichuan Province

Shaanxi Archaeological Institute, Xi'an, Shaanxi Province

Shaanxi History Museum, Xi'an, Shaanxi Province

Shaanxi Provincial Administrative Bureau of Cultural Heritage, Xi'an, Shaanxi Province

Shandong Provincial Bureau of Cultural Heritage, Jinan, Shandong Province

Shanxi Provincial Bureau of Cultural Heritage, Taiyuan, Shanxi Province

Shanxi Provincial Institute of Archaeology, Taiyuan, Shanxi Province

Sichuan Provincial Bureau of Cultural Heritage, Chengdu, Sichuan Province

Xi'an Municipal Institute of Archaeology and Preservation of Cultural Relics, Xi'an, Shaanxi Province

Yanshi City Museum, Yanshi, Henan Province

Zhejiang Provincial Bureau of Cultural Heritage, Hangzhou, Zhejiang Province

Zhejiang Provincial Institute of Archaeology, Hangzhou, Zhejiang Province

Zhouyuan Administrative Office of Cultural Relics, Fufeng, Shaanxi Province

Acknowledgments

Five years ago, when I first discussed the idea of organizing this exhibition with Marc F. Wilson, director of The Nelson-Atkins Museum of Art, I received his enthusiastic encouragement. Earl A. Powell III, director of the National Gallery of Art, agreed not only to participate but to accept, on behalf of the Gallery, responsibility as the principal organizer, owing to a conflict presented by the simultaneous expansion of The Nelson-Atkins Museum of Art. I cannot find words to convey my gratitude to Mr. Powell and Mr. Wilson for their foresight, determination, and leadership.

The project has benefited immeasurably from the cooperation of the State Bureau of Cultural Relics, The People's Republic of China; museums and archaeological institutions throughout China; many Chinese scholars and archaeologists; the Chinese Embassy to the United States of America; and the American Embassy to The People's Republic of China. I would like to express my deep appreciation to the State Bureau of Cultural Relics, particularly to General Director Zhang Wenbin and his colleagues, Mr. Ma Zishu, Ms. Wang Limei, Mr. Lou Bojian, and Mr. Song Xinchao; the Advisory Committee of the State Bureau, particularly Professors Su Bai, Yu Weichao, Zhang Zhongpei, Xu Pingfang, Huang Jinlüe, and Sun Ji; Art Exhibitions China, particularly the exhibition team of Messrs. and Misses Yang Yang, Yin Jia, Zhang Jianxin, Zhu Shumin, Zhao Gushan, and Chen Shujie; and the photography team of Messrs. and Misses Fan Shenyan, Li Fan, and Zhang Yulian; and the transportation team of Messrs. Zhang Yake and Yang Guangming. Ms. Wang Limei enthusiastically participated in this project from the early stages and effectively coordinated work at the various museum and archaeological institutions in China. Mr. Yang Yang was the team leader of Art Exhibitions China and supervised related preparations in the agency. Ms. Fan Shenyan traveled throughout China to make the beautiful photographs published here, even managing to satisfy my request for numerous details and excavation photographs. Additional photographs were made by Messrs. Gao Yuying, Jiang Cong, Qin Ziyu, Wang Baoping, and Wang Mengxiang. I am grateful to Ambassador Li Zhaoxing and the staff at the Chinese Embassy to the United States; to Messrs. Li Gang and Zhan Yucheng at the Ministry of Culture of The People's Republic of China; and to Messrs. Paul Blackburn and William G. Crowell at the United States Embassy to The People's Republic of China. I am also appreciative of James J. Lally, who lent his expertise in reviewing the values provided for indemnity and insurance purposes.

Since 1997, I have worked with the excellent staff at the National Gallery of Art, perhaps most closely with D. Dodge Thompson, chief of exhibitions, whose professionalism and cooperative spirit I admire greatly. Sincere thanks are owed to the many other staff who tirelessly gave of their time and expertise to the realization of this project, including Alan Shestack, deputy director; Carol Kelley, deputy to the director; Ann B. Robertson and Jennifer Bumba-Kongo, department of exhibitions, who provided administrative support; Susan M. Arensberg, Isabelle Dervaux, Carroll Moore, Rolly Strauss, and Yu-wen Wu, department of exhibition programs, who prepared educational texts and produced the brochure and audio-visual program; Mervin Richard, Michael Pierce, and Judy Ozone, conservation division, together with Michelle Fondas and Andrew Krieger, in the registrar's office, who organized and supervised the packing and shipping of the works; Mark A. Leithauser, Donna Kwederis, Gordon Anson, John Olson, and Bill Bowser, department of design and installation; Joseph Krakora, Sandy Masur, Ruth Anderson Coggeshall, and Melissa McCracken, office of external affairs; Philip C. Jessup, Jr., Nancy R. Breuer, and Montrue V. Conner, office of the secretary-general counsel; Deborah Ziska and Nancy Starr, information office, and Faya Causey, department of academic programs, who organized the symposium.

The process of assembling this catalogue presented enormous challenges. Twenty-four specialists in Chinese art and archaeology agreed to contribute texts, despite our schedule. Their wide-ranging scholarship has enriched our understanding of the history of ancient China and the experience of many thousands of readers and visitors to the exhibition. We are grateful to Richard M. Barnhart, Albert E. Dien, Lothar von Falkenhausen, Louisa G. Fitzgerald-Huber, Donald Harper, David N. Keightley, Ladislav Kesner, Michael Knight, Dieter Kuhn, Colin Mackenzie, Elinor L. Pearlstein, Jessica Rawson, Edward L. Shaughnessy, Zhixin Sun, Robert L. Thorp, Alain Thote, Roderick Whitfield, and Xia Mingcai. We are especially fortunate to be able to publish essays by Professors Su Bai, Yu Weichao, Zhang Zhongpei, Zou Heng, and Xu Pingfang, who are among the most senior and foremost archaeologists in China. In the selection and collection of photographs and illustrations for the catalogue, I was assisted by Misses and Messrs. Fan Shenyan, Gua Dashun, Wu En, Wang Shimin, Feng Haozhang, Huang Qingchang, and Peng Hao; I also thank Messrs. Gao Wei and Wang Jihuai for supplying critical excavation data.

The production of the catalogue was a joint effort by the editors office at the National Gallery of Art, and the department of Asian art, The Nelson-Atkins Museum of Art. In Washington, I am grateful to Frances Smyth, Mary Yakush, Chris Vogel, Charles Dibble, Jennifer Wahlberg, Maria Shay, Margaret Bauer, Allison Needle, and Andrew Christenson. Ms. Yakush skillfully managed the editorial side and ensured that the contributions would be consistent, in collaboration with Mr. Dibble. Mr. Vogel created an elegant design. In Kansas City, I am grateful to Yuling Huang, Lingen Lu, Jason Steuber, Theresa Stock, Zhijun Zhao, and Dan Chaffee. While they all shared duties and gathered information for the authors, Jason Steuber was my principal aide, assisting in all communications; compiling the English bibliography; and performing countless essential tasks. I thank Zhijun for translating Professor Zhang Zhongpei's article; Lingen for translating the contributions by Professors Su Bai, Yu Weichao, Zou Heng, and Xu Pingfang, and compiling the concordance; Yuling for compiling the Chinese bibliography and translating Mr. Zhang Wenbin's foreword, Theresa for her multi-faceted administrative work, Dan for creating drawings of some of the works exhibited, and Wang Hui for her assistance at the later stages.

To all those who have helped bring our project to its successful conclusion, I extend my deepest gratitude.

Xiaoneng Yang

Archaeological Sites

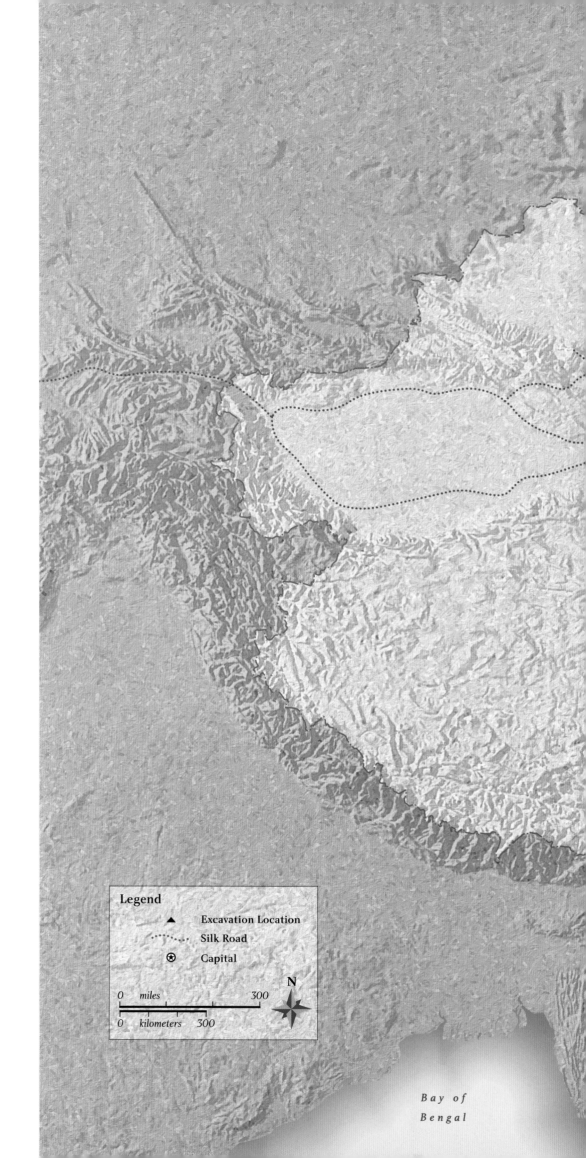

Legend

▲ Excavation Location

⋯⋯ Silk Road

⊛ Capital

0 miles 300

0 kilometers 300

N

Bay of Bengal

Aohanqi
Fuxin
Jianping
Lingyuan Kazuo

⊛ Beijing

Mancheng
Quyang
Pingshan

Qingzhou
Linqu

Anyang

Datong

Xiangfen
Quwo

Longxi Qin'an Chunhua
Baoji
Tianshui Wei River Lintong
Fufeng Xi'an
Chang'an

Yanshi
Linru

Mengcheng

Xichuan
Huai River
Shouxian

Taihu
Lake

Suixian
Yuhang

Jingmen
Jiangling
Yangzi River

Guanghan

Dongting
Lake

Poyang
Lake

Xin'gan

Liao River

Yellow River

Yellow
Sea

East
China
Sea

Yangzi River

Pearl River

Guangzhou

South China Sea

5000   4000   3000

Yangshao Culture
c. 5000 – 3000 BCE

Dawenkou Culture
c. 4300 – 2500 BCE

Majiayao Culture
c. 3300 – 2050 BCE

Taosi Longshan
Culture
c. 2500 – 1900 BCE

Hongshan Culture
c. 4700 – 2920 BCE

Liangzhu Culture
c. 3300 – 2200 BCE

Shandong Longshan
Culture
c. 2500 – 2000 BCE

cat. 6

cat. 1

cat. 14

cat. 24

BRONZE AGE CHINA

CHU AND
OTHER
CULTURES

EARLY IMPERIAL CHINA

| 2000 | 1000 | 1 CE | 1000 |

Erlitou Culture
c. 1900 – 1500 BCE

Lower Xiajiadian Culture
c. 2000 – 1500 BCE

Shang Dynasty
c. 16th – 11th century BCE

Spring and Autumn Period
770 – 476 BCE

Western Zhou Dynasty
c. 11th century – 771 BCE

Warring States Period
475 – 221 BCE

Qin Dynasty
221 – 207 BCE

Northern Wei Dynasty
386 – 534 CE

Western Han Dynasty
206 BCE – 24 CE

Eastern
Wei
Dynasty
534 – 550 CE

Northern Qi Dynasty
550 – 577 CE

Tang Dynasty
618 – 907 CE

Later
Liang
Dynasty
907 – 923 CE

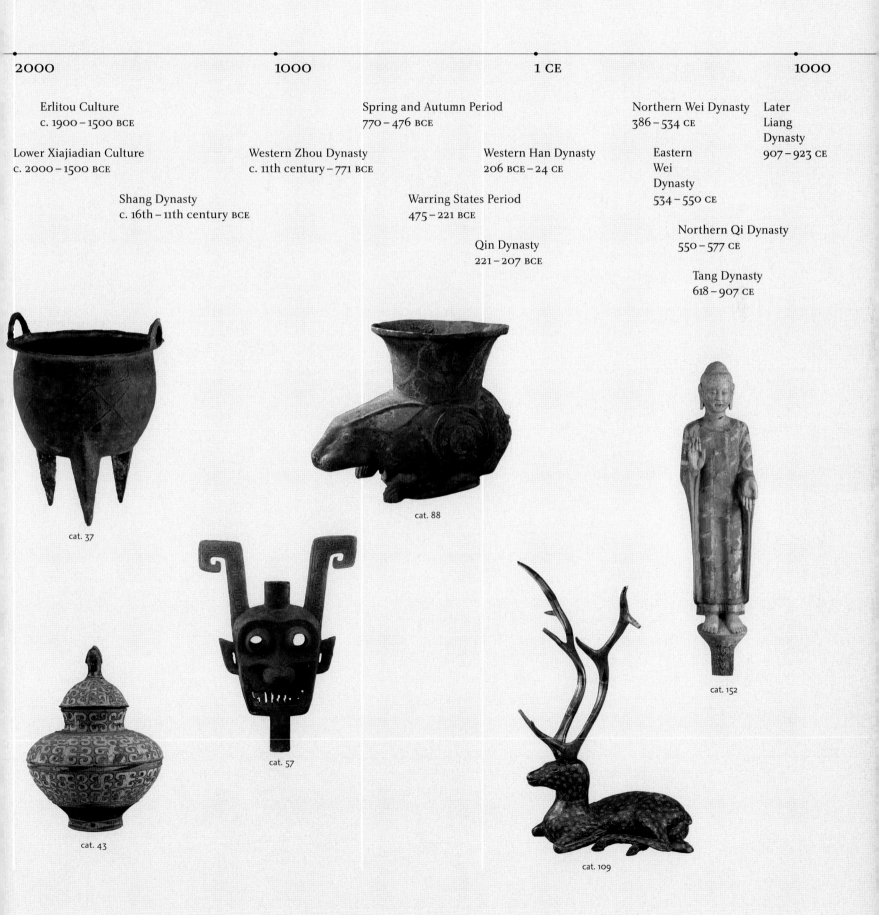

cat. 37

cat. 88

cat. 152

cat. 57

cat. 43

cat. 109

Note to the Reader

The works of art included in the exhibition are representative of four periods, corresponding to sections of this catalogue: Late Prehistoric China (c. 5000–2000 BCE), Bronze Age China (c. 2000–771 BCE), Chu and Other Cultures (c. 770–221 BCE), and Early Imperial China (221 BCE–924 CE). The order of presentation is chronological, with exhibited works from the same culture or find site presented in groups.

The Pinyin system of romanization has been used throughout. Chinese characters, which appear in the concordance beginning on page 556, are written in nonsimplified characters.

For some matters treated here, a unified terminology does not exist; for instance, authors' usage of terms such as the "upper," "middle," or "lower" Yellow or Yangzi River may sometimes be subjective and may not follow a strict geographic designation.

Hardstone objects from China traditionally described as "jade" (*yu*), and particularly carvings dated after the second millennium BCE, are usually nephrite. Neolithic hardstone carvings were made from a variety of hard, compacted minerals that assume a high luster when polished: nephrite, serpentine, fluorite, and other minerals not always easily distinguished by visual inspection. For this reason, the designation "jade" is used throughout the titles in the exhibition.

Dimensions of the objects are given in centimeters, followed by equivalent inches in parentheses. Weights, to the extent germane, are given in kilograms, followed by equivalent pounds in parentheses.

While every effort has been made to present the most current scholarship, it goes without saying that some of the views published here may one day be superseded by future discoveries.

CONTRIBUTORS TO THE CATALOGUE

RB   Richard M. Barnhart
AD   Albert E. Dien
LvF   Lothar von Falkenhausen
LF-H   Louisa G. Fitzgerald-Huber
DH   Donald Harper
DNK   David N. Keightley
LK   Ladislav Kesner
MK   Michael Knight
DK   Dieter Kuhn
CM   Colin Mackenzie
EP   Elinor L. Pearlstein
JR   Jessica Rawson
ES   Edward L. Shaughnessy
ZS   Zhixin Sun
RT   Robert L. Thorp
AT   Alain Thote
RW   Roderick Whitfield
SB   Su Bai
XM   Xia Mingcai
XP   Xu Pingfang
XY   Xiaoneng Yang
YW   Yu Weichao
ZZ   Zhang Zhongpei
ZH   Zou Heng

CHINESE HISTORICAL PERIODS AND DYNASTIES

Palaeolithic Period
c. 1,700,000 – 8000 BCE

Neolithic Period – Chalcolithic Period
c. 8000 – 2000 BCE

Xia Dynasty
c. 21st – 16th century BCE

Shang Dynasty
c. 16th – 11th century BCE

Zhou Dynasty
c. 11th century – 221 (256) BCE

    Western Zhou Dynasty
    c. 11th century – 771 BCE

    Eastern Zhou Dynasty
    770 – 221 (256) BCE

        Spring and Autumn Period
        770 – 476 BCE

        Warring States Period
        475 – 221 BCE

Qin Dynasty
221 – 207 BCE

Western Han Dynasty
206 BCE – 24 CE

Eastern Han Dynasty
25 – 220 CE

Three Kingdoms Period
220 – 265 CE

Western Jin Dynasty
265 – 316 CE

Eastern Jin Dynasty
317 – 420 CE

Southern and
Northern Dynasties
420 – 589 CE

Sui Dynasty
581 – 618 CE

Tang Dynasty
618 – 907 CE

Five Dynasties
907 – 960 CE

Song Dynasty
960 – 1279 CE

    Liao Dynasty
    916 – 1125 CE

    Jin Dynasty
    1115 – 1234 CE

Yuan Dynasty
1279 – 1368 CE

Ming Dynasty
1368 – 1644 CE

Qing Dynasty
1644 – 1911 CE

Xiaoneng Yang

A History of Modern Chinese Archaeology

XIAONENG YANG | Traditional Chinese antiquarianism, particularly the *jin shi xue* (the study of ancient Chinese bronzes and stone stelae), has endured for one thousand years.[1] In contrast, modern field archaeology has come to be practiced in China only recently, starting in the early twentieth century. It is a young sibling if compared with Roman, Greek, and Egyptian archaeology.[2] Modern Chinese archaeology is distinguished from previous efforts to investigate physical remains by its scientific methodology of field surveys and excavations.

A series of momentous discoveries during the first decade of the twentieth century — in particular, the Shang oracle-bone inscriptions at Anyang in Henan province and the Han-Tang manuscripts, paintings, textiles, and wooden slips from Dunhuang and Jiuquan in Gansu province, stimulated modern Chinese archaeology.[3] Evolving from traditional sinology, after the political revolution of 1911 it absorbed the Western disciplines of palaeontology and geology. Initiated and first practiced in China by Japanese, Russian, and Western scholars and explorers, most of them self-taught, Chinese archaeology would eventually come to be a province of Chinese intellectuals.

Despite the interruptions imposed by political and social turmoil,[5] the discipline developed rapidly over the course of less than a century, and much of China's early history has been rewritten as a result. The achievements of Chinese archaeologists have drawn attention and admiration from around the world. Chinese archaeology has in fact entered a golden age,[6] the result of a developmental process comprising four stages: initiation (1890s – 1910s); formation (1920s – 1940s), institutionalization (1949 – 1976), and maturation (1977 to the present).

1890s – 1910s: INITIATION

Long known as the "Central Kingdom," China was battered during the nineteenth century and the first decade of the twentieth century by totalitarianism, poverty, and foreign invasion. In 1911, Chinese intellectuals and patriots engineered the overthrow of the Qing dynasty, and the Republic of China was established.[7] One of their foremost goals was the pursuit and importation of science and democracy from the West, epitomized by the May Fourth Movement of 1919.[8] If the door of China was first cracked by foreign forces, it was the Chinese people who enthusiastically swung it wide open.

Chinese intellectuals eagerly embraced foreign scholarship, including that of Western archaeologists. Liang Qichao (1873 – 1929), a key reformer and a leading scholar, was among the first to apply Western archaeologists' periodization of the prehistoric era to China. His 1901 essay summarizing Chinese history refers to three successive prehistoric periods — delineated by the use of stone, bronze, and iron tools — a chronology established by the Danish archaeologist Christian Jürgensen Thomsen (1788 – 1865). Although the periods vary in length in different regions, Liang suggested that the sequence applies to prehistoric China, and he further posited the existence of a Stone Age before the legendary figure Shen Nong and a bronze age

Cat. 126, detail

since Shen Nong, or Yan Di — the first legendary Emperor Yan. Today, the Chinese people consider themselves the descendants of the Yan Di and Huang Di emperors.[9] Liang pioneered the use of Western archaeological concepts and ideas to investigate ancient Chinese history.

During the same period, foreign scientists and archaeologists began to visit China, either on their own or in the company of missionaries.[10] Torii Ryuzo (Japanese, 1870–1953) may have been the first trained archaeologist to work in China. In 1895, Torii surveyed sites dating from the Neolithic to the Han period and found polished stone axes and spearheads in the Liaodong peninsula of northeastern China. After surveying the region in 1905 and 1908, he published a report describing his travels and research, and the anthropological, archaeological, geographical, and topographical information that resulted.[11] Torii and other Japanese archaeologists continued to survey sites throughout China and occupied Taiwan, covering a wide temporal and geographic range of subjects, ranging from prehistoric burials, ancient architecture, Buddhist caves, and imperial mausoleums.[12]

American, English, French, German, Russian, and Swedish explorers also organized expeditions to China. They left their footprints throughout the northwestern regions and along the Silk Road, especially in the provinces of the Xinjiang and Gansu.[13] Among them was Aurel Stein (1862–1943), a Budapest-born citizen of Great Britain who conducted large-scale geographic and archaeological surveys in Gansu, Inner Mongolia, and Xinjiang (1900–1901, 1906–1908, and 1913–1916). These surveys yielded valuable information on sites and cemeteries such as the Mogaoku Grottos at Dunhuang, Gansu; Xixia (Tangut) Yuan dynasty cities at Heicheng, Inner Mongolia; and the ancient city of Gaochang at Turfan, Xinjiang.[14] Stein is chiefly remembered for the more than ten thousand paintings, textiles, prints, manuscripts, and other objects that he removed from the Mogaoku Grottos (the artifacts are now in the British Museum, London; the British Library, London; and the National Museum, New Delhi).[15] French, Japanese, and Russian explorers also acquired a large number of the remaining Mogaoku treasures. Paul Pelliot (French, 1878–1945), procured several thousand works, the second-largest group ever to leave China (now mostly in the Musée Guimet, Paris).[16] Langdon Warner (1881–1955) of the Fogg Art Museum, Harvard University, Cambridge, removed more than twelve fragments of wall paintings and a kneeling bodhisattva (now in the Arthur M. Sackler Museum, Harvard University, Cambridge) from the Mogaoku Grottos and transported them to the United States in 1924[17]; Warner's second expedition to Dunhuang in 1925 was less successful. In 1930, the Fogg trustees persuaded Stein to conduct yet another "survey" under the Fogg's aegis, in northwestern China. When Chinese academics protested, this survey also failed.[18] Many Chinese archaeologists characterize Stein's and others' activities in China as plunder and *dao jue* (unlawful excavations).

Geographer and explorer Sven Anders Hedin (Sweden, 1865–1952) approached exploration from a different perspective. He conducted archaeological, geographic, meteorological, and palaeontological surveys from 1893 to 1935 in Xinjiang, Qinghai, Gansu, Ningxia, Inner

Bodhisattva as guide of souls. Ink and colors on silk; height 80.5 (31⅞); Tang dynasty; from Dunhuang, Gansu province. Stein painting 47, ch. LVII.002. Courtesy of the British Museum (left).

Kneeling attendant bodhisattva. Molded clay stucco over wooden armature, gesso-covered surface with polychomy and gilding; height 122 (48); Tang dynasty; from Dunhuang, Gansu province (Fogg China expedition, 1923-1924). Courtesy of the Arthur M. Sackler Museum, Harvard University Art Museums (right).

Mongolia, and Tibet. During an expedition that lasted from 1899 to 1902, he discovered the Loulan site at Xinjiang, an abundant source of historical data.[19] Most of Hedin's surveys were well documented by maps, photographs, drawings, and site descriptions. His last and most important joint venture with Chinese scholars, the Northwestern Scientific Investigation Group, or Sino-Swedish Expedition, was led by Xu Bingxu (1888–1976)[20] and lasted from 1927 to 1935. The cooperative nature of this expedition resulted from protests by Chinese academics, especially members of the faculty at Peking (Beijing) and Ts'inghua (Qinghua) Universities,[21] who were unwilling simply to act as observers in archaeological excavations. Hedin agreed that all artifacts discovered would remain in China. With ten Chinese and seventeen European scholars at its start, Hedin's expedition remains the largest joint Chinese-Western archaeological project ever undertaken.[22]

The Geological Survey of China, an agency of the Republic's Ministry of Agriculture and Commerce, and its founding director Ding Wenjiang (Chinese, 1887–1936)[23] played vital roles in the early years of archaeological investigations in China. A British-trained geologist who sought to promote Western science in China, Ding was appointed by the government to the Survey in 1916 to locate mineral deposits. Ding recruited several distinguished Western scientists to assist in the effort. The most influential and well-known were Amadeus William Grabau

(American, 1870 – 1946), chief palaeontologist of the Survey and editor of *Paleontologia Sinica*; Johan Gunnar Andersson (Swedish, 1874 – 1960) who was hired by the Chinese government to survey coal and iron resources; Davidson Black (Canadian, 1884 – 1934) and J. Franz Weidenreich (German, 1873 – 1948), respectively professor of anatomy and director of the Cenozoic Laboratory at Peking Union Medical College (founded by the Rockefeller Foundation); and Pierre Teilhard de Chardin (French, 1881 – 1955), a Jesuit priest, theologist, and palaeontologist who also practiced archaeology.[24] Under Ding's leadership, the Survey expanded its work of locating ore to include several palaeontological and prehistoric archaeological projects. The projects initiated and arranged by the Survey and its members not only transmitted new knowledge and educated a generation of Chinese scientists and surveyors in related fields but also contributed to the birth of Chinese archaeology.

The earliest expeditions and the later, more rigorous geological and palaeontological surveys all centered on northern China. Whereas the early expeditions had favored relics of historical periods and especially Buddhist art, interest in prehistoric archaeology grew steadily, and almost all were associated with the Survey. In this era, the work was undertaken by foreigners or by Chinese nationals who had been educated abroad and had returned to China. Most of the resulting reports were published at the highest standard of the time and remain essential references for today's readers, though the excavation techniques often seem primitive to modern eyes.

During the 1910s, Chinese institutions of higher learning such as Peking University created departments of geology whose curricula introduced students to fieldwork. That textual scholars came to appreciate fully the value of archaeological materials is evident in studies by Luo Zhenyu (1866 – 1940) and Wang Guowei (1877 – 1927) of Han dynasty wooden slips and Shang dynasty oracle-bone inscriptions. In 1908, upon learning that oracle bones had been discovered in Anyang, Henan province, Luo sent his brother to collect the bones. Luo identified Xiaotun, Anyang, as Yinxu, the Late Shang capital (c. thirteenth-eleventh century BCE), and linked oracle bones to the religious and ritual practices of the Shang royals. In 1915, Luo personally went to Anyang to investigate the site first-hand; he recovered oracle bones, as well as other objects. Later, Wang Guowei used oracle-bone inscriptions to verify historical documents regarding the genealogy and history of the Shang dynasty and demonstrated that the "Yin ben ji" of the *Records of the Historian* (*Shi ji*, c. 104 – 86 BCE) was for the most part accurate.[25] Luo and Wang not only inherited the traditional textual research of the Qian Jia School (School of the period of the Emperors Qianlong and Jiaqing, 1796 – 1820), but also made great contributions toward the development of *jin shi xue* as a major branch of Chinese archaeology. The groundwork for the formation of field archaeology in China was firmly in place.[26]

The Swede Johan Gunnar Andersson (was impelled by the uncertain political climate of the early 1900s to shift his attention from geology to palaeontology in 1917. With Ding Wenjiang's unfailing encouragement, as well as his own fund-raising skills, Andersson secured support from both China and Sweden for publicity, financial assistance, and staff for palaeontological and archaeological undertakings.[27]

In 1921, Andersson was responsible for three major discoveries: the Neolithic cave at Shaguotun, Jinxi area, Liaoning province; the Neolithic settlement at Yangshao village, Mianchi county, Henan province (Yangshao culture [c. 5000–3000 BCE]); and the Palaeolithic cave at Zhoukoudian, Beijing, which led to the discovery of Peking Man, or *Sinanthropus pekinensis* (700,000–200,000 BP).[28]

The Yangshao excavation best represents modern Chinese archaeology in its inaugural phase. It took several years to complete the Yangshao excavation. Although Andersson had collected vertebrate fossils from Yangshao village as early as 1918, it was not until his assistant assembled several hundred stone artifacts from the site that Andersson himself returned to Yangshao. In April 1921 he found some painted pottery but did not realize its importance until he returned to Beijing and read a report on the American geologist Raphael Pumpelly's 1903–1904 exploration to Anau, in present-day Turkmenistan, which referred to protohistoric painted pottery.[29] With the permission of the government and the support of Ding Wenjiang, Andersson organized a team and launched an excavation from October to December of the same year.[30]

Andersson believed that the painted Yangshao pottery had been brought to the Yellow River valley in prehistoric migrations from Eastern Europe. Therefore he searched for the roots of the Yangshao culture in the Gansu and Qinghai provinces, in northwestern China. During explorations in 1923–1924 he discovered the remains of six regional prehistoric and Bronze Age cultures, including the Majiayao (Machang) (3300–2050 BCE) and the Qijia (2000–1700 BCE). He identified and distinguished the characteristics of these cultures and then established a chronology of prehistoric cultures in the upper Yellow River area.[31] Andersson's nomenclature was adopted and remains in use today, though his chronology is not entirely accurate. Although he and his teammates had been trained in geology and palaeontology by Walter Granger (American, 1872–1941) of the American Museum of Natural History, New York,[32] their excavation skills and experience were in developmental stages. Few comparative data and no carbon-14 tests were then available. For all that, his achievement — the discovery of a Stone Age in the "cradle area" of Chinese civilization — was remarkable. Andersson's work revealed that a previously unknown civilization, which used polished stone tools, painted pottery, and an advanced system of agriculture, had inhabited the Central Plains, the eventual seat of the dynastic cultures.

Andersson's early hypothesis that Chinese civilization had been transmitted from the West may have been influenced by the cultural diffusion theory prevalent among Western intellectu-

Hardstone owl; height 34.1 (13 ⅜); Shang dynasty; excavated in 1935 from Tomb 1001, Houjiazhuang, Anyang, Henan province. Courtesy of the Institute of History and Philology, Academia Sinica, Taipei.

als in the 1920s. His idea of the origin of Chinese civilization in alien cultures, on the basis of certain similarities between them, is understandable, but, we now know, incorrect.[33]

Andersson also initiated and guided the Zhoukoudian excavation, a find that drew international attention. At the suggestion of J. Megregor Gibb, professor of chemistry at Peking University, Andersson visited Zhoukoudian, Peking, in 1918. Andersson did not find the actual site and did not arrange the excavation until he sent his new assistant, the Austrian palaeontologist, Otto Zdansky, to Zhoukoudian in 1921. During another visit in 1921, Andersson noticed flakes of quartz, and, guessing that they might have been used as cutting implements, he asked Zdansky to complete the excavation. Zdansky unearthed two hominid molars during short-term excavations that same year and in 1923. The Zhoukoudian excavations lasted much longer than Andersson initially anticipated and eventually uncovered the world's richest and most comprehensive early Palaeolithic remains.[34]

In 1926, Andersson announced this discovery at a reception to welcome the Crown Prince of Sweden, Gustaf VI Adolf (1882 – 1973).[35] Andersson suggested that the Zhoukoudian excavation should be taken over by the Survey, in cooperation with Davidson Black of the Cenozoic Laboratory at Peking Union Medical College, and financed by the Rockefeller Foundation. This rewarding Sino-foreign enterprise lasted more than ten years until it was halted in 1937 by the Japanese invasion. The Zhoukoudian excavation spawned the first generation of Chinese palaeolithic archaeologists, which included Pei Wenzhong (1904–1982), who had excavated the first almost intact cranium of Peking Man at Zhoukoudian in 1929 and discovered *in situ* stone tool artifacts and evidence of the use of fire by the Peking Man in 1931.[36] Tragically, the more than forty fossil remains of Peking Man which had been kept by several Americans in China, were all lost in December 1941.[37] After Black's death in 1934, Weidenreich was hired to continue anatomical studies on the Peking Man. Weidenriech published most of his own research, and his publications, as well as those of Black, proved to be vital records after the fossils' disappearance.[38]

Andersson established the practice of gathering experts from different disciplines to research and excavate archaeological sites. For example, Yuan Fuli (Chinese, 1893–1987), an American-educated geologist,[39] and Zdansky were the principals in the Yangshao excavation and topographical survey. At Andersson's invitation, Black studied the human skeletons at Yangshao, identifying them as proto-Chinese, similar to those of the present-day northern Chinese.[40] Such collaborative strategies remain the method of choice for interpreting the findings of archaeological excavations.

While archaeological work continued, academics in other related fields had come to be called the "Questioning Antiquity" school *(yi gu pai)*. Headed by Gu Jiegang (1893–1980), they determined that the chronicles of the three *huang* "emperors" and five *di* "emperors" of pre-dynastic China (before 2000 BCE) had been created by Confucians and other schools that arose only after the Eastern Zhou period. Records of the early dynastic epoch (or Xia and Shang dynasties, c. the 21st–11th century BCE), moreover, were extremely sparse, and those that recount the history of the Xia and early Shang were also found to be unreliable, to the point that some even doubted the existence of the Xia.[41] More than two thousand years of received wisdom and Chinese historiography were being challenged: suddenly an entire corpus of history—and the legendary sages of antiquity, model rulers, and early dynasties—had been subverted. China itself seemed to have lost its roots. Who but the Chinese archaeologist would be able to reconstruct early Chinese history?

Locating Yinxu (the Ruins of Yin) at Anyang, the purported Late Shang capital, became the first priority of Chinese scholars. The archaeologists' objective was the same as that of traditional Chinese historiographers and antiquarians: to test the veracity of the classics and their annotations and, in so doing, to fill in the lacunae of history *(zhengjing bushi)*. In 1928, the Institute of History and Philology of Academia Sinica founded an official Archaeological Section, which embarked on its initial field work at Anyang in the fall of that same year under Fu Sinian (1896–1950), the director of the institute and an eminent historian. Dong Zuobin (1895–1963), a gifted palaeographer of oracle-bone inscriptions despite a lack of university or archaeological training, was the engineer. Dong's intention was to explore whether oracle bones might still survive in underground Yinxu after thirty years of exhaustive hunting had turned up little. The field work yielded nearly eight hundred pieces of inscribed oracle bones.[42]

Soon after, two young Chinese scholars trained at Harvard University became key figures in the Anyang excavations. Li Ji (1895–1979), who modestly described himself as an anthropologist by training and an archaeologist through opportunity,[43] was selected as the first head of the section in December 1928, and assumed the direction of the Anyang excavations. Li had taught at Qinghua University from 1925 to 1928, and worked with the archaeological team of the Freer Gallery of Art until 1930. Li is acknowledged as the first native Chinese archaeologist because of his work, assisted by Yuan Fuli, on the excavation of a Yangshao culture site at Xiyin, Xiaxian, Shanxi, in late 1926. The Anyang excavations continued for fifteen seasons from 1928 to 1937. With Li Ji's arrival at the Anyang project in the second season, the team began to pay attention to stratigraphic sequences of remains, traces of pits, tombs and buildings.[44] Numerous artifacts and oracle bones, architectural foundations made of pounded earth, sites of Shang palaces and temples, and Shang royal mausoleums, were excavated.

The Anyang team continued to meet with success. Liang Siyong (1904–1954), son of Liang Qichao and the earliest academically trained Chinese field archaeologist (in the strictest sense of the word) joined the Anyang team in 1931. He discerned that the Shang culture was later than the Longshan culture, and the Longshan culture later than the Yangshao culture, by distinguishing the three stratigraphic orders of the Yangshao, Longshan, and Shang at Hougang, Anyang, in the same year.[45] During the 1934–1935 seasons, Liang headed the excavations of eleven Shang royal tombs (one unfinished) at Xibeigang, Anyang. These excavations were the culmination of the Anyang undertaking, not only because its team was the best organized and engaged five hundred workers per day (a record high), but also — and more important — because of its discovery of structures, scales, and burials of the mausoleums.[46] The Anyang excavations confirmed that the Yinxu at Anyang was the true Late Shang capital, and also that Chinese archaeology had come to be guided by Chinese archaeologists.

In the early 1920s, Emile Licent (French, 1876–1952) and Pierre Teilhard de Chardin uncovered three palaeolithic sites at Ningxia, Shaanxi, and Inner Mongolia, including the Ordos Man (a human incisor) and thousands of stone implements.[47] Wu Jinding (Chinese, 1901–1948) found the Longshan culture at Longshan, Licheng, Shandong, in 1928[48] — a discovery that immediately inspired the investigation of the relationship among the Yangshao, Shang, and Longshan cultures. In 1936–1937, Shi Xigeng (Chinese, 1912–1939) of the Xihu Museum unearthed black pottery and jade and stone objects at Liangzhu, Hangxian (currently Yuhang), Zhejiang. Shi's classification of the Liangzhu as the Longshan culture was accepted by scholars at that time[49]; since 1959, archaeologists have identified these remains as those of the Liangzhu culture. In 1945, Xia Nai (Chinese, 1910–1985) corrected Andersson's sequence of prehistoric cultures in the upper Yellow River valley. Through his fieldwork and analysis of data Xia demonstrated that the Qijia culture was later than the Yangshao culture.[50] This achievement presaged his critical role in Chinese archaeology from the 1950s to the 1980s.

In 1928, the Central Committee of Antiquities Preservation was established, charged with

Site photograph of the 1935 excavations at Tomb 1001 (Shang dynasty), Houjiazhuang, Anyang, Henan province. Courtesy of the Institute of History and Philology, Academia Sinica, Taipei.

the protection of ancient cultural relics and the prevention of unauthorized digging. Its enforcement authority was strengthened by the enactment in 1930 of the Law on the Preservation of Antiquities and by the promulgation in 1931 of regulations concerning the excavation and export of antiquities.[51]

During the formation period, Chinese and foreign archaeologists, guided by their convictions that the origins of Chinese culture were to be found in the environs of the Yellow River — or, alternatively, that Chinese culture was originally transmitted from the West — concentrated most of their efforts on the Yellow River valley and on northern China. "Palaeolithic" and "Neolithic" were accepted as designations for China's early periods, a usage that has continued to the present day.[52] Human and institutional resources were decidedly limited: fewer than twenty professional archaelogists were engaged in fieldwork through the whole of China. The formation of Chinese archaeology, however, benefited significantly from the training of its practitioners in the West, as well as from the work of the leading international specialists.[53]

Between 1937 and 1949, large-scale excavations by Chinese archaeologists were suspended as a result of the Japanese occupation and civil war in China. Some archaeological activities such as surveys continued in the northwestern and southwestern regions. While Japanese archaeologists took advantage of the occupation to render excavation-site surveys from northeastern China to Taiwan, Western scholars were forced to withdraw from Chinese archaeology for a period.[54]

1949–1976: INSTITUTIONALIZATION

When the People's Republic of China was formed in October 1949, archaeological work was reenergized. Administration, excavation, research, and education were systematized and gradually extended nationwide. Since 1950, Chinese archaeology has been a state-regulated enterprise with steady, though modest, financial support from the government. Guo Moruo (Chinese, 1892–1978) launched these initiatives, while Xia Nai implemented them.

Guo Moruo, a renowned man of letters and a leading spirit of Chinese history, literature, and epigraphy (all mastered by self-study), was more than a patron of archaeology. Vice Premier of the State Council and President of the Chinese Academy of Sciences from 1950 until 1978, he proposed and received approval from Premier Zhou Enlai (1898–1976) to establish the Bureau of Cultural Relics (now the State Bureau of Cultural Relics) under the Ministry of Culture. He also proposed an Institute of Archaeology under the Academy, which became part of the Chinese Academy of Social Sciences in 1977. Both were established in 1949 and 1950.[55] The former is the government branch that administers the affairs of archaeologists and museums, while the latter is the national academic agency for excavation and research. Zheng Zhenduo (Chinese, 1898–1958), a noted scholar, was the founding director of both.[56] Guo also selected Liang Siyong and Xia Nai as deputy directors for the Institute of Archaeology. Zheng, who was not a field archaeologist, devoted himself to the administration of archaeological affairs until his death in 1958 (Liang, incapacitated by severe tuberculosis, had died in 1954). In 1962 Xia became director of the institute by default but emerged as a major policymaker from the 1950s through the mid-1980s.

Xia Nai had been an intern under Liang Siyong in field archaeology during the Anyang excavations and had studied at the University of London from 1935 to 1939. There, one of his advisors was Mortimer Wheeler (British, 1890–1977). Liang's studies abroad greatly benefited him later.[57]

When Xia assumed the leadership of the Institute in 1950, he quickly organized and dispatched a team of his young protégés to Huixian, Henan province, in the Yellow River valley. Xia taught each one how to conduct field work, and in the depths of winter he personally excavated remains of nineteen chariots dated to the Warring States period (475–221 BCE) — an exceedingly laborious and intricate task. Xia cultivated a generation of core archaeologists for the institute while continuing to achieve such discoveries as the Shang culture remains at Huixian and Zhengzhou, both in Henan province, which antedated those from Anyang. Features of Chu tombs in Changsha, Hunan province, were preliminarily observed through large-scale excavations that laid the foundation for further research into Chu culture.[58] These projects expanded our knowledge of the sequence and regional distribution of the Shang culture and extended controlled archaeological excavations into the Yangzi River reaches. From the 1950s through the 1970s, under the direction of Xia, the Institute was at the center of most major archaeological excavations.

In the early 1980s, Xia Nai was the greatest authority in Chinese archaeology, and I was inspired by his gentle, amiable, and approachable manner. A man of principle and integrity, he did not hesitate to state his beliefs or even to oppose his supervisors or high government officials. The story of the excavation from 1956 to 1958 of one of the imperial mausoleums of the

Ming dynasty (1368–1644) near Beijing is often related. Wu Han (1909–1969), vice mayor of Beijing and a famed historian of Ming history, had proposed to excavate the mausoleums but was rebuffed by Zheng Zhenduo and Xia Nai. Wu was insistent, and eventually the excavation plan of the Wanli mausoleum was approved by the State Council. Xia Nai headed the assignment, unwillingly. The excavation ultimately confirmed Xia's belief that existing conditions presented a major impediment to excavation, and the plan to excavate the largest of the Ming mausoleums was abandoned. In 1961, the State Council forbade excavation of imperial tombs on the basis of Xia's reports. Later, Guo Moruo wanted to excavate a Tang dynasty mausoleum, but when Xia Nai objected, Moruo capitulated. Xia frequently exhorted colleagues not to be motivated by the possibility of exhuming treasures. Although settlements or residential sites often contained only pottery fragments, their research value often surpassed that of many tombs. The achievement of an archaeologist, Xia argued, should be measured not by what has been recovered but rather by how the site has been excavated.[59] Xia's words still guide archaeological practices today.

In the 1950s, Marxism-Leninism-Mao Zedong Thought became the mandatory theoretical guideline for Chinese archaeology. Marxist historical materialism and the social evolutionary model proposed by anthropologist Lewis Henry Morgan (American, 1818–1881)[60] and further elaborated by Friedrich Engels (German, 1820–1895)[61] informed the interpretations of archaeological data. (Guo Moruo had in fact advocated Marxist historical materialism and Morgan's theory long before 1949.) In 1930, Guo published *A Study of Ancient Chinese Society (Zhongguo gudai shehui yanjiu)*, the first scholarly interpretation of ancient Chinese history under the Marxist model of social evolution with an emphasis on the forces and relations of production. Adapting Engels' and Morgan's ideas, Guo classified ancient China as having primitive, successive slave societies.[62] Guo's fresh approach not only won recognition from academic circles but dominated archaeological studies from 1949 until very recently.[63] Marxist historical materialism captivated archaeologists because it proposed that social development was the consequence of techno-economic and techno-environmental evolution, data manifested in archaeological findings.

The politicization of archaeological research during this period did not change the data, and dicta of Morgan, Engels, or Mao Zedong (1893–1976) were often confined to conclusions or interpretations. One of the paradigms was the attempt to match archaeological discoveries to the Marxist model of kinship and social organization, such as matriarchal or patrilineal societies, and no one dared to criticize these efforts. Overall, the objective description and analysis of archaeological data were not affected, as Chinese archaeologists continued to study the typology, stratigraphy, and chronology of cultures—an approach that originated in traditional historiography.[64]

Yet, between 1949 and the early 1970s, no practical or theoretical exchanges took place between China and the West. Scholarly and cultural dialogues between Chinese and foreign archaeologists were scarce and superficial if they occurred at all. Except for a brief period when China and its archaeologists were in the Soviet orbit during the 1950s, they were isolated from developed nations in the West. All progress depended upon Xia Nai and archaeologists of his generation, as well as the younger generation of archaeologists.

In 1952, Peking (Beijing) University established the Archaeological Specialization or Division (called the Department of Archaeology since 1983) under the Department of History, built upon the foundation established as early as 1922 under the leadership of Ma Heng (1881–1955), an epigrapher. Ma and his colleagues organized archaeological surveys and excavations during the 1920s and 1930s, but as his expertise was not field work, systematic and professional field training was not offered until 1952.[65]

As the training of an archaeologist takes at least four years, formal university programs could not satisfy the immediate demand for more archaeologists in the field. Trained archaeologists were needed for rescue excavations engendered by the nationwide large-scale construction of railways, roads, irrigation works, canals, reservoirs, factories, and buildings. Accordingly, the Institute of Archaeology, Peking (Beijing) University, and the State Bureau of Cultural Relics jointly organized a series of accelerated courses — two months in the classroom and two months of fieldwork — and from 1952 to 1955 aspiring archaeologists were trained in this way. During the four years of short-term training courses, 341 students were selected from all over China. They returned to their original locations or provinces after graduation.[66] Many served as core archaeologists and leaders of provincial and local institutions until their retirement. These archaeologists were nicknamed "Huangpu classes," a reference to the Huangpu (Whampoa) Military Academy (1923–1930) located at Huangpu, Guangzhou City. During the early twentieth century, most senior school-trained generals were educated at this school and later served in the armies of the Nationalist and Communist parties of China.[67]

American-style anthropology, encompassing archaeology, physical anthropology, cultural anthropology, art history, and linguistics, was not encouraged until 1980. Until then, archaeology and ethnology were regarded as separate disciplines and taught in different university departments;[68] Chinese academic officials considered archaeology an essential constituent of the science of history rather than the science of anthropology.[69]

Eventually an efficient network for administration and research was established in China. In addition to the State Bureau of Cultural Relics and the Institute of Archaeology, another national archaeological research agency, the Institute of Vertebrate Palaeontology and Palaeoanthropology, was established under the Chinese Academy of Sciences. It became responsible for palaeolithic archaeology. Archaeological teams in the provinces, autonomous regions, and special municipalities (hereafter collectively called "provinces") were formed in affiliation with either a provincial museum, cultural bureau, or cultural relics administrative commission. Departments of cultural relics, organized under the provincial cultural bureaus, were established in many cities and prefectures. When it was revealed that cultural relics had

Bronze canister with gilt bronze rider; height 50 (19 ⅝); Western Han dynasty; excavated in 1956 from Tomb 10, Shizhaishan, Jinning, Yunnan province *(left)*.

Silk banner; length c. 212 (83 ½); Han dynasty; excavated in 1972 from Tomb 1, Mawangdui, Changsha, Hunan province *(right)*.

been discovered accidentally in some localities, regional authorities were given the responsibility for reporting and collecting discoveries and archaeological materials found by farmers, construction workers, and surveyors. They also participated in excavations, although the more important field excavations were directed by the Beijing-based institutions. Over several decades, the network for administration has evolved, and now also provides locations for the study, preservation, and display of cultural properties.

In 1950, the State Council issued provisional statutory measures prohibiting the unauthorized excavation and export of precious cultural relics, including works of art and rare books. In 1953, the Council further required that all ancient tombs and sites discovered during construction be excavated by teams operating under the authority of the State Bureau of Cultural Relics and the Chinese Academy of Sciences.[70] As a result of effective and strict enforcement, smuggling and the illegal export of artifacts almost ceased between the 1950s and early 1970s. Archaeologists were able to work without fear of interference by intruders or plunderers.

Cultural relics, especially those already above ground and those in private collections, were hardly exempt from politics, though. Many works of art were lost, particularly during the

Cultural Revolution (1966–1976).[71] For example, the Ming dynasty city walls of Beijing were demolished between the 1950s and the early 1970s, despite the outcry of scholars, in order to widen roads and build new construction. Protests by Liang Sicheng (Chinese, 1901–1972), a leading authority on ancient architecture and elder brother of Liang Siyong, were ignored.[72]

Still, beginning in the 1950s, the Chinese government subsidized archaeological publications, including monographs and three major periodicals: *Wenwu (Cultural Relics)*, *Kaogu (Archaeology)*, and *Kaogu xuebao (Acta Archaeologica Sinica)*. The first is produced by the Wenwu Press (Cultural Relics Press) with the State Bureau's sponsorship, while the latter two are published by the Institute of Archaeology. These journals ensure the promulgation of research and data of archaeological discoveries and works of art, and are the most prominent and scholarly national journals on the subject today. Archaeologists refer to them as the "Three Great Magazines." In 1966, however, publication was suspended. In 1972 publication resumed, with Zhou Enlai's permission, and at Guo Moruo's request.[73]

While the metropolitan centers of the ancient Chinese dynasties remained the preeminent planned archaeological projects (field stations of the Institute of Archaeology were established in the region of the Yellow River capitals — in particular, in the precincts of Anyang, Luoyang, and Xi'an), archaeological activities occurred in nearly all of China's provinces.[74] With the resumption of palaeolithic archaelogy in 1949 at the Zhoukoudian site, new hominid fossils and cultural remains from all periods continued to be discovered throughout China, at Yuanmou, Yunnan; Liujiang, Guangxi; Lantian, Shaanxi; Dingcun, Shanxi; and even in Tibet.[75] Neolithic archaeologists refined prehistoric chronology in the Yellow River valley, while also obtaining fresh knowledge of the Yangzi River basin by unearthing cultural remains at Daxi (4400–3300 BCE), Qujialing (3000–2600 BCE), and Songze (3900–3300 BCE).[76] The 10,000-square-meter excavation of the moated Yangshao culture village at Banpo, Xi'an, and the 5400-square-meter excavation of the Dawenkou culture (4300–2500 BCE) cemetery at Dawenkou, Tai'an, Shandong, expanded knowledge of social and material life and the patterns of settlements in northern China.[77] Across the Taiwan Straits, several prehistoric vestiges were excavated, and were found to share, with cultures in other southeast provinces of Fujian, Guangdong, and Jiangxi a tradition of coarse cord-marked pottery.[78]

Besides the discovery of the Early Shang culture at Erligang in Zhengzhou, a Bronze Age culture that antedated the Erligang was found at Erlitou, Yanshi, Henan province, in 1959.[79] This find supplied a missing link between the Shang dynasty and prehistoric China. Many scholars now believe that the Erlitou culture was the relic of the first historiographical Chinese dynasty, Xia (c. 2000–1500 century BCE). An idiosyncratic Bronze Age culture (c. the fifth BCE to first century CE), strikingly different from the Yellow River cultures, was uncovered in the Dianchi Lake area, Yunnan province, in southwestern China.[80] Its sculptural bronzes revealed the daily and ritual life, economy, custom, and other social aspects of the Dian people. Ancient capitals from the Eastern Zhou to the Yuan dynasties, at Luoyang, Xi'an, and Beijing, were surveyed and excavated, and ancient cities, architectural plans, scales, and technology were documented, all since the 1950s.[81]

Although planned archaeological activities were infrequent or sporadic during the Cultural Revolution, extraordinary accidental discoveries and rescue excavations continued to occur. The jade shrouds from the tombs of Prince Liu Sheng and his wife at Mancheng, Hebei (second century BCE); a bronze galloping horse from Leitai, Wuwei, Gansu (186 CE); an almost intact corpse of a noblewoman, textiles, silk paintings and documents, and lacquers from Mawangdui, Changsha, Hunan (second century BCE); and the life-size terra-cotta army from the burial pits (third century BCE) near the First Emperor's mausoleum at Lintong, Shaanxi, were all unexpected discoveries.[82] These finds confirmed the prodigious capability of the ancient Chinese people to create astonishing works of art. Gradually, exhibitions were organized and sent abroad, beginning in 1972. These have attracted huge numbers of visitors, and have increased interest in and understanding of Chinese culture and art. Perhaps more important, such exhibitions heralded China's eventual reopening to the world.

1977 TO THE PRESENT: MATURATION

The arrest of the Gang of Four in late 1976 marked the end of the Cultural Revolution.[83] In the wake of sweeping reforms initiated by Deng Xiaoping (1905–1997), China has fundamentally changed. Under this favorable climate, archaeology in China has achieved maturity, owing in part to the diverse means of scientific chronometric dating (and particularly the full utilization of radiocarbon and carbon-14 dating techniques).

In 1977, Xia Nai used the information provided by carbon-14 dating to produce a chronological framework for prehistoric cultures in seven regional clusters. He substantiated his 1962 thesis that several cultural systems had coexisted in the Yellow River and Yangzi River areas — rice cultures flourished in the south, and millet cultures in the north.[84] In 1984, Xia further suggested that a sophisticated and highly stratified society had emerged prior to the Shang period (and no later than the Erlitou period).[85] Xia spurred rethinking of when, how, why, and from where Chinese civilization was formed and developed. Xia Nai's 1977 study had recourse to a mere ninety-four items dated by radiocarbon analysis; by 1991, radiocarbon dates had been established for more than 2,100 objects.[86] Chronometric dating techniques other than radiocarbon dating — amino-acid racemization, archaeomagnetism, dendrochronology, fission track, obsidian hydration, potassium-argon, thermoluminescence, and uramium series — began to be employed.

Epochal archaeological discoveries of early and middle Neolithic cultures in the Yellow River watershed and the lower Yangzi River delta were realized in the 1970s. In the north, Neolithic cultures dated to the sixth millennium BCE were excavated at Dadiwan, Qin'an, Gansu province; Peiligang, Xinzheng, Henan province; and Cishan, Wuan, Hebei province.[87]

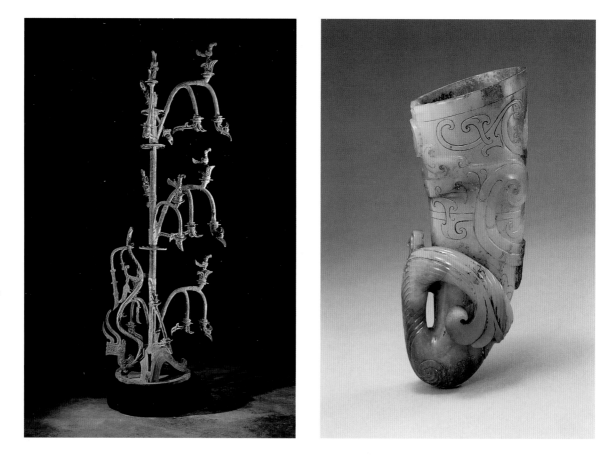

Bronze spirit tree; height 384 (151 ⅛); Shang dynasty; excavated in 1986 from Pit 1 at Sanxingdui, Guanghan, Sichuan province *(left)*.

Jade rhyton; height 19.4 (7 ¼); Western Han dynasty; excavated in 1983 from the tomb of the King of Nanyue at Xianggang, Guangzhou, Guangdong province *(right)*.

In the meantime, another culture that had existed between the sixth and fifth millennia BCE (c. 5400 - 4400 BCE) was unearthed at Beixin, Tengxian, Shandong province.[88] These relics of millet-based cultures have been universally recognized as predecessors of the Yangshao and Dawenkou cultures. In the south, cultural remains from 5000 to 3300 BCE, which seem to parallel those of the Yangshao culture, were excavated at Hemudu, Yuyao, Zhejiang province.[89] This rice-based culture is extraordinary because of its bone tools and above-ground log houses constructed with mortise-and-tenon joints.

Beginning in 1981, Su Bingqi (1909 – 1997) identified at least six major independent co-evolving regional traditions throughout prehistoric China, and proposed that "archaic cities" and "archaic states" had emerged during the late prehistoric period.[90] Since then, the concept of coexisting and interactive multicultural sequences has emerged as a prevalent theoretical approach in contemporary archaeology. Founding chair of the Archaeology Specialization (now Department of Archaeology) at Beijing University, Su Bingqi was also an esteemed typologist of ancient pottery. He was capable of picking up random pot sherds and immediately identifying each by culture, utilizing touch alone. During my last visit with him in Beijing, in October 1996, he discussed topics ranging from the formation of the "Chinese archaeological school" to his optimistic prospects for future Chinese archaeology.[91]

During the 1980s, Jilin, Nanjing, Shandong, Shanxi, Sichuan, Wuhan, Xibei, and Zhengzhou universities added an Archaeological Specialization within their departments of history. Jilin University established a Department of Archaeology in 1988. Zhongshan and Xiamen Universities in southern China also established archaeological programs, although they are contained within their departments of anthropology, as they tend to be in the United States. Political connections are no longer prerequisites to participation in intellectual endeavors. Various schools and theories of archaeology have been introduced from the West and discussed in China.[92] Chinese archaeologists and students are eager to embrace the ideas, theories, methodologies, and trends followed by archaeologists from other countries.

The Cultural Relics Law of China was promulgated in 1982, and in the years since, excavations have benefited from protection by Chinese law. By the 1990s, most provinces had established institutes of archaeology independent of parent museums or cultural relics administrative commissions. More than one thousand professional archaeologists are employed by archaeological institutions and universities throughout China. Several large and important projects have been staffed by archaeologists associated with provincial and city institutions. They have developed techniques to preserve excavated artifacts such as the bamboo and wood articles, costumes, and silk paintings and documents from the Mawangdui Han tombs; lacquer and textiles from the Mashan grave of the Warring States period (cats. 111–112); and lacquer from the tomb of Marquis Yi of the Zeng state (cats. 107–109).[93]

Social reform and administrative decentralization since 1980 have created opportunities for archaeologists to publish outside of the "Three Great Magazines," and periodicals published by the provincial institutions, with a regional focus or specialization, have flourished. *Nongye kaogu (Agricultural archaeology)* has been published in Jianxi province since 1981; a national gazette, *Zhongguo wenwubao (China Culture and Relics Newspaper)*, instituted in 1986, focuses on archaeology and museums.[94]

Prompted by the discovery and subsequent sale of a quantity of Ming dynasty porcelain discovered under the South China Sea in 1986, a unit of underwater archaeology was created by the Museum of Chinese History in 1987. Japanese specialists were invited to China to give lectures; Chinese archaeologists were sent to Holland, Japan, and the United States to study related techniques. In 1989, a Sino-Japanese team conducted an underwater archaeological survey of a shipwreck near Taishan, Guangdong province.[95] Proposals for joint archaeological ventures have been advanced by both Chinese and non-Chinese archaeologists.

On 22 February 1991, the State Bureau of Cultural Relics adopted twenty-two regulatory articles governing cooperative archaeological investigations. Having been prohibited from participating in archaeological work for more than forty years, American, British, Canadian, French, Israeli, Japanese, and Korean archaeologists, specialists, and students are once again working in China on projects investigating the palaeolithic through dynastic periods.[96] Experts in archaeology, archaeobotany, archaeozoology, archaeological conservation, geomorphology, palynology, physical anthropology, remote sensing, and topography have worked together, employing geological coring, electrical resistivity, the Fourier Transform Infrared spectrometer, ground-penetrating radar, the Geographic Information System, the Global Positioning System, proton magnetomerty, aerial and satellite image analysis, botanical specimens through soil flotation, chemical analyses, faunal remains analysis, collection and analysis of phytoliths, isotopic analysis of ancient human bone, micromorphological analysis, mineralogical analysis, and uranium-series dating. Investigations are continuing on early hominid populations, distribution, chronology, and behavior; the distribution of microlithic sites; prehistoric diet, settlement and subsistence patterns; the evolution of landscape and topography; climatic and environmental variations; cultural adaptations and tool technologies; the commencement and development of sophisticated societies; the origins and evolution of rice agriculture; early Bronze Age sites; early Shang civilization; and prehistoric and ancient cultural interaction between East and West in the pivotal region of Xinjiang province. Archaeological collaborations have extended into conservation and restoration. Among the great achievements of the past decade are discoveries of hominid occupation of China around one million years ago; early domesticated rice cultures; prehistoric walled towns; and the earliest known Buddhist sanctuaries.[97]

Our knowledge of ancient China, once purely speculative, is now based on a systematic, scientific history encompassing nearly two million years. Two male *Homo sapiens*, one a well-preserved cranium unearthed at Dali, Shaanxi province, in 1978, another a relatively complete human fossil, including the cranium dated to 280,000 BP were found at Jinniushan, Yingkou, Liaoning province, in 1984.[98] The two finds provided data on the transition from *Homo erectus* to *Homo sapiens*. For the late prehistoric period, the momentous discoveries of jade works of the Liangzhu culture (cats. 29 – 36) in the lower Yangzi delta and of the Hongshan culture (cats. 10 – 22) in northeastern China have revealed a high level of skill in the crafting of hardstone materials, and corroborated the theory that Chinese civilization arose in many places. Along with the Taosi and Shandong Longshan, these cultures employed stratified burials (cats. 24 – 28). Additional evidence of walled towns and pictographs (cat. 23) has led many scholars to believe that China emerged as a state-organized society in the third millennium BCE.[99]

The great historian Sima Qian (c. 145 – 86 BCE) documented dynastic China from the Xia dynasty (c. 2100 BCE) to his era, but he was unable to reconstruct a year-to-year chronology prior to 841 BCE. Archaeological finds have now made it possible to create a temporal and spatial framework of early bronze cultures that corresponds with the first "Three Dynasties" (Xia, Shang, and Zhou). A very early Shang city located at Shixianggou, Yanshi, Henan province, provides crucial information to ascertain the nature of the Erlitou culture and the distinction between Xia and Shang.[100] Modern archaeology has revealed, in areas traditionally described as backward, advanced and complex cultures that created objects of surpassing beauty. This is perhaps most evident in the works included here from the Yangzi River watershed (cats. 57 – 75).[101] The extraordinary bronze figures, masks, human heads, and spirit trees from Sanxingdui, Guanghan, Sichuan province, and Dayangzhou, Xin'gan, Jiangxi province, are unlike those found in the Shang metropolitan or the Yellow River area, but, almost all contemporaneous bronze cultures shared the Shang dynastic ritual bronze vessels and motifs.[102]

The material and artistic features of ancient Chinese cultures were poorly described in historical documents. The record was silent on the huge underground terra-cotta army of the First Emperor of the Qin dynasty (221 – 206 BCE). Today, however, Song dynasty paintings can be compared with their excavated antecedents, which date more than one thousand years

Excavation photograph of Tomb 1, Mawangdui, Changsha, Hunan province, showing submerged wooden figurines and lacquer vases. The tomb (which dates to the Western Han dynasty) was excavated in 1972.

earlier.[103] Ming dynasty porcelain can be traced back to glazed ceramic antecedents from the eleventh century BCE. The set of sixty-five bronze bells from the tomb of Marquis Yi of the Zeng state, with a range of move than five octaves of twelve semi-tones each, rivals a modern-day piano.[104] Archaeology in China, moreover, is not limited to underground excavations: archaeological techniques have been applied to the study of Buddhist caves and works of art in Xingjiang, Central China, and Tibet, in order to establish their regional and temporal distributions.

The progress of Chinese archaeology over the last hundred years mirrors the opening of twentieth-century China; it has opened to view the richest and most abundant cultural remains in the world. Yet the ancestral legacies revealed by archaeology are finite, and great care must be exercised, regardless of other considerations, in the practice of archaeology. Ensuring the well-being of Chinese archaeology in the twenty-first century will require overcoming some grave obstacles, such as organized looting and smuggling of archaeological treasures.[106] Archaeologists have achieved great things in times of prosperity as well as turmoil. The future of Chinese archaeology, too, is certain to be fruitful.

1 The *jin shi xue* was formally established during the Northern Song dynasty (960–1127). See Wei 1937; and Rudolph 1963. Although early antiquarian activities in China are often treated as "archaeology," in this article the term is used narrowly to describe scientific excavations and surveys, as well as related research, undertaken since the late nineteenth century.

2 Roman, Greek, and Egyptian archaeology were established earlier than Chinese archaeology; for related history, see Daniel 1975.

3 For discoveries of oracle-bone inscriptions, see Li Ji 1977, 3–31; for a related comprehensive study, see Keightley 1978. For the Dunhuang discoveries, see Chavannes 1913; Pelliot 1920–1924; Waley 1931; Luo 1914; and Whitfield 1982–1985.

4 Chinese academics generally consider the *jin shi xue* the predecessor of Chinese archaeology. See Xia 1979; Xia and Wang 1986; and Wang 1986.

5 These include the Japanese invasion and the Second World War (1937–1945), the Civil War (1945–1949), the Anti–Rightists Campaign (1957–1958), and the Cultural Revolution (1966–1976). For accounts of modern Chinese history and related events, see Fairbank and Feuerwerker 1986, 519–550; MacFarquhar and Fairbank 1987, 138–152, 253–258; and 1991.

6 Since the late 1970s, people in the field have termed the present stage of Chinese archaeology the "Golden Age." For example, see Chang 1977, 623; Zhongguo 1984b; and Dien 1999.

7 For related history and social background, see Fairbank 1978 and 1983.

8 The May Fourth Movement originated with a Beijing University student demonstration against a treaty signed by the Beijing leadership that favored foreign interests. It soon developed into a movement against imperialism and feudalism and generated the New Culture Campaign, which sought to reassess the Chinese cultural and intellectual heritage while advocating Western science and democracy. During this period, classical language and writing were superseded by the vernacular. For Western and Marxist views of the May Fourth movement and phenomenon, see Hua 1952; Chow 1960; Lin, 1978; and Fairbank 1983, 464–504.

9 Liang 1959, 8. For contributions of other Chinese scholars during that period, see Yu 1983. For Liang Qichao's history, thought and scholarship, see Levenson 1959; Chang 1971; and Huang 1972.

10 Several foreign expeditions can be traced back to the mid-nineteenth century. For instance, John Andersson, an Englishman who worked in India, went to Yunnan province and collected some polished stone objects around 1860. See Andersson 1871.

11 Torri 1910.

12 For more detailed accounts, see Mizuno, 1948, 6–37; and Chen 1997, 43–45.

13 For a comprehensive account of the foreign expeditions, see Hopkirk 1980.

14 For Stein's accomplishments, see Stein 1907, 1912, 1921, 1928, and 1933; and Mirsky 1977.

15 Waley 1931; and Whitfield 1982–1985.

16 Pelliot 1920–1924; and Giès and Cohen 1995.

17 For accounts of Warner's activities, see Bowie, 1966, 114–122, and Hopkirk 1980, 209–222. Russian archaeologists as well removed works of art in the course of their expeditions during the late nineteenth and early twentieth centuries. In 1898, D. Klementz organized the first Russian archaeological expedition to Turfan, Xinjiang. During this venture, he removed some wall paintings from temples. For this expedition's report, see Klementz 1899. In addition, Russian K. Koslov (1863–1935) went to Xinjiang, Qinghai, Tibet, and Inner Mongolia regions six times between 1883 to 1926. His most important achievement was the discovery and excavation of the ancient cities at Heicheng, Inner Mongolia, in 1907–1909. Meanwhile, he took more than eleven thousand pieces of manuscript and works of art to Russia; they are now in the collections of the Institute of Oriental Studies and the State Hermitage Museum. Between 1902 and 1914, the German Albert von Le Coq (1860–1930) went to Xinjiang. He collected and removed many documents, frescoes, and sculptures and took them to Germany. Many were destroyed during the Second World War. See Hopkirk 1980, 114–146, 200–202, and 229–231.

18 Hopkirk 1980, 223–227.

19 Hedin 1943–1945.

20 For Xu Bingxu's (Xu Xusheng) history and scholarship, see Huang 1981.

21 Xu 1931; and Hedin 1943–1945.

22 Yuan 1983. In fact, some objects remained in Sweden after related research was completed.

23 For the biography of V. K. Ting, see Hu 1956

24 Li Ji 1977, 35–48.

25 Luo 1910; Luo 1914; Wang 1959; and Zhongguo 1994, 1–6.

26 Xia 1979.

27 Andersson summarized his accomplishments in geology and palaeontology thus: "By a series of fortunate circumstances I was on several occasions the pioneer. In 1914 I was the first to stumble upon the organic origin of stromatolite ore. In 1918 I discovered the Collenia nodules and recognized their connection with similar 'fossils' in the pre-Cambrian area of North America. In the same year we discovered the first Hipparion field in China made known to science. In 1919 we found the beaver fauna at Ertemte in Mongolia." See Andersson 1934, foreword, xviii.

28 See Andersson 1934, xviii.

29 Pumpelly 1908. According to current knowledge, the cultural remains at Shaoguotun belong to the Hongshan and the post-Hongshan (Xiaoheyan culture) cultures. See Liaoning 1997d, 3–4.

30 Andersson 1923 and 1934, 163–187.

31 Andersson 1924, 18–20; 1934, 224–276; and 1943, 295.

32 Andersson 1934, 97; and 1943, 17–19.

33 For comprehensive evaluations of Andersson's scholarship, see Chen 1991a; and Zhang 1998.

34 Andersson stated that "I have a feeling that there lie here the remains of one of our ancestors and it is only a question of your finding him. Take your time and stick to it till the cave is emptied, if need be." See Andersson 1934, 101.

35 Grabau designated the discovery Peking Man. Black named it *Sinanthropus Pekinensis* after his exhaustive study in 1927. See Andersson 1934, 104; and Black 1927.

36 For reports of these discoveries, see Pei 1929 and 1931;

and Black 1931.

37 For the history of the Zhoukoudian discovery, see Andersson 1934, 94 – 126; and 1943, 20-26. Jia 1950.

38 For example, see Weidenreich 1936, 1937, 1939, and 1943.

39 For the archaeological contribution of Yuan Fuli, see An 1998.

40 Black 1925, 98; Andersson 1934, 331; and 1943, 32.

41 Gu 1926 – 1941, especially vol. 1, 1926.

42 Li Ji 1977, 49 – 54.

43 Li Ji 1977, 38.

44 Li Ji offered a detailed description of the Anyang excavations. See Li Ji 1977, 49 – 119.

45 Liang Siyong 1933.

46 For the formal archaeological reports of these excavations, see Liang and Gao 1962 – 1976.

47 Boule 1928; Andersson 1934, 146 – 155; and Teilhard de Chardin 1941.

48 This site was later excavated by the Archaeological Section during 1930–1931. See Wu 1930; and Li Ji 1934.

49 Shi 1938.

50 Xia 1948.

51 Shi 1993.

52 This distinction warrants continuation, since palaeolithic archaeology requires knowledge of geological stratigraphy and index fossils whereas knowledge of artifacts and cultural deposits are essential for Neolithic archaeology.

53 Besides those mentioned in the text, Henri-Édouard-Prosper Breuil (1877 – 1961), a prominent French archaeologist, studied Palaeolithic discoveries from Zhoukoudian and northern China. See Breuil 1931.

54 For more information, see Chen 1997, 264 – 275.

55 Xia 1978, 221; and 1982, 454.

56 For a brief biography of Zheng Zhenduo, see Xie 1993.

57 Throughout his life as a student, Xia's talent and diligence deeply impressed his advisor Stephen Glanville (1900 – 1956). In 1938, Glanville described Xia's prospects "I have not the least doubt that he is a man of real ability who will make a name for himself in China if he is ever allowed to work there again...." See Field and Wang 1997, especially 39.

58 Wang 1985, 408 – 409.

59 Wang 1985, 408 – 410.

60 For his evolutional series, see Morgan 1877.

61 Further explications are contained in his classic work, see Engels 1884.

62 For a detailed discussion on Guo's study, see Dirlik 1989, 137 – 179.

63 Tong 1995, 177 – 183.

64 Chang 1986a, 5 – 8; and Olsen 1987.

65 For a brief history of the Department of Archaeology, Beijing University, see Li 1995.

66 Guo, 1956, 6; and Zheng 1956, 10.

67 For a brief history of the Huangpu Military Academy, see Wang 1990.

68 For the situation of Chinese anthropology since the 1950s, see Guldin 1990, especially 3 – 29; and 1994.

69 Xia 1990.

70 Murphy 1995, 81 – 83 and 183 – 184.

71 For the history of the Cultural Revolution, see MacFarquar and Fairbank 1991.

72 Luo 1998, 296 – 305.

73 Xia 1978, 222.

74 For English summaries of archaeological discoveries during this period, see Chang 1977; and Watson 1981.

75 For more information, see Wu and Olsen 1985, especially 4 – 14.

76 Sichuan 1961; Shanghai 1962; and Zhongguo 1965b.

77 For example, see Zhongguo 1963; and Shandong 1974.

78 Chang 1969.

79 Henan 1959; and Zhongguo 1965c.

80 Yunnan 1959.

81 As a result of those excavations and surveys, see Zhongguo ziran 1985.

82 Zhongguo 1980b; Gansu 1974; Hunan 1973; and Shaanxi 1988b.

83 Mao Zedong's wife, Jiang Qing, together with her three closest partners, held great political power during the Cultural Revolution. For more information regarding the Gang of Four, see MacFarquhar and Fairbank 1991, 336 – 370.

84 Xia 1977. Xia Nai introduced the carbon–14 dating method to his Chinese colleagues in 1955, only a few years after its invention (see Xia 1955). In 1965, Xia built the first carbon–14 laboratory in China at the Institute of Archaeology.

85 Xia 1985, 79 – 101.

86 Zhongguo 1992.

87 Gansu 1983a, and 1983b; Kaifeng 1978; and Handan 1977.

88 Zhongguo Shandong 1984.

89 Zhejiang 1978; and Hemudu 1980.

90 Su and Yin 1981; Su 1984a, 225 – 234; 1986; 1991; and 1994, 236 – 251.

91 For the "Chinese archaeological school," see Su 1995. For more information on Su's contributions, see Wang 1997c; and Cao 1998.

92 A representative example was offered by Yu Weichao and Zhang Aibing. Their 1992 article treats ten theories and methodologies, including stratigraphy, environmentalism, settlement patterns, and metrology; see Yu and Zhang 1992.

93 Hunan 1973; Hubei 1985a; and Hubei 1989.

94 For a summary of these publications, see Falkenhausen 1992.

95 Zhang 1990a, 72 – 73.

96 Olsen 1992, 3 – 4; and Murphy 1995, 123 – 124, and 195.

97 For a comprehensive summary of recent Sino–foreign archaeological collaborations in China, see Murowchick 1997.

98 Wu and Olsen 1985, 91 – 106; and Wenwu 1990, 60.

99 For a summary of major views on this issue, see Zhongguo 1998b.

100 Wenwu 1990, 178 – 180.

101 Sichuan 1987b and 1989; Sichuan 1994; and Jiangxi 1997.

102 For more information, see Yang Xiaoneng 1999.

103 For silk paintings of the Warring States period and silk banners and paintings of the Western Han period, see Hunan 1983, pls. 52 – 53 and 79 – 86.

104 Hubei 1989, 1, 108 – 118.

105 Su 1996.

106 The activities of two gangs at Houma, Shanxi province, exemplify the serious looting and smuggling situation in China. See Yang 1997b. For related laws and enforcement, see Murphy 1994a and b, and 1995.

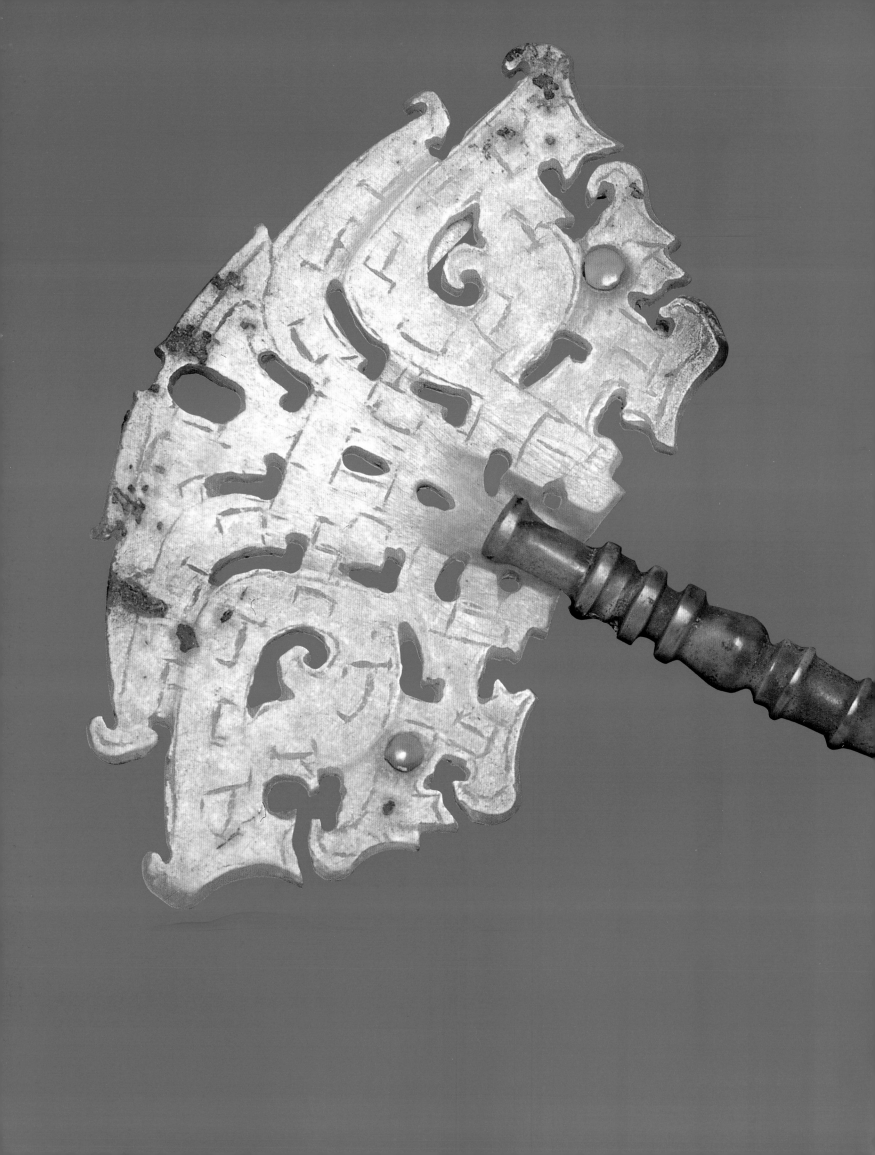

LATE PREHISTORIC CHINA

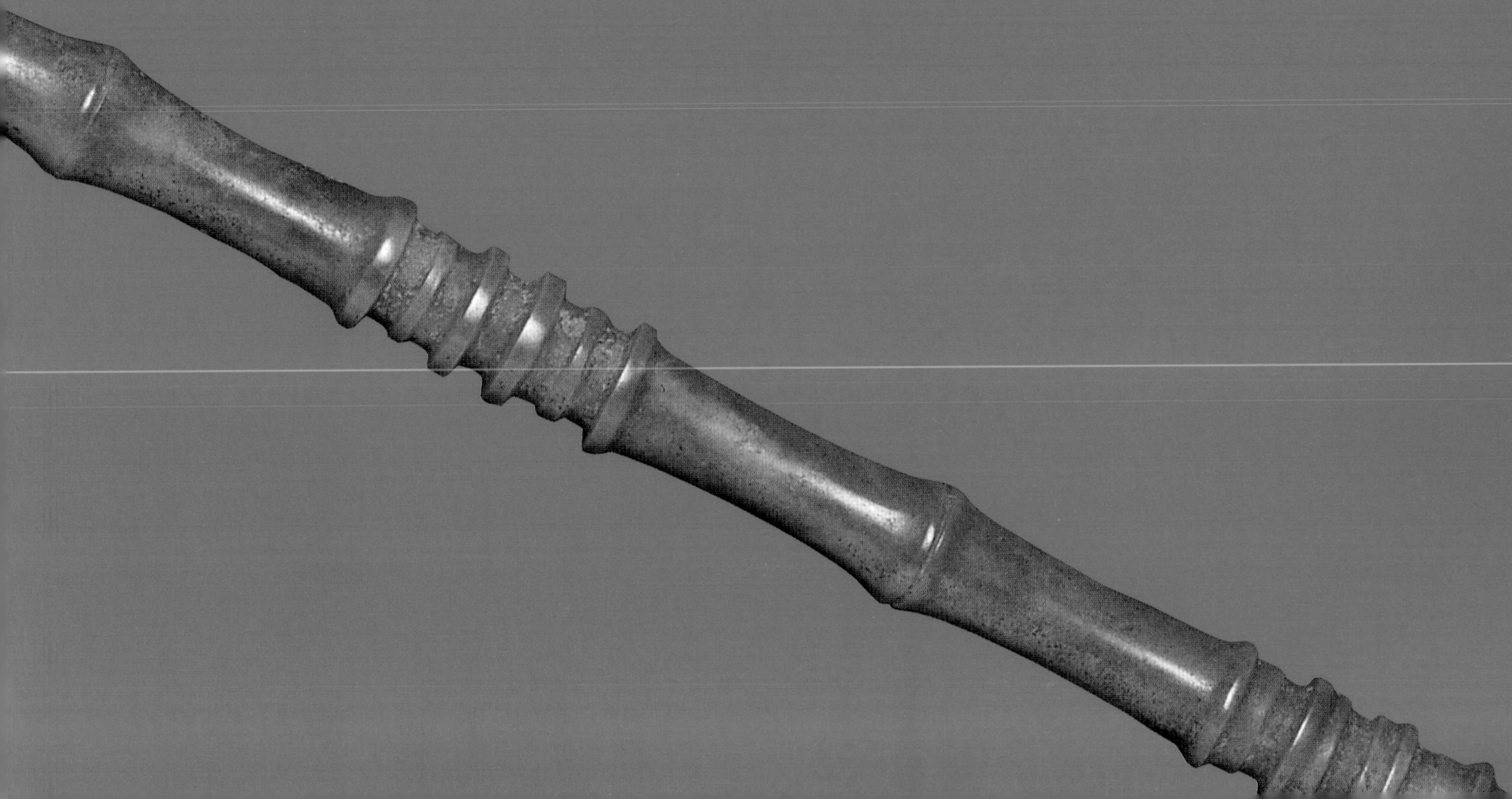

The Foundation of Chinese Civilization

LATE PREHISTORIC CHINA (C. 5000–2000 BCE)

Prior to the birth of modern Chinese archaeology, the best accounts of China's prehistory were the learned sagas contained in the *Shi ji* (Records of the historian) by Sima Qian (c. 145–86 BCE) or the narratives in the *Yue jue shu* (c. 40 CE) by Yuan Kang (c. first century CE). The latter mentions an Eastern Zhou philosopher who claimed that the Iron Age had been preceded by the Stone Age, the Jade Age, and the Bronze Age.[1] Few people took this four-fold periodization of human history seriously; most dismissed it as vagary, a position that was maintained even into the early twentieth century. In the 1910s, for example, the Japanese archeologist Torii Ryuzo discovered what we now know to be Neolithic artifacts in northeastern China but attributed their manufacture to "barbarian" peoples or minorities inhabiting the peripheries of China during the dynastic era.[2] Today, after nearly a century of archaeological investigations, we can discern a panorama of prehistoric China spanning nearly two million years. Surveys and excavations performed in the Yellow and Yangzi River regions and in northeastern China have yielded a framework of six coevolving regional traditions that ranges from the Neolithic to the Chalcolithic Age.

Five of these six regional traditions, representing the late stage of China's prehistory (c. 5000–2000 BCE), are represented in this exhibition. They comprise the following: in the middle Yellow River basin, the Yangshao culture, distinguished by its polychrome painted pottery (cats. 1–5), and one of its late continuations — the Taosi Longshan culture, with a distinctive painted ceramic style of its own (cats. 25–27); in the upper reaches of the Yellow River, the Majiayao culture (which also developed out of the Yangshao culture), whose splendid ceramics incorporate abstract and, more rarely, figural designs (cats. 6–9). The Dawenkou and Shandong Longshan cultures inhabited the lower Yellow River area; they are represented here by pottery incised with pictographs and elegant jadework (cats. 23–24). The Hongshan culture, manifested in its jades, a terra-cotta torso, and ceramics (cats. 10–22), was situated in northeastern China. The lower Yangzi River delta was peopled by the Liangzhu culture, associated with jades that feature exquisite miniature carvings (cats. 29–36). The last established nexus (not included in this exhibition) is in the middle Yangzi River basin, and its late-period culture, Shijiahe, produced well-known, small-scale animal and human sculptures in terracotta and jade.[3] These cultures, whose artifacts manifest distinctive characteristics, were the main forces in the formation of Chinese civilization; each bequeathed its heritage to the later dynastic cultures.

The most significant contributions of archaeology to our understanding of prehistoric China are the following: (1) in the absence of reliable written records, archaeology created a framework for the prehistory of China; (2) it established that the Chinese dynastic civilization did not originate solely in the Yellow River valley (as had previously been thought), but that it was formed by a confluence of cultures inhabiting the lands bordering the Yangzi River, northeastern China, and other areas. The peoples of each region, while interacting with those from

Cat. 30, detail

Terracotta head; height 22.5 (8⅞); Hongshan culture; excavated in 1983 from Niuheliang, Jianping, Liaoning province.

other regions, formed distinctive cultures—each at a different pace, certainly, but developing along similar trajectories.

The objects themselves do not allow us to distinguish the artistic superiority of one culture over another. Beginning in the fourth millennium BCE, jade was used extensively to make ritual objects, exemplified by the Hongshan culture in the north and the Liangzhu culture in the south. During roughly contemporaneous periods, monochrome pottery became prevalent in most regions, while polychrome ceramics flourished among the Majiayao and the Taosi Longshan cultures. The phenomenon of exchange among regional cultures is manifested in their works of art. Dragon motifs, for example, although they assumed diverse forms, were shared by the Hongshan, Taosi Longshan, and Liangzhu cultures (compare cats. 10, 25, and 35); animal masks appear in the Hongshan and Liangzhu cultures (compare cats. 13 and 29 – 30).[4]

Archaeology has demonstrated that these prehistoric cultures were more complex and interconnected than had previously been thought. Ceramics from the Jiahu site at Wuyang (Henan province) in the middle Yellow River region, dating to between 7000 and 5800 BCE, exhibit similarities to those of the Peiligang culture in the same area; the use of tortoise-shell and river deer (*Hydropotes inermis*) tusks among the Jiahu peoples is mirrored in objects of the Dawenkou culture in the region of the lower Yellow River; the cultivation of rice at Jiahu re-flects the influence of Yangzi River cultures.[5] This discovery challenged the conventional ap-proach of characterizing cultures by primary reliance on excavated artifacts.

Over time, the cultural position of the Central Plains (located in ancient "central" China)[6] became more prominent. The region's geographic advantages enabled the cultures that inhab-ited it to take on an increasingly assimilative and intermediary character during the course of China's prehistory. During that period, societies experienced fundamental changes, elaborated herein by Professor Zhang Zhongpei (pages 519–525). These changes ushered China into the dynastic era. XY

1   Sima Qian, juan 1 "Wu Di ben ji" in the *Shi ji* (for English translation and notes see Watson 1961); and Yuan Kang, juan 11 "Waizhuan ji baojian" in the *Yue jue shu.*
2   See Torii 1910.
3   See, for example, Yang Xiaoneng 1988.
4   For further discussion of this subject, see Yang Xiaoneng 1999.

5   Yu 1999.
6   The term "Central Plains," narrowly defined, corresponds to the present-day province of Henan. Under a broader definition, which we use here, it extends to the reaches of the middle and lower Yellow River.

During the fifth millennium BCE, all across northern China, along the fertile loess terraces bordering the Yellow and Wei Rivers and their tributaries, small Neolithic agricultural settlements were coming into being. These settlements belong to the Banpo culture, which takes its name from the site discovered in the early 1950s near the present-day city of Xi'an, in eastern Shaanxi province.

The Banpo people were not the first agriculturalists in this area, nor the first to make pottery. They were preceded in the sixth millennium by a cultural horizon of millet farmers who produced a distinctive corded-ware pottery. Many of the Banpo villages were built in exactly the same locations first occupied by their corded-ware predecessors, and there is sufficient similarity between these two cultural groups to suggest a degree of continuity between them.[1]

The Banpo culture belongs to a broad category of northern Neolithic cultures, called the Yangshao horizon, conventionally defined by their use of pottery with painted decoration. The Yangshao period lasted from the early fifth millennium until Longshan times, beginning in the early fourth millennium, when the production of painted wares came virtually to an end in north China. By the Longshan period, when undecorated gray wares were the ceramics of choice, other important cultural changes had taken place. The population had increased substantially beyond its level during Yangshao times, social organization had become more complex and more highly stratified, and for the first time we see evidence of strife among the settlements as they vied for more limited resources. Apart from Banpo, the Yangshao culture is represented in the exhibition by Majiayao vessels (cats. 6–9), and by a single, atypical example from the Dahecun phase in Henan (cat. 5).[2]

The three Banpo sites known in greatest detail are Banpocun; Jiangzhai at Lintong, not far from Xi'an; and Beishouling at Baoji in western Shaanxi province.[3] All three sites were occupied for long periods of time, and they must have been established landmarks, familiar to generations of Banpo people in their travels from one location to another. These villages covered areas as large as 50,000 square meters, and the layout of each was essentially the same. The main component was a dwelling area, usually surrounded by a ditch measuring about five meters wide and five meters deep. The houses within this area faced an open common at the center, where traces of animal pens have been discovered.

The houses themselves were either round or square in plan, and their foundations were constructed at ground level, or slightly below. The walls were of wattle and daub, and wooden posts supported their thatched roofs. Many had covered ramps leading to the interior. Inside was a central hearth, and in some cases banquettes made of clay were constructed along the inner walls. At Jiangzhai the houses were arranged in five clusters, each made up of a single large dwelling, about twenty meters square, surrounded by a number of smaller dwellings. According to K. C. Chang, this layout indicates that the village was organized according to lineage affiliation.[4]

The burial fields and the kilns were located outside the dwelling area, beyond the confines of the ditch. In the Jiangzhai cemetery, the archaeologists discovered close to fifty burials from the first Banpo phase, nearly all of them simple rectangular pits containing a single individual in dorsal position. Later, however, the burial procedure must have undergone a radical change. The majority of the three hundred Phase II graves were found to be secondary burials containing some twenty individuals, both male and female, of various ages, arranged neatly in rows. There are also rare cases where the remains seem to have been haphazardly tossed into the grave pit. Both primary and secondary burials are typical of the broader range of Banpo sites, as was the habit of burying infants, placed in pottery urns, close to their families in the dwelling area. The uniformly small number of grave goods that accompany the Banpo burials indicates a relative lack of rigid social stratification.

In fields peripheral to the settlements the inhabitants grew millet and vegetables. They relied on slash-and-burn agriculture, which entailed the progressive cutting away of the surrounding wooded areas to prepare new ground for cultivation. To supplement their diet, the Banpo people raised domesticated pigs and fished in the river; in the outlying wooded areas, they hunted wild animals. All these activities required the specialized production of stone and bone implements. The craft involving the highest level of specialization, however, was pottery making. Kilns have been found at all the major sites, and judging by the abundance of pottery at these settlements, they must have been frequently in use. Alone among the artifacts that have been preserved, the pottery provides an insight into the aesthetic sensibilities of the Banpo people.

Despite the very large numbers in which they have been found, the pottery vessels are confined to three basic types: tall, wide-mouthed jars tapering toward the base, which were used for storing grain; containers for liquids (large water jars, usually with a pointed bottom, requiring a stand of some sort, and smaller gourd-shaped flasks, possibly for millet ale); and, finally, bowls, as well as larger basins with everted rims.

Painted decoration is restricted almost entirely to the small number of vessels used at meals. The decoration was applied exclusively in black pigment, which contrasts with the reddish color of the ware. At the onset of the decorative tradition, the patterns were alternatively geometric, consisting mainly of multiple zigzag lines, used primarily for flasks, or composed of small, more or less realistic images of animals and fish, which are painted on the inner surfaces of bowls. The fish are often paired with mysterious masklike human faces, with fishlike appendages extending from the sides of their mouths. Subsequently, larger and progressively more stylized images of fish make their appearance on the outer surfaces of the bowls, and from then on, the interiors are left plain. In the final period, contorted versions of these stylized fish are added to the small flasks in sophisticated designs that leave the original image almost unrecognizable. In general, however, the key to an appreciation of the Banpo decorative style resides less in a perception of specific images, such as the fish or masklike faces, than in an awareness of the careful and eloquent balance of painted and unpainted surface and the configurations and elements of pure design thus engendered — characteristics inherent to this style since its beginning.

1

Painted pottery *hu* vessel

Height 15.6 (6), width 24.8 (9 ½)
Neolithic Period, Banpo Culture
(c. 4500 – 4000 BCE)
From Beishouling, Baoji, Shaanxi Province

The National Museum of Chinese History, Beijing

Like many of the Neolithic vessels included in this exhibition, which are exceptional either in shape or decoration, this water container is a rare and atypical form.[1] Water containers characteristic of the Banpo culture are normally shaped as jars with a narrow neck and flat base, or as tall, slender vessels that come to a point at the bottom. The present version is found at only a few Banpo sites in western Shaanxi province dating from an early phase in the culture's development.[2] While its cup-shaped mouth is in keeping with those on other water containers, the overall appearance of the vessel suggests that it was modeled on a sack-like container made of animal skin that was tied off at the two corners. Cords passing through the rounded lugs attached to the vessel's sloping shoulders enabled it to be lowered into the water and to be more easily transported.

The burnished reddish tan surface is decorated at the center by a rectangular field of intersecting diagonal lines painted in a brownish black pigment. Each of the lateral edges is bordered by a row

of triangles pointing outward. The pattern, which seems to take its inspiration from a woven fabric, is of special interest because it is among the earliest examples of Neolithic painted decoration.

The tradition of painted wares associated with the Banpo tradition (cats. 2–4) was preceded by another, almost equally widespread tradition of unpainted ceramics that lasted more than a millennium. The earliest evidence of painted decoration occurs at the end of this pre-Banpo phase in the form of a single band painted around the outer surface of small bowls beneath the mouth. Other patterns present from the beginning of the Banpo phase that may derive from woven materials include simple rows of zigzag lines, alternately painted and left in reserve.[3]

On the interiors of somewhat later bowls from the Xi'an site of Banpocun in eastern Shaanxi province, geometricized human faces with fishlike appendages sometimes appear with the images of fish or with small diamond-shaped fields filled with intersecting lines, which probably represent fishing nets.[4] It is unlikely, however, that the pattern on the present vessel had such a specific connotation. LF-H

1 Excavated in 1958 (M 98:3); published: Zhongguo 1983b, 100, fig. 82: 3; color pl. 2: 1; Yang 1991, 1, no. 7; Wenwu jinghua 1993, pl. 14, fig. 2; Zhang 1990b, cat. no. 1501.
2 This water container was recovered from a grave (M 98) in the middle stratum at Beishouling, identified as belonging to the early period in the Banpo culture. A second, undecorated vessel of the same type was unearthed from M 5 at the same site, but the stratigraphical position of this burial was uncertain. A third example, again without decoration, comes from an early Banpo burial (M 295) at Longgangsi, near Nancheng, south of Beishouling (Zhongguo 1983b, 161; pl. 52: 1; Shaanxi 1990, 123, fig. 87: 6; 167, fig. 109: 3; pl. 85:5).
3 Compare Zhongguo 1983b, pl. 45: 2–3.
4 Zhongguo 1963, pls. 114–115.

2

Painted pottery *pen* basin

Diam. 51 (19 ¾)
Neolithic Period, Late Banpo Culture
(c. 4000 – 3500 BCE)
From Dadiwan, Qin'an, Gansu Province

Gansu Provincial Museum, Lanzhou

The exceptionally large size of this *pen*[1] suggests
that it may have been used for ceremonial functions, perhaps, for ritual ablutions. The vessel was
unearthed from the same site as a flask (cat. 3),
within the confines of one of the square dwelling
foundations (F 1) at the settlement. There, a smaller
basin, decorated in patterns similar to those on
the flask, was also found, indicating that the flask
and the present vessel are closely contemporary.[2]

The decoration on the outer wall of the basin,
rendered in black crescent-shapes and fine parallel
lines against the red surface, has much in common
with the patterns repeated in the three registers on
the flask. But unlike the patterns on the flask, those
on the basin retain a direct reference to the representations of fish that were fairly common motifs

during the preceding phases of Banpo pottery.
They are seen in the earlier strata at Dadiwan and
at sites to the east throughout Shaanxi province.

The derivation of this design is apparent in the
trailing finlike forms and in the motif of the vertically placed crescent and bowed line, which origi-
nates from the older imagery of the fish's gill (fig. 1).
The head of the fish and its pectoral fins have been
eliminated. The allusion to the fish has receded in
importance in these more fully evolved designs, and
the emphasis has shifted to the purely aesthetic
qualities of the painted configurations themselves.
By late Banpo times, the hitherto discrete images
have been altogether transformed by a more cursive
style of painting. LF-H

1 Excavated in 1979 (F 1); published: Gansu 1983c, color pl.
  1:3; Zhang 1990b, cat. no. 48; color pl. 6.
2 Gansu 1983c, pl. 3:4.

FIG. 1. Fish design on a
pottery *pen* from Dadiwan,
Qin'an, Gansu province;
Late Banpo culture. After
Gansu 1983c, 30, fig. 19:2.

3

Painted pottery ping *flask*

Height 31.8 (12.40), diam. at base 6.8 (2 ½),
diam. at mouth 4.5 (1¾)
Neolithic Period, Late Banpo Culture
(c. 4000–3500 BCE)
From Dadiwan, Qin'an, Gansu Province

Gansu Provincial Museum, Lanzhou

The head modeled from the vessel's short neck
is remarkable as an early testament to the interest
in human physiognomy and to the Neolithic artist's ability to represent the human form in plastic
terms.[1] The face, described with broad cheeks and
a small chin, is probably intended to portray a boy
or young man. The slightly slanting plane of the
face shows three short horizontal incisions marking
the eyes and mouth. The carefully shaped nose
has two small holes indicating the nostrils, and
the protruding ears are pierced by a circular hole
at the center. The hair, shown by vertical grooves,
is combed forward over the brow and trimmed in
an even line across the forehead and around the
back of the neck. At the level of the vessel's mouth,
the head is abruptly cut off, but the full shape of
the crown may originally have been supplied by
a lid or stopper, possibly secured by cords tied
through the holes in the ears.

   Vessels adorned with plastic renditions of human heads are a rare occurrence. They have been
found for the most part in Gansu and Qinghai
provinces in association with the Banshan and Machang cultures of the late third millennium.[2] One
other example datable to Banpo times was discovered at Luonan in eastern Shaanxi.[3] The Luonan
head, apparently that of a young girl, is more completely and sensitively articulated than the one in
the exhibition, and counts as a small masterpiece
of its genre. Its discovery so far away from Dadiwan
suggests that heads such as these may have been a
subspecialty in pottery workshops across the entire
Banpo settlement area.

   The designs painted on the red-slipped body
of the vessel are unrelated to the human head and
comply with the decorative conventions current in

such as the combination of the crescent and bowed line. The chief distinction between them is that the patterns on the flask retain no allusions to the images of the fish, which had so long informed the Banpo designs. While the balance of painted and unpainted forms within a given design, which is intrinsic to the earlier Banpo patterns, was maintained, the designs themselves are transformed by the late Banpo painters into ones that are entirely geometric. This vessel thus combines a new venture in realistic sculptural form with a style of painted decoration that had become virtually abstract. LF-H

1 Excavated in 1973; published: Gansu 1983c, color pl. 1:2; Yang Xiaoneng 1988, pl. 2; Yang 1991, no. 17; Jin 1988, no. 8; Zhang 1990b, color pl. 12; Murowchick 1995, 45, figure at lower right; Wu 1996, pl. 26.
2 Examples of Banshan and Machang heads are illustrated in Andersson 1943, pls. 186–187; Qinghai 1980, no. 43.
3 See Hao 1984, 103; Yang Xiaoneng 1989, color pl. 1:1. The Luonan jar is analogous in shape to examples from Jiangzhai Period II at Lintong.

eastern Gansu at the end of the fourth millennium. The patterns, repeated in each of the three registers, consist of large oval shapes seen in red reserve, outlined by the converging arcs of two segmental triangles, one of which extends to the lower edge of the register, and the other toward the upper edge. Bisecting each oval horizontally is a crescent shape with a narrow, bowed line above it. The space between one oval and the next is filled by a series of diagonal lines bordered on either side by two crescent shapes, alternately painted and left in reserve.

This complex and formulaic decorative scheme is associated with the final phase of the Banpo culture at sites in the upper Wei River valley. The general conformity between this design and the one on cat. 2 is recognizable in the curvilinear quality of the lines, contrasting with the deep red color of the ground, and in specific design elements,

4

Painted pottery *hu* jar

Height 20.8 (8 ⅛)
Neolithic Period, Late Banpo Culture
(C. 4000 – 3500 BCE)
From Wangjiayinwa, Qin'an, Gansu Province

Gansu Provincial Museum, Lanzhou

This water jar,[1] like the basin (cat. 2), was recovered from one of the late Banpo settlements in the vicinity of Qin'an, north of the Wei River in eastern Gansu province. Its painted decoration similarly reflects an advanced phase in the evolution of the Banpo ceramic tradition, in which hitherto distinct images, such as those of fish, become subsumed within complex, integrated decorative schemes that move uninterrupted across the surface.

The design on the present vessel, applied in a thin brown pigment, has been convincingly interpreted as the image of a pig's face, which is repeated three times around the shoulder.[2] The snout is represented at the center of each face by an oval in reserve, containing two circles that indicate the nostrils. Two crescent shapes, also in reserve, serve as the eyes, while the wavy line below and the angled line above represent the jaw and furrowed brow. The design is arranged so that the eyes belonging to one face are also shared with the two adjacent faces. The baluster-shaped neck ends in a sloping upper section, which echoes the curvature of the shoulder. Four pairs of back-to-back triangles surround a circular perforation at the top.

Unlike the fish on cat. 2, which had once existed as discrete and easily recognizable images,[3] the pig seems to have been added to the design repertoire during the final phase of the Banpo tradition and has no prehistory as an independent image. The particular design on cat. 4 is also rare, and finds its single close parallel in the designs painted on the two registers of a bottle-shaped water container from the Banpo site of Jiangzhai, near Xi'an, in Shaanxi province, located 300 kilometers east of Qin'an.[4] Although domesticated pigs *(Sus domestica)* and wild boar *(Sus scrofa)* are both found among

5

Painted pottery *gang* urn

Height 47 (18 ⅓), diam. at mouth 32.7 (12 ¾),
diam. at base 19.5 (7 ⅝)
Neolithic Period, Henan Yangshao Culture
(c. 3500–3000 BCE)
From Yancun, Linru, Henan Province

The National Museum of Chinese History, Beijing

The realistic images painted on this vessel[1] are a surprising — and seemingly unique — departure from the geometric patterns that had dominated painted ceramics in the Central Plains area during the preceding millennia. This vessel is from the very end of the Henan Yangshao period, when painted pottery, supplanted by a new tradition of unpainted gray and black wares emphasizing silhouette, had all but vanished throughout the region. This vessel from Linru, just south of Yanshi, also takes us eastward along the Yellow River into the area where the earliest Bronze Age settlements were later to arise.

Nearly the full height of the vessel's wall is occupied by the separate images of a long-legged white wading bird, probably a heron, shown with a fish hanging from the tip of its beak, and, to the right, a large, hafted axe (fig. 1). The remarkably natural, lifelike appearance of the bird owes in part to its being depicted without the heavy black contour lines seen on the fish and the axe, and to the particular care with which the long beak and knees are portrayed. An incised line dividing the upper and lower mandibles adds to the realistic effect. The only unnaturalistic element — the treatment of the eye as a large black circle with a dot inside — conveys a sense of watchful alertness and engages us directly in its line of vision. The axe, on the other hand, is described with a view to technical detail, and even includes a description of the woven leather grip wrapped about the haft.

But the highly descriptive nature of these images should not lead us to mistake them as mere decoration. The combination of these two ostensibly incongruous images suggests instead that they were symbolic in intent. In all probability, the image of the white heron signified a place name or the

the faunal remains at Banpo sites, the lack of tusks on the faces on the Wangjiayinwa and Jiangzhai vessels indicates that these images are pigs, rather than boars.[5]

The graves at the Wangjiayinwa settlement, unlike those at other Banpo sites, have a small, rounded compartment extending outward from the burial pit on the occupant's left side.[6] These compartments were designed to hold the ceramic vessels, which normally would have been placed in the burial pit itself. The unusual nature of these burials suggests the emergence of local variations in the westernmost regions of the Banpo cultural system during its final phase. LF-H

1   Excavated in 1981 (M 53:7); published: Gansu 1984b, 1–17, 58; pl. 2:2; Zhang 1990b, cat. no. 23; color pls. 5; 25, far left.
2   Gansu 1984b, 7; Xi'an 1988, 1:243; Wagner 1992, 1:32–33; 2: pl. 3:2–3.
3   See Zhongguo 1963, color pl. 1:2.
4   Xi'an 1988, 2: color pl. 10. Two water jars with baluster-shaped necks from late Banpo burials (M 262 and M 315) at the site of Longgangsi, near Nancheng, in southwestern Shaanxi province, exhibit similar designs, except that the faces on these vessels seem to be human; see Shaanxi 1990, 119, fig. 84:1–2; 169, fig. 111:4–5; pl. 80:1–3.
5   Zhongguo 1963, 257–258; Zhongguo 1983b, 146–150; Xi'an 1988, 1, 521–525.
6   Gansu 1984b, 4, fig. 7; 5, fig. 11.

FIG. 1. Bird-fish-axe design on the urn. After Yan 1981, 79, fig. 1.

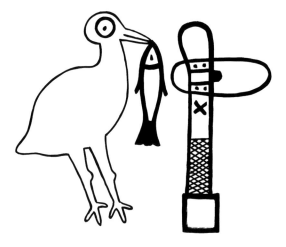

name of a clan associated with it.[2] The axe likely served as an honorific attribute, indicating rank or status. Taken together, the axe and heron may have identified the vessel's owner, or the person for whom it was made.

The images painted on the Yancun vessel appear to be related to the pictographs occasionally incised on vessels of approximately the same date associated with the Dawenkou culture of Shandong province (compare cat. 23). On vessels from two high-status Dawenkou burials at the Juxian site of Dazhujia (M 17, M 26), and from other burials at the nearby site of Lingyanghe, there occur two sorts of graphs. The first type shows a circle above a crescentlike shape, which may also be combined with a third element, which is either flat or rounded at the bottom and rises to three or five symmetrical peaks at the top. Based on their similarities to characters in the Shang oracle-bone texts, these elements are generally read as "moon," "fire," and "mountain," respectively, and they are generally regarded to make up a place name. The second category, which may occur singly or in association with the first type, is made up of graphs that represent ritual implements, including hafted axes and hafted adzes, and others that appear to be scepters.[3] Archaeological evidence of cultural transmission between Yancun in Henan and the Dawenkou sites in Shantong is sufficient to suggest an actual link between the kind of images painted on the

Yancun *gang* and those incised on the Dawenkou vessels. [4]

The Yancun and Dawenkou images bear a striking similarity to some of the earliest inscriptions on bronze vessels, which date to the period of the first-generation rulers at Anyang, around 1300 BCE. Several of these bronze vessels recovered from the large royal tomb M 1 at Wuguancun at Anyang carry an inscription consisting of a central graph, equivalent to the modern character for *dan*, flanked on either side by two back-to-back human figures in profile, which make up the character *bei*, or "north." These two combined graphs are followed by another, depicting a hafted bronze halberd, with the modern reading *ge*. On the evidence of the oracle-bone texts, the first part of the inscription is read Bei Dan, or Northern Dan. Although Bei Dan itself is only rarely mentioned in the oracle-bone texts, Western Dan, Eastern Dan, and Southern Dan occur with some frequency.[5] The identification of the first element in the Wuguancun inscriptions as the name of a place (or a clan) lends credence to the interpretation of the Yancun and Dawenkou images as place names. The hafted axes and adzes on the Yancun and Dawenkou vessels, like the hafted halberd on the Wuguancun bronzes, would seem to function as honorifics. The importance of the heron and the axe on the Yancun vessel thus resides not only in the naturalistic rendition of the images, but in the evidence they provide for a nascent stage in the history of graphic notation in China.[6]

The vessel, of a reddish buff ware, was finished on a slow wheel and then coated with a thin white slip before it was painted. Six hook-shaped lugs below the rim, two of which have been broken off, enabled a lid to be tied in place. LF-H

1 Excavated in 1978; published: Linru 1981, 4, fig. 1:1; pl. 1 (showing repairs); frontispiece (color); Zhang 1981, 21 – 24; Zheng 1982, 48 – 51; Fan 1983, 8 – 10; Tokyo 1986, no. 30; Chang 1986b, 130 and 137, fig. 98; Yang 1991, no. 14; Yan 1989, 303 – 307; pl. 12:1; Chang 1990, cat. no. 1682; Wu 1996, pl. 20.

2 The view that the heron signifies a place name has been proposed by several scholars, including Zheng Jiexiang, who notes that the word *guan* (heron) occurs in a much later text known as *Shan hai jing* (Classic of mountains and seas), referring to the "land of the *guantou* (or *huantou*) people," who in early times had been displaced to the south from the Linru region of Henan (Zheng 1982, 50). Although it is pleasant to imagine that some 5000 years ago the Linru area might have been a habitat known for its waterfowl, all we can say for certain on this point is that the artist who painted the heron on the Yancun *gang* was deeply familiar with his subject.

3 Shandong 1974, 118, fig. 94. Several Yancun vessels are closely analogous to examples belonging to Period IV at the Zhengzhou site of Dahecun, in Henan, which has been dated on the basis of radiocarbon analysis to the late fourth millennium. Finds from Dahecun include an un-decorated *gang* (W3: 1), the same size and shape as cat. 5, along with distinctive curve-sided *ping* with pointed bottoms (W1: 1; W2), compatible with one from Yancun (Zhengzhou 1979, 344, fig. 36:1 – 2; 346, fig. 39:5; pls. 11:6, 13:9; compare Linru 1981, 4, fig. 1: 10; also see Zheng 1982, 49, fig. 2). Both types of vessels have also been recovered from Zhangshanzhai, another site in the Linru vicinity (Fang 1978, 138, fig. 2:12 – 13). The four dendrochronologically calibrated radiocarbon dates for Dahecun IV are: 3506±3342 BCE (WB-03); 3072±2902BCE (ZB-09); 3493±3109 BCE (ZB 84 – 21) and 3371±3101 BCE (ZB 84 – 22) (Zhongguo 1991, 165).

4 Shandong 1974, 118, fig. 94:3 – 4. The emblematic designs on the Dawenkou pottery and others incised on Liangzhu jades are discussed by Wu 1985, 34 – 36; Li Xuegin 1987, 75 – 80, 85; and Keightley 1989, 197 – 198. The long-legged wading bird painted on the Yancun *gang* is not to be confused with the "sunbirds" inscribed on Liangzhu jades.

5 The inscriptions on the Bei Dan Ge vessels probably identify the person for whom the vessels were cast. More complete discussions of the Wuguancun M 1 inscriptions may be found in Fitzgerald-Huber 1983, 24 – 25; Bagley 1987, 52, 429 – 435. The vessels were previously published by Guo Baojun 1951, 1 – 61; pls. 1 – 44; and Chen 1956, 268 – 269, 314; Illustrations of some of the vessels appear in Henan 1981, nos. 272 – 274.

6 The Yancun and Dawenkou inscriptions were examined more fully in a paper titled "Where Have All the Documents Gone," delivered by the present author at the Multiple Origins of Writing Symposium, held at the University of Pennsylvania, 26 – 27 March 1999.

THE YANGSHAO

CULTURE:

MAJIAYAO

Although the Majiayao culture was first identified by the Swedish archaeologist J. G. Andersson in the early 1920s, much remains unknown about it, and it continues to yield surprises.[1]

In Gansu, as elsewhere in China, Majiayao enjoys a unique position because of the extraordinary quality of its painted wares. These ceramics, which comprise a wide range of shapes, from tall wide-mouthed storage jars and slender water containers to basins with gracefully everted rims, are of an unrivaled elegance. Even more remarkable are their highly dynamic painted designs, applied to the smooth, finely burnished surfaces. These designs are executed in multiple parallel lines, often involving spiral-based configurations, and they are used to decorate all manner of things, even children's pottery rattles.[2] Figural decoration, seen on three of the Majiayao vessels in the exhibition, is, however, exceptional (cats. 6, 8, 9). Concentric markings visible around the inner surfaces of the rims indicate that the vessels were finished on a fast wheel. The wheel may also have been employed in the application of the painted decoration.

Less is known than we might wish about the culture that sustained this exceptional ceramic tradition and about the people in whose daily lives these vessels played a role. Generally speaking, they were agriculturalists who lived in small villages and tilled their fields on the loess terraces above the rivers and streams that cut through the area. Their dwellings, implements, and the shapes of many of their vessels have much in common with the broad continuum of fourth-millennium painted pottery cultures stretching eastward as far as present-day Henan province. The cultural distinctiveness of Majiayao, on the other hand, is readily perceptible in the straw-colored ware of their ceramics, which contrasts with the red ware typical of this region, and in the distinctive designs that decorate them.

The Majiayao sites are distributed from Lanzhou eastward along the Wei River roughly to Shaanxi province, and westward along the upper reaches of the Yellow River and its tributaries into Qinghai province. The combined evidence of stratigraphical sequences at several sites in the Tianshui area has established that the Majiayao culture in this region was preceded by a series of earlier cultures, including Banpo, as well as Miaodigou and Shilingxia. Majiayao, in turn, was replaced at the end of the third millennium by the roughly contemporary and interrelated cultures known as Keshengzhuang II and Qijia.[3] The radiocarbon dates for the Majiayao finds in this region cover a broad span of time, from the mid-fourth millennium to the early centuries of the third millennium.[4]

One of the most instructive Majiayao sites is Linjia, in Dongxiang, southwest of Lanzhou, where excavations in 1977, revealed the foundations of some twenty-seven dwellings and a number of ashpits.[5] The settlement was occupied, continuously or repeatedly, for a considerable period of time, during which dwellings were abandoned and replaced by ones that were generally larger and more substantial.

The house foundations are roughly square in shape with a central hearth and a single doorway leading to a small vestibule built at the front. During the earlier period, the founda-

Painted pottery *pen* basin; height 12.5 (5), Majiayao culture; excavated in 1995 from Zongri, Tongde, Qinghai province (M 157).

tions were somewhat below ground level, and the vestibules contained steps leading down to the floor level. In the later period, the houses were built at ground level, but the vestibule was still retained. Most of the houses during both periods are oriented northwest, toward the river.

Several thousand artifacts, including pottery, bone, and stone implements were unearthed at Linjia. Some of these items were found within the confines of the house foundations, apparently left behind when the dwellings were deserted. A collection of especially beautiful ceramics was recovered from the late-phase dwelling designated as F 16, among them a *guan* and two tall water-jars with refined decoration and a well-shaped *pen* basin with a rounded bottom and a broad sloping rim.[6] In two of the vessels from another late-phase dwelling (F 8) were discovered the carbonized remains of hemp (*Cannabis sativa*).

The ashpits located around the dwellings were also rich in artifacts, including the fragments of countless ceramic vessels. One of these ashpits (H 19) contained a large amount of carbonized broom-corn millet (*Panicum miliaceum*), the grain that evidently formed the agricultural basis of the Linjia economy. Apart from the stone knives used in harvesting the millet, bone arrowheads, and spears, some with their edges inset with microlithic blades, indicate that the diet of the Linjia people was supplemented by the meat of wild animals. Stone axes and adzes, used in felling trees and in woodworking, were also found in abundance.

A particularly surprising find at Linjia was knife blade made of bronze, said to have been uncovered from beneath the foundations of a late-stage dwelling (F 20), as well as bits of slag removed from an ashpit (H 54). These finds have been questioned by scholars as probable later intrusions, because it is generally believed that metalworking was unknown in Gansu province until about the year 2000 BCE, when it appears in association with the Qijia culture. For the present, however, the possibility of some form of metalworking during the late phase at Linjia is an issue perhaps best left open.

More is known about the Majiayao dwellings than about their cemeteries. One Majiayao burial, however, located at Hetaozhuang, near Minhe, in Qinghai province (M 1), has attracted considerable attention because of its unusually large size and the quantity of artifacts it contained.[7] The burial pit itself was square, rather than rectangular, and measured four meters on each side. On the chamber floor, at the depth of two and one-half meters, were discovered the traces of a coffinlike construction made of wooden planks, which was about three meters square — almost as large as the pit itself. For several reasons, including the fact that the skull was missing from the skeletal remains, the archaeologists have concluded that M 1 was the secondary interment of an individual who had been removed from an earlier grave and given a final (and presumably more opulent) burial. In all, the Hetaozhuang burial contained 36 pottery vessels, many of them closely similar in their decoration to those unearthed from Linjia, along with 215 bone beads, and 10 of turquoise. The remains of a sacrificed sheep and the skulls of several pigs were also found in the grave.

Further discoveries of Majiayao ceramics have been made only very recently at Zongri, near Tongde, in eastern Qinghai province.[8] This site, which is of great interest, has yielded over 200 burials and a number of ash pits. Some of these graves contained the traces of timber coffins large enough to accommodate four or five pottery vessels, in addition to the human remains.

The contents of the tombs were surprising in several regards. In many of the tombs, including M 157 and M 192, finely potted basins and storage vessels decorated in the Majiayao style were accompanied by other vessels of a totally distinct type with regard to their ware, their shapes, and their decoration. These vessels, called "Type C" by the archaeologists, are made from a coarse siliceous clay and coated with a clay slip. They take the form of often imperfectly shaped amphora-like storage vessels, simple rimless bowls, and one-handled jugs. Their comparatively crude decoration, executed in a purplish red pigment, consists chiefly of parallel rows of zigzag or scalloped lines, and other designs resembling tassels painted around the vessel below the neck. The same patterns are used to decorate the interiors of bowls.[9]

The coexistence of these two types of wares in the same Zongri burials points to the presence of two separate cultural groups in this region, which must have been in close contact. The most unexpected aspect of the M 152 and M 192 burials, however, is the very early date assigned to them. The calibrated radiocarbon dates ascertained for tombs M 157 and M 192 are 3700 BCE ±140 and 3735 BCE ±225, respectively.[10] If these dates can be trusted, they would indicate that the Majiayao culture was in existence fully five hundred years earlier than has been previously assumed on the basis of radiocarbon dates determined for the Majiayao strata at sites in Gansu province, such as Shizhaocun, and, in turn, they would require a reassessment of the relationships between Majiayao and other fourth-millennium cultures in the Gansu-Qinghai area.

The shapes of the "Type C" vessels, the use of purplish red pigment, and the dentate bands discernible in their decor, moreover, are characteristic of the later Banshan pottery tradition, which flourished in Gansu during the second half of the third millennium. An understanding of the relationship between these two ceramic groups and the cultures they represent is a further-challenge posed by the discoveries at Zongri. The Zongri finds thus provide tantalizing new evidence bearing on the genesis and interrelationships of several of the important painted pottery traditions in western China that succeeded the earlier Banpo phase. Much will depend upon obtaining further radiocarbon dates for the Zongri sites against which the validity of the present early dates can be judged. LF-H

1 Andersson 1943, 88–99; pls. 45–57, 181–185; Sommarstrom 1956, 55–138; pls. 1–60.
2 Sommarstrom 1956, pl. 9:1a–c.
3 Zhongguo Gaqing 1990, 577–586; pl. 1; Guo 1958, 36–49.
4 Zhongguo 1991, 274, 279, 281–284, 287.
5 An extensive report on the Linjia finds is published in Gansu 1984a, 111–161; pls. 15–25.
6 Gansu 1984a, pls. 20:2; 23:3–4.
7 Qinghai 1979, 29–32.
8 Qinghai 1998, 1–14, 35; pls. 1–5; Chen 1998, 15–26.
9 The mixture of Majiayao and Zongri "Type C" wares occurs at many sites along the upper reaches of the Huanghe from Guide southwest to Tongde (Chen 1998, 20, fig. 4; 23–26).
10 Chen 1998, 19.

6

Painted pottery *pen* basin

Height 14.1 (5 ½), diam. at mouth 28 (11)
Neolithic Period, Majiayao Culture
(c. 3900 – 3500 BCE)
From Shangsunjiazhai, Datong, Qinghai Province

The National Museum of Chinese History, Beijing

The interior of the basin is decorated with a frieze organized in three panels, each containing a line of dancing figures holding hands with one another.[1] The figures are described in minimal detail, with round heads, oval bodies and sticklike limbs. Short braids hang from the top of their heads. Despite the simplicity of their treatment, a degree of motion is conveyed by the slightly different positions of the legs, while the figures at the end of the line seem to sway, or pull away from the three in the middle. The figures are bordered above by a line along the inner edge of the rim, and by a series of circumferential lines below. The sides of the panels framing the figures are formed by clusters of parallel vertical lines, whose bowed shapes owe to the curvature of the vessel wall. The spaces separating the panels are divided diagonally by a band of even width or by one that tapers to both sides. The rounded, slightly

everted rim is edged with fine diagonal lines, interspersed with clusters oriented radially. The outer wall of the vessel is encircled by three parallel lines gathered together on one side into a single hook-like flourish.

Recent excavations at Zongri, a second site in eastern Qinghai province, located to the southwest of Datong, near Tongde, provide new insight as to the meaning of the vessel's decoration and also point to a need for a revised assessment of the chronology of the Gansu Majiayao pottery tradition.[2]

The representations of human figures on two basins unearthed from separate burials at Zongri have direct bearing on the vessel exhibited here from Shangsunjiazhai. The example from M 157 shows a row of comparable stick figures — thirteen in all — holding hands in the same manner. The chief difference is that these figures have round abdomens, suggesting that they represent pregnant females. If the decoration on this Shangsunjiazhai vessel and the one from Zongri M 157 (see page 69) are indeed related in meaning, then the figures that decorate it are probably those of ithyphallic males. On the vessel from M 192, the figural panels are narrower and contain only two figures, shown fac-

ing one another and holding between them a large round object. This object, taken in conjunction with the representations on the other two basins, may be a child. If the interpretation of these representations is correct, then the decor of the three vessels counts as one of the few cases during the Chinese Neolithic in which the subject of human fertility makes itself known.

Calibrated radiocarbon dates for the two Zongri burials around 3900–3500 BCE indicate that all three *pen* with figural decoration are earlier than would previously have been believed. The dating suggests that an initial phase of the ceramic tradition, which is represented in these burials by other vessels as well, may be considerably older than the period of the late fourth and early third millennium to which it has been ascribed on the basis of the Gansu sites, such as the middle and late phase at Dadianzi and Shizhaocun V, where Majiayao ware has been found in greater abundance.[3] LF-H

1 Excavated in 1978; published: Qinghai 1980, color pl. 6; pl. 11; Li 1982, fig. 16; Zhang 1983, 49, fig. 3: 6; Chang 1983a, 152, fig. 117; Yang 1991, no. 20; Murowchick 1994a, 62, lower right; Wu 1996, pl. 21.

2 Qinghai 1998, 1–14, 35; pls. 1–5; Chen 1998, 15–26.

3 Radiocarbon dates for M 157 and M 192 are provided in Cheni 1998, 19, table 1. For diagrams of the M 157 and M 198 burials and the vessels found in them, see Qinghai 1998, 3, figs. 6–7. The presence in these two burials of decorated amphora-shaped storage vessels unrelated to the Majiayao style vessels found with them would seem to indicate the commingling of two separate cultures at the Zongri sites (see Qinghai 1998, 3, fig. 6:4–5; fig. 7:3; pl. 2:3–6; pl. 3:1–2, 5–6; color pl. 4; Chen 1998, 17, fig. 2).

7

Painted pottery *ping* container

Height 26 (9 ¾), diam. at mouth 7 (2 ¾)
Neolithic Period, Majiayao Culture
(c. 3000 – 2500 BCE)
From Lijiaping, Longxi, Gansu Province

Gansu Provincial Museum, Lanzhou

The purely geometric decoration on this water container[1] is more fully representative of Majiayao than the other three examples in the exhibition, insofar as the vessels belonging to this tradition rarely show figural designs. It is also the single example where the calligraphic quality of the lines, one of the most remarkable aspects of this style, can be adequately appreciated.

The designs consist of radial spirals composed of a series of circular nuclei centered along the front and back of the vessel, and others along the sides, which incorporate the ring-shaped lugs. Circumferential lines at the base of the neck and those at the bottom of the register function as additional nuclei, so that the bundles of spiral arms that radiate from the top of one nucleus to the bottom of the next involve the entire decorated surface in an endless spiralling motion. Filling the interstices between the bundles of spiral arms are smaller circles in reserve formed by the converging arcs of three segmental triangles painted in black.

The full measure of this ceramic tradition can only be realized among the thousands of other vessels in this style — the gracefully shaped bowls and handsome storage jars, created of this same fine ware, whose carefully smoothed and burnished surfaces are decorated in a seeming endless variety of similar monochrome patterns rendered in multiple parallel lines. Arguably the finest of all the early Chinese ceramics, these remarkable vessels are easily a match for Neolithic wares found elsewhere in the world.

While the earliest datable evidence for this ceramic tradition is presently found at the sites of Shangsunjiazhai (cat. 6) and Zongri in Qinghai province, it seems mainly to have been centered at sites to the south of Lanzhou in the Dongxiang and Linxia areas, and to the east along the upper reaches of the Wei River.[1] The present example from Longxi finds a close parallel in a fragmentary *ping* with the same shape and decoration recovered farther downstream along the Wei River, at the Tianshui site of Shizhaocun. The *ping* was recovered from the second stratum at Shizhaocun, as was the following small bowl (cat. 8).   LF-H

1   Excavated in 1971; published: Gansu 1979, no. 13; color pl. 6; Fitzgerald-Huber 1981, pl. 38, fig. 99; Li 1982, 5, upper left; Zhang 1990b, cat. no. 133.

8

Painted pottery *bo* bowl

Height 5 (2), diam. 16.5 (2 ½)
Neolithic Period, Majiayao Culture
(c. 3000–2500 BCE)
From Shizhaocun, Tianshui, Gansu Province

The Institute of Archaeology, CASS, Beijing

Within this small, rounded bowl[1] is the figure of
a froglike creature, who is seen from above, as
if it had been captured and put inside. The vessel
and its figural decoration are thus integral to each
other, the one serving playfully as a setting or context for the other. The creature's back is shaped as
a broad oval containing a large circle at the center,
which is divided down the middle by three lines
into two hemispheres, filled by a dense network of
intersecting diagonal lines. The small rounded head
is almost entirely black, save for the circular eyes
and the mouth, which appear in reserve. The two
front legs, ending in three toes each, curve forward,
seeming to press against the vessel wall; the rear
legs mirror them, turning back toward each other.
The asymmetrical relationship between the oval
outline of the figure and the circular shape it contains, as well as the fact that the oval is placed
slightly aslant in relation to the head, endows the
creature with a hint of animation. In an equally
subtle manner, the lines separating the hemi-

spheres of the circle follow an almost imperceptible
curve from one side to the other, producing the
effect of a dome-shaped surface. The design is
completed by multiple tangential lines painted
just beneath the rim, which converge at three equidistant points along the wall's circumference. The
point of convergence to the right of the figure's
head is marked by a hooklike flourish. A section on
the left side of the bowl, where the frog's front foot
is located, and a smaller section on the right have
been restored.

Whether the figure at the center of the Shizhaocun bowl is meant to be a frog or a turtle is not
entirely certain. While the round body and possibly
the head might suggest a turtle, the legs and the
three-toed feet do not. Two similar images painted
on the interior of a Banpo bowl from the Jiangzhai
site at Lintong, in Shaanxi province, are clearly
those of spotted frogs.[2]

This vessel and the following *guan* jar (cat. 9)
were both excavated in the 1980s from the important stratified site of Shizhaocun, near Tianshui,
located just south of the Wei River in eastern
Gansu. The site revealed six superposed strata,
documenting a sequence of cultural phases and
their associated ceramic traditions spanning
a period of three millennia, from approximately
5000 to 2000 BCE. The present bowl was recovered
from the second stratum, along with a pointed-
bottom water flask decorated in the same manner
as cat. 6. Both these vessels are regarded as somewhat older than the *guan*, which was unearthed
from a different location at the site.[3] LF-H

1 Excavated in 1982 (T 244.3:16); published: Zhongguo
   Ganqing 1990, 577–586, pl. 1:3–4; Goepper 1995, no. 5;
   Rawson 1996, no. 4.
2 See Xi'an 1988, 2: color pl. 1.
3 Zhongguo Ganqing 1990, 577–586.

9

Painted pottery *guan* jar

Height 21.7 (8 ⅓)
Neolithic Period, Majiayao Culture
(c. 3000–2500 BCE)
From Shizhaocun, Tianshui, Gansu Province

The Institute of Archaeology, CASS, Beijing

The single most arresting feature of this vessel's decoration is the human face, in relief, centered on one side.[1] The body is represented below, in painted lines alone. The sensitivity with which this face is modeled, and the refinement and sweetness it conveys, set it entirely apart from its earlier and less expressive counterpart from Dadiwan (cat. 3).

The oval face, tilted a little to one side, is slightly dished below the forehead. Although modeled from the same buff-colored ware as the rest of the vessel, the face has been coated with a pinkish slip to enhance its lifelike appearance. The eyes and the half-opened, faintly slanting mouth are rendered as shallow depressions, which are shaded gray. The finely modeled ridges of the arched eyebrows are accented by almost imperceptible black lines. Three fine vertical lines drawn from the nostrils downward to the tip of the chin probably indi-

cate tattooed markings or the cosmetic application of face paint.[2] The top of the brow is indicated by a low ridge curving upward from the temples, and above, the figure's hair is twisted into a high chignon at the front. The head is encircled by a brownish black band on the surface of the vessel and by broad painted strips that radiate away from the face, ending in triangular pointed tips. Lower down on the vessel, on either side of the chin, appear two circles in reserve, each filled by a cross.

The figure's outstretched arms and small, splayed fingers appear below. The body itself is shown as a skeleton, with its spine and ribcage framed as an oval shape in reserve, bordered by a series of horizontal and diagonal brushstrokes. The area of the pelvis at the base of the vessel is blurred and less easy to distinguish. This skeletal figure with its contrasting, delicately modeled face and poignant half-smile, seems mysteriously poised between this world and a world beyond. In all probability, the vessel was exclusively intended for a role in the rites of burial.

The surfaces flanking the figure are painted with contrasting designs: the one to the right exhibits a more open pattern of crosses seen against the lighter ground of the ware; the one to the left shows a denser pattern of triangular serrations in vertical strips pointing in the opposite direction to the smaller triangles left in reserve. Beneath the rim, two broad horizontal bands frame a zone of narrow circumferential lines. LF-H

1 Excavated in 1982; published: Zhongguo Ganqing 1990, 583, fig. 9: 2; pl. 1:1, 2; Wenwu jinghua 1993, 81, fig. 1; Goepper 1995, no. 4; Rawson 1996, no. 3.
2 Similar striations appear on the faces of the Banshan lids acquired by the Swedish archaeologist J. G. Andersson in Gansu earlier this century (Andersson 1943, pls. 186:1, 187:1). Human heads shaped from the necks of Machang vessels unearthed from sites in Gansu and Qinghai provinces often exhibit a series of parallel vertical lines painted beneath the eyes and down the cheeks, suggesting a form of face painting that may have been associated with mortuary rites (compare Zhang 1993, pl. 7:1 and Elisseeff 1986, no. 4). The Banshan and Machang cultures both date to the third millennium BCE.

THE HONGSHAN

CULTURE

During the fifth and fourth millennia BCE, a prehistoric culture, currently known as the Hong-shan, developed in northeastern China and coexisted with the Yangshao culture.[1] Concentrated in present-day western Liaoning province and southeastern Inner Mongolia, its geographic range extended east to the western edge of the Liao River in Liaoning province, west to northern Hubei province, south beyond the line now formed by the Great Wall, and north past the Xilamulun (or Western Liao) River as far as the Mongolian Steppe. Evidence from the southern and western peripheries shows that there were contacts between the Yangshao and the Hong-shan cultures.[2]

The identification of the Hongshan culture has been a process spanning nearly a century. In the early 1900s, Japanese and French expeditions conducted surveys in what we now know to have been the culture's geographic periphery.[3] In 1921, the Swedish archaeologist J. G. Anders-son recovered remains from a cave at Shaguotun (in the area of Jinxi, Liaoning province), which he identified as a Neolithic sacrificial site.[4] In 1935, Japanese archaeologists under the supervision of Kōsaku Hamada (1881–1938), excavated ruins at a site in Chifeng, Inner Mongolia, called Hongshanhou (literally, "the rear area of the red mountain") that yielded stone tools and pottery vessels identified by Japanese scholars as prehistoric relics;[5] Chinese archaeologists of the 1940s believed that these finds were those of a "blended culture" that reflected interactions between the Yangshao of central China and northern microlithic cultures.[6] In the 1950s, Chinese archaeologists began to identify such remains as those of a distinct culture, which they termed Hongshan after the type site.[7] The finds suggested to some scholars that the Hongshan had developed under the influence of the Yangshao culture — even that they represent a phase of the Yangshao (although the latter identification remains the subject of debate).

Finds from the late 1970s and early 1980s dramatically broadened our understanding of the Hongshang culture. Rescue surveys and excavations conducted in Liaoning province during the 1970s discovered various type of jade carvings — coiled dragons, owls, turtles, cloudlike plaques — and painted pottery cylinders, which archaeologists have dated to the Hongshan culture.[8] Planned surveys and excavations rendered since 1979 at Dongshanzui of Kazuo, and Niuhelian (both in Liaoning province) have yielded similar jades from stone tombs, as well as terra-cotta figures placed near a circular altar, and clay sculptures from what is believed to have been a female spirit temple (Nüshenmiao).[9] Jades and human sculptures constitute the predominant artifacts of the Hongshan culture.

So far, more than four hundred Hongshan sites have been identified in the region of Inner Mongolia, while more than one hundred sites have been discovered within Liaoning province.[10] Large-scale excavations and surveys at Niuheliang (where the counties of Lingyuan and Jianping meet) of Liaoning province have found more than twenty sites dated to the late period of the Hongshan culture — the fourth millennium BCE; sixteen of these sites have been designated "localities"; thirteen of these localities are stone-covered burial mounds. The mounds, built on top, or on the high slopes of small hills — sometimes one to a hill, sometimes several — often contain

Aerial view of the female spirit temple at Niuheliang, Jianping, Liaoning province; Hongshan culture.

numerous stone tombs and a few stone altars. The three other localities comprise the female spirit temple, a pyramid-shaped artificial hill (constructed of pounded earth and covered with stone) that occupies a surface area of 10,000 square meters, and a stone structure foundation.

Excavations at four of the localities (2, 3, 5, and 16) have brought to light sixty-one tombs constructed of stone and covered by stone mounds; these comprise five basic types: large central tombs, stepped tombs, Type A tombs, Type B tombs, and auxiliary tombs. They are distinguished by their form, their size, their placement above or below ground, and by the presence (or absence) of artifacts made of particular materials—principally jade and pottery. Type B tombs and auxiliary tombs generally contain no artifacts; large central tombs and stepped tombs do not include pottery objects. Of the tombs excavated thus far, thirty-one contained burial objects, and the specific material of the artifacts assigned to the graves seems to have had a particular, albeit unknown, significance. Most often, the burial objects were jade (twenty-six graves); one grave contained jades and objects made of stone, three graves contained pottery alone, and only one grave contained both jades and pottery.[11]

Stone artifacts used by the Hongshan people reveal aspects of their economic life. Tools fall into three categories defined by the manufacturing technique: chipped and unpolished tools, microlithic pieces, and polished implements; the types normally reflect the developmental sequence, although they were produced and employed by the Hongshan people concurrently. Agricultural implements were large and simple, suited to basic farming; tools for hunting were carefully manufactured.[12]

Relatively thin deposits of cultural remains suggest that the Hongshan people moved more frequently than would a community whose economic basis was entirely agricultural, and the abundance of wild and domestic animal bones recovered from Hongshan sites strengthens this inference. They were not, however, a wholly transient community: six kilns have been found thus far, yielding various types of painted and unpainted pottery that the reflect influence of northeastern Chinese and Asian cultures as well as the Yangshao culture.[13] The Hongshan culture was based in a region that falls between steppe and agricultural zones; it was a transitional society, poised between steppe and farming cultures. By the late period, the Hongshan culture

Excavation photograph of Tomb 4, Mound 1, Locality 2, at Niuheliang, Jianping, Liaoning province; Hongshan culture.

seems to have become somewhat more rooted. They also made use of metal-casting technology, disclosed by a small copper ring unearthed from a tomb at Niuheliang (Tomb 1, Mound 4, Locality 2) and two small molds excavated from the foundation of a house at Xitai, Aohanqi, Inner Mongolia in 1987.[14]

Jade — normally contained exclusively in larger tombs — seems to have been a more prestigious material than pottery; the latter is associated with the smaller tombs, or placed around the tombs.[15] In contrast to the jades of the Liangzhu culture (cats. 29–36), Hongshan jades were more simply carved and without miniature motifs; while other cultures used the material lavishly in their burials, the Hongshan were more frugal: the richest burial found thus far produced a mere twenty jades, and the most important burials — the so-called central tombs — contained fewer than ten.[16] The type of jade seems to have been a more important consideration than its quantity.

One of the most significant discoveries associated with the Hongshan culture is the so-called female spirit temple. Its identification as a temple is debated; some scholars identify it as a repository. Twenty-two meters long from north to south, and nine meters at its widest, the chambered subterranean structure was constructed of earth and thatch applied to a wood framework.[17] The walls were painted with red and white geometric patterns, and the temple was filled with unbaked clay sculptures depicting human figures and animals, as well as sacrificial pottery objects; seven female figures — life-size, twice-life-size, and triple-life-size — arranged by size and set off by dragons and birds of painted clay, have been recovered.[18] Only one image of the eponymous female spirit — a clay head — has been excavated. If it in fact served as a temple, the building's modest size indicates that it was not intended to hold many worshippers. Guo Dashun suggests this temple was built for and used by a few, elite individuals and argues that the graduated female sculptures may indicate a hierarchical form of ancestor worship.[19] The difficulties in distinguishing the unbaked clay from the surrounding earth have prompted archaeologists wisely to halt further excavation and cover the site with earth until the development of more refined equipment and skills.

The complex of pyramid-shaped structures, temples, mounds, and altars at Niuheliang was built on a series of hilltops or high hillsides over an area measuring approximately fifty square kilometers, within a band measuring one kilometer from north to south; the female spirit temple was located at center of the complex, which ingeniously incorporates the geographic features of the area. Su Bingqi has suggested that Niuheliang represents a precursor to late imperial complexes incorporating a mausoleum, temple, and altar.[20] Some archaeologists have detected the emergence of a ritual system in the Hongshan culture on the basis of stratified burials and the systematic use of jade and pottery in the tombs.[21]

The extensive use of sophisticated ritual jades in China during its late prehistory — exemplified by the Hongshan culture in northeastern China and the Liangzhu culture in the lower Yangzi River delta — has prompted some scholars to identify the period as the Jade Age.[22] The jade's primary use in ritual and decoration rather than for tools, however, renders that terminology somewhat suspect.[23] xy

1   Calibrated carbon-14 data date the Hongshan culture to between 4710 and 2920 BCE. See Yang Hu 1989, 222; and Yang Hu 1994, 46 and 49.
2   Wenwu 1990, 27. Guo Dashun has outlined a regional context for the Hongshan culture in an essay published in English: see Nelson 1995a, 21–64.
3   Torii visited Chifeng, Inner Mongolia in 1908; Licent examined the site in 1924. See Torii 1914, 31; Licent 1932, 27.
4   Andersson 1934, 188–199. Guo Dashun suggests that it is a Hongshan and post-Hongshan site and functioned primarily as a cemetery, but that it was used for sacrifice as well. See Liaoning 1997d, 4.
5   Hamada and Mizuno 1938.
6   See, for example, Pei 1948.
7   Yin Da 1955; and Lü 1958.
8   Fang and Liu 1984; Li 1986a; Wengniute 1984.
9   Guo and Zhang, 1984; and Liaoning 1986.
10 Guo 1989, 203; and Liaoning 1997d, 14.

11 Liaoning 1997d, 16–25.
12 Liaoning 1994, pls. 77–88.
13 Liaoning 1994, pls. 55–73; and Liaoning 1997d, 6–10.
14 Yang Hu 1994, 47.
15 Liaoning 1997a, b, and c.
16 The central tomb at Niuheliang Mound 1, Locality 5, for example, contained only seven jades. See Liaoning 1997a.
17 This temple is composed of two separate structures; the main structure is 18.4 meters long, and the minor one is 2.65 meters long. Stone was not used in the temple's construction. See Liaoning 1986, 2–3; and Liaoning 1997d, 30.
18 Liaoning 1986, 1–6.
19 Liaoning 1997d, 35.
20 Su 1994, 91–92.
21 Liaoning 1997d, 39–42.
22 For a geo-archaeological investigation of early jades, see Wen and Jing 1997.
23 Xie 1994.

10

Jade coiled dragon

Height 10.3 (4 ⅛)
Hongshan Culture, c. 4700 – 2920 BCE
From Niuheliang, Jianping, Liaoning Province

Liaoning Provincial Institute of Archaeology, Shenyang

11

Hollow cylindrical jade object

Height 18.6 (7 ⅜), diam. 10.7 (4 ¼)
Hongshan Culture, c. 4700 – 2920 BCE
From Niuheliang, Jianping, Liaoning Province

Liaoning Provincial Institute of Archaeology, Shenyang

Two jade coiled dragons found back-to-back on the chest of a male, and a hollow cylindrical jade object positioned underneath his skull were excavated from Tomb 4, Mound 1, Locality 2 at Niuheliang in 1984 (see page 80, plate).[1] These two different types of carvings embody the spirit and style of the Hongshan jade repertoire. Although earlier excavations in Liaoning province had suggested a connection between jades such as these and the Hongshan culture, the controlled excavation at Niuheliang in 1984 was the first to scientifically assign these objects to the Hongshan culture and to document their positions in the burial.[2] Fifteen years of subsequent excavations at the site have yielded no other examples of jade dragons.

The position of cat. 10 on the body, as well as the drilled hole, indicates that the object was hung on the chest of the deceased. The rarity of jade dragons in burials testifies to the fact that they were reserved for an exclusive group of the Hongshan, and they may have served as elements of ritual (perhaps involving pigs or boars[3]), tokens of status, or fertility symbols.[4]

The jade creature combines a coiled, serpentine body with a head resembling that of a pig or a bear; on that basis, such objects have conventionally been identified as "pig-dragons" or "bear-dragons."[5] Tusks on dragons from the Zhaobaoguo culture, as well as on a clay sculpture from the female spirit temple at Niuheliang, however, suggest that the head more likely represents that of a boar.[6] Hongshan representations of dragons took a variety of forms and were carved of various types of jade — cream colored, light green (as in this example), or blackish green. A larger jade from Sanxingtala, Wengniuteqi, Inner Mongolia illustrates one such variant: here, a decorative mane extends from the top of the head to the elongated body (fig. 1).[7] Its form is thought by some scholars to derive from the earlier form (exemplified by cat. 10),[8] but more archaeological evidence is required to establish that derivation with any certainty.

Archaeological evidence has demonstrated that the dragon was an image common to a number of prehistoric cultures, including the Hongshan, the

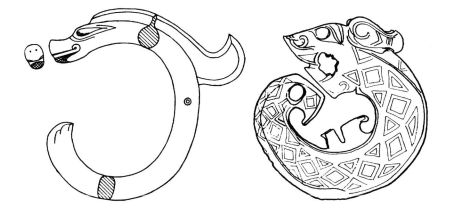

FIG. 1. Jade coiled dragon; height 26 (10 ¼); Hongshan culture; excavated in 1971 from Sanxingtala, Wengniuteqi, Inner Mongolia. After Wengniute 1984, 6, fig. 1 (left).

FIG. 2. Jade coiled dragon; height 7 (2 ¾); Shang dynasty; excavated in 1976 from the Fu Hao tomb, Anyang, Henan province. After Sun 1984, 7, fig. 1 (right).

11

Yangshao, and the Taosi Longshan (see cat. 25).[9] Dragon images from later periods are evidence of the enduring impact of these cultures, as well as regional influences: the plastic form of dragons from the Shang period (c. 1600–1100 BCE) such as one from the Fu Hao Tomb at Anyang (fig. 2), resembles both the Hongshan and Taosi dragons.[10]

With a form resembling that of a horse's hoof, the hollow cylinder, cat. 11 represents the most common type of jade object excavated from the Niuheliang tombs, although they are not invariably a component of the central tombs' burial objects. Though identified by some scholars as arm or wrist ornament or a tool of some sort,[11] the position of these objects in the tombs — placed horizontally underneath or above the skull of the dead[12] — has led to a consensus that they were used as hair ornaments.[13] Objects from the later period, such as a jade excavated from Dayangzhou (Xin'gan, Jiangxi province),[14] depict figures with towering, braided hair held in place with cylindrical objects, a hair style that may have been associated with individuals of particular status, or participants in rituals or ceremonies. The identification of the Hongshan cylinders with such ornaments is uncertain. Furthermore, the function of the symmetrically drilled holes, as well as the significance of the objects' horizontal placement remains unknown. The jade bears a resemblance to Hongshan pottery vessels with sloping edges, but whether the two forms are related has not been established.[15] Whatever their function, jade cylinders had a long use; one was found in the same region in a grave dating some fifteen hundred years later, hung at the back of the deceased.[16] xy

1 Two-thirds of the mound had been heavily damaged by the construction of a sewer system. The find was nonetheless an unusually rich one that included twenty-six tombs, fifteen of which contained jade objects, while the rest contained no artifacts. Several of the tombs, arranged in a row, shared a stone wall with one another — an unusual feature. See Liaoning 1986, 7 and 9 – 10; and Guo 1997, 20.
2 Sun 1984; Sun and Guo 1984.
3 Nelson 1995b.
4 Childs-Johnson 1991, 93.
5 Sun and Guo 1984, 15 – 16; Liaoning 1997d, 50.
6 Zhongguo Neimenggu 1987, 491 – 496; Liaoning 1997d, 91.
7 Wengniute 1984, 6.
8 Sun 1984.
9 Yang 1999, chap. 3.
10 Zhongguo 1984a, 158.
11 Hayashi 1990; Liaoning 1997d, 26.
12 Liaoning 1986, 9; Liaoning 1997b, 10.
13 Yang 1993b, 47 – 48; and Liaoning 1997d, 26 – 53.
14 Jiangxi 1997, 156 – 157.
15 Yang Hu 1994, 13.
16 Zhongguo 1996, 171 and 174.

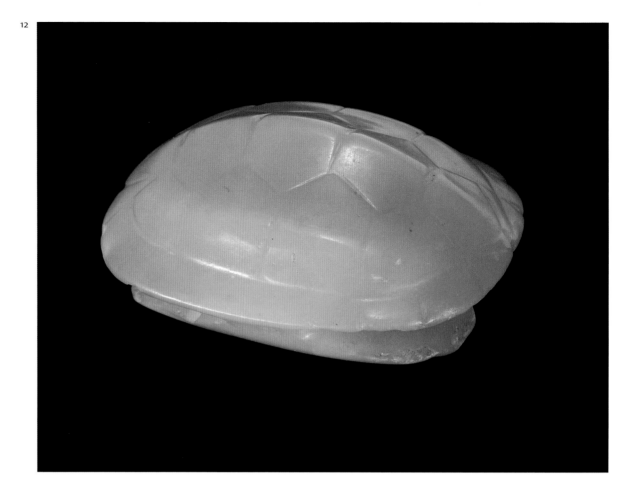

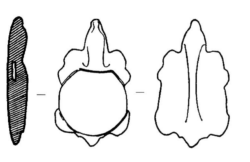

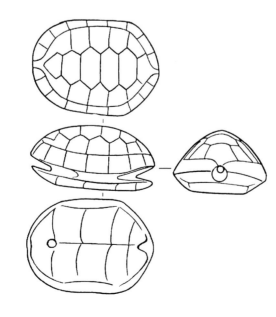

FIG. 1, Jade turtle; length 4.8 (1 ⅛); Hongshan culture; excavated in 1973 from Tomb 1, Hutougou, Fuxin, Liaoning province. After Fang and Liu 1984, 3, fig. 7:5 *(top)*.

FIG. 2. Jade turtle; length 5.4 (2 ⅛); Western Zhou; excavated in 1993 from Tomb 63, Beizhao, Quwo, Shanxi province. After Shanxi 1994b, 19, fig. 28:1 *(bottom)*.

12

Jade turtle carapace

Height 2.7 (1 ⅛), width 5.3 (2 ⅛), depth 4.1 (1 ⅝)
Hongshan Culture, c. 4700 – 2920 BCE
From Niuheliang, Jianping, Liaoning Province

Liaoning Provincial Institute of Archaeology, Shenyang

13

Jade animal mask

Height 10.2 (4.02), width 14.7 (5.79),
depth 0.4 (0.16)
Hongshan Culture, c. 4700 – 2920 BCE
From Niuheliang, Jianping, Liaoning Province

Liaoning Provincial Institute of Archaeology, Shenyang

In 1989, archaeologists excavated a single large tomb designated as Tomb 21, Mound 1, Locality 2 at Niuheliang. Built into the rock of the hill and covered with rocks and stone slabs, the tomb contained the body of an adult male, as well as twenty jade objects. Though not one of the largest or more

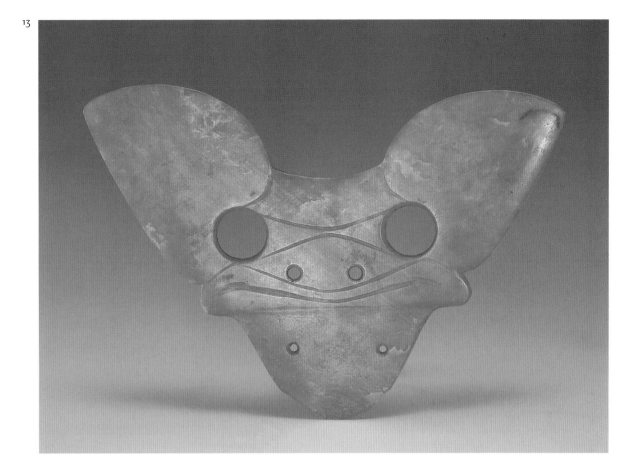

impressive of the Niuheliang tombs, Tomb 21 has yielded the richest complement of jades of any Hongshan tomb excavated thus far. The tomb had never been disturbed, a fact that permitted archaeologists to map the original positions of its jades and to obtain a better understanding of their possible use and functions. The jades include ten square-and-round-cornered *bi* disks, two double *bi*-shaped disks, one hollow cyclindrical object, and a cloudlike pendant, as well as a jade turtle carapace and a jade animal mask.[1] The latter two — elaborate and unique items — are included in this exhibition.

The turtle carapace was placed on the left side of the chest of the deceased. Unlike other jade turtles of the Hongshan culture (fig. 1), this example is painstakingly carved to represent the carapace itself. Holes and tenons on the bottom of the jade suggest that it was originally combined with other materials or objects. The tradition of making images of turtles, or of using the actual shell for specific ritual or decorative purposes, has a long history in China. Recent archaeological discoveries at Jiahu, Wuyang, Henan province have revealed that as early as 6000 BCE turtle plastrons were incised with marks.[2] The two large central graves at Hutougou and Niuheliang yielded additional turtle- or tortoise-shaped jades of the Hongshan culture.[3] At Niuheliang, two

larger jade turtles were placed in the hands of the deceased. Other prehistoric cultures also produced turtle-shaped jades, such as the one discovered at Lingjiatan, Hanshan, Anhui province.[4] During the Shang period, turtle shells were frequently employed for divinatory purposes (see cat. 56), while turtles were common subjects for sculptors, who rendered lifelike, detailed versions in hardstone (cat. 54). Even so, few examples survive of jade turtle carapaces, although the tradition endured for several thousand years over successive generations; one late but almost identical example was recovered from a Western Zhou tomb at Beizhao, Quwo, Shanxi province (fig. 2).[5]

The turtle in China is an auspicious symbol, associated with longevity, but whether this associations extends back in time to the Hongshan people remains an open question. In any case, the secular and sacred associations of the turtle motif and of the carapace itself — a tradition that has continued for 8,000 years — indicate the lasting importance of the image.

The jade animal mask (cat. 13) is a plaquelike abstraction of an animal head. The two eyes and the nostrils are hollowed in the round. The two symmetrical small perforations in the animal's jowls, with traces of wear on the bottom edges of the mask, and the mask's position in the burial — on the waist of tomb's occupant — indicate that it was probably the upper part of a composition or an important element of a belt. The archaeological report states that Tomb 21 overlapped with Tomb 4 (the find-site of the coiled dragons and the hollow cylindrical jade [cats. 10, 11]) and Tomb 14,[6] an indication that it is an earlier burial. Like the turtle carapace, this animal mask probably is the earlier form of such representations in the Hongshan culture. The animal mask constitutes a dominant motif in Shang ritual bronzes (see cats. 57, 70), and its origin, meaning, and function have long been a focus of scholarly inquiry. The discovery of jades of the Liangzhu culture carved with animal motifs (see cats. 29, 30), has led some scholars to trace the origin of Shang animal masks back to the Liangzhu culture of the lower Yangzi River delta, but animal masks appear among other prehistoric as well, including the Hongshan culture,[7] and it is likely that the later form of the motif drew inspiration from various sources in ancient China. XY

1 Excavated in 1989; reported: Liaoning 1997b.
2 Henan 1989, 12.
3 Fang and Liu 1984, 3; and Liaoning 1997a, 6.
4 Anhui 1989, 6.
5 Shanxi 1994, 18.
6 Liaoning 1986.
7 Yang 1999, chap. 3.

14

Jade plaque with animal design

Height 9.5 (3 ³/₄), width 28.6 (11 ¹/₄)
Hongshan Culture, 4700 – 2920 BCE
From Niuheliang, Jianping, Liaoning Province

Liaoning Provincial Institute of Archaeology, Shenyang

This plaque, the largest jade of the Hongshan culture excavated thus far, was positioned vertically in the tomb, with its back facing up.[1] Thin and finely engraved, the object produces a clear, ringing tone when struck. Both sides are carved with patterns resembling tiles, although the front is more elegantly and delicately worked. At center, openwork and engraving allow the upper part to look like a pair of round eyes and eyebrows of a bird or animal; immediately below, five striations suggest birds' feet, or perhaps animal teeth. Extensions from the middle to the two sides resemble wings in flight; the tilelike patterns on the jade may represent feathers — perhaps those of an owl, a frequent image in prehistoric China (along with abstract or mythical birds) that became quite popular by the Shang period (c. 1600 – 1100 BCE). The precise iconography, however, remains disputed: other scholars have argued that it represents a phoenix, a dragon, the tusks of a boar, deer antlers — even a rose.[2] Burials of the Hongshan culture have yielded many jade animals and birds whose iconography is less enigmatic than that of this example; the most plausible interpretation of the image is that it combines elements of certain birds or animals in an abstract manner, but the uniqueness and this abstractness of this plastic form make the precise identification of the image — much less its meaning — hypothetical. While several jades resembling this example appear in collections, this is the sole example recovered by archaeological excavation. XY

1 Excavated in 1995 from Tomb 27 Mound 1, Locality 2. The tomb has not been fully reported, but see Liaoning 1997d, 71.
2 Deng 1992, 8; Du 1998, 62; Liu 1998, 77; and Liaoning 1997d, 71.

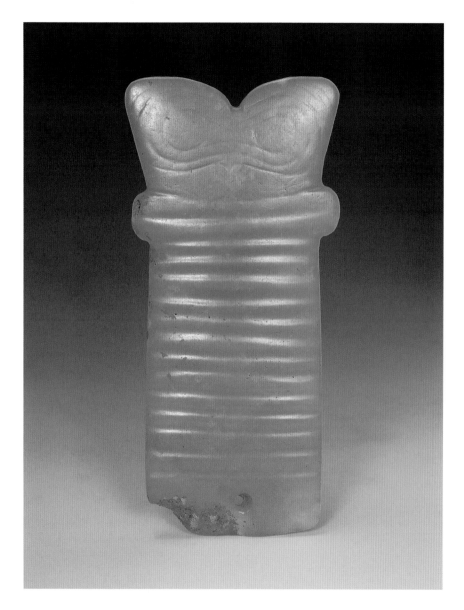

15

Jade Y-shaped object with animal mask

Height 12.1 (4 ³/₄), width 6 (2 ³/₈), depth 0.3 (¹/₈)
Hongshan Culture, c. 4700–2920 BCE
From Fuxingdi, Fuxin, Liaoning Province

Liaoning Provincial Institute of Archaeology,
Shenyang

This Y-shaped jade, recovered in 1981 from the
Fuxingdi site during an archaeological survey,[1]
resembles two jade objects in the collection of the
Liaoning Provincial Museum.[2] There is at present
no counterpart available from controlled archaeological excavation. The most striking element of the
jade is the abstract animal or owl mask, dominated
by two large, round eyes at its upper end. Animal-
like mask motifs, consistently depicted facing front
and with enormous eyes, appear throughout prehistoric China, an indication that their meaning and
significance transcended specific cultures. A handlelike extension, perforated at the bottom, projects
from the mask, and there are traces of wear at the
bottom edges — evidence that the object was originally tenoned to another object or into a stand.

A form of handlelike jades appears in Bronze
Age cultures such as the Erlitou and during the
Shang and Zhou periods;[3] they are commonly
identified as ritual instruments. These later jades
may represent a formal synthesis of objects represented by this Y-shaped jade and the rod-shaped
fittings of the Liangzhu culture (cat. 34). XY

1   Published: Sun 1984, 10.
2   Mou and Yun 1992, pls. 15–16; and Liaoning 1994, pl. 54.
3   Zhang Changshou 1994.

16

Jade owl

Width 3.8 (1 ½)
Hongshan Culture, c. 4700 – 2920 BCE
From Hutougou, Fuxin, Liaoning Province

Liaoning Provincial Museum, Shenyang

17

Three-holed jade object with animal heads

Height 2.8 (1 ⅛), width 9.2 (3 ⅝)
Hongshan Culture, c. 4700 – 2920 BCE
From Sanguandianzi, Lingyuan, Liaoning Province

Liaoning Provincial Museum, Shenyang

In 1973, along the river at Hutougou (in Fuxin county, Liaoning province), farmers found a stone tomb, part of which had been washed away by the current.[1] They recovered several jades, including the owl exhibited here (cat. 16), as well as two turtles, a bird, another owl, a *bi* disk, and a cloudlike plaque. (Archaeologists subsequently conducted a systematic excavation of the tomb and found another grave.) Although the precise positions of these particular objects remain unrecorded, discoveries such as these, as well as systematically excavated finds, have have enabled archaeologists to identify jade carving as one of the attributes of the Hongshan culture.

The Hongshan jade animal figures are uniformly small (turquoise was also used to create small-scale animal sculptures); holes drilled into the back of the objects indicate that they may have been attached to certain articles — perhaps clothing — or that they served as pendants. These jade turtles and birds exhibit a more naturalistic approach to representation than do other Hongshan jades such as the jade plaque with animal design and the Y-shaped object (cats. 14, 15). Particular cultures or periods do not necessarily exhibit a uniform artistic style; indeed, abstract and realistic approaches to representation coexisted in the Hongshan culture.

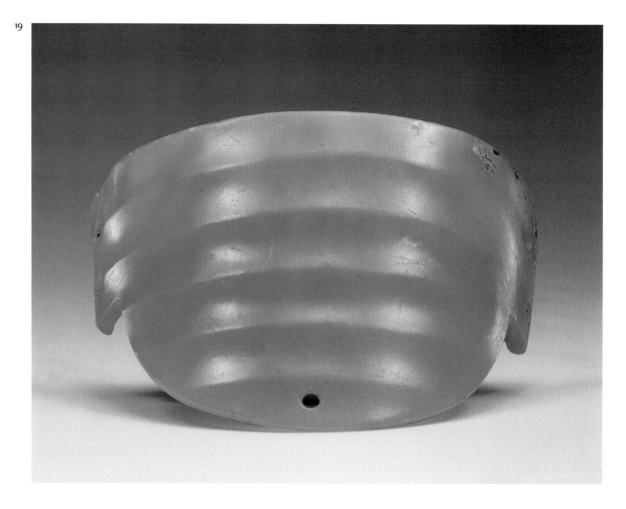

19

19
reverse

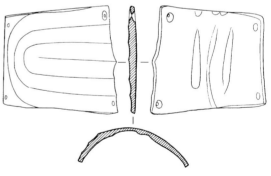

FIG. 1. Jade arm orna-
ment; length 7.1 (2 ¾);
Lower Xiajiadian culture;
excavated in 1977 from
Tomb 659, Dadianzi,
Aohanqi, Inner Mongolia.
Adapted from Zhongguo
1996, 172, fig. 82:2.

down on the right side of the abdomen overlapping
the braceletlike jade.[2] Four pairs of shallow openings at the back of the plaque suggest that it was
attached to another object — although probably
not fabric or clothing, since such attachments commonly have sharp edges and protrusions. Though
the object is often identified as a pendant, an alternative hypothesis identifies its function as ceremonial and relates it to the ritual *fu* or *yue* axes.[3] Its
conspicuous position on the body and its size (it is
largest jade in the burial) suggests that it surpassed
the other jades in importance.

The jade arm ornament (cat. 19) and a jade
bracelet were excavated in 1986 from Tomb 9, Locality 3. Originally reported to have been found on the

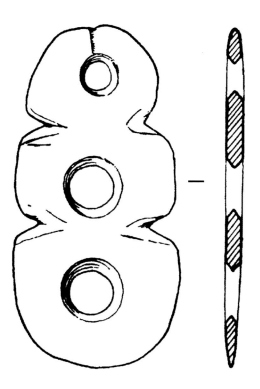

20

FIG. 2. Triple-*bi*-shaped jade pendant; length 6.4 (2 ½); Hongshan culture; excavated in 1973 from Tomb 3, Hutougou, Fuxin, Liaoning province. After Fang and Liu 1984, 4, fig. 9:3.

right side of the chest of the deceased, a more recent publication places it on the tomb occupant's upper arm[4] — a position that indicates a function for which we have evidence of a long tradition. Several tilelike patterns decorate the surface of the object; two holes are pierced on opposite sides, and a single hole is pierced through the curved end. Three examples of similar jades dating fifteen hundred years later than the Hongshan jades (one of these resembles the cloudlike plaque, and one resembles the arm ornament [see fig. 1]) have been excavated from tombs of the Lower Xiajiadian culture.[5]

The double-*bi*-shaped pendant (cat. 20) was dug out by farmers from a tomb at Locality 2, Niuheliang and retrieved by archaeologists in 1981.[6] Two much smaller double-*bi* pendants of a different shape were unearthed at Tomb 21, Mound 1, Locality 2 at Niuheliang in 1989.[7] Another smaller triple-*bi*-shaped pendant was excavated at Hutougou, Fuxin, Liaoning province in 1973 (fig. 2).[8] The *bi* — a

flat disk with a hole in the center — was a cherished image in China from prehistoric through imperial times. It had a ritual function, and later texts, such as the *Zhou li* (The rites of Zhou), dating from the Warring States to Western Han periods, remark that the *bi* might symbolize heaven, or that it served as a ritual instrument for sacrifices to heaven. In fact, the diverse forms and sizes of the Hongshan *bi*-shaped pendants are an indication that they probably served several purposes — decorative, ceremonial, or ritual. XY

1 For example, see Yang 1993a; Du 1998; Liu 1998.
2 Liaoning 1997a.
3 Liaoning 1997d, 27 and 56.
4 Reported: Wei 1994, 11 – 12; Liaoning 1997d, 61.
5 Zhongguo 1996, 171 – 172.
6 Reported: Sun and Guo 1984, 13 – 14.
7 Liaoning 1997b, 10 – 11.
8 Fang and Liu 1984, 4.

21

Terra-cotta torso of a pregnant woman

Height 5 (2)
Hongshan Culture, c. 4700 – 2920 BCE
From Dongshanzui, Kazuo, Liaoning Province

Liaoning Provincial Institute of Archaeology,
Shenyang

In 1979, archaeologists excavated a round, altarlike stone structure and a square stone structure at Dongshanzui. Surrounding the round stone structure, 2.5 meters in diameter, nearly twenty fragments of terra-cotta figures were discovered, including a half-life-size figure, sitting cross-legged with its hands clasped together in front of the body, and this terra-cotta torso of a small, naked pregnant woman[1]; the latter and a similar torso in particular have intrigued scholars.[2] In 1963, a tiny pottery sculpture of a naked torso was excavated at Xishui-quan, Chifeng, Inner Mongolia,[3] but attracted little attention. The Chinese did not, apparently, have a tradition of sculpting naked figures comparable, for example, to classical Greek and Roman sculpture. Anatomically detailed, naked pottery or wooden funerary figures were fashioned during the Han dynasty, but their bodies were clothed.[4] Sculptures from this period exhibit subtle differences in facial features that served to distinguish one figure from another. Among the most famous of these are the terra-cotta figures from the pits near the Qin First Emperor's mausoleum (cats. 123 – 128).

The artist of the Hongshan torsos stands out in his adept representation of the human form. In comparison, other contemporary sculpture is more primitive and naive (fig. 1). Perhaps because of the artist's skill and the uniqueness of sculpted representations of nudes, this figure and another (not exhibited here) have been admired as China's own version of Venus; she is sometimes identified as a fertility goddess.[5]

An unbaked clay female head excavated from the female spirit temple also relates to the Hongshan sculpture.[6] The head's proportions are realistic and her expression affable. Her eyes were inlaid with turquoise, while her slightly opened lips con-

vey the impression that she is talking. Considered as a group, the Hongshan human sculptures represent an artistic achievement of the highest level for the period.[7] XY

1 Excavated in 1979; reported Guo and Zhang 1984, 1–11.
2 Guo and Zhang 1984, 8–9.
3 Zhongguo Neimenggu 1982, 187, 196.
4 For example, see Shaanxi 1992, 5–8; and Zhongguo Hanchengdui 1994, 120–122.
5 For example, see Yu 1984, 13, 17.
6 Sun and Guo 1986.
7 For a survey of prehistoric sculpture, see Yang 1988.

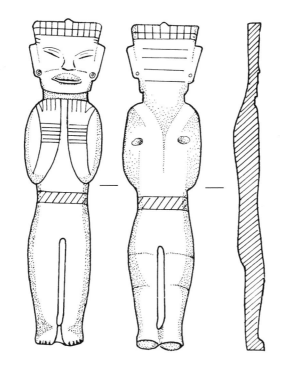

FIG. 1. Jade human figure; height 9.6 (3 ¾); Neolithic period; excavated in 1987 from Tomb 1, Lingjiatan, Hanshan, Anhui province. After Anhui 1989, 8, fig. 22.

Decoration and cross
section of cat. 22. After
Liaoning 1997c, 18, fig. 5:1.

22

Painted pottery *lei* jar

Height 41 (16 ¹⁄₈), diam. at mouth 12.6 (5),
diam. at base 11.6 (4 ¹⁄₂)
Hongshan Culture, c. 4700–3000 BCE
From Niuheliang, Jianping, Liaoning Province

Liaoning Provincial Institute of Archaeology,
Shenyang

Among the sixty-one Hongshan stone tombs excavated so far in the Niuheliang zone, only four included pottery vessels among the burial objects —
in each case, a single painted pottery *lei* jar with a
lid.[1] This *lei*[2] was found near the feet of the occupant
of a smaller tomb (Tomb 5, Mound 4, Locality 2)
designated by the excavators as a Type A tomb.[3] Pottery vessels (whose function may have been sacrificial
rather than utilitarian) are limited to smaller tombs;
the furnishings of larger tombs, by contrast, are
exclusively jade (see p. 80), but it remains uncertain
whether the distinction in the material of the furnishings was generated by the tomb occupant's
social, material, or occupational status.

The Hongshan burials were often encircled with
large numbers of painted pottery cylinders, open at
both ends, positioned in a single ring. One hypothesis, which takes into account the fact that the
cylinders are bottomless, is that these objects
served as vessels for communicating between
heaven and earth; other scholars have argued that
the cylinders were sacrificial devices, perhaps prototypes of the stone mound.[4]

Pottery of the Hongshan culture comprises two
principal types: painted red vessels with geometric
decorations, and unpainted gray or red-brown
cylindrical vessels with zigzag patterns. The red-
painted pottery (of which this *lei* is an example)
reflects the influence of the Yangshao culture; the
unpainted vessels represent an indigenous regional
heritage and style. XY

1   Guo 1997, 20, 22. One of the four tombs contained a jade
    object.
2   Excavated in 1992; reported: Guo 1997.
3   Liaoning 1997c, 17–18.
4   Liaoning 1997d, 81; Liaoning 1997c, 19.

Before China advanced into the Bronze Age, two successive cultures, the Dawenkou and Shandong Longshan, occupied a prominent position in the lower Yellow River valley during the late prehistoric period. The core area of the Dawenkou culture (c. 4300 to 2500 BCE) was in the present-day provinces of central and southern Shandong, northern Jiangsu, and Anhui, while the Shandong Longshan culture (c. 2500 to 2000 BCE) dominated the central and eastern Shandong peninsula and the northern Huai River region of Jiangsu province. With nearly identical geographic distributions, the two cultures spanned a regional continuity of approximately twenty-three hundred years, and along with contemporaneous prehistoric cultures in other areas of ancient China, their social, economic, and cultural evolution contributed to the formation of dynastic civilization in Bronze Age China.

THE DAWENKOU CULTURE

Named after the type site at Dawenkou, Tai'an, Shandong province, excavated in 1959,[1] the Dawenkou culture is sometimes referred to as the Qinglian'gang culture on the basis of an earlier excavation (1951) at Qinglian'gang, Huai'an, northern Jiangsu province.[2] By general agreement, however, the term Dawenkou is generally accepted and widespread.

The climate in which the Dawenkou people lived was temperate and warmer than today, like most of the Yellow River valley, and millet was the staple crop. The Dawenkou employed sickles made of bone, tooth, and shell, as well as polished and often bored stone axes and hoes. Built either at or half-below ground level, houses were either square or round and probably had eaves and conical roofs. The Dawenkou people wore hair ornaments, necklaces, and bracelets made of jade, stone, bone, tooth, ivory, and pottery. They had a distinctive custom of head deformation and tooth extraction. Their burial etiquette presented another distinctive attribute of the culture: the larger rectangular graves included second-level ledges (*ercengtai,* or narrow earthen platforms, usually for holding funerary goods), wooden coffins and burial chambers furnished with the heads and lower jaws of pigs, the teeth of river deer *(hydropotes inermis),* and turtle shells. In the late period of the culture — the early third millennium BCE — a disparity is evident between the funeral articles of the rich and poor and even in the placement of their tombs.

The artistic achievement of the Dawenkou culture is manifested in works of carved ivory and bone (engraved tubes and combs), fine "white" pottery ("baggy legs" *gui* pitchers and *he* tripods), and thin-walled black pottery (goblets or stemmed cups). The thin black pottery preceded the production of the Longshan eggshell black pottery. In general, most pottery of the Dawenkou culture was red. Many pottery vessels, painted with beautiful geometric patterns, have been found from the early period, but few from the late period have been recovered. The late period is represented mostly by pottery *zun* urns with incised pictographs (see cat. 23), ritualized stone and jade items (*ben* and *yue* axes), and animal-shaped pottery vessels. Most clay vessels were made on potter's wheels.

In the late 1970s, Tang Lan (1901 – 1979) suggested that pottery pictographs of the Dawenkou culture were already standardized and simplified and therefore quite advanced. These pictographs, commonly identified as one of the distinctive traits of the Chinese civilization or state-organized society, are comparable to bronze and oracle-bone inscriptions from later periods. Tang believed that the Dawenkou culture was indeed already a slave or state-organized society, but that argument has proved controversial.[3]

Despite the fact that more than two hundred Dawenkou sites have been identified and more than ten cemeteries have been excavated, the site at Yuchisi, Mengcheng, Anhui, has been regarded as one of the most important. Covering approximately 100,000 square meters, it is one of the largest residential settlements of this culture ever discovered. Archaeologists categorized the Yuchisi site as a different regional type of the Dawenkou culture. At Yuchisi, remains of row houses and more than one hundred and fifty tombs of a later period were excavated. About half of the *zun* burial urns were for children. Yuchisi was the first site where coffinlike apparatuses were also incised with pictographs,[4] expanding our knowledge of the function and meaning of early pictographs.

THE SHANDONG LONGSHAN CULTURE

Most of the archaeological cultures of the Shandong Longshan age, even the now renowned Liangzhu culture, were once called the Longshan culture. The Longshan culture was first discovered at Longshan, Licheng, Shandong, in 1928.[5] According to the practice of the time, similar cultural remains took the name of the type site: Longshan. Since then, archaeological excavations and research have greatly expanded our understanding of the Longshan culture, which is now subdivided geographically into the Shandong Longshan, Henan Longshan, Shaanxi Longshan, Hubei Longshan, Hunan Longshan, and Taosi Longshan cultures.

The Shandong Longshan culture is distinguished from the Dawenkou culture by its high-stemmed, eggshell-thin, black pottery goblets (less than 1 millimeter thick), town walls of pounded-earth *(hangtu),* copper and bronze tools, oracle bones for divination, and thunder-cloud patterns and animal-mask designs.[6] Contrasting sharply with the painted pottery of the Yangshao and Majiayao cultures, black pottery epitomizes the Shandong Longshan culture — to such an extent, in fact, that the culture was also termed "Black Pottery Culture." The culture also produced elaborate works in jade that were as sophisticated in craftsmanship as those of the neighboring Liangzhu culture. A jade hairpin adorned with an openwork animal mask, excavated in 1989 from Tomb 202 at Zhufeng, Linqu, Shandong province (cat. 24) is from one of the largest burials of the Shandong Longshan culture. The tomb was furnished with painted wooden coffins and chambers, an *ercentai* ledge, painted wooden containers, pottery vessels (including several eggshell pottery goblets), ritual jade objects, stone and bone tools, turquoise ornaments, and dozens of alligator scutes (probably the remains of alligator drums).[7] The size of the tomb and its lavish contents indicate that the occupant might have been a ruler of the region.

The advancements of the Shandong Longshan culture seem to have extended beyond art, style, and technology. War and ritual became institutionalized, social stratification developed, and regional states were very likely established. The works of art exhibited here are only one visual index to that society. XY

1 Shandong 1974.
2 For more information, see Zhongguo 1984a, 86–97; Chang 1986a, 156–169.
3 Tang Lan 1977, 1978, and 1979. For a summary of the argument (and opposing opinions) see Shandong 1979. Western scholars usually refer to the period as the Bronze Age, rather than Slave Age.
4 Liang 1995; Wang 1995. For general information regarding this site, see Zhongguo Anhui 1994; Wang 1997.

5 Wu 1930; Li Ji 1934.
6 Liu 1972.
7 Zhongguo Shandong 1990, 587–594. Du Jinpeng suggested that the animal mask was the image of a deity wearing a crown and originated with the Dawenkou and Liangzhu cultures. See Du 1994.

23

Pottery *zun* urn with incised pictograph

Height 59.5 (23 ¼), diam. 29 (11 ⅜)
Dawenkou Culture, c. 4300–2500 BCE
From Yuchisi, Mengcheng,
Anhui Province

The Institute of Archaeology, CASS, Beijing

For students of the origins of Chinese civilization,
the pictographs on the *zun* urns of the Dawenkou
culture are an important source of information.
Their similarity to Early Bronze Age inscriptions has
made these pictographs especially significant to
scholars working on the emergence of writing. If
the Dawenkou pictographs are true writing, they
would make it possible to ascertain the nature of
the Dawenkou culture.

In 1973, Yu Xingwu (1896–1984) first construed
the pictograph on a *zun* urn of the Dawenkou
culture as the character *dan*, meaning daybreak
or sunrise.[1] The 1974 Dawenkou archaeological
report published six pictographs from Dawenkou,
Lingyanghe, and Qianzhai, all in Shandong
province.[2] Since then, a series of similar discoveries
— at Lingyanghe, Dazhujia, and Hangtou in Shandong province have been reported.[3] An excavation
at Yuchisi, Mengcheng, Anhui province, is underway at this time. Several different pictographs on
burial *zun* urns unearthed at this site are identical
to those found in Shandong province, including the
typical "sun-fire (or moon)-mountain" seen here.
The furnishings that accompanied this *zun*, excavated from Tomb 215 in 1995, included pottery *ding,*
guan, and *hu* vessels.[4]

To date, more than twenty individual pictographs have been found,[5] all dating to the late stage
of the Dawenkou culture — the third millennium
BCE.[6] Some pictographs were found outside of the
Shandong area. Their stylized form is advanced —
well beyond simple pictures, marks, or decoration
— and they are very close to bronze or oracle-bone
inscriptions, which are indisputably recognized as
true early Chinese writing. The meaning of these
pictographs must have been widely known within
the Dawenkou culture.

groups, each with distinct customs. Archaeological analyzes of the remains at Yuchisi have identified the site as a local subtype of the Dawenkou culture.[12] Accordingly, these pictographs, although identical, were not clan signs; they were probably emblems or names for certain sacrificial rituals.[13] XY

1   Yu Xingwu 1973, 32.
2   Ren 1974; Shandong 1974, 72–73 and 116–119.
3   Major reports of these discoveries are Huang 1979; Wang Shuming 1986, 1987, and 1991; Li Xueqin 1987; Shandong 1991.
4   Unpublished, according to Wang Jihuai, the excavator.
5   Shandong 1991, 206. For additional pictographs, see Liang 1995; Wang 1995.
6   Gao 1979, 115–116; Shandong 1991, 202.
7   For example, Qiu 1978b; Gao 1984; Li 1986b; Cheung 1981. For the opposite view, see Wang 1981, 28 and 42; Wang 1991.
8   Keightley 1989, 197–198; Boltz 1994, 44–52.
9   Wang Shuming 1989, 371–372; Shandong 1991, 206.
10 Shao 1978; Gao 1979, 114.
11 Wang Shuming 1989 and 1991.
12 Liang 1995; Wang 1995. For general information on the site, see Zhongguo Anhui 1994; Wang 1997a.
13 For a full discussion of this suggestion see Yang Xiaoneng 1999.

After two decades of research and debate, most scholars now agree that the Dawenkou incised symbols are true pictographs.[7] The interpretation of individual pictographs is still underway. Some specialists have argued that the Dawenkou pictographs are akin in form and nature to "clan emblems" of later bronze inscriptions and the forerunners of Chinese writing, while rejecting the characterization of the pictograph as true "writing."[8]

The urns excavated in the Shandong region, were all from medium- and large-size tombs and were prominently positioned in the graves.[9] Their placement suggests a significant function, although the precise purpose of the vessels, which are identified by some scholars as components of ritual sacrifice[10] and by others as wine-making utensils,[11] remains the subject of debate. The urns at Yuchisi served as burial containers, used primarily for children. People of the Dawenkou culture, in the two different areas, belonged to two separate clans or

24

Jade hair ornament inlaid with turquoise

Overall length 23 (9 ½), width 9 (3 ½)
Neolithic Period, Shandong Longshan Culture
(c. 2000 BCE)
From Zhufeng, Linqu, Shandong Province

The Institute of Archaeology, CASS, Beijing

To create this elegant accessory,[1] the lapidary combined a long, tubular pin of mottled gray-green and
a thin, curved plaque of creamy white jade. The pin
head is drilled with a V-shaped notch, which slips
over a concavity hollowed in the base of the plaque.
Gradually tapered to a softly pointed tip, this pin
is exquisitely crafted in the round. Two bamboolike
sections, each composed of two gently concave
cylinders joined at a central node, alternate with

bands of ridges and curves of lathelike precision.
The plaque is symmetrically carved with hooked
contours and vermiform perforations, the latter
formed by drilling adjacent sections. One pair of
circular perforations is inlaid with turquoise beads;
another pair along the lower edge may have been
used to thread a binding to the pin. Sketchy incisions — some echoing the contours of the openwork plaque, others rendered as simple curves and
intersecting lines — may represent preparatory,
unfinished designs.

This ornament was excavated from a large, rectangular tomb in north-central Shandong province.

images — the excavated examples among them found mostly in eastern-central China (Anhui and Hubei provinces) — stimulate ongoing scholarly debate as to their symbolic significance and possible relation to jade designs of the Liangzhu culture of the east coast area near present-day Shanghai.

Throughout the third millennium BCE, a vast complex of late Neolithic cultures occupied eastern and central China. The types of wheel-thrown pottery found in this tomb appear to be distinctive to the late phase of the Longshan culture in Shandong province. Two openwork pieces (variously identified as jade or kaolinite) unearthed in 1991 from a tomb in Sunjiagang, Lixian, in northern Hunan (near the Hubei border) suggest that the Shandong Longshan style of jade carving exemplified by this head ornament may have extended farther south than previously realized.[4] Although technically analogous to this openwork plaque, the Hunan pieces incorporate clearly zoomorphic silhouettes, such as a bird or dragon. Whether these delicate openwork carvings attest to a general diffusion of styles or to a widespread distribution of styles originating from geographically concentrated workshops remains to be discovered. EP

Originally, the tomb's single occupant lay encased in a wood coffin within an outer wood coffin. The plaque and pin lay beside the skeleton's head and neck. The coffin also contained a creamy white jade pin of a finely articulated, hooklike form beside the shoulder and three jade ritual weapons (one blade, two axes) near the hips. Other grave goods included approximately 980 very thin turquoise plaques, bone implements, and black and gray earthenware tripods, jars, and handled cups.

Whether this composite ornament was worn in life or made exclusively for burial, whether intended as a separate hairpin or as an insert in a fabric headpiece, is unknown. Whereas the form of the pin is so far unique, the plaque's attenuated, hooked silhouette and vaguely masklike decoration invite comparison with an intriguing variety of jade images. These include goggle-eyed motifs incised on a blade previously unearthed in Liangchengzhen, Rizhao, in southeastern coastal Shandong province (fig. 1),[2] as well as human and monsterlike faces depicted on plaques and blades in several Chinese and Western collections.[3] Generally dated to the third millennium BCE, these diverse facial

1 Excavated in 1989 (M 202); reported: Zhongguo Shandong 587–594. See also Wenwu Jinghua 1992, pls. 60–61; Rawson 1996, 58–59 (no. 21); Tang 1998, 3: pls. 73–74.
2 Liu 1972, 56–57, figs. 1–2.
3 Du 1994, 55–65.
4 Wenwu Jinghua 1993, pls. 45–46.

THE TAOSI

LONGSHAN

CULTURE

When the cemetery at Taosi was first uncovered, the startling riches discovered there gave rise to speculation that this was a site of the legendary Xia, referred to in historical texts as the predecessors of the Shang.[1] But much of the material excavated at Taosi bears little direct relation to Erlitou, now considered by many archaeologists as a Xia capital city, and, moreover, the radiocarbon dates for Taosi place it somewhat earlier, in the final centuries of the third millennium BCE.

The Taosi site, north of the Yellow River in the Xiangfen region of southern Shanxi province, was excavated between 1978 and 1985. Although remains from this same culture have been reported from numerous other locations in the area, only Taosi has been extensively excavated and published in any detail. Traces of dwellings, storage pits, and kilns have been noted, but the archaeological investigation has focused on the cemetery alone. Many tantalizing questions therefore remain about this distinctive late Longshan culture.

The cemetery itself, however, is of great importance. It is estimated to contain several thousand burials, of which nearly a thousand have already been excavated. The large number of burials suggests that the area was densely populated, and the fact that many of the graves overlap indicates that the cemetery was in use for a long period of time. Archaeologists have classified the burials according to their size. The majority of graves were small, measuring roughly two meters in length and a half to one meter in width, and for the most part they were unfurnished. The medium-size tombs, a little more than two meters long and a meter wide, numbered fewer than a hundred. They contained wooden coffins and a variety of burial objects, such as pottery and wooden vessels, jade axes, *cong*, and personal ornaments, as well as pig mandibles. One of the medium-size tombs (M 3296) yielded the surprising discovery of a small cast copper bell. The bell is assumed to have been made in a place other than Taosi because, so far, no evidence of either smelting or metalworking has come to light in the vicinity of the site.

At least four of the objects in the exhibition come from the large tombs, which are the burials of the elite members of the Taosi community.[2] As far as can be ascertained, the large burials, generally about two meters in length and two to three meters wide, are exclusively those of adult males. The coffin, fashioned of wooden planks, was placed at the center of the tomb, surrounded by as many as nearly two hundred burial objects. One of the most lavishly provided of the tombs at Taosi, M 3015, gives us a sense of the wealth and variety of objects destined for an elite burial. In all, the tomb contained 178 objects, including 14 pottery vessels, 23 wooden objects, 130 items of jade and stone, and 11 bone implements. Among the pottery vessels were examples of handsomely shaped corded gray-ware containers, and even a small ceramic stove, all of which are the recognizable descendants characteristic of the older Miaodigou II culture that once thrived in this area. The tomb also yielded a small number of painted earthenware vessels, including a *hu* (cat. 26a).[3]

Even more remarkable for the very fact of their preservation were a number of wooden objects, such as caskets and vessels. Some of the wooden vessels, like those from other tombs,

Painted pottery *pen* basin; height 20.5 (8); Taosi Longshan culture; excavated in Tomb 2103 at Taosi, Xiangfen, Shanxi province.

appear originally to have been painted in a wide-ranging palette of red, white, yellow, black, and green. More significantly, the surfaces of many of these vessels bore decoration in lacquer.

The surprisingly large number of ritual jade objects, which may have functioned in the ceremonial life of the Taosi court as insignia of rank and office, included *bi* disks, finely shaped axes, large harvesting knives, and adzes. Stone and bone arrowheads were also found. Tomb M 3015 was, moreover, provided with a small orchestra, consisting of two large, elaborately and brightly decorated wooden drums with alligator skin coverings, and with what are thought to be their tuning devices still intact, and a stone chime measuring some eighty centimeters in length. The tomb occupant was also accompanied by three of his dogs.

The magnitude of M 3015 and the abundance and quality of objects that have been recovered from other burials in the Taosi cemetery hint at the prosperity of this society and the advanced nature of its organization, which was both highly stratified and specialized; and they likewise attest to the refined taste of its cultured elite. A fuller assessment of this culture and its interrelationships with other societies of the late Longshan world, as well as its possible link to the early phases of the Erlitou culture, will depend on identifying and excavating the neighboring settlement areas, once populated by this impressive society.

The evidence of the Taosi finds, moreover, has important implications for more general issues bearing on the long-term preservation and transmission of visual language. It has been commonly assumed that the Yangshao tradition of painted pottery and its complex decorative syntax had been completely extinguished by the Longshan period, when a new tradition of unpainted gray wares came to predominate throughout the China heartland area. The discovery of a thriving and sophisticated tradition of painted ware at Taosi has begun to alter this perception. The painted vessels at Taosi ware differ from the Yangshao ceramics in many ways, notably that they were fashioned of low-fired earthenware decorated only after firing. The use of spiriform patterns, however, suggests that elements of the older tradition of painted decoration had continued uninterrupted as an ancillary tradition, at least in some areas of the Central Plains, throughout Longshan times. The excavations at Dadianzi (cats. 41–45) demonstrate that the tradition of painted wares survived even into the early days of the Bronze Age. The existence of this continuing and evolving tradition of painted decoration, in evidence at Taosi and later at Dadianzi, begins to shed light on the question of how the decorative programs of some of the earliest bronzes of the late Erlitou and Zhengzhou periods came to include spiriform patterns and to maintain something of the more ancient syntax.

The presence of lacquerware at Taosi is especially noteworthy, because it may well be that the colorful palette of the painted ceramics, distinguished from the monochrome painting tradition of the earlier Yangshao ceramics, originated under the influence of lacquer painting. LF-H

1   No complete report of the Taosi excavations has as yet appeared. The present text is based on the information provided in Zhongguo Shanxi 1983, 30–42, pls. 4–7. An initial report on the site was published in Zhongguo Shanxi 1980, 18–31, pls. 4–6. The metal bell from M 3296 and two pottery bells found elsewhere at the site are discussed in Zhongguo Shanxi 1984, 1069–1071, pl. 3. Color illustrations of the Taosi site and some of the burial objects are available in Wenwu jinghua 1993, pls. 35–40.

2   Two of the basins (cats. 25, 27a) and the *hu* (cat. 26a) are known to have come from large tombs (M 3072, M 3073, and M 3105, respectively). The size of the tombs that contained the other three objects exhibited here is not clear from the archaeological report.

3   Zhongguo Shanxi 1983, pl. 5:1.

25

Painted pottery *pan* basin

Height 8.8 (3 ½), diam. 37 (14 ½)
Late Neolithic Period, Taosi Longshan Culture
(c. 2500–2000 BCE)
From Taosi, Xiangfen, Shanxi Province

The Institute of Archaeology, CASS, Beijing

The Taosi cemetery is remarkable for its lavishly furnished elite burials, and it is from one of these that the present earthenware basin was recovered.[1] Its painted decoration, consistent with the other ceramics in the exhibition from this site, was not applied until after the vessel had been fired. It shows around the sloping inner surface a red serpent, seen against a jet-black ground, which uncoils clockwise from a bulge at the vessel's center. Two rows of scales, half red and half in black

reserve, extend the full length of its body in slightly staggered alignment, creating a checkerboard effect. The head, marked by a tiny black eye, shows two lappet-shaped appendages above and below, and a long dentated snout and lower jaw. The pinnate sprig emanating from between the teeth is a puzzling aspect of the image, which must once have served as an important key to the figure's symbolic meaning. The serpent is encircled by a band of red paint around the upper edge of the wall and the canted rim.

The serpent motif in China reaches far back in history, but it occurs infrequently before the Anyang period. It makes its first, and so far unique, appearance during the early Neolithic, in the form of an eared or crested serpent painted on the shoulder of a *hu* from the Banpo level at Beishouling, Baoji, in Shaanxi province, dating to the fifth

millennium.[2] On the Beishouling *hu*, the figure of
the serpent is chased by a bird, apparently nipping
its tail.

At the beginning of the Bronze Age, the image
of the coiled serpent reappears, on a pottery lid
from the site of Dadianzi, located far to the north in
the Aohan district (Aohanqi) of Inner Mongolia.[3]
The body of the Dadianzi serpent, like that on the
Taosi *pan*, is composed of alternating red and black
scales, in colors suggesting the influence of lacquer
painting. In the Late Shang and Early Western Zhou
periods, the image of a serpent-bodied creature
becomes the dominant motif decorating the interior
of cast bronze *pan*. On the bronze vessels, however,
the serpent's head is replaced by a larger tigerlike
head in profile, or by an equally formidable *taotie*
face, which is positioned at the center of the vessel,
with its body reconfigured to form a full circle
around it.[4]

Although some form of continuity between
the image of the serpent on the Taosi vessel and
the corresponding images on the later bronze *pan*
might be expected in light of their obvious similarities, there is no evidence from the intervening
period to substantiate this connection. LF-H

1   Excavated in 1980 (M 3072:6); published: Zhongguo
    Shanxi 1983, pl. 4:1; Wenwu jinghua 1992, 74, no. 61;
    Zhongguo 1993, fig. 36:1; Sugaya 1993, 137, no. 1; Goepper
    1995, no. 13; Rawson 1996, no. 7.
2   The lid is illustrated in Zhongguo 1996, 137, fig. 73: 6.
3   See Zhongguo 1983b, 105, fig. 86:1.
4   Both versions are represented by *pan* from Tomb 5 at
    Xiaotun (Zhongguo 1980a, 33, fig. 21; 34, fig. 22).

26a

26

Two painted pottery *hu* vessels

a. Height 19.2 (7 ½)
b. Height 28.2 (11 ⅛)
Neolithic Period, Taosi Longshan Culture
(c. 2500–2000 BCE)
From Taosi, Xiangfen, Shanxi Province

The Institute of Archaeology, CASS, Beijing

The spiraling designs on the shoulder of the first of these two vessels (a)[1] carry echoes of the monochrome designs of a much earlier period (compare cat. 7). Yet by comparison the effect of the designs is quite different, conditioned by the warm pastel hues of pink and ocher now added to the design and by the softer appearance of the unpolished surface, as well as the slowed and more graceful tempo of their clockwise progression around the surface.

Black lines, fluctuating in width as they descend from the top of one configuration to join the next from below, and the S-curved bands in ocher, which float free at the bottom, create the appearance of scarves blown lightly back, suspended in air as the progression of spirals moves steadily forward. Together, they bring to the overall design a new sense of buoyancy. With a similar subtlety, faint black lines in the guise of additional spiral arms extend upward at the front of each spiral. These seem to define the contours of the S-shaped bands in red, equal in width to those in ocher. In this way, an element of ambiguity is introduced into the design,

26b

syncratic and even whimsical. These forms do not reflect the strict symmetry of those on the other vessel, and instead take shape as heavily outlined, larger and smaller units painted in pink, which move across the surface in waves, slowly following one another. The erstwhile spiral nuclei, shaped as squared ovals, hang like pastel bubbles under the crests of the larger units. Against the open, whitish ground above, smaller squared circles in the same pastel hue float high up on the vessel wall. Together with the smaller dark ovals between them these shapes conceivably had meaning as celestial forms. LF-H

1 Excavated in (a) 1981 (M 3015:42) (b) 1979 (M 3002:49); published: (a) Zhongguo Shanxi 1983, pl. 1:1; (a and b): Sugaya 1993 19, pl. 2:1-2; (b) Zhongguo 1993, pl. 4:2; Zhongguo 1993, 45, fig. 36:2.
2 Zhongguo Shanxi 1983, pl. 5:1.
3 Zhongguo Shanxi 1983, pl. 5:1, 4. Examples of ceramic stoves and the containers that fit them are known in the same Shanxi area as early as Yangshao times (Zhongguo 1959, pl. 39:1 – 3, 5 – 6).

as the area of red paint begins to function simultaneously as ground and as an integral part of the spiraling configurations.

A narrow band of ocher at the base of the broad, flaring neck marks the upper limit of the decorated frieze. Both the neck and the inner edge of the rim are painted black. The strongly canted base is left plain, revealing the buff-colored ware. The vessel comes from tomb M 3015, one of the most richly furnished of all the Taosi burials.[2]

The second vessel (b), a larger version of the first, has the same dramatic silhouette created by the oblique planes of the shoulder and the base and the sharp angle where they join. The strongly receding base indicates that these vessels were designed to rest in the circular openings of specially made ceramic stoves, which are found in the same burials.[3]

The painted designs on (b) have a character all their own, which might be described as ideo-

27a

27

Two painted pottery *pen* basins

a. Height 18.2 (7¼), diam. at mouth 46.5 (18⅜)
b. Height 21 (8¼), diam. at mouth 31.5 (12⅜)
Late Neolithic Period, Taosi Longshan Culture
(c. 2500–2000 BCE)
From Taosi, Xiangfen, Shanxi Province

The Institute of Archaeology, CASS, Beijing

The final two vessels from Taosi introduce painted designs unlike any seen before on Neolithic Chinese ceramics. These additions to the common fare reflect a prosperous society able to indulge the demands of a sophisticated elite clientele with a taste for innovation and a wider range of decorative modes.

The first vessel (a)[1] comes from a large, high-status burial, which was located next to the one that contained the *pan* decorated with the figure of a coiled serpent (cat. 25).[2] The pattern on the outside of the basin consists of juxtaposed, diagonally oriented units alternating in black and white, each the mirror-reverse of the one adjacent. They interlock with the pink ground like pieces of a jigsaw puzzle. The effect of these patterns is made more dramatic by the fact that the remaining surface — the interior, rim, and base — are all painted black. The unusual size of the basin suggests that it may have been intended for a ceremony at which a large number of people were present. A *pen* of the same shape but of slightly smaller diameter was recovered from another large, richly furnished grave discovered at the cemetery (M 1111).[3]

The pattern on the second vessel (b)[4] consists of adjacent sets of ribbonlike bands, again oriented

27b

on the diagonal, that continue uninterrupted across the vessel's upper and lower sections. The bands are shown in white against a pinkish red ground, but some of the units appear to be tinted pale green. These designs possibly take their inspiration from painted fabrics. LF-H

1 Excavated in 1982 (M 3073:28); unpublished.
2 Zhongguo Shanxi 1983, 33, fig. 4.
3 Zhongguo Shanxi 1983, pl. 6:3.
4 Excavated in 1983 (M 2035:1); unpublished.

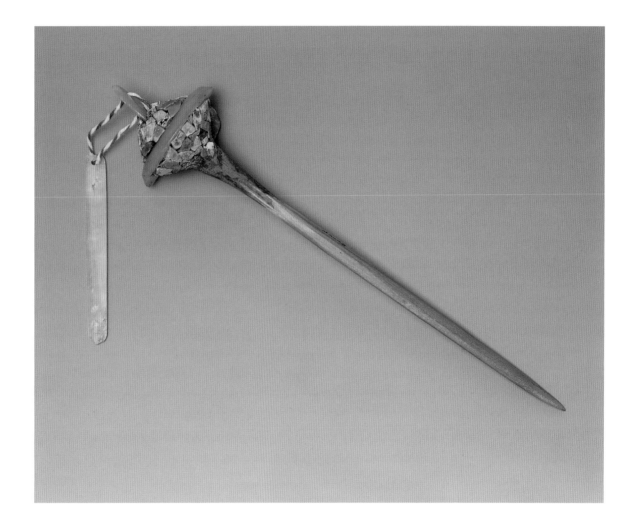

28

Jade and bone hair ornament inlaid
with turquoise

Length 22.5 (8 ⅝)
Neolithic Period, Taosi Longshan Culture
(c. 2500–2000 BCE)
From Taosi, Xiangfen, Shanxi Province

The Institute of Archaeology, CASS, Beijing

None of the objects associated with the Taosi culture speaks quite so eloquently of the refined and courtly ambiance surrounding the elite members of these communities as do the personal ornaments. In a direct and intimate way these ornaments reveal the dimension of a wealthy and high-status social stratum, unheralded at other contemporary late Neolithic sites in the Central Plains area.

The ornament exhibited here[1] was designed to be pinned in the hair. It combines in a fanciful display a variety of precious materials, including nephrite and turquoise. The polished bone stem is surmounted by a spherical section inlaid with turquoise chips and further embellished by a wedge of white jade through the center, which projects beyond the sphere on one side. Mounted at the top of the sphere is an upright finial of pale olive green jade with a pointed extension above. The final element of the assemblage is a slender rectangle of the same olive green nephrite, which would originally have been fastened in place by

Cat. 32a, detail showing a human face rendered in profile and wearing a feathered headdress.

dam lay between the river and the houses — probably to control flooding during the rainy season. Farther away, excavators found the remains of a small pier, constructed of wooden posts and boards, extending onto the shore. Excavations at other sites have uncovered fragments of a boat and oars, providing further evidence of water transportation.[6] Finds from Qianshanyang suggest that Liangzhu residents may also have built their houses on stilts — a very common form of domestic architecture in the marshy areas of southern China.

Since the mid-1970s, archaeologists have excavated hundreds of Liangzhu burials, ranging from small graves that contain few (if any) burial goods to large, lavishly furnished tombs. The most extravagant of these, presumably those of the social elite, were found in Middle Liangzhu sites at Fanshan and Yaoshan in northern Zhejiang province.[7] Excavations at the Fanshan site — a man-made earthen mound approximately 82 meters long, 27.5 meters wide, and 3.5 meters high — revealed eleven tombs, which together yielded more than three thousand jades as well as fine pottery vessels and stone implements. A mound of similar dimensions at Yaoshan was more elaborately structured than the Fanshan site: it comprised a central, square platform of red earth encircled by a six-foot-wide ditch filled with loose gray soil and surrounded by a U-shaped platform of yellowish brown earth; the entire structure was covered with gravel. Twelve tombs arranged in two rows were found on top of the mound, eleven of them miraculously intact at the time of excavation. All yielded a large quantity of burial goods, including several hundred jades, and some tombs apparently held double coffins that included a storage compartment between the inner and outer coffins. The absence of either architectural remains or traces of human habitation has led scholars to speculate that this had once been an important and sacred site (probably reserved for public meetings or religious rituals), subsequently abandoned and turned into a cemetery.

Of all Liangzhu achievements, jade carving reveals an unparalleled artistic sophistication and technical virtuosity.[8] The antecedents of Liangzhu jade carving can be traced to its parent culture, the Majiabang culture, which arose in the fifth millennium BCE. Majiabang jades, limited to earrings, beads, bracelets, and small pendants, are technically crude, shaped by pecking and then ground to a polish; many show pitted surfaces and bear clear scars of abrasion. Over the subsequent two thousand years, jade carving witnessed tremendous advances, and by the middle of the third millennium BCE, Liangzhu craftsmen were producing works of unprecedented quantity, variety, and artistic sophistication. The most distinctive forms include *bi* disks, *cong* tubes, axes, bracelets, beads, pendants, fittings, and ornamental plaques, many of which have complex shape, fine and elaborate surface decoration, and exceedingly lustrous finish.

Until recently, insights into the carving techniques of Liangzhu jade craftsmen have remained elusive, largely because most of the recovered jades are finished products; traces of tool marks, which might reveal how the jades were carved, have been smoothed out by polishing. The discovery of roughly made *bi* disks at various sites and of jade fragments and quartz drill bits at Mopandun (Dantu county, Jiangsu province), however, have begun to shed light on the techniques of Liangzhu jadework.[9] Liangzhu lapidaries used rotating wheel-saws to slice jade or extract it from large boulders, and some type of rotating mechanism for drilling and plane grinding. (The extensive use of the potter's wheel in the Liangzhu pottery industry attests to a mastery of rotary tools.) They seem to have shaped the jades from slabs with bowstring saws (probably made of leather straps), as well as with thin stone blades and bamboo slips. Drills — both solid and hollow — were used to bore holes; the jades were polished with leather and pieces of bamboo and brought to a high luster with elutriated quartz sand whose grade approximates that used in the modern jade industry.

The sources of the nephrite that constitutes the raw material of the Liangzhu jades remain uncertain; mineralogical analyzes have eliminated all presently known nephrite deposits in China and neighboring countries as possible sources for the Neolithic industry. Several scientists suggest that local sources of nephrite existed in Liangzhu times but have since been exhausted. A recent identification of nephrite deposits in Xiaomeiling, Liyang county, Jiangsu province — well within ancient Liangzhu territory — lends support to this theory.[10] Although the Xiaomeiling nephrite has proved to be mineralogically distinct from that of Liangzhu jades, it nevertheless confirms the existence of nephrite-forming conditions in this area.

The splendor of Liangzhu jades not only reveals a flourishing material culture but also sheds light on the social, political, and religious life of its people. Because jade is much harder than metal and can be shaped only by grinding with abrasives, jade-working is extremely laborious and time-consuming and requires specialized skills. The enormous quantity of refined jades in lavishly furnished tombs points to a stratified society, in which the elite class could deploy large numbers of specialized workers for their extravagant, conspicuous consumption of a precious material. The construction of the Fanshan mound (estimated at 180,000 cubic feet of earth) confirms the existence of both an elaborate social organization that was able to plan, manage, and sustain such a formidable project, and a large labor force. Finally, although many Liangzhu jades (notably beads, pendants, and bracelets) are clearly ornamental, some large objects — particularly *bi* disks and *cong* tubes — appear to have served no practical function. The staggering amount of labor expended in their manufacture and the archaeological context in which they were found suggest that these forms probably served as ritual paraphernalia for those of privileged status.

With the beginning of the second millennium BCE, the Liangzhu culture fell into decline. Although its cultural attributes seem to have had little influence on its immediate successors, the Liangzhu jades inspired later artistic traditions. Many Liangzhu jade shapes were adopted as standard ritual objects in the cultures and dynasties that arose afterward. One of its representative forms — the *bi* disk — constituted a vital element of official paraphernalia through the fall of the last imperial dynasty in the beginning of the twentieth century. Jade itself has remained a highly valued and prestigious material for over five thousand years, and the many practices associated with jades that originated in the Liangzhu culture have remained integral to Chinese civilization. zs

1 Shi 1938, 4 – 5. For additional discussion and bibliography on the Liangzhu culture, see Sun Zhixin 1993, 1 – 40.
2 For additional discussion of Liangzhu agriculture, see An 1988, 235 – 245.
3 Zhejiang 1960, 73 – 91.
4 Zhejiang 1988b, 32 – 51.
5 Suzhou 1990, 1 – 27.
6 Nanjing 1985, 1 – 22; Zhejiang 1960, 73 – 91.
7 Zhejiang 1988a, 1 – 31; Zhejiang 1988b, 32 – 51.
8 For additional discussion of Liangzhu jades, see Sun Zhixin 1993, 18 – 21.
9 Wang 1984, 23 – 35; Zhou and Zhang 1984, 46 – 50.
10 Wen 1990, 136.

29

Jade *cong*

Height 10 (3 7/8), exterior diam. 8.4 cm (3 3/8),
interior diam. 6.6 (2 5/8)
Liangzhu Culture, c. 3200 – 2000 BCE
From Fanshan, Yuhang, Zhejiang Province

Zhejiang Provincial Institute of Archaeology,
Hangzhou

Of all the diverse jade objects associated with the
Liangzhu culture, the *cong* displays the most complex form: a cylindrical tube encased in a square
prism that gently tapers from top to bottom, usually
divided into evenly spaced tiers by horizontal
grooves. *Cong* vary in size, from short examples with
one or two tiers to large, pillarlike examples that

stand as high as 30 centimeters tall with as many as
fifteen tiers.[1] Their projecting collars span a range
of thickness and rotundity, and their corners are
variously rounded or sharply angled. Each of the
four corners is generally decorated with a face
motif sculpted in low relief or engraved in fine lines;
these motifs range from simple masks comprising
only circular eyes and a bar-shaped mouth to complex faces with intricate scrollwork. Most *cong* have
a glossy finish; finely polished examples may be
quite lustrous.

The function and meaning of *cong* remain enigmatic. Centuries of speculation have focused on
theories proposed in Late Zhou and Han texts that
postdate the Liangzhu culture by two or three thousand years and are for that reason irrelevant to
how these objects were used in Neolithic times.
(The term *cong* itself derives from texts of the Late
Zhou period and, though descriptively useful, is
archaeologically meaningless.) In recent years
some scholars have attempted to relate the *cong*
to totemism and shamanism by applying Western
anthropological theories to the study of jades;[2]
others warn that such analogies should be treated
with great caution.[3]

Given their impressive size and weight, most
cong could not have been worn as personal ornaments. Their discovery in predominantly large,
lavishly furnished tombs suggests that *cong* probably signified wealth and privileged social status.
However, they may have served other functions as
well. In a tomb at Sidun, Jiangsu province, numerous *cong* lay in a circle around the tomb occupant,
suggesting that they had been arranged for a
specific religious or ritual purpose.[4]

The recurring motif of superimposed faces, as
seen on this *cong*,[5] probably grew out of an image
combining a human figure with a monster's face, of
which the decoration on a *cong* recently unearthed
at Fanshan, Yuhang, Zhejiang province, provides a
detailed example.[6] The upper part of the image
seems to represent a human figure wearing a fan-
shaped feather headdress. A band of incised angular spirals encircles its trapezoidal face; two pairs of
concentric circles and two superimposed rectangles

form the subject's beady eyes, broad nose, and toothy mouth; horizontal lines on either side of the circles suggest the canthi. The figure seems to be riding on a fearsome monster which has large circular eyes, a gaping mouth with protruding tusks, and two clawed feet. This double image mirrors the more abbreviated face motifs commonly found on Liangzhu jades.

The significance of these face motifs is highly controversial. While generally agreeing that these faces carry symbolic meaning, scholars differ in their interpretations of the image. Some argue that they depict the animal assistants of shamans, while others suggest that they represent deity figures, ancestor spirits, or even phallic symbols.[7] Although archaeological evidence does not yet allow further speculation on the specific meaning of these faces, we can reasonably postulate that they represented religious icons of some sort. zs

1 For examples of *cong* of various heights and proportions, see Zhejiang 1989, pls. 6 – 58.
2 Liu 1990, 30 – 37; Chang 1989, 37 – 43.
3 Rawson 1995, 124.
4 Nanjing 1984, 113 – 114.
5 Excavated in 1986 (M 12:97); reported: Zhejiang 1988a, 14. For an updated interpretation of the archaeological contents see Wenwu 1990, 103.
6 Zhejiang 1988a, 10 – 14, figs. 19, 20; for detailed photographic reproductions, see Zhejiang 1989, pls. 6 – 9.
7 Chang 1989, 39; Hayashi 1988a; Mou 1989b, 193; Teng 1988, 37; Xiao 1992, 54 – 56.

30

Jade *cong*

Height 4.5 (1 ¾), exterior diam. 7.9 (3 ⅛),
interior diam. 6.7 (2 ⅝)
Liangzhu Culture, 3200 – 2000 BCE
From Yaoshan, Yuhang, Zhejiang Province

Zhejiang Provincial Institute of Archaeology, Hangzhou

Unlike the common type, this short *cong*[1] has a circular wall resembling a bracelet. A large monster face is incised in fluent lines on each of the four decorative panels, its circular eyes, bar-shaped nose and mouth sculpted in low relief. Between the eyes, vertical lines form a fan shape, echoing the feather headdress of the human figure in the more elaborate human-monster configuration. In contrast to the fine spirals and curls that fill the background, the eye circles are cut in deep grooves, giving the face a threatening aspect.

While most *cong* have a square cross section and circular central hole, round, bracelet-shaped forms have been found at several Middle and Late Liangzhu sites, including Fanshan in northern Zhejiang province, Fuquanshan in Shanghai city, and Sidun in southern Jiangsu province.[2] The slightly raised angle that appears in some examples along the median line of the decorative panel nonetheless suggests an affinity to the typical *cong* shape.

It is likely that the *cong* developed out of the bracelet form, perhaps reflecting lapidaries' search for an effective means to present the face motif. The close resemblance between the bracelet and the earliest known example of the *cong* — datable to the Early Liangzhu period (c. 3000 BCE) — suggests such an evolution.[3] The cong differs from the bracelet by having four rectangular panels, on which simple, monsterlike faces are incised. These are the earliest known examples of face motifs, but they consist of exactly the same pictorial elements as the later ones — a pair of gogglelike eyes joined by an arched bar and a wide-open mouth with protruding tusks. As the surface decoration grew more elaborate in the Middle Liangzhu period (c. 2800 – 2400 BCE), the craftsmen accentuated

the motif by elevating it into relief with a slightly bulging median axis. It is in this experiment that they found the potential of transforming the two-dimensional image into a three-dimensional one. Consequently, the *cong*'s cross section evolved from circular to rectangular. This represented a turning point in the developmental sequence of the *cong*, when the emphasis shifted from surface decoration to formal structure. The *cong* subsequently grew much taller and assumed monumental forms, while the face motifs became noticeably abbreviated. However, the old form did not die out with the invention of the new form; indeed, it continued for a long period. zs

1 Excavated in 1987 (M 9:4); reported: Zhejiang 1988a, 36–37.
2 Zhejiang 1988a, 14, fig. 23; Zhejiang 1988b, 36–37, fig. 9, pl. 6; Shanghai 1984, 3, color pl. 1: 2; Nanjing 1984, 117–119, pl. 4: 3; for detailed photographic reproductions, see Zhejiang 1989, pls. 10, 11, 14; Shanghai 1992, pl. 88.
3 Nanjing 1982, 29, fig. 6; for a detailed photographic reproduction, see Zhejiang 1989, pl. 12.

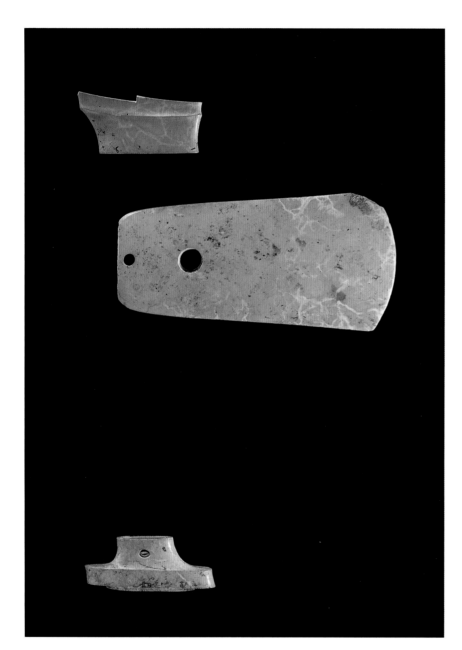

31

Jade *yue* axe and haft fittings

axe: length 16.7 (6 ⅝), height 8.2 (3 ¼)
fittings: top, height 3.6 (1 ⅜);
bottom, height 3.1 (1 ¼)
Liangzhu Culture, c. 3200–2000 BCE
From Fanshan, Yuhang, Zhejiang Province

Zhejiang Provincial Institute of Archaeology,
Hangzhou

This large axe, carved from a cream-colored nephrite fretted with white veins and brown speckles, has a gracefully curved cutting edge and two straight sides, all gently and thinly beveled.[1] Two drilled holes pierce the axe's butt, the larger of them bored from both sides, as evidenced by a small ridge in the aperture. The surface of the blade is polished to a glossy luster, while the butt, which would have been fitted into a haft and thus would not have been visible, is unfinished.

Evidence suggests that finely crafted jade axes evolved from functional weapons and hacking tools of ordinary stone. The earliest stone examples, dated to the fifth millennium BCE, come from the cultures of the eastern coast. Thick and lenticular in cross section, these perforated stone axes (many of which have cracks and chips along their edges, suggesting that they were in fact used as implements) closely resemble their unperforated counterparts. It is the perforation, by which the blade is mounted to the handle, that distinguishes the two types of axes.[2] Whereas the blade of an ordinary axe would have been positioned in the split end of the handle and then tied with a cord, the butt of a perforated axe blade was inserted into a groove cut in the handle and then tied through the hole (fig. 1). This simple hole ensured a much stronger bond between the blade and the handle, and it may be that this superior, reinforced hafting led to the exclusive use of the perforated axe as a weapon, for the secure mounting of a blade would have made a fatal difference in battle. Over the fourth millennium BCE, the perforated axe became increasingly large and flat. Many are smoothly polished and have an exceedingly thin blade.

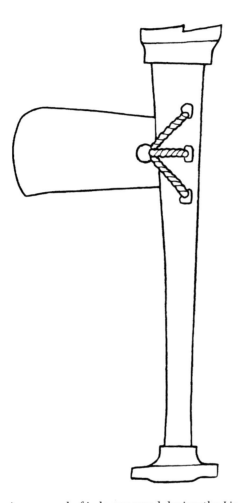

wooden handle was originally inlaid.[4] The fine
material, extraordinary workmanship, and, above all,
the imposing form of these jade axes command
power and respect. Indeed they probably served
exclusively as symbols of political and military authority, for few, if any, show signs of wear.

The axe served this symbolic function throughout the Bronze Age and during the early centuries
of imperial China. Several bronze axes resembling
the jade form have been found in royal tombs of
the Shang period.[5] Two axes of impressive size
and decoration (see cat. 52) were found in the tomb
of Fu Hao (d. c. 1200 BCE) — an eminent female
general and the consort of King Wu Ding — who
led the Shang armies in several military campaigns.[6]
Ancient documents also record that the king held
the axe as he directed his armies in battle and
delegated his military authority to his general by
presenting him with the axe.[7] As this practice subsequently diminished in later periods, the axe became a ceremonial weapon in the regalia and was
illustrated on the royal banners. It remained an
emblem of the sovereignty until as late as the sixteenth century, when its image was embroidered
on the emperor's dragon robe, an allusion to its
functions in remote antiquity.[8] zs

Axes carved of jade appeared during the Liangzhu period and had by then become larger and
flatter than their stone predecessors. The many jade
axes found at Liangzhu sites vary considerably in
size and proportion, but all have a thin, flat blade,
one or two perforations near the butt, and a curved
cutting edge beveled on both sides. Found exclusively in large and richly furnished tombs — generally one to a tomb — the axes were placed next
to the left hand of the tomb's occupant, with the
cutting edge pointing outward. The handles, made
of wood or other organic material, have rarely survived, but those that have show evidence of lavish
decoration. An ivory handle found at Fuquanshan,
Shanghai, entirely covered with complex engrav-
ings, is among the most exquisite works of Liangzhu
art.[3] Small bits of jade found between two ornate
end fittings in a tomb at Fanshan suggest that the

1   Excavated in 1986 (M 20:144); reported: Zhejiang 1988a,
    16. The two jade haft fittings were excavated from M 20
    along with the axe. See Zhejiang 1988a, 16.
2   Fu 1985, 820–829.
3   Shanghai 1984, 3, fig. 18; for a detailed photographic
    reproduction, see Shanghai 1992, pl. 92.
4   Zhejiang 1988a, 14–15, fig. 25.
5   Fu 1985, 820–829.
6   Zhongguo 1980a, color pls. 13:1, 2.
7   Lin 1965, 311–312.
8   For an illustration, see Fong 1996, pl. 162.

32a

32b

32

a. Jade trapezoidal plaque

Height 5.2 (2), width 10.4 (4 ⅛), depth 0.3 (⅛)
Liangzhu Culture, c. 3200 – 2000 BCE
From Fanshan, Yuhang, Zhejiang Province

Zhejiang Provincial Institute of Archaeology,
Hangzhou

b. Jade trapezoidal plaque

Height 3.4 (1 ⅜), width 6.4 (2 ½), depth 0.3 (⅛)
Liangzhu Culture, c. 3200 – 2000 BCE
From Yaoshan, Yuhang, Zhejiang Province

Zhejiang Provincial Institute of Archaeology,
Hangzhou

In addition to large *bi* disks and *cong* tubes, the
Liangzhu culture created a diverse variety of small
jade objects, among which trapezoidal plaques are
a standard form. Although they are fairly consistent
in shape, their decorative schemes, all derived from
the monster-and-human-face image, vary considerably: some plaques have only a simple face represented by a pair of circular eyes and a bar nose,
while others (in particular those from the Fanshan
and Yaoshan sites) are extravagantly embellished.
The vocabulary of the plaques' surface decoration
comprises three primary elements: face motifs,
ribbons, and scrollwork. The face motif is usually
abbreviated to a pair of circular eyes and a bar-
shaped nose and mouth but is occasionally
extended to include the feather headdress. Ribbons
and scrollwork, which were introduced in the Middle Liangzhu period (c. 2800 – 2400 BCE), add
complexity to designs and textural detail to otherwise spare surfaces. The talent and imagination of
the Liangzhu craftsmen are evident in their ability
to create a rich variety of patterns within a limited
decorative repertoire.

Painstakingly shaped and elaborately embellished, the first plaque (a)[1] displays a high level of
technical and aesthetic virtuosity. Together with
neatly hollowed openwork, twisting and winding
ribbons form a monster face with circular eyes, a
broad nose, and a large mouth with sharp fangs.

A pair of clawed feet, also represented by winding ribbons, extends from beneath the jaws. Two human faces, rendered in profile and wearing feather headdresses, flank the central image, while ribbons and spirals interweave to create an intricate network that links the monster and human faces. Fluent engraved lines lend a tactile quality to the lustrous surface.

Among numerous jade plaques excavated over the past twenty years, those from Fanshan and Yaoshan in northern Zhejiang province are the most ornate.[2] No two examples bear identical designs, and it may be that their distinctiveness served to define the individuality of their owner. The context and function of these plaques are still unknown. The plaques are characteristically worked down to a stepped edge at the bottom and pierced with a row of small holes, perhaps to attach the plaque to a piece of garment or an object made of perishable material. They may also have been components of a larger assemblage such as headgear, an interpretation suggested by the discovery of plaques among beads and pendants in the Fanshan and Yaoshan tombs.[3] Given the diverse shapes of Liangzhu jades, a large variety of combinations can be made by arranging the trapezoidal plaques with various beads, pendants, and fittings.

The second plaque (b)[4] is precisely symmetrical and consistent in thickness. Exact lines and sharp edges delineate its contour, testimony to the craftsman's skillful and assured hands. Amid interlaced ribbons and spirals, a monster face emerges — with large circular eyes, a broad nose, and a wide-open mouth with protruding tusks, all executed in fine engraved lines. As in earlier examples, the lines are formed of repeated short cuts, but here more finely and fluently executed. Above the monster face, an oval opening has been cut with great precision; four small holes are drilled at regular intervals along the stepped lower edge. The surface of the plaque is finished to a soft gloss.

This plaque is an excellent example of Middle Liangzhu jades, which are characterized by their exact and fluent lines, precise cuts, smoothly polished surfaces, and, above all, intricate surface decoration. Several theories have been proposed to explain the remarkable advances in carving technology that these middle-period plaques display. A plausible hypothesis suggests that Liangzhu craftsmen developed a heating process to soften the surface of jade, and that the creamy white color of Middle Liangzhu jades is not the result of burial but rather of heating the stone to more than 900 degrees Celcius (a temperature achievable in pottery kilns of the period).[5] A simulation test found that while the composition and structure of the jade remains constant after heating, its specific gravity and hardness are reduced — the latter by three to four degrees on the Mohs scale. This significant reduction in the stone's hardness would have facilitated carving to a great extent, improving the shaping process as well as permitting the extensive use of incised scrollwork. zs

1   Excavated in 1986 (M 16:4). No complete reports have yet been published on these excavations; only two brief reports (on major tombs and significant objects) have so far appeared. See Zheijiang 1988a, 1–31. This jade is not included in the report.
2   Zhejiang 1988a, 19–21, figs. 31, 35, 36, 39–44; Zhejiang 1988b, 40–43, figs. 20, 24. for more detailed photographic reproductions, see Zhejiang 1989, pls. 112, 115, 120, 121, 122.
3   Zhejiang 1988a, 19–21, fig. 4; Zhejiang 1988b, 40–43, figs. 2, 25.
4   Excavated in 1987 (M 11:86); reported: Zheijiang 1988a, 20–21.
5   Wen and Jing 1992, 266.

33

a. Jade plaque

Height 3.9 (1 ½), width 7.1 (2 ⅝)
Liangzhu Culture, c. 3200–2000 BCE
From Yaoshan, Yuhang, Zhejiang Province

Zhejiang Provincial Institute of Archaeology,
Hangzhou

b. Jade plaque

Height 6.2 (2 ½), width 8.3 (3 ¼)
Liangzhu Culture, c. 3200–2000 BCE
From Yaoshan, Yuhang, Zhejiang Province

Zhejiang Provincial Institute of Archaeology,
Hangzhou

Although both these plaques were excavated from a Middle Liangzhu site at Yaoshan, they are technologically centuries apart. The rather primitive-looking monster face on the first plaque (a)[1] is represented by a pair of circular eyes and a cross-shaped mouth, all executed in openwork. The carving technique — clearly at an early stage in its evolution — is evident in the Y-shaped cutouts that represent the corners of the eyes: having first drilled a hole, the carver cut lines radiating outward (the bore is detectable where the lines meet). The cuts are rough and clumsy, implying the use of a soft saw-blade possibly made of a leather strap, as are the engraved lines that describe the eyebrows and nose. The archaic appearance and crude manufacture of this plaque exhibit an affinity with a small openwork pendant unearthed from an early Liangzhu site at Zhanglingshan in Jiangsu province and raise the possibility that the two objects may have been created contemporaneously,[2] but the plaque's smooth finish and the two beautifully drilled holes that represent the eyes suggest that it was probably reworked and refinished at a later time.

The image depicted on the second plaque (b)[3] — a variant of the conjoined human figure and monster face — is far more complex than that of the first. A square-faced and unusually long-necked human figure, wearing a feather headdress flanked by two winglike shapes covered with curls and spirals, appears to merge into a fearsome monster face below. The monster face has two large bulging eyes, two prominent nostrils, and a large mouth, incised along the bottom edge of the plaque, with neatly aligned teeth. The carving technique is far more advanced than that of the first plaque: the contour is smooth, the engraving fluent, and the openwork precise. The surface is carefully modulated to accentuate the monster's face and smoothly polished to a soft luster.

The function of these plaques remains unknown. They have been found exclusively in Middle Liangzhu tombs at Yaoshan positioned among pottery vessels near the feet of the deceased.[4] Although their half-disk form resembles that of neck pendants *(huang)* found near the chest of the deceased, their position and the absence of suspension holes indicate that they may have served other functions. Small, connected holes on the back of plaques suggest that the objects were probably sewn onto clothing or sheets of fabric, which decomposed over the centuries of burial. zs

1 Excavated in 1987 (M 7:55); reported: Zheijiang 1988a, 46.
2 Nanjing 1982, 30, fig. 4:13, for a photographic reproduction, see Zhejiang 1989, pl. 203.
3 Excavated in 1987 (M 10:20); reported: Zheijiang 1988a, 46–47.
4 Zhejiang 1988b, 46–47.

34

a. Jade rod-shaped fitting

Height 6 (2 ⅜)
Liangzhu Culture, Middle Period
(c. 2800–2400 BCE)
From Yaoshan, Yuhang, Zhejiang Province

Zhejiang Provincial Institute of Archaeology, Hangzhou

b. Jade rod-shaped fitting

Height 18.4 (7 ¼)
Liangzhu Culture, Middle Period
(c. 2800–2400 BCE)
From Fanshan, Yuhang, Zhejiang Province

Zhejiang Provincial Institute of Archaeology, Hangzhou

Square in cross section and gently tapering to a point, these rod-shaped fittings are decorated with face motifs and incised striations that date them to the middle period of the Liangzhu culture (c. 2800–2400 BCE). The monster faces on the smaller fitting (a)[1] are in high relief with dished eyes and sculpted mouth; the faces on the larger one (b)[2] are somewhat abbreviated and cut in low relief.

Rod-shaped fittings were made throughout the Liangzhu period; the developmental sequence of the form largely parallels that of the *cong*. Examples datable to the early period (3200–2800 BCE) are round in cross section, taper gradually to a point, and are drilled through the broad end with a small conical hole.[3] By the middle period, such fittings become thicker and longer, often square in cross section, and were decorated with complex face motifs. The monster-and-human images, similar to those on the *cong*, are executed in modulated relief, and finely engraved lines and characteristically span the two adjacent sides of the corner. The butt is often worked down to a stepped tab, which is drilled with a small hole. Rod-shaped fittings of the Late Liangzhu period (2400–2000 BCE) are much longer and more angular in form. One example found at Fuquanshan in Shanghai measures 34

34a

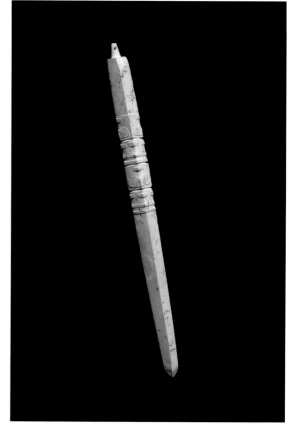

34b

centimeters and has sharp corners.[4] Its surface decoration is drastically abbreviated: low-relief bars and bands of parallel lines spanning the corners vaguely allude to the face motifs of the distant past.

Rod-shaped fittings are thought to have been used as components of necklaces; certainly short ones could plausibly have served that function, but examples from Late Liangzhu sites seem to be too long to have been worn as necklace pendants. Some were probably mounted with their tips pointing upward, so that the face motifs would have been oriented right side up, but the diversity of their positioning at the burial sites — near the head, the hands, or the chest of the deceased — renders archaeological evidence for their function inconclusive.

Rod-shaped fittings have also been found at the Dawenkou site in Shandong province.[5] Round in cross section and pointed at one end, they closely resemble and are contemporaneous

with Early Liangzhu examples. They were made throughout the Middle and Late Dawenkou periods (3500–2500 BCE), during which their form remained unchanged. It is likely that they were introduced from Liangzhu during the early third millennium BCE with the strengthening interactions between the two cultures.[6] zs

1 Excavated in 1986 (M 9:7); not recorded in the brief report.
2 Excavated in 1986 (M 20:73); reported: Zheijiang 1988a, 23.
3 Nanjing 1982, 25–35, for a detailed photographic reproduction, see Zhejiang 1989, pl. 140.
4 Shanghai 1986, 23, for a detailed photographic reproduction, see Zhejiang 1989, pl. 139.
5 Shandong 1974, 96, pl. 97: 9.
6 For discussion of the interactions between prehistoric cultures in the Lake Tai region and those in the Shandong region, see Gao 1986, 42, 47.

35

Jade *zhuo* bracelet

Height 2.6 (1), exterior diam. 7.4 (2 ⅞),
interior diam. 6 (2 ⅜)
Liangzhu Culture, c. 3200–2000 BCE
From Yaoshan, Yuhang, Zhejiang Province

Zhejiang Provincial Institute of Archaeology,
Hangzhou

This thick-walled bracelet[1] is beautifully formed,
elaborately decorated, and polished to a soft luster.
Four monsterlike faces carved in high relief encircle
its exterior, each featuring a pair of round eyes
with bulging pupils and a wide, straight mouth with
neatly aligned teeth. Thin, sunken lines define the
arched eyebrows, round nose, and prominent jaws.
Unlike the awesome expression of most Liangzhu
monsters, these faces appear rather playful.

The jade is creamy white, but scattered spots
and fine streaks of olive color suggest that the
stone was originally translucent green. The form of
this bracelet, as well as the symmetrical arrangement of the monster faces at the four corners, exhibits a close affinity with that of the *cong*, which
indeed may have been its inspiration.

Bracelets number among the earliest Liangzhu
jade forms; their antecedents can be traced to the
very beginnings of eastern-coast jadework during
the fifth millennium BCE. Examples from Liangzhu
display a rich variety of shapes and designs —
slim, thick, or convex walls and surface patterns
engraved in intaglio or raised in relief. Decorative
motifs primarily comprise face images and scrollwork, but twisted-rope patterns occasionally appear.
A bracelet found on the arm of the deceased in a
Fuquanshan tomb in Shanghai consists of two half-

Cat. 35, incised and carved decoration. After Zhejiang 1988b, 46, fig. 35:3.

rings, drilled along the short edge so that they could be joined at the perforations.[2]

Although varied in shape and decoration, jade bracelets are ubiquitous among prehistoric cultures, and their distribution spans the Liao River valley in northeastern China to the Zhujiang River valley in the far south.[3] It is still too early to assign a common origin to jade bracelets; pottery and bone antecedents dating back much earlier than the jade forms have been found among many of these cultures, and these exhibit a wide variety of idiosyncratic formal features; bracelets of the Late Yangshao culture, for example, have a triangular cross section. The fact that in later periods bracelets were made of other materials (including gold, silver, agate, ivory, and lacquer) apparently did not diminish the value attached to jade: for thousands of years after the Liangzhu culture — even to the present day — jade bracelets have been the most prevalent and favored items of personal adornment in Chinese society. zs

1   Excavated in 1987 (M 1:30); reported: Zheijiang 1988a, 48.
2   Shanghai 1984, 2, pl. 1:7; for a detailed photographic reproduction, see Shanghai 1992, pl. 83.
3   Liaoning 1986, 11 – 13, figs. 14, 16, 18, 20; Zhongguo 1963, 194; Xi'an 1988, 315 – 316; Zhongguo Shandong 1979, 12 – 13; Sichuan 1961, 18, fig. 35; Zhongguo 1965b, 67; Anhui 1982a, 313 – 315; Anhui 1989, 1 – 9; Zhu 1984, 90 – 95; for a full bibliography, see Sun Zhixin 1996, 137 – 166.

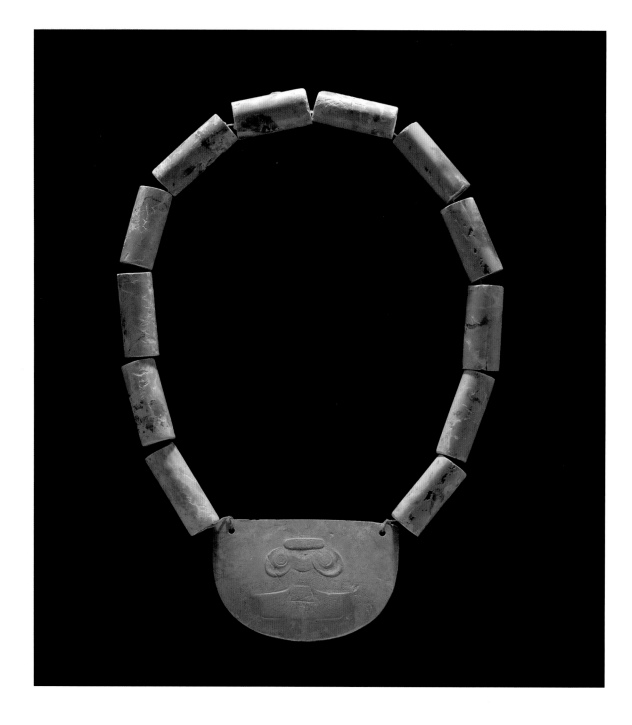

36

Jade beads and plaque

Beads: length 2.7 – 3 (1 – 1 ¼)
Plaque: height 4.2 (1 ⅝), width 6.3 (2 ½)
Liangzhu Culture, c. 3200 – 2000 BCE
From Yaoshan, Yuhang, Zhejiang Province

Zhejiang Provincial Institute of Archaeology,
Hangzhou

By quantity, beads dominate the inventory of Liangzhu burial goods — some tombs contain more than
a hundred — and they are the oldest form of jade
objects among cultures of the eastern coast, with
examples dating back to the fifth millennium BCE.
Jade beads were carved in tubular, spherical, and
barrel-shaped forms; tubular beads are by far the
predominant type. Most beads are undecorated,
but some tubular forms bear face motifs similar
to those cut in sunken lines on the *cong,* often so
finely executed that the details are visible only
under magnification. Despite their modest, undeco-

rated surfaces, spherical beads — with their precisely round contours and brilliant luster — testify
to the skill of Liangzhu lapidaries.[1] Although beads
could be carved from lumps of raw jade, they were
more likely made from drill cores or other off-cuts
of larger objects.

Beads are most often found clustered in
burials — sometimes together with plaques and
pendants — as components of necklaces or other
assemblages that were originally strung together.
Determining the original arrangement of dislocated
beads is a formidable, perhaps impossible, task
and all reconstructions are for that reason conjectural. The fact that the beads and the plaque
of this reconstructed necklace were found in close
proximity to one another, for example, does not
necessarily imply that they were strung as part
of a single assemblage.[2]

This plaque takes the form of a half disk with
a gently curved and smoothly finished surface.
The carving on the front of the disk, executed in
extremely fine, sunken lines, depicts a human
figure, arms at his side, wearing a feather headdress; he appears to be riding on a monster with
large circular eyes, a bar-shaped mouth, and two
clawed feet. Two small holes are drilled near the
straight edge, one in each corner.

Semicircular plaques constitute a standard
category among Liangzhu jades.[3] Some are decorated with face motifs and scrollwork, others are
plain-surfaced; several examples are drilled at
the back with connecting holes, which suggests
that they were probably attached or sewn onto
garments of fabric or leather. zs

1   For photographic reproductions, see Zhejiang 1989,
    pl. 185; Shanghai 1992, pl. 73, 90.
2   Excavated in 1986 (M 22:8); the beads and plaque are not
    recorded in the excavation report (Zheijiang 1988a, 1–29).
3   Zhejiang 1988a, 22, fig. 23; 1988b, 46–47, figs. 28, 33 for
    photographic reproductions, see Zhejiang 1989, pls. 151,
    152, 153; Shanghai 1992, pl. 62.

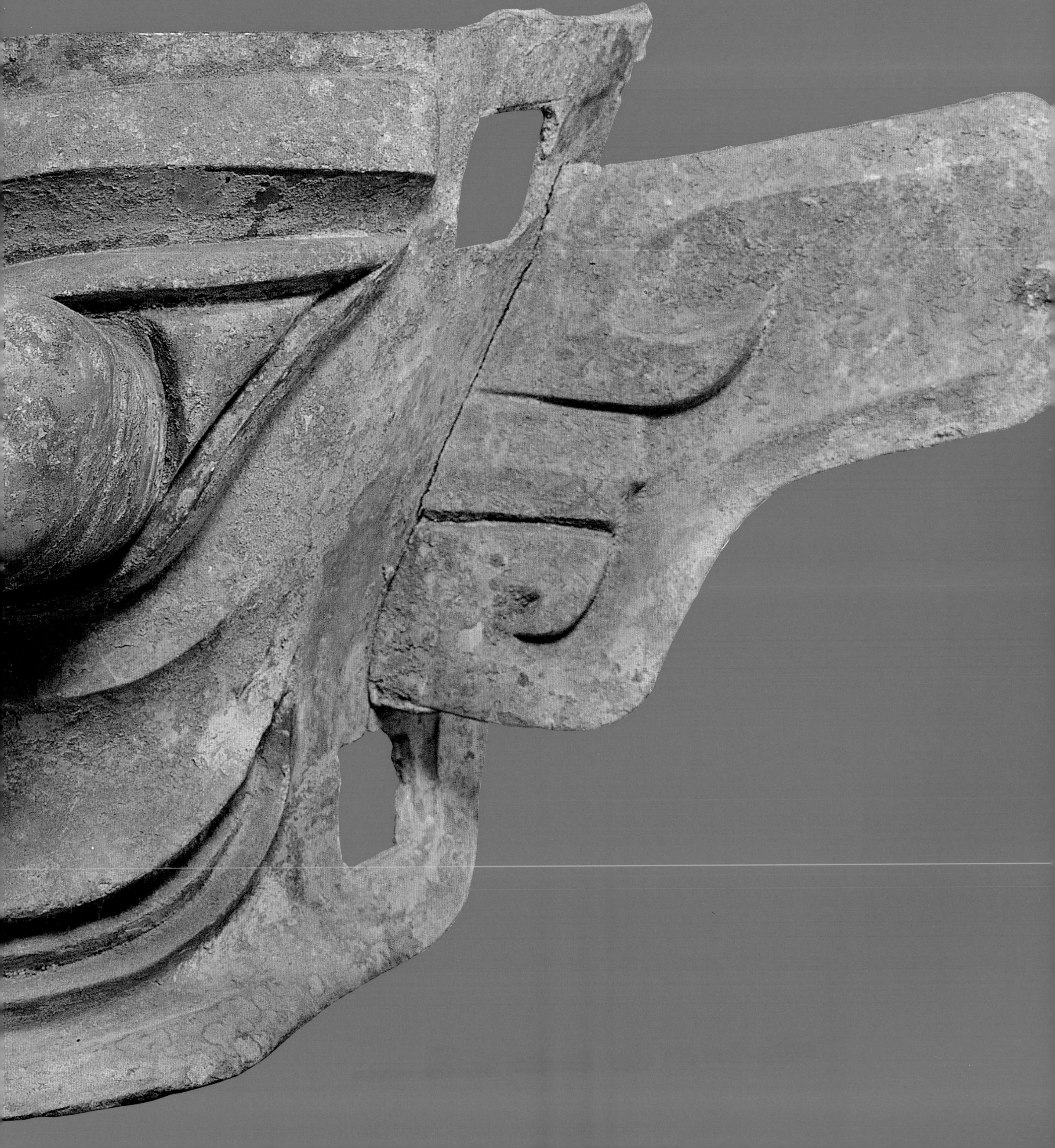

The Epic of the Three Dynasties

BRONZE AGE CHINA (C. 2000–771 BCE)

According to traditonal historiography, the first three successive dynasties — the Xia, Shang, and Zhou — ruled parts of northern China during the period to which the archaeological finds described in this section can be dated. While various ancient texts document the deeds of the Three Dynasties' kings (including King Yu, the first king of the Xia dynasty, and by extension, the first king of China, who directed his people to build irrigation systems to prevent floods[1]), there was no physical evidence to verify such legends. The early writings situate the capitals of the Three Dynasties in the present-day provinces of Henan and Shaanxi — the region long believed to be the cradle of Chinese civilization; locating the remains of the Three Dynasties has been a consistent priority of Chinese archaeologists. As a result of the efforts of several generations of archaeologists, the Xia, Shang, and Zhou dynasties have begun to emerge from their cloud of mystery; the progress of these investigations itself comprises a trilogy of sorts.

The first episode was the 1928–1937 Anyang excavations, which proved the existence of the Shang dynasty and identified Anyang as the area of the Late Shang capital.[2] The Anyang project continues to this day; one of the most unexpected recent discoveries has been the undisturbed tomb of Fu Hao. The Shang dynastic culture is represented by highly advanced objects and writing — ritual bronzes, jades, oracle-bone inscriptions — as well as the foundations of palaces, cities, and large royal mausoleums. Exhibits from the Anyang area, including items from the Fu Hao tomb, exemplify the dynasty's artistic achievements (cats. 46–56). The Anyang excavations, moreover, have demonstrated that some accounts of early China in ancient Chinese historiographical works are in fact reliable and helpful in the planning of archaeological projects.

The second episode in the investigation of the Three Dynasties was the search for the Xia in western Henan, which ancient texts identified as the dynasty's seat. Since the 1950s, archaeologists have conducted field work at the Erlitou site, Yanshi, Henan province.[3] These excavations brought to light the earliest bronze culture in China (see cats. 37–40). The Erlitou culture's temporal and geographic range falls within the parameters of the Xia dynasty described in texts. While the Erlitou excavations were underway, a Shang city at Zhengzhou was discovered and identified as earlier than the Anyang Shang culture and later than the Erlitou culture.[4] The prevalent view identifies the Erlitou relics with the Xia culture — a position argued herein by Professor Zou Heng — but no writings have been discovered that definitively confirm this hypothesis. While the nature of the Erlitou culture remains the subject of some debate, there is consensus that the Erlitou culture was a state-organized society that appeared earlier than the Zhengzhou and Anyang Shang cultures.

Investigations of the Western Zhou dynasty were performed contemporaneously in the Shaanxi area. Excavated ritual bronzes, especially those with long inscriptions, have greatly benefited our understanding of the ritual and lineage system of that period (see cat. 81). The Zhou people had close ties to the Shang culture, from whom they inherited the major elements of their culture, to the point that many Late Shang and Early Western Zhou bronzes are so

Cat. 82, detail

Bronze plaque inlaid with turquoise; length 16.5 (6 ½); Erlitou culture; excavated in 1984 from Erlitou, Yanshi, Henan province.

similar that there are few recognizable standards to distinguish between them. This exhibition includes bronzes and jades from the Western Zhou metropolitan area (cats. 76–77), the Zhou's homeland (cats. 78–83), and the state of Jin, established by a member of the Zhou royal family, in Shanxi province (cats. 84–90). Traditional historians believe that the Three Dynasties represent the mainstream of cultural and artistic development during the years in which they flourished; recent archaeological finds, however, have shown that the situation may not be so simple. As was the case during the preceding Neolithic period, distinctive regional cultures continued to thrive thoughout the Bronze Age in the areas adjacent to the territories of the Three Dynasties.

The third episode in the investigation of Early Bronze Age China was the extension of archaeological investigation into the regions beyond the political scope of the Three Dynasties. In northeastern China, the discovery of the Lower Xiajiadian culture in Inner Mongolia revealed that many elements of the Erlitou culture were assimilated by the northeastern Chinese peoples: *jue* and *jia* vessels in the Erlitou style were commonly employed in the Lower Xiajiadian culture (cats. 44–45), and artifacts of both cultures display shared decorative elements, such as animal-mask motifs and cloud-and-thunder patterns (compare, for example cats. 38 and 41–43). These shared characteristics show cultural influences from the Central Plains extended into distant areas as early as the first half of the second millenium BCE. In southern China, findings from Sanxingdui (Guanghan, Sichuan province) along the upper

Yangzi River (cats. 65–75) and Dayangzhou (Xin'gan, Jiangxi province) along the middle Yangzi River (cats. 57–64) are testimony to the extensive development of Bronze Age cultures all over China proper.

The artistic achievements of the southern Bronze Age cultures parallel those of the Shang dynasty. Certainly, the Sanxingdui and the Dayangzhou cultures adopted a tradition of bronze ritual vessels from the Shang (cats. 59–62, 74), but bronzes from these southern Chinese cultures also display local, indigenous features. The Sanxingdui human, animal, and mythical sculptures, for example, contrast sharply with the northern dynastic tradition (see cats. 65–73). Bronzes from Dayangzhou contain local features, but these are often manifested in minor ways — in the animal ornaments on the handles of objects or in certain decorative patterns (cats. 59–62). Its musical instruments, such as the bronze *bo* bell (cat. 64), nevertheless demonstrate salient regional characteristics. On the other hand, cultural exchanges were mutual. These discoveries have proved that advanced bronze cultures inhabited both the south and the north of China; the long-held prejudice among scholars that the south was a backwater is no longer tenable. No writing from Shang period China has been discovered in the two southern cultures (except pictographs and dedicatory inscriptions in the Shang dynastic style from the Hunan provincial area); whether that fact reflects differences between the northern dynastic culture and the bronze cultures of the south is a question that remains to be answered. XY

1   See, for example, Sima Qian, "Xia ben ji" in the *Shi ji* (Records of the historian).
2   For the history of the early Anyang excavations, see Li Ji 1977.
3   For achievements of the early-stage investigations, see Zhongguo 1965c.
4   Henan 1959.

THE ERLITOU

CULTURE AT

YANSHI, HENAN

PROVINCE

The luster of the "Erlitou culture" derives from unique finds characteristic of the type site. First identified as the result of a deliberate effort to discover material remains of the Xia dynasty (the first of the Three Dynasties [*san dai*] of traditional Chinese historiography), the Erlitou site in Yanshi county, Henan province, lies in the eastern suburbs of the great city of Luoyang.[1] Excavations have yielded a large quantity of a gray pottery dated as intermediate between that of local Neolithic cultures and Early Shang period pottery from such key sites as Zhengzhou. Moreover, the Erlitou site may hold upward of a dozen pounded-earth foundations conventionally regarded as "palaces" by their excavators. The two palaces already uncovered reveal courtyard plans of a kind fundamental to all later Chinese architectural practice.[2] Over the last two decades, many richly furnished graves have been excavated, yielding, in addition to hardstone objects, the earliest bronze vessels in China proper. Most Chinese scholars now confidently equate this archaeological culture with the Xia, relying on its general correspondence in time (c. 1900–1500 BCE) and place (western Henan province) with the expectations of historiographical tradition.

The confidence of many Chinese scholars has not, however, persuaded all researchers. The lack of a worldwide consensus on the identity of the Erlitou type site (compared with the general acceptance of the Zhengzhou and Anyang sites as Shang) illustrates some of the competing assumptions and agendas of archaeologists and historians, both inside and outside China today. For many Chinese scholars, especially those who conceive of archaeology as an essentially historiographic discipline, the recovery of the Erlitou culture marks a major breakthrough in the reconstruction of the past and the reconciliation of historiography and "scientific evidence." As such, the work at Erlitou is considered important as the excavations at Anyang (cats. 46–54) and the Plain of Zhou (cats. 78–83). In each case, modern archaeology verifies a received historical tradition, complementing and correcting that record.

Among scholars who embrace a different orientation, such as the North American view of archaeology as anthropology, the evidence from Erlitou appears less revelatory: The absence of any writing (save a few signs on pottery sherds) and the lack of any putative royal burials (with one disputed exception), combined with the piecemeal publication of the finds, raises many doubts about what has been recovered at the site itself. So far, the type site is exceptional in its own right; no other sites of this archaeological culture compare in their material inventories. The absence of any references to a Xia people or to Xia kings in the Shang oracle-bone inscriptions from c. 1200 BCE (see cats. 55–56) also makes the equation of the Erlitou culture with the Xia dynasty problematic. Other archaeological cultures could be championed as putative Xia remains, including, for example, the remarkable cemetery at Taosi in Xiangfeng county (Shanxi province).

In general, more data generated over time will help promote greater clarity in disputes regarding the identity of particular archaeological cultures or finds, even if they are not conclusively resolved by the latest discovery. Resolving the status of the Erlitou culture can only

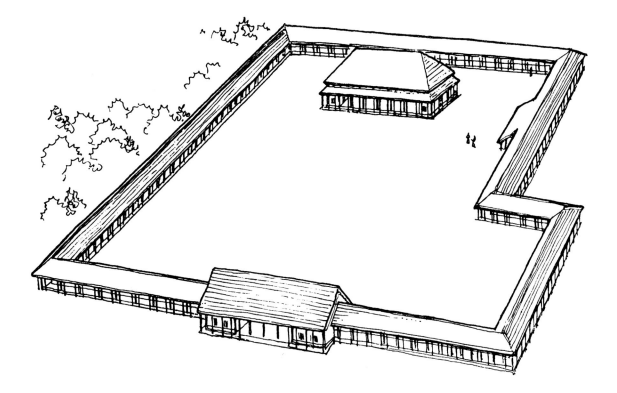

Conjectural reconstruction of one of the "palaces" at Erlitou, Yanshi, Henan province. After Yang 1987, 75, fig. 5.

result from a broader consensus on other issues — theoretical and practical. How do we choose to define a "state" and its archaeological traces? How do we imagine the interaction of peoples and their collectivities over space and across time? What is the meaning of a concept such as "the Xia kings" for excavators? Only within a paradigm that assumes certain answers to these and related questions can one posit solutions. It remains to be seen whether researchers will endeavor to establish such a broad paradigm of common goals and assumptions. RT

1   Thorp 1991a.
2   Thorp 1983b.

37

Bronze *ding* tripod

Height 20 (7⅞), diam. at mouth 15.3 (6)
Erlitou Culture, Period IV or Lower Erligang Period
(1600–1400 BCE)
From the Erlitou site at Gedangtou, Yanshi,
Henan Province

The Institute of Archaeology, CASS, Beijing

The *ding* tripod, a type ubiquitous throughout the
Chinese Bronze Age, has come to symbolize the
ritual vessels of the Shang and Zhou dynasties.
This particular vessel[1] complements the more common *jue* pouring cups (of which about a dozen are
known) and *jia* and *he* wine warmers in the repertoire of ritual vessels from this site. The vessel was
intended for practical use; later examples suggest
that it might have been used to cook a meat stew,

outer mold sections would have been formed to render the everted rim and to leave space for the two loop handles. This *ding* has a simple pattern of crossed relief lines in a band around its waist, an effect that takes advantage of the piece-mold technique. The interior of outer molds could easily be scored, carved, or even stamped with decorative designs to create relief on the surface of the cast object.

This *ding* was recovered through the efforts of the local public security bureau after it, a *jia* tripod and a *gu* goblet were unearthed by workers at a factory near the Erlitou site. Since the archaeological context was never properly documented, or related artifacts (such as pottery) collected, the assignment of this *ding* to the Erlitou culture (rather than to the subsequent Lower Erligang [Early Shang] Phase) is at best hypothetical. Several vessels with similar decoration have been recovered from other sites in Henan: a *jue* was found at Zhengzhou in 1958, and a *jia* was found in Xinzheng in 1975.[2] These related examples are usually assigned to the Early Shang period (c. 1600 – 1300 BCE).[3] RT

1   Recovered in 1987; reported: Zhongguo Erlitou 1991, 1138 – 1139, and pl. 8.
2   Henan 1981, nos. 61 and 91.
3   Thorp 1985.

and the tripod's pointed legs would have allowed the vessel and its contents to be placed directly into a bed of hot charcoal or some other fuel. This *ding* is of a modest size that permits easy manipulation by one pair of hands; presumably the two loop handles at the rim were used to lift it off the fire.

The vessel still bears traces of seams between the ceramic piece-molds used for its casting, as well as signs of an early repair. The mold assembly required for such a vessel presented no great challenges, and surely the object was less demanding to cast than the more common *jue*. A spherical clay core (with three pointed stumps to create a hollow in each conical leg) formed the vessel's interior. Outer mold sections formed the body of the vessel, their joins aligned at regular intervals around the vessel — probably in three sections extending from one leg to the next. If the *ding* was cast upside down (as generally seems to have been the practice) the

38

Bronze plaque inlaid with turquoise

Height 14.2 (5 ½), width 9.8 (3 ⅞)
Erlitou Culture, Period II (c. 1800–1700 BCE)
From the Erlitou site at Gedangtou, Yanshi,
Henan Province

The Institute of Archaeology, CASS, Beijing

Unprovenanced objects closely resembling this
bronze plaque were catalogued some years ago
as horse "frontlets," and indeed their size, shape,
and loops for attachment plausibly suggested this
identification;[1] their use of turquoise inlay, on
the other hand, was reminiscent of finely crafted
weapons from Anyang and other Late Shang contexts. Only in 1981 was a plausible archaeological
source for this kind of object reported, with the excavation of the grave at Erlitou that contained the
plaque shown here.[2] This example was found near
the chest of the deceased in a burial distinguished
by the richness of its furnishings, which included
fragments of lacquerware as well as bronzes and
jades. Since its discovery, other rich burials at the
site have yielded similar plaques. However, there
is no evidence at Erlitou for horses or their trappings, and chariots cannot be attested in northern
China prior to the Anyang occupation several
centuries later. Thus, the function of this and the
other plaques remains a matter for conjecture.

All of these plaques measure about 15 centimeters in length, with rounded corners, small loops
on each long side, and raised bands that contain
small fragments of turquoise. Turquoise has been
found in other contexts at Erlitou, such as the inlay
on a bronze disk (possibly a mirror) and strings of
beads. The stone was not native to the region, however, and must have been acquired through some
kind of trade from distant points. We have little if
any evidence for the use of turquoise with bronze
after the Erlitou culture period in northern China
until it reappears in the Late Shang, as for example
in objects from the tomb of Fu Hao (cats. 46–54).

This design is often interpreted as a mask on
the visual evidence of what appear to be two round
eyes peering over a snout and two jaws surmounted

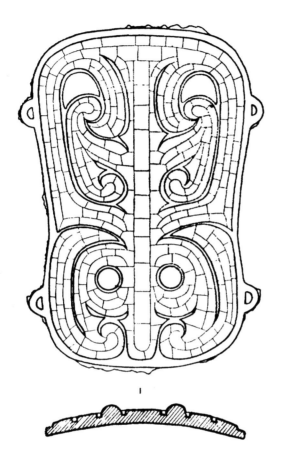

by large ears or horns (fig. 1). Eyes on these plaques come in two shapes, either unframed circles (as here) or circles within pointed sockets. The upper "horns," however, vary in every example. If the image anticipates the motifs that play so large a role in later bronze decoration (for example, the *fangding*, cat. 46), and for which the anachronistic term *taotie* has been employed since premodern times, it nonetheless differs in a number of respects. No consensus has emerged as to the significance of such motifs, but their ubiquity in so many media (bronze, stone, lacquer) and varied contexts — even as early as the Erlitou culture — makes the question worth pursuing.

Two plaques have been recovered at the Sanxingdui site in distant Sichuan province.[3] They may be roughly contemporaneous in date, a fact that would point to the possibility of exchanges between the bronze-using cultures of northern China and the upper Yangzi River region in the early second millennium BCE. Since hardstones also suggest this possibility, the character of such exchanges deserves attention. RT

1 Loehr 1965, no. 19 and Poor 1975, no. 13.
2 Excavated in 1981; reported: Zhongguo Erlitou 1984, 37–40, and pl. 4.
3 Zhao 1994, nos. 63–64.

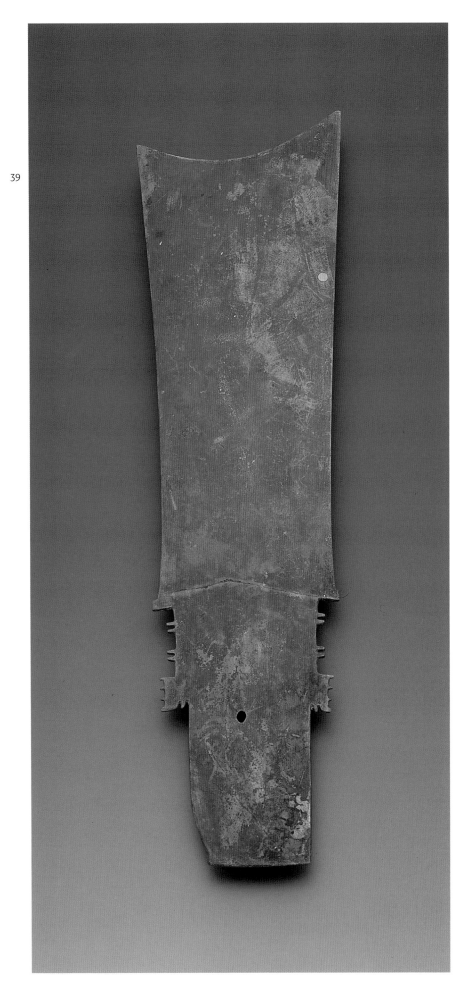

39

39

Hardstone *zhang* ritual blade

Height 54 (21 ¼), maximum width 14.8 (5 ⅞)
Erlitou Culture, Period III (c. 1700 – 1600 BCE)
From the Erlitou site at Gedangtou, Yanshi,
Henan Province

The Institute of Archaeology, CASS, Beijing

40

Hardstone *yue* axe

Height 21 (8 ¼), maximum width 23 (9 ¼)
Erlitou Culture, Period IV (c. 1600 – 1500 BCE)
From the Erlitou site at Gedangtou, Yanshi,
Henan Province

The Institute of Archaeology, CASS, Beijing

The shapes of hardstone objects recovered from
rich burials at Erlitou suggest specialized, perhaps
ceremonial or ritual, purposes. Blades or scepters
(*zhang*) are a form not established in the Neolithic
period and, like the dagger-axe (*ge*), may actually
depend on bronze prototypes.[1] Such blades
would normally have been hafted at a right angle
to handles — in the case of this *zhang*,[2] perhaps
through the small perforation in its tang (although
its length and thinness would have rendered it too
fragile for any use except as an insignia or token
of rank); we have no physical evidence, however,
that such elaborate hardstone blades were ever
actually hafted and displayed. The stone *zhang* from
Erlitou was found in a grave, placed pointing north
on the chest of the deceased, and was paired with
a similar but smaller blade pointing in the opposite
direction. It seems unlikely that the blades were
attached to handles at the time of the burial.

Broad flat axes (*yue*), on the other hand, were
widespread in Neolithic cultures of the eastern
coast and the mouth of the Yangzi River.[3] Two variants documented at Erlitou are more elaborate: one
shown here is a conventional flat axe with a circular
perforation, four segments to the cutting edge,
and six small "teeth" on each side.[4] The other variant (called a *qi* or *qibi*) is a disk with a large central

40

perforation, the same four segments to the putative cutting edge, and teeth above and below. If the disk variant was used actually as an axe blade, it must have been hafted, but no obvious method of attachment is apparent from the Erlitou examples. Like the *zhang* blade, this well-crafted stone may have been carried as regalia or insignia.

The main affinities between the large Erlitou hardstone blade types and outlying cultures are found in the Northwest macroregion (present-day Shaanxi) and the Upper Yangzi macroregion (the Sichuan basin). The Sanxingdui site (cats. 65–75) has yielded copious quantities of similar blades. Just as the use of imported turquoise as inlay in Erlitou bronzes implies contacts with other areas (see cat. 38), it may be argued that the Erlitou type site was in communication with distant regions — in this instance at the receiving end of a tradition of fashioning hardstones. As yet, it appears unlikely that Erlitou was itself a center for such craft. RT

1 First suggested by Jessica Rawson; see Bagley 1980, 76.
2 Excavated in 1980 (VM3:4); reported: Zhongguo Erlitou 1983, 199–205, 219 and pl. 1.
3 Shao 1993.
4 Excavated in 1981 (81YLVM 6:1); reported: Zhongguo Erlitou 1984, 37–40 and pl. 3.

TOMBS OF

THE LOWER

XIAJIADIAN

CULTURE AT

DADIANZI,

AOHANQI,

INNER MONGOLIA

The Lower Xiajiadian culture, dating to the early Bronze Age, was located far to the northeast of the Erlitou metropolitan centers in the area roughly coinciding with the territory once populated by the earlier Hongshan culture (cats. 10–22). It is represented in the exhibit by ceramic vessels from the Inner Mongolian site of Dadianzi, in the vicinity of Chifeng, but its wider distribution extended both north and south of the Yan mountains, well into what are now Hebei and Liaoning provinces.[1]

The Xiajiadian sites are situated for the most part on the table lands above the rivers that wind through the region. Often these sites seem to occur in pairs, facing each other across the rivers, or in clusters near the mouths of rivers. The settlements with closer access to the rivers were apparently the preferred location, while those situated at a greater elevation tend to be smaller and less rich in artifacts. Dadianzi, itself a large and important site, was surrounded by smaller settlements and guarded by a sentry post built in the mountains overlooking it.

One of the most renowned features of the more sizable Lower Xiajiadian settlements are the defensive walls that surround them, which were constructed of pounded earth or of stone. A series of walled settlements stretching along the Daling and Laoha Rivers provides a very early prototype for the Great Wall, erected in this same area during the Warring States period. At Dadianzi, the walls seem to have been largely of pounded earth, although the gateways were faced in stone. Walled enclosures also surround the mud-brick dwellings at some of the Xiajiadian sites.

The Xiajiadian cemeteries, including the one at Dadianzi, were located beyond the defensive walls. The burial field at Dadianzi was unusually large, and the well-preserved graves found there, nearly 800 in all, can be considered as typical for the culture as a whole. While most of the graves are relatively small, the larger burials of the elite members of the community, which are dug to an exceptional depth, are the more interesting for the artifacts they contained and for what they reveal about the Dadianzi society and its connection with other, often distant cultures.

M 612, the tomb from which all but one of the pottery vessels in the exhibition were recovered, is an example of a fairly typical large, high-status burial at Dadianzi (fig. 1). It was located at the northern edge of the cemetery. The burial pit measured over two meters in length and almost a meter in width, but its most surprising aspect was its depth of fully six meters. Preserved in the walls of the pit were the foot holes used for climbing up and down it.

At the bottom of the pit were the partial remains of a skeleton, identified as a male, approximately forty-five years old. Under his left ear lay a pair of turquoise beads, and between his thighbones were some forty stone beads, perhaps once sewn to the ends of a sash tied at his waist. Traces of a fabric belonging to his garment or to his shroud were also detected. Although the wooden coffin had disintegrated, its imprint was left in the soil.

The burial objects were found not in the burial chamber but on the ledges of a niche cut into the sides of the pit more than two meters above the floor of the chamber. In the side of the

FIG. 1. Plan of Tomb 612 at Dadianzi, Aohanqi, Inner Mongolia. After Zhongguo 1996, 55, fig. 29.

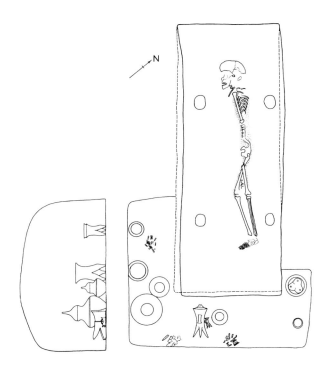

niche aligned with the foot of the coffin were placed the *gui* and *jiao* (cats. 44, 45), along with a number of pig's feet. On the ledge to the right was a *li*, emptied of its contents and placed upside down. The majority of the pottery vessels and other items were deposited in the niche to the left, including a large *li* (cat. 41), a second, smaller *li*, a *hu* (cat. 43), and a small covered jar. In the same section of the niche were found the remnants of lacquerware objects, a jade pendant, and more pig's feet. One of the *li* vessels contained several cowrie shells, which must have been acquired through long-distance trade, as well as pieces of turquoise.

Evidence that the burial rites continued as the tomb was being repacked with earth is indicated by the discovery at the depth of about three meters of two separate sacrificial burials, which had consisted of dogs, and also of pigs which had their feet removed.[2]

The excavation of the Dadianzi site is important not only because it revealed a hitherto relatively unknown culture in the northeast, but because it provides evidence of long-distance connections with the early Bronze Age urban centers far to the south in the Henan area of the Yellow River valley. Among the most significant objects recovered from the Dadianzi burials are the *gui* and *jiao* ceramic vessels, used for pouring ritual libations (cats. 44, 45). These vessels are seen only in the large, high-status burials and are considered to represent prestige goods. As vessel types, they have no prehistory in the northeast, but at the Erlitou sites in Henan they are very common.

While the presence of these two vessel types at Dadianzi can be considered as proof of the influence from the distant Erlitou urban centers, it raises many unanswered questions about the actual nature of the interaction between the two cultures. That these two vessels were found in the burials alongside the other ceramic vessels suggests their incorporation into the ceremonial rites of burial, indicating that this interaction may have involved more than casual trade relations. One possibility is that individuals made their way from Erlitou to the northeast, and that the local Xiajiadian elite were sufficiently impressed by the newcomers to emulate their vessels and the rituals for which they were designed. The quite distinctive nature of the Dadianzi culture, however, dispels any suggestion of a wider Erlitou presence within these communities.

A number of the *gui* and *jiao* vessels from Dadianzi exhibit what appear to be imitation rivets, lending support to the theory that a tradition of sheet-metal vessels may have existed at Erlitou before the development of cast-bronze technology.[3] Other metal artifacts found at Dadianzi, however, suggest no influence from Erlitou, but point instead to cultural transmissions from a very different source, namely the Eurasian steppe. These artifacts include trumpet-shaped earrings and larger annular nose rings, which have been recovered from roughly contemporary finds scattered all across the northern periphery of present-day China, from Gansu eastward to Liaoning province.[4] Earrings of the same kind are associated with the Andronovo and other nomadic peoples who had begun to make their way east across the steppelands from as far away as Western Central Asia.[5] Other types of metal objects from Dadianzi include cast-bronze accouterments for weapons, among them finials that were secured to wooden hafts by metal nails. Although a clay casting-mold has been recovered from a related Lower Xiajiadian site, implying the existence of local bronze production, the ultimate prototype for these finials is possibly to be found as far away as the Bactrian-Margiana area in what is now southern Turkmenistan and Afghanistan.[6]

These finds tell us that Dadianzi was a crossroads for cultural transmissions from very different cultures. The site may well have been one of the important transit points from which Eurasian metalwork was carried south to the Erlitou urban centers, where its influence is especially visible in the shapes of bronze knives and other implements.[7] In exchange, other goods deemed of equal value were evidently transported to the north. These commodities probably included textiles and, almost certainly, lacquerware. Evidence from the elite burials at Dadianzi reveals that the *gui* and *jiao* ritual pouring vessels were accompanied by lacquered wooden beakers *(gu)*, just as they were at Erlitou, and it is fair to assume that these three vessel types arrived in the north as a set.[8]

The presence of lacquerware at Dadianzi and the likelihood that it was imported from the south raise a number of issues regarding the painted decoration on the Dadianzi vessels (cats. 41, 42, and 43). The pervasive syntax of these designs, based on complex interconnected and re-curving C-shapes, as well as such distinctive designs as quasi-zoomorphic faces, are also perceptible in the designs on the turquoise inlaid bronze plaques from Erlitou (cat. 38). Because the pottery and the bronze vessels at Erlitou are either undecorated or embellished only with simple striations, it is generally assumed that the decorative systems we associate with the early Shang bronzes did not arise until after the Erlitou period. The inlaid plaques are the exception. The evident paucity of decorated objects from Erlitou and the elaborate repertory of painted designs at Dadianzi, known from no other culture at this period, have led to speculation that some design elements later seen on bronzes — including most importantly the *taotie* image (see cat. 42) — may have appeared first at Dadianzi.

The shared characteristics of the designs on the Dadianzi pottery and those on the inlaid plaques from Erlitou may, however, be susceptible of a somewhat different explanation. The patterns on the Dadianzi ceramics, outlined in black against a red ground, call to mind nothing more strongly than carved lacquerware. We also know from the archaeological reports that lacquer was used at Erlitou to decorate not only wooden vessels but a wider range of objects, including coffins.[9] Although virtually none of this material has been made available in illustration, the drawing of a single fragment of lacquered wood from an Erlitou burial shows the carved design of two oval eyes with C-shaped curls above, reminiscent of an early form of the *taotie*.[10] The abundance of lacquered objects at Erlitou and the evidence that some of them bore carved decoration suggest that the patterns on the inlaid bronze plaques and the Dadianzi ceramics may both reflect a tradition of carved lacquer decoration current at Erlitou.[11]

Given the fact that we do not yet know in any detail what forms the lacquered decoration at Erlitou took, it would seem a rush to judgment to assign the priority of such important designs as the *taotie* to the Dadianzi culture. Real answers to the sources of the painted designs on the Dadianzi ceramics and to the broader issue of the relationship between these two early Bronze Age cultures await further information that only future archaeological excavations may be able to provide. LF-H

1 A complete report of the excavations at Dadianzi is provided in Zhongguo 1996. A convenient synopsis of the Lower Xiajiadian culture by Guo Daoshun, translated into English, is available in Nelson 1995b, 147–181.
2 M 612 is described in Zhongguo 1996, 54–56.
3 Examples of *gui* and *jiao* vessels showing imitation rivets are illustrated in Zhongguo 1996, 82, fig. 41:1–3, 5; 84, fig. 42:4; Zhongguo 1993, 133, fig. 105:1–2. See Fitzgerald-Huber 1995, 20–21.
4 Zhongguo 1996, 188–191; pl. 56:3; Zhongguo 1993, 134, fig. 106:2. The earrings are discussed in Fitzgerald-Huber 1995, 65–66, n. 111; Bunker 1998, 607–609, 611.
5 Compare Kuzmina 1998, fig. 5:10–18.
6 The Dadianzi cast-bronze fittings are illustrated in Zhongguo 1996, 190, fig. 86:1–5; pl. 56:1–2, 4. A reconstruction of how two of these fittings were placed on a haft is shown in Zhongguo 1993, 134, fig. 106:3. A Bactrian finial similar to one from Dadianzi (Zhongguo 1996, 190, fig. 86:3; pl. 56:4) is shown in Ligabue 1988, 165, fig. 8g; Pottier 1984, 177, fig. 43:316.

7 Lin 1986, 250; Fitzgerald-Huber 1995, 24–25.
8 The best preserved of the Dadianzi lacquered *gu* is illustrated in Zhongguo 1996, color pl. 20:1.
9 Lacquerware from Erlitou burials is noted in Zhongguo Erlitou 1983, 203–205; and Yang 1984, 39–40.
10 Zhongguo Erlitou 1983, 203, fig. 9:9 (80 YL III M 2:2).
11 The painted designs on the Dadianzi ceramics also share certain similarities with the older tradition at Taosi (cats. 25–26). At Taosi, where fragments of lacquer have been found, the palette of red and black is sometimes present, but more striking are specific design motifs later seen at Dadianzi, among them the running spiral, and, even more surprisingly, the motif of the coiled serpent (Zhongguo Shanxi 1983, 42; Zhongguo 1996, 1124, fig. 65:2–4; color pl. 16:3 [spirals]; 137, fig. 73:6; color pl. 12:3 [coiled serpent]). A question arises whether designs similar to the ones on the Taosi pottery may have had a wider currency in the Central Plains area in lacquerware and whether they may have been transmitted to Erlitou and ultimately to Dadianzi in the north.

of the tomb floor. The *li* were usually placed upside-down above a *guan* jar, but the example from M 612, found in an upright position, is an exception.

Unlike the much earlier painted pottery of the Yangshao Neolithic, the Dadianzi vessels were decorated after firing. This characteristic, which they share with the painted ware from the late Neolithic site of Taosi (cats. 25–27) results in a tendency for the paint to flake off, especially when one layer of paint is applied over another. The chalky white pigment is the most vulnerable of all. In the present case, it would appear that the entire outer surface of the vessel, with the exception of the feet, was first coated with black paint. The primary decoration in white and red was added subsequently, leaving a narrow line of the underlying black pigment visible along the edges of the designs.

The image of a single eye delineated in red can be made out above the juncture of two of the legs, like those visible on other vessels of this type from M 612.[1] The remainder of the decoration seems to be largely a free invention of the artist, who has transformed the more customary bands of curling forms into an exuberant assemblage of flamelike forms rising on the surface, unconstrained by the rules of symmetry that govern most of the decorative schemes associated with Dadianzi. The painting on this vessel thus contrasts with the orderly arrangement of patterns seen on the *hu* (cat. 43), recovered from the same burial (M 612).

The patterns encircling the inner side of the rim are more restrained and conventional. Painted to a smaller scale and meticulously executed, the configurations of white curls, in repeated units aligned radially and circumferentially, are outlined by minute black lines, ending in dots at the tips of the curls. LF-H

1 Excavated in 1977 (M 612:14); published: Zhongguo 1993, 129, fig. 101:1; Zhongguo 1996, 204, fig. 94: 10.

41

Painted pottery *li* jar

Height 25 (9 ¾)
Early Bronze Age, Lower Xiajiadian Culture
(c. 2000–1500 BCE)
From Dadianzi, Aohanqi, Inner Mongolia

The Institute of Archaeology, CASS, Beijing

Li vessels shaped like the present example[1] have been found in almost all the furnished burials at Dadianzi. In the larger and more important burials they were placed with other ceramics in the niches cut into the wall of the tomb high above the level

42

Painted pottery *lei* jar

Height 30 (11 ⅝)
Early Bronze Age, Lower Xiajiadian Culture
(c. 2000 – 1500 BCE)
From Dadianzi, Aohanqi, Inner Mongolia

The Institute of Archaeology, CASS, Beijing

Lacking the spirited flamboyance of the designs seen on some Dadianzi vessels and the disciplined control of others, the painted decoration on this vessel[1] has a wild and unruly aspect, and an importance all its own. It is on this vessel that we en-

counter one of the earliest known occurrences of the *taotie* face which was to become the preeminent image on bronze vessels during the Shang period and into the early years of the Zhou.[2]

Centered on the shoulder of the vessel above the level of the ear-shaped lugs, the *taotie* is readily identified by its two oval eyes, surmounted by curving eyebrows. Beneath the nostrils, the double lines of its bar-shaped mouth end at both sides in C-shaped curls. Evenly spaced pairs of short vertical lines indicate the teeth. The lower jaw, running parallel to the mouth, is drawn up at the side into reversing curls, which in turn touch the lines reaching upward to form the *taotie*'s "crest." The alert and menacing appearance of the face suggests that the image was probably apotropaic.

The *taotie*, moreover, is accompanied by other creatures. Lower down on the right side is another, more attenuated face, found amid the swirling, vaporous lines that fill the surface. Two sweeping S-curved shapes form the face, one the mirror-reverse of the other, with narrow, slanted lines representing the eyes. A second face of the same kind appears below, to the right. This particular type of face is also seen on one other vessel recovered from the same tomb as the *lei*.[3]

To the left of the *taotie* can be discerned a final figure, which reaches to the bottom of the painted register. The head is rendered only as a horizontally placed C-shape with a point at the center, but the rest of the form seems humanlike, with pointed shoulders, its arms bent to the chest, and a long spinelike body, with what at the bottom resemble legs drawn up as if the figure were squatting. Wing-like appendages are apparently hinged to its arms.[4] This figure, no less cryptic than the *taotie* and the other faces, seems to be presented as the apparition of a mysterious, almost dreamlike world.

The *taotie* on the *lei* is reminiscent of the demonic faces with large eyes seen on the slightly older Liangzhu jades.[5] The two faces on the right side, on the other hand, compare with those on the turquoise-inlaid bronze plaques from the contemporary site of Erlitou (cat. 38).[6] While a link almost certainly exists between these images, the story behind their transmission from one culture to another remains sketchy. A satisfactory explanation is also needed for the apparent relationship between the endlessly twisting convolutions forming the context for the figures on the *lei* and the curvilinear patterns associated with the Bronze Age *taotie* and other images, which by Anyang times become compressed to form the *leiwen*.

This *lei*, in contrast to the other Dadianzi vessels exhibited here, comes from the burial M 371. It was found in a niche cut into the wall of the tomb almost two meters above the foot of the coffin. Placed on top of it was a *li* vessel resting upside down. The niche also contained other vessels and traces of red lacquer, jade and stone ornaments, cowrie shells, and pigs' feet. The skeleton, estimated to have been about forty years old, was poorly preserved; but a staff point and thirteen bone arrowheads unearthed nearby indicate that it was a male. Across his shinbones was found a lacquer *gu* vessel inlaid with turquoise. In the fill above the tomb chamber were the remains of several dogs and pigs, including one pig with an arrow lodged between its cervical vertebrae and its shoulderblades.[7] LF-H

1   Excavated in 1976 (M 371:10); published: Zhongguo 1996, 105, fig. 54:1; pl. 11, fig. 3.
2   The only other *taotie* to vie in age with the one on the Dadianzi *lei* is a fragmentary image carved in lacquered wood from Erlitou (Zhongguo Erlitou 1983, 203, fig. 9:9). Related images are seen on other Dadianzi vessels; for example, Zhongguo 1996, 105, fig. 54:3.
3   Zhongguo 1996, 105, fig. 54:4; pl. 5:1.
4   A figure of the same type shown in profile occurs on an Early Shang bronze fitting from Xiaoshuangqiao accompanied by a serpent and a tiger; see Henan 1993, 247, fig. 7:2.
5   Compare Mou 1989a, 91, fig. 119.
6   Zhongguo Erlitou 1984, 38, fig. 5:1; pl. 4:1; Zhongguo Erlitou 1986, 321, fig. 6, top; pl. 7:1.
7   Zhongguo 1996, 56; 57, fig. 30.

43

Painted pottery *hu* jar

Height 40.5 (15¾)
Early Bronze Age, Lower Xiajiadian Culture
(c. 2000 – 1500 BCE)
From Dadianzi, Aohanqi, Inner Mongolia

The Institute of Archaeology, CASS, Beijing

This magnificent globular jar[1] swells outward from
a narrow ring foot of approximately the same diameter as the taller, slightly flaring neck. The vessel
is surmounted by a high dome-shaped cover with
a finial rising above.

In contrast to the previous *li* vessel, which
comes from the same burial at Dadianzi (cat. 41),
the designs on the present vessel are painted in
a chalky white pigment outlined by fine black lines

against a red ground. The decoration on the body is arranged in two horizontal registers, bordered by narrow bands edged in rounded relief. Diagonal strips within the bands encircle the vessel in alternating colors. Executed with utmost discipline, the principal configurations in white, ending in paired curls, are organized in parallel rows with the larger units occupying the zone of the vessel's widest circumference. The units in each row are the mirror-reverse of those above and below. Horizontal strips marked by pairs of small black squares link the rows of smaller and larger units within each register, while others lead to the curls on the right of each unit. Similar units in single file circumscribe the neck.

The patterns on the lid, organized in a somewhat looser, but no less rigorous manner, are oriented along horizontal lines, and, vertically, by lines of fluctuating width reaching to the upper and lower borders. The finial above appears to represent a snake's head, with its mouth modeled in relief.

The narrow band of white lozenges around the foot, different in character from the rest of the decor, is shown in fine lines of red reserve against a black ground. At the center each lozenge is studded with a black dot. LF-H

1   Excavated in 1977 (M 612:22); published: Zhongguo 1993, 130, fig. 102, center; Zhongguo 1996, 117, fig. 61:5; 204, fig. 94:7. The excavation report identifies the vessel as a *guan*.

44

Pottery *gui* vessel

Height 27.2 (10 ⁵/₈)
Early Bronze Age, Lower Xiajiadian Culture
(c. 2000 – 1500 BCE)
From Dadianzi, Aohanqi, Inner Mongolia

The Institute of Archaeology, CASS, Beijing

This vessel[1] and its smaller counterpart the *jiao* (cat. 45) were found in the niche of M 612, lying side-by-side. These two vessel types, intended for the pouring of libations, have been recovered only from the larger high-status burials at Dadianzi, and they invariably form a pair. Evidence indicates that in most, if not all cases, they were accompanied by a lacquered wooden goblet shaped as a flaring cylinder, which lay nearby. Together the three vessels evidently formed a specific ritual set. Only one complete example of the *gu* has survived (M 726:7), but we know of their presence in other tombs like M 612 by the remaining traces of their lacquer shell.[2] Apparently the three vessels were deposited in the niche at the conclusion of the libation rite, after their contents had been emptied.

The *gui* from M 612 is fashioned of a buff-colored ware, largely obscured by the black paint that covers its surfaces. Its three hollow, tapering legs support a cylindrical body that widens toward the rim. The radius of the rim is approximately equal to that of the splayed legs at their tips, which accounts for the vessel's well-balanced appearance. The rim rises at the front to form a short, upright pouring channel. A small knob at the opposite side of the rim may originally have served to secure a cover in place. At the back of the vessel, a broad strap handle reaches from the midsection to the upper part of one leg.

Gui vessels of this type recovered from Dadianzi are closely analogous to examples from the Erlitou Period II, and along with the *jiao,* establish the existence of long-distance cultural transmissions from the Central Plains region to the far northeast at the beginning of the Bronze Age.[3] Despite the clear dependence of the Dadianzi *gui* on a Henan prototype, its surface decoration indicates that

the vessel was locally produced. Although the Erlitou ceramic vessels sometimes show incised decoration,[4] the band of triangles around the vessel's midsection and the diagonal lines that fill the narrow bands above and below are pricked into the surface, penetrating the layer of the black paint to the clay body below. Pricked designs, rare at Erlitou, are regularly seen on Neolithic pottery across a broad area of the northeast, including the Hongshan wares, which come from the same geographical region where the Lower Xiajiadian culture later developed. LF-H

1. Excavated in 1977 (M 612:10); published: Zhongguo 1993, 132, fig. 104:2; Zhongguo 1996, 204, fig. 94:1.
2. Zhongguo 1996, color pl. 20:1.
3. A *gui* closely comparable to cat. 44 was recovered from M 49, a Period II burial at Erlitou (Zhongguo Erlitou 1992, 297, fig. 4:3).
4. For example, a *gui* from M 33 at the Erlitou site of Yichuan Nanzhai (Henan 1996, 39, fig. 6:8; 1. 4:3).

45

Pottery *jiao* vessel

Height 18 (7 ⅛)
Early Bronze Age, Lower Xiajiadian Culture
(c. 2000 – 1500 BCE)
From Dadianzi, Aohanqi, Inner Mongolia

The Institute of Archaeology, CASS, Beijing

This small pouring vessel[1] stands delicately poised
on three legs tapering to pointed tips. Its body,
smooth and undecorated, rises from the low bulging section as a slender flute that widens at the rim.
The rim sweeps upward at the front and back to a
pointed apex. A long tubular spout extends forward
in a slight curve from the vessel's midsection. Seen
in combination, the spout and the tops of the rim
fan out in space, forming an elegant configuration
across the top of the vessel. The broad strap handle
on the vessel's left side curves outward from a point
above the spout and rejoins the bulging lower section of the vessel above one of the legs. The several
sections of the vessel were fashioned separately and
luted together. The grayish buff ware is covered by
a thin coat of black pigment. Unlike the larger *gui*,
this vessel is elliptical in cross section.

The *jiao*, like the *gui*, finds its prototype among
examples recovered from Erlitou Period II.[2] Rare
instances of this vessel type cast in bronze are also
known from approximately the same time.[3] The *jiao*,
however, is much less common at Erlitou in both
media than the *jue*, which has a long open pouring channel instead of a spout, and lacks its high
neck. LF-H

1 Excavated in 1977 (M 612:10); published: Zhongguo 1993,
   132, fig. 104:1; Zhongguo 1996, 204, fig. 94:5. The excavation report identifies the vessel as a *jue*.
2 Zhongguo Erlitou 1992, 297, fig. 4:9; Henan 1996, 65,
   fig. 3:5.
3 Guo Baojun 1981, pl. 8:2.

TOMB 5

AND OTHER

DISCOVERIES

AT XIAOTUN,

ANYANG,

HENAN PROVINCE

The Anyang excavations of 1928–1937 created "Shang archaeology," simultaneously restoring the second of the traditional Three Dynasties to history.[1] In conjunction with studies of the oracle-bone inscriptions (cats. 55–56), archaeologists substantiated the last segment of Shang dynastic history, when eight or nine self-styled kings (wang) divined at Anyang. However, the Anyang excavations posed many questions that were unanswerable given the limited evidence: Where had the Shang come from? How had their culture and their state developed over time? What were their relations with other, contemporaneous groups, presumably the descendants of the Xia and the ancestors of the Zhou?

One of the main achievements of Chinese archaeologists working since 1950 has been a range of plausible responses to many of these important questions. We now have at least a general understanding of the long-term growth of the culture that became the "Late Shang." Most Chinese scholars believe that remains of the Xia have been identified at the Erlitou type site (cats. 37–40), and many discoveries over the breadth of China proper have gone a long way toward defining an "Early Shang culture" and the Late Shang state's position in relation to other contemporaneous groups.

All the Anyang sites had been so badly looted that it seemed to some observers in the 1930s that the "ruins of Yin" (Yinxu) were nearly exhausted, at least with respect to the most precious items. That expectation has been proved wrong several times, first by a large find of oracle bones in 1973 and continuing in 1976 with the richest royal tomb ever excavated at the site: Tomb 5. Both discoveries were made within a few steps of the Anyang Work Station, where a permanent archaeological team assigned to the site resides. Still more recent finds, again including oracle bones and richly furnished burials, testify to the long-term potential for archaeology of all kinds at Anyang.[2]

Subsequently known as the tomb of Fu Hao from more than one hundred inscriptions of that name on bronze vessels, the assemblage in Tomb 5 can be dated to the reign of the first Shang king certain to have reigned at Yin, Wu Ding (c. 1200 BCE).[3] Most scholars believe Fu Hao was a royal consort or queen of Wu Ding — one of the king's three consorts now known from archaeological remains; she apparently died before the king. Fu Hao is the first truly historical Shang figure well documented both through material remains and contemporary inscriptions. Her tomb held more than 200 bronze ritual vessels (6 of which are included in this exhibition); about 250 other bronze objects, including bells, tools, and weapons; some 750 jades; more than 100 stone and semiprecious stone carvings; more than 560 bone carvings; 3 ivory goblets; 11 ceramics; and 6,800 cowries. As the only unlooted royal burial from the Shang center at Anyang, Fu Hao's tomb has opened a unique window on the life of the Shang elite.

The assemblage of more than two hundred bronze ritual vessels found in the Fu Hao tomb has revolutionized our understanding of Shang bronzecasting.[4] Many of the vessels, presumably made during the lifetime of this consort, were inscribed with her name. Others bear inscriptions indicating they were made for and belonged to other contemporary lineages and may

Conjectural reconstruction of the edifice above Tomb 5 at Xiaotun, Anyang, Henan province. After Yang 1987, 140, fig. 18.

have been given to the deceased at the time of her funeral. Some may have been given to her prior to her death or even confiscated booty. In any case, most of the vessels appear remarkably consistent in design and style, testifying in all probability to the range and quality of bronze production at the Anyang foundries. As a group, these vessels represent a cross section of the royal bronze industry of the period, documenting the stylistic characteristics of a number of vessel types, as well as varying approaches to decoration. Many vessels were made as constituents of matched sets but vary slightly in dimension and weight, while still other types are extremely unusual, perhaps even unique. All were cast using ceramic piece-molds that were finished by individual detailing, the same technology already in evidence at Erlitou (see cat. 37). The assemblage also demonstrates the character of ritual in Fu Hao's time and the relative emphasis placed on offerings of wine (actually fermented grain), millet, and meat. While one cannot deduce a strict code prescribing the composition of this ritual set, the Fu Hao assemblage does suggest that the Zhou custom of graded perquisites tied to social or ritual status developed from Shang norms. RT

1   Li Ji 1977 and Chang 1980 review the history of the Anyang excavations.
2   The best overview of Anyang archaeology is Zhongguo 1994.
3   Zhongguo 1980a. See also the review of these issues in Thorp 1981–1982b.
4   Zhongguo 1985 and Thorp 1988a.

46

Bronze *fangding* vessel with flat legs

Height 42.3 (16 ⅝), weight 18 (39 ⅝)
Late Shang Yinxu Period II (c. 1200 BCE)
From Xiaotun Locus North, at Yinxu, Anyang,
Henan Province

The Institute of Archaeology, CASS, Beijing

Round, tripod *ding* (cat. 37) are emblematic ritual
vessels of the Shang and Zhou; four-legged variants
with rectangular bodies (*fangding*) may well have
been royal perquisites. While this type is not documented in metal prior to the Early Shang (c.
1600–1300 BCE), when *fangding* do make their

appearance it is as large-scale paired vessels whose
size and shape distinguish them from other types.[1]
The assemblage at Dayangzhou in Jiangxi province
held one such large *fangding* (cat. 59), but several
pairs from Zhengzhou are the best evidence to link
this variant with Shang royal patrons. At Anyang, a
pair of large *fangding* were among the very few vessels found in place in the royal tombs at Xibeigang
(they were overlooked by looters in Tomb 1004), and
Tomb 5 likewise held an impressive pair inscribed
"Mu Xin" — the posthumous appellation of Fu Hao.
Indeed, the largest Shang vessel presently known,
weighing 875 kilograms, is a solitary *fangding* recovered from the east end of the royal cemetery bear-

ing a dedicatory inscription to another of Wu
Ding's consort, designated posthumously Mu Wu.

This *fangding* vessel,[2] however, is modest in
scale, one of a pair notable for their fine decoration. Each of the four flat sides carries a large, high-
relief rendering of the prototypical animal mask.
The rendition is remarkably complete in anatomical
terms, with snout, jaws, eyes in their sockets, ears,
and horns. The thick flanges that transfix the masks
run from the nose ridge up to a crest with no obvious anatomical rationale. The raised surfaces of
these masks are embellished with sunken lines for
necessary details (such as eye sockets and nostrils)
or hooked spirals that fill space. The surrounding
ground, by contrast, is covered entirely by fine-
lined, squared spirals, crisply cut into the molds.

The vessel is also notable for its flat legs,
aligned at a diagonal under each corner, and given
attributes of the so-called *kui* dragon. This dragon
motif often complements masks in the main bands
of decoration, as seen here, and also appears in
lesser bands on ring feet, necks, and other surfaces.

Here the *kui* is poised with snout and jaws upward,
its single eye in relief, and its long body and curled
tail filling the vessel leg. The flat leg was already
established as a formal element in the Early Shang,
but its use in vessels produced at Anyang remained
limited.[3] Present information suggests that flat
legs were more common during the Late Shang
(c. 1300 – 1050 BCE) in foundry production outside
Anyang. RT

1   See Fong 1980, 108.
2   Excavated in 1976 (M 5:812); reported: Zhongguo 1980, 38.
3   In an unpublished database of 690 published vessels I
    compiled in 1992, only 11 of 116 *ding* from Yinxu sites had
    flat legs.

47

Bronze *yan* steamer with three vessels

Height of *yan* 63 (24 ³/₄), width 103.7 (40 ⁷/₈),
depth 27 (10 ⁵/₈), weight 138.2 (304 ⁵/₈)
Late Shang Yinxu Period II (c. 1200 BCE)
From Xiaotun Locus North, at Yinxu, Anyang,
Henan Province

The Institute of Archaeology, CASS, Beijing

Claims of an archaeological object's uniqueness
are prone to eventual contradiction, and not simply
because of the "risk" of new discoveries. Most
objects made in large workshop settings, including
Shang bronze foundries, are in fact elements of
groups, either true sets made at one time to a
shared design, or simply common types and varieties. Nonetheless, the triple steamer (*yan*) from
Tomb 5[1] is an isolated example without obvious
analogues. It suggests the broader range of creative
designs that the foundries sometimes pursued.
Objects such as this steamer set were probably

Cat 67 from above and side: decoration and cross section. After Zhongguo 1980a, 45, fig. 30.

made rarely (perhaps only for Shang kings and queens). The ability to study them, in turn, is mediated by accidents of preservation and discovery.

The assemblage consists of a large, six-legged table with three bowls (zeng) held in position by collars that encircle openings on the top of the table. The table itself is a box that held water for steaming when a fire was laid amid the legs, and residues of soot suggest that the table was in fact employed for this purpose. Each zeng is open at the bottom; an insert of woven bamboo or the like must have been used to hold the grain and to allow the steam to penetrate the contents. The contents of the zeng would likely have been transferred to bowls and served at the altar. The design is flawed: the loop handles of the zeng block one another when all three are in position.

The decoration of the yan is somewhat improvisatory. The upper register on the sides of the table displays a band of dragons in profile and whorls; triangular lappets form a second band below. The collars and the zeng are decorated with bands of repeating motifs. Diamondback dragons loop around the openings on the top of the table, but here the decoration is less formally balanced: while the heads and tails of two dragons come together at one side of the center collar, only one dragon lies on the other side; lest the surface remain undecorated, however, a frontal animal mask and miniature dragon motif fill this area. RT

1   Excavated in 1976 (M 5: 790 [yan], 768, 769, 770 [vessels]; reported: Zhongguo 1980, 44 – 46.

48

Bronze owl-shaped *zun* vessel

Height 46.3 (18 ¼), weight 16.7 (36 ¾)
Late Shang Yinxu Period II (c. 1200 BCE)
From Xiaotun Locus North, at Yinxu, Anyang,
Henan Province

The Institute of Archaeology, CASS, Beijing

The artisans of Shang bronze foundries had a grasp
of metallurgy that was probably informed by traditional attitudes and practices learned from their
elders, but bronze production was commanded by
an elite whose ritual needs, and ritual specialists,
dictated many salient characteristics of the objects.
Whether individual patrons dictated specific requirements as well is probably impossible to determine: even with many hundreds of excavated
objects from the Yinxu sites, few if any patterns

linked to patron identity are visible in the designs.
In any event, after satisfying all stipulated requirements, artisans making molds had at most a limited
ability to make objects look as *they* saw fit.

Yet, in spite of all of these presumed strictures,
works of considerable novelty emerged from the
foundries, whether on the initiative of the foundry
or the patron. The two owl-shaped wine containers
inscribed "Fu Hao" are key examples — at once
aesthetic objects and useful containers for holding
alcoholic spirits. Other sculptural vessels in bronze
are known, including smaller but otherwise similar
birds.[1] The most telling comparison, however, is to
an owl carved in white marble from Tomb 1001 at
Xibeigang. Given that this tomb may have been the
burial of King Wu Ding, Fu Hao's mate, the many
similarities in design would seem to relate to one
period and narrow social circle.

The Fu Hao owl[2] stands on two plump, drum-
stick legs; a downturned fan of tail feathers forms
the vessel's third "leg." The body of the owl is an
elongated oval that rises to a round neck. The owl's
beak and face are cast as one piece with the neck,
while the rear part of the head forms a removable
lid with miniature bird and dragon as knobs. The
strap handle at the back is aligned opposite the
beak at front, which forms the spout of the vessel.
A pair of hornlike appendages (actually curved
serpents with bottle horns) stands perpendicular
to the axis of beak and handle. An owl thus takes
shape from various details woven into the fabric of
the body. The marble owl from Tomb 1001 is similar
in many ways, although its details are necessarily
informed by the properties of stone rather than
those of metal. For example, the standing horns
of the bronze owl become flattened horns on the
marble bird, while the open space between the legs
and tail of the Fu Hao vessel is adumbrated by the
grooves cut into the base of the stone. RT

1 Bagley 1987, 406 – 411, reviews many related examples.
2 Excavated in 1976 (M 5:785); reported: Zhongguo 1980,
   56 – 59.

49

Bronze animal-shaped *gong* vessel

Height 22 (8 ⅝), weight 3.35 (7 ⅜)
Late Shang Yinxu Period II (c. 1200 BCE)
From Xiaotun Locus North, at Yinxu, Anyang,
Henan Province

The Institute of Archaeology, CASS, Beijing

New types of vessels and variants associated with
wine consumption proliferated in Anyang bronze
production. Older types derived from ceramic
prototypes, such as *lei, pou, hu,* and *you,* were made
in bronze in considerable numbers and also modified to yield variants with different body shapes.

Among the new types without ceramic prototypes
are the *gong* or *guang* service vessel type shown
here and the *fangyi,* a square-section wine storage
vessel with a lid resembling a miniature hipped
roof. Anyang assemblages customarily include large
numbers of vessels dedicated to wine offerings; the
Fu Hao tomb contained an abundance of storage
vessels, warming vessels, and serving and drinking
vessels. The purported fondness of Late Shang kings
for alcoholic spirits became a stinging point of
criticism in the propaganda of the Western
Zhou *Book of Documents.*[1]

This vessel[2] offered a convenient way of pouring
spirits into drinking goblets or warming cups (*gu*

Cat. 49 from above and
side. After Zhongguo
1980a, 63, fig. 42.

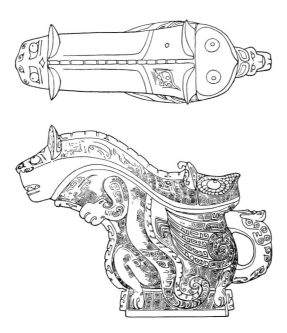

vessel (cat. 48), one is tempted to find rebuslike
messages in this combination of familiar animals,
both of which appear in other contemporaneous
decoration. RT

1   Karlgren 1974, 43 – 46, quoting Tsiu Kao (*Jiu gao,*
     "Announcement on drunkenness").
2   Excavated in 1976 (M 5:802); reported: Zhongguo 1980,
     59 – 63.
3   Bagley 1987, 412 – 420.

and *jue).* The ring foot elevates the elongated oval
bowl, which in turn extends upward in one direction to form a large trough pouring spout. The
loop handle affixed opposite the spout allows a user
to direct and control the flow of liquid, possibly
cradling the spout with one hand while manipu-
lating the handle with the other. The lid fits tightly
over the rim, sealing in warmth and keeping the
liquid free of contamination, while allowing the
contents to breathe through open teeth in the
tiger's head.

This vessel and others like it in collections
outside China have been celebrated, and rightly
so, for their astute design, in which two animals are
placed back-to-back, their bodies extending from
the two ends of the lid down to the ring foot.[3] A
tiger forms the front of the *gong;* its squared head,
with standing ears, relief eyes, and bared fangs, is
rendered on the vessel's lid. The feline's body occupies the front half of the vessel proper (spout and
bowl), its limbs raised in relief, the rear paw and
curling tail hanging down onto the foot. At the
rear of the *gong,* an owl with pointed beak and large
eyes stares up from the lid; its body is suggested
with wings on the rear of the bowl and legs that
run down onto the foot. As with the owl-shaped *zun*

50

Bronze *fangjia* vessel

Height 67 (26 ⅜), weight 19.2 (42 ¼)
Late Shang Yinxu Period II (c. 1200 BCE)
From Xiaotun Locus North, at Yinxu, Anyang,
Henan Province

The Institute of Archaeology, CASS, Beijing

In addition to innovative animal-shaped vessels, the Anyang foundries produced vessels in new, square-section (*fang*) shapes. While *ding* made as rectangular vessels appear in other periods, square-section vessels are limited to the Late Shang. Such vessel types include pod-base vessels for warming or serving wine (*jue, jia, he*) and several ring-base types for drinking and storing wine (*gu, lei, zun, hu*, as well as the new *fangyi*). The attraction of this shape for potters in foundries might have included the ease of making outer mold sections from a square model or core, the opportunities that the wide, flat field presented for decoration with large, graphic imagery, and possibly the implied distinction from ceramic, wheel-made prototypes. (Square-section vessels were not produced as pottery.) While an interest in *fang* vessels was apparently widespread, it does not seem to have endured: The *fangjia* from Tomb 5 are the only examples from the period (Yinxu II) at Anyang; another pair from Tomb 160 (Yinxu III) are the only later traces of this variant among excavated examples.[1]

The formal innovations introduced by the designers of this vessel[2] include a body and tall neck in square-section complemented by relief decoration and fairly thick flanges. Other details, however, might be deemed less successful aesthetically: the four squared legs are very thick and create a congested appearance where they join the flat base. The square posts and caps dominate the rim and detract from the visual buoyancy of the *jia's* usually sleek form.

The masks that fill the four sides of the body are composed of disparate elements in relief rather than the unified face that decorates the *fangding* (cat. 46). These elements are covered with the same tight, squared spirals that appear in the back-

ground, an ornament that undercuts the readability or integrity of the mask motif. Altogether, the assemblage of vessels made for Fu Hao shows a considerable variety of decoration, belying the notion of any simple and predictable evolution over time from one characteristic decorative style to another.

This vessel is one of three large *fangjia* made for Fu Hao. It was found with another, round-section vessel of similar scale and other *jia* bearing the names of other lineages; it may be that the gift of *jue* and *gu* from the Si Tu Mu, Ya Qi, and Shu Quan lineages included these warming vessels, as well as the serving vessels. The tomb assemblage also held large containers with two of these inscriptions identifying their owner's lineage. The true nature of the gifts from these lineages therefore may well have been both a large quantity of alcoholic spirits and the equipment to use it. RT

1 Zhongguo 1998a, 93 – 94.
2 Excavated in 1976 (M 5:752); reported: Zhongguo 1980, 67 – 68.

51

Bronze *jue* vessel

Height 37.3 (14 ⅝), weight 4.4 (9 ⅝)
Late Shang Yinxu Period II (c. 1200 BCE)
From Xiaotun Locus North, at Yinxu, Anyang,
Henan Province

The Institute of Archaeology, CASS, Beijing

From the heyday of the Erlitou type site until some
time in the Western Zhou period, the *jue* pouring
vessel was one of the most common types of bronze
ritual vessels. About a dozen small, thinly cast, and
plain *jue* have been recovered to date at Erlitou;
at Early Shang sites, *jue* are commonly found paired
with *gu* wine goblets. This pairing is typical of all
stages in the Anyang occupation, when hundreds
of examples from period burials are documented.
The paired *jue* and *gu* constitute the "lowest common denominator" among Shang bronze vessels
and ritual sets.

   Tomb 5 held forty *jue* altogether, but this example[1] and its mate stand apart by virtue of their size
and thick casting. This is an exceptionally large *jue*
— at almost 38 centimeters, nearly twice as tall as
other examples from the tomb, which range from 20
to 26 centimeters. The complement of *jue* in Tomb 5
corresponds to four sets of vessels, each component
inscribed with a different clan-sign that indicates
its origin. The Fu Hao *jue* comprise the large pair
represented by the exhibited example, and ten
others of smaller size and different shape. Three
other lineages (Si Tu Mu, Ya Qi, and Shu Quan)
are represented by three sets of nine *jue* each,
paired of course with *gu* goblets (eleven, ten, and
ten, respectively). The sets of goblets and pouring
vessels were probably gifts or offerings made to
Fu Hao at the funeral; they may even have been
used for drinking or libations at the grave during
the rites, a custom known as early as the prehistoric
Dawenkou and Longshan cultures (fourth – third
millennium BCE) of Shandong.

   Its three flared legs and trough spout and tail
extending well beyond the vessel body, this *jue* is
nonetheless a stable and solid vessel. The evident
thickness of the vessel walls is matched by thick

flanges that mark the waist band and the underside
of the spout. The animal head on the strap handle
and the masks at the waist are in fairly high relief;
most of the other decoration is less readable. RT

1   Excavated in 1976 (M 5:1579); reported: Zhongguo 1980, 85.

52

Bronze *yue* axe

Height 39.5 (15 ½), maximum width 37.3 (14 ⅝),
weight 9 (19 ¾)
Late Shang Yinxu Period II (c. 1200 BCE)
From Xiaotun Locus North, at Yinxu, Anyang,
Henan Province

The Institute of Archaeology, CASS, Beijing

Large, flat axes (*yue*) appear in bronze in the Early
Shang, although they have precursors in hardstone
that date much earlier. While not as common as the
ge dagger-axe and *mao* spear-point, more than three
dozen examples of bronze *yue* are known.[1] Only a
few are classified as "large *yue*," including four examples from Fu Hao's tomb, of which this is one.[2]

The large axe is associated in traditional texts with
the granting of military authority, as when a lord
was invested with the power to wage a campaign,
but it was also evidently used for the punishment of
decapitation; several graphic attestations to the
practice appear in oracle-bone and bronze inscriptions. Transmitted texts tell us that the last Shang
king, the evil Zhou Xin, was beheaded with a "yellow *yue*" by the victorious founder of the new dynasty, Wu Wang. Many scholars believe that the
logograph for "king" *(wang)* originated in a picto-
graphic representation of such large axes; such an
etymology suggests that flat axes may have served as
royal insignia.

The shape of this example is characteristic of
its type: the wide tang is flanked by a pair of slots

for binding the axe to the shaft; the blade itself is broad and ends in a curved cutting edge. The decoration, however, is unusual: a diminutive human head flanked by a pair of animals, usually identified as tigers. The meaning of this iconography is uncertain and much debated: a number of parallels exist, both on objects from Anyang (including the enormous Si Mu Wu *fangding*) and others more widely dispersed.[3] Most speculation identifies the head as that of a "shaman," flanked by his "familiars" — animals who aid him in his tasks; few examples of these juxtaposed motifs are known, however, and they seem a rickety foundation for any broad theory for the interpretation of Shang iconography generally. The mate to this axe features an altogether different decoration — an animal mask with bottle horns, flanked on either side by flattened bodies. This said, it is worth remembering that the two examples of the human face-and-tiger motif from Anyang are both linked directly through inscriptions on the objects to consorts of Wu Ding. One must wonder whether the motif relates to the status or identity of these consorts. RT

1   Yang and Yang 1986, 128 – 138.
2   Excavated in 1976 (M 5:799); reported: Zhongguo 1980, 105.
3   Chang 1983, 61 – 78, and Allan 1991, 124 – 170.

53

Ivory goblet inlaid with turquoise

Height 30.3 (11 $^{7}/_{8}$) diam. at rim 11.3 (4 $^{1}/_{2}$)
Late Shang Yinxu Period II (c. 1200 BCE)
From Xiaotun Locus North, at Yinxu, Anyang,
Henan Province

The Institute of Archaeology, CASS, Beijing

The durability of hardstones and bronzes has given
them an unwarranted prominence in our understanding of Shang material culture. Few items of
wood are known, but evidence for carved wooden
chambers, sometimes featuring inlay and painted
surfaces, was identified in the royal tombs at
Xibeigang. Wooden and lacquered objects have also
been detected from impressions in undisturbed
areas of these tombs, such as a drum and chime
stand in Tomb 1217. Many lacquered objects, as well
as textiles and basketry, probably accompanied the
bronze vessels that composed an altar set; they
probably played a significant role as serving vessels
for a ritual feast. Carved bone and ivory were also a
part of these arrays, but rarely have intact vessels
such as this ivory goblet[1] been recovered.

Drinking goblets (gu) are among the most common Shang bronze vessel types, paired as a rule
with small pouring vessels (jue). Fu Hao's tomb
contained fifty-three bronze gu, but her three ivory
goblets represent a more exhalted level of craft
enjoyed by some of the elite. The form of this
goblet's body resembles that of biconical bronze
examples; here, however, the waist is larger in
diameter relative to the base and mouth; the rim
as well does not flare so dramatically as it normally
does in bronze goblets. A large handle is mounted
at one side, with a prominent beak at top and a
grip in the middle, and the surface is carved with
fine lines tracing motifs and ground patterns that
conform with elements of bronze decoration. The
motifs are inlaid with small pieces of turquoise,
creating a color and image-to-ground contrast
more pronounced than is found in bronze vessels;
inlay is attested in lacquered objects and wooden
surfaces as well. The stylistic choices available to
artisans working ivory, lacquer, and wood were

much affected by the achievements of the bronze
foundries, but surely the reverse is equally plausible: the consistency of Shang style suggests that the
artisans responsible were not limited to any single
medium. RT

1   Excavated in 1976 (M 5:100); reported: Zhongguo 1980, 217.

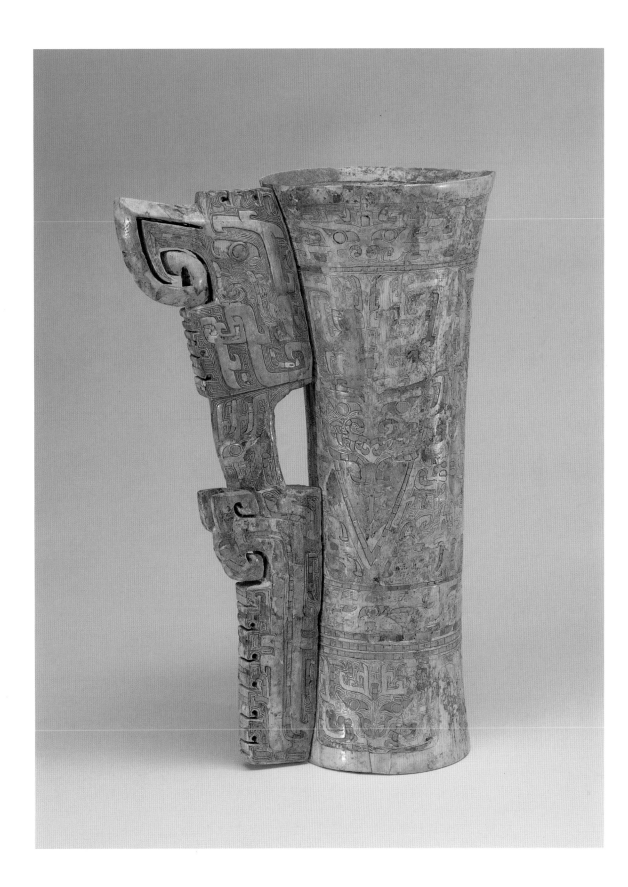

54a

54c

54b

54

a. Jade crane

Length 12 (4 ¾)
Late Shang Yinxu Period II (c. 1200 BCE)
From Xiaotun Locus North, at Yinxu, Anyang,
Henan Province

The Institute of Archaeology, CASS, Beijing

b. Turquoise dove

Length 6.4 (2 ½)
Late Shang Yinxu Period II (c. 1200 BCE)
From Xiaotun Locus North, at Yinxu, Anyang,
Henan Province

The Institute of Archaeology, CASS, Beijing

c. Hardstone tortoise

Length 5.8 (2 ¼)
Late Shang Yinxu Period (c. 1200 – 1050 BCE)
From Xiaotun Locus North, at Yinxu, Anyang,
Henan Province

The Institute of Archaeology, CASS, Beijing

The Fu Hao tomb has yielded an abundance of
hardstone carvings; more than 750 examples are
enumerated in the formal excavation report.[1] Many
of these objects are ritual types *(zong, bi, gui)* —
forms attested as early as the Neolithic period —
and the tomb included a good number of weapons
and other shapes thought to be ceremonial. One
ge dagger-axe bears an incised text understood to
indicate that the blade was one of five presented
by a statelet called Lu. It may be that important
personages such as Fu Hao were presented with
raw stone or carved products as gifts from subordinate groups. Many of the hardstones have been
tested in recent years and prove to be minerals
subsumed under the rubric nephrite. At least some
are thought to come from the region of Khotan in
Central Asia (modern Xinjiang), a legendary source
of jade throughout Chinese history.

Over half of the carvings (426 items) are decorative objects. Many are flat plaques shaped as real
animals (such as this long-necked crane[2]) or as
imaginary beasts; the plaques frequently include
perforations for suspension or attachment. The
most appealing objects, however, are carved in the
round, as are this dove and tortoise. The dove[3]
is a smoothed nugget of turquoise that irresistibly
invites holding in the hand. The tortoise[4] shows
the ability of jade artisans to utilize features of the
natural stone. In this instance, a dark layer within
the stone forms the tortoise's carapace, while the
body and limbs are rendered from lighter material.
This technique is rarely if ever found prior to the
Late Shang.   RT

1   Zhongguo 1980, 114 – 195. See also Chen 1986, 210 – 219 and
    Zheng 1989, 315 – 325.
2   Excavated in 1976 (M 5:516); reported: Zhongguo 1980, 163.
3   Excavated in 1976 (M 5:416); reported: Zhongguo 1980,
    204.
4   Excavated in 1975 (75 AST F11:18); reported: Zhongguo
    Anyang 1976, 272. The tortoise was recovered from a
    foundation (Foundation 11) not far from Tomb 5. This
    subterranean house may have served as a jade workshop
    and in any case held such rarities as traces of painted
    walls, lacquer-painted pottery, and glazed ware. The ar-
    chaeologists also recovered an inscribed bronze lid that
    they date to Yinxu Period IV.

As early as the fourth millennium BCE, the inhabitants of Neolithic China and its border regions had sought to foretell the future by cracking animal bones — applying high heat to the bones and interpreting the resulting stress cracks as lucky or unlucky. By the Late Shang dynasty (c. 1200–1045 BCE) such pyromantic divination had become institutionalized to a remarkable degree.

The Shang diviners prepared the shoulder blades of cattle or the shells of turtles by planing away their rough surfaces and boring hollows into their backs; they then applied some utensil such as a red-hot poker to the edge of the hollow so that the thinned bone cracked to form a characteristic T-shaped crack on its front surface. (The modern Chinese character *bu*, meaning "to divine," is a picture of such a crack.) After the cracking had taken place, the diviners numbered the cracks sequentially, and engravers then carved some or all of the following information into the bone: the crack-number, a record of the date, the name of the presiding diviner, the subject matter of the divination (referred to as the divination "charge"), and, sometimes, the forecast itself and a record of what had eventually happened. Occasionally, red or black pigment would be rubbed into the cracks and the inscriptions to enhance their visibility, and, perhaps, their mantic potency. Modern scholars have identified the names of well over a hundred Shang diviners (including the king himself) who presided over the rituals involved.

These oracle-bone inscriptions provide one striking example of archaeological discoveries that have added much to our understanding of China's past. It was only at the very end of the nineteenth century that Chinese scholars began to collect and decipher the "dragon bones" that peasants from the village of Xiaotun (near present-day Anyang, in the northern Henan panhandle) had been finding in their fields. The political and military upheavals that followed the fall of the Qing dynasty in 1911 delayed the study and scientific excavation of these valuable materials. With the reunification of China in 1927, a series of scientific excavations was conducted at Anyang in the late 1920s and 1930s, but the work was again disrupted by the start of the Sino-Japanese War in 1937 and resumed only in 1950. The process of assembling and deciphering the earliest Chinese writing has continued down to the present, and more than forty-five thousand pieces of inscribed oracle bone — some large and complete, some badly fragmented and incomplete — have to date been published. The recent publication in China of a comprehensive thirteen-volume collection of oracle-bone rubbings indicates the importance attached to these materials.[1]

The inscriptions, together with the temple-palace foundations, bronze workshops, bronze ritual vessels, ornamental jades, and impressive burials that modern scholars have excavated near Anyang reveal that the site was the major cult center of the late Shang dynasty kings. This was where they buried their royal ancestors, offered sacrifices to them, and performed the divinatory rites that were thought to ensure the dynasty's success. The oracle-bone inscriptions are particularly valuable to historians because the existence of the objects was unknown for some three thousand years; for that reason, the information they record comes down to us

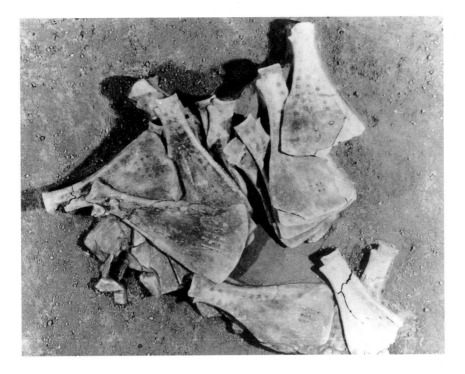

Bovid scapulas excavated in 1971 from Huayuanzhuang, Anyang, Henan province; Shang dynasty.

untouched by the hands of copyists and editors. The inscriptions reveal that divination was one of the central institutions of the Shang state, for it demonstrated the king's contact with the powers that ruled the Shang world. The king, known as "I, the one man," was usually the person who interpreted the cracks, and his forecasts (the recorded outcomes carved into the bones almost invariably proved him correct) served to legitimate his position and reassure his supporters. A king such as Wu Ding (the twenty-first Shang king, who died c. 1189 BCE) divined about most aspects of his life: harvests, rainfall, settlement building, his hunts and excursions, the mobilization of conscripts, military campaigns and alliances, enemy invasions, the birth of his children, his health, the meaning of his dreams, the good fortune of the coming ten-day week and of the night to come, the harm caused by ancestors and other powers (usually in the form of illness or crop damage), and the successful offering of reports, prayers, rituals, and sacrifices to his ancestors. Many of the divinations end with the wish that there will be "no disasters" or "no fault," others with the hope that the powers will provide spiritual assistance.

The oracle-bone inscriptions form the earliest body of writing yet found in eastern Asia. The Shang engravers employed a repertoire of more than three thousand oracle-bone characters, many of which exemplify the traditional principles of logographic script and prefigure specific Chinese characters in use to this day. Many of the Shang values and practices that the inscriptions document — the concern with ancestor worship and with the powers of nature, respect for senior generations and kinship ties, the keeping of bureaucratic records, the ability to mobilize large numbers of workers in the service of the elites, and the close association between divination, spiritual insight, and worthy leadership — continued to play a strategic role in later Chinese history. The Shang kings appear to have placed their oracle bones in storage pits once their usefulness had been exhausted. But the divination inscriptions recorded on them represent a remarkable legacy, providing us with an intimate sense of the Shang kings' daily activities, their decision making, and their hopes and fears across a span of over three thousand years. DNK

1   Guo Moruo 1978–1982.

55

Inscribed bovid scapula

Height 40.5 (15 7/8), width 22.5 (8 7/8)
Shang Dynasty, twelfth century BCE
From Xiaotun, Anyang, Henan Province

The Institute of Archaeology, CASS, Beijing

In December 1971 Chinese archaeologists found
a group of twenty-one complete bovid scapulas in
a test trench some 160 meters west of Xiaotun.
This scapula[1] bears twenty-two preparatory hollows
on the lower front surface and over thirty hollows
on the upper back surface.[2] After the divinatory
crackings had been performed, the Shang engravers recorded eight inscriptions on the front
of the bone.

One of the longest divination charges is recorded in seventeen characters that, starting at
the top, form the far-left column on the bone (ten
characters) and then, at the bottom of the column,
run to the right (seven more characters). It may
be tentatively translated as follows: "In performing
the lustration ritual for the Herdsmen [officers],
to Ancestress Yi offer a fine [?] pig, to Ancestress
Gui a boar, to Ancestress Ding a pig, to Ancestress
Yi a pig." Another charge (recorded as the last
eleven characters of the third column from the
right edge of the bone) was addressed, by contrast,
to the ancestors: "In performing the lustration
ritual, to Ancestor Gui offer a pig, to Ancestor Yi
a boar [?], to Ancestor Wu a pig."[3]

The other six charges on the scapula involve
other offerings, mainly of various kinds of pigs
(also of a dog), and lustrations to various ancestors
and ancestresses. Curiously, the engravers erased
the heads of all the "pig" characters, a practice
(found occasionally on other bones) that must
have had some significance.[4] The "temple names"
of the ancestresses (Yi, Gui, and Ding) and ancestors (Gui, Yi, and Wu), were conferred upon them
posthumously. The Shang selected these names
from a list of ten counters or "stems" (a later term)
that they also used to name the ten days of their
week. The Shang were thus able to schedule their

ancestral sacrifices, so that they offered sacrifices to Ancestress Yi on a *yi* day, to Ancestor Gui on a *gui* day, and so on.

The purpose of divinations such as these was to ensure that the various rituals and offerings would be acceptable to the ancestral spirits. The inscriptions on this scapula are unusual in several respects: the engravers have not recorded the day-date of the divinations or the name of the diviner, nor have they numbered the cracks; the ancestors themselves do not appear to be the usual kings and consorts who regularly received ancestral sacrifices. These features suggest that the divinations were performed by diviners other than those who normally divined the king's affairs. The archaeological context and the affinities with other diviner groups of inscription style and content suggest that these diviners were probably active during the reign of Wu Ding (d. c. 1189 BCE) or slightly later. DNK

1 Excavated in 1971; reported: Guo Moruo 1972, 2–11 (no. 12); Guo Moruo 1978–1982, no. 31993; Zhongguo 1983a, Fu [supplement] 3.
2 Zhongguo 1983a, 1161.
3 In both charges translated, the final character for "pig" is, unusually, repeated; perhaps two pigs were to be offered.
4 See Zhongguo 1983a, 1161.

56

Inscribed turtle plastron

Height 19.5 (7 ⅜), width 12 (4 ¾)
Shang Dynasty, twelfth century BCE
From Huayuanzhuang, Anyang, Henan Province

The Institute of Archaeology, CASS, Beijing

In October 1991 the Anyang Work Team of the Institute of Archaeology excavated 1,583 oracle-bone fragments, found in layers, from a well-made storage pit in the eastern section of Huayuanzhuang, located some three hundred meters south of the village of Xiaotun. Of the fragments that bore writing, 574 were turtle plastrons (557 fragments) and carapaces (17 fragments); 5 were bovid scapula fragments. The onerous task of reconstituting some of the original bones — the turtle shells, in particular, were badly fragmented — was completed in June 1992. The main topics divined on the bones found in this pit involved sacrifices, hunts, weather, and sickness.

Eight divination charges are recorded on this plastron.[1] The first (top right, to be read from the center out, then down) may be translated as follows: "Crack-making on *yiyou* [day 22 in the 60-day cycle]: 'Prince You [?] goes to the foothills of Xinnan [?]; if he nets pigs, he will catch some.'" This charge, expressed in the positive future tense, was paired with a negative abbreviated charge inscribed on the left side of the shell (reading from the center out, then down): "Crack-making on *yiyou*: '[Prince You] may not catch some.'" This balancing of positive and negative charges, with the undesired charge expressed more weakly than the desired charge, was a common feature of divinations performed on plastrons during the reign of Wu Ding; it presumably reflected some early sense of *yin-yang* balance that the Shang perceived in the workings of the world. The symmetry of the turtle plastrons, which permitted opposing divination charges to be carved on either side of the central spine, encouraged such balanced formulations.[2] In the present case, the engravers numbered five cracks on the right side of the plastron and five cracks on the left side,

showing that the topic had been cracked ten times in all.

The other divinations on the plastron concern the chance of encountering other game, such as pig and deer, at other locations; their intent was to ensure that the various hunts had a successful outcome. The inscription at the bottom left ends with an auspicious prognostication: "The prince read the cracks and said: 'We will encounter [game].'" Some of these other divinations, as the numbers indicate, were cracked four times, some only twice. The inscriptions should probably be dated to the time of Wu Ding, but the fact that a prince, rather than the king, made the prognostication, is one of several indications that, as in the case of the scapula (cat. 55), this plastron was not divined by the king's court diviners but by another group. DNK

1   Excavated in 1991 (H3:52); reported: Zhongguo Anyang 1993, 488–499, fig. 11; Rawson 1996, no. 37a.

2   Keightley 1988.

Descendants of the early Bronze Age cultures of the North China macroregion produced the Shang ceremonial center at Yinxu, but the long-term cultural history of other macroregions remains obscure. Cultures of the mid- to late second millennium BCE shared many of the same material assets — pounded-earth construction, gray pottery and proto-porcelain, and bronze metallurgy with a distinctive repertoire of vessels and weapons. In the Wei River valley of the northwest, a people called the Zhou expanded their territory over time and eventually overwhelmed the Late Shang center at Yinxu, establishing the third of the Three Dynasties. But what of the inhabitants of the Yangzi River areas, or of more distant realms such as the Gan-Yangzi macroregion (largely present-day Jiangxi province)? The development of Bronze Age cultures in these regions is the focus of two groups of objects: those from Dayangzhou (Xin'gan county in Jiangxi province) and those from Sanxingdui (Guanghan county in Sichuan province).

By the 1970s, archaeologists working along the Yangzi River system had accumulated considerable evidence for Bronze Age cultures in contact with the Erligang Phase, Early Shang culture of Henan. The first major site to be documented in this enormous region was a small walled settlement at Panlongcheng (Huangpi county, Hubei province), north of the Yangzi River, where the culture in evidence was in all essentials identical to that known from Henan.[1] This settlement could plausibly be interpreted as an outpost of the northern culture, possibly an extension of the early Shang state. Its decline seemed to correspond with the settlement of Yinxu in the north, and perhaps indicated a general retrenchment of Shang rule. Other finds were less informative. The Middle Yangzi macroregion of present-day Hunan yielded, among other discoveries, isolated vessels and large bells. In some cases these objects seemed to be products from the north, but in other instances they were sufficiently distinctive to suggest local manufacture. Thus the model of a "metropolitan" Shang culture centered in the north and contemporaneous "provincial" outliers took shape.[2]

On the heels of the discovery of Panlongcheng, however, came reports of a walled settlement well south of the Yangzi River, at a site called Wucheng located west of the Gan River in Jiangxi province. Material remains here included many characteristic Shang features mixed with so many local variants that from the outset scholars preferred to see this as a hybrid culture, possibly created through interaction of a local group with the north.[3] It was far too distant from Henan to sustain interpretation as a Shang dynasty outpost, and moreover the Wucheng site flourished at the same time as Yinxu. Little evidence for bronzecasting was reported before 1989, when on the east bank of the Gan River peasants repairing dikes unearthed a quantity of bronzes from the soil of a relic sandbar called Dayangzhou. When this find was cleared that fall, the contents corresponded with the Wucheng type site's culture but far exceeded all previous finds of bronzes and jades. This single discovery has revised our understanding of the archaeological context of an entire region, a body of knowledge that had taken shape slowly and haphazardly over several decades.

Excavation photograph of the tomb at Dayangzhou, Xin'gan, Jiangxi province.

Although preservation conditions were poor, the excavators believe the find at Dayangzhou comprised the durable contents of a large burial chamber (about 10 by 3.6 meters).[4] Human remains were sparse — only two dozen human teeth were recovered, and these were attributed to three individuals: a young female and two infants. Most Chinese scholars identify these individuals as sacrificial victims who accompanied the tomb's occupant in death. The grave goods consisted primarily of bronze objects (475 items), especially weapons (232 items) and tools (51 items), but also copious ceramics (139 items), including characteristic Wucheng "proto-porcelains." The ceramics are sufficient to date the burial to Period II at Wucheng, which in turn is generally correlated to an early phase of the Late Shang (the period of Fu Hao). The array of bronzes, including ritual types, spans a somewhat broader period, starting with the Erligang Phase (c. 1600 BCE) and continuing through Yinxu Periods I–II (c. 1200 BCE). RT

1 Bagley 1977.
2 Kane 1974–1975. For a synthesis of the data and critique of previous views, see Thorp 1985.
3 Li 1998a, 218–230.
4 Jiangxi 1997. See also Bagley 1993 for a discussion that emphasizes the affinities of the bronzes.

57

Bronze two-sided mask

Height 53 (20⅞), width 38.5 (15⅛), weight 4.1 (9)
Late Shang Period (c. 1200–1050 BCE)
From Dayangzhou, Xin'gan, Jiangxi Province

Jiangxi Provincial Museum, Nanchang

The ever-increasing number of archaeologically recovered objects is steadily eroding many of the simple facts that once constituted our understanding of the Chinese Bronze Age. It has been a commonplace, for example, that human imagery played only a minor role in the period, with no significant tradition of portraiture or other human sculpture. A recent survey of artifacts from the Shang and Western Zhou periods, however, compiled dozens of

only surface detail — a decoration of intaglio curls. An open tube at the top of the head may have served as a socket, but its diameter is far larger than would be required to hold a plume or similar ornament.

Several writers have pointed to a find of nearly two dozen small bronze masks in southern Shaanxi province (the northern periphery of the Upper Yangzi macroregion) as the closest parallel to the Dayangzhou example.[3] These masks are much smaller, however — about 15 – 20 centimeters in length — and were most likely affixed to a surface, such as a shield. The differences notwithstanding, their design is similar: round eyes that bulge from round sockets, large noses with open nostrils, squared teeth in open mouths, and flat, squared ears. Although related images are known, most human faces in the Shang period feature eyes set into sockets with pointed canthi. Full lips are more common than teeth. Another relevant comparison is the splayed figure on the sides of a bronze drum said to come from the south and now in the Sumitomo Collection, Kyoto.[4] The shape of the head, most of its features, and especially the horns are similar to the Dayangzhou mask. Had the mask been mounted on a torso, the assemblage may have resembled the figure depicted on the drum. RT

1   Xu 1996a, 334 – 352.
2   Excavated in 1989 (XDM: 67); reported: Jiangxi 1997, 131.
3   The find was at Chenggu, Shaanxi province; see Tang 1980 and Li 1998b. The small masks are illustrated in Shaanxi 1979c, no. 116.
4   Li Xueqin 1985, no. 129.

examples of anthropomorphic images — in bronze and jade; bodies, heads, and faces; large freestanding works as well as miniatures.[1] The many masks and heads from the Sanxingdui pits (cats. 65 – 75), moreover, have significantly increased the total number of examples, and the importance of human imagery can no longer be downplayed.

This double mask[2] evidently was fitted into a stand (or perhaps a torso) at its square stem. The head itself was cast in two parts: the top half from the ears upward was joined to the lower portion to create an enclosed form with perforations at eyes and mouth. Flat ears extend from each side of the face, as do large right-angled horns bearing the

58

Bronze tiger

Height 25.5 (10), width 53.5 (21 ⅛), weight 6.2 (13 ⅝)
Late Shang Period (c. 1200 – 1050 BCE)
From Dayangzhou, Xin'gan, Jiangxi Province

Jiangxi Provincial Museum, Nanchang

Bronze foundries specialized in the production of weapons and ritual vessels. Nonetheless, by the beginning of the Late Shang, metal was being used for other objects, including helmets, masks and heads, and animal figures. Such objects retain the surface decoration common on ritual vessels and rely on the same piece-mold casting process. These less typical castings may also represent exercises

in creative design, combining several media and synthesizing imagery found in other contexts. The bronze tiger[1] in the Dayangzhou tomb exemplifies many of these trends.

The animal was cast, but with three flat sides and open bottom resembles a folded plate of bronze; the design is reminiscent of the carved marble tiger from Tomb 1001 at Xibeigang.[2] The bronze tiger's face is composed of conventional elements: fangs in the upper jaw and the short ears suggest the species. The body, on the other hand, is less specific to the animal itself. Two large limbs (whose surfaces are not descriptive of a feline's coat) originate from relief shoulders and end in what must be claws. The curled tail is rendered as two halves, one on each side, hanging behind the animal's haunches and separated by an empty slot that runs through the animal from head to tail. The top surface — the animal's neck and back — is decorated as a separate panel; an innocuous bird rests on the animal's spine.

Given the peculiarities of its form, it is likely that this bronze tiger was placed on or over some other object, covering and ornamenting it. In this respect, it recalls the marble tiger and owl from Tomb 1001 at Xibeigang (see cat. 48), each of which has a vertical slot at the back, suggesting that they served to anchor a vertical element. The Xin'gan tiger also resembles several bronze tigers, inlaid with turquoise at front and rear, from the tomb of Fu Hao.[3] The head and forelegs of the Fu Hao tigers are cast as one piece, and two of these bronzes originally had jade tubes affixed to the heads. The Fu Hao tigers have no very obvious practical use, but they may have been displayed near Lady Hao in life or death. A pair of bronze tigers in the Freer Gallery of Art, Smithsonian Institution, Washington, dated to the Western Zhou period may represent the continuation of such a tradition; their open backs suggest that they were the base for some kind of standing object.[4]

Tigers are the most common animal motif among the bronzes in the Dayangzhou tomb. The miniature renderings affixed to the handles of *ding* and *yan* seem to be distinctive representations of this local tradition, but tiger imagery is known from other regions, including Anyang (see cat. 49). The ferocity attributed to this animal in later literary sources may have been recognized in the Shang period, and on this basis it might have been associated with warriors, martial valor, and the like. We should not be surprised to find this image in the regalia of kings and lords (and perhaps their consorts as well) who sought to celebrate their courage and prowess.[5] RT

1 Excavated in 1989 (XDM:68); reported: Jiangxi 1997, 131.
2 Li Ji 1977, pl. 5.
3 Zhongguo 1980a, pl. 76.
4 Freer Gallery 1946, pls. 26 – 27.
5 Allan 1991.

59

Bronze *fangding* vessel

Height 97 (38 ⅛), width 58 (22 ⅞), depth 49.2 (19 ⅜),
weight 49 (107 ⅞)
Transitional Period (c. 1400–1200 BCE)
From Dayangzhou, Xin'gan, Jiangxi Province

Jiangxi Provincial Museum, Nanchang

Whoever was interred at Dayangzhou—perhaps a local chief or the lord of a statelet *(fangguo)*—the burial accorded him some of the trappings and status symbols of a Shang noble. On the other hand, the assemblage as a whole was quite different from norms familiar from finds in Henan. This tomb held forty-eight ritual vessels, but a selection heavily skewed toward pod-base types (thirty-eight items) for cooking meat offerings *(fangding, ding,* and *li)* and for steaming grain *(yan)*. The remaining

ten vessels were wine containers *(hu, you, lei, pou),* a large serving ladle, and two food vessels (a *pan* or *gui* and a *dou).* Conspicuously absent are the most common types of northern Bronze Age vessels: *gu* goblets and *jue* and *jia* tripods. It may be that the rites in which these vessels were used emphasized the preparation and service of meat and grain offerings; individual consumption of wine (the purpose of *gu* and *jue)* — at least using bronze vessels — was apparently not part of the ritual.

The single large *fangding*[1] was among the bronze vessels removed from the site by peasants before proper excavation was initiated. It originally stood northwest of the supposed coffin area, at what may have been the foot of the coffin. It is the largest of six *fangding* in the assemblage; one measuring 13 centimeters in height is best regarded as a miniature. Large *fangding* had previously been found in the north as paired vessels, including several sets at Zhengzhou and a pair in the tomb of Fu Hao. Like most northern examples, this vessel carries

a distinctive order of decoration: a plain central panel bordered by bands of bosses and crossed below the rim by a register of mask motifs with paired eyes. The cylindrical legs are topped by relief ram heads placed diagonally to the corners of the body. The loop handles are hollow and surmounted by profile tigers aligned with the short sides of the vessel. Both the relief of the ram heads and the tigers set this example apart from northern *fangding,* and, together with the slightly different proportions of the body and of legs to body, suggest this *fangding* may postdate Erligang Phase examples (c. 1600–1400 BCE) from the North China macroregion.

As with specimens from the north, the vessel was cast in stages, with the base cast onto the legs, the walls cast into the base, and the tigers cast onto the handles. RT

1 Recovered in 1989 (XDM:8); reported: Jiangxi 1997, 32.

60

Bronze *ding* tripod

Height 62.4 (24 ½), diam. 15 ½, weight 28.5 (62 ¾)
Transitional Period (c. 1400 – 1200 BCE)
From Dayangzhou, Xin'gan, Jiangxi Province

Jiangxi Provincial Museum, Nanchang

Fourteen round *ding* with flattened legs in the form of animals were found at Dayangzhou. This vessel[1] is the largest, and takes pride of place among the eight others, all of which feature zoomorphic legs; six of those vessels also have tigerlike creatures cast onto the handles. Ranging in height from this example's 62.4 centimeters down to 19 centimeters, the vessels seem to adumbrate a set of *ding* in graduated sizes, a feature of ritual assemblages first associated with the Western Zhou period. Although the tomb of Fu Hao has many pairs and sets of vessels, none was created as a gradually diminishing

series utilizing a common design. (The third largest of the Dayangzhou flat-legged *ding* features a different decoration and to that degree does not fit the set.)

This *ding* is impressive both for its design and for the quality of its execution. The three legs are slightly modeled in cross section, and their dramatic silhouettes (plausibly representing dragons) are enlivened by many hooks and curls. The animal's mouth is spread open at the point where the foot meets the shallow bowl; a row of sharp teeth is clearly seen on the lower jaw; the upper jaw seems to be elaborated as a trunk. The register on the bowl is given over to more conventional mask motifs within a circle band; hooked flanges are aligned with the legs and at each midpoint. The swallowtail motif seen on the *yan* steamer (cat. 61) encircles the rim of this *ding*.

Two *ding* with animal-shaped legs and handles that incorporate animal forms were among the first bronze vessels associated with the Wucheng culture.[2] Like the Dayangzhou vessels, their legs, flanges, and standing ornaments were separately cast and then mounted in the ceramic mold assembly used to cast the bowl; casting locked these elements in place. The Dayangzhou tomb also contained three stone legs of similar shape; it has been suggested that they were used for a *ding* made from some perishable material such as lacquer.[3] RT

1 Excavated in 1989 (XDM:14); reported: Jiangxi 1997, 18.
2 Fong 1980, no. 17.
3 Jiangxi 1997, 153.

61

Bronze *yan* steamer

Height 105 (41¼), diam. 61.2 (24⅛),
weight 78.5 (172¾)
Transitional Period (c. 1400–1200 BCE)
From Dayangzhou, Xin'gan, Jiangxi Province

Jiangxi Provincial Museum, Nanchang

Among vessels in the Dayangzhou find, only this
four-legged steamer (*yan*)¹ surpasses the large
fangding in height and weight. It too was placed
near the coffin, and like the *fangding* was removed
by peasants before proper excavation began. Both
of these vessels would have towered over other
bronze and ceramic objects on an altar or in the
tomb chamber. Both were made to appear thickly
cast (in particular, the loop handles and rim of
the steamer), and both display animals on their

handles. These truly are the "imposing vessels" (zhong qi) mentioned in later texts.

While four-legged steamers are extremely rare, the three-legged type, which originated in bronze forms during the Erligang Phase, had become relatively more common by the Late Shang. *Yan* (or *xian*) steamers are most frequently either bereft of decoration or given only a minimal treatment of "bowstrings" on the bowl and a few relief elements from an animal mask on the legs. This vessel, however, combines extensive intaglio decoration on the base with relief eyes, ox horns, and mouth. A single register of mask motifs bordered by circles wraps around the upper bowl, while a monocular band occupies the outer edge of the rim. The loop handles have swallowtail chevron motifs that can also be found on Wucheng ceramics. Flanges at the median line of each leg are echoed above by flanges set into the wall of the bowl. Four-legged creatures with small ears, no horns, and a scale pattern covering their bodies form the handles. A good analogue of the Dayangzhou *yan* is a three-legged example found in 1977 in Liquan county, Shaanxi.[2] The disposition of decoration is almost the same, but the

Liquan *yan*, at 70 centimeters and 25 kilograms, is slightly smaller. This *yan* is one of a number of linkages between the Gan River culture and the Wei River valley of the Zhou.

The Fu Hao tomb contained a singular steaming box with three bowls (cat. 47), also a large and impressive vessel. The cooked grain may have been presented in ceramic vessels, which were plentiful in the Dayangzhou find. No bronze types, with the possible exception of the *dou,* appear suitable for this function. RT

1   Recovered in 1989 (XDM:38); reported: Jiangxi 1997, 53–57.
2   Shaanxi 1979, no. 59.

62

Bronze *fangyou* vessel

Height 27.8 (10⅞), diam. at mouth 7.3 (2⅞),
weight 2.3 (5⅛)
Late Shang Yinxu Period II (c. 1200 BCE)
From Dayangzhou, Xin'gan, Jiangxi Province

Jiangxi Provincial Museum, Nanchang

Bronze vessels for the storage, preparation, or
service of wine are sparsely represented in the
Dayangzhou assemblage. This *you* wine container
with a bail handle[1] is one of three examples of its
type. The assemblage also included a pair of *hu*, a
lei, a *pou*, and a large serving ladle. These vessels are
not of a matched set, and this *you* and one *hu* are
the most advanced stylistically when judged against
developments known from the north. In both cases,
squared spirals *(leiwen)* fill the ground over the
entire surface. Most of these wine vessels are unex-
ceptional renderings of common types and variants;
this *fangyou*, by contrast is decidedly unusual.

The square-section *(fang)* body is punctured by
two large open channels that run from side to side
and cross in the interior. If the vessel were dipped
into a larger container of hot or cold water, the
water would immediately flow through these openings to warm or cool the liquid contents of the
vessel. Another example of this design is known,
a Late Shang vessel (now in the Beijing Palace
Museum) of similar size with, however, only a single
channel running from front to back.[2] As in the
Dayangzhou example, decoration surrounding the
channel literally frames the opening. The Palace
Museum vessel has a plain neck and differs from
the Dayangzhou example in other details of the
handle and lid.

Many features of this *fangyou* link it to Late
Shang examples from Anyang, including vessels
from the tomb of Fu Hao and the pre–World War II
excavations. *You* vessels with tall necks are attested
in both round- and square-section varieties, but
their decoration varies considerably. A somewhat
smaller round *you* from Xibeigang Tomb 1022 shares
many features with the Dayangzhou *fangyou* —
dense decoration on all surfaces, a bail handle

ending in animal heads, a link joining handle
and lid — but exhibits a surprising innovation.[3]
Its "neck" is actually a separate *gu* vessel placed
upside-down atop the belly of the *you*. The wine
container thus carries a drinking goblet. One might
argue that this innovation and designs such as
the Dayangzhou *fangyou* are more likely to have
emanated from the Shang foundries at Anyang than
from the culture of the Gan River tomb. If so, this
vessel (like the bronze helmet [cat. 63]) would
be one of few imports that testify to interaction
between Jiangxi and the north. RT

1   Excavated in 1989 (XDM:47); reported: Jiangxi 1997,
    62–69.
2   Weng and Yang 1982, 120.
3   Li and Wan 1972, pl. 43.

63

Bronze helmet

Height 18.7 (7 ³/₈), weight 2.21 (4 ⁷/₈)
Late Shang Period (c. 1200–1050 BCE)
From Dayangzhou, Xin'gan, Jiangxi Province

Jiangxi Provincial Museum, Nanchang

An extraordinary quantity of bronze weaponry
— spear points, dagger-axes, arrow points, knives —
sets the Dayangzhou find apart from most Shang
period tombs (the supposed royal tombs of Anyang
are exceptional in this respect). For example, at
Tomb 1004 at Xibeigang, within a large undisturbed
area several levels below the juncture of the shaft
and the south ramp, the excavators found two large
fangding, a collection of 360 spear points, and still

rior's own features, the mask must have presented a fierce countenance to any adversary. At the rear, a small tube on the ridge probably held a plume.

The helmets from Tomb 1004 follow the same overall design, but vary considerably in detail.[3] Two examples in American collections (the St. Louis Art Museum and The Nelson-Atkins Museum in Kansas City[4]), share the same traits, and could well have originated from Anyang. Outside the cache in Tomb 1004, however, bronze helmets are very rare in Shang finds. RT

1   Liang and Gao 1970, 30–35, pls. 23–30.
2   Excavated in 1989 (XDM:341); reported: Jiangxi 1997, 115.
3   Yang Hong 1980, 8–12.
4   For the St. Louis helmet, see Kidder 1956, 94–96; the Kansas City helmet is unpublished.

farther below, 141 bronze helmets.[1] The Xibeigang context provides sufficient grounds to argue that bronze weaponry was an important perquisite of a Shang king, and perhaps of local chiefs or lords as well. The single helmet found in the Dayangzhou tomb[2] may well have constituted part of a local lord's personal regalia.

This example, like the bronze helmets from Anyang, is almost round in section and was made using two mold-sections that join at the ridge running from front to back. The front edge is cut away over the warrior's forehead, while the sides and back hang down to afford protection to the ears and neck. Above the warrior's face are attributes of a mask: squared eyes, curled nostrils, a pair of ears in relief, and a pair of horns sweeping to each side in still higher relief. In combination with the war-

64

Bronze *bo* bell

Height 33 (13), weight 12.6 (27 ¾)
Late Shang Period (c. 1200 – 1050 BCE)
From Dayangzhou, Xin'gan, Jiangxi Province

Jiangxi Provincial Museum, Nanchang

During the Zhou period, chimes of bronze bells assumed a key role in the elaborate web of status and ceremonial relations governing the lives of the elite. The Shang period prototypes for these musical bells include two products of mid-Yangzi and Gan Yangzi regional cultures: a large bell standing on its shank with mouth open at the top *(nao)*, and the much rarer type seen in the example here.[1] This bell type, conventionally called *bo,* was designed to be hung from its loop; it may have had a clapper suspended within through the opening in the top. By contrast, the large *nao* type was mounted on a stand; its tones were produced by striking the

exterior lip with a mallet. The bells that assumed greatest prominence in the subsequent Zhou period, *yongzhong,* combined features of both earlier southern types. *Yongzhong* were suspended in the same orientation as the *bo,* mouth down, but retained the shank and striking method of *nao.* Loop suspension bells descended from Shang *bo* were made throughout much of the Zhou period, albeit less commonly than *yongzhong.*

This *bo*[2] is elliptical in cross section and wider at the mouth than at the top. Its two convex faces are decorated with a horned mask below a whorl device; intaglio lines trace curls and spirals, while fragments of a dragon's body float to either side. The edges feature large, hooked flanges; a bird facing outward rests on the top flange at each side. The swallowtail motif observed on the four-legged *yan* and round *ding* (cats. 60 – 61) frames the top and bottom margins and encircles the whorl as well (see fig. 1).

Most published Shang period *bo* have been unearthed in present-day Hunan province; a few others, with unknown provenances, reside in collections. This *bo* and the three *nao* that accompanied it may be the earliest bells found to date in a formal burial. The shape of the Dayangzhou bell differs from other examples in several respects: The mouth of the bell lacks a broad band below the decorated panel; wider at the base relative to total height, its proportions are more compact than those of other *bo*. The loop is also short and wide, unlike those that imitate the body shape of the bell itself. Most *bo*, moreover, give greater prominence to the bulging "eyes" of the masklike motifs that figure in their decoration. Here, by contrast, it is the central whorl and enframing horns that command attention. RT

1   Falkenhausen 1993b reviews musical bells in Shang and Zhou culture; see also cat. 91.
2   Excavated in 1989 (XDM:63); reported: Jiangxi 1997, 73–80.

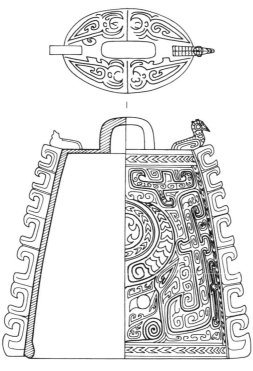

FIG. 1. Cat. 64 from above and side: decoration and cross section. After Jiangxi 1997, 81, fig. 43.

After archaeological contexts become well known through repeated excavation and analysis, investigators can make many plausible inferences from physical evidence. In Shang archaeology, burials constitute the most frequent context for bronze ritual vessels and jades, yielding a considerable range of data for establishing periodization, the social identity of the deceased, the ritual process that accompanied the interment, and many other features of the society that created the tombs. An exceptional archaeological context, however, means that archaeologists have few rules of thumb to guide their interpretations. When a find is made within an archaeological culture only recently recognized, the challenges are greater still. "Common knowledge" does not exist, and each new report may alter even basic information. This perplexing situation characterizes our understanding of the Sanxingdui culture of the Upper Yangzi macroregion (Sichuan province) and most particularly the contents of the two pits discovered in summer 1986.

The area near Sanxingdui (located in Guanghan county to the north of Chengdu) was recognized as a rich archaeological zone in the 1930s. Archaeologists of the Sichuan Institute have worked there for decades, and a major investigation of a large site began in 1980/1981.[1] The site name has recently been applied to an archaeological culture that spans the late Neolithic to the Zhou period. In July and August 1986, two pits were discovered by brick-factory workers in the southern part of the Sanxingdui site, near sections of a large, pounded-earth wall that once defined the ancient settlement. The site's excavators date these two pits to Period III at Sanxingdui, and correlate that period in turn with the early segment of the Late Shang period (Yinxu I – II).[2] They identify the two finds as "sacrificial pits" — debris from two large burning sacrifices presumably conducted by the community that resided in the nearby walled settlement. That the site had specific associations with the elite is entirely plausible given the richness of the finds: more than sixty ivory tusks, hundreds of hardstone blades and other objects, bronze ritual vessels, more than fifty life-size bronze heads, more than twenty bronze masks, a life-size standing bronze figure, as well as various gold objects.

Even a basic description of these objects, however, is handicapped by the lack of a final excavation report. The brief reports in print are synoptic, and much material remains unpublished. Several conferences convened to investigate these finds have yielded interpretive essays on broad topics rather than substantive additions to the data, and the pictorial record as well is incomplete. Under these circumstances, many basic facts remain unresolved. For example, the excavators argue that Pit 2 was later in date than Pit 1, but the rationale for this dating appears open to question; the pits apparently held almost no ceramics, which might have allowed a dating relative to the site occupation. The supposed wider range and more evolved features of objects in Pit 2 attest only the richer contents of that find, as Sun Hua has pointed out.[3]

Arguments about the "sacrificial" character of these pits and about their supposed connection to the Shu culture of the first millennium BCE offer still more opportunities for disputation. While the large volume of charred animal bones and other debris testifies to some kind of conflagration, the contents and the pits themselves may correspond less to burning sacrifices

Excavation photographs of Pit 2 at Sanxingdui, Guanghan, Sichuan province.

than to disposal pits. Indeed, compared to the much fuller data from Late Shang sites such as Anyang, several particularities of the pits warrant notice: the lack of sacrificial human victims, the presence of valuable ivory, and the unprecedented bronze heads, masks, and standing human figure. While many of the contents of the two pits were deliberately broken, it is not certain that a ritual inflicted that damage. Likewise, the connections between this culture and the Shu culture are only sketchily demonstrated at present, although that link has become an article of faith among many Chinese archaeologists, especially in Sichuan. RT

1   Sichuan 1987a; Bagley 1990; Yan and Linduff 1990.
2   Sichuan 1987b, 1989; Bagley 1988.
3   Sun 1993.

65

Bronze standing figure

Height 262 (103⅛)
Late Shang Period (?) (c. 1300–1100 BCE?)
From Pit 2 at Sanxingdui, Guanghan,
Sichuan Province

Sanxingdui Museum, Guanghan, Sichuan Province

Until the discovery of the underground army of
the Qin First Emperor (d. 210 BCE) near Xi'an (see
cats. 123–128), it was a commonplace that large-
scale human sculpture did not exist in ancient
China. This may continue to hold true for the
Bronze Age cultures of northern China, but it
cannot encompass the Sanxingdui culture of the
Upper Yangzi. This life-size, bronze standing figure[1]
has become the signature object of the pits at
Sanxingdui. While unique in that context, it was
in fact found among more than fifty bronze heads
and more than twenty bronze masks, all closely
related in style to the standing figure. Many of
the individual heads and masks could have been
installed on torsos like that of the full-scale bronze
example seen here. The elite of the Sanxingdui
culture seem to have placed great importance on
anthropomorphic sculpture.

The figure stands atop a large, two-part base—
a plain cube with sloping sides at the bottom with a
small plinth supported by four animal heads above.
The animal heads face outward at a diagonal to
the plinth's corners and have exaggerated snouts, a
row of squared teeth in their upper jaws, large eyes
in pointed sockets, and horns or ears. The plinth
itself features conventional Shang motifs along its
edge: a single "eye" in a field of squared spirals
between circle bands. These motifs quote Shang
bronzes known in the north as well as in the Middle
Yangzi and Gan Yangzi regions.

The figure itself, however, offers few traits that
can be connected so directly to the imagery and
styles of the Shang. It stands squarely on two bare
feet, and the elongated body is hidden within a full-
length garment that masks the shoulders, chest,
waist, and hips. The figure's arms are raised at right
angles to the torso at shoulder level; the right is

held up to the level of the nose, the left at chest level. Each sleeved arm ends in an oversize hand with a circular grip, suitable perhaps for grasping a cylindrical and curved object (perhaps an ivory tusk).

The thick neck supports a small head, the features of which may be intended to represent a mask and a large headdress. The figure's facial features are of a piece with most of the individual bronze heads from the site: wide slanted brows, almond-shaped eyes with a median ridge, a pronounced nose with cheek ridges extending from the nostrils, a straight, tightly closed mouth, and a square jaw. The large ears are squared and have holes (possibly for earrings) in the lobes. The band that encircles the head resembles that found on another bronze head, which also features paired loop motifs.[2] Above the band are petal forms, but the center portion suggests an eyed mask or horns to some observers. At the back of the head are two

openings that might have held an ornament, perhaps resembling those of the two individual heads (cats. 66, 67).

The surface of the body seems to represent a three- or four-piece garment.[3] A long skirt hangs below the knees, a separate rear panel ends in tails. An upper garment covers the body from the waist up but seems to have only a single (right) sleeve; this garment has a flap at the figure's right with its own patterning. Beneath this outer garment is an inner jacket with long sleeves (and perhaps a middle jacket with medium-length sleeves). A band affixed behind the right armpit wraps over the shoulder, crosses the chest, and is affixed again just behind the left armpit. RT

1   Excavated in 1986; reported: Sichuan 1989, 3–6.
2   K2/2:90; see Sichuan 1989, 7.
3   Wang and Wang 1993.

66

Bronze human head with gold leaf

Height 48.5 (19 ⅛)
Late Shang Period (?) (c. 1300–1100 BCE?)
From Pit 2 at Sanxingdui, Guanghan,
Sichuan Province

Sanxingdui Museum, Guanghan, Sichuan Province

67

Bronze human head with gold leaf (flat top)

Height 42.5 (16 ¾)
Late Shang Period (?) (c. 1300–1100 BCE?)
From Pit 2 at Sanxingdui, Guanghan,
Sichuan Province

Sanxingdui Museum, Guanghan, Sichuan Province

68

Bronze human head with hair ornament

Height 49.4 (19 ⅜)
Late Shang Period (?) (c. 1300–1100 BCE?)
From Pit 2 at Sanxingdui, Guanghan,
Sichuan Province

Sanxingdui Museum, Guanghan, Sichuan Province

The head of the standing figure (cat. 65) mirrors
the features of most of the fifty-four bronze heads
found in the two Sanxingdui pits. Those that have
been documented fall into a range of 36 to 49
centimeters in height, roughly approximating the
head of the standing figure. The heads have several
features in common: broad, slanted brows; almond-
shaped eyes with a median ridge; a pronounced
nose, with cheeklines extending to each side; a
tightly closed, straight mouth; a square jaw; and
squared ears with holes for earrings. Several examples are smaller (ranging from 13 to 29 centimeters
in height) but retain the basic physiognomy.

The heads may be distinguished as various
"types" on the basis of their headgear. The most
common type (no fewer than thirty-eight examples

separates forehead from cranium, and a notch centered over the nose ridge must have held an object in place over the front of the skull. On the back of the skull, a raised band (resembling headgear of some sort) hangs down between the ears. Mounted to the back of the skull of cat. 68 is a curved, flaring tube, open at both ends, intended perhaps to hold an element of a headdress.

All the bronze heads have extensions at the front and back of the neck that terminate in triangular points. Seen from the side, the heads seem to have been designed to be mounted onto a support — possibly a torso of another material such as stone, clay, or wood. Thus mounted, these heads may have been bronze components of large statues comparable to the standing figure. The contents of the two pits (assuming a rough contemporaneity) may have been part of a large ritual precinct or temple, with more than fifty human images installed as an ensemble. If the human heads and the standing figure indeed constitute an ensemble, several roles or statuses might have been implied by the varied headgear; only one head bears headgear matching that of the standing figure. How the

by one count, including cat. 67[1]) has a broad forehead, a flat cranium — interpreted by some as a representation of a flat cap — and a braided pigtail that extends down the back of the head and neck; other types (to the extent published) apparently lack the distinguishing hairstyle. (Some writers have argued that the other types conceal the "hair" beneath the headgear.) At least one other example features a mask of applied gold leaf that covers the entire face, except for the brows and eyes. Three of the heads from the Sanxingdui pits (including cats. 66 and 68[2]) may be distinguished as another type on the basis of their rounded skulls. A curved line

different types might have been arranged or intended to interact symbolically remains unknown. Nothing comparable is attested at present from any other Bronze Age culture within the boundaries of present-day China.

Do these figures represent kings or ancestors of the people of the Sanxingdui culture? At Anyang, deceased kings and remote ancestors were the focus of intense cultic activity. Are these images of gods, spirits, or totems of the Sanxingdui people? Many scholars assume that the complex pantheon of deities and spirits documented in Late Zhou and Qin-Han texts (such as *Shan hai jing* [Classic of mountains and seas] or *Chu ci* [Songs of Chu]) must have had ancient roots among the many different peoples of the earlier Bronze Age, especially in the south. Are the images susceptible of some other explanation? The faces and masks are consistent,

drawn (it would seem) from a single type. Compared with the many permutations of the so-called *taotie* known from Shang tradition, this is a relatively stable imagery. The people of the Sanxingdui culture certainly knew of the Shang image (see cat. 74), yet they devised a distinctly different set of symbolic representations for their purposes, which on present evidence did not include rites involving bronze vessels and offerings of the kind documented in the north. RT

1 Excavated in 1986; published: Zhao 1994, nos. 21–22.
2 Excavated in 1986; published: Sichuan 1989, 2; Zhao 1994, nos. 23–24; Rawson 1996, no. 23.

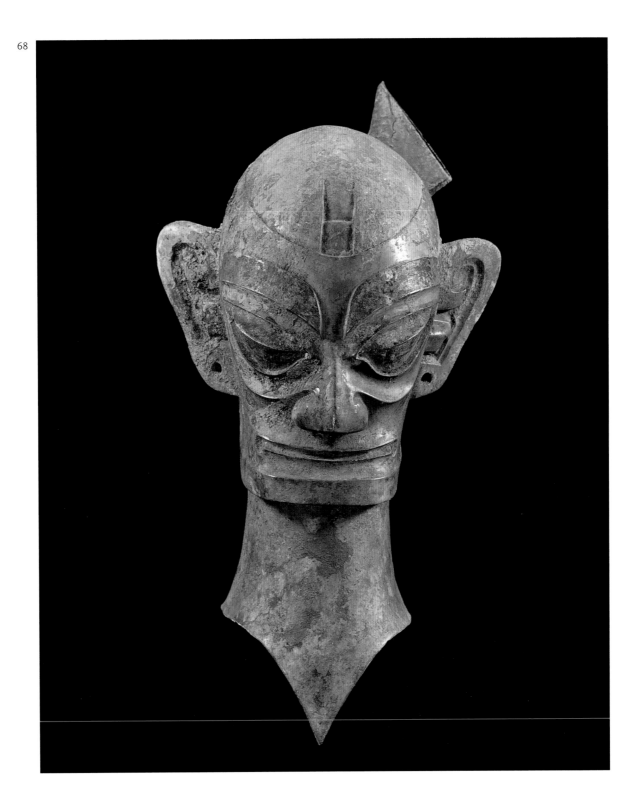

69

69
side

69

Bronze mask with hooked-cloud ornament

Height 85.4 (33 ⅝)
Late Shang Period (?) (c. 1300 – 1100 BCE?)
From Pit 2 at Sanxingdui, Guanghan,
Sichuan Province

Sanxingdui Museum, Guanghan, Sichuan Province

70

Bronze mask

Height 40.5 (15 ⅞)
Late Shang Period (?) (c. 1300 – 1100 BCE?)
From Pit 2 at Sanxingdui, Guanghan,
Sichuan Province

Sanxingdui Museum, Guanghan, Sichuan Province

Pit 2, which contained the standing figure and the
most of the bronze heads, also held about fifteen
bronze masks, distinguished from the heads in
lacking necks, backs, and tops. Most are somewhat
larger than the heads, and all have small square
openings at their sides that must have been used
to attach them to some kind of support. Lines
visible across the forehead, behind the ears, and
under the jaw suggest that the bronze heads themselves may represent beings wearing masks, but
the basic physiognomy of the masks themselves
mirrors the facial features of the standing figure
and many of the Sanxingdui heads.

Three masks from Pit 2 stand apart, however,
distinguished from the heads and other masks
by a number of details: their cylindrical eyes protrude grotesquely from elongated sockets and are
bounded by narrow lids; the tops of their ears are
drawn out at right angles and end in single points,
while their upturned mouths, ridged in the middle,
bestow an almost Archaic smile. Cat. 69,[1] which
bore traces of black pigment around the eyes and
red on the mouth, has an ornament over the nose
resembling a hooked-cloud motif, composed of a
pair of spirals curling inward at the base and the
top and a blade-shaped device in the middle. Other

masks, some of which are pieced at the forehead, may have originally included similar attachments.

Like the heads, these masks may have been mounted on torsos to create large statues akin to the standing figure or on stands that did not otherwise incorporate human features; some Chinese authors have even suggested that the masks may have been constituents of totem poles. They may also have been elements of architectural decoration or large furniture used in a ritual precinct, perhaps serving as part of a gateway, altar, or hall; thus installed, these masks would have dominated their immediate surroundings with their enigmatic countenances.

The motif of the almond-shaped eyes with their median ridges (which characterizes the majority of the pits' masks and heads) has been interpreted as a representation of closed eyes; the notion that eyes are somehow compelling — intended to provoke fear or awe (as "eyed-masks" around the world often are[2]) — is weakened with respect to the masks from the Sanxingdui pits by the possibility that most of these masks and heads actually are "blind." All the Sanxingdui masks and heads in any event lack the physical attributes conventionally associated with eliciting such emotions — fangs, teeth, or tongues. RT

1   Excavated in 1986; published: Zhao 1994, no. 30; Rawson 1996, no. 25.
2   Wu 1997a.

71

Bronze figure with headdress

Height 42.6 (16 ¾)
Late Shang Period (?) (c. 1300 – 1100 BCE?)
From Pit 2 at Sanxingdui, Guanghan,
Sichuan Province

Sanxingdui Museum, Guanghan, Sichuan Province

While the large standing figure (cat. 65) has become the signature object from the Sanxingdui
pits, a number of smaller bronze figures offer
glimpses into the culture's representation of the
human form. Pit 1 contained at least one diminutive (15-centimeter) kneeling bronze figure
"dressed" only in a waistband that seems to prefigure the *mawashi* of Japanese sumo.[1] This same
figure wears its hair in long locks that run from the
forehead to the back of the skull. Pit 2 held at least
eight small bronze figures; the figure published in
the initial report has a twisted pose with its right
knee touching the ground and its torso and head
aligned in the same plane.[2] The head (approximately 4 centimeters high) is a miniature rendering
of the features known from the full-size heads and
masks.

One of these pits also held the partial (or broken) human figure exhibited here, which as yet has
not been reported by the excavators.[3] The head
resembles the full-size heads and masks, and the
arms are raised at the sides in a pose similar to that
of the large standing figure. Unlike the small figures
from Pit 2, here the arms and chest are covered
with relief motifs that may indicate designs on a
garment. Unlike all the other figures, this example
wears an elaborate headdress that rises from a band
above the forehead. The iconography of the headdress remains uncertain; some have identified it as
an elephant on the basis of the large opening (perhaps representing a mouth) below a curled trunk
and a pair of large pointed ears. RT

1 Excavated in 1986; reported: Sichuan 1987b, 4 – 5;
   published: Zhao 1994, no. 25.
2 Excavated in 1986; reported: Sichuan 1989, 6; published:
   Zhao 1994, no. 26.
3 See Asahi 1998, no. 77.

72

Bronze raptor ornament

Height 43.3 (17)
Late Shang Period (?) (c. 1300 – 1100 BCE?)
From Pit 2 at Sanxingdui, Guanghan,
Sichuan Province

Sanxingdui Museum, Guanghan, Sichuan Province

73

Bronze dragon-shaped ornament

Height 40 (15¾)
Late Shang Period (?) (c. 1300 – 1100 BCE?)
From Pit 1 at Sanxingdui, Guanghan,
Sichuan Province

Sanxingdui Museum, Guanghan, Sichuan Province

These objects were recovered singly from the two
Sanxingdui pits. Each must originally have served
as a covering or finial of some kind in combination
with pieces, perhaps including perishable materials, that either were not deposited in the pits or
did not survive burial. It remains uncertain which

by strong modeling; the surface is otherwise un-decorated.

The Sanxingdui pits contained components of "spirit trees" — complex bronze stands as high as 4 meters tall, festooned with branches whose tips support perching birds. While this head is consid-erably larger in scale than the spirit-tree birds, one cannot rule out the possibility that it was a compo-nent of such a stand or a similar object.

The "dragon" is perhaps a less arbitrary identi-fication. It too is a hollow tube, increasing slightly in diameter from its open bottom to its closed top.[2] Four half-circles and holes at the base of the object presumably served to attach it to a shaft. A large hook mounted at the front of the tube calls to mind the ornament on the nose ridge of the bronze mask (cat. 69). The dragon that boosts itself onto the top of the tube rests on its forward limbs, neck ex-tended, and jaws open; its elongated body extends down the back of the tube, while the hind limbs clutch at the sides. A billy-goat beard, small horns, and large ears complete the head. Motifs conven-tionally denominated "dragons" on Shang objects (such as the small dragon on the lid of the owl-shaped vessel from Tomb 5 [cat. 48]) have little in common with this creature, which anticipates later representations of dragons. RT

1 Excavated in 1986; published: Zhao 1994, no. 47; Rawson 1996, no. 29.
2 Excavated in 1986; reported: Sichuan 1987b, 6.

other objects (if any) from these pits might in fact be related to these ornaments.

The conventional zoomorphic identification of the "eagle" ornament[1] is at best arbitrary, though its large beak suggests some type of raptor. The object is circular in cross section, with small holes at the bottom edge that might have served to attach the object to a shaft or other insert. The assem-blage that this head completed would presumably have been of considerable size, assuming that the head was scaled naturalistically with the remainder. Its beak and large squared eyes are accentuated

74

Bronze *lei* vessel

Height 54 (21 ¼)
Late Shang Period (?) (c. 1300 – 1100 BCE?)
From Pit 2 at Sanxingdui, Guanghan,
Sichuan Province

Sanxingdui Museum, Guanghan, Sichuan Province

Ritual vessels constitute only a small percentage of the bronze objects recovered from the Sanxingdui pits, overshadowed in number (and in sheer weight) by the bronze heads, masks, and the standing figure — all emblematic of a distinctive tradition. In rich burial assemblages in the north, such as the tomb of Fu Hao (cats. 46 – 54), by contrast, ritual vessels predominate; with the notable exception of weapons, other uses for bronze are far less important.

Both of the Sanxingdui pits yielded *zun* and *lei* wine containers, vessel types that flourished during the Upper Erligang Phase and the Transitional Period prior to the occupation of Anyang. Bronze had long been used to create vessels for cooking meat offerings, steaming and serving grain, and warming and serving the alcoholic drinks favored in Shang rites, but large, metal containers intended to store wine appeared only later. It may be that stoneware vessels had been used to hold alcoholic spirits prior to the appearance of bronze types — indeed, the *zun* shape itself derives from ceramics. The *zun* and *lei* share a structure in common: a ring foot, more or less tall in proportion to the overall height of the vessel; a body wider than the foot, with an expanding profile; and a sharply defined (carinated) shoulder break. The types are distinguished by the treatment of their necks and mouths. *Zun* have wide, trumpet-shaped mouths, while *lei* have cylindrical necks with everted lips.

Three *lei* and nine *zun* are reported from the Sanxingdui pits. At the time of their excavation, their exteriors were covered by a red pigment (possibly ochre). The vessels themselves contained cowries and hardstone carvings; Jessica Rawson has suggested that the vessels may have served as "precious containers" for such objects rather than for storing wine, their presumed original function in the north.[1] It remains uncertain whether any of these vessels was produced by the Sanxingdui culture; all may well have been imports. Indeed, the *zun* from Sanxingdui have close stylistic parallels with examples recovered from sites in Hunan in the Middle Yangzi macroregion, and recent studies of lead isotope ratios strongly suggest that the bronzes at Sanxingdui and those at Dayangzhou (cats. 57 – 64) utilized the same lead ores.[2]

The Sanxingdui *lei* reflect two distinct styles. Two of the three *lei* have flush surface decoration, and animal heads in relief at the shoulder edge are centered over prominent *taotie* masks on the body. (The two vessels differ, however, in height and in the treatment of particular decorative elements — the horns on the animal heads, as well as the flanges and motifs in secondary registers.) Both *lei* resemble an example unearthed at Yueyang on Lake Dongting in Hunan province. The third *lei*, shown here,[3] is a tall vessel with an especially high ring foot. Thin, hooked flanges divide the exterior into four identical sections: masks at the foot are surmounted by larger masks on the body and relief ram heads. The shoulder has a band of simple decoration, while the neck is bare except for "bowstring" lines. The ram heads at the shoulder appear to have been attached to the body after its casting, possibly by using a tenon on the vessel. The treatment of the two levels of mask decoration is distinctive: many parts of the masks are in relief and "exploded" so that the elements float apart from each other. Relief surfaces and ground are decorated with intaglio lines tracing curls and quills; image and ground as a result are weakly contrasted. RT

1 Rawson 1996, 70.
2 Zheng 1995.
3 Excavated in 1986; published: Zhao 1994, nos. 68, 69.

75

Incised gold sheath

Length 142 (55⅞), diam. 2.3 (⅞)
Late Shang Period (?) (c. 1300–1100 BCE?)
From Pit 2 at Sanxingdui, Guanghan,
Sichuan Province

Sanxingdui Museum, Guanghan, Sichuan Province

Carbonized fragments of wood found within this
unalloyed gold tube[1] suggest that it served as the
sheath for a wooden staff; a dragon ornament
found near in the pit may have also been a part
of the original assemblage. The material itself suggests that this staff was associated with an individual of high status among the people of Sanxingdui
—a king, a chief, or a shaman.

The sheath carries incised decoration at one
end: a terminal ring of "happy faces" beneath which
fish (whose scales are carefully detailed) and birds
are skewered by two bands of arrows. Bird imagery
appears in the spirit trees from Pit 2; the arrows
and fish, however, are uncommon in decorative
repertoires known from the Sanxingdui site. The
faces may have an association with human figures
displayed on several stone scepters from Pit 2,
motifs that might themselves be shorthand representations of the standing figure or its ilk.

Gold was an important resource of the southwest, so it is not surprising that the community
at Sanxingdui utilized this precious metal. Shang
centers of the north, by contrast, have yielded
very few gold artifacts. RT

1   Excavated in 1986; reported: Sichuan 1987b, 4.

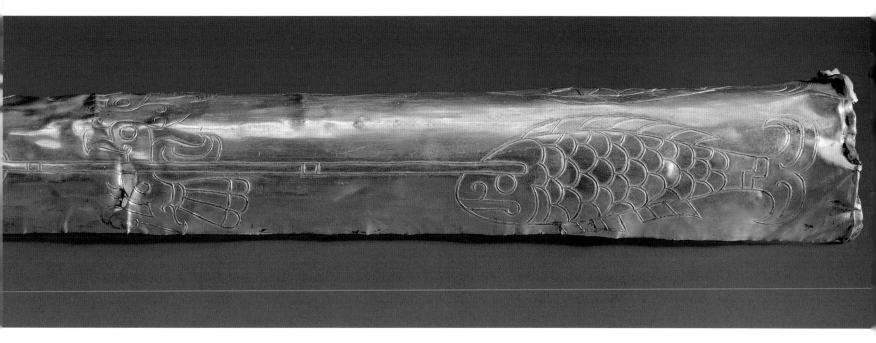

The bronzes from Tomb 163 are somewhat heterogeneous stylistically; the animal-shaped vessels seemingly are of somewhat earlier date than the bells, but all the bronzes fall within the Middle Western Zhou period (c. 950–850 BCE). Whereas the inscriptions on the bells mention the name Xing Shu — presumably referring to the lineage of the tomb occupant's husband — the animal-shaped vessels are inscribed with another name, Deng Zhong.[9] In theory, Deng Zhong ("second-born of Deng") could be the name of a person, but it is more probably the name of a lineage — a branch of the house of Deng, probably the natal lineage of the woman buried in the tomb. The Zhangjiapo finds have shown beyond doubt that Xing Shu ("junior of Xing"), a similarly ambiguous name, is the name of a branch lineage and not of an individual.[10] It is precisely during the Middle Western Zhou period that major lineages increasingly split up into branches, possibly in response to demographic pressure.[11]

Zhou custom prescribed clan exogamy; since the Xing were affiliated with the Ji clan (the clan of the Zhou royal house) and the Deng with the Man clan, we know that members of these two lineages would have been eligible to marry. Aristocratic women often brought sacrificial vessels from their own families into marriage. The animal-shaped vessel in this exhibition may be one such example — part of the dowry of a Deng woman marrying into the house of Xing. LvF

1   Zhongguo Fengxi 1962; Zhongguo 1962; Zhongguo Fengxi 1963; Zhongguo Fengxi 1981; Zhongguo 1984a, 253–257; Bao 1979; Hu 1982; Shaanxi 1995.
2   From its foundation in 1950 until 1977, the Institute of Archaeology was part of the Chinese Academy of Sciences.
3   Zhongguo Fengxi 1962; Zhongguo 1962; Zhongguo Fengxi 1965; Zhongguo Fengxi 1980; Zhongguo Fengxi 1981; Zhongguo Fengxi 1984; Zhongguo 1984a, 253–257; Zhao 1984.
4   Zhongguo 1986, Zhongguo Fengxi 1990; Zhang Changshou 1990.
5   Such proximity decreased from generation to generation: if the first Xing Shu lineage head was the brother of a

Zhou king, his son would have been the first cousin and his grandson a second cousin of the king in their respective generations, and so forth.
6   Zhang and Zhang 1994.
7   Zhang Changshou 1990, 1991, 1992, 1993, 1994; Zhang and Zhang 1992.
8   Liang and Feng 1963; Zhongguo 1965a; Zhongguo Fengxi 1983; Shaanxi 1977.
9   The inscription on the two vessels reads *Deng Zhong zuo bao zun yi* ("Deng Zhong made [this] precious ritual vessel").
10 Zhang Changshou 1990.
11 Hayashi 1983; Falkenhausen 1997.

76

Bronze *ding* tripod with five handles

Height 122 (48⅛), diam. at mouth 83 (32⅝)
Latter Phase of the Early Western Zhou Period
(c. 1000–975 BCE)
From Tomb 1 at Shijiayuan, Chunhua,
Shaanxi Province

Chunhua County Cultural Relics Museum,
Shaanxi Province

This *ding*,[1] weighing 226 kilograms, is the largest
and heaviest Western Zhou bronze vessel on record,
though fragments exist of even larger ones.[2] Together with two much smaller *gui* vessels found in
the same tomb, it formed part of an assemblage of
ritual bronzes, now incomplete because the tomb
was looted before excavation.

Chunhua is located on the loess plateau at the
northern edge of the Western Zhou metropolitan
core. Tomb 1 at Shijiayuan was part of the cemetery

of an aristocratic lineage, whose members had
presumably resided at a large Early to Middle Western Zhou settlement discovered nearby. Since no
inscribed bronzes have been found at this site
so far, the name of the lineage remains unknown.

The bowl of the *ding* has a slightly sagging
profile and an everted rim from which two large,
outward-bent handles rise. The three handles laterally attached to the vessel body are a feature unique
to this specimen. They have no discernible practical
use (the *ding* was lifted by the rim handles), but
they enhance the object's silhouette and effectively
frame its decoration.

The principal decorative motif, repeated three
times around the vessel body, consists of a symmetrical pair of single-legged dragons converging toward a central flange. Raised in high relief against
a background of fine spirals, the dragon bodies are
accentuated by widely spaced sunken-line curls.
As is often the case in Shang and Early Western

Zhou bronzes, the motif is deliberately ambiguous and can be read either as two dragons represented in profile, or as one central horned mask *(taotie)* with two dragon bodies — or the spliced body of a single dragon — emerging from it. The frontal "mask" aspect of the motif is enhanced by the addition of a three-dimensionally sculptured miniature buffalo head below the central flange.

This constellation of dragons in profile and a frontal buffalo head recurs in slightly different form on the face of the rim handles. Here the buffalo head is reduced to an abstract chiffre placed between — and thus separating — the two dragons ascending toward it. Like their counterparts on the vessel walls, these dragons have curled tails, sinuous bodies, and mushroom-shaped horns, but each sports two legs instead of one.

The slightly bulging legs of this *ding* feature relief animal masks with pointed spiraling ram's horns. A different type of mask adorns the three lateral handles, notable for its wide, upright horns, which — like the small buffalo heads on the vessel body — must have been precast and inserted in the mold assemblage; the rest of the vessel would have been cast around them.

The combination of bold relief and sculptural elements is characteristic of the bronze style of the latter phase of the Early Western Zhou period (c. 1000 – 950 BCE).[3] Its confident execution may indicate that this is a product of a workshop attached to the Zhou royal house. LvF

1   Excavated in 1979; published: Chunhua 1980; Hayashi 1984, 2:17, fig. 191; Higuchi and Enjōji 1984, no. 44; Li Xueqin 1986, 1: nos. 135 – 136; Rawson 1990, part 1:31, fig. 23; Wenwu jinghua 1990, no. 51.
2   For example, a dragon-shaped handle, 60 (23 ⅝) in length, from Julianghaijia, Fufeng, Shaanxi province (Gao 1994).
3   Hayashi 1984.

77

Bronze animal-shaped *zun* vessel

Height 38.8 (15 ¼), width 41.4 (16 ⅜)
Middle Western Zhou Period (c. 975–875 BCE)
From Tomb 163 at Zhangjiapo, Shaanxi Province

The Institute of Archaeology, CASS, Beijing

Shang and Zhou animal-shaped vessels are not pure
sculpture. Each vessel can be viewed both in terms
of the animal (or animals) it resembles and in terms
of the standard ritual vessel type (*you, ding, hu, zun,*
or *gong*) that its maker used as his point of departure. In some instances, the "animal" aspect eclipses
the "vessel" aspect; in others, the "vessel" aspect

predominates. The present specimen[1] is quite typical in manifesting a tension between these dual
derivations. The raised cover and the bulge below it
detract from the object's overall animal likeness in
the effort to create a standard vessel of ambiguous
typological affiliation, possibly a *you.* Perhaps in
part because of the need to accommodate the standard vessel shape, the animal embodied by the
vessel is of uncertain zoological identity. It has a
sheeplike muzzle, large round eyes, narrow pointed
ears, and columnar horns; its long, thick neck contrasts with the short, thin legs; the feet have toes
rather than hooves; and a pointed protrusion from
the lower belly may intimate a wing or fin. Most

of these elements have parallels elsewhere in the Western Zhou bestiary,[2] but the specific combination is unique.

The staid demeanor of this composite creature is enlivened by a crest of four handles shaped as rambunctious animals: a long-tailed bird and three different kinds of dragons. Dynamic tension is introduced as well by the surface ornament, which accentuates the object's animal features. The animal's breast, belly, and hindquarters are adorned with symmetrical pairs of S-shaped dragons that, when viewed frontally, can be read as animal masks. This motif frequently appears on ritual bronzes; its deployment on the belly, with a prominent bird-shaped flange as its central axis, accentuates the derivation of that portion of the object from a standard vessel type.

As is typical for Middle Western Zhou bronzes, the main elements of the decoration are executed as wide, flat, empty bands with jagged outlines that barely emerge from their background of thin spirals. A Middle Western Zhou date is also suggested by the specific resemblance of the vessel's cover to Middle Western Zhou *you* covers.[3] The cover's surface features two sinuous dragons merging into a single head — or, alternatively, a spliced depiction of both sides of a single dragon.

The original name for animal-shaped vessels is unknown;[4] it may be that there was no uniform name, and that, during rituals, each vessel was used for the same function as the standard vessel on which it was based. If so, this vessel may have been used as a *you*. Like many Western Zhou *you*, in fact, the vessel was paired with a slightly smaller vessel of identical shape. LvF

1 Excavated in 1984 (M 163:33); published: Zhongguo Fengxi 1986, pl. 1; Rawson 1990, part 2:709–710, fig. 119.3; Zhongguo 1993, 182.
2 Hayashi 1986, 128–129.
3 Hayashi 1984, 2:280–285.
4 Since the eleventh century CE, convention has subsumed all animal-shaped vessels under the term *zun*, now sometimes amended to *xizun* to differentiate them from trumpet-mouthed *zun* vessels.

Zhuangbai, a hamlet situated approximately 100 kilometers west of the city of Xi'an, between the Wei River (25 kilometers to the south) and the Qi Shan mountains (25 kilometers to the north), was recognized as an important archaeological site in December 1976, when farmers clearing a field turned up an ancient bronze vessel; subsequent excavation revealed a pit containing 103 bronze vessels dating to the Western Zhou period (c. 1100 – 771 BCE) — the so-called Hoard 1. Zhuangbai lies in the Zhou Yuan — the Plain of Zhou — the ancestral homeland of the Zhou people prior to the establishment of their dynasty in the middle of the eleventh century BCE. Even after the political capital had been moved to the vicinity of present-day Xi'an, many important Zhou families continued to maintain households in the Zhou Yuan.

Although the plain covers a small area (approximately 10 square kilometers), it has yielded more Western Zhou bronze vessels than any single locality in China. In the 1800s, when archaeological finds in China began to become systematically reported, several important Western Zhou bronze vessels were discovered within the plain's perimeter in the two counties — Qishan and Fufeng — whose border bisects the Zhou Yuan: the Mao Gong *ding*, found in the 1840s in Jingdang (Qishan) and now in the collection of the National Palace Museum in Taipei, Taiwan; the Da Yu *ding*, discovered at around the same time in Licun (Qishan) and now in The National Museum of Chinese History, Beijing; and the Da Ke *ding*, discovered in 1890 in Renjia (Fufeng) and now in the Shanghai Museum. In the 1970s, the Zhou Yuan was the focus of a concerted archaeological investigation, with important discoveries of other hoards made at Dongjia (thirty-seven vessels, found in 1975, belonging to the Lü lineage); Hejia (two vessels of the San lineage, discovered in 1973, complementing another hoard of eleven San vessels that had been unearthed about 2 kilometers to the east in Shaochen in 1960); Qiangjia (seven vessels, belonging to the Guoji lineage, discovered in 1974); as well as the tomb of Bo Dong at Zhuangbai (fourteen important vessels found in 1975) — about one hundred meters from where Hoard 1 was discovered a year later.

Tombs usually contain ritual implements that either belonged to the deceased during his lifetime or were made expressly for his burial. By contrast, hoards are groups of objects secreted in haste to preserve them from marauders and often contain the accumulated heirlooms of a family. The Zhou Yuan hoards indicate that the old families of the Zhou Yuan owned bronze ritual vessels and other treasures produced over the course of several generations. By the early eighth century BCE, however, the Zhou dynasty was coming to an end; it is likely that most of the hoards of the Zhou Yuan date from about the year 771 BCE, when the region of the Zhou capital — including the Zhou Yuan — was finally overrun by the invading Quan Rong and the families were forced to flee.

The 103 bronzes of Hoard 1 derive from at least five generations of the Wei, a family related to the ruling house of the previous Shang dynasty. The lengthy inscription on the most famous of the hoard's bronzes, the Shi Qiang *pan* (cat. 81), recounts how the High Ancestor of the Wei family presented himself to King Wu of Zhou after the Zhou defeat of the Shang

(c. 1045 BCE) and was rewarded with a plot of land in the Zhou Yuan. It goes on to mention three subsequent generations of the family—Ancestor Yi, Grandfather Xin, and the deceased-father Duke Yi—before finally mentioning Shi Qiang himself, who served as a scribe *(shi)* at the Zhou court of King Gong (r. c. 917–900 BCE). These three immediate ancestors of Qiang seem to have made some of the bronzes found in the hoard. Ancestor Yi probably corresponds to an individual named Shang, the patron of a set of vessels comprising a *zun* and *you*. An inscription on these two vessels indicates that Shang was married to a woman from the ruling house of Zhou. Grandfather Xin is almost certainly the person named Zhe, the patron of the Zhe *jia* tripod (cat. 79), as well as a *gong* server, a *fangyi* square casket, and a *zun*. Inscriptions also seem to confirm that Duke Yi, the father of Qiang, was the posthumous temple name of a man named Feng, the patron of the Feng *zun* (cat. 80), as well as a corresponding *you* and four *jue*. Qiang himself also made two *jue* in addition to his eponymous *pan*.

The Wei family history does not by any means end with Qiang. Indeed, by far the most prolific patron of bronze vessels in the family (as reflected by the family hoard) was Qiang's son, Xing. Xing is named as the patron in the inscriptions of at least 36 of the 103 vessels in the hoard, including the Sannian Xing *hu* (cat. 82). Some of these inscriptions clearly indicate that Xing was a son of Qiang. One other individual, Bo Xianfu, named as the patron of a set of ten *li*, may have been Xing's son. Although no specific inscriptions confirm this affiliation, if it is true (as seems likely), then Bo Xianfu may represent the last generation of the Wei family.

Hoard 1 is important not only because of the large number of bronze vessels it contained nor because of the obvious beauty of many of the individual vessels. What is of surpassing importance is that these bronzes were produced over five or more generations, a legacy that can be delineated with certainty on the basis of the inscriptions on the bronze vessels. The Wei family vessels chronicle the development of bronze styles, generation by generation, over the course of much of the Western Zhou period. Aptly described as a yardstick with which to measure other Western Zhou bronze vessels,[1] these bronzes have resolved questions about dating particular bronze vessels and vessel styles (see cat. 79), and they attest to important changes that took place over the course of the Western Zhou period in the culture's social organization, ritual performance, and poetic expression—changes that in large measure contributed to the classical expression of what it meant to be Chinese. ES

78

Lü Fu Yi bronze *gu* vessel

Height 25.2 (10), diam. at mouth 13.2 (5 ¼)
Early Western Zhou Period, late eleventh – early
tenth century BCE
From Zhuangbai, Fufeng, Shaanxi Province

Zhou Yuan Administrative Office of Cultural Relics,
Fufeng, Shaanxi Province

Notable for its long, narrow neck and the elegant
smoothness of its upper body, this *gu*[1] is decorated
only at its base, with a wide ribbonlike band sand-
wiched between two narrower bands of *yunwen*
(cloud pattern). Its shape dates it to the end of
the Early Western Zhou period — the first half of
the tenth century BCE — but the calligraphy of
its simple inscription (which reads "Father Yi of the
Lü [lineage]") suggests an earlier date. Whatever
its absolute date, this *gu* and four others that the
excavators have grouped with it are doubtless the
latest examples of this vessel type from Hoard 1.[2]

The *gu,* traditionally classified as a wine vessel,
was one of the standard vessel types of the Shang
period. Although it continued to be used through
the Early Western Zhou period, it became rare after
the beginning of the Middle Western Zhou period
(roughly the reign of King Mu [r. c. 956 – 918 BCE]).
The disappearance of this specific vessel type may
well prefigure the apparent abandonment of almost
all wine vessels in the "ritual reform" of the Middle
Western Zhou period. This reform saw a dramatic
change in the composition of sets of vessels used
in rituals: food vessels, especially *ding* and *gui,* often
in multiples, came to dominate ritual assemblages.
The Xing vessels of Hoard 1 are representative of
the composition of such a set after the reform: two
xu, four *hu,* eight *gui,* three *jue,* five *li,* and at least
four different sets of *zhong.*

The family name in the inscription, Lü, is identified with a hoard of thirty-seven vessels discovered
in 1975 in Dongjia, Qishan, Shaanxi province —
about 3 kilometers northwest of Zhuangbai. Although the character is written differently on the
Dongjia vessels, the appearance of this vessel in
the Wei family hoard may reflect marriages between

these two neighboring families; other inscribed vessels discovered in the Zhou Yuan provide considerable evidence of intermarriage among many of the families that resided there.[3] ES

1   Excavated in 1976 (6); reported: Shaanxi 1978, 17, fig. 34.
2   Shaanxi 1980, 2: nos. 7–10.
3   For a discussion of these intermarriages, see Shaughnessy 1998.

79

Zhe bronze *jia* vessel

Height 34.1 (13 ¾), diam. at mouth 18.6 (7 ⅜)
Early Western Zhou Period, second quarter of the tenth century BCE
From Zhuangbai, Fufeng, Shaanxi Province

Zhou Yuan Administrative Office of Cultural Relics, Fufeng, Shaanxi Province

This *jia*[1] is one of four vessels commissioned by Zhe, a scribe of the Zhou court, titled *Zuoce* — "Maker of Strips" (court records were written on bamboo or wooden strips at the time). The Zhe *jia* bears a simple inscription: "Zhe makes for Father Yi this treasured offertory vessel. [Clan-sign]." Zhe's other vessels — a *gong*, a *fangyi*, and a *zun* — are inscribed with a longer text (identical on all three) that commemorates an award from the Zhou king:

> It was the fifth month; the king was at An.
> On *wuzi* [day 25], [the king] commanded
> Maker of Strips Zhe to grant the land of
> Wang to the Lord of Xiang; awarded metal
> and awarded retainers, [he] extols the king's
> beneficence. It is the king's nineteenth
> year. [He] herewith makes for Father Yi
> this offertory; may he eternally treasure it.
> [Clan-sign]

The "Father Yi" (Fu Yi) to whom the vessels are dedicated is almost certainly the Ancestor Yi (Yi Zu) named in the Shi Qiang *pan* inscription (see cat. 81). The genealogy traced in the *pan* inscription also shows that Qiang, who was active at the court of King Gong (r. c. 917–900 BCE), was almost certainly Zhe's grandson; Zhe can thus be reasonably placed about fifty years prior to Gong's reign — roughly to that of King Zhao (r. c. 976–957 BCE).

The Zhe vessels have provided decisive new evidence for dating Western Zhou bronze vessels. One of the Zhe vessels, the Zhe *fangyi*, is strikingly similar to a vessel in the Freer Gallery of Art, Washington, the Ling *fangyi*. A lengthy inscription on the Ling *fangyi* mentions the duke of Zhou (Zhou Gong), known to have served as regent for seven

years at the beginning of the dynasty (c. 1042 – 1036 BCE)[2]; most scholars, on that evidence, dated the vessel to the very beginning of the dynasty — certainly no later than the reign of King Cheng (r. c. 1035 – 1006 BCE). However, the inscription also mentions a temple — the Kang Gong — that one scholar argued must have been dedicated posthumously to Cheng's son, King Kang (r. c. 1005 – 978 BCE); its mention suggested that the Ling *fangyi* could date no earlier than the reign of King Zhao, the son of King Kang.[3]

The debate about the date of the Ling *fangyi* extended to the dating of scores of Early Western Zhou period bronze vessels — indeed, in some ways to the entire development of bronze styles through the first hundred or so years of the dynasty. The discovery in 1976 of the Zhe *fangyi*, a virtual double of the Ling *fangyi*, has resolved the debate conclusively: since the inscription of the Shi Qiang *pan* leaves no doubt that the Zhe *fangyi* dates to the reign of King Zhao, it is now almost universally agreed that the Ling *fangyi* and many other vessels that had heretofore been dated to the reign of King Cheng must date to the reign of his grandson, King Zhao — or at least to the second half of the Early Western Zhou period.[4] ES

1   Excavated in 1976 (17); reported: Shaanxi 1978.
2   This dating was first advanced by Guo Muruo and Chen Mengjia, two of the greatest authorities on Western Zhou bronze vessels and their inscriptions: see Guo Muruo 1930; Chen 1936. It was accepted by almost all Western scholars writing on Western Zhou bronzes. For a summary of the debate see Shaughnessy 1991, 193 – 216, and for citations to Western-language scholarship, 200 n. 20.
3   The argument was made by Tang Lan in Tang 1962.
4   See, for example, Rawson 1990, part 1:63.

80

Feng bronze *zun* vessel

Height 16.8 (6⅝), diam. at mouth 16.8 (6⅝)
Middle Western Zhou Period, middle of the
tenth century BCE
From Zhuangbai, Fufeng, Shaanxi Province

Zhou Yuan Administrative Office of Cultural Relics,
Fufeng, Shaanxi Province

The Wei vessels from Hoard 1 — particularly those
that trace the generations of the family — chronicle
important stages in the development of Western
Zhou bronzework, including the evolution of decorative designs. The Feng *zun*,[1] together with the
Feng *you*, with which it would have been paired in
the set of ritual vessels, is an excellent example of a
facing long-tailed crested bird design, which for a
brief while seems to have displaced the stylized
animal-face design that had dominated Chinese
bronze ornamentation through the end of the Early
Western Zhou period.

The first documented appearance of this facing-
bird design is on the Hui *gui*; its inscription dates
the vessel to the very end of the reign of King Zhao
(r. c. 976 – 957 BCE).[2] Within a generation the design had reached its mature form, as exemplified
by the Feng *zun*. It appears as well in the Dong *gui*
discovered in a tomb one hundred meters to the
west of Hoard 1; the *gui*'s lengthy inscription, which
recounts its patron's repulse of an invasion of the
Zhou central state by enemies from the Huai River
region, dates the vessel to the thirteenth year of
King Mu (944 BCE) — about the date of manufacture of the Feng *zun* and Feng *you*. Surprisingly, as
beautiful as the facing-bird design is, it seems
to have remained in vogue only very briefly: under-
stated remnants of it appear in narrow descriptive
bands beneath the lip of vessels manufactured over
the next generation or two (see, for example, the
Shi Qiang *pan*, cat. 81); by the end of the Middle
Western Zhou period, however, it seems to have
disappeared almost completely.

The inscription on the Feng *zun*, identical to
that on the Feng *you*, is dedicated to one "Father
Xin" — the temple name, according to the Shi
Qiang *pan*, of Qiang's grandfather:

> It was the sixth month, after the growing
> brightness, *yimao* [day 52]; the king was at
> Cheng Zhou, and commanded Feng to meet
> with Da Ju. Da Ju awarded Feng metal and
> cowries, and [Feng] herewith makes for
> Father Xin this treasured offertory vessel.
> [Clan-sign]

This inscription shows that Feng was almost certainly the father of Qiang; since Qiang served at
the court of King Gong (r. c. 917 – 900 BCE), Feng
must have been active two or three decades prior,
c. 940 – 930 BCE. ES

1 Excavated in 1976 (18); reported: Shaanxi 1978, 3.
2 For the Hui *gui*, see Shaanxi 1986.

81

Shi Qiang bronze *pan* vessel

Height 16.2 (6 ⅜), diam. 47.3 (18 ⅝)
Middle Western Zhou Period, end of tenth
century BCE
From Zhuangbai, Fufeng, Shaanxi Province

Zhou Yuan Administrative Office of Cultural Relics,
Fufeng, Shaanxi Province

The Shi Qiang *pan*[1] is without question the most
important of the 103 vessels found in Hoard 1.
Indeed, in a little more than two decades after
its discovery and first publication, it has already
come to be regarded in many respects as the most
important of all Western Zhou bronze vessels,
a position attributable almost entirely to its 270-
character-long inscription, which might justly be
described as the first conscious historical writing
in China. In two balanced halves, it juxtaposes
an outline of the first seven Western Zhou kings
(including the reigning *Tianzi* [Son of Heaven], who
is not named but who must have been King Gong
[r. c. 917–900 BCE]) with a similar genealogy of
four generations of the Wei family. The inscription
concludes with a prayer that Qiang's own merits be

acknowledged and that he be granted a long life so
that he may continue to serve the Zhou kings.

The genealogy given in the Shi Qiang *pan* inscription has made it possible to date the rest of
the Hoard 1 vessels and is an important historical
document in itself. The inscription is equally important as evidence for the rise of poetry in China,
being stylistically identical to the four-character
rhyming line structure of the *Shi jing* (Classic
of poetry).[2] ES

Inscription of the Shi Qiang *pan*

Accordant with antiquity was the Cultured
  King!
He first brought harmony to government.
Di on High sent down fine virtue and great
  security.
Extending it above and below,
he joined the ten thousand countries.

Capturing and controlling was the Martial
  King!
He proceeded and campaigned through the
  four quarters,

piercing Yin and governing its people.
Eternally unfearful of the Distant Ones,
oh, he attacked the Yi minions.

Model and sagely was the Completed King!
To the left and right he cast and gathered
his net and line,
therewith opening and integrating the Zhou
country.

Deep and wise was the Vigorous King!
He divided command and pacified the
borders.

Vast and substantial was the Radiant King!
He broadly tamed Chu and Jing;
it was to connect the southern route.

Reverent and illustrious was the Stately
King!
He patterned himself on and followed the
great counsels.

Continuing and tranquil is the Son of
Heaven!
The Son of Heaven strives to carry on
the long valor of the Cultured and Martial
kings.
The Son of Heaven is diligent and without
flaw,
faithfully making offerings to the spirits
above and below,
and reverently making glorious the great
plans.

Heavenly radiant and incorruptible,
Di on High, Hou Ji, and the witch protectors
give to the Son of Heaven an extensive
mandate,
thick blessings, and an abundant harvest.
Among the borderland *man*-savages, there
are none who do not hasten to present
themselves.

Pure and retiring was the High Ancestor!
He was at the numinous place of Wei.
When the Martial King had already
defeated Yin,
the Wei scribes and valorous ancestors
then came to present themselves to the
Martial King.
The Martial King then commanded
the Duke of Zhou to dispense to them
domicile
at a low place of Zhou.

Happy and helpful was Ancestor Yi!
He assisted and served his ruler,
distantly planning with belly and heart his
sons' acceptance.

Clear-eyed and bright was Grandfather Xin
of the branch lineage!

Transferring and nurturing sons and
grandsons,

he had abundant good fortune and many
    blessings.
Even horned and redly gleaming,
appropriate were his sacrifices.

Extending and even was my cultured
    deceased-father!
Duke Yi was strong and bright,
obtaining purity without debts:
the agriculture was well ordered.

It is the servant filial and friendly
Scribe Qiang morning and night does not
    fail;
may he daily have his merits acknowledged.
Qiang does not dare to stop,
and in response extols the Son of Heaven's
illustriously beneficent command,
herewith making this treasured offertory
    vessel.

Would that his valorous grandfather and
    cultured deceased father grant favor,
and give Qiang vibrant freshness,
fortunate peace, blessed wealth,
a yellowing old age, and a prolonged life
so that he may be worthy to serve his ruler.
May he for ten thousand years eternally
    treasure and use it.

1   Excavated in 1976 (24); reported: Shaanxi 1978, 4.
2   The translation that follows is largely adapted from
    Shaughnessy 1991, 3–4, 183–192. For a reconstruction
    of the rhymes and a presentation of the rhyme scheme,
    see Behr 1996, 199–204.

82

Sannian Xing bronze *hu* vessel

Height 65.4 (25 ¾), diam. at mouth 19.7 (7 ¾)
Middle Western Zhou Period, first half of the
ninth century BCE
From Zhuangbai, Fufeng, Shaanxi Province

Zhou Yuan Administrative Office of Cultural Relics,
Fufeng, Shaanxi Province

Xing (or Wei Bo Xing, as he also referred to himself in the bronze inscriptions) commissioned more
bronzes by far than any other member of the Wei
family. The inscription on one of his fourteen bells
discovered in Hoard 1 establishes that Xing was the
son of Qiang, patron of the Shi Qiang *pan*.[1] In addition to these bells, Xing also commissioned at least
twenty-two other inscribed bronze vessels, spanning
the reigns of several Western Zhou kings: the earliest of the Xing bronzes probably date to the reign
of King Gong (r. c. 917–900 BCE); the Shisannian
Xing *hu* (Thirteenth-year Xing *hu*), for example, was
probably made in 903 BCE.[2] At the other extreme, a
notation corresponding to 862 BCE probably dates
Xing's *xu* vessel to the reign of King Yi (r. c. 865–
858 BCE).[3]

The Sannian Xing *hu*, or Third-year Xing *hu*,[4]
was probably made late in Xing's life. Two aspects of
the inscription suggest that Xing was by this time
an elder — and a distinguished one at that. The
inscription commemorates two banquets at which
Xing was invited to join the king, a rare honor. More
important, it indicates that Xing's father had died
by the time of its manufacture (the vessel is dedicated to Xing's "august grand-father and cultured
deceased-father" [*huang zu wen kao*]); the father
seems to have been alive when the Shisannian Xing
hu was made.

The style and especially the ornamentation of
other Western Zhou bronze vessels, moreover, cor-
roborate the dating of this vessel to about 870 BCE.
The Sannian Xing *hu* is completely decorated with
what is usually referred to as a wave pattern *(boqu
wen)*, which also appears on the *ding* cauldrons
made for Ke — the Da Ke *ding* — and seven smaller
Xiao Ke *ding*. These famous vessels bear inscriptions

that show them to have been commissioned by the grandson of a minister who served King Gong, putting their date of manufacture about the time of King Xiao (r. c. 872? – 866 BCE). Although relatively rare on Western Zhou bronze vessels, the wave pattern proved to be very influential in later bronze ornamentation, especially during the Spring and Autumn period (770 – 476 BCE).[5] Its distinctive pattern of continuous lines marked a shift away from designs symmetrically arranged along a vertical axis (where two pieces of a mold joined) toward the sort of flowing design that encircles later Chinese bronze vessels. ES

1   For this bell see Shaanxi 1980, 2: no. 54; the bell inscription is translated in Falkenhausen 1993b, 41 – 43.
2   For the date of the Shisannian Xing *hu*, see Shaughnessy 1991, 255 n. 70.
3   For the date of the Xing *xu*, see Shaughnessy 1991, 261 n. 81.
4   Excavated in 1976 (32); reported: Shaanxi 1978b.
5   See Rawson 1990, part 1:91: "The wave pattern, with its insistent impression of movement created by the continuous line, and broad areas of texture created by concave or relief bands, had an impact such as none of the earlier designs had achieved."

83

Bronze *fangding* vessel

Height 17.8 (7)
Middle Western Zhou Period, c. late tenth – early ninth century BCE
From Zhuangbai, Fufeng, Shaanxi Province

Zhou Yuan Administrative Office of Cultural Relics, Fufeng, Shaanxi Province

This *ding* vessel[1] is certainly the most eccentric of all the bronze vessels found in Hoard 1. The cauldron itself is oblong in shape, roughly similar to several cauldrons from the reigns of Kings Mu (r. c. 956 – 918 BCE) and Gong (r. c. 917 – 900 BCE), such as the Dong *fangding jia*, recovered from a Middle Western Zhou period tomb at Zhuangbai, and the Fifteenth-year Jue Cao *ding*. The climbing dragons at the corners turn their heads (crowned by two prominent bottle-horns) away from the vessel. The creatures at the corners of the square base extend into the vessel's legs; they are chimerical beasts, with "eyes resembling those of a monkey, a beak like that of an eagle, curling horns like those of a ram, and a neck like that of a deer."[2] The hollow, square base would have held combustible materials to cook or warm the contents of the cauldron above it; at either end are windows that serve a utilitarian function as well as a decorative one by providing air for the fire within. The most striking feature of the *ding*, however, is the "gatekeeper" figure, which serves as a latch to close the two doors at the front of the base. He is portrayed naked, in a kneeling position, with his left foot amputated.

Two other known bronze vessels from the Western Zhou period also feature images of a gatekeeper with an amputated foot or leg. One, in the Palace Museum in Beijing, resembles the vessel featured here, but the gatekeeper (whose left leg is amputated at the knee) is portrayed standing, supporting himself with a cane in his left hand.[3] The other gatekeeper vessel, a model of a cart (perhaps a toy) discovered in 1989 in Wenxi county (Shanxi province), is even more fanciful than the Zhuangbai *ding*: the gatekeeper clings to one side, while four birds and a monkey perch on the roof of the cart,

six animals climb its sides, and two crouching tigers
and two wheels lie beneath it — fifteen movable
parts in all. The gatekeepers are figural evidence of
one of the "five punishments" of ancient China —
amputation (*yuexing*) of the foot or of the leg at
the knee. The *Zhou li* (Rites of Zhou) states that
those who had suffered such amputations were
to be employed to guard the royal parks (*you*),[4]
presumably — given their obvious physical handi-
cap — as gatekeepers, perhaps as they are depicted
here.   ES

1   Excavated in 1976 (77); reported: Shaanxi 1980, 2:10, fig. 77.
2   Shaanxi 1980, 2:10, fig. 77.
3   Regarding this vessel, see Wang 1974, 7, 29.
4   For a discussion of the punishment (as well as of the
    vessels), see Skosey 1996, 87 – 91, 144 – 145.

In about 1050 BCE, the Shang state was overthrown by a people known as the Zhou. They established their capital near the present-day city of Xi'an. A ritual center, today called Zhou yuan, was located in the present-day counties of Fufeng and Qishan to the west of Xi'an. Here many aristocratic families kept sets of ritual vessels and presumably used them for offerings to their ancestors. Attacked and driven out of Shaanxi in 771 BCE by tribes known as the Quanrong, the Zhou buried their ritual bronzes in pits at Zhou yuan, hoping, it would seem, to return to claim them at a later date. Modern farmers and archaeologists discovered some of these large caches. Contemporary inscriptions on some of the bronzes provide partial histories of particular families and accounts of their relationships with the Zhou king.[1] Some textual evidence on the history of the Zhou also exists.[2]

A network of kin relationships was the key to Zhou rule of an immense territory, stretching from Baoji in western Shaanxi to beyond Beijing in the northeast. Beneath the Zhou king, his relatives ruled as lords in the different small states. Among the remarkable features of the burials of these lords is the way in which similar inscriptions (implying a shared language) and similar ritual objects (implying shared beliefs) created coherence and order. The peoples over whom the Zhou ruled must have had diverse languages and customs, but the sense of organized control that the Zhou achieved through a strong elite presence was to set a model of a unified state that endured even to the twentieth century.

The bronze ritual vessels provide a point of reference for dating these Zhou tombs. Members of the Zhou elite from Shaanxi who controlled far-flung areas such as the Yan state near Beijing seem to have had bronzes similar to those found in Baoji or Zhou yuan. What is more, the vessels excavated in Zhouyuan are particularly important, as the inscriptions made it possible to establish reasonably reliable chronological sequences of ritual vessel development.[3] For instance, the early Zhou vessels follow closely, in both shape and ornament, those of their Shang predecessors. The Zhou probably emulated the Shang in order, through their offerings, to establish in the eyes of the spirits their political claims to rule what they saw as the world. Some time in the early ninth century BCE, a major change in vessel types took place, almost certainly coinciding with and reflecting some sort of greater ritual, or possibly, political reform.[4] Large flasks for wine *(hu)* and sets of tripods *(ding)* and basins *(gui)* for food were the principal components of such sets. Sets of bells also date from this period. The Jin state tombs contained vessels characteristic from before and after the ninth century BCE.

The Jin state was established by Tangshu Yu, a brother of the Western Zhou king Cheng. The area occupied lay in the region of present-day Houma at the bend of the Yellow River in southern Shanxi province. Known since the 1960s, this site has been extensively investigated in the last decade by archaeological teams from Beijing University.[5] A large cemetery of approximately 3800 by 2800 meters revealed more than 600 burials as well as five horses and chariot pits. The tombs are of a type standard in the Yellow River area, consisting of a deep shaft with a coffin chamber at the bottom. Inside the coffin chambers were wooden coffins. To enable the body of the dead and his or her possessions to be properly installed in the tomb, a long access ramp of between 18 and 20 meters was provided to the south. Alongside the principal burials of the Jin lords are the tombs of the lords' consorts.

Tomb M 8, in which a vessel in the shape of a hare (cat. 88) was found, yielded bronze vessels inscribed with the names of Marquis Pi and Marquis Su of Jin. Dating the objects in the Jin tombs is controversial, especially since Tomb M 8 contained vessels whose shapes are typical of the latter part of the Western Zhou period.

The Jin lords seem to have adhered to the ritual practices of Xi'an in the sense that they used the same types and numbers of ritual vessels during the period down to the ninth century BCE. From the ninth and early eighth centuries BCE, their customs changed quite markedly. As well as standard Late Western Zhou ritual vessels, the Jin lords acquired or commissioned small, unusual bronzes (cats. 89, 90). The shapes are borrowed from vessels in other materials, perhaps even of wood, for they have little or nothing in common with the basin and tripod shapes of the principal Zhou ritual vessels, which originally derived from ceramics. Around the same period, the casters of Jin and their neighbors in the Ying state also made vessels that reproduced the forms of much more ancient bronzes. It seems possible this development reflected a deliberate return to the past. It may be that members of the Jin state had lost vessels during the eighth century BCE, as the Quanrong and other tribes encroached on the ritual centers in the west. Perhaps the Jin felt impelled to make these inferior copies for burial to replace lost originals.

Apart from the bronzes, the most striking feature of the Jin tombs is the wealth of ancient jade buried in them, including carvings that may date to the Late Shang and Early Western Zhou periods — from the twelfth to the tenth century BCE. The tombs also contained magnificent coverings for the body in jade and agate (cats. 85, 86). Systematic decoration of the dead with face plaques that indicated the features of eyes, mouth, and ears (cat. 84) seems to have become a standard feature of burials in the Jin state around the same date that a similar practice developed at the capital of the Zhou kingdom near Xi'an in the ninth century BCE. From the quantity of jades found in the Jin tombs, it seems possible that the practice was more fully developed in the Jin state than in other areas. The Jin must have had both a special regard for jade and unusual access to quantities of ancient pieces and raw material. JR

1   For a survey of scholarship on Western Zhou bronze inscriptions see Shaughnessy 1991.
2   For an account of archaeological finds of the Western Zhou period, see Rawson 1999.
3   Rawson 1990, part 1:15 – 22.
4   Rawson 1990, part 1:92 – 110.
5   For an account of the archaeological finds in English, see Xu 1996b, 193 – 231.

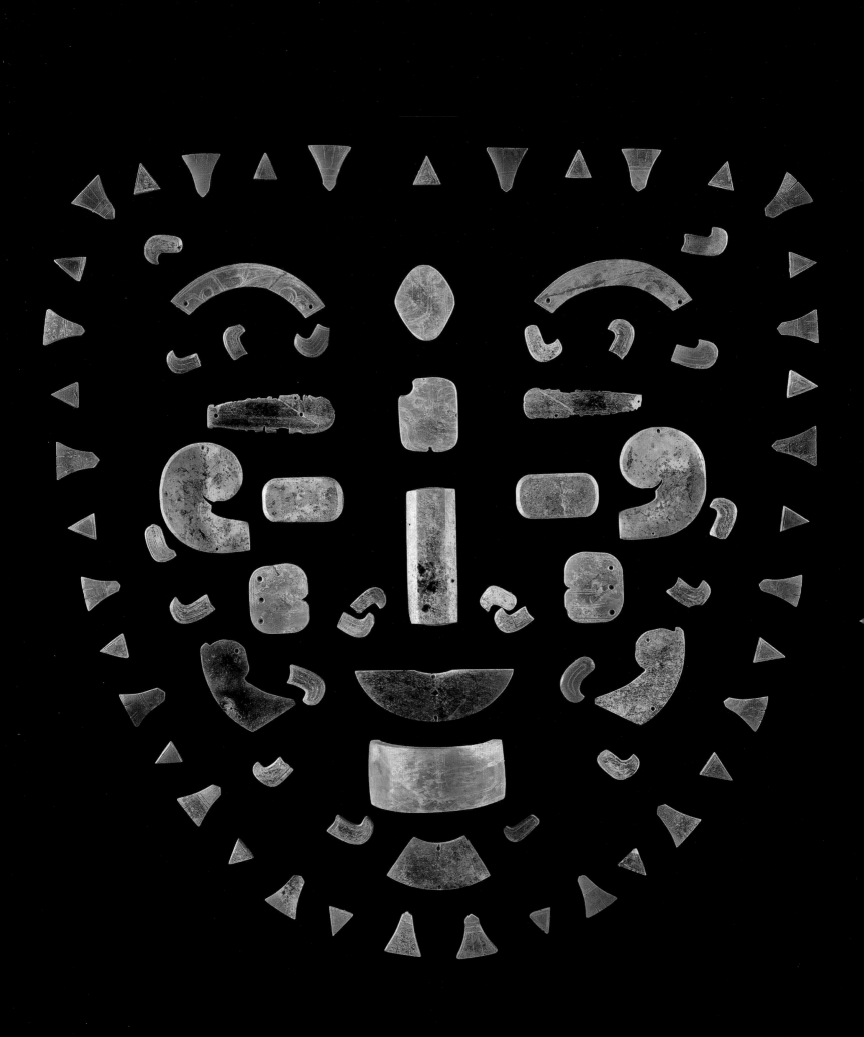

84

Jade and hardstone face covering

Late Western Zhou Period, ninth to
eighth century BCE
From Tianma-Qucun (Beizhao, Quwo),
Shanxi Province

Shanxi Provincial Institute of Archaeology,
Taiyuan

These seventy-nine plaques, which were combined
with agate or faience beads to form a schematic
face, covered the head of the person buried in
Tomb M 31 (possibly the consort of the Jin ruler
buried in Tomb M 8; see cats. 129–137).[1] It is likely
that the individual plaques were sewn onto a textile
to form a complete covering.

The plaques include a variety of different forms.
Small pieces — triangles alternating with three-
pronged shapes — form a circular or rounded rectangular border. The jade is cut to imitate the
features of the face (mouth, nose, eyes, eyebrows,
and ears), and plaques fill the spaces between the
strongly carved eyebrows and areas below the eyes,
at the cheeks, and around the mouth. The varied
carving on the plaques, some of which were clearly
broken or cut for their new function, is evidence of
reuse; it is likely that jade was scarce and that every
available piece was precious.

The tombs at Tianma-Qucun are remarkable for
the large number of jades that they contain. This
face covering is one of a number of similarly complex jade compositions, which seem to have been a
speciality of this area. While earlier examples may
be recognized in jades found at Chang'an, at sites
in Fengxi, south of present-day Xi'an, none of those
jade groups is as elaborate as the face coverings
from the Jin state tombs.[2]

The face coverings were accompanied by
arrangements of beads and arc pendants (*huang*),
many of great complexity (see cats. 85, 86); the
pendants seem to have come into fashion in the
ninth to eighth centuries and were undoubtedly important components of burial costumes,
esteemed both for the value of the material and
for the properties ascribed to jade.[3] Certainly, the

choice of a material that was traditionally employed
for highly valued objects suggests that these coverings were, in themselves, intrinsically important.
The emphasis on the features of the face suggests
that they were intended to protect the person in
the afterlife by creating a sense of awe in those who
might approach the wearer, whether living people
or spirits. In combination with the complex array
of beads and arcs distributed over the body, the
plaques may also have been intended to suggest the
rank and power of their owners.

It has been argued that these face coverings,
together with their associated tiered arrangements
of plaques and beads, were predecessors of Han
period jade shrouds (see cats. 129 and 139), but an
unbroken continuity between the two forms of
burial apparatus is unlikely. The use of jade face
coverings came into being and then declined and
indeed almost disappeared well before the Han
period. For that reason, it is more likely that the
jade ornaments of the Jin state constitute a tradition peculiar to the Late Western and Early Eastern
Zhou periods in this part of China. The convention
of linking tiers of jade plaques with agate and
faience beads (see cat. 85) may have been introduced to the Zhou area by peoples who lived on the
western and northern peripheries of the Yellow
River system. JR

1   Excavated in 1993 (M 31:73); reported: Shanxi 1994a.
2   See Zhang Changzhou 1993, pl. 6:3.
3   For a discussion of the sources of jade pendants, see Sun
     Ji 1998.

85

Jade *pei* pectoral

Length c. 50 (19 ⁵⁄₈)
Late Western Zhou Period, eighth century BCE
From Tianma-Qucun (Beizhao, Quwo),
Shanxi Province

Shanxi Provincial Institute of Archaeology,
Taiyuan

This pectoral,[1] part of a complex array of jades, was suspended from the wearer's neck. It is composed of a jade ring joined with two pairs of arc-shaped pendants and a small bar by sets of beads; a second jade ring is thought to have been part of this ornament. The two rings and two of the arcs are relatively plain, although one of the arcs retains traces of lines that have been worn (or smoothed) away. The two arcs at the ends of the ornament carry incised designs of dragons with interlacing ribbon-shaped bodies, a pattern developed during the Middle to Late Western Zhou period. It seems likely that the jades were originally carved for other uses; the same probably holds true for the other jades that compose the burial apparatus.

A notable feature of all such complex ornaments is the use of beads in several materials, particularly in agate or carnelian and in varieties of faience. Beads, especially hardstone beads, are surprisingly rare in the history of Chinese decorative art; only a few of the Neolithic peoples who inhabited the Chinese landmass before the advent of the Shang used these ornaments to any appreciable extent (the fine tubular beads of the Liangzhu peoples are outstanding examples).[2] Inhabitants of the southern areas (notably the peoples of Xin'gan in present-day Jiangxi) used jade and turquoise beads in the latter part of the second millennium BCE.[3] Beads were used only rarely by the Shang at Anyang, nor were they common during the first centuries of Zhou rule.

Beads came into more widespread decorative use during the tenth to ninth centuries BCE. Among the earliest of the assemblages that include beads are those from Western Zhou period tombs at Liulihe, Fangshan near Beijing,[4] where turquoise was favored over faience, popular in western Asia. Beads that might be regarded as forms of faience, that is, fired mixtures of silica and pigment, have been found in Middle Western Zhou tombs at Rujiazhuang near Baoji in western Shaanxi province.[5] That beads were used as decorative ornaments in two so widely separated corners of the Western Zhou kingdom during approximately the same period suggests that they were not a local invention, but rather reflected the influence of peoples in the border areas, a development that figures in other decorative arts as well. It seems possible that these beads demonstrate an interest in decorative jewel-like ornaments shared by peoples on the periphery in China, a feature that was perhaps also common to other parts of Central Asia.

Beads used in this pectoral are of considerably later date than those found at Fangshan or Rujiazhuang. Complex pendants should be treated as part of a relatively late phenomenon. The association of pectorals with face plaques (cat. 84) suggests an intent to create a formidable display. It is likely that the jades illustrated here and in cat. 85 manifest a completely new approach to the world of spirits and the afterlife that developed in the latter part of the Western Zhou period. JR

1   Excavated in 1992 (M 8:114 – 124); reported: Beijing 1994.
2   For beads of the Liangzhu culture, see Ma and Ho 1992, nos. 80, 81, and 82.
3   For beads from Xin'gan in Jiangxi province, see Ma 1994, nos. 88 and 94.
4   For ornaments from Liulihe, see Rawson 1996, no. 56.
5   For beads from Rujiazhuang, see Lu and Hu 1988, color pl. 25.

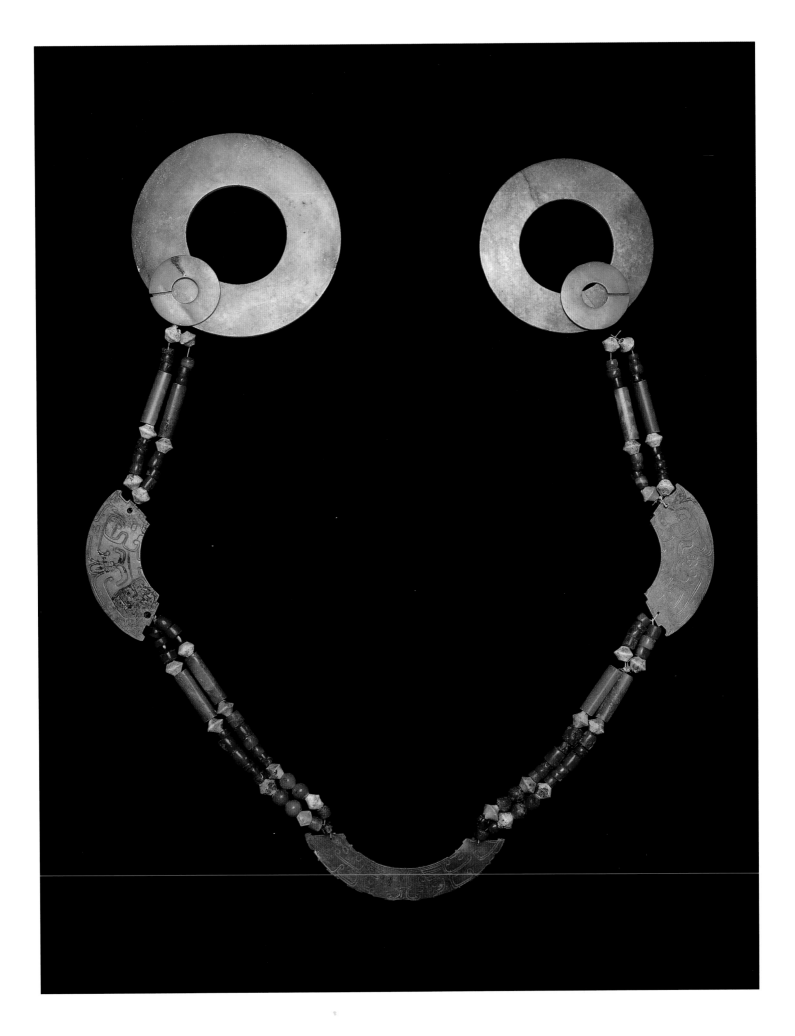

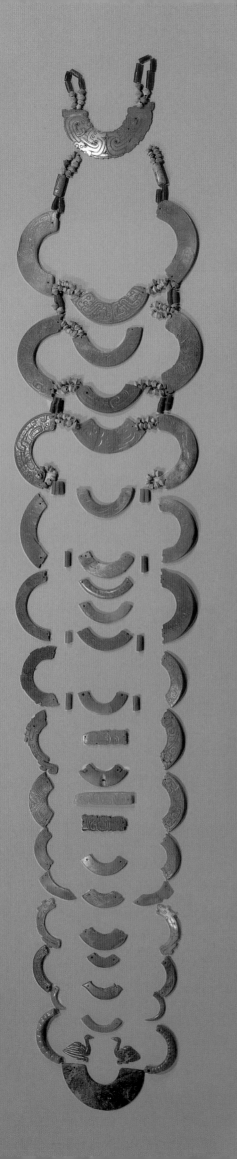

86

Jade *pei* pectoral

Length c. 150 (59 ⅛)
Late Western Zhou Period, eighth century BCE
From Tianma-Qucun (Beizhao, Quwo),
Shanxi Province

Shanxi Provincial Institute of Archaeology,
Taiyuan

This complex assembly of jade plaques and beads,[1]
more than twice as long as the pectoral ornament
described in cat. 85, comes from Tomb M 63, as
does a bronze vessel also exhibited, cat. 90. Such
bronzes date to the very end of the Western Zhou
period, around the time of the collapse in 771 BCE
of the Zhou kingdom and the loss of its capital at
Xi'an. While these bead-and-jade coverings similarly date to the eighth century BCE, the constituent
jade carvings themselves date from a number of
different periods and were obviously amassed over
a long stretch of time.

Here, threads holding short groups of faience
and agate beads join jade *huang*, which dominate
the composition. The brown color of the arcs is the
result of burial; the arcs were originally a translucent gray or green. Many have a schematic animal
head at each end; others carry finely incised decoration, which permits approximate dating of the
individual pieces. One such *huang* displays patterns
typical of tenth-century BCE bronzes and jadework,
suggesting a date of manufacture one hundred or
more years prior to the burial itself. This *huang*
features a pair of dragons, each with two heads and
sinuous bodies that intertwine at the center; birds
with long, sweeping plumes were characteristic of
this period, and such dragon designs may have
developed by analogy. Jade craftsmen seem to have
adapted their designs from contemporaneous
bronzework, interlacing the creatures' plumes,
crests, and bodies to fit the limitations of their
inherently smaller work surface. From such small
beginnings arose an entire genre of jade (and later,
bronze) design.[2]

Many of the jades found in Tomb M 63, like
those from Tomb M 8 (cat. 85), were originally

carved for another purpose, and date from the tenth or ninth century,[3] others even earlier — back to the Shang period. It is likely that the Zhou (and their vassals in the minor states) acquired such pieces when they conquered the Shang in the mid-eleventh century; the looting of the royal tombs may have occurred at that time or at a later date.

The more difficult question is why these jades came to be buried in the eighth century and not earlier. Perhaps in a time of political and economic uncertainty, when the Zhou were destabilized by attacks from border peoples, it seemed more prudent to bury jades for the afterlife than to risk their immediate loss; or perhaps equipping the bodies of rulers, their consorts, and their nobles with jades reflected a change in how the afterlife was conceived among the Zhou and their Jin dependents. A direct relation between Zhou burial practices and the Han's elaborate shrouds, pectorals, and face coverings for their dead (see cats. 139 – 146) is implausible, however, for Han burial appurtenances were created in a culture separate in both time and place from the Jin state of the Zhou period. JR

1   Excavated in 1994 (M 63:41); reported: Shanxi 1994b.
2   For a discussion of the sources of interlace on Western Zhou bronzes, see Rawson 1990, part 1:113 – 123. Interlace appears on the lids of *hu* from Tomb M 8 at Tianma-Qucun (Beijing 1994, 20, fig. 26).
3   See Rawson 1995, 22 – 28.

87

Jinhou Pi bronze *gui* vessel

Height 38.4 (15 ⅛)
Late Western Zhou Period, ninth century BCE
From Tianma-Qucun (Beizhao, Quwo),
Shanxi Province

Shanxi Provincial Institute of Archaeology,
Taiyuan

Following the changes in ritual during the ninth century, lords of the Late Western Zhou period acquired sets of ritual food basins *(gui)* that comprised an even number of vessels, often fitted with lids (as in this example). This *gui*[1] with its substantial square base, S-shaped profile, and two handles, is a typical example. (Less common during the Early Western Zhou period, the squared base of the *gui* became a standard feature in the ninth to eighth centuries.) The handles bear large animal heads with rounded horns or ears, and a flange contains a trunklike extension. Abstract angular S-shaped motifs fill two borders on the body and two on the lid, the handle of which is composed of an everted ring. Other semi-abstract designs form borders around undecorated panels within each of the four sides of the base. The bronze has a gray-green sheen, with traces of bright green and reddish corrosion.

One of a pair surviving from a group of four, this basin is inscribed inside the body and lid dedicating the bronze by an individual titled Jinhou, or Marquis of Jin, for ritual offerings to his ancestor. Jinhou is not the occupant of the tomb, however. The character for the name of the lord has been transcribed in several different ways by various scholars, however, and these identifications remain controversial.[2]

While many Shang period bronzes were inscribed, often with the characters of the owner's names, the form of the inscription on this vessel is typical of the Zhou period. It is likely that these inscriptions were intended to be read by both the living and the dead, for it was expected that the ancestors would be drawn to the feast by the aroma of the food and wine prepared for them in these vessels. The inscriptions may have been placed inside the vessels so that the ancestors would read them as they consumed the contents. In addition to the dedications seen here, some bronzes contain longer inscriptions that memorialize the honors accorded the owners of the vessels. Such achievements may have been recorded in these inscriptions precisely because the living lords wished to inform their ancestors of these honors, which presumably raised the status of the living and might raise the ranking of the ancestors as well.[3]

Inscriptions such as those on this vessel and, much later, on seals (cat. 138) are among the many elements of daily life that were carried into the realms of the ancestors and spirits. By the Han period, the afterlife had come to be viewed as including a large bureaucracy that required the paraphernalia of officialdom, including seals and records, to authenticate the positions of the dead and to receive similarly important information across the boundary of death. That view of the afterlife was altogether different from that of classical Greece and Rome, which prized individualism in the afterlife as it did on earth, and it was also far removed from that of the early Christians, whose Kingdom of God had much in common with the court of a small European state of the day. JR

1   Excavated in 1992 (M 8:30); reported: Beijing 1994.
2   See Xu 1996b, especially table 2.
3   For a full discussion of Western Zhou period bronze inscriptions, see Shaughnessy 1991. For a critique of this view, see Falkenhausen 1993a.

88

Hare-shaped bronze *zun* vessel

Height 31.8 (12 ½), width 22.2 (8 ¾),
diam. at rim 18.4 (7 ¼)
Middle to Late Western Zhou Period,
ninth century BCE
From Tianma-Qucun (Beizhao, Quwo),
Shanxi Province

Shanxi Provincial Institute of Archaeology,
Taiyuan

Examples of animal-shaped bronze ritual vessels
are rare at all periods of ancient Chinese history,
and this hare-shaped wine vessel,[1] called a *zun* for
the trumpet-shaped mouth rising from the animal's
back, is a unique example of the form.

    Zun have been found in many Middle Western
Zhou tombs of the tenth century, usually in the
form of a round-bodied vessel on a small oval-
ringed foot, with a trumpet-shaped mouth emerging from a low shoulder. Here the globular body has
been replaced by that of a hare, modeled very accu-

rately, with many lifelike features. The head strains forward, the ears are folded back against the animal's body, and the crouching legs almost conceal the oval ring foot. Cast relief roundels on the animal's flanks are decorated with fine, spiraling intaglio lines. The vessel is heavily patinated and corroded and shows signs of repair. It was found together with two cast hare-shaped boxes of similarly lifelike design.[2]

Animal-shaped containers were not typical of the Yellow River ritual bronze tradition. During the Shang period, peoples inhabiting the south, particularly along the Yangzi River and in Hunan province, employed vessels in the shapes of animals; famous pieces include a boar, an elephant, and two addorsed rams.[3] It would seem that, from time to time, these animal-shaped bronzes were exchanged or traded, from south to north, perhaps by way of the tributaries of the Yangzi River. Very elaborate versions of such animal vessels seem to have been made around 1200 BCE at the Shang precursor to the present-day city of Anyang in Henan province, for high-ranking members of the Shang court. Fu Hao, the consort of one of the most powerful Shang kings, Wu Ding, had a pair of bird-shaped vessels and a pair of vessels in the shape of strange imaginary animals.[4]

During the Early Western Zhou period, animal-shaped bronzes became known to the Zhou inhabiting the region of the Wei River. Bronze creatures have been found both near the capital at Xi'an and further west at Baoji,[5] and this hare-shaped *zun* appears related to pieces imitative of Yellow River animal bronzes. The fact that this bronze has unmistakable elements of contemporaneous bronze ritual vessels, "obscured" by the figure itself, suggests that these hares were not ancient pieces handed down through several generations but that they were cast in the Middle or Late Middle Western Zhou period. It is likely that they were made in some part of the Zhou territory or within the confines of the Jin state, but their shape and their style suggests that they are older than the ninth- or even early eighth-century bronzes found with them in Tomb M 8. While the typology of animal-shaped bronzes links south and north, it does not define their significance to their owners in either region. JR

1 Excavated in 1992 (M 8:20); reported: Beijing 1994.
2 For a brief report on the excavation of the tombs, see Beijing 1994.
3 For a description of Shang animal-shaped bronzes, see Bagley 1987, 30–36.
4 Fong 1980, nos. 29, 30.
5 Rawson 1990, no. 119.

89

Bronze *he* vessel

Height 34.6 (13 ⅝); body: height 21.8 (8 ⅝),
width 20.6 (8 ⅛)
Late Western Zhou Period, ninth to
eighth century BCE
From Tianma-Qucun (Beizhao, Quwo),
Shanxi Province

Shanxi Provincial Institute of Archaeology,
Taiyuan

Ritual pouring vessels *(he)* are generally thought to
have accompanied water basins *(pan)*; both this
vessel[1] and a circular *pan* (with decorative features
that suggest an earlier date) were found in a Jin
state tomb thought to have belonged to the consort of the marquis interred in Tomb M 8 (see cats.
87, 88).[2]

He vessels of the Early and Middle Western
Zhou period were generally composed of a tri-
lobed body on three legs, with a short neck, a small
domed lid and handle, and a straight spout; they
reflect a tradition carried over from much earlier
Shang ritual-vessel castings.[3] While its function
may have been similar to these earlier examples, the
distinctive shape of this vessel dates it to the later
Western Zhou period.

The body of the vessel is disk-shaped, resembling the cross section of a log supported on the
backs of two stooping human figures. The spout
consists of an S-shaped projection that terminates
in a small animal head with round eyes, horns, and
a little crest; another imaginary animal decorates
the handle at the back. The lid, in the shape of a
bird, is linked to a loop on the body of the vessel by
a small creature. The animal appendages and the

coarse ribbon decoration of the piece are typical of Late Western Zhou period bronzes. The shape is extremely unusual but is paralleled by an example from Shaanxi province (the county of Fufeng in the Zhouyuan).[4]

This vessel and cat. 90 are representative of a new tradition of shapes that came into being during the latter part of the Western Zhou period. Prior to this period, human forms rarely (if ever) appear in the decoration of ritual vessels from the Yellow and Wei River areas, although examples are found occasionally on chariot fittings and weapons. Human faces and figures are slightly more prevalent among cast bronzes from the south (although their style is quite different from Western Zhou representations illustrated in this example and cat. 90), and well-known examples have been found in the east (Anhui province), the central region (Hunan province), and the west (Sichuan province).[5] The weakening of Zhou power and the growing independence of specific territories such as the Jin state may have been paralleled by the easing of ritual control over bronzecasters, permitting a greater variety in design. JR

1 Excavated 1993 (M 31:8); reported: Shanxi 1994a.
2 For a brief report on the tomb see Shanxi 1994a.
3 For a discussion of the type, see Rawson 1990, part 1, nos. 112 – 115.
4 Rawson 1990, part 1: fig. 152.
5 Bagley 1987, figs. 80, 187, and Bagley 1990, 52 – 67, fig. 28.

90

Cylindrical bronze vessel with pedestal base

Height 23.1 (9 ⅛), diam. 9.3 (3 ⅝)
Late Western Zhou Period, ninth to
eighth century BCE
From Tianma-Qucun (Beizhao, Quwo),
Shanxi Province

Shanxi Provincial Institute of Archaeology,
Taiyuan

This small, unusually shaped bronze vessel[1] comes
from a tomb thought to have been that of the consort of a Jin state lord buried in Tomb M 64. While
the relative dating of the principal tombs has been
the subject of debate,[2] it is reasonably certain that
this bronze and other pieces from Tomb M 63 are
from the Late Western Zhou period or even somewhat later.

The small, box-shaped base is supported by four
human figures topped by a lidded cylinder. A bird
stands on the lid, whose small cast-in loops are
paired with loops on the vessel's body. Within its
base hangs a pair of small bells. This decorative
feature is typical of some Early Western Zhou
period food basins *(gui)* in which the bell was suspended from a loop attached to the underside of
the basin and concealed by the pedestal.

The decoration consists of narrow strips of
relief demarcated by parallel intaglio lines. The
waved-shaped motifs on the base and the body of
the cylinder are typical of the late Middle and Late
Western Zhou period, coinciding with the change
in vessel types that took place in the early ninth
century. Whether this piece had a direct connection with the ancestor offerings associated with
other ritual vessels remains unknown, as does the
question of what it was intended to contain.

Tombs in the Jin state burial ground have
yielded both standard ritual bronzes and many
small pieces of highly individual character. The fact
that no pieces precisely comparable to these unusual bronzes have been discovered in the Zhou
centers in present-day Shaanxi province points to
the development of an independent style in the Jin
state. Indeed, it seems that while the Zhou aristo-

crats who controlled the area of the capital south of present-day Xi'an standardized the ritual vessels used for ancestor offerings, the lords of the Jin state took another direction, developing ritual practices that made use of vessels of unusual form, as well as vessels that replicated much older shapes. Tomb M 63, for example, contains not only innovative and unusual vessels, but also archaizing forms, such as a square vessel described as a *fangyi* in traditional writings. It is possible that both the unusually shaped bronzes and the archaistic vessels were made during the last decades of Zhou rule, and that their forms reflect contemporaneous political and social upheaval. Similar vessels and jades have been found in the states of Guo and Ying in Henan province.[3] JR

1 Excavated 1993 (M 63:86); reported: Shanxi 1994b.
2 For a discussion of the dating of the principal tombs in the Jin state burial ground, see Xu 1996b.
3 For brief reports see Henan 1995b and Henan 1988.

90, bottom interior

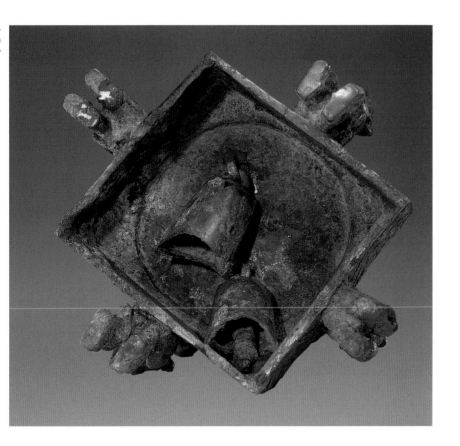

The Flamboyance of Eastern Zhou

CHU AND OTHER CULTURES (C. 770–221 BCE)

In 770 BCE, King Ping of Zhou moved his capital east to Luoyang; the five and a half centuries of the Zhou dynasty that followed, comprising two consecutive phases — the Spring and Autumn period (770–476 BCE) and the Warring States period (475–221 BCE) — are generally called the Eastern Zhou period. The Western Zhou kings had wielded considerable power; the kings of the Eastern Zhou period, by contrast, were largely puppet figures: during their reign several regional kingdoms, including Qi, Chu, Jin, and Qin, successively exercised hegemony over the region and waged frequent wars — both internally and with one another.[1] Remarkably, the political turmoil did not impede the progress of art, literature, and philosophy; to the contrary, they flourished, to the point that the extraordinary cultural prosperity of the Eastern Zhou period has customarily been characterized as the "hundred schools of thought contending" (baijia zhengming), and the "hundred flowers blooming" (baihua qifang). Archaeological excavations have revealed several thriving, unique cultures that radiated from present-day Yunnan province in the southwest into the Mongolian steppe in the northeast. One of these — the Chu culture — dominated southern China and formed one of the most influential cultures of the Eastern Zhou period.

"Chu culture" as defined here is not limited to the people or their kingdom but extends to the cultural attributes and influence of Chu. Over time, through the annexation of more than forty smaller states, the territory of the Chu kingdom expanded; Chu culture as a result was a rich amalgam of diverse cultures and groups.[2] Its richness is manifested in literature such as the Chu ci (Songs of Chu), an anthology that dates to the Late Warring States and the Han periods, but what of its material culture? A century of archaeological investigation has yielded remains covering a vast zone that includes the present-day provinces of southern Henan, Hubei, Hunan, and Anhui, and has considerably expanded our knowledge of the culture. A distinctively Chu culture seems to have emerged around the sixth century BCE, although archaeologists have traced its origins back to the Early Western Zhou period on the evidence of bronzes and oracle-bone inscriptions; Professor Yu Weichao situates the origins of Chu culture even farther back in time—to the Early Shang period — on the evidence of ceramic li vessels (see his essay herein).[3]

Objects associated with the Chu culture in this exhibition include their signature artifacts — lacquerware, textiles, and bronzes — from Henan, Hubei and Anhui provinces, ranging from the Middle Spring and Autumn period to the Warring States period (cats. 91–122). These objects represent the contents of burials identified with the Chu kingdom but also artifacts associated with other states. The bronzes and lacquerware from the tomb of Zenghou Yi, for example (cats. 92–102) show the intensity of Chu influence over states that were politically independent of Chu. The form and the decoration of ritual bronzes from the Chu burials at Xiasi in Henan province testify to the formation of distinctive artistic characteristics (as does the technique of lost-wax casting); a chime of bronze bells from the same locality (cat. 91), indi-

cates the pervasiveness of Zhou forms and fashions, although its surface decoration points to
an emerging Chu style; thereafter, Chu culture assumed a distinctive and individual identity.

Chu art, characterized by lush interlaced openwork decoration (particularly on the appendages or flanges of objects) often incorporated themes associated with shamanism or spirit
worship, evidenced in bronzes such as the cranelike figure with deer antlers (cat. 100) and a
lacquered wood guardian animal that incorporates a crown of real antlers (cat. 101). Although
chimerical combinations of animals or entirely imaginary creatures were characteristic elements of Shang art as well, Chu representations disclose an impassioned spiritual flamboyance;
the Shang creatures, by contrast, suggest a more somber, religious introspectiveness.

Ensuring a comprehensive representation of Chu culture in this exhibition to some extent
takes place at the expense of other contemporaneous cultures whose artifacts offer added testimony to the glory of the Eastern Zhou period. The burial artifacts from the tomb of the King
of Zhongshan in northern China shed some light, however, on the depth and the range of the
era's cultural efflorescence. The Zhongshan kingdom was much less powerful than Chu, but it
did produce works that rival those of Chu artisans and constitute an artistically coherent mar-

riage of Zhou and nomadic traditions (the latter are echoed in a bronze sculpture of a tiger attacking a deer[4]). Zhou culture was likely a model for the kingdoms that surrounded it; certainly, Zhou writing and rituals (including bronze and jade ritual implements) were adopted by neighboring cultures. From an aesthetic perspective, moreover, these cultures were the equal of those that inhabited the Central Plains. Long held in disfavor by Zhou historians and orthodox historiographers, Chu and Zhongshan emerged from the "barbarian" south and north to constitute major forces, together with the states of Wu, Yue, Qi, Jin, Yan Qin, and Shu, in the formation of what we know today as "the Chinese." Ironically perhaps, it was another "barbarian" state — Qin in the northwest — that united ancient China in 221 BCE. XY

1   For an English-language text that provides additional background regarding this period, see Li Xueqin 1985.
2   Zhang Zhengming's eighteen-volume study (1995a) provides an overview of the Chu kingdom and its culture.
3   For a comprehensive discussion of Chu culture see Zhang Zhengming 1991; for an examination of Chu bronzes, see Mackenzie 1991, 107 – 157.
4   Illustrated in Hubei 1985a, 2: color pls. 32 – 33.

Now normally submerged under the Danjiang Reservoir, the nine large tombs at Xiasi in Xichuan county (Henan province), together with two tombs at the adjacent locality of Heshangling, represent six generations of a high-ranking aristocratic lineage in the Chu kingdom. They date from the second quarter of the sixth to the third quarter of the fifth century BCE. Each lineage head was buried in a large tomb with an associated horse-and-chariot pit; in some cases, their principal consorts were buried in separate large tombs nearby. Besides the main occupant, each large tomb contained one or several additional skeletons, possibly human victims chosen from the main occupant's own relatives. Tomb 2 at Xiasi, much larger and more lavishly appointed than the others, was surrounded by fifteen small tombs containing possibly lower-ranking human victims.

The large tombs, some of which had been looted before excavation, contained abundant assemblages of ritual bronzes and funerary jades. The constellation of bronze vessels reflected the ritual rank of the deceased person. Tombs of females lack the weapons and horse-and-chariot items seen in those of their husbands, and they contain fewer vessels. None of the tombs yielded any trace of "useful" items such as ceramics.

Despite some looting, Tomb 2 at Xiasi contained thirty-six bronze vessels and a set of twenty-six bells, which is shown in this exhibition. Its exceptionally lavish furnishings, to some extent echoed by those in the three consorts' tombs clustering around it (Tombs 1, 3, and 4), testify to privileges far exceeding those enjoyed by either previous or succeeding generations of the same lineage. This cluster of tombs yielded a number of bronze vessel types not encountered in the others, such as flat-bottomed tripods (sheng) and other vessels of archaic form, harking back to the mid-ninth century BCE. Possibly, these vessels testify to their owners' participation in special kinds of rituals restricted to the royal family and its immediate entourage. In their execution, as well, many of the bronzes from Tomb 2 and its cluster are far more luxurious than those seen elsewhere at the cemetery. Highlights include some of the earliest vessels with metal inlay found anywhere in China and a unique altar stand with intricate decoration executed in the lost-wax casting technique, which was very rarely used in Eastern Zhou bronzework.

In their bronze inscriptions, the lineage heads buried at Xiasi-Heshangling refer to themselves as Chu Shuzhisun ("Descendants in a Junior Line of Chu"), indicating that they were descended from an earlier king of Chu but only distantly related to the king of their own time. The inscriptions give the name of the occupant of Tomb 2 at Xiasi as Peng. This individual has been identified with Yuan (or Wei) Zi Feng, chief minister of Chu from 552 until his death in 548 BCE.[1] Feng was a descendant of Sunshu Ao (fl. 598 – 597 BCE), who had been chief minister under King Zhuang of Chu (r. 613 – 591 BCE), and whose descendants hereditarily governed the territory surrounding present-day Xichuan. Some scholars assume the earliest capital of the Chu kingdom to have been located in this area,[2] but in the sixth and fifth centuries BCE, the Chu capital had long been moved southward to the environs of present-day Jiangling (Hubei province), and Xichuan had become a border domain. The inscriptions on bronzes found in the Xiasi-Heshangling tombs indicate that these objects had been brought along by princesses from surrounding states marrying into Sunshu Ao's lineage, an indication that the heads of that lineage were considered equal in rank to local rulers outside the Chu kingdom. Such inter-marriages may have been part of an overall political strategy aiming at establishing the king of Chu as in every respect the equivalent of the Zhou king, for Zhou court ritual ranked the heads of ministerial lineages at the royal court on a par with local rulers.

Yuan Zi Feng rose to office as a result of a political shift in the mid-sixth century BCE. Previously, key ministerial positions at the Chu court had been occupied by the powerful uncles and brothers of the reigning king. In an effort to strengthen their own position, King Kang of Chu (559 – 545 BCE) and his followers began appointing members of lesser-ranking lineages such as Yuan Zi Feng.[3] The office of chief minister did not remain in Feng's lineage after his death. These historical circumstances, which can be reconstructed by combining evidence from inscriptions and historical texts, may explain the exceptional lavishness of Yuan Zi Feng's and his consorts' tombs and their contents. LvF

1   Li Ling 1981.
2   Shi 1988; Blakeley 1988; Blakeley 1990.
3   Blakeley 1992.

91

Chime of twenty-six bronze *zhong* bells

Height 23.6 – 120.4 (8 ⅜ – 47 ⅜), width at lower
lip 14.8 – 59.7 (5 ¾ – 23 ½), weight 2.8 – 152.8
(6 ⅛ – 336 ⅞)
Middle Spring and Autumn Period (c. 550 BCE)
From Tomb 2 at Xiasi, Xichuan, Henan Province

Henan Museum, Zhengshou

This is the largest continuous bell-chime so far
known from the Chinese Bronze Age,[1] though other
contexts — e.g., the tomb of Marquis Yi at Leigudun,
Suixian (Hubei province) — have yielded multiple
chimes totaling larger numbers of bells. The twenty-
six bells *(yongzhong)* were arranged on a two-tiered
wooden rack; each bell was suspended from two
ropes, connected by a bronze pin through the bell's
suspension loop.[2] To minimize acoustic interference from the vibrating suspension ropes, the ropes
were made of lead.

Long and massive octagonal shanks counterbalance the bell bodies; the suspension rings are
affixed laterally, causing the bells to tilt toward the
player and permitting greater accuracy in striking
than in vertically suspended bells — an important
feature, since each *yongzhong* can emit two notes,
depending on whether it is struck in the center
or midway to the side. (The interval between the
two notes usually approximates either a minor or
a major third.) Long forgotten and not rediscovered
until 1978, this acoustic phenomenon is caused by
the bell's almond-shaped (pointed-oval) cross section. The inscriptions that identify the tones on
Marquis Yi's bells show that Eastern Zhou bellcast-
ers could determine the pitch of both tones in
advance — a skill that they must have developed
through assiduous experimentation, since the
mathematics then available did not permit casters
to calculate an exact formula for the relation between size and pitch.[3]

This chime still emits tones similar to those
heard during the Bronze Age. Its range extends over
five octaves, with up to ten different notes per oc-
tave (sometimes, the same note can be played on
more than one bell). One can play a pentatonic

scale in E in three consecutive octaves. The overall distribution of notes is less regular than in earlier and contemporaneous chimes made in northern China, possibly indicating that mid-sixth-century Chu casters were just beginning to cast acoustically sophisticated bell-chimes.[4]

The symmetrical groups of bosses on each *yong-zhong* probably served to dampen the nonharmonic overtones emitted by the upper part of the bell, thus emphasizing the two fundamental notes. The enclosed panels between the bosses, as well as on the shank, are ornamented, in typical Chu style, with tiny dragons raised in jagged relief.[5] Larger versions of the dragon motif appear on the flat head and in the center of the striking platform.

The inscribed text, repeated seventeen times,[6] identifies the individual for whom this chime was made as the grandson of a Chu king. Though unknown from historical sources, this Wangsun Gao may have been the son of Wangzi Wu (d. 552 BCE), a royal prince and Yuan Zi Feng's predecessor as chief minister of Chu. Feng's tomb contained a magnificent set of seven bronze tripods made for Wangzi Wu. How such royal bronzes came into Feng's possession is unclear; perhaps they were a gift from the Chu king, symbolizing Feng's appointment as chief minister and, simultaneously, the ouster of Wangzi Wu's branch of the royal lineage.[7] LvF

Inscription[8]

It was the first month, in the first quarter, day *dinghai*. I, Wangsun Gao, selected my auspicious metals and for myself made [these] harmonizing bells. They are long-vibrating and sonorous, and their fine sound is very loud. With them, sternly and in a very dignified manner, I reverently serve the king of Chu.

I am not fearful and make no mistakes. I am gracious in my administrative demeanor. I am thoroughly familiar with the awe-inspiring ceremonies. I am greatly respect-

ful and am at ease and composed. I am
fearful and very careful; earnestly planning
[my actions], I am good at defending [my
ruler]. For this I am known in the Four
States. I respectfully keep my treaties and
sacrifices, and as a result forever obtain
happiness. Martial in warfare, I consider
and carefully plan [my strategies] and am
never defeated.

Glistening are the harmonizing bells.
With them feast in order to please and to
make happy the king of Chu, the various
rulers and the fine guests, our fathers and
brothers and the various gentlemen. How
blissful and brightly joyous! For ten thousand years without end, forever preserve
and strike them.

1 Excavated in 1979; published: Henan 1980, pl. 1.3;
   Zhao 1986; Thorp 1988b, no. 9; Henan 1991: 140–179,
   pl. 58–60; So 1995, 31, fig. 32.
2 The rack is a reconstruction, the original having decomposed in the ground. Only twenty-four of the original
   twenty-six connecting pins were found; they are not
   depicted in the excavation report.
3 Falkenhausen 1993b, 72–97; Falkenhausen and Rossing
   1995, 469–470.
4 Falkenhausen 1993b, 256–260; Falkenhausen and Rossing
   1995, 466 and 471.
5 Compare Hayashi 1988b, 383–391.
6 The twelve largest bells each feature a complete version of
   the text; the following four bells each feature one-half, the
   next following six each one-third, and the final four each
   one-quarter of the text.
7 This interpretation partly follows suggestions in Zhang
   1985 and Chen Wei 1983. The authors of the excavation
   report (Henan 1991) attempt to identify Wangzi Wu as the
   occupant of Tomb 2, a claim that cannot be correct
   (Li Ling 1996c).
8 Translation after Falkenhausen 1988, 1080–1083, and
   Mattos 1997, 100–101.

vessel.[5] The decoration consists of rows of stylized dragon heads with angular, interlaced bodies executed flush with the surface. Such decorations evoke the style of the sixth century. They can be contrasted with the more dynamic schemes of curling relief elements seen on the *hu* (cat. 96) and *jian-fou* (cat. 97). CM

1   Excavated in 1978 (C 96); reported: Hubei 1989, 1:189 – 193, figs. 91, 92:1, and 2: pl. 50:1. Inscribed on the interior wall of the vessel, on the rings of the lifting handles, and on the bowl of the spoon: "Marquis Yi of Zeng commissioned [this vessel]; may he possess it and use it for eternity."
2   Such vessels are identified as *yu ding* on their inscriptions; two *yu ding* were found in Tomb M 1 (mid-sixth century BCE) at Xiasi, Xichuan, Henan province. See Henan 1991, 55 – 57, figs. 44 – 46 and pl. 23:1. A list of grave contents inscribed on bamboo slips found in a Chu state tomb at Baoshan near Jiangling, Hubei province (Tomb 2, late fourth century BCE) describes the vessels as *huo ding*. See Hubei 1991, 1:98. For a full discussion of the nomenclature of *ding*, see Yu and Gao 1978 – 1979.
3   For the hooks (C 155), see Hubei 1989 1:193, fig. 94, and 2: pl. 50:1. Other hooks were found at Xinyang Changtaiguan Tomb 1 (see Henan 1986, pl. 37:2), and Shanxian Houchuanzhen (see Guo Baojun 1981, pls. 94:1 – 2 and 86:3). Four lifting hooks, identified as *mu* [?] in the lists of the tomb's contents, were found in Baoshan Tomb 2. See Hubei 1991, 1:102, fig. 59, and 2: pl. 29:4.
4   For the ladle (C 183), see Hubei 1989, 1:215 – 216, fig. 114:2 and 2: pls. 60:1 – 2. *Sheng ding* were used for serving rather than cooking. For a discussion of *sheng ding*, see Yu and Gao 1978 – 1979.
5   Handles were often cast-on during the Shang dynasty — legs only rarely so. See Bagley 1987, 42.

93

Bronze *gui* vessel with pedestal

gui: height 31.8 (12 ½), diam. at mouth 22.2 (8 ¾)
pedestal: height 10.0 (3 ⅞), width 23.2 (9 ⅛),
depth 23.0 (9)
Warring States Period (C. 433 BCE)
From Leigudun, Suixian, Hubei Province

Hubei Provincial Museum, Wuhan

Whereas *ding* were ritual vessels for meat and fish, *gui* served as containers for serving grain. This example[1] is one of a set of eight matching *gui* found in the central chamber of the tomb next to a row of nine *sheng ding* with flat bases. Starting in the Middle Western Zhou period, *gui* and *ding* were made in closely matched sets (probably inspired by the already established fashion for chimes of bells); the number in each set indicated the rank of their owner.[2] Nine *ding* and eight *gui* are said to have been an entitlement reserved for the Zhou ruler, but archaeological evidence shows that by the end of the Western Zhou period the rulers of some of the increasingly independent states had usurped this right.[3]

The reappearance of the pedestaled *gui* is one instance of a revivalism that pervaded Eastern Zhou culture beginning in the fifth century BCE. *Gui* with square pedestals had been introduced at the start of the Western Zhou period and enjoyed intermittent popularity during the remainder of the period; by the Early Eastern Zhou period, however, the form had become rare (except in the east and southeast), and by the eighth and seventh centuries BCE, it had gone into complete eclipse within the Chu-Zeng sphere. Its appearance in Marquis Yi's tomb may reflect eastern influence. A set of eight pedestaled *gui* discovered in the tomb of Marquis Zhao of Cai (r. 518 – 491 BCE) at Shouxian in Anhui province suggests a roughly contemporaneous intermediary source for the form, for the Cai state had ties to states further east. The Cai and the Zeng vessels share specific features — in particular, the square opening on the pedestal and the petaled knob on the lid; the traditional masked handles of the Cai *gui*, however, are replaced in this example by ser-

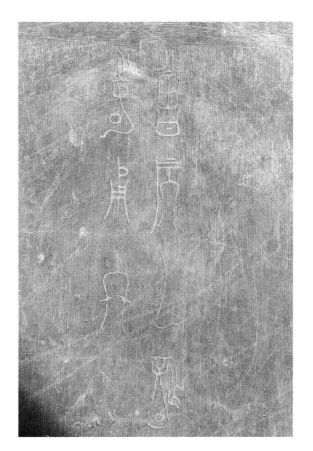
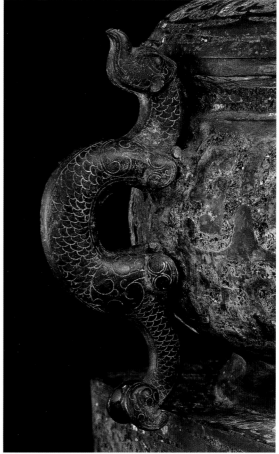

pentine creatures in a style that is characteristically Zeng. By the fourth century, pedestaled *gui* had become part of the Chu repertoire of ritual vessels and endured as a form until the state's demise in 223 BCE.[4]

The *gui*, its pedestal, and lid were originally inlaid with turquoise, a few fragments of which still survive in the cast-in arabesques and abstract bird shapes. The practice of inlaying bronze vessels with other materials began in the late seventh or early sixth century BCE; inlays were primarily copper during the early period, and sparing use was made of such decoration. This vessel, by contrast, in which turquoise was used lavishly to cover the entire surface, is characteristic of the exuberant decorative scheme of many of Marquis Yi's food vessels (see cat. 94). CM

1 Excavated in 1978 (C 108); reported: Hubei 1989, 1:207–209, and 2: pls. 58:1–2. Inscribed on both the inside wall of the vessel and on the lid: "Marquis Yi of Zeng commissioned [this vessel]; may he possess and use it for eternity."
2 For a discussion of vessel sets, see Yu and Gao 1978–1979; Rawson and Bunker 1990, 37–38.
3 See, for example, the set of nine *ding* and *li* and seven *gui* from Jingshan Songhequ Sujialong. Hubei 1972, 47–53 and pls. 9–10.
4 See, for example, the *gui* from Shouxian Zhujiaji Lisangudui, illustrated in So 1995, 70, fig. 128.

94

Bronze *dou* vessel inlaid with turquoise

Height 26.4 (10 ⅜ in), diam. at mouth 20.6 (8 ⅛ in)
Warring States Period (c. 433 BCE)
From Leigudun, Suixian, Hubei Province

Hubei Provincial Museum, Wuhan

Bowl-shaped forms with a domed lid on a tall stem
are conventionally termed *dou,* while flatter, dish-
shaped forms lacking a lid are termed *bian* or *fu.*
In the *Zhou li* (Rites of Zhou) the *dou* is defined as
a container for sauces, while the *bian* is a container
for dried meats.[1] In the *Yi li* (Book of ceremonial)
they are often listed following one another, indicating that they performed related functions.[2] This is
confirmed by the placement in the tomb of the
dou[3] next to two *bian.*

Although the ritual texts indicate that stemmed
vessels were indispensable components of a com-

plete ritual repertoire of forms, they were only
intermittently fashionable in bronze, and it was
in ceramic, wood, or basketry that they were more
popular. Bronze forms often show a dependence
on ceramic, wood, or basketry models. Flat, dishlike
forms became fashionable during the Late Western
Zhou period, but grew rarer and eventually disappeared in the course of the Early Eastern Zhou
period. A more rounded form with a domed lid,
imitative of ceramic examples, began to appear during the sixth century in the north and was popular
throughout the fifth century. In the Chu sphere,
on the other hand, bronze stemmed vessels are
rare in the sixth and fifth centuries BCE.[4] None was
found in the Xiasi tombs, and only three — this *dou*
and two *bian* — were present in Marquis Yi's tomb.
By contrast, twenty-three lacquered *dou* were found
in the tomb, and it is in this material, rather than
bronze, that the *dou* form is usually found in the

95

Bronze *zun-pan* vessels

zun: height 30.1 (11 ¾), diam. at mouth 25 (9 ⅞)
pan: height 23.5 (9 ¼), diam. at mouth 58 (22 ¾)
Warring States Period (c. first half of fifth
century BCE)
From Leigudun, Suixian, Hubei Province

Hubei Provincial Museum, Wuhan

This remarkable composite vessel[1] represents the
culmination of the fashion for festooning ritual
vessels with elaborate sculptural ornaments. This
flamboyant style is characteristic of bronzecasting
in the Chu sphere during the sixth and fifth centuries BCE and stands in contrast to the simpler
profiles of vessels preferred in northern regions
such as the Jin state.[2]

Beneath the encrustations of ornament lie two
vessel types whose functions, according to the
ritual commentaries, were unrelated: a *pan* basin
(conventionally used for ritual ablutions) and a
zun goblet (used for libations). The consistent style
of their decoration and fact that the vessels were
found placed one inside the other suggest that they
were nonetheless designed as a unit. While their
placement in the tomb's central chamber, near the
wine vessels, suggests that they were wine containers, the mass of intricate and fragile decoration
would have hindered any practical function; it
would, in fact, have been impossible to pour liquid
from the *zun*. The value of these vessels therefore
probably lay less in their use in ritual than in their
ornament.

Imaginary creatures, in astonishing profusion,
clamber over the vessels: the authors of the excavation report counted more than one hundred and
seventy "dragons" among the sculptural elements.
On the large handles of the *zun*, they take the
form of felines with reverted heads and lolling
tongues; the beasts that clench the rim of the *pan*
in their mouths seem more amphibian. A writhing
energy animates all of these creatures, echoed in
the fields of tiny curls that cover the walls of the
two vessels.

Chu sphere. The marquis' bronze *dou*, however, does
not closely match the wooden *dou* from the tomb
and seems instead to have been based on northern
bronze *dou*.

Unlike most of the marquis' bronzes, this *dou*
has retained much of its turquoise inlay.[5] The decoration on the bowl of the piece consists of stylized
pairs of addorsed birds with reverted heads, identifiable by the eyes at the top of the frieze and claws
at the bottom. These evoke the design schemes
on Early to Middle Western Zhou period bronzes,
and may have been a deliberate revival of the older
style. CM

1 *Zhou li* in Lin 1983, 54 – 56.
2 See, in particular, the *Pin li* (Education of a mission) in
   Yi li, Yang 1982, chap. 21.
3 Excavated in 1978 (C 194); reported: Hubei 1989, 1: 211 –
   212, fig. 111:2, and 2: pl. 59:2 – 3. Inscribed inside the bowl
   and the lid: "Marquis Yi commissioned [this vessel]; may
   he possess and use it for eternity."
4 A pair of bronze *dou* were excavated from the tomb of
   Marquis Zhao of Cai (r. 518 – 491 BCE) in Shouxian, but
   they are not very close in form to the Marquis Yi example.
   See Anhui 1956, pl. 6:4.
5 So 1995, 51, plausibly suggests that the fine intaglio bordering lines may originally have held a metallic inlay.

body of the vessel by digging sockets into the appendages, which were fitted over tongues protruding from the vessel. Analysis of the solder used to fix the four monsters to the foot of the *zun* has established that it contained 53 percent tin, 41 percent lead, and 2 percent copper.[4]

While many of the individual elements were probably cast using the traditional ceramic section-mold technique, the bands of openwork at the mouth of the *zun* and *pan* represented a much sterner challenge. This discontinuous "surface" of this multilayered openwork is formed of individual C- and S-curls, each supported by one or more stalks rising from a mesh below. The intricacy of this openwork would most certainly have required the use of a fusible model such as wax. The lost-wax method of casting had been used in China's border regions as early as the Shang period, but it began to be exploited for vessel ornaments only in the seventh century BCE.[5] The technique was most advanced in the Chu state, as demonstrated by a mid-sixth-century BCE vessel stand (*jin*) that makes extensive use of the technique.[6] The delicacy of the filigree work on the *zun-pan*, however, far surpasses that on the *jin* and represents the apogee of lost-wax casting as an ornamental technique.

While the vessel would undoubtedly have been valued for its technical virtuosity, it is likely that the ornamentation held symbolic meanings as well. The clambering amphibian figures with bifurcated tails that clench the rim of the *pan* in their jaws seem to derive from the serpent-devouring-frog motif common on bronzes south of the Yangzi River; such figures occur intermittently in Chu woodcarving as well.[7] Although the creatures cannot be identified with any zoological or iconographic certainty, they can be read as three-dimensional counterparts of the creatures painted on the sides of Marquis Yi's coffin; these undoubtedly fulfilled a religious role.[8]

The vessel is one of a small number of bronzes from the tomb that were apparently not made for Marquis Yi himself. Beneath the inscription in the *pan* that identifies the object as commissioned by the marquis, an earlier, partly erased inscription names a different Zeng figure — Marquis Yu —

As a tour de force of multiple casting, this piece stands unrivaled by any metalwork from the ancient world: the vessels themselves were cast using the traditional ceramic section-mold technique, modified to exploit the more recently invented pattern-block technology.[3] Individually cast components were then soldered to the vessels and to each other using a tin-lead solder — fifty-six soldering points have been identified on the *zun* and forty-four on the *pan*. The heads, tongues, and bodies of the *zun* handle figures, for example, were all cast separately, then soldered together. They were attached to the

generally believed to have been one of Marquis Yi's predecessors (probably his father or grandfather).[9] The vessel thus probably dates from the first half of the fifth century BCE and was an heirloom when it entered Marquis Yi's tomb.

The early date of the piece may explain how two vessels of unrelated ritual function came to be combined into a single unit. Although no precedent for this combination (nor even for the *zun* itself as a vessel type) is known from the Chu or Zeng repertoire of forms, a *zun-pan* set has been excavated from the tomb of Marquis Zhao of Cai (r. 518–491 BCE), a small state located between Zeng and the southeastern states of Wu and Yue. The Cai *pan* and *zun* bear virtually identical inscriptions stating that they were made for the dowry of a Cai princess on her marriage to a Wu monarch; the inscriptions imply that the objects were made to function as a unit.[10] Although no *zun-pan* combinations have been found in Wu territory, single *pan* and *zun* were extremely important there well into the Eastern Zhou period; in fact, as a number of scholars have pointed out, this was the only region where *zun* survived after the middle of Western Zhou period.[11] It seems likely, therefore, that the idea of combining *pan* and *zun* into a single, composite unit first arose in the Cai or the Wu state and that the idea was then briefly taken up in the Zeng state. However, the combination does not seem to have taken hold, either in the Zeng or the Chu state.[12] The only other bronze vessel that could tentatively be advanced as a derivative of Marquis Yu's *zun-pan* is a vessel from a late fourth-century BCE hoard at Yuyi Nanyaozhuang in Jiangsu province. Although it is conventionally identified as a *hu*, the vessel has four zoomorphic handles (unusual in a *hu*) reminiscent of Marquis Yu's *zun*, and a strange, dishlike foot that may be a vestige of the *pan*, now fused with the *zun* into a single vessel. CM

1 Excavated in 1978 (C 38); reported Hubei 1989, 1:228–234, figs. 127–128 and 2, color pl. 10 and plates 69–74. The neck of the *zun* is incised with the inscription "Marquis Yi commissioned [this vessel]; may he possess it and use it for eternity." An inscription cast into the inside of the *pan* reads "The [ ] vessel of Marquis Yu of Zeng." A later incised inscription, partly obliterating the original one, reads "Marquis Yi commissioned [this vessel]; may he possess and use it for eternity."
2 For a discussion of the origins of this style, see So 1983, 64–71; Rawson 1987a, 49–52; Mackenzie 1991, 132–141; and So 1995, 21–36.
3 The pattern-block technique differed from traditional casting methods in that an ornament was pressed into sections of clay, which were then set into the interior of the vessel mold. For a full discussion of this technique, see Bagley 1995, 46–54. For a discussion of the use of pattern blocks in Zeng bronzes, see So 1995, 52–53.
4 See Hubei 1991, 1:177.
5 For a discussion of the lost-wax method of casting in China, see Bagley 1987, 44–45; So 1980, 266; and Mackenzie 1991, 136–139.
6 The *jin* was excavated from Tomb 2 at Xiasi, Xichuan Xian, southern Henan province. See Henan 1991, 126–128, fig. 104, and pl. 49.
7 Mackenzie 1984–1986, 31–48.
8 See Hubei 1991, 1:28–45, figs. 18–22, for a discussion of the motifs on the coffin.
9 See Hubei 1991, 1:229–230 and note 1 above.
10 For a discussion of these pieces, see foreword by Tang Lan to Wu Sheng 1958, and pl. 45 (*zun*) and pl. 50 (*pan*), 3–4.
11 See Kane 1974–1975, 77–107; Rawson 1987a, 45–49.
12 The only other *zun* recovered from an Eastern Zhou period Chu site is an unprepossessing funerary ceramic, completely devoid of decoration, from Tomb 2 (fourth century BCE) at Changtaiguan, Xinyang, Henan province. See Henan 1986, pl. 98:8.

96

Pair of bronze *hu* jars with stand

hu: height 99 (39)
stand: height 13.2 (5 ¼), width 117.5 (46 ¼),
depth 13.2 (5 ¼)
Warring States Period (c. 433 BCE)
From Leigudun, Suixian, Hubei Province

Hubei Provincial Museum, Wuhan

With its highly articulated profile, sharp angles,
and heavy appendages, this monumental set of
ritual wine vessels[1] epitomizes an architectonic
approach to form characteristic of many of Marquis
Yi's bronze vessels. Two lidded *hu*, with detachable

"crowns," fit into circular openings in the stand
(*jin*). Horizontal ridges inside the vessels are evidence that each was cast in three pours of metal.[2]
The vessel handles and the supports for the stand
were cast separately and attached with a tin-lead
solder.

   The set was found in the central chamber, next
to the *jian-fou* wine coolers (cat. 97) and the *zun-
pan* (cat. 95). Depictions of ritual scenes on fifth-
century BCE pictorial bronze vessels show *hu*, with
ladles, placed on stands or low altars; descriptions
of *hu* in the *Yi li* (Book of ceremonial) also prescribe
ladles and *jin* as part of the ritual paraphernalia.[3]
It seems possible that the ladles placed on the

traditionally associated with the *hu* are here transferred to the *jin*.

The most impressive decorative feature of the *hu* are the large handles in the form of sinuous monsters whose heads and tails sprout antler forms.[10] Antlered monster figures appear on Xiasi and Xingzheng *hu*, and these creatures seem to be descendants of such figures. Belief in the magical efficacy of antlers seems to have been particularly important in the Chu sphere, where they were a prominent feature of carved wood tomb guardians (see cat. 100).[11] The antlers decorating this vessel were no doubt intended to enhance the ritual aura of the *hu*. The textured surface of the *hu*, on close inspection, reveals a dazzling number of small fantastical creatures. CM

adjacent *jian-fou* would have been used to decant the wine from the *hu* into the *jian*. Three other bronze *jin* are known, including a famous example with openwork decoration from Xiasi Tomb 2,[4] but the vessel from Marquis Yi's tomb is the only example found with its associated *hu*. *Jin* were probably more often made of less costly materials, such as stone, ceramic, or (in the Chu state and its sphere) lacquered wood.[5] Its appearance here in bronze exemplifies the extravagant use of the material in the marquis' ritual paraphernalia.

Antecedents of these *hu* can be traced back to the Middle Western Zhou period, when paired *hu* began to displace wine vessels such as *zun*.[6] During the Early Eastern Zhou period, *hu* were particularly favored in the Chu and Zeng states, where they were cast on a monumental scale and assumed a more articulated profile.[7] By the seventh century BCE, monster-shaped handles had replaced the traditional mask design, and decorative straps (which appear on examples dating from the Western Zhou period) had become more prominent; celebrated examples from Xiasi and Xinzheng[8] exemplify this trend. The vessels from the tomb of Marquis Yi differ from these immediate predecessors in two respects: circular sections (which may derive from Western Zhou examples[9]) substitute for the rectangular outline, and the zoomorphic feet

1   Excavated in 1978 (C 132, 133, 135); reported: Hubei 1989, 1:219 – 222, figs. 119 – 120 and 2: pls. 63 – 64. A cast inscription inside the neck of each *hu* reads "Marquis Yi of Zeng commissioned [this vessel]; may he possess and use it for eternity."
2   According to the excavation report (Hubei 1989, 1:221), the neck and foot were cast first, then joined to the belly.
3   *Hu* vessels are depicted on a *yi* from Changzhi Fenshuiling in Shanxi province, a *dou* in the Walters Art Gallery, Baltimore, and a *hu* in the Musée Guimet, Paris: Weber 1973, figs. 21d, 66d, and 67e. In each case, the ladle is depicted floating above the *hu*. *Hu* with ladles are described in the Xiang Yin (District Symposium) section of the *Yi li*. See also Steele 1917 (1966 repr.), 52.
4   See Henan 1991, pl. 49
5   A square, lacquered wood *jin* found in the central chamber of Marquis Yi's tomb may have been a stand for *dou* rather than *hu*; a rectangular table that may have originally held lacquered *hu* was found in the northern chamber (Hubei 1989, 1:374 – 376, figs. 233 – 234). Both examples have legs taller than those of the bronze version. Another version in lacquered wood has been found in the fourth-century BCE Tianxingguan Tomb 1 at Jiangling: see Hubei 1982, 102, fig. 26 and pl. 22:5.
6   See Rawson 1990, 74, 102 – 103.
7   See So 1983, 64 – 71.
8   See Guan 1929, 1: pl. 38.
9   The combination of the *hu*'s rounded forms with a rectangular stand may have reflected cosmological concerns. The L-shaped raised borders on the stand echo similar L-shapes used as part of a cosmological diagram on the lacquered wood clothes-chests in the Marquis Yi's tomb. See Hubei 1989, 1:357, fig. 217.
10 The complexity and undercutting of the antler forms indicate that they were cast using the lost-wax method.
11 See Mackenzie 1991, 107 – 158.

97

Bronze *jian-fou* cooler and ladle

jian: height 63 (24 ⅞)
fou: height 51.8 (20 ½)
ladle: length 84 (33)
Warring States Period (c. 433 BCE)
From Leigudun, Suixian, Hubei Province

The National Museum of Chinese History, Beijing

Houston and San Francisco only

A pair of *jian-fou* were found in the central chamber of the tomb next to the other vessels associated with the serving of wine — the *zun-pan* (cat. 95), the pair of large *hu* (cat. 96), and the filter (cat. 98). Lying across the top of each *jian-fou* was a large ladle *(shao)* used to extract the wine.[1] Each weighing approximately 170 kilograms, the *jian-fou* are the largest of the Marquis Yi ritual vessels (fig. 1), and the impression of immense mass is accentu-

ated by the top-heavy profile of the vessels: large slabs overhanging the edges of the vessels bear down on the heads of the serpentine handles, while the small creatures that support the vessels appear to sag under the weight of their burden.

Each comprises an outer vessel *(jian)* and a much smaller inner vessel *(fou)*. A removable grate with a square opening holds the neck of the *fou*. The base of the *fou* is secured at the bottom by L-shaped prongs that protrude from the inside of the *jian*'s base and fit into square openings in the foot of the *fou*; a hinged lock on one of the prongs holds them in position (see fig. 1). The composite form of these vessels suggests that they were used to cool wine by filling the space between the two containers with ice. The provision of ice for cooling wine seems to have been important in ceremonies and banquets during the summer months. A passage in the *Zhou li* (Rites of Zhou) refers to the

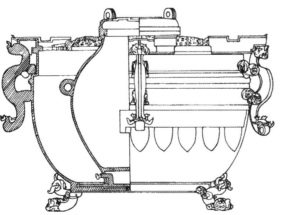

FIG. 1. Profile and cross section of a *jian-fou* from the Zenghou Yi tomb. After Hubei 1989:1, 224, fig. 122.

provision of a "*jian* for ice,"[2] and several passages in the *Chu ci* (Songs of Chu) refer to cool wine.

The idea of combining *jian* basins and *fou* into composite wine coolers developed during the sixth century BCE, probably in the south. Basins were a common form of vessel from the beginning of the Eastern Zhou period; by the early sixth century their size had increased dramatically, sometimes approaching 60 centimeters in diameter. Although the basins probably fulfilled a variety of functions, the discovery of a *jian* and *fou* placed side by side in a mid-sixth-century BCE Chu tomb suggests that by this time the two types were already on occasion used in combination,[3] and by the end of the century the association had become formalized. In the tomb of Marquis Zhao of Cai at Shouxian in Anhui province, two paired, square basins were found with matching square-sectioned *fou* placed inside them.[4]

Since no earlier square *jian-fou* are known, it seems likely that the Cai versions inspired the basic form of the Marquis Yi *jian-fou*. Once adopted into the Zeng repertoire of vessels, this essentially plain vessel-type was transformed by the addition of heavy appendages — elaborate zoomorphic handles and feet and angular outcrops over the rim — into a much more elaborate form consonant with the Chu-Zeng style. Certain aspects of this style may derive from woodcarving techniques: a lacquered wood *jin* stand from the central chamber exhibits the same contrast between sinuous zoomorphic form and the angularity of the outcrops present on the *jian-fou*. These blocks may have been purely decorative features, but it is also possible that they possessed some as-yet unrecognized symbolic significance.[5] CM

1   Excavated in 1978 (C 139); reported: Hubei 1989, 1:223–228, figs. 122–125, and 2: color pl. 9:3–4, pls. 66–68; for the ladle (C 138), see Hubei 1989, 1:235–236, fig. 133:1 and color pl. 9:3 and pl. 66. Inscriptions incised on the interior of the *jian* (outer vessel) and *fou* (inner vessel) read: "Marquis Yi commissioned [this article]; may he possess and use it for eternity." The same inscription, much more elegantly written and probably cast rather than incised, appears on the interior of the ladles.
2   Lin 1983, 53.
3   See Tomb M 3 at Xichuan Xiasi. Henan 1991, 213, fig. 156, nos. 19 *(jian)* and 21–22 *(zun fou)*.
4   Rings on the inside of each wall of the *jian* may have served to secure the *fou* in some way or may have supported a grating on which the ice was placed. Similar rings appear on the inside of two *jian* cast for King Guang of Wu also found in the Cai tomb, indicating that these also were intended to be used with internal vessels. See Anhui 1956, pl. 15:3.
5   The L-shaped corners of a cosmological diagram on a lacquered wooden clothes chest from Marquis Yi's tomb are tantalizingly reminiscent of the corner blocks on the *jian-fou* and *jin* (see Hubei 1989, 2: pl. 121). On the chest, these L-shapes are clearly not decorative features but serve to delineate the shape of the cosmos. On another chest, linked cruciform shapes are also reminiscent of the layout of the top of the *jian-fou* and *jin* (Hubei 1989, 2: pl. 124:1).

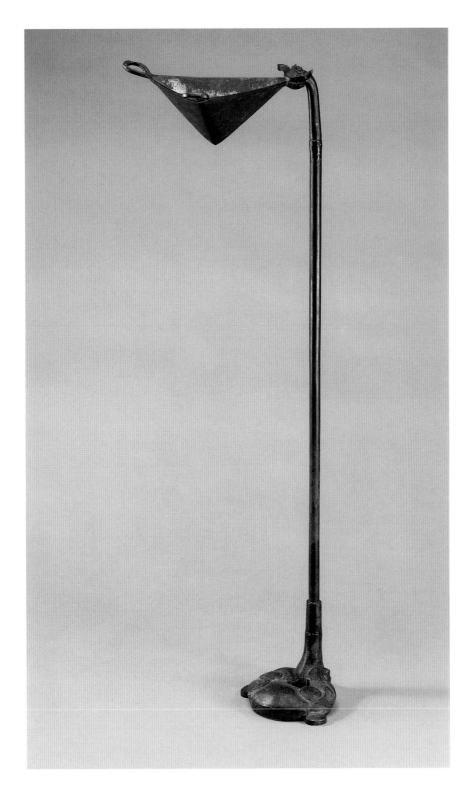

98

Bronze filter

Height 88.5 (34 ¾)
Warring States Period (c. 433 BCE)
From Leigudun, Suixian, Hubei Province

Hubei Provincial Museum, Wuhan

This unusual object consists of a triangular funnel clenched in the mouth of a monster-head, which forms the top of the stand; a curled monster in profile forms the base.[1] The funnel itself is undecorated; twelve small holes are cast in the bottom, and two loop handles are soldered to the side of the funnel opposite the monster-head. The funnel shape and the holes — as well as the object's placement in the central chamber next to the square *jian-fou* wine coolers — suggest that it was intended to strain wine or medicinal potions (possibly in conjunction with a cloth liner). Although no other bronze versions are known, a small triangular funnel woven in bamboo was found in a late fourth-century BCE Chu tomb at Baoshan near Jingmen (Hubei province).

The frequent mention of spiced wine in the *Chu ci* (Songs of Chu) implies that straining filters would have been in common use; a passage in the *Zhao hun* (Summons of the soul) explicitly refers to the straining of wine:

> Jadelike wine, honey-flavoured, fills the
>   winged cups;
> Ice-cooled liquor, strained of impurities,
>   clear wine, cool and refreshing;
> Here are laid out the painted ladles,
>   and here is the sparkling wine.[2]

CM

1   Excavated in 1978 (C 23); reported: Hubei 1989, 1:234 – 235,
    figs. 131 – 132:1, and 2: pl. 75:2 – 4. Inscribed at the top
    of the stand: "Commissioned by the Marquis Yi of Zeng
    for his use."
2   Hawkes 1985, 228.

99

Bronze brazier, charcoal shovel, and dustpan

brazier: height 14 (5½), diam. 43.8 (17¼)
shovel: length 38.6 (15¼)
dustpan: length 29.0 (11⅜)
Warring States Period (c. 433 BCE)
From Leigudun, Suixian, Hubei Province

Hubei Provincial Museum, Wuhan

The shovel *(chan)* and dustpan *(qi)* were discovered stacked inside the brazier *(lu)*,[1] which was placed in the central chamber between the two large *huo ding* (cat. 92). From this placement, it seems possible that the brazier was actually used to cook the contents of the *ding*. Chain handles on either side of the brazier would have allowed it to be lifted while the fuel was alight.

An inlaid copper scroll of avian forms encircles the sides of the brazier, and a similar scroll, incorporating dragonlike figures, decorates the shovel. In both cases, the inlay was cast separately and affixed to the vessel mold's interior; molten bronze was then poured in to form the object.[2] The shape and decoration of the dustpan faithfully imitate basketwork, the conventional medium for such implements; an example in bamboo from the Chu state was found in Tomb 2 at Baoshan near Jingmen in Hubei province.[3]

A perforated shovel found in the tomb of Fu Hao at Anyang may have been used for charcoal and suggests that braziers may have been in use, although not consigned to tombs, as early as the Shang period.[4] Examples begin to appear in tombs during the sixth century BCE, and their forms are particularly prominent in the south and southeast. The earliest known example is a brazier from Lijialou, Xinzheng in Henan province identified with the Chu prince Yingci, who was active during the first decades of the sixth century BCE.[5] The decoration of that example is closely related to styles popular in the southeast.[6] A brazier excavated from Jing'an Shuikou in Jiangxi province is in-

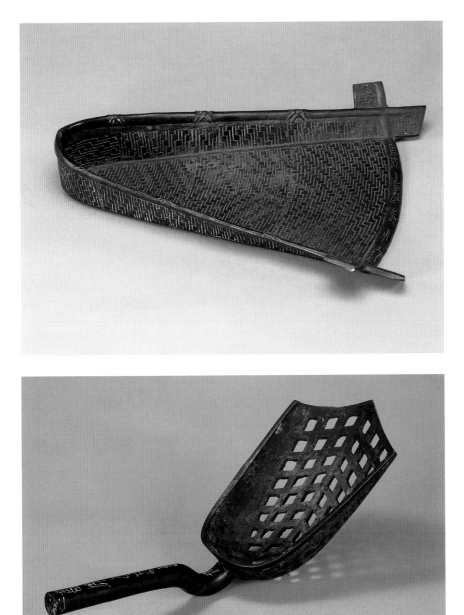

scribed with the name of King Yichu of Xu, who is mentioned in the *Zuo zhuan* (Chronicle of Zuo) in the sixth year of Zhao Gong (536 BCE).[7] All this evidence suggests that bronze braziers may have been a southeastern invention. By the fifth and fourth centuries BCE, however, braziers are common elements of tomb paraphernalia in both north and south.[8] A brazier from a Chu state tomb at Xinyang Changtaiguan, whose form resembles that of the Marquis Yi example, still contained charcoal.[9] CM

1   Excavated in 1978 (C 166 – 168); reported: Hubei 1989, 1:244 – 247, figs. 141:1, 142:2 – 3; 143 – 144, and 2: pl. 81:1 – 3. Inscribed on the base of the brazier, the handle of the shovel, and the mouth of the dustpan: "Marquis Yi of Zeng commissioned [this article]; may he possess and use it for eternity."

2   The technique is discussed in Weber 1973, 105 – 106. See also Rawson 1987b, 52 – 53.

3   See Hubei 1991, 2: pl. 53:1. A bronze dustpan (not, however, imitative of basketwork) was also found in the tomb (pl. 34).

4   See Zhongguo 1980b, pl. 63:2 – 3. A bronze shovel was discovered in a mid-seventh-century BCE tomb at Pingxi near Xinyang in southern Henan province. See Xinyang 1989b, 22, fig. 4:5.

5   See Guan 1929, 1: pl. 54. For a discussion of the Xinzheng bronzes and their dating, see So 1995, 22 and 422.

6   See So 1995, 422. As So points out, this piece is closely related to the decoration on a bronze jar from Gushi Hougudui. See Gushi 1981, 1 – 8, pl. 3:3.

7   See Jiangxi 1980, 13 – 15, pl. 2:2 – 3. Like the example from Marquis Yi's tomb, the brazier was accompanied by a perforated shovel. An Early Eastern Zhou period dish with openwork sides from Tunxi Yiqi M3 (implausibly identified as a *pan* in Chinese publications) may be an early form of such braziers. See Anhui 1987, no. 39.

8   A brazier was excavated from an early fifth-century BCE tomb at Gushi Hougudui in southern Henan province. See Gushi 1981, pl. 2:4. For a brazier from Jixian Shanbiaozhen in Henan province, see Guo Baojun 1981, pl. 82:1. A brazier with chain handles, dated to the late sixth century BCE, was excavated from Changzhi Fenshuiling Tomb 26: see Shanxi 1964, 120, fig. 9:3. For fourth-century BCE Chu examples from Baoshan and Jiangling, see Hubei 1991, 2, pl. 34:4, and Hubei 1996, pl. 13:4.

9   Henan 1986, pl. 43:1; the dustpan is illustrated in pl. 41:4.

100

Bronze cranelike figure with deer antlers

Height 143.5 (56 ½), base: width 45 (17 ⅝),
depth 41.4 (16 ⅜)
Warring States Period (c. 433 BCE)
From Leigudun, Suixian, Hubei Province

Hubei Provincial Museum, Wuhan

Washington only

The bronze sculpture, conventionally identified as
an antlered crane,[1] is composed of eight separately
cast elements: a nearly square stand, two legs, two
wings, a body that extends into a small head, and
two antlers. The stand, which resembles the lid of
a vessel, has four rings, one on each side, probably
intended to attach the stand to another object or
to hold it in position.

The surface decoration of the object has many
affinities with the style of several other bronzes cast
for the marquis.[2] The antlers, head, neck, and front
part of the body, as well as the legs, are decorated
with triangles, scrolls, and volutes. These incised
motifs are inlaid with gold, much like those on
a bronze stand for stone chimes (*qing*) found at
Leigudun.[3] The body and the upper part of the
wings are covered with relief comma patterns; the
rims of the wings were inlaid with turquoise, most
of which is now lost. The stand is decorated in
abstract motifs in low relief and was originally
inlaid with semiprecious stones. All of the object's
ornamental motifs are in fact characteristic of fifth-
century BCE bronze decoration — with an important exception: four tiny snakes, cast in the round,
that hold the rings at the base of the object. Fourteen bronzes from the tomb of Marquis Yi are decorated with the same ornament, which is otherwise
almost unknown in the Chinese bronze repertoire.[4]
The object's composite ornamentation therefore
reflects the varying artistic trends of the Chu kingdom, as well as a close association with the Chu
royal bronze foundries of the fifth century BCE.

While often identified as a crane, the figure
incorporates elements of other animals: two snakelike dragons emerge from the bird's rounded sides

to hold the wings, and a crown of deer antlers emerges from its head. Wooden sculpture of antlered creatures often served as tomb guardians in Chu culture; the antlers of this figure and its placement next to the double coffin of the marquis have prompted many specialists to identify the object as an auspicious creature intended to protect the tomb and its owner from evil spirits.[5]

Wooden sculpture of long-necked birds, sometimes crowned with antlers, resting on tigers were common in the Chu kingdom from the fifth century

to the end of the fourth century BCE. They were carved for use in funerary ritual, generally as drum stands.[6] Although the shape of the present sculpture differs somewhat from the wooden models carved by the Chu craftsmen (or at least from known, published examples [see fig. 1]), its mortise-and-tenon joinery links the object to Chu wooden sculpture.

This object was probably a drum stand.[7] The antlers have a decidedly unnatural round shape, while their tips and the beak of the bird are approx-

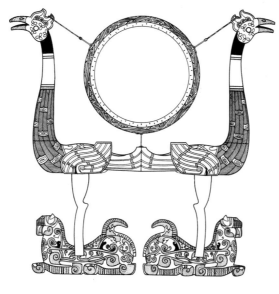

imately equidistant from one another; rings passing through the beak and the tips of the antlers would likely have held a hanging drum. Moreover, a hanging drum with three rings, but without a stand, was discovered in the funerary chamber of the marquis' tomb; its dimensions (diam. 42 [16 ½]) and the position of the rings attached to its wooden frame strongly suggest that this drum was originally suspended from the bronze sculpture.

The functional and the magical properties of this sculpture are by no means mutually exclusive: to the contrary, the complex iconography that melds various animals into a hybrid being probably reflected local beliefs, while the sound produced by the beating drum would have animated this supernatural being. AT

1 Excavated in 1978; inscribed on the right side of the beak: "Made for the eternal use of Marquis Yi of Zeng"; published: Suixian 1979, pl. 7.1, Hubei 1989, 1:251, fig. 147; 2: color pl. 11.5, and pl. 83; Tokyo 1992, no. 32; Goepper 1995, no. 62; Rawson 1996, no. 63.
2 Thote 1987, 49.
3 See Hubei 1989, 1:134–136.
4 Three *ding* tripods with snakes holding movable rings were found in Tomb 1 at Hougudui, Gushi, southern Henan province. None have been published to date.
5 Hubei 1989, 1:250; Li Xueqin 1979b, no. 24; Rawson 1996, 137. It has also been suggested that the bird was placed in the tomb to accompany the spirit of the marquis through the afterlife. See Goepper 1995, no. 62.
6 See Hubei 1996a, 91, fig. 62 (Tomb 1 at Wangshan, Jiangling, Hubei province); Hubei 1995, 304, 309, fig. 206 (four drum stands at Jiudian, Jiangling, Hubei province); Henan 1986, 93–94, 95, fig. 67 (Tomb 2 at Changtaiguan, Xinyang, Henan province); Hubei 1984a, 105, 108 and 106, fig. 82; 112, fig. 90 (fifteen drum stands and six sculptures at Yutaishan, Jiangling, Hubei province). See also Chen 1980a.
7 Thote 1987.

101

Bronze drum stand

Height 54 (21 ¼), diam. 80 (31 ½)
Warring States Period (c. 433 BCE)
From Leigudun, Suixian, Hubei Province

Hubei Provincial Museum, Wuhan

Washington only

Constructed of a central tube linked to a ring base by an openwork web, this drum stand[1] shows eight pairs of writhing and twisting serpentine dragons (cast in the round and originally inlaid with turquoise), over whose torsos, tails, and heads smaller dragons clamber in great profusion. The excavators have identified twenty-two separately cast sections, linked together by casting-on and by soldering with copper and a tin-lead alloy.

A pole inserted into the tube of the stand originally supported a barrel-shaped drum 106

centimeters wide and approximately 90 centimeters in diameter, made of maple (*pterocarya stenoptera*). (The pole had broken, and the drum had fallen to the floor of the tomb.) The drum originally stood approximately 1 meter above the stand, and the pole protruded a further 1.5 meters above the drum. Together with the drum itself and the stand, the total height of the assemblage would have been almost 4 meters. Positioned at the end of the shorter arm of the bell rack, the drum clearly formed part of the ritual orchestra. It has been plausibly identified with the *jian gu*, or "supported drum," mentioned both in the *Zhou li* (Rites of Zhou) and the *Yi li* (Book of ceremonial), the latter in connection with the Great Archery Contest *(Da she)*.[2]

This type of drum is probably descended from barrel-shaped drums, supported on small feet or low stands, in use as early as the Shang period. The ghost of a barrel-shaped drum, preserved in the earth in Houjiazhuang tomb HPKM 1217, clearly

ponent of the rituals is confirmed by their depiction in conjunction with bell-chimes and stone chimes on a number of pictorial vessels from the north and west.[5] A lacquered wood box in the form of a duck found in the western chamber of Marquis Yi's tomb (cat. 107) depicts a figure playing a hafted drum *(jian gu)*.

Only two other drum stands are known — one from the Leigudun Tomb 2 (possibly the tomb of Marquis Yi's consort or of a close descendant)[6] and another from a late sixth- or early fifth-century BCE tomb at Shucheng Jiulidun in Anhui province. Composed of intertwined serpents (like the marquis' drum stand), the Jiulidun stand suggests that drums may have had a particular association with serpents. Although the frequent depiction of the *jian gu* on the pictorial vessels, as well as its mention in the ritual texts, indicate that the instrument was widely used, the fact that all known examples of bronze drums or drum stands are associated with the south probably reflects not only the plentiful supplies of copper and tin in the region, which allowed a wider range of articles to be cast, but also the local prestige of the item itself. CM

1   Excavated in 1978 (C 67); reported: Hubei 1989, 1: 152 – 154, fig. 68:1 and 2: pl. 43. Inscribed at mouth of center tube: "Commissioned by Marquis Yi of Zeng for his possession."
2   Chap. 16 in *Yi li*, Yang 1982.
3   Liang and Gao 1968, pl. 16.
4   See Bagley 1980, 123, for a discussion of these two drums.
5   See Weber 1968, figs. 66d, 67e, 68e, and Fong 1980, 290 – 292, and 316 – 317, no. 91.
6   Hubei 1985b, 16 – 36, 29, fig. 36 (M2:79) and pl. 3:3.

shows that the skin used for the tympanum was reptilian; the scales left a visible impression in the soil.[3] The barrel drum may have been particularly important in the south, since the only two bronze versions known — one in the Sumitomo Collection and the other excavated from Wangjiazui Baini, Chongyang, in southern Hubei province — are of southern manufacture.[4]

By the Eastern Zhou period, such drums were conventionally raised on hafts fixed into heavy bases. That drums constituted an important com-

102

Bronze triple *ji* halberd

Length (including spearhead and shaft) 325 (127 ⅞)
Warring States Period (c. 433 BCE)
From Leigudun, Suixian, Hubei Province

Hubei Provincial Museum, Wuhan

This halberd consists of three bronze blades and
a spearhead attached to a long haft.[1] The blades
vary slightly in length (the longest, excluding its
tang, is 18.3 centimeters) and exhibit the slender,
curving profiles characteristic of the period. Each
blade extends down the haft approximately 15 centimeters. This lower part *(hu)* provided a firm attachment to the haft by means of thongs threaded
through perforations in the *hu* and bound to the
haft. The upper blade extends into a tang, which
anchors the unit through a slot cut into the haft.
The haft itself, ovular in cross section, is made of
wood veneered in strips of bamboo bound with silk
and coated in red and black lacquer. A horn ferrule
is attached to the base of the haft.

This is one of thirty halberds found in the
northern chamber, named in their inscriptions as
ji. The term *ji* has been traditionally applied to halberds that include a spearhead, but as only three of
these weapons have spearheads the evidence of this
group suggests that *ji* may be more correctly defined
as two or more blades attached to long hafts. The *ji*
hafts average 3.3 meters in length — much longer
than the single-bladed *ge* halberds (which average
1.3 meters) in the tomb. The greater reach of the *ji*
suggests that it was a charioteer's weapon; the
shorter *ge* was the mainstay of footsoldiers.

Most of the *ji* from the tomb are inscribed with
names other than those of the tomb's occupant
(Yue is the most common, followed by Yu); these
are generally believed to be names of Marquis Yi's
predecessors.[2] CM

1   Excavated in 1978 (N 139); reported: Hubei 1989, 1:264, fig.
    154 and 2: pl. 90:1 – 2.
2   Hubei 1989, 1: 460.

103

Bronze *shu* spear

Overall length 328 (129 ⅛), length of blade 11 (4 ⅜)
Warring States Period (c. 433 BCE)
From Leigudun, Suixian, Hubei Province

Hubei Provincial Museum, Wuhan

The northern chamber of Marquis Yi's tomb contained seven spearlike weapons; inscriptions on
three of the objects identify them as *shu*.[1] They
are distinguishable from conventional spears *(mao)*
by a number of characteristics: the blades of conventional *mao* have a flat leaf-shaped profile; this
weapon exhibits a tri-star cross section similar to
that of arrowheads of the period; a thick collar,
decorated with interlaced serpents, encircles the
blade at the base, paired by a similar collar further
down the haft. These collars would have slowed the
weapon had it been used as a projectile and suggest
that the *shu* was more likely a thrusting or slashing
weapon.[2] *Mao* hafts are conventionally made of
plain wood and circular in cross section; *shu* hafts,
by contrast, are octagonal in cross section and
veneered with bamboo strips — a feature that
would have enhanced the resilience of the long
haft when wielded laterally. The length of its haft
suggests that the *shu*, like the *ji* (cat. 102),
was primarily a charioteer's weapon.

   Shu are mentioned in several classical Chinese
texts, including the *Zhou li* (Rites of Zhou) and
the *Shi jing* (Classic of poetry);[3] commentaries on
these texts indicate that the *shu* lacked a blade:
fourteen long poles with bronze ferrules found in
the tomb's north chamber seem to correspond to
those descriptions.[4] The bladed form seems to have
been a relatively rare variant of the *shu*, associated
particularly with the southern states of Chu, Zeng,
and Cai. Two weapons with features that closely
resemble this example — a tri-star blade, octagonal
socket, and separate collar — were excavated from
the tomb of Marquis Zhao of Cai (r. 518 – 491 BCE)
at Shouxian in Anhui province.[5]   CM

1   See Hubei 1989, 1:292, fig. 178:1 (N 290). The exhibited
    example is uninscribed. See Hubei 1989, 1: 292 –294,
    fig. 178:2, and 2: pl. 97:2 (N 155).
2   An array of long spikes that springs from the collar of one
    of the *shu* would have made it a formidable weapon when
    wielded laterally. See Hubei 1989, 1: 292, fig. 178:3.
3   The discussion that follows is based on the excavation
    report. See Hubei 1989, 1:293 – 295.
4   Hubei 1989, 1:295. Two types of *shu* are listed in the bam-
    boo slips buried in the tomb: seven *shu* and nine *jin shu*.
    The report suggests that the bladed *shu* should be identi-
    fied with the *shu* and the bladeless form with the *jin shu*.
5   Anhui 1956, 11 and pl. 22:4 – 5. A variant of this type,
    distinguished by a row of spikes at the base of the blade,
    was found in a late sixth-century BCE Chu tomb at
    Caojiagang, Dangyang county, Hubei province (Hubei
    1988, 482 – 483, fig. 30, pl. 18:3). This type seems to have
    been the precursor of a *shu* with long spikes found in
    Marquis Yi's tomb (Hubei 1989, 1:292, fig. 178:3).

104

Two bronze mat weights

Height 8.0 (3 ⅛), diam. 11.8 (4 ⅝)
Warring States Period (c. 433 BCE)
From Leigudun, Suixian, Hubei Province

Hubei Provincial Museum, Wuhan

These are two of a set of four weights (zhen) found
in the eastern chamber of Marquis Yi's tomb.[1] Each
depicts eight intertwined dragons in high relief.
Attached to the arched body of one dragon is a ring
handle; circular sockets between the bodies of the
dragons would originally have held inlay. The high
degree of undercutting of the dragons' bodies implies that the weights were cast using the lost-wax
method.

These weights were probably used to secure
mats woven of bamboo or reed. Remains of mats
have been frequently found in Chu tombs and
clearly constituted an indispensable household
article.[2] Carved stone reliefs from the Han period
show figures seated on low platforms or on what
seem to be mats placed on the floor. Mats are often
mentioned in the Yi li (Book of ceremonial) as part
of the paraphernalia of ceremonials, and their
correct placement in ritual use seems to have
been a matter of some concern.

These are the earliest bronze zhen recovered.
They exemplify the broadening scope of the
bronzecaster, who increasingly was commissioned
to produce not only ritual vessels and weapons
but everyday articles as well. A number of similarly
shaped bronze objects have been found in tombs of
the Warring States and Han periods,[3] and the Chu ci
(Songs of Chu) makes reference to "weights of white
jade with which to hold the mats."[4] It is unlikely,
however, that jade mat weights existed outside the
imagination of poets; all examples of such objects
recovered thus far are of bronze or lead. CM

1 Excavated in 1978 (E 4, E 94, E 109, E 138); reported:
   Hubei 1989, 1:244 – 247, fig. 141:3, and 2: pl. 81:4 – 5.
2 See Hubei 1989, 1:387, fig. 241:4, and 2: pl. 146. Six mats
   were found in the fourth-century BCE Chu Tomb 1 at
   Xinyang Changtaiguan in southern Henan province; most
   were about one meter wide and bound with silk at the
   edges. See Henan 1986, pl. 68:1 – 3.
3 A pair of domed-shaped, bronze objects, 8.6 (3 ⅜) wide,
   with ring handles was excavated from Tomb 1 at Sihui
   Niaodanshan in Guangdong province. See He 1985, 362,
   fig. 3:8. A set of four square weights filled with lead was
   found in a tomb at Beiling Songshan near Zhaoqing in
   Guangdong province. See Guangdong 1974, 73, fig. 13.
   Four zhen in the form of leopards inlaid with gold, silver,
   and agate were excavated from the tomb of Dou Wan
   (d. c. 113 BCE) at Mancheng. These have been identified
   as either paper or mat weights. Zhongguo 1980b, 1:265
   and 2: color pl. 26.
4 Lady of the Xiang, trans. Hawkes 1985, 108.

105

Gold *zhan* bowl and *bi* spoon

zhan: height 11.0 (4⅜), diam. at mouth 15.1 (5⅞)
bi: length 13 (5⅛)
Warring States Period (c. 433 BCE)
From Leigudun, Suixian, Hubei Province

Hubei Provincial Museum, Wuhan

Unlike the bronze ritual vessels and bell chime, which were placed in the main chamber, this covered bowl and spoon were found with other gold objects in the tomb's eastern chamber.[1] The location suggests that these objects were not for ritual purposes, as were many of the objects placed in the chamber, but intended for the marquis' personal use and enjoyment. The spoon was found inside the bowl, indicating that they composed a set. Perforations in the bowl of the spoon suggest

that it might have been used to scoop meat or vegetables from a broth or to serve grain.[2]

Unlike the majority of the ritual bronzes from the tomb, the vessel does not bear an inscription; nevertheless, certain aspects of the style indicate that it was cast in Zeng foundries. The S-shaped zoomorphic feet are simplified versions of the creatures that support some of the bronzes from the tomb, such as the *jin* stand for the *hu* (cat. 96). The decoration — dragon interlace on the bowl and squared spirals and rope twist on the cover — echoes that on a bronze *ding*, inscribed with Marquis Yi's name, from the tomb's central chamber.[3]

The spoon is made of electrum (87.45 percent gold and 12.55 percent silver), a naturally occurring alloy.[4] The bowl has not been analyzed but is undoubtedly of similar composition. The thickness of the metal indicates that the piece was cast rather than hammered from sheets, the conventional method of forming vessels in precious metals in other parts of the ancient world.[5] Casting, whether using ceramic section-molds or the lost-wax method, requires a more extravagant use of metal than does hammering; the piece thus testifies to the application of traditional Chinese bronzecasting techniques to vessels in precious metals despite their relative wastefulness of the metal. Hammering was, however, commonly used to create precious-metal plaques. Over nine hundred such plaques, probably appliqués for armor,[6] were found in Marquis Yi's tomb, mostly in the northern chamber; Tomb 2 at Xiasi, Xichuan (sixth century BCE) contained similarly hammered precious-metal plaques. Solid gold vessels, on the other hand, are virtually unknown in pre-Han period China, presumably because of the material's cost. The only other excavated piece is an oval bowl with jade handles from Tomb 306 (early fifth century BCE) at Shaoxing in Zhejiang province;[7] the piece is considerably smaller, however, than Marquis Yi's bowl.

Identification of this bowl as a *zhan* rests on its similarity to a bronze bowl-and-cover type identified in their inscriptions as *zhan* or *yu*.[8] Such vessels were important in the Chu state and apparently were derived, over the course of the seventh century BCE, from *gui* grain containers. In its new form, the vessel assumed a more spherical shape; the *gui*'s massive handles were reduced in size, and the ring foot was replaced by three small zoomorphic legs. During the sixth century, these appendages were often cast in openwork, as exemplified by a *yu* of Chu Wang Xiong Shen (Gong Wang, r. 590–560 BCE);[9] the elaborate openwork of these sixth-century examples shows that they were clearly important vessels, but it is not certain whether they continued to serve a ritual function during that period. The placement of a gold *zhan* in the central chamber of Marquis Yi's tomb, as well as the absence of bronze forms of such vessels from the tomb's central chamber, suggests that by the second half of the fifth century this ritual object had become private treasure. CM

1   Excavated in 1978 (E 2); reported: Hubei 1989, 1:390–392, figs. 242–243:1, and 2: color pl. 17. The objects were discovered beneath the marquis' coffin near a gold goblet and two gold lids that may originally have covered vessels made of now-decomposed organic materials. Four gold belt hooks were found within the marquis' inner coffin. See Hubei 1989, 1: 392–393 and 399, figs. 243–244.
2   A similar openwork bronze spoon was found in Tomb 1 at Mashan in Jiangling Province. See Hubei 1985a, pl. 33:1.
3   See Hubei 1989, 1: 200, fig. 101.
4   Hubei 1989, 1: 393, table 45. See *Dictionary of Art*, s.v. "metalwork"; *Encyclopaedia Britannica*, s.v. "electrum."
5   Thomas Chase states that the piece was cast, although he cites no evidence for this (see Chase 1991, 31). For a discussion of casting versus hammering techniques, see Bagley 1987, 16–17.
6   See Henan 1991, 203–208 and pls. 73–76; Hubei 1989, 1:390–399 and pls. 148–149.
7   See Jiangsu 1984, 10–28, pl. 5:1.
8   See the Chu Wang Xiong Shen *yu* (Metropolitan Museum of Art, New York, Accession no. 199–165.24a–b) and the X yu Wei (?) *zhan* from Yidigang, Suixian: Cheng and Liu 1983, no. 1, 75, fig. 3. See Tan and Bai 1986, no. 3, 58.
9   See also an example of this type from Tomb 2 at Xichuan Xiasi: Henan 1991, pl. 32.

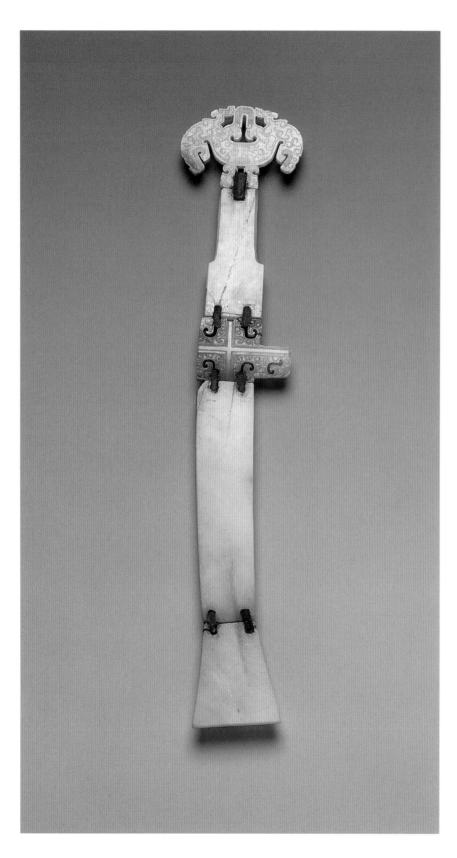

106

Jade pendant in the shape of a sheathed dagger

Length 33.6 (13 ¼), width 5.1 (2)
Warring States Period (c. 433 BCE)
From Leigudun, Suixian, Hubei Province

Hubei Provincial Museum, Wuhan

This unique belt pendant[1] was found in the inner coffin of the marquis, placed next to his waist; it may have originally been attached to a belt of organic material, now decomposed. The object is composed of five thin jade slices approximately 0.5 centimeter thick, joined by metal clips to form a gently curved profile. Unlike some composite jades formed of movable parts joined by links, the clips that join these pieces do not allow the parts to swivel. The impression of silk weave visible on the clips indicates that the piece was originally in contact with silk.[2]

The most elaborate part of the object is the pommel, composed of two addorsed downward-facing dragons, whose foreheads and necks form the outer profiles of the piece. Their bodies join at the center in a broad U, and their claws form the top of the pommel. Three perforations give the impression of two eyes and a mouth joined to a nose; fine incising and striations decorate the object's surface.

The hilt is formed by a plain narrow section, which widens to indicate the top of the scabbard. The middle element of the assemblage, slightly convex in cross section, has an integrally carved hook on the back, possibly to attach the object to a belt; the tongue projecting to the right may have been intended to represent a sword-guard.[3] The assemblage terminates in a flaring section that anticipates jade scabbard chapes from the latter part of the Warring States period.[4]

This object raises intriguing (but as yet unanswerable) questions about the symbolic role of swords and daggers during the Eastern Zhou period. Short swords had been introduced from northwest regions during the Middle Western Zhou period; by the Early Eastern Zhou period, they were in common use in the central plains area. In the southeast, swords developed independently — from short daggers that may themselves have developed out of spear blades. Swords associated with kings of the Wu state were widely known by the end of the sixth century BCE and were given as gifts to friendly neighboring states. In the Chu sphere, however, swords were rare until the fourth century BCE.[5] It is noteworthy that no swords appear among the thousands of weapons contained in the tomb of Marquis Yi (although the soldier caryatids supporting the bell rack are depicted wearing swords). Moreover, this pendant's curved profile seems to imitate not a sword but rather a type of curved knife with ring handle known as *xiao*. (There is no evidence, however, that such knives were furnished with scabbards.[6]) This object may therefore represent a fusion of two different types: the curved knife familiar in Zeng and Chu territory and the more prestigious Wu sword, examples of which may not have been available to the marquis. CM

1 Excavated in 1978 (EC 11:99); reported: Hubei 1989, 1:419–421, and 2: color pl. 20:2, pl. 160:1, 2.

2 Hubei 1989, 1:421. The report does not state whether the clips are gold or bronze. The fact that they have corroded suggests the former.

3 It is not clear why the tongue projects only to one side. This section may be a partly recarved fragment of an existing blade.

4 Jessica Rawson observes that jade chapes were a relatively late addition to the repertoire of jade sword fittings. See Rawson 1995, 298, no. 21:8.

5 Only two swords were found among the Chu tombs at Xichuan, Xiasi. Excavated from the Late Warring States period Tomb M 11, they were probably imports. See Henan 1991, 306, fig. 233:6–7.

6 For a *xiao* from Marquis Yi's tomb, see Hubei 1989, 2: pl. 84. The earliest surviving wooden scabbard was found in a seventh-century BCE tomb of a noble of the Huang state. It sheathed a straight sword rather than the curved knife that is represented by the Marquis Yi jade. See Xinyang 1989b, 26–32, figs. 5:4, 7, and pl. 3:4.

Lacquer is a natural substance extracted from a tree indigenous to the Far East, *rhus verniciflua,* that grows in areas of up to five hundred meters in altitude with an average temperature of 8 to 20 degrees Celsius and an average annual rainfall of more than 60 millimeters.[1] Even under ideal conditions, mature lacquer trees produce a very small quantity of the substance. Once collected, raw lacquer (a highly toxic substance) needs to be clarified and processed before being stored in airtight containers. Application of the lacquer to the underlying object and the drying period between coats require specific conditions of temperature (between 25 and 30 degrees Celsius) and humidity (between 75 and 85 percent). The processing of lacquer and manufacture of lacquerware thus required a succession of operations, and workshops included highly skilled and specialized craftsmen.

The two present-day provinces that compose the approximate geographic area of the Chu kingdom — Hunan and Hubei — have yielded an abundance of lacquerware dating back three centuries prior to the advent of the Qin empire in 221 BCE. Several major discoveries were made in the area during the twentieth century. In the 1930s, Hunan was celebrated for the splendid lacquerware discovered in uncontrolled digs around Changsha; some of these pieces are now in museums and private collections in the West. In the 1960s, a construction boom associated with Hubei's rising population led to the discovery of several important sites in the Jiangling area; in the years since, hundreds of tombs (some of them very large) have been excavated.

Recovered objects, often perfectly preserved, have yielded a wealth of information about the development of lacquer techniques and decoration during what appears to have been the most important period in the evolution of this craft.[2] The evidence suggests the development of two independent traditions in lacquerware — one in the Chu kingdom, the other in the Qin kingdom — prior to the formation of the empire.

Discoveries from Hunan and Hubei indicate that several categories of objects were lacquered to take advantage of specific properties of the substance — the decorative aspect of its glossy surface, its durability, its imperviousness to liquids, and its protective qualities. The contents of Marquis Yi's tomb testify to the extensive and varied use of lacquer during the fifth century in domestic objects (containers and utensils for daily life, furniture), musical instruments (zithers, flutes, drums, mouth organs), weapons (shields, armor, halberd shafts), funerary items (coffins, carved wooden figures), chariots, and architectural elements.[3] Lacquer was most often applied to a wood base, but also to leather and bronze. The range of colors — at least until the Han period — was limited; black and red lacquers, the latter made with cinnabar or a substitute, were the most common. Motifs painted with two additional colors — yellow and brown — begin to appear, however, on a few pieces of lacquerware from the fifth century BCE, including items from the tomb of Marquis Yi. The tomb evidence (in particular, cats. 107 and 111) also testifies to the development of pictorial subjects in lacquerwork by the fifth century BCE.

A succession of innovations during the fourth century furthered the exploitation of the decorative and technical properties of lacquer. Improvements in wood carving, together with advances in joinery techniques, gave rise to the manufacture of highly refined objects (cat. 108). The invention of the lathe made it possible to create thin-walled, round containers, and a technique, developed in the fourth century BCE, of curving thinly sliced pieces of wood by exposing them to fire, hot water, or steam permitted the manufacture of delicate cylindrical shapes. In the fifth or fourth century BCE, lacquer artisans devised a process — the so-called dry-lacquer technique — for the manufacture of luxury objects: pieces of fabric, such as hemp, were joined over a clay model, and the cloth was coated with layers of lacquer, sometimes mixed with ash powder; after each coating, once the lacquer had dried, the surface was finely sanded, and the process repeated as many times as necessary to obtain a perfectly smooth finish. Finally, the use of new pigments extended the range of lacquer decoration. These were ground to a very fine powder, mixed with oil (rather than directly into the raw lacquer, which makes many colors turn black), and applied to the surface of the lacquerware. At least ten colors, including shades of orange, turquoise, and green (the latter two being particularly difficult to manufacture) were used to decorate a circular toilet box discovered in Tomb 2 at Baoshan.[4] These innovations took place within a short period — a century or so — probably in response to patrons' demands.[5]

Lacquerware developed its own aesthetic, and it had a profound influence on all the other applied arts from the same period, including bronzework (cat. 115). As the kingdoms and principalities strengthened their relations with one another through commercial exchange and military alliances during the fourth and third centuries BCE, cultural interactions and cross-influences developed to a far greater extent than previously — and particularly so in the arts and crafts. Comparisons of lacquerwork from Chu tombs in Hubei (before 278 BCE) and Hunan (fourth to third century BCE) with pieces from the Qin sites of Qingchuan in Sichuan (late fourth to early third century BCE) and Shuihudi (Yunmeng) in Hubei (c. mid-third to mid-second century BCE) illustrate the geographic development of lacquer craftsmanship.[6] New production processes — in particular, the use of curved wood in bronze fittings and dry-lacquer techniques — seem to have been much more highly developed and widely used among the Qin than in Chu culture, where their application was limited to luxury items. AT

1   Regarding the processing of lacquer and the manufacture of lacquerware, see Garner 1979.
2   Hou 1995; Hubei 1994; Thote 1990.
3   Hubei 1989, 45–55, 151–175, 252–390.
4   Hubei 1991, 1:144–146; 2: color pl. 7–8.
5   Thote 1990.
6   See, respectively, Hubei 1994, Shang 1957, Beijing 1954, Sichuan 1982, 1–21; Yunmeng 1981.

107

Duck-shaped painted lacquer *he* box

Height 16.5 (6 ½), length 20.1 (7 ⅞), width 12.5 (4 ⅞)
Warring States Period (c. 433 BCE)
From the tomb of Zenghou Yi at Leigudun, Suixian,
Hubei Province

Hubei Provincial Museum, Wuhan

Washington only

This box[1] was discovered in the tomb's western
chamber, which contained the remains of thirteen
sacrificial victims resting in lacquered coffins. Compared to the contents of the other chambers, the
objects buried with these young girls were both scant
and modest, but this box is remarkable for the high
quality of its execution and its unusual shape. Carved
in the round, it is composed of three separate pieces:
the bird's head and neck, the body (formed of two
glued halves), and the lid of the box. Two openings
are carved into the top: one to accommodate the
rectangular lid; the other, cut at the front, within
which the bird's head is secured by means of a tenon.
Two small wooden nails anchor the tenon; they also
allow the head to move left or right.

The entire surface of the piece is lacquered
in black and decorated with paintings in red and
yellow. The features of the bird are carefully detailed; the remaining decoration comprises an
assortment of motifs largely unrelated to the representation of the bird itself — scales, zigzag lines,
and dots. Panels on the sides of the object depict
musicians. On one side, a human figure strikes a
yongzhong chime bell with a long mallet; the bell is
suspended (together with a larger bell and two
chime stones) on a stand in the shape of two birds
confronting each other. On the other side of the
box, a warrior dances, while a musician plays a
drum positioned on a vertical pole placed in an
animal-shaped pedestal. The three figures represented in the images bear strange features: apparently naked, with disproportionately small heads,
they may be men (perhaps shamans) wearing masks
for ritual or ceremonial purposes, or, as seems
more likely, supernatural beings.

The naturalistic sculptural representation of
the object itself is somewhat at odds with the
execution of its painted images. Ignoring correct
proportions or otherwise lifelike representation,
the artist's main concern seems to have been to
create recognizable images within a small frame:
accordingly, he emphasizes the most important
details. The bird that supports the right side of the
stand is represented in full, but only half of its

complement on the left is portrayed — we can guess the form of the second figure from the first. The musician's long mallet is bent (rather than straight as it would have been in reality) to illustrate the musician striking the bell. Bells and chime stones are here suspended together on the same stand, a representation belied by archeological evidence: the Leigudun chimes, as well as chimes from other known sites, indicate that bells and stones were invariably hung on separate stands.

Only one other piece comparable to the bird-shaped box has been found — a stemmed *dou* with a lid found at Yutaishan, Jiangling (Hubei province).[2] The decoration of the cup itself is more naturalistic in style than that of the Leigudun box, and the motif that decorates the stem — diagonal lines ending in spirals — is typical of the latter part of the fourth century BCE. AT

1   Excavated in 1978; published: Hubei 1989, 1:363–365, figs. 222–224, and 2: color pl. 14 and pl. 130; Tokyo 1992, no. 13; Goepper 1995, no. 72; Rawson 1996, no. 65; Tokyo 1998a, no. 11.
2   Hubei 1984a, 102, fig. 77.1; color pl. 1 and pl. 61.

108

Painted lacquer *dou* container

Height 24.3 (9 ⅝)
Warring States Period (c. 433 BCE)
From the tomb of Zenghou Yi at Leigudun, Suixian,
Hubei Province

Hubei Provincial Museum, Wuhan

One of a pair of identical cups from Marquis Yi's
tomb, this *dou*[1] was discovered in the burial chamber, together with a pair of similarly shaped, but
slightly taller and differently decorated stemmed
cups. The placement of these objects suggests that
they were intended for the marquis' personal use
and not for ritual.

This *dou,* which presents a massive, even architectural profile, is composed of two parts: the body

and the lid, each carved from a single piece of
wood (fig. 1). The domed lid has an almost oval
section, compressed on two sides to accommodate
the two large handles supported by the rim of the
cup. The walls of the shallow cup flare out smoothly
and rest on a massive stem, which tapers evenly to a
wide, flared base. Given its shallow interior, the cup
was apparently not intended to hold much food.

The decoration of the object is based on contrasts of colors and technique. The top of the lid
and the entire surface of the handles are carved in
raised relief, with motifs so intricate as to be individually nearly indiscernible. In the middle of the
lid, an oval medallion represents three dragons
facing outward and swallowing up other dragons;
only the claws, eyes (represented by two red dots),
and mouths of the creatures are clearly outlined;

the dragons' bodies are composed of abstract ornaments with no zoomorphic attributes. The handles draw the dragon motif out to an even greater level of complexity: only two heads, staring at each other with almond-shaped eyes, can be clearly seen. Each seems to be holding the rim of the cup in its mouth — or perhaps trying to get at food inside.

In contrast, the surface decoration of the object, composed of geometric designs rendered in various contrasting techniques, seems less fluid — even static. Some of these designs are engraved and their lines filled with red color against a black background; others are simply painted on. A few intertwined motifs are outlined in black against a background composed of thin, parallel red lines that intersect at right angles. The remaining designs, flat and plain, are set in red against black, or in black against red. The diversity of the design does not, however, entirely mask a fundamental coherence: even the most abstract motifs are based on the dragon pattern.

Clearly, the *dou* presented a number of technical challenges to its craftsmen — challenges that they met with remarkable skill and inventiveness. Even had lathe turning been available to the artisans (it was not introduced until the very end of the fifth century or the beginning of the fourth), the oval shape of the cup and the lid would have precluded use of the technique. Though mortise-and-tenon joinery was a common technique in the Chu lacquerware workshops of the period, and might have been used to attach separately carved handles to the cup, the object was carved out of a solid piece of wood. The limited palette available to lacquer artisans of the period (essentially, red and black) was overcome by using a combination of techniques for ornamentation — engraving, carved relief, and painting; indeed the craftsmen seem to have made use of all possible solutions within their limited range of decorative possibilities. A yellow lacquer may have been used as well for the cup's surface decoration; the excavators of the site report that traces of a gold (or gold-yellow) pigment were visible on the *dou* when it was found but vanished soon afterward. Certainly, the color was available: yellow lacquer appears in the paintings on the inner and outer coffins of Marquis Yi.[2] AT

1   Excavated in 1978; published: Hubei 1989, 1:368 – 369, fig. 227; 2: color pl. 15 and pl. 132; Tokyo 1992, no. 12; Hubei 1994, no. 9; Tokyo 1998a, no. 12.
2   Hubei 1989, 1:28.

109

Painted lacquer deer

Height 77 (30), length 45 (17 ⅝),
height of torso 27 (10 ⅝)
Warring States Period (c. 433 BCE)
From the tomb of Zenghou Yi at Leigudun, Suixian,
Hubei Province

Hubei Provincial Museum, Wuhan

Placed in the marquis' burial chamber, this figure of a recumbent deer[1] is the more elaborate of two deer found in Tomb 1 at Leigudun; the other sculpture was placed in the central chamber with the ritual bronzes. The head and the body are separately carved from single pieces of wood, and the head rotates left and right on the neck so that the animal can be positioned to look straight ahead or to the side. The sculpture evidences an artistic sensibility that was quite new in the fifth century BCE: the deer reclines on its legs in a natural posture, and its head seems to have been copied from nature (the antlers are in fact real deer antlers, fixed in holes carved into the wood). Black lacquer covers the entire surface of the wood, and against this background, small, almond-shaped designs, together with myriad tiny dots, are painted in red lacquer to imitate fur. The antlers are decorated

with black triangles and scrolls. The materials and the quality of the workmanship indicate that this was a luxury object; pieces of lower quality were usually coated with ink.

A square hole is cut into the back of the deer, probably to attach an object such as a drum; several deer-shaped drum stands have been found over the years in Chu tombs in the Jiangling district of Hubei province and, to a lesser extent, in Hunan province.[2] Some stands were made to support real drums (fig. 1); others supported replicas in plain wood. The drum found in the eastern chamber of the marquis' tomb was not associated with this stand; the three rings attached to the drum strongly suggest that it originally hung from the antlered cranelike figure (cat. 100) found in the tomb.

In many cases, however, wooden figures of reclining deer did not serve as stands but rather as auspicious figures intended to protect the tomb and the deceased.[3] Most, if not all, such guardian objects were placed at the head of the outer coffin, as evidenced in the seven tombs at Yutaishan, Jiangling.[4] AT

1 Excavated in 1978; published: Hubei 1989, 1:381, fig. 238; 2: color pl. 16, pl. 142; Tokyo 1992, no. 11; Tokyo 1998a, no. 21.
2 Several tombs in the Jiangling district contained such drum stands, in particular, Tombs 2 and 11 at Paimashan (see Hubei 1973, 158, fig. 12, and pl. 9.1); Tomb 7 at Xi'eshan (see Hubei 1984b, 525, fig. 14); and Tomb 10 at Wuchangyidi (see Jiangling 1989, 49, fig. 38.1).
3 Tomb 1 at Tengdian, Jiangling, Hubei province (see Jingzhou 1973, 12, pl. 4.1); Tomb 1 at Liuchengqiao, Changsha, Hunan province (see Hunan 1972, pl. 10); and three tombs from the cemetery at Jiudian, Jiangling, Hubei province (see Hubei 1995, 306, fig. 208.3 and pl. 93.3).
4 Hubei 1984a, 108a, and 111, fig. 89.2.

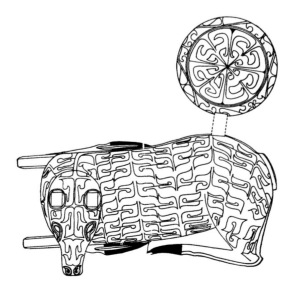

FIG. 1. Painted lacquer deer-shaped drum stand from Tomb 7 at Xi'eshan, Jiangling, Hubei province; Warring States period; length 45 (17 ¾). After Hubei 1984b, 525, fig. 14.

110

Painted lacquer screen

Height 15 (5⅞), width 51.8 (20⅜)
Middle Warring States Period, c. middle or second
half of the fourth century BCE
From Tomb 1 at Wangshan, Jiangling,
Hubei Province

Hubei Provincial Museum, Wuhan

This small screen, which stands on two nearly
square feet, is made of a rectangular frame set with
various animals carved in the round.[1] The somewhat static composition of two symmetrical groups
of figures is enlivened by the figures themselves:
All the animals, even the smallest, are engaged in
combat, and they are rendered with an attention
to proportion and detail likely taken from direct
observation. Deer, frogs, and two different species
of birds — the main figures in the composition —
battle intertwined serpents; the snakes bite or
menace the deer and the frogs, while the birds
aggressively seize the snakes with their claws or
grasp them in their beaks as if to swallow them. At

the base of the stand (probably intended to represent the subterranean world), intertwined snakes,
densely massed, are caught in the act of smothering
small birds. Such reptilian iconography was particularly developed in the art of the Chu kingdom.[2]

The images of attack and escape are imaginatively presented to pull the viewer into the scene.
Attacked from behind, one of the frogs in each of
the panels faces out, while the other is seen from
the rear; deer are captured in flight as they seek,
vainly, to escape the serpents. The composition can
be interpreted as a representation of life and death
— and particularly of violent (albeit natural) death.

Animal combat scenes from pre-imperial China
only rarely display such naturalism and keen observation. Probably influenced by animal representations from the steppe regions,[3] Chinese artists
made use of the theme from the sixth century BCE on.

The screen can be viewed from any angle —
even the narrow sides and areas normally obscured
from sight are decorated with interlaced serpents
— evidence of the high quality of this refined
sculpture (fig. 1). The figures are carved separately

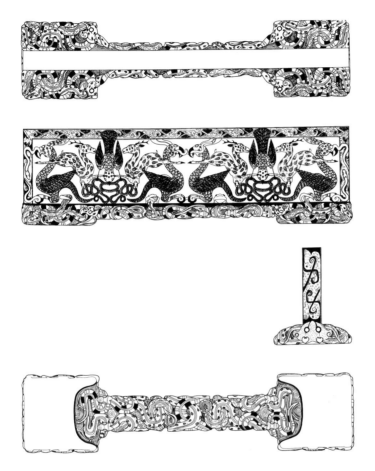

and secured within the wooden frame; layers of black and brown lacquer cover the frame and part of the animals, while details of the carvings are picked out in colors, including red, blue, silver-gray, and yellow. Some of the colors have faded in the years since the discovery of the screen, and the original decoration probably included other pigments that have not survived (though the date of this screen coincides with the practice of mixing pigments in oil — rather than directly into raw lacquer — to ensure the stability of the color). The level of the screen's artistry and craftsmanship is representative of the works of art made for the elite of the Chu kingdom, and even perhaps for members of the royal family. AT

1   Excavated in 1965; published: Hubei 1966, 47, fig. 19; pls. 2 and 3; Juliano 1975; Hubei 1994, no. 1; Hubei 1996, fig. 66, color pl. 2 and pls. 33–34; Tokyo 1998a, no. 28.
2   Thote 1993.
3   Jacobson 1988.

FIG. 1. Cat. 110: from above; horizontal view; from side; from below. Adapted from Hubei 1996, 94, fig. 66.

111a

111

Two painted lacquer *erbei* cups

a. Length 15.7 (6 ⅛), maximum width 12.6 (5)
b. Length 18.1 (7), maximum width 13.3 (5 ¼)
Late Warring States Period, c. early third
century BCE
From Tomb 1 at Mashan, Jiangling, Hubei Province

Jingzhou Prefecture Museum, Hubei Province

These two oval cups[1] (*erbei*, or ear cups, so called because of the two earlike extensions at the rim) are part of a large set of eating and drinking vessels found in a compartment at the head of the outer coffin from Tomb 1 at Mashan. Carefully packed inside a bamboo casket, the set is composed of several lacquered pieces (twelve *erbei*, two boxes) and bronze vessels (two *erbei*, one *hu* wine container, two tripod *ding*, a large ladle and spoon, as well as a *yi* and a *pan* basin for washing the hands).

The earliest *erbei* known to date were excavated from an eighth-century BCE tomb in Hubei province.[2] During the Warring States period, at least two main types were in use within the Chu kingdom: the shape of the vessel is the predominant criterion for defining the typology. The first is characterized by quite large angular and pointed projections, while cups of the second type (represented by these examples) have small rounded "ears." In both cases, these appendages are generally raised. The projections on the larger cup are beveled rather than raised, a subtype represented only rarely among burial vessels and of later date than the two conventional forms.[3] That this beveled *erbei* is the sole such example among the Mashan lacquerware earcups (as well as its larger size) suggests that it was reserved for a specific use (or user) during meals.

Both cups are decorated with unusual motifs in somewhat heterogeneous styles. The first cup is painted with cinnabar red, yellow, and pale yellow. Touches of gold decorate a dark red background on the inner surface; the outer surface is painted in black background (the colors have changed since the excavation). Two large birds symmetrically frame a quatrefoil motif at the center, an

unusual arrangement executed with great elegance; each bird is composed of four volutes that curve alternately in opposite directions. The remaining decoration is composed of scrolls and diagonal lines — traditional motifs in the repertoire of Chu lacquer decoration from the fourth century BCE to the third.

The second cup has an entirely abstract decoration — unsymmetrical at first glance (and for that reason unusual in pre-imperial China), but in fact forming a composition similar to the bird-and-quatrefoil motif of the other *erbei*. This example is one of the earliest known objects to make use of these design innovations, created at the very end of the fourth century BCE and fully developed in the third century. The range of the artists' skills displayed by these two cups is remarkable — spanning figures taken from nature (albeit not naturalistic) rendered with painstaking attention to detail, to large and purely abstract designs. The red and black volutes on the second *erbei* are rendered so that they may be viewed as red ornaments on a black background or, alternatively, black-on-red — an ambiguous and apparently deliberate visual effect. Whatever their meaning, such effects were clearly valued by the artists and by their patrons. AT

1　Excavated in 1982 (17-1, 17-2); published: Hubei 1985a, 78, figs. 64.1, 64.4; color pls. 29.1, 29.3, 29.4, and pl. 36.
2　Tomb 1 at Anju, Suizhou, Hubei province. See Suizhou 1982, 53.
3　The earliest known example was excavated from Tomb 1 at Shazhong, Jiangling, in Hubei province. See Hubei 1996, 189, fig. 126.3.

TOMB 1

AT MASHAN,

JIANGLING,

HUBEI PROVINCE

In 689 BCE King Wen moved the capital of Chu from Danyang to Ying (near present-day Jiangling in Hubei province). Traces of its surrounding wall are all that remain of the ancient city, but until its conquest by the Qin state in 278 BCE, Ying was center of political and cultural life in central China.[1] The twenty-eight hundred tombs discovered between 1961 and 1982 on the site of the city and its environs are an indication of its importance.[2] Nearly a third of these tombs were each furnished with a large wooden outer coffin (*guo*) and one or more inner coffins (*guan*); well-preserved tombs from the sites at Baoshan,[3] Yutaishan[4] and Mashan[5] have yielded a dazzling array of tomb furnishings: bronze ritual vessels, bells, and weapons; horse armor and trappings; chariot fittings; leather and jade objects; sculptures of imaginary beasts rendered in bronze or wood; funeral inventories and other documents written on bamboo slips; colorfully decorated lacquerware; coffin mats; and exquisite silk clothing and shrouds.

Tomb 1 at Mashan was discovered in January 1982 in the brickyard of the Mashan commune, located approximately sixteen kilometers north of the present-day city of Jiangling and eight kilometers north of Ji'nan. The tomb — an oblong pit with vertical walls containing an outer coffin and a single inner coffin placed along an east-west axis — was a comparatively modest type common among low-ranking aristocrats known as *shi* (knights).[6]

The tomb's "outer coffin" — a chamber (*guoshi*) 248 centimeters long, 106 centimeters high, and 149 centimeters wide — was built of massive, 18-centimeter-thick boards cut from the center of a Chinese variety of zelkova (*ju; Zelkova schneideriana*). A herringbone-patterned mat (*renziwen*), 330 centimeters long and 189 centimeters wide, lined the interior; lime mortar sealed the coffin and preserved its contents from the depredations of water, insects, tomb robbers, and, to some extent, decay.[7] The outer coffin comprised three separate compartments: the largest compartment contained the inner coffin, which held the corpse of the deceased; a long side-compartment held grave goods, bamboo baskets and mats, a variety of pottery vessels, grave figurines, and the skeleton of a small dog. The third compartment, located at the head of the corpse, contained an extraordinary imaginary beast carved from a root, a neck-rest of woven bamboo, two bamboo boxes containing bronze and lacquer vessels, and several wooden figurines of attendants dressed in silk.

The inner coffin (200 centimeters long, 67 centimeters wide, and 61 centimeters high) was made of Chinese catalpa (*zi, Lindera zimu, Hemsl.*). The lid and sides were covered by a dark brown plain silk casing (*huangwei*)[8] ornamented with lozenge-pattern trimmings, held in position by three hemp bands. A twig of bamboo, still green when the outer coffin was opened, and a piece of fine, plain silk (originally painted) lay on top of the casing.

The unnamed woman buried in Mashan Tomb 1 died between the age of forty and forty-five, sometime between 340 and 278 BCE. She was approximately 160 centimeters tall, and her outstretched body (of which only the skeleton and hair, covered by a wig, remain), was wrapped in cloth, placed on a board carved with geometrical patterns, and encased in a woven bamboo mat. She belonged to the lower aristocratic class of *shi*, who probably were not entitled to wear

FIG. 1. Brocade bands securing the wrapped body.

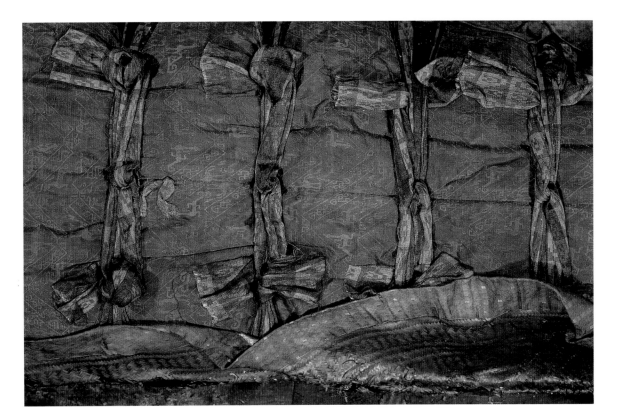

patterned silk garments, yet she was buried with thirty-five astonishingly well-preserved pieces of silk clothing, shrouds, and other articles of excellent quality. Her burial outfit is the earliest known example of its kind from China,[9] and it ranks among the best and most spectacular early textile finds ever made.

The body was tightly wrapped in layer on layer of shrouds and garments (figs. 1 and 2). Over a pair of open-seat trousers (the earliest example of underwear found in China[10]), she was dressed in, successively: a skirt; a lined robe; a short, embroidered gown; and a lozenge-patterned *shenyi* (the long, padded robe worn by aristocratic men and women for ritual and official ceremonies) (cat. 112a). Dressed in the garments that she would have worn in life, her upper and lower body were covered with special burial textiles *(mao* and *sha)*, and she was wrapped in a silk cloth, two shrouds *(qin)* of embroidered and weave patterns; and a padded coverlet of woven brocade[11] in a pattern depicting dancers and imaginary creatures (cat. 112b). The coverlet was secured by nine woven silk brocade bands in the so-called pagoda pattern (cat. 112c), wrapped in a shroud, and, finally, covered with another padded coverlet.

Several features are striking but unexplained. The woman's arms were fixed at breast level with a ribbon, her thumbs were tied to each other with red cord, and her big toes were tied with yellow cord; the ribbons and cords may been intended to keep the body intact.[12] Her hands held small silk rolls, fastened with strings to her middle fingers. (The use of such black-and-crimson silk rolls is described as "hold tight" [*wo*] in the ancient ritual texts.[13]) Her face

FIG. 2. The body, wrapped
and tied.

was covered by an unusual trapezoidal cloth of dark brown silk with *jin*-brocade trimming and a
dark yellow lining; openings for the eyes and nose had been cut in the fabric. (Normally face
covers [*mingmu*] were square, made of black silk with red lining, and did not have openings.[14])
A silk belt, from which jade and glass pendants were suspended, adorned the woman's waist.

The silk wardrobe, the silk shrouds, and other silk textiles — as well as the other burial
objects of high quality that were found in the coffin — are evidence of the custom of lavish
burials practiced by the aristocratic upperclass; the patterned silk fabrics themselves document
a flourishing regional silk weaving industry that catered to the tastes of a fashion-conscious
society. DK

1   Yu 1995, 130 – 131.

2   Kuhn 1992a, 40 – 65.

3   Hubei 1991. Five tombs were excavated at the Baoshan
    site.

4   Hubei 1984a. Five hundred and fifty-eight tombs were
    found at the site between November 1975 and February
    1976; 349 of these are dated to the Warring States period.

5   Hubei 1985a.

6   At the site of Yutaishan in Jiangling county alone, 248
    tombs of this type have been excavated: see Kuhn 1992,
    41; a typology of Chu tombs in the county of Jiangling was
    suggested by Guo 1982, 158; on the social ranking of this
    tomb see Peng Hao 1982, 12.

7   Kuhn 1996b, 16 – 17.

8   The coffin's silk casing is most probably the *shazhao*, used
    to conceal the coffin on its way to the grave site; it may
    have been placed on top of the coffin in the grave. For
    class differentiations in the use of silk, see Zhang Chang-
    shou 1992, 49 – 52; Kuhn 1995c, 65 – 66.

9   Rawson 1996, 144.

10 Hubei 1985a, 17, 23: fig. 24, pl. 16:1.

11 The typical *jin* brocade weave of the Warring States
    period was a polychrome two- or three-series warp-faced
    compound tabby.

12 Goepper 1995, 342.

13 Kuhn 1995b, 217.

14 Hubei 1985a, 97.

112

a. Embroidered *luo* gauze weave sleeve
Length 114 (44 ¾), width at cuff 32 (12 ½),
width at shoulder 49 (19 ¼)

b. Fragment of *jin* brocade body shroud
Length 73 (28 ¾), width 50 (19 ⅝)

c. *Jin* brocade band with woven "pagoda"
pattern
Length 84 (33 ⅛), width 23 (9 ½)

Late Warring States Period
(between 340 and 278 BCE)
From Tomb 1 at Mashan, Jiangling, Hubei Province

Jingzhou Prefecture Museum, Hubei Province

This sleeve (cat. 112a)[1] was originally part of an
unlined robe tailored from grayish white silk gauze
and embroidered with a complex design of dragons,
phoenixlike birds, and tigers *(longfenghu wenxiu)*
against a background of lavish, almost zoomorphic,
flowering tendrils.[2] The partially damaged robe

(196 centimeters long and opening to a width of
276 centimeters), trimmed with lozenge-patterned
jin brocade at the cuffs, neck, and lower hem,
composed the sixth layer of the Mashan tomb
occupant's body wrappings.

The robe's design of real and imaginary animals
embroidered in various colors — reddish brown,
brown, yellowish green, yellowish brown, black, gray,
and a radiant orange — is the only gauze-weave
embroidery from the tomb; the other embroideries
were stitched on a tabby ground. The robe is evidence of a demand for intricate motifs, executed in
luxurious materials, that could only be created by
hand. Although other fabrics from the tomb testify
to remarkable advances in weaving, such delicate
patterns of rich color and material diversity could
not have been produced on a loom, nor could a
loom have produced the lively and formally balanced rhythmic patterns of the hand embroidery.[3]

Gauze fabrics *(luo)* are light, very delicate, and
almost transparent weaves with many netlike holes.
(*Luo* originally meant a net for catching birds, a
meaning transferred to the gauze fabric with its
hexagonal holes.) The complex weaving technology
of gauze weaves can be traced back as early as the
Shang period.[4] Such translucent and lustrous silk
was a luxury clothing material in China, and, a few
centuries later, in classical Rome, where its price
matched that of gold.

A single pattern-unit measures 29.5 centimeters
by 21 centimeters. The silk threads used for the
chain stitches[5] range between 0.2 and 0.4 millimeters in diameter; the stitches themselves vary
from 2 to 2.4 millimeters in length and from 1 to
1.2 millimeters in width. The excavation report
describes this four crossed-warp plain gauze
(sijingjiao suluo) as a weave composed of groups of
four comparatively coarse (0.15 millimeters) warp
threads repeating the weave structure over the
entire width of the fabric.[6] The weft thread was
fine and untwisted. The warp and weft threads were
given an S-twist of 3,000 to 3,500 turns per meter,
which added to the elasticity needed in the weaving
process. In Han and pre-Han times the four
crossed-warp threads consist of two fixed ends

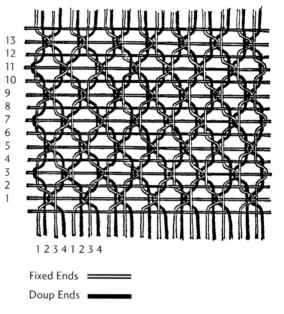

13
12
11
10
9
8
7
6
5
4
3
2
1

1 2 3 4 1 2 3 4

Fixed Ends ═══════
Doup Ends ▬▬▬▬▬

(dijing) and two doup ends *(jiaojing)*. At regular intervals (weft entry no. 1, 5, 9, 13 or no. 3, 7, 11) one of the doup ends of each group is drawn to the left by doup heddles, crosses under its corresponding fixed end and is lifted (fig. 1).[7] The weft entry (no. 1, 3, 5, 7 . . .) binds the doup end in its position. The following weft entry (no. 2, 4, 6, 8 . . .) is woven in tabby weave. After four weft entries (no. 1–4, 5–8, 9–12), the weaving process started to repeat.

The outermost wrapping of the occupant of Tomb 1 at Mashan was composed of five matching *jin*-brocade panels (of which one is represented in this exhibition [cat. 112b]), lined with a dark yellow, tabby-weave silk, and pieced together to form a shroud measuring 333 by 233 centimeters.[8] The two central pieces of the shroud measure the full length, the remaining three are approximately 166 centimeters long.[9]

A vertically repeating pattern of symmetrically paired figures — human dancers and imaginary creatures *(wuren dongwu wen)* — extends over the entire width of the fabric between zigzagging patterned rectangles. From right to left, these comprise (1) dragons with elongated necks; (2) singing dancers in robes and headdresses, swinging their long sleeves above their heads (compare cat. 146); (3) phoenixes with wings extended and elaborate

FIG. 1. Weave structure of four cross-warped plain gauze (cat. 112a). Drawing by D. Kuhn. *(left)*

tails; (4) crawling, amphibian-like dragons with long tongues; (5) unicorn-like creatures; (6) upside-down phoenixes with raised wings; (7) addorsed dragons; and (8) another pair of crawling dragons.

The *jin* brocade of the Warring States period was a polychrome, warp-faced compound tabby weave. The warp in this textile is composed of threads slightly twisted in an S-direction (the ground warps are dark yellow and brown; the patterning warp is dark red); the weft is dark brown. The thread count of the warp and weft amounts to 156:52 per centimeter, which means that the pattern unit in weft direction comprises approximately 7,660 ends over a width of 49.1 centimeters. The pattern unit in warp direction repeats after 286 picks, or 5.5 centimeters. A small weaving flaw (an error in preparing the loom) runs consistently through the patterned rectangles that divide the seventh from the eighth figural scene, evidence that a mechanical device was used to make the pattern during the weaving.[10]

Technologically, as well as artistically, the Mashan Tomb 1 *jin* brocade constitutes one of the most complex woven figural designs thus far excavated in China. Stiff and angular geometric patterns — imposed to some extent by the limitations of early loom technology — here give way to designs

that imitate embroidered textiles and incorporate images, both human and imaginary, derived from other media, as well as from literary sources. Translating hand-executed embroidery designs into a loom pattern meant that these designs could be repeated almost endlessly — reproducing the size, shape, and color of a given pattern. This translation of handwork to loom technology was a remarkable step toward the large-scale production of fabrics with sophisticated and complex weave designs.[11]

Nine silk bands (cat. 112c),[12] woven in *jin*-brocade in a "pagoda" pattern *(taxingwen)* and measuring between 211 and 227 centimeters in length and between 45 and 49 centimeters in width, secured the outer textile shroud of the tomb's occupant.[13] Each "pagoda," composed of small geometric shapes, measures approximately 3.7 centimeters high by 1.4–1.6 centimeters wide; nineteen such pagodas (alternating in orientation) extend symmetrically across the weft of the fabric from a central pagoda that forms the axis for nine pagodas to the left and nine to the right. The same pattern alternates vertically — along the warp — after two pagoda rows (that is, every 7.4 centimeters). The thread count of the warp and weft amounts to 88:24 per centimeter. This means that the pattern unit in weft direction comprises at a minimum approximately 2,024 ends, and in warp direction repeats after approximately 178 picks. Three combinations of threads in two colors were used to weave the brocade: light brown and yellowish brown, dark brown and yellowish brown, and vermilion and yellowish brown; the weft thread is dark brown.

The pattern of the band testifies to the highly developed geometrical style in silk weaving — a style mastered as early as the late fourth century BCE. The design's enduring role in fashion is evident in the silk pagoda bands that ornament the clothes of wooden female figures packed in the compartment at the head of the inner coffin (fig. 2).[14]   DK

1 Excavated in 1982 (N 9); reported: Peng 1982, color pl. *xia*.
Published: Hubei 1985a, color pls. 3.1, 28.3, 28.4, page 70,
fig. 59; Huang 1985, color pl. 24; Zhang 1988, 32, 33: color
pl. 23; Kuhn 1991, 227: fig. 25.3; Zhao 1992, color pl. 1.1;
Goepper 1995, 345, 346: pl. 78,6; Rawson 1996, 146: pl. 67c;
148: pl. 67.5.

2 The description of the sleeve, the original garment (N9),
its weave, and composition is mainly based on information provided in Hubei 1985a, 20, 29 (fig. 29.1), 33 – 34,
56 – 57, 63, 66, 71, and in Chen and Zhang 1982, 9 – 11.

3 Kuhn 1995a, 82 – 83.

4 Wang 1979, 49; Kuhn 1982, 384 – 385.

5 The chain-stitch technique may have been used as early
as the Shang dynasty and the Western Zhou period; see
Sylwan 1949, 119, and Huang 1985, pl. 2.

6 The description of the weave structure of the textile (N 9)
given in Hubei 1985a, 33 – 34, contradicts the description
in Chen and Zhang 1982, 10, who argue that after three
weft (shuttle) entries in plain weave, one weft is inserted
to fix the doup end.

7 The structure of the weave as it is drawn in Hubei 1985a,
29, fig. 29.1, suggests that all four warp ends may have
been used as doup ends as well. This is highly improbable,
and resolution of the question awaits a technical analysis
of the weave. For the time being, we accept Peng Hao's
argument (1982, 5) that the ground structure of the weave
is the same as that of the gauze (No. 340-17) from Tomb 1
at Mawangdui. The drawing of fig. 2 is reconstructed on
the assumption that the observation of Peng Hao is valid.

8 Excavated in 1982 (N 4); reported: Jingzhou 1982, 6, fig. 11,
pl. 3:2 – 4. Published: Hubei 1985a, color pls. 14 – 17;
Huang 1985, pl. 15; Huang 1988, 14 – 17, color pl. 13; Kuhn,
1991, 226, fig. 25.2; Wu 1992, pls. 2 – 4; Zhao 1992, color pl.
1:2; Kuhn 1995a, 89; Goepper 1995, 343 – 344; Rawson
1996, 145, 147 – 148.

9 The description of this part of the body shroud *(qin)*,
identified by some Chinese archaeologists as a coverlet
(jin), is based on information in Hubei 1985a, 12, 25 – 26,
31, 41 – 43; Kuhn 1995a, 88 – 90; Goepper 1995, 344; Rawson 1996, 148.

10 A precise description of the weaving flaw awaits publication of the technical analysis of Chinese textile historians.

11 Kuhn 1995a, 106.

12 Excavated in 1982 (N 3); published: Hubei 1985a, color pl.
9.4; 38: fig. 3.11; Huang 1985, 22: pl. 18 and 8: fig. 18; Goepper 1995, 343, 344: fig. 78.4; Rawson 1996, 145: fig. 67a; 147:
fig. 67.3.

13 The description is based on the information provided
in Hubei 1985a, 12, 35, 37, 38, 71; Huang 1985, 8:18.

14 Hubei 1985a, 81: fig. 66.

TOMB 2 AT

BAOSHAN,

JINGMEN,

HUBEI PROVINCE

The archaeological site of Baoshan is located to the northeast of Jiangling in the vicinity of the ancient capital of the Chu kingdom.[1] Tomb 2 was the largest in a small burial ground of five tombs dating to the Middle and Late Warring States period (475–221 BCE). Excavated between late 1986 and early 1987, Tomb 2 remains the most important discovery to date in the Jiangling area, not only for its size and content, but also for its historical value. Written records found inside the tomb have enabled Chinese archaeologists to identify the tomb's occupant as Shao Tuo, a high-ranking official in the Chu kingdom who died in 316 BCE.

At its mouth, the tomb shaft measured 34.4 meters long from east to west and 31.9 meters wide from north to south. It was dug on a hilly site and covered with a mound 5.8 meters high and 54 meters in diameter at the time of the discovery. The tomb shaft was sunk to a depth of 12.45 meters and shaped in an inverted pyramid, with fourteen descending steps on each of its four sides. The middle section of the eastern side of the shaft opened onto a large ramp, initially built to give access to the tomb itself during the funeral ceremonies. The tomb was breached at some point prior to excavation, but the thieves were apparently interrupted in the midst of their work, and the burial contents were nearly complete and well preserved when the tomb was excavated. The integrity of the tomb's contents, as well as their condition, reflects the care that the Chu devoted to protecting their dead; indeed the Chu, to a greater extent than other Zhou cultures, unceasingly refined the art of burial over a period that began in the eighth century BCE.

At the bottom of the shaft lay a large wooden structure (guo) that measured 6.32 meters long, 6.26 meters wide, and 3.1 meters high, built entirely of heavy wood beams from the floor to the roof. Eight bamboo mats were placed on top of the guo, and the entire structure was enveloped with a thick layer of sticky fine clay. The shaft was then filled with layers of pounded earth up to the mouth of the tomb. The tomb itself was composed of four chambers surrounding a central burial room in which four graduated coffins were placed — one inside the other; the remains of the deceased were placed in the last and smallest coffin. Each of the four chambers was filled with furniture and objects — nearly two thousand items — situated according to their function in ritual and daily life. The ritual bronzes and a large set of vessels that contained food and probably beverages were placed in the main chamber, near the head of the deceased. The southern chamber contained weapons and chariot fittings; the western chamber contained objects for travel, while the northern chamber held the necessities of everyday life.

The contents of Tomb 2 reveal that important changes had taken place at the end of the fifth century BCE in a tradition of burial practices that had been followed for centuries. Entire categories of vessels that were commonly included among the set of ritual bronzes do not appear in their usual complement; some are of low quality — defective in their casting, unimaginative in their ornamentation, even undecorated. By contrast, objects for daily use display superior craftsmanship and lavish decoration (cat. 144). Until the end of the fifth century, tombs of high-ranking officials and members of the aristocracy contained a wealth of musical instruments, including sets of bells and chime stones; their number and quality probably reflected the status of the tomb's owner. By contrast, Tomb 2 at Baoshan contained only one bell — a *zheng,* intended for signaling rather than musical performances, a zither for personal use, and a small suspended drum. Jade objects, so abundant in earlier tombs, are sparsely represented in that of Shao Tuo. By contrast, the tomb was amply stocked — and notably more so than tombs of earlier date — with nonritual objects: wooden mannequins wearing swords, pieces of furniture (a folding bed, low tables, plates, lamps, chests, and cabinets), objects for the owner's personal use (fans, mirrors, and toilet boxes) and for his adornment. Sixty-nine bamboo caskets accompanied the deceased; some of them still contained the remains of fruit (jujubes, persimmons, plums, and pears), as well as lotus rhizomes and ginger, when the tomb was excavated. One noteworthy continuation of earlier practices is the large amount of armor (for men and horses) and weapons placed in the tomb.

Writings found in the tomb have shed light on aspects of Chu social and religious life. Four hundred and forty-eight bamboo strips, two hundred and seventy-eight of them inscribed with characters, were distributed among the four chambers surrounding the burial room. Most of the strips were originally tied to one another by string (now rotted) to compose documents; the fact that they were found in their original positions has permitted the reconstruction of the documents. The writings from Tomb 2 fall into one of three categories. Most are reports by the local administration to the central government on issues of law. Another group of texts deals with divination, and a small number are inventories of the tomb's contents; the latter have proved particularly valuable for identifying the ancient names of some of the objects deposited in the tomb. The writings reveal a handsome calligraphy in several hands, but the fact that many of the characters employed are unknown (some are variants, others long-obsolete characters or even errors) has made the texts difficult to decipher. AT

1   Hubei 1991.

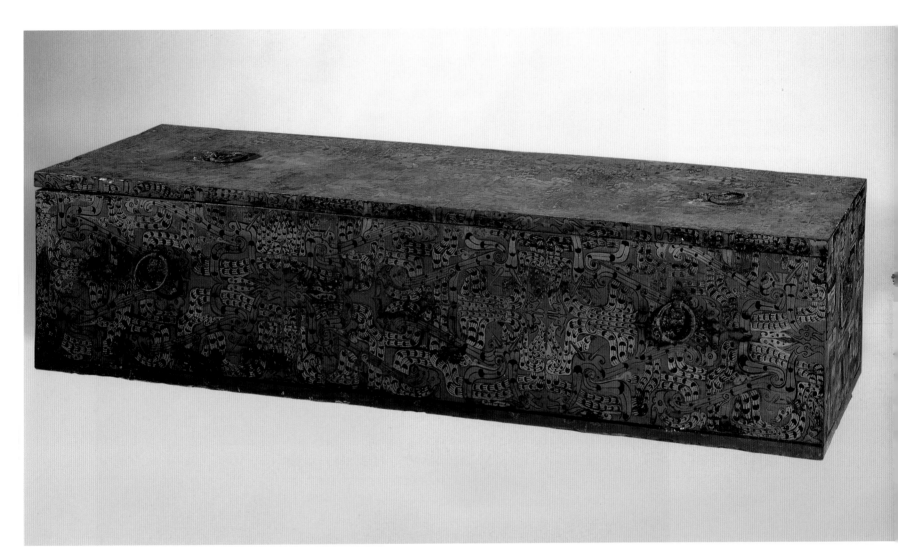

113

Painted lacquer coffin

Height 45 (18 ⅛), width 184 (72), depth 45 (18 ⅛)
Middle Warring States Period, c. second half of
fourth century BCE (before 316)
From Baoshan, Jingmen, Hubei Province

Jingzhou Prefecture Museum, Hubei Province

This coffin is the innermost of three nested coffins
from the central chamber of the tomb.[1] A number
of ancient texts indicate that sumptuary laws governed the number of coffins permitted to each rank
of the aristocracy. Although the accounts are not

consistent, it seems that three coffins were the preserve of feudal lords or high ministers (qing). However, the presence of three coffins in this tomb of a
lower-ranking minister (zuo yin) suggests that these
regulations were not strictly observed in Chu.[2]

The bottom, sides, and end-panels of the coffin
are each made from single planks, joined by swallow-
tailed mortises and tenons; the joints are sealed with
lacquer. Mask-and-ring bronze handles, originally
gilded, are attached to the sides, the end-panels,
and the lid of the coffin. The coffin was originally
wrapped in a textile, but this had largely decomposed
when the tomb was opened. Silk gauze (sha) was

115

Bronze *zun* vessel inlaid with gold and silver

Height 17.5 (6 7⁄8), diam. at mouth 24.8 (9 7⁄8)
Middle Warring States Period, c. second half of the
fourth century BCE (before 316)
From Baoshan, Jingmen, Hubei Province

Jingzhou Prefecture Museum, Hubei Province

This lidded vessel,[1] one of a pair, was found in the
eastern chamber of Tomb 2, along with most of the
ritual bronzes and a group of lacquered containers
for eating and drinking. Chicken bones, presumably
offerings for the deceased, were found in one of
the two vessels.

The vessel's shape is unusual for pre-imperial
bronzes. With slightly flared circular walls, and a
lid topped by a flat circle, the container is modeled
on lacquerware, and like its lacquer counterparts,
has three small feet (here ornamented with eyes)
and two movable rings attached to animal masks
(pushou). Reversed, the lid rests on its four bird-
shaped rings to serve as a food receptacle. The
vessel's ornaments and fittings were cast on; traces
left by mortise-and-tenon joinery to attach them to
the interior of the mold are still visible inside the

box and beneath the lid. Mortise-and-tenon joins
were used in precisely the same manner to attach
metal fittings to wooden boxes.

The bronze's decorative motifs as well strongly
resemble the painted decoration of contemporaneous lacquerware. Color contrasts are rendered by
gold and silver inlaid in the recesses of the bronze
surface, and the fluid and curvilinear ornaments
are imitative of brushwork. The imitation of lacquerware, in fact, approaches the literal: the inner
walls of the bronze are coated with red lacquer. This
luxury vessel clearly illustrates the artistic dominance of lacquerware over bronzework, a phenomenon that first appeared at the turn of the fourth
century BCE and developed progressively through
the Han dynasty. The phenomenon reflects less the
influence of one form of production on the other
than the progressive decline in the importance of
ritual bronze decoration.

Along with another vessel discovered in Tomb 1
at Jiangling (Hubei province), this vessel and its
complement from Tomb 2 at Baoshan were manufactured by workshops specializing in luxury bronze
items inlaid with precious metals and, in some
cases, accented with lacquer, turquoise, or other

1   Excavated in 1987; published: Hubei 1991, 1: 190–191, fig. 120; 2: color pl. 11.1 and pl. 56.1.
2   See Guangdong 1974, 71, fig. 5; Lawton 1982, no. 9; Hubei 1996, 135–136, figs. 91–92, and color pl. 4.

FIG. 1. Bronze *zun* inlaid with lacquer from Tomb 2 at Wangshan, Jiangling, Hubei Province; Warring States period; height. 17.1 (6¾): from above; cross section. After Hubei 1996, 135, fig. 91.

materials (fig. 1). Archaeological discoveries have suggested that these workshops were located near or even within the Chu capital, close to the present-day city of Jiangling. These workshops, which produced wine vessels *(hu* or *lei),* as well as round bronze food containers,[2] probably ceased operations when the capital was destroyed by the Qin army in 278 BCE.

The highly complex — almost abstract — designs on the lid and vessel body are based on dragon-and-bird motifs. Their zoomorphic forms are concealed in the ornament: eyes, marked by circular dots, stare out of heads that emerge from intricate bodies, which flow into the forms of other, similarly abstract creatures. Four units of the motif can be seen on the main register and, in a different rendering, at the center of the lid; another motif is repeated six times on the sides of the vessel. Though organized in repeating units, the animals are intricately configured to create an impression of endless movement and to suggest that they are, in fact, alive. AT

116

Horn carved with three dragons

Height 10.2 (4), diam. at widest point 1.9 (⅝)
Middle Warring States Period, c. second half of the
fourth century BCE (before 316)
From Baoshan, Jingmen, Hubei Province

Jingzhou Prefecture Museum, Hubei Province

This rare piece was made from a single antler, from
which it takes its pointed shape.[1] Three dragons are
carved in the round, their snakelike bodies twisting
together into a spiral as each bites the body of
another. Each deeply carved figure in the composition is mutually independent, secured to the others
at the points of dramatic contact: the two larger
dragons grip each other with their front legs; having none, the smallest dragon must make do with
his mouth. This miniature sculpture exemplifies the
deep roots of tour-de-force work in the Chinese
applied arts; such work was highly valued, if not
continuously throughout the history of the arts,

then at least periodically, and as early as remote
antiquity.

The sculpture was discovered in the northern
chamber of Tomb 2 at Baoshan, preserved in a bamboo casket that contained several items for personal
adornment, including a wig, four jade and bone
ornaments, and a tiny sculpture of mythical animals
carved from a root. The antler sculpture likely
served a similar function and was perhaps worn on
a hat or in the hair. AT

1   Excavated in 1987; published: Hubei 1991, 1:261,
    fig. 174.2; 2: pl. 87.1.

BRONZE EJUN QI

JIE TALLY FROM

QIUJIAHUAYUAN,

SHOUXIAN,

ANHUI PROVINCE

Shouchun, at present-day Shouxian on the middle course of the Huai River, was an important political center for brief periods on two occasions during the Eastern Zhou period (770–221 BCE). The last capital of the state of Cai was situated in this area at the turn of the fifth century BCE; later, in 241 BCE, Shouchun became the last capital of the once mighty kingdom of Chu, which had suffered a series of crushing military defeats. During the 1930s, a large Chu tomb at Zhujiaji, in Shouxian, was repeatedly looted, yielding plentiful bronze vessels, including some of the largest and heaviest found in China up to that time. The inscriptions on some of these bronzes indicate that this tomb belonged to a Chu king, who has been tentatively identified as either King Kaolie (r. 262–238 BCE) or King You (r. 237–228 BCE).[1] In 1955, the tomb of Marquis Zhao of Cai (r. 518–491 BCE) was discovered by farmers inside the west gate of the modern town of Shouxian, followed by rescue excavations that yielded more than five hundred objects of bronze, jade, bone, and gold leaf. The inscriptions on many of the bronzes found in the tomb show that, during the reign of Marquis Zhao, Cai had become a client state of Chu, whose royal capital was then located at Ying in the Middle Yangzi region. The inscriptions on other bronzes from the same tomb attest to intermarriage between the rulers of Cai and those of the emergent southeastern kingdom of Wu.[2]

Because of these important discoveries, an archaeological survey team was organized in 1957 to explore the surrounding region. Members of the survey team obtained four bronze tallies (*jinjie*) that had been found by farmers during an irrigation project at the locality of Qiujiahuayuan. According to the initial report, an iron hammer, a small piece of Chu gold currency, and sherds of pottery were discovered at the same time.[3] The sherds were thrown away, the gold piece was sold to the county bank and the hammer was lost later; the bronze tallies were kept by two local people. An additional bronze tally carrying the same inscription as one of the four tallies from Qiujiahuayuan was acquired at Xinji, Mengcheng county, Anhui province, in 1960.[4] It was said that this tally had also been found in Shouxian, and scholars have commonly assumed that it came from Qiujiahuayuan, but this is by no means certain.

Since the tallies are dated to 323 BCE, they predate the removal of the Chu capital to this region by almost a century. At that time, the state of Cai had already ceased to exist, and the Shouchun area had come under the direct administration of the Chu kingdom. In all probability, the discovery of the five tallies attests to the activity of Chu merchants and the commercial statutes of the Chu court in this region during a period when the Shouchun area was still located at the periphery of the Chu realm. XY

1 Most of the looted bronzes are now in the collection of Anhui Provincial Museum. Anhui 1987, pls. 80–94.
2 Anhui 1956; Anhui 1987, 62–78.

3 Yin and Luo 1958, 8. The postscript to this article reports that during a follow-up visit local people denied that a gold piece had been found. See Yin and Luo 1958, 11.
4 Anhui 1987, pl. 79 caption.

117

Bronze Ejun Qi *jie* tally

Height 31 (12 ⅛), width 7.3 (2 ⅞)
Middle Warring States Period,
late fourth century BCE
From Qiujiahuayuan, Shouxian, Anhui Province

The National Museum of Chinese History, Beijing

This bronze tally[1] (*jinjie*) exempted merchants from road tolls or excise along certain explicitly defined trading routes within the Chu kingdom. Issued at the royal capital and renewed annually, they were to be shown to local representatives of the Chu government. Similar documents made for persons of lower rank than the beneficiary of this tally were probably engraved on bamboo,[2] and the vaulted shape of the bronze tablets, with a "node" in the center mimics that of bamboo tablets. Their cast inscriptions, inlaid in gold, are to be read in eight vertical lines starting in the upper right, ignoring the "node." Their lengths differ according to that of the inscribed text, but all the tallies are equal in width. They were almost certainly manufactured in sets of five; when joined together, the five tallies would have formed a complete cylinder (fig. 1).

The tallies found at Qiujiahuayuan comprise two "boat tallies" and two "wagon tallies," which probably came from two distinct sets (see fig. 2). Their inscriptions refer, respectively, to trading expeditions along water and land routes. The texts refer to boats and wagons in groups of fifty (with the understanding that clearly specified equivalents could substitute for one standard-size "boat" or "wagon"), and each tally in a set of five may have covered ten boats or wagons moving together; groups of ten may have been more manageable than flotillas of fifty boats or convoys of fifty wagons. The goods that were transported are not specified, though they seem to have included livestock, at least on the boat expeditions.

The person to whom these tallies were issued, Ejun Qi ("Qi, Lord of E"), was not himself a merchant but a high-ranking Chu administrator.[3] The location of E, his place of residence, is uncertain; it may have been either at present-day Wuhan — at the confluence of the Yangzi and the Han Rivers — or further to the north, near Dengxian in southwestern Henan province. The tallies recorded the royal privilege for official trading activities administered by Ejun Qi. Their royal origin and the high status of the beneficiary no doubt account for their luxurious execution. Whether the merchants were themselves government officials or private individuals who conducted their business under some arrangement with Ejun Qi's administration is unclear; in any case, the tally inscriptions explicitly state that the merchants were not to be lodged and fed at government expense — presumably in contrast to traveling administrators.

The reconstruction of the routes described in the inscriptions (see fig. 3) is tentative because all places mentioned have not been securely identified. Some place names are still in use today (as are most of the river names), but they may not designate the same locations as they did in antiquity. What does seem clear is that the trade routes for both boats and wagons led Ejun Qi's merchants to the outermost reaches of the Chu state. Conducted under government auspices, these expeditions may well have had the character of inspection tours. Moreover, the fact that both boat and wagon expeditions were to end at the Chu capital of Ying, near present-day Jiangling (Hubei province), suggests that one purpose of these far-flung commercial operations may have been to supply the royal court.

The boats of Ejun Qi's merchants traveled all over the Middle Yangzi basin. A northwesterly route took them up the Han River, across central Hubei into southern Shaanxi. An easterly route then led them down the Yangzi, past Lake Poyang into Jiangxi and to southern Anhui. A southern route went up the Xiang River deep into the interior of Hunan, an area into which Chu had only recently begun to penetrate; the inscription mentions five rivers without giving names of settlements, probably indicating that no Chu administrative centers had yet been set up here. Finally, the boats proceeded up the Yangzi to the Chu capital.

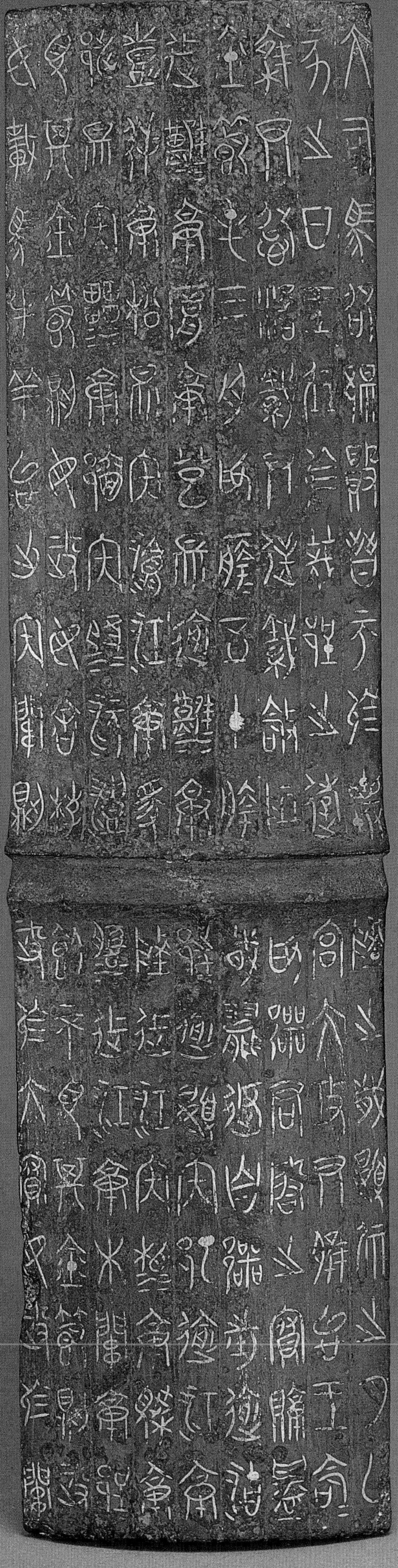

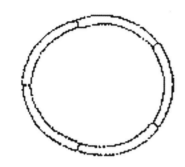

FIG. 1. Five joined tallies in cross section. Adapted from Yin and Luo 1958, 9, fig. 1.

FIG. 2. Boat tally *(left)*; wagon tally *(right)*. Adapted from Yin and Luo 1958, 9, figs. 1 and 2.

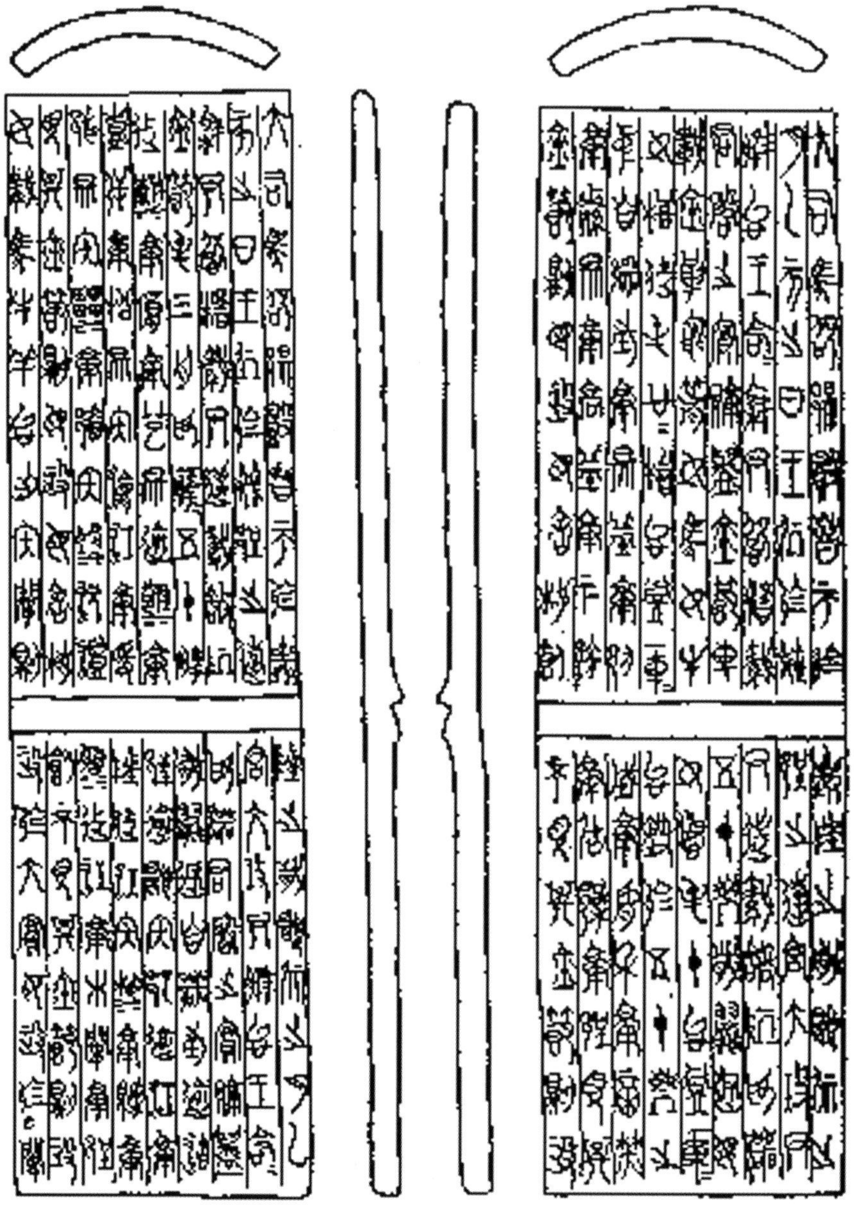

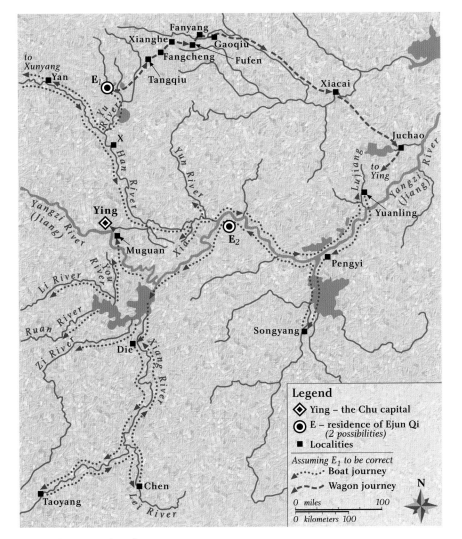

FIG. 3. Reconstruction of
the land and water routes
described in the Ejun Qi *jie*
tallies. Adapted from Fu-
nakoshi 1972: 78, fig. 2.

The land route proceeded from E to the northern border areas of the Chu state—first to the
Nanyang basin (southwestern Henan) and from
there down the Huai River valley into northern
Anhui. These areas, conquered by Chu since the
early seventh century BCE, remained contested
territory. Perhaps for this reason, the wagon tallies
prohibit trading in materials liable to be put to
military use.

Following the convention for official documents,
the inscription texts begin with a date. The year is
specified by reference to the defeat of the Jin army
at Xiangling, which is known from historical sources
to have occurred in 323 BCE (the sixth year of the
reign of King Huai of Chu); the month is given in
terms of the Chu calendar; the day is the twelfth in
the ever-repeating Cycle of Sixty. The administrators
involved with the issuance of the tallies are named
(some of their titles are still poorly understood),
followed by stipulations for the use of the tallies and
the descriptions of the travel routes.

While the tallies' elegantly written characters
exemplify the Chu script, a literate person from outside Chu would have been able to make sense of the
tally inscriptions without difficulty, for the several
regional scripts current before the Qin unification in
221 BCE were variants of a single writing system. Characters for specific words might differ from kingdom
to kingdom and even within a kingdom, but such
variations reflect differing dialects or terminologies
rather than differing writing systems.

Since the bronze tallies are unique, the extent
to which they are representative objects of their
kind is uncertain. Nevertheless, their importance as
documents for the economic history of the Warring
States period cannot be overstated. LvF

Boat Tally Inscription[4]

In the year when the Great Minister of War
Shao Yang had defeated the army of Jin at
Xiangling, in the Xiayi month, day *yi hai,*
when the king dwelled in the pleasure
palace at Jieying, the Great Intendant of
Public Works Shui took a royal order to

command the Jiyin [?] official Dao [X], the Jianyin official Ni, and the Jianling official Qi to cast these metal passports for the merchants from Ejun Qi's treasury. Add up three boats to make one large boat; fifty large boats a year will [make the journey] one by one and return.

They will depart from the E market-office, traverse the lake [?], go up the Han River, stop at Yan, stop at Xunyang, go down the Han River, stop at [X], traverse the Xia River, enter the Yun River; traverse the Jiang [i.e., the Yangzi River], stop at Pengyi, stop at Songyang, enter the Lujiang River, stop at Yuanling; go up the Jiang, enter the Xiang River, stop at Die, stop at Taoyang, enter the Lei River, stop at Chen, and enter the Zi, Ruan, Li, and You Rivers; ascend the Jiang, stop at Muguan, stop at Ying.

When they show their metal tallies, they will be exempt from excise, [though] they will not be lodged or be given food. When they do not show their metal tallies, they will be assessed excise. If they transport horses, oxen, and sheep in and out of the gates, then they will be assessed excise at the Great Treasury but not at the gates.

Wagon Tally Inscription

In the year when the Great Minister of War Shao Yang had defeated the army of Jin at Xiangling, in the Xiayi month, day *yi hai*, when the king dwelled in the pleasure palace at Jieying, the Great Intendant of Public Works Shui took a royal order to command the Jiyin [?] official Dao [X], the Jianyin official Ni, and the Jianling official Qi to cast these metal passports for the merchants from Ejun Qi's treasury. Fifty wagons a year will [make the journey] one by one and return.

Do not transport metal, leather, or bamboo for making arrow shafts. If [they use] horses, buffaloes, or oxen, add up ten as the

equivalent of one wagon; if [they use] human carriers, add up twenty as the equivalent of one wagon, and subtract these [wagon equivalents] from the total of fifty wagons.

They will depart from the E market-office, stop at Tangqiu, stop at Fangcheng, stop at Xianghe, stop at Fufen, stop at Fanyang, stop at Gaoqiu, stop at Xiacai, stop at Juchao, stop at Ying.

When they show their metal tallies, they will be exempt from excise, [though] they will not be lodged or be given food. When they do not show their metal tallies, they will be assessed excise.

1 Excavated in 1957; published: Yin and Luo 1958; Guo Moruo 1958; Zhongguo 1961, pl. 53.1; Shang 1963, 16, 50; Zhongguo Lishi 1984, no. 68; Li Xueqin 1985, 167–168; Li Xueqin 1986, 5: no. 139; Ma 1986, pl. 73.
2 Cf. Chen 1995, 306–312; Chen Wei 1989.
3 Since the seventh century BCE, the title *jun* indicated royally appointed governors or satraps governing territories newly annexed to the Chu state. Whether their position was hereditary is unknown.
4 These translations are based on Yin and Luo 1958; Guo Moruo 1958; Tan 1962; Yu 1963; Shang 1963; Funakoshi 1972; Huang 1982: 263–288; Liu Hehui 1982; Li Ling 1983, 368–372; Chen Wei 1986; Liu 1987; Liu 1989: 176–182; Xie 1991; Zhu and Li 1995, Liu 1995, 343–347; Li Ling 1996a. An X indicates a character of unknown transcription.

TOMB 1 AT

TIANXINGGUAN,

JIANGLING,

HUBEI PROVINCE

Tianxingguan Tomb 1, at Jiangling in Hubei province, was excavated between January and March of 1978. Like many other vertical-shaft burials of the Middle Warring States period in the region, the tomb was built as a multi-chambered wooden crypt placed at the bottom of a pit (12.2 meters deep), with three internested coffins in the central chamber, surrounded by side-chambers filled with burial goods. Although the tomb had already been robbed at the time of excavation, archaeologists recovered more than 2,500 artifacts, including well-preserved bronzes and lacquerware. The distribution of the burial goods in the various chambers did not follow a strict division by category, but the eastern chamber held the majority of the many musical instruments placed in the tomb, and the western chamber contained most of the weapons and military equipment. The fantastic lacquered wood figure (cat. 118) was found in the southern chamber along with a second lacquered figure — a bird standing on a tiger-shaped base with a pair of antlers jutting from its body just above the wings.

One of the two bamboo-slip manuscripts found in the western chamber is a tomb inventory. From it we learn that the deceased was named Pan Cheng, a man who held aristocratic rank as Lord of Diyang. The inventory further reveals that many of the burial goods were gifts from relatives, friends, and colleagues of Pan Cheng. The second manuscript — a record of turtle divination, milfoil divination, and sacrificial offerings performed by specialists on behalf of Pan Cheng during his lifetime (cat. 119) — provides information that suggests a mid-fourth-century BCE date for the burial. DH

118

Painted lacquer guardian animal with antlers

Height including antlers 170 (66⅞)
Warring States Period (c. mid-fourth century BCE)
From Tianxingguan, Jiangling, Hubei Province

Jingzhou Prefecture Museum, Hubei Province

This large, carved-wood figure of a monster was excavated from the southern chamber of the tomb, together with bronze ritual vessels and bells.[1] The assemblage is composed of three main parts: the square base, the twin bodies and heads (each with gogglelike eyes and a long, lolling tongue), and the antlers.[2] The entire figure is painted in black, red, and yellow lacquer: S-shaped dragons with long tongues, interspersed with small star shapes, decorate the figure's curving necks; abstract mask motifs cover most of the base. The fluidity of these motifs contrasts with angular zigzag patterns (echoing designs current in Chu textiles) on the joints of the necks and body and the lower panel of the base.

Abstract scrolls decorate the antlers where they fork, and the tips are also painted.

This figure ranks among the largest and most impressive of the more than two hundred carved wood monster figures (conventionally termed *zhen mu shou* [tomb guardians]) that have been found in medium- and large-scale Chu tombs of the late fifth or fourth century BCE in the Jiangling region of Hubei province.[3] The concentration of these figures in the region — the site of the Chu capital of Ying — suggests that they were central to Chu burial customs at this time. A smaller number have been excavated from other Chu sites in the provinces of Hunan and Henan, but so far none has been reported from outside Chu territory.

Woodcarving, together with sophisticated joinery techniques, seems to have been exceptionally advanced in Chu. A wide variety of lacquered wood artifacts, including various articles of furniture, have been recovered from Chu tombs, whose waterlogged conditions permitted their survival. Unlike other lacquered wood articles, which fulfilled a real-life use prior to being buried, the monster figures were probably made specifically for burial. Almost invariably, they are placed in the chamber of the tomb closest to the head of the tomb occupant and face inwards toward the occupant. Among the various identifications of these figures with imaginary creatures mentioned in ancient texts that have been proposed, the most plausible identifies them as representations of Tu Bo, Lord of the Underworld.[4] The *Zhao hun* (Summons of the soul), one of the *Chu ci* (Songs of Chu), describes Tu Bo as "nine-coiled, with dreadful horns on his forehead, and a great humped back."[5]

Although the twin-headed version from Tianxingguan Tomb 1 is by no means unparalleled, the majority of the surviving figures possess only single heads. These seem to have evolved during the course of the fifth century BCE from much simpler supports for antlers. The earliest known example, excavated from a sixth-century BCE Chu tomb at Dangyang Caojiagang, lacks eyes or tongue. Even simpler are a small number of bases in bronze that may also have had a similar function. The earliest of

FIG. 1. Painted lacquer bird with antlers from Tomb 1 at Tianxingguan, Jiangling, Hubei province; Warring States period; height 108 (42½). After Hubei 1982, 103, fig. 27.

these comes from a mid-seventh century BCE tomb of a ruler of the small state of Huang (in Guang-shan county in southern Henan province); another example was found in a fifth-century BCE tomb at Shaoxing in Zhejiang province.[6] The widespread distribution of these stands, as well as the occasional finds of antlers in tombs in Shanxi and Shandong provinces, implies that belief in the magical efficacy of antlers enjoyed a broad currency in ancient China.[7] The cult of antlers, however, seems to have been particularly strong in the Chu region: carved wood deer sculptures with real antlers are frequently found in the larger Chu tombs, and antlers are also frequently applied to carved wood figures of birds (fig. 1).[8] Frequent mention in the *Shan hai jing* (Classic of mountains and seas) of horns or antlers as attributes of imaginary beasts suggests that antlers were regarded as sources of magical power, a belief that was widespread in the ancient world.[9] CM

1 Excavated in 1978; reported: Hubei 1982, 104–105, fig. 28, pl. 23:7.
2 Similar antlers from tombs at Jiudian near Jiangling have been identified as those of *Elaphurus davidianus*. See Hubei 1995a, Appendix 10, 535.
3 The most extensive publication of these figures is Hubei 1984, 107–111, figs. 88–89 and pl. 67–68:1–3, Hubei 1995a, 298–308, figs. 196–205, and pls. 91–93:2. A few have also been discovered in Chu tombs in Hunan and Henan province. See Chen and Ruan 1983, 63–67.
4 See Chen and Ruan 1983, 63–67.
5 Hawkes 1985, 225. It should be noted, however, that the continuation of the passage quoted describes Tu Bo as having a tiger's head with three eyes and a bull's body, features that do not appear on these figures.
6 For the Guangshan stand, see Henan 1984, pl. 3:3. The Shaoxing stand is illustrated in Jiangsu 1984, 23, fig. 34, pl. 2. See also Mackenzie 1991, 127–128 and note 58.
7 A number of Early Western Zhou period bronzes are decorated with heads bearing antlerlike horns (see, for example, the *you* in the Freer Gallery of Art illustrated in Rawson 1990, IIB: 364, fig. 38.4). Two antlers were found along with Western Zhou period bronzes in a pit near Jiangling. See He 1994, 90, fig. 12:1–2. A bronze ornament in the form of antlers was excavated from a seventh-century BCE tomb near the site of the ancient capital of the state of Xue near Tengzhou in southern Shandong province. See Shandong 1991b, pl. 15:6.
8 See, for instance, the figure of a bird standing on the back of a tiger from this tomb (Hubei 1982, pl. 3:2). See also the bronze figure of an antlered crane from the tomb of Marquis Yi of Zeng (cat. 100) and the miniaturized antler-

like excrescences on the monster handles of the pair of *hu* (cat. 96) from the same tomb.
9 The symbolism of antlers in both Chu and the broader Asian context is explored in Salmony 1954.

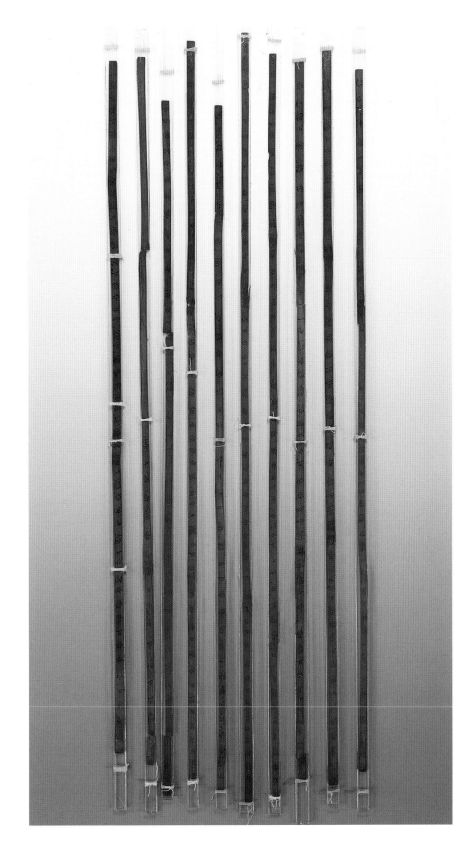

119

Ten bamboo slips

Length 64–71 (25–27 5/8), width 0.5–0.8 (1/8–1/4)
Warring States Period (c. mid-fourth century BCE)
From Tianxingguan, Jiangling, Hubei Province

Jingzhou Prefecture Museum, Hubei Province

Written with brush and ink, in the script current in
Chu during the fourth century BCE, the Tianxingguan manuscripts take their place among a growing
collection of similar objects excavated from Chu
tombs of the Warring States period. Seventy-four
unbroken bamboo slips vary from 64–71 centimeters in length and from 0.5–0.8 centimeters in
width; the slips are notched in two places on the
left side, upper and lower, to facilitate binding the
slips together with cords. The binding cords had
disintegrated long ago, leaving the unbroken slips
in a jumble when they were discovered between
January and March 1978 in a compartment on the
west side of the burial chamber. Their original
order in the manuscripts must be reconstructed
by Chinese archaeologists and paleographers.
This information is not yet formally published.[1]

One set of slips is a funerary document, an
official record identifying the deceased and listing
the burial goods, many of which were presented by
relatives and members of the Chu elite. It is from
this tomb inventory that we know the deceased
was named Pan Cheng, a man who held aristocratic
rank as the Lord of Diyang. Such inventories have
been found in many tombs of the Warring States,
Qin, and Han periods. For the deceased, the document must have served in part as a declaration of
status in the other world to which he had been
transferred; for archaeologists, it is an invaluable
key to names for many of the artifacts, which allows
the matching of words in classical literature with
their corresponding material objects and deepens
our knowledge of early Chinese civilization.

These bamboo slips are from the second
manuscript, a record of divination and sacrifice
performed on behalf of Pan Cheng over a period of
years. Based on the more than half-dozen divination-sacrifice records discovered since the 1960s

States elite in Chu and elsewhere since turtle and milfoil divination were a shared inheritance from Shang and Zhou religious tradition.[2]

The Tianxingguan divination-sacrifice record documents the routine of divination to obtain judgments from the spirits and their approval of sacrificial offerings — continuing the pattern of divination coupled with propitiatory and exorcistic acts that is first recorded in the Shang oracle-bone inscriptions (cats. 55–56). Among the ten bamboo slips exhibited, nos. 8 and 5 (in that order) contain nearly an entire entry from the original record. The translation, followed by an explanation, follows.[3]

1. In the year that the Guest from Qin, Gongsun Yang, inquired after the King at Ying [the Chu capital]; in the tenth month; on the day *bingxu*. Gu Ding divines for the Lord of Diyang, Pan Cheng, with the Long Treasure [turtle]: "In serving the King [[from the tenth month extending to the tenth month of the coming year, would that during the entire year [Pan Cheng] himself experience benefit and concord." (Divination with the turtle plastron is performed.) The prediction:]] "The divination is ever auspicious. As there is slight concern for [Pan Cheng's] person, there is to be a rite of expulsion. According to the cause, let the rite expel it."

2. "Select a lucky day in the Cuan [eleventh] month to pledge in prayer to Grand One, one perfect ox; to the Director of the Life-mandate and to the Director of Faults, one ewe each; to the Lord of the Earth, one black sheep; and to pledge in prayer to Great Water, one perfect ox.[4] Select a lucky day in the Xianma [twelfth] month to re-quite [[the pledge to the royal ancestors from Sire Zhuo to Sire Hui. Entertain them with the Great Animal Sacrifice [ox, sheep, pig], offering one hundred [animals]." (Divination is performed.) The prediction: "Auspicious. Throughout the term of the entire year there will be happiness."]][5]

in other Chu tombs, it is thought that such records are a selection of the acts of turtle divination, milfoil divination, and sacrifice performed during the several years preceding death. Perhaps the copies of such divination-sacrifice records were compiled specifically for burial in the tomb; this might be one explanation for the discovery of tomb inventories together with divination-sacrifice records in a number of Chu tombs. It is certain that men like Pan Cheng — an elite patron of religious specialists — kept such records throughout their adult lives, however. The tomb copies provide a vivid first look at the daily religion of the Warring

Pan Cheng employed several turtle and milfoil diviners, each of whom possessed his own divination materials; for example, Gu Ding's turtle plastron is called Long Treasure. The turtle diviner Fan Huozhi is named in another divination-sacrifice record from Wangshan Tomb 1 (also at Jiangling), showing that diviners provided their services to an array of clients in the region around the Chu capital at Ying.[5]

Excavated Chu divination-sacrifice records all follow the same basic formula. The exact date is first, with the year identified according to significant Chu events for that year. In the translated entry, the Gongsun Yang from Qin who pays his respects to the King of Chu might be none other than the famed Shang Yang, the Qin minister who reorganized Qin government in the mid-fourth century BCE. If this identification is accepted, the date of the Tianxingguan tomb should be closer to the middle than to the end of the century. The divination itself proceeds in two stages (as numbered in the translation). In the first stage, the subject of divination is stated — the words in quotation marks represent the statement uttered aloud at the original event. The act of divination follows. When the diviner uses milfoil stalks, hexagrams are written in the text (the hexagrams in the excavated divination-sacrifice records are written as numbers, not as solid and broken lines). Then comes the diviner's prediction based on examination of the turtle plastron or hexagrams. And the prediction includes the recommendation for a ritual expulsion to avert any spiritual or demonic harm that might befall Pan Cheng.

This leads to the second stage, which entails a second divination to verify which spirits are to receive what sacrifices. The statement concerning sacrifices is followed by the diviner's prediction (invariably, the proposed sacrifices are judged by the spirits to be auspicious). The offering of sacrifices is a two-part process. Initially, sacrifices are "pledged" *(dao)* to the spirits pending positive signs of spiritual assistance; subsequently, the sacrifices are actually given, thus "requiting the pledge" *(sai dao)*. Any entry in the manuscript may include a combination of new sacrificial pledges and requitals of pledges made in previous divinations.

The excavated Chu divination-sacrifice records bear witness to the vitality of religious belief and practice among the Warring States elite. Contrary to the conventional wisdom that a kind of intellectualized humanism espoused by the philosophers had supplanted their active belief in the world of spirits and demons, the manuscript evidence reveals the elite engaged in daily religious activity and details the spirits worshiped by them. Manuscripts such as these truly shed new light on early Chinese civilization. DH

1   Excavated in 1978. An excavation report on Tianxingguan Tomb 1 has been published by the Jingzhou Prefecture Museum: Hubei 1982, 71 – 116.

2   For further discussion of the excavated Warring States divination-sacrifice records, see Harper 1998 and Li Ling 1990, 71 – 86. Much of our present knowledge of this type of manuscript comes from the reproduction and transcription of the divination-sacrifice record from Baoshan Tomb 2 at Jingmen, Hubei province, published in Hubei 1991, 1:364 – 369.

3   I must emphasize that this translation is tentative pending the full publication of the Tianxingguan manuscripts. For this translation, I have relied on the transcription of the two slips, nos. 8 and 5, prepared for this exhibition by Peng Hao of the Jingzhou Prefecture Museum, as well as on a preliminary reconstructed facsimile prepared by Wang 1989b. Peng Hao has noted that slip no. 8 was originally broken, and it is not certain that the lower section of slip no. 8 has been restored correctly. I enclose this part of the translation in double brackets.

4   Li Ling 1995 – 1996, summarizes the archaeological and textual data concerning the supreme deity Grand One in popular religion of the Warring States, Qin, and Han periods. Among the other spirits named, the Director of the Life-mandate and the Lord of the Earth are well-known in received sources; Great Water may be a Yangzi River spirit.

5   This section of the translation placed in double brackets represents what is written on a third bamboo slip not exhibited here; the translation is based on Wang Minqin's facsimile and transcription and is tentative.

6   For the reproduction and transcription of the Wangshan divination-sacrifice record, see Hubei 1995b.

THE TOMB OF

KING CUO OF

ZHONGSHAN

AT SANJI,

PINGSHAN,

HEBEI PROVINCE

Zhongshan was a minor kingdom situated on the sides of the Taihang Mountains. Its rulers were descended from the Di tribes, regarded as "barbarians" by their Zhou neighbors. Seldom mentioned in the historical texts, Zhongshan was apparently founded sometime before 530 BCE and flourished for approximately two centuries. By 323 BCE at the latest, its rulers had adopted the title of king, like virtually all territorial rulers in China during the Warring States period. The course of Zhongshan's history was largely determined by its relations with its more powerful neighbors; the state was temporarily annexed by Wei from 406 to 378 BCE, participated successfully in a coalition war against Yan in 312 BCE, and was finally annihilated by Zhao in 296 BCE.[1]

Archaeological investigations during the 1970s revealed extensive remains of the Zhongshan capital of Lingshou and the royal cemeteries on the north bank of the Hutuo River at Sanji, Pingshan (Hebei province). The capital consisted of several adjacent enclosures with pounded-earth walls and moats and resembled the capitals of neighboring kingdoms. The city's total area has not thus far been determined, and the settlement itself remains unexcavated; excavations have focused instead on the numerous cemeteries in the area.

Archaeologists located two regularly aligned complexes of royal tombs, one inside the walls of Lingshou, the other some two kilometers to the west. Following a custom introduced during the Warring States period, each ruler's tomb featured a large pounded-earth mound atop a subterranean pit. In antiquity, these mounds were covered by wooden buildings, concentrically arranged on different levels around the mound's earthen core to give an impression of multistoried architecture.[2] In an undoubtedly intentional analogy to the palace compounds in the center of a walled capital, each necropolis was enclosed by several layers of walls. Remains of similar tomb complexes are still today a prominent feature of the landscape near several Warring States capitals; they are China's earliest remains of truly monumental architecture (figs. 1, 2).

The tomb buildings — the so-called *xiangtang* — were places of sacrifice, reflecting a new custom distinct from the rituals that had long been conducted in ancestral temples. Such sacrifices were directed to the soul of the deceased, which, according to some modern scholars' reconstruction, was thought to reside in or near these buildings.[3] The notion that each person had a soul — or, according to later formulations, several souls — was new to China during the Warring States period and may have derived from areas to the west. It was linked to the evolving conception of an afterworld directed by a host of lesser gods and demons, whose hierarchy mimicked the increasingly complex bureaucracy of the Warring States period.[4] These ideas constituted a major departure from the ritual regime of traditional Zhou culture, in which the main emphasis had been on kin relationships and lines of succession. From this point forward, tombs were fashioned in the image of the world of the living in order to provide an attractive dwelling for the deceased person's soul. The ritual paraphernalia and symbols of status that had dominated earlier funerary assemblages, though still present in tombs of the elite, were no

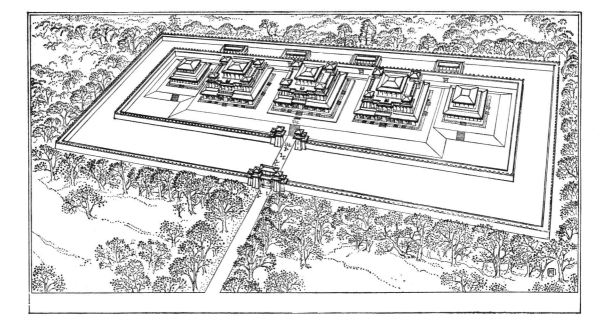

longer paramount. Instead, these tombs contain an unprecedented array of luxury items for use in daily life, as well as objects that testify to an increased preoccupation with ensuring the soul's well-being by means of magic and the occult.

A unique inlaid-bronze diagram found in Tomb 1 in the western necropolis outside Lingshou shows the plan of a necropolis in which the tomb of a king was to be symmetrically flanked by those of two queens and two first-degree consorts; only two of the five tombs were ever built. The central tomb (Tomb 1) is that of King Cuo,[5] the second-to-last king of Zhongshan, who died around 308 BCE. Its mound, which originally rose to some 20 meters (including the height of the foundation platform) and measured some 60 meters on each side at the base, had eroded over time, and archaeologists salvaged only scanty remains of the colonnades surrounding a central offering hall constructed on three levels. The tomb itself stretches a length of 97 meters underground — far beyond the perimeter of the mound and its foundation platform. Two sloping passages lead into a tomb chamber measuring 25 meters square at the bottom. Looters had virtually emptied the stone-lined central burial chamber prior to the tomb's excavation; three wooden boxlike storage compartments, however, were found on the second-level ledge surrounding the burial chamber, and two of them contained an abundance of bronze and pottery vessels, jades, and musical instruments, as well as traces of objects made of organic materials such as lacquered wood.

Aside from the main tomb pit, the underground portions of King Cuo's tomb also included six subsidiary tombs, probably of persons closely associated with the king in life; two horse-and-chariot pits, each containing twelve horses and several chariots with their associated paraphernalia; a pit containing ten sheep and six horses; and a pit containing three boats, ap-

FIG. 2. Excavation photo-
graph of the tomb of King
Cuo.

parently linked to the Hutuo River by a narrow underground canal. Of these, the second horse-and-chariot pit, located to the southwest of the entrance to King Cuo's tomb chamber, was the least disturbed.

Inscriptions on several vessels found in the western storage compartment defend the king's participation in the 312 BCE war against the Yan. Couched in the sententious ritual language of the Zhou, complete with stock phrases from classical texts, these texts extol the political values that were being propounded by Confucian philosophers during the period. They show that, in spite of its relative obscurity and its "barbarian" origins, Zhongshan oper-ated fully within the contemporaneous cultural mainstream. In layout and size, as well, King Cuo's tomb is typical of that of a Warring States period ruler, and its assemblage of funerary goods is the most comprehensive preserved from the highest level of society during the late fourth century BCE. LVF

1 Hebei 1995, 1:3–5; Li Xueqin 1985, 93–107.
2 Fu 1980.
3 Wu 1988.
4 Poo 1998.
5 The name Cuo is sometimes transcribed as Xi.

120

Two bronze three-pronged objects

Height 119 (46 ⅞), width 74 (29 ⅛)
Middle Warring States Period,
late fourth century BCE
From Tomb 1 at Sanji, Pingshan, Hebei Province

Hebei Provincial Cultural Relics Institute,
Shijiazhuang

Two sets of large unornamented three-pronged
bronze objects were unearthed from the royal
Zhongshan tombs. Those exhibited[1] belong to a set
of five from one of two horse-and-chariot pits at
the tomb of King Cuo. Unlike the specimens from
Tomb 6 (at the eastern necropolis inside Lingshou),
whose hollow stems were cast separately from the
flat portions, those from Tomb 1 were each cast as
one piece. The stems contain wood remains of up
to 48 centimeters in length, indicating that these
objects were mounted on poles, presumably for display; enigmatic symbols on the stems may indicate
their placement. Two of the five specimens are
inscribed, but these inscriptions merely give the

to weigh down the mat on which the king was seated. (Chairs came into common use in China only during the tenth century CE.)

These beasts combine the features of several animals — tigers, reptiles, and birds.[4] The ornamentation, inlaid in gold and silver, serves in part to accentuate the zoomorphic features; the exuberant feather pattern on the wings is especially noteworthy. Elsewhere, abstract spiral designs predominate; in the center of the back, these spirals take the shape of two symmetrical, curled, bird-headed animals.

Winged dragons and felines first occur in Chinese art during the mid-fifth century BCE. Jessica Rawson has suggested that they derive from the Near East (see cat. 133); they may have reached China by way of Iranian or Scythian intermediaries. By the time of King Cuo, in any event, this iconography was well established all throughout the area of Zhou culture, and it would be erroneous to tie its occurrence in this tomb to the "non-Chinese" identity of the Zhongshan kings. In artistic terms, the elegant, dynamic shape of these winged beasts is light-years away from any known western Asian prototypes, unmistakably indicating a Late Zhou sensibility. The aggressive stance of the animals — clawed feet spaced far apart, front lowered and

hindquarters raised — and their open wings and grimacing mouths suggest that the beasts are ready to spring at some imaginary attacker. Such creatures are the fountainhead of a long tradition of winged protecting beasts (bixie) placed inside or in front of tombs. As part of a demonic iconography that began to evolve during the Warring States period, they may also have been associated with immortality and travel through limitless space. LvF

1 Excavated in 1978 (M1 DK:36); published: Hebei 1979, pl. 3.1; Tokyo 1981, no. 43; Li Xueqin 1986, 2: no. 108; Thorp 1988b, no. 63; Hayashi 1988b: 295, fig. 3–297; Hebei 1995, cover, 1:139–141, 143, fig. 51, and 2: color pl. 16.1, pl. 94.1; So 1995: 66, fig. 121.

2 The inscriptions on the four winged mythical beasts are as follows: 1. "Fourteenth ritual cycle, Official Treasury of the Right, Petty Officer Guo Ying, Worker Jie, Weight." 2. "Fourteenth ritual cycle, Official Treasury of the Right, Petty Officer Guo Ying, Worker Jie." 3. "Fourteenth ritual cycle, Official Treasury of the Left, Petty Officer Sun Gu, Worker Xi, Weight." 4. "Fourteenth ritual cycle, Official Treasury of the Left, Petty Officer Sun Gu, Worker Cai" (Hebei 1995, 1:413 and 414–415, figs. 171.3–6 and 172.1–2). The same names also appear on various other objects from King Cuo's tomb.

3 In spite of the excavators' assertions (Hebei 1995, 1:404), the treasuries mentioned in the inscriptions consequently cannot be identical with the workshops in which these items were manufactured.

4 Hayashi (1988b, 295) classifies them as "running dragons."

122

Bronze mythical animal inlaid with gold
and silver

Middle Warring States Period,
late fourth century BCE
Height 12.1 (4 ¾), length 21.8 (8 ½)
From Tomb 1 at Sanji, Pingshan, Hebei Province

Hebei Provincial Cultural Relics Institute,
Shijiazhuang, Hebei Province

Two bronze beasts, differing from each another only
in the shape of their tails, were found in the east
storage compartment flanking King Cuo's burial
chamber.[1] Both objects were partly encrusted with
an unknown black material and show visible signs
of wear. The excavators speculate that the paired
objects may have been supports for a paneled
screen or low table or used to weigh down a mat.

Like the winged beast (cat. 121), the animal here
depicted displays hybrid characteristics: its muzzle
resembles that of a tiger, but it has two short horns
near the ears, while its cloven hooves are bovine, as
is shape of the body. The sophisticated inlaid ornamentation, which accentuates some of the animal's
features, consists principally of abstract spirals in
gold and silver on a red ground; the spiral patterns
are interrupted by a band around the animal's neck
that resembles the numerous dog collars discovered
in King Cuo's tomb. The collar design may indicate
that these supernatural beasts had been tamed and
brought under the king's control. LvF

1   Excavated in 1978 (M1 DK:38); published: Hebei 1979,
    pl. 5.1; Hebei 1995, 1: 138 – 139, 142, fig. 50; 2: color pl. 15.1;
    pl. 93.

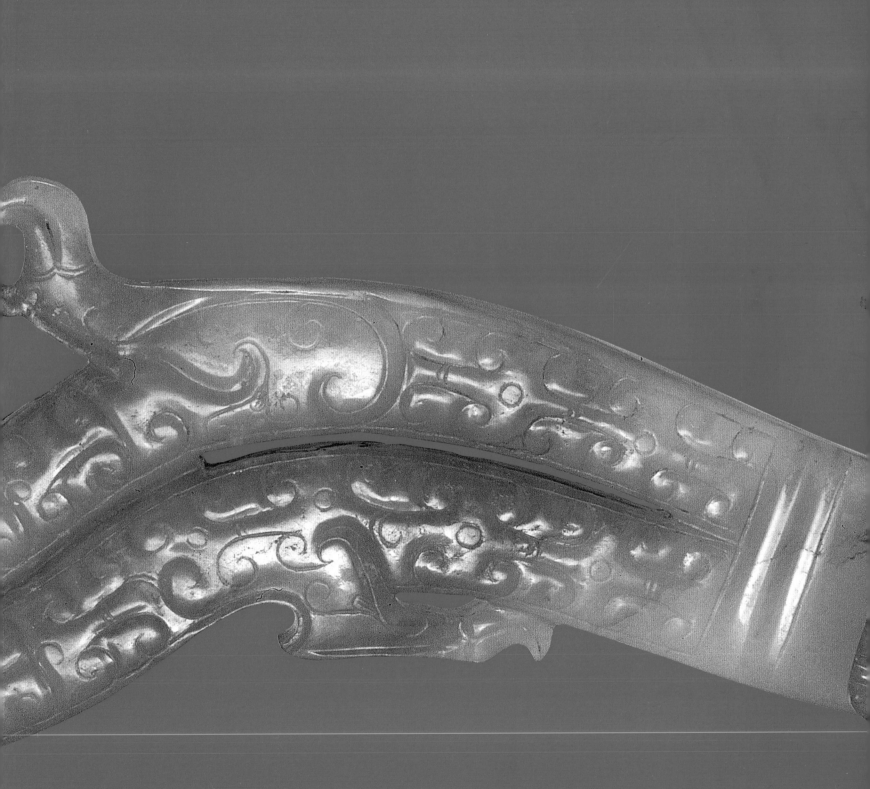

The Grandeur of Empires

EARLY IMPERIAL CHINA (221 BCE – 924 CE)

The history of imperial China, lasting more than two thousand years, has been amply documented in officially sponsored dynastic chronicles, supplemented by classic literature and *yeshi* — unofficial histories — that provide valuable information on particular states, cultures, peoples, customs, and events. These records, however, devote little attention to art and aesthetics, and tracing that history has largely fallen to archaeology. While in many cases, the historical records have pointed excavators in specific directions or have assisted in identifying the owners of particular tombs, the texts are more often silent on the wonders of recently discovered imperial art. Sima Qian's *Shi ji* (Records of the historian), for example, contains a detailed account of the First Emperor's mausoleum, and places it near the present-day city of Xi'an. Archaeological surveys located the necropolis, but even Sima Qian's extravagant description of the splendors of the mausoleum did not prepare archaeologists for an astonishing discovery a few hundred meters from the tomb: the First Emperor's underground army, comprising more than seven thousand life-size terra-cotta statues of officers, footsoldiers, archers, charioteers, and horses (cats. 123 – 128).

The grandeur of the underground army mirrors the ambitions and accomplishments of the First Emperor, who united squabbling, disparate kingdoms in 221 BCE to create China's first centralized government. The unification of China during his reign and its consolidation during the ensuing Han dynasty resulted in a cultural and artistic synthesis, manifested by stylistic similarities that often surmount great distances. The Han prince Liu Sheng, buried at Mancheng in the northern province of Hebei, and the King of Nanyue, buried at Xianggang in the southern province of Guangdong — separated by 3,500 kilometers as the crow flies — were encased in remarkably similar armorlike shrouds composed of thousand of pieces of jade (compare cats. 129 and 139).

Cultural exchange and assimilation, facilitated by diplomacy and trade, opened China to the outside world, and Chinese art of the imperial era provides tangible evidence of these contacts. The most celebrated of the trade routes — the Silk Road — extended from continental China to Western Asia (and ultimately to Europe), but there were other routes to other regions as well. Trade through the South China Sea — the "Ocean Silk Road" — linked the mainland to southern and western Asia, and the influences of these regions are embodied in burial artifacts from the King of Nanyue's tomb (see cats. 138 – 150).[1] A second route, which connected the present-day southwestern regions of Sichuan, Guizhou, Yunnan, Tibet, and Guangxi to southeastern Asia and India,[2] was an additional avenue for social and artistic contacts. Buddhism, which originated in the Indian subcontinent, was embraced by the Chinese (prior to the twentieth century, it was in fact the only "foreign" religion that truly took root throughout China[3]), and objects discovered in the crypt of the Famen Monastery pagoda (cats. 160 – 168) testify to its profound influence. Buddhist imagery — in particular, painted stone sculptures of sinicized Buddhas and bodhisattvas discovered at Qingzhou in Shandong province (the farthest reaches

Cat. 168, detail

Excavation photograph of
Pit 1 at Xiyangcun, Lintong,
Shaanxi province

of eastern China) (cats. 151–153)—is evidence of the extent to which "non-Chinese" religion
and aesthetics informed the art of imperial China.

In the early stages, Chinese art and civilization evolved from indigenous cultures; with the
development of trade and social contracts, however, elements of foreign cultures became increasingly apparent. Gold and silver objects from the Tang dynasty (cats. 154–166) epitomize
the integration of Chinese and foreign styles. The art of the Tang dynasty, one of the most prosperous and liberal periods in Chinese history, shows that exotica was cherished for its own sake:
a bronze ewer (cat. 169), so highly valued that it was enshrined in a reliquary cache along with
the sacred relics of the Buddha, was probably exported from India; glass dishes (cat. 168) found
in another reliquary deposit likely came from Iran. During the Tang era many foreigners lived,
studied, or worked in China; ceramic funeral figures depicting native Chinese women and
clearly non-Chinese men engaging in sport or hunting (cat. 170) portray a climate of cultural
exchange and coexistence.

While it provides vivid evidence of a nation engaged in the world that lay outside of its vast
borders, the art of imperial China nonetheless reflects the evolution of an indigenous culture.
The Han scripts on a bronze *hu* vessel (cat. 132) and on the seal of "Emperor Wen" (cat. 138), for
example, trace their origins back to prehistoric pictographs (cat. 23), mediated by Shang oracle-
bone inscriptions (cats. 55–56), Western Zhou bronze inscriptions (cats. 77–83), and inscribed
Eastern Zhou bronze tallies (cat. 117) and bamboo slips (cat. 119). Tang representations of the
human form (cats. 170–175) hearken back to a prehistoric terra-cotta torso (cat. 21), to bronze
statues, masks, and heads of the Shang period (cats. 65–71), to the life-size terra-cotta warriors

of the First Emperor's army (cats. 123–127), and to a miniature jade dancer (cat. 146). The material culture of imperial China reflects technological advancements that extended the range of artistic media, but even here continuities link China of the Common Era to its prehistoric antecedents. To be sure, particular materials are associated with the artifacts of specific periods: prehistoric China had a rich tradition of pottery vessels, the Three Dynasties favored bronze and lacquer, while gold, silver, and porcelain were creatively mingled with the art of imperial China. We can nonetheless trace a continuity that stretches from the Hongshan culture through the entirety of imperial China in the use of jade to create some of the most cherished — indeed, revered — works of art.

The art of imperial China embodies a distinctively humanistic, even modern, sensibility. Art that was primarily sacred, religious, ritualistic, and imaginary in its early stages, is transformed here into a secular, realistic, practical, and ultimately human aesthetic. Two examples show the extent to which the aesthetic had changed. A chime of bronze bells from the Chu culture (cat. 91) served as an element of ritual and as a mark of social status; an orchestra depicted on a Tang marble relief (cat. 175), by contrast, points to a view of the afterlife that resounds with enjoyment. XY

1 An extraordinary jade rhyton (not in this exhibition) from the King of Nanyue's tomb, reflects Central and Western Asian influence; horn-shaped cups were not traditionally made in China or its dependencies. See Guangzhou 1991, 2:202 and color pl. 15.
2 Wang Binghua argues that there were two continental trading routes: the grassland route and the oasis route,

which is the better-known Silk Road. See Wang 1993. For the southwestern silk road, see Jiang 1995.
3 In the twentieth century, however, Marxism was transmitted to China from Europe and was embraced by the socialist society.

THE TERRA-

COTTA ARMY

NEAR THE FIRST

EMPEROR'S

MAUSOLEUM,

LINTONG,

SHAANXI

PROVINCE

The terra-cotta army of the first Chinese emperor, Shihuangdi (r. 246 – 210 BCE), while undeniably a dramatic find, constitutes but one element of an enormous and complex necropolis, the construction of which reportedly began with the emperor's accession to the throne.[1] Its massive scale sets it apart from other burials, but the Lintong necropolis nonetheless represents a continuation of more than five centuries of Qin funerary structures and beliefs, and its design integrated elements of non-Qin funerary structures.[2]

At the center of the necropolis, enclosed within two sets of walls lies an as-yet unexcavated underground tomb chamber, marked by an enormous tumulus. According to a famous passage in Sima Qian's (c. 145 – 86 BCE) *Shi ji* (Records of the historian) the tomb chamber was built as a microcosm of the universe, with waterways made of mercury and depictions of celestial constellations and terrestrial topography. Excavated components of the Lintong necropolis, however, indicate that the microcosm extended beyond the tomb itself. Nearly one hundred pits, containing hundreds of horse skeletons and kneeling terra-cotta figures of grooms, were discovered to the east of the compound's outer wall; inscriptions identify these pits as "imperial stables." Nineteen tombs located near the tumulus have yielded human remains, possibly those of officials and retainers to accompany the emperor in death. Two half-size models of chariots, each pulled by a team of four horses and manned by a driver — all carefully rendered in bronze — were buried to the west of the tumulus within the inner wall of the necropolis; they were probably intended as transport for the emperor in the afterlife.[3] In the same pit, large quantities of the organic remains of hay were found, suggesting that these structures represented depots. Between the inner and the outer wall on the west side of the tumulus, a cluster of small pits contained clay models and the remains of various birds and animals; the pits may have been intended to represent the emperor's parks and forests.

The terra-cotta army was found in three pits — underground wooden structures — located about 1.25 kilometers east of the tumulus. Pit 1 contained approximately six thousand warriors and horses, as well as several chariots, in battle array in eleven parallel trenches. Pit 2 contained some fourteen hundred figures — cavalrymen, infantry, and horses — as well as ninety wooden chariots. Pit 3 contained sixty-eight soldiers, one chariot, and four horses. A fourth pit, much shallower than the other structures, was empty. The contents of the first three pits were looted and the structures burned, apparently by the army of Xiang Yu, soon after their completion.

Various theories have been proposed regarding the configuration of the underground vaults. A standard view maintains that Pit 1 represents the right (or main) imperial army, Pit 2 the left army, Pit 3 the command, and the unfinished fourth pit the central army.[4] Another theory suggests that the pits themselves were not constructed merely as an *ersatz* army, but rather as a staging of typical situations in which the Qin army might be engaged. Pit 1 thus depicts the deployment of the Qin imperial guard in battle formation; Pit 2 represents the army's barracks; Pit 3 depicts a scene at military headquarters; Pit 4 — the "unfinished pit" — is the ground of battle.[5] Under this reading, the group of pits might have represented the Qin forces symbolically defending the imperial city against invaders or, alternatively, mounting an aggressive campaign of conquest. The terra-cotta army should in any event be viewed as a complex representation — both a substitute for a "real army" and a theatrical enactment.

The sculptures have often been characterized as masterpieces of naturalistic art. However, far from being simply realistic, the significance of the figures lies in the interplay of the stylized rendering of human body with the close transcription of details of body parts and outfits, such as belts and belt hooks, boots, armor, and coiffures. The effect of verisimilitude is further enhanced by veristic painting and the real bronze weapons which the figures carried. These components literally transcribed the appearance of each figure's attributes. Together with postures and gestures, which spatially define and therefore differentiate the function of individual figures within the entire configuration, they represent the specific rank and function of each soldier.[6]

The First Emperor's terra-cotta army constitutes the first known instance of the massive deployment of tomb figures in early China. The use of figurines and models in the mortuary context developed during the Middle and Late Eastern Zhou periods, particularly within the territory of Qin state. Small anthropomorphic clay figures have been unearthed from several Qin tombs that predate the Lintong necropolis; pottery models of granaries have been found in late sixth-century BCE Qin tombs.[7] A separate tradition of wooden tomb figures developed toward the end of the Eastern Zhou period in another area with distinct cultural traits — the state of Chu.[8] Such figures and models and other miniature or nonfunctional objects are collectively termed *mingqi* ("spirit articles"), and they have been traditionally viewed as substitutes for the animals and human victims sacrificed at burials, as well as surrogates for objects of value placed in the tombs.[9] Research based on recent archaeological finds, however, suggests that these objects in fact constitute an integral part of the strategy to re-create — in the tomb — the earthly dwelling of the deceased. This concept of a tomb as a living environment modeled on the mundane world gained currency during the Late Eastern Zhou period; it may have originated within the territory of the Qin state and evolved more quickly in this region than in the Zhou territories.[10]

The replication of the living world in tombs and the widespread use of *mingqi* models and figures to furnish and populate that environment have been interpreted by some scholars as reflecting a new religious trend that emphasized the separation of the dead from the living,[11] or the material manifestation of new religious ideas motivated by structural changes in Late Eastern Zhou society.[12] The Lintong necropolis suggests a slightly different possibility: it made sense for the designer, whoever he was, to use different modes of representation and to employ elements with varying degrees of verisimilitude. It contained both "real" things — sacrificed humans and animals, actual weapons, hay — that were, properly speaking, *presented,* and elements such as the terra-cotta army that were *re-presented.* The goal of the ritual specialists and artisans responsible for the First Emperor's posthumous abode was not to illustrate or to follow

Excavation photographs of
the terra-cotta army pits.
Top left and bottom: Pit 1;
top right: Pit 2.

some precise metaphysical idea but to produce a self-sustaining version of the world — a fictive and efficacious reality. The practical constraints of such image-making must have played a decisive role in the creation of the First Emperor's necropolis. For how, after all, does one reproduce "all the myriad waterways,"[13] or the requisite personnel and matériel of an entire army? How does one supervise the countless logistic, technological, and aesthetic problems implicated in re-creating the world?

Supported by the unparalleled power and economic resources of the state and using all available representational modes and strategies, the First Emperor's necropolis could have been created as a comprehensive replica of the real world. Chinese tombs and burials signified the power and status of their builders and occupants: during the Bronze Age, the ability to sacrifice the lives of retainers, soldiers, concubines, or animals, or to put precious articles into the tomb constituted a sign of power; by the Qin period, the ability to have them *depicted* — possessing the aesthetic, cognitive, technological, and economic resources to reproduce the world — became a more efficient way of asserting power and status.

The terra-cotta army and the Lintong necropolis show that complex representation is not a result or fulfillment of some preconceived religious doctrine, nor a mirror of Qin ideology. Rather, the most consistent ideas regarding the afterlife are to be found in the tombs and monuments themselves, where current metaphysical and religious conceptions intersected with personal wishes and anxieties and were transformed by the practical constraints and conditions of making the afterlife a material reality.[14] LK

1   For a detailed treatment of the various aspects of the terra-cotta army, see the report on the excavation of Pit 1, Shaanxi 1988b; Yuan 1990; Wang 1994a; Ledderose and Schlombs 1990, and Kesner 1995, all of which contain extensive references to further sources.

2   Wu 1995, 114 – 17. For a reconstruction of the Lishan necropolis see Yuan 1990, 1 – 63; Wang 1994b; Yang 1985; Thorp 1983a and bibliographies therein.

3   Shaanxi 1991.

4   Yuan 1990, 36; Wang 1987, 41 – 42.

5   Wang 1994a, 1 – 24.

6   The stylistic aspects of the figures are discussed in Kesner 1995.

7   See Hu 1987 and Sun 1996. For granaries see Ledderose and Schlombs 1990, 164 – 77.

8   See, for example, Hubei 1984, pls. 69 – 71; Henan 1986, pls. 106 – 108.

9   For the concept of *mingqi*, see Cai 1986 and discussion in Kesner 1995, 116 – 117, with further references.

10   Falkenhausen 1990; Falkenhausen 1994; Poo 1998, 157 – 177.

11   Poo 1998, 176 – 77.

12   Falkenhausen 1994.

13   Poo 1988, 176 – 177.

14   This is more fully developed in Kesner 1995 and Kesner 1996.

123

Terra-cotta figure of a high-ranking officer

Height 192 (75 ½)
Qin Dynasty, third century BCE (c. 210)
From Pit 1 at Xiyangcun, Lintong, Shaanxi Province

Qin Terra-cotta Museum, Lintong, Shaanxi Province

The height, clothing, and headgear of this officer[1] all indicate his high rank. He wears a double-layered tunic under a fish-scale armor apron, and a rectangular cap tied with ribbons under the chin. His sleeves are half-rolled and his hands are folded across his belly, his left index finger raised as if resting on a long sword. One of seven similar figures found in Pits 1 and 2, it was positioned directly behind one of the chariots in the second column of Pit 1, as if riding into battle. The seven figures have been identified as generals *(jiangjun)*, but it is more likely that they represent officers *(gongcheng)* of the eighth of the Qin army's twenty grades. The highest-ranking commanders of the Qin forces are not represented in the terra-cotta army.[2]

The production of the figures that compose the army was a large-scale, workshop operation that involved standardized, prefabricated components.[3] The torsos were modeled from the bottom up using coiled strips of coarse clay. Heads and hands were usually made in composite molds (as were individual elements such as ears) and assembled to form the figure, which was then covered with a fine clay slip; separately cast details (such as belt hooks) were then attached to the slip-coated figure. Armor and physiognomy were detailed by low-relief carving and incised lines. The figures were fired (at temperatures of around 1000 degrees Celsius) and subsequently painted with pigments suspended in a lacquer base. Only faint traces of the original color remain, but it is clear that the craftsmen sought to reproduce the colors of the armor and garments worn by specific ranks of warriors.[4]

Creating the terra-cotta army must have posed formidable technological and logistical challenges, and it stands as a monument to administrative efficiency as much as an artistic achievement.

Cross section of one of the pits, showing wood supports and the disposition of the figures. After Shaanxi 1988b, 44, fig. 19.

No written record regarding its production has survived, but simply procuring and transporting the large volume of requisite raw materials and supervising the manufacture must have involved meticulous planning and coordination — although administrative efficiency was characteristic of Qin society. The use of prefabricated (often molded) components or modules, which rationalized production to a great degree, can be viewed as another instance of the pervasive standardization efforts that characterized other areas of Qin society.[5]

The human body had played a relatively minor role in Bronze Age Chinese art. Creating the tomb as a microcosm, however, provided an impetus for the development of figural art. While there are precedents for the use of anthropomorphic clay models in Qin tombs prior to the First Emperor's burial, the Qin sculptures represent a quantum leap from these small, stylistically rather simple works.[6]

The First Emperor's terra-cotta army was emulated on a more modest scale in Han mortuary art. In several terra-cotta armies excavated from second-century Western Han tombs (the twenty-five hundred soldiers from Yangjiawan near Xi'an, or figures from pits around the tomb of the Han emperor Jingdi), the monumentality of the Qin army figures gives way to a more organic, three-dimensional style.[7] LK

1 Excavated in 1976; reported: Shaanxi 1988b, 1:51–53; 2: figs. 44–45.
2 Several authors have sought to associate particular figures with specific Qin military ranks recorded in contemporary texts. The most exhaustive treatment is provided by Wang (1994a, 168–208), who suggests that the eighth rank is the highest rank represented in the First Emperor's terra-cotta army. See also Chen and Lu 1985.
3 Regarding mass-production with respect to Chinese artistic practices, see Ledderose 1992.
4 Details of production are discussed in Yuan 1990, 330–352; Shaanxi 1988b, 163–192, pls. 154–158; Schlombs 1990.
5 Bodde (1986, 52–64) discusses Qin efforts at standardization.
6 For tomb figures predating the Qin army see Cai 1986; Sun 1996; Yuan 1990, 365–367. Wu Hung (1998, 108) explicitly links the terra-cotta army to earlier Qin clay figures.
7 For the Yangjiawan terra-cotta army, see Shaanxi 1977; for the figures from the Jingdi mausoleum, see Mou 1992; for the relationship between the Qin terra-cotta figures and their Han antecedents, see Wang 1994a, 450–471.

124

Terra-cotta figure of a middle-ranking officer

Height 190 (74 ¾)
Qin Dynasty, third century BCE (c. 210)
From Pit 2 at Xiyangcun, Lintong, Shaanxi Province

Qin Terra-cotta Museum, Lintong, Shaanxi Province

A member of an infantry formation accompanying a chariot, this middle-ranking officer[1] is distinguished from the lower-ranking soldiers by his armor of overlapping rectangular plates (representing lacquer-coated leather), joined with cords and rivets; épaulières cover his shoulders and upper arms. A tunic extends below his knees, and he wears squared shoes. The figure's left hand probably originally held a sword; the fingers of the right hand grasp another weapon (now lost). The hands of the Qin army figures were created through a combination of molding and modeling and then inserted into the hollow arms. Their manufacture exemplifies the module system, which rationalized and speeded the production process: using double- or single-section molds, the artisans created palms, to which fingers (usually separately modeled) were then attached. Working with a limited number of prefabricated variations, the sculptors created several basic forms — hands with fingers bent or with fingers outstretched — that could be fitted to various types of bodies.[2]

The officer's face, with its elaborately styled mustache and beard, displays a remarkably vivid, attentive expression; individualized features include the incised wrinkles that crease his forehead. The detailed treatment of the Qin warriors' faces has led some scholars to identify the figures as portraits of individuals;[3] others have divided the physiognomies into types and identified these with particular regions from which the ranks of the Qin army were drawn.[4] The faces, however, are to a large extent stereotypical, a fact directly related to their mass production. The artisans used a variety of standardized, molded components to create the heads of the figures; combinations of particular elements and hand finishing "individualized" the figures.[5] That the terra-figures do not convey distinct, indi-

vidual physiognomies is not merely the consequence of constraints imposed by serial production; rather such methods of production fitted well with the intended purpose. There was no need to replicate the specific individuals who composed the army — only their functions, since their personalities were fully subsumed by their roles within the organization. Nonetheless, particularizing the individual soldiers enabled the artisans to differentiate figures within groups of the same type (the cavalry, archers, infantrymen).[6] LK

1 Excavated in 1976; reported: Shaanxi 1988b, 1:61–63; 2: fig. 55.
2 Ledderose 1992 discusses the modular production technique in relation to the terra-cotta army. The construction of the hands is detailed in Shaanxi 1988b, 2: pls. 143–144.
3 See, for example, Cotterell 1981, 28–29; Wang 1984, 70–73; Nie 1986, 57.
4 Wang 1984, 73.
5 Shaanxi 1988b: 1:176–181, pls. 156–157; Schlombs 1990.
6 For detailed treatment, see Kesner 1995.

125

Terra-cotta figure of a standing archer

Height 186 (47.24)
Qin Dynasty, third century BCE (c. 210)
From Pit 2 at Xiyangcun, Lintong, Shaanxi Province

Qin Terra-cotta Museum, Lintong, Shaanxi Province

This standing archer[1] was found in the outermost
left rank of a formation of archers that protected
the infantry in the pit's nine central trenches. The
figure is lightly dressed in a long, belted tunic and
short trousers; his shoes are tied to his feet with
knotted strings, and his hair is braided into a topknot. The position of the archer's hands and the
downward-pointing position of his bow suggest
that he is engaged in shooting exercises.

thigh, holds the arm of the crossbow, while his right hand is positioned near the bow's trigger — perhaps in the act of shooting, or, alternatively, awaiting a command.[2]

The posture of this kneeling archer, based on an organic interplay of planes, eschews the strict frontal stance of most of the standing figures. The most striking and significant stylistic feature of Qin sculptures lies in the linking of a conceptually conceived human form with details of painstaking visual accuracy. There is no precedent in Chinese art for this massive deployment of verisimilitude. Here, the construction of the jacket, composed of lamellae joined by thongs and rivets, mimetically depicts lacquered leather armor. Details of the archer's coiffure — three braids plaited into a chignon — as well as the texture of the sole of his shoe and the folds on his left sleeve and collar, are transcribed into plastic form. The realism extends to such details as the bending of the right foot on which the weight of the body rests, the texture of the sole, and the folds on the inner side of the left sleeve.

More than five hundred figures from the three pits bear stamped or incised characters. While most are numerical symbols, probably associated with the assignment of figures into "groups," characters on approximately eighty-five of the figures have been identified as signatures of master potters, who would have directed teams composed of approximately ten workers.[3] LK

1   Excavated in 1997; unreported.
2   Wang (1994a, 220 – 223) discussing a similar figure from Pit 2, raises several interpretations of the archer's stance.
3   The inscriptions are described in Shaanxi 1988b, 1:194 – 207, figs. 112 – 119.

127

Terra-cotta figure of a charioteer

Height 193 (76)
Qin Dynasty, third century BCE (c. 210)
From Pit 1 at Xiyangcun, Lintong, Shaanxi Province

Qin Terra-cotta Museum, Lintong, Shaanxi Province

This figure of a charioteer[1] was found positioned behind one of the chariots in Pit 1, accompanied by one soldier at his left and another at his right. Other groupings suggest variations in how such vehicles were manned — in some cases a driver, an officer, and a soldier; in others only a driver and a soldier. The charioteer is clad in full armor. The figure's square-shaped bonnet, tied beneath the chin, suggests a high rank within the army.

The verisimilitude of most Qin sculptures has prompted a number of commentators to identify their style as "realistic" or "naturalistic,"[2] a claim that ignores the marionette-like artificiality of the figures. This characteristic inheres in the subject matter itself: the warriors had to be represented in specific postures and gestures defined by their function. The conceptual aspect of their style occasionally makes these figures appear rigid — sometimes even frozen in exaggerated postures. In so doing, however, it captures the stances that embody and define — and thus differentiate — the specific function of a specific warrior within the army as a whole. The descriptive style of representation then literally transcribes each warrior's attributes — his headgear, armor, outfit, boots, weapons — and also differentiates his function and rank within the army. Both stylistic approaches, organically intertwined, delineate aspects of the model of the figure, and establish its status as a functional component of the army.

The chariots found in the First Emperor's necropolis are uniformly two-wheeled vehicles with a rectangular carriage linked by a single shaft to a team of four horses. Chinese archaeologists have distinguished variations among the chariots;[3] those in Pit 2 are primarily lightweight models that presumably would have been used by an army on the offensive. Chariots were the preeminent symbol of

status during the Western Zhou period (c. 1100–771 BCE) and, together with teams of horses, were placed in the tombs of aristocrats; their use in combat during that period was probably secondary to their symbolic role. By the end of the Eastern Zhou period (770–211 [256] BCE), however, their function as a symbol of status had declined, and they played an important role in the strategy of the Qin army. LK

1   Excavated in 1976; unreported.
2   Shaanxi 1988b; Yuan 1990; Wang 1994a, 423–430; Ledderose and Schlombs 1990, 277–78, and others.
3   Wang 1994a, 123–130; a reconstruction of a chariot appears in Ledderose and Schlombs 1990, 288–292.

128

A group of four terra-cotta chariot horses

Height 170 (67)
Qin Dynasty, third century BCE (c. 210)
From Pit 1 at Xiyangcun, Lintong, Shaanxi Province

Qin Terra-cotta Museum, Lintong, Shaanxi Province

This team of four horses,[1] ears pitched forward, eyes bulging, and nostrils dilated, compose a team pulling one of the Qin army's chariots. They are sturdy, broad-necked animals, well-suited for their role in combat; their tails are curled to avoid interfering with the harness. An estimated five hundred sculptures of horses have been excavated from Pits 1 and 2, together with their bronze trappings and remnants of their yokes and bridles. Isolated examples of horse sculptures appear in pre-Qin

Excavation photograph of Pit 1, with traces of chariot remains.

Excavation photograph of Pit 1 (*right*).

dynasty art, but the formal and technical sophistication of these representations, which effectively balance realistic depiction and stylization (for example, in the rectangular form of the mane) are unprecedented.

Each sculpture is composed of several parts: the animal's trunk was formed in three sections, each made of coiled clay strips; the legs, the neck, the head and the tail (the latter two formed in molds) were then attached to the trunk, and the entire sculpture coated with a fine clay slip. Details (the eyes, the muzzle, striations in the mane) were in-

cised before firing, after which the horses were painted in bright colors.

Horses, represented in conjunction with human figures or individually, had become a staple element of the tomb *mingqi* by the Western Han dynasty (206 BCE – 24 CE). During the Tang dynasty (618 – 907 CE), the presence of horse figures in tombs reflected the passion of the aristocracy for these animals rather than a military function. LK

1   Excavated in 1976; reported: Shaanxi 1988b, 1:183 – 192; 2: figs. 145 – 153; 158.

129

Jade shroud sewn with gold wire, and
set of plugs

Length 188 (74), width at shoulder 44.1 (17 ⅛)
Western Han Dynasty, late second century BCE
(c. 113)
From the tomb of Liu Sheng at Lingshan,
Mancheng, Hebei Province

Hebei Provincial Museum, Shijiazhuang

The jade shroud of Liu Sheng[1] is the most famous
example of this extraordinary category of object.
Since its discovery in 1968, approximately forty
complete or fragmentary shrouds have been found;
few are in such good condition as this example and
that of Liu Sheng's consort, Dou Wan, both of
whom were buried in tombs carefully hollowed out
of a mountainside at Lingshan, Mancheng, Hebei
province.[2]

Prior to their discovery, such jade shrouds were
known from a number of texts. One of the fullest
descriptions is found in the *Han jiuyi buyi* (Ancient
rites of the Han dynasty) by Wei Hong, first century
CE: "When the Emperor died, a pearl was placed
in his mouth; his body was wrapped around with
twelve layers of reddish yellow silk. Jade was used
to make the garment. It had the shape of armor
and the jade pieces were stitched together with
gold threads."[3]

These jade shrouds have been treated as a Han
development arising out of jade face coverings and
pectorals in use as early as the Western Zhou period
(see cats. 84, 85). Found primarily in eastern China,
the shrouds in fact have little direct connection
with the earlier tradition. The pectorals are most
often found in the western provinces, and the most
elaborate are at least three or four hundred years
older than the shrouds. Shrouds differ markedly
from one another in the details of their construction, but they are more or less uniformly composed
of twelve sections: the face, the head, the front and
back parts of the tunic, the arms, the gloves, the
leggings and the feet (fig. 1), each consisting of
closely fitting plaques drilled at the corners and
sewn together with wire. In the later centuries

of the Han period, different metals — gold, silver,
or copper — were used to indicate the rank of the
shroud's owner, but most of the examples dating
from the early period were sewn with gold. The
shroud made for the King of Nanyue (cat. 139) exemplifies a lesser level of refinement: only certain
sections contain drilled plaques; in these instances,
silk rather than metal was used to attach the pieces
to one another. Despite such variations, it seems
that the design of such shrouds followed a widely
disseminated model.

Liu Sheng's shroud incorporates a Neolithic
jade *cong* tube (see cats. 29, 30) to hold his genitals.
From this and other such examples, we may infer
that the Han had discovered Neolithic tombs,
which they mined for jade; the large quantities of

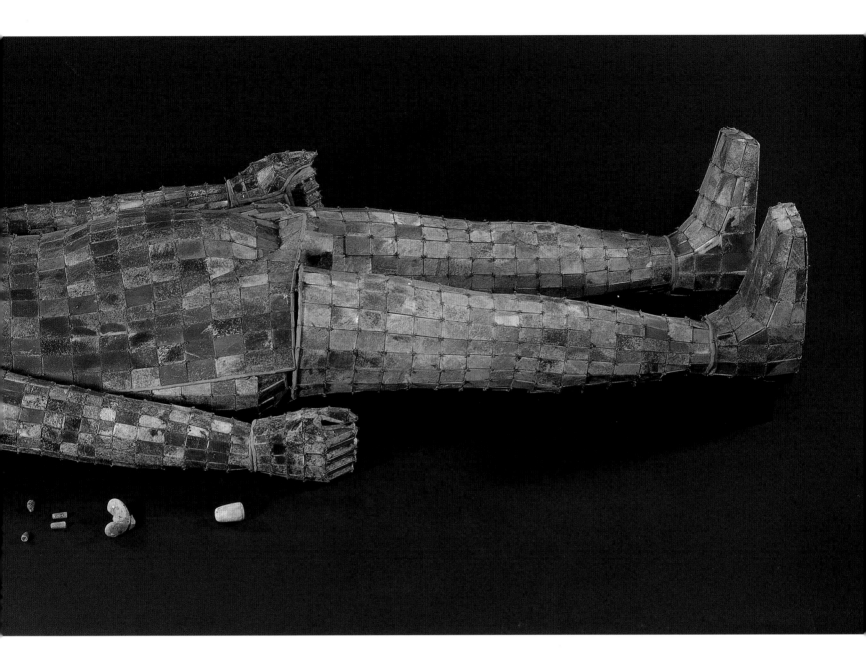

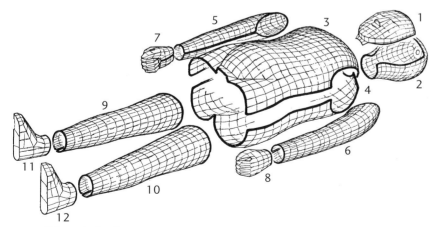

FIG. 1. Schematic drawing of the sections of Liu Sheng's jade shroud. After Zhongguo 1980b, 1:348, fig. 227.

disks in such burials may even have intrigued the Han and inspired them to place disks within the jade shrouds, as was done both for the King of Nanyue (cat. 140) and Liu Sheng.

It has often been suggested that these shrouds were intended to effect the transformation of their owners' bodies into jade.[4] A more plausible interpretation is that such shrouds served as armor to protect the bodies of the elite from the attacks of evil demons and forces thought to cause illness, corruption, and decay. Tombs of other members of the Liu family were sometimes also equipped with jade-bladed weapons,[5] which were probably intended for protection. Liu Sheng was also supplied with a set of plugs to block the body apertures; their function may have been similar to that of the

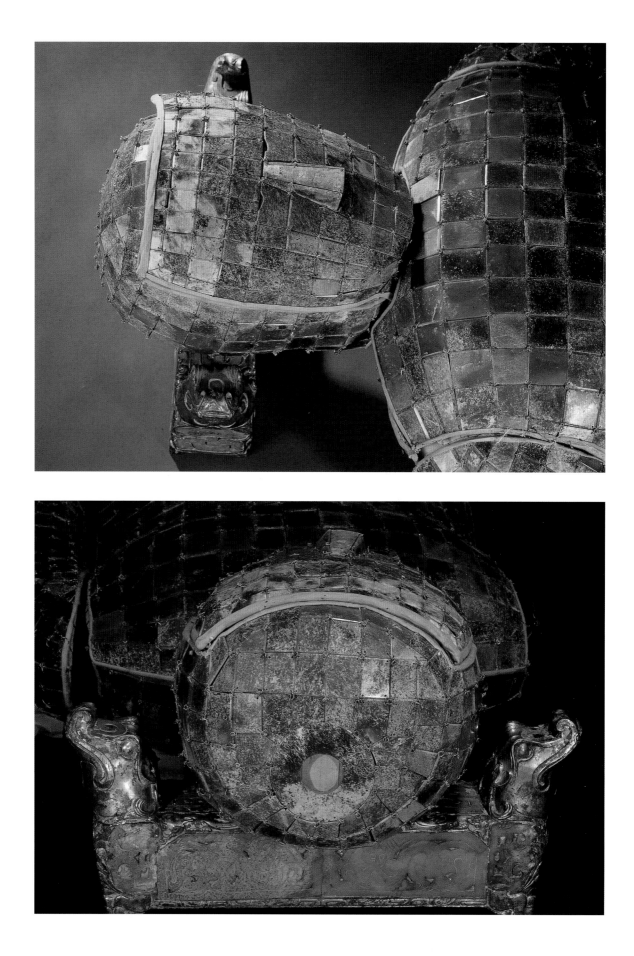

earlier face coverings. Liu Sheng was also supplied with an exceptionally attractive headrest (cat. 130).

Jade shrouds were apparently made almost exclusively for members of the Liu family, the family that supplied the rulers of the Han empire. Members of the Liu family were installed as kings in small states, primarily on the eastern side of present-day China. Their large rock-cut tombs, tunneled far into the sides of small hills, were an extraordinary innovation. Generally, they consisted of a long access passage, branching into small and large chambers, and terminating in the main burial room. Liu Sheng's had two major chambers: the front chamber, equipped with tents or canopies and vessels, may have been intended for feasting and ceremonial observances. The rear chamber was lined with stone slabs. At right stood the coffin; in the center, fine tables and utensils for eating and drinking; and at left, a preparation area in which stood stone figures of attendants. Thus, the tomb held all the necessities for daily and ceremonial life. While the artifacts suggest an afterlife of feasting and enjoyment, the jade shroud and the protective apparatus point to the anticipation of danger as well. JR

1 Excavated in 1968 (M 1:5188); reported: Zhongguo 1980b, 1:346–349.
2 Thorp 1991b, 26–39.
3 Wei 1935–1936, 7.
4 Wu Hung 1997b, 147–169.
5 See a Chu kingdom tomb at Shizishan, Xuzhou, Jiangsu province, reported and illustrated in Shizishan 1998, 4–33, color pl. 1.

130

Gilt bronze headrest inlaid with jade

Height 17.6 (6 7/8), width 44.1 (17 3/8), depth 8.1 (3 1/4)
Western Han Dynasty, second century BCE (c. 113)
From the tomb of Liu Sheng at Lingshan, Mancheng, Hebei Province

Hebei Provincial Museum, Shijiazhuang

Gilt bronze headrests inlaid with jade appear to have been standard items in tombs prepared for members of the Liu family and their close relatives or associates. Three examples have been well published: the one exhibited here,[1] a comparable piece from the tomb of Liu Sheng's consort, Dou Wan, and one from a tomb at Houloushan in Xuzhou.

All three consist of a rectangular framework with three-dimensional animal heads at the two ends. The beasts flanking Liu Sheng's headrest have a piglike yet somewhat reptilian appearance; each head points sharply upward, with a curling snout, two bulging eyes, two small ears, and the traces of some sort of horn or crest scrolling behind the ears. Small spirals inlaid with jade fragments lie behind the nostrils and between the lower part of the two eyes. Eight jade plaques decorate the two long sides of the headrest, two small plaques make up the two short sides, and a large and highly complex carved jade fills the upper surface.

Their diverse style suggests that some of the jades were made for other purposes and reused to compose this headrest. The beautifully carved jade on the upper surface has the appearance of an Eastern Zhou carving, although it likely dates from the Han period. Two S-shaped dragons, embellished with small incised scrolls, confront each other around a central point and are paired with dragons facing outward at the two ends; their long, curling snouts echo those of the beasts that form the ends of the headrest. The angular form of the dragons is reminiscent of renderings in bronze, and the small scrolls and hooks along their bodies suggest the cloud patterns that developed out of such motifs.[2] The undulating surface and varied textures of this jade section complement the fine scrolling relief of the two upper gilt bronze edges.

The high relief of the bronze and jade on the upper surfaces of the headrest contrasts with the markedly flatter designs on the side plaques. Each of the four larger rectangular plaques, two on one side, two on the other, with angled upper corners, frames an S-shaped tigerlike creature twisting to face the viewer. These creatures, displayed in profile with striated, curling tails, closely resemble the feline dragons depicted in other works in this exhibition (cats. 141, 145). It seems likely that these feline creatures derive from animal representations on gold or bronze plaques and harness ornaments from present-day Inner Mongolia and southern Siberia. Transformed into jade, they have been fully assimilated into their new context.[3]

The four smaller plaques that form the bodies of the main creatures of the headrest are D-shaped and have narrow slots carved within them; it seems likely that they were originally parts of pendant sets. Each comprises two S-shaped dragons backing onto each other; their contours form the curved edge of the plaque, and a small flattened disk-shaped object lies between their tails. The plaques at each end of the headrest also seem to represent varieties of S-shaped dragons. One bears traces of a suspension hole, and the head of a dragon looking back over its body can be discerned; it is possible that this piece and its simpler tandem at the other end of the headrest were originally intended for other uses. Such an interpretation is supported by jades in the headrest of Dou Wan, a similar (albeit much less elegant) example. The two long sides include sections of *bi* disks cut to fit the rectangle, and squared fragments similarly compose the top and two ends; the original patterns (criss-crosses, animal scroll borders) and composition of these constituent pieces remain clearly evident in this adaptation.

A somewhat more complex composition can be observed on the headrest from the Houloushan tomb (fig. 1). In this example, four creatures form the metal framework, their feet supporting the headrest itself, while their heads decorate the corners of the upper surface. Fragments of two S-shaped dragon pendants compose the top, and a piece of another dragon pendant forms one of the sides; jade plaques have been used to fill in extra space. The headrest is particularly interesting for the small, framelike device at the center of one side, flanked by two monster faces with ring handles. JR

FIG. 1. The top, underside, and two sides of a gilt bronze and jade headrest; length 31.2 (12¼); Western Han period; excavated in 1991 from Houloushan, Xuzhou, Jiangsu province. After Xuzhou 1993, 43, fig. 33.

1 Excavated in 1968 (M 1:5188); reported: Zhongguo 1980b, 1:78 – 81.

2 Long scrolls, often called cloud scrolls, had several sources, including (as here), the dragon patterns originally developed for bronzes and adapted to jade. A lacquer painted form related to such jade and bronze designs appears on the coffin of the wife of the Marquis of Dai, buried at Mawangdui (Hunan 1973, 1: fig. 26).

3 A clear example of a jade plaque based upon a bronze ornament from the north or northwest is illustrated by So and Bunker 1995, no. 79.

131

Bronze *ding* tripod with bear-shaped legs

Height 18.1 (7 ¹⁄₈), diam. 20 (7 ⁷⁄₈)
Western Han Dynasty, late second century BCE
(c. 113)
From the tomb of Liu Sheng at Lingshan,
Mancheng, Hebei Province

Hebei Provincial Museum, Shijiazhuang

Numerous bronze vessels were found in the tomb
of Liu Sheng, most of them plain utensils — basins,
cauldrons, steamers, and flasks — intended for the
day-to-day preparation of food. This example,[1]
however, evokes an ancient tradition of ritual *ding*
food vessels. Between each of the two U-shaped
handles on either side of the body, fastened on a
small pin, an animal-like peg can be slotted beneath
two of the four animals standing on the lid to hold
the lid in position, or removed from this locking
position and lifted backward.

It seems unlikely that this *ding* and the *hu* from
the tomb of Liu Sheng (cat. 132) were intended for
ritual ancestor offerings, although late Zhou and

Han practices have yet to be fully explored. It may
be that the plain *ding* and *hu* found in many tombs
were intended for this purpose.

While this bronze has many similarities with
earlier Eastern Zhou *ding* vessels, particularly those
from the Jin state in Shanxi and its successors, it
also has several characteristics that point to a later
manufacture: the locking device (which suggests
that the container was filled with something important that merited extra security in cooking or serving) is not seen during the earlier period, while
the bear-shaped feet are a feature common to many
Han bronzes. (Freestanding bear-shaped feet seem
to have been intended to support lacquered vessels
that have since decayed and disappeared.[2])

Bears are somewhat unusual in the repertoire
of ancient Chinese animal motifs, and no bronze
examples are known from the Shang or the Zhou
periods. While the bear figure may have been a Han
innovation, part of a repertoire of new designs, two
other sources for the image have also been proposed. It may have been borrowed from Western
Asian, Central Asian, and Siberian images of "the

fierce creatures." In western regions, such figures usually took the form of lions; in the Far East (where lions were unknown), the creatures were generally rendered as tigers or bears. On the other hand, bears may have been considered important spiritual forces in Siberia, where they were probably more prevalent than they were in China; it may be that, in seeking out practices from lands adjacent to them, the Han learned of the powers of the bear. Certainly the spiritual force of the bear was deployed in exorcism rites. The *Zhou li* (Rites of Zhou) contains a famous passage describing an exorcist: "In his official function, he wears [over his head] a bearskin having four eyes of gold, and is clad in a black upper garment and a red lower garment. Grasping his lance and brandishing his shield, he leads the many officials to perform the seasonal exorcism *(no)*, searching through houses and driving out pestilences."[3]

Bears also appear in a number of texts that describe landscapes, particularly in *fu* poetry, and in descriptions of animal combats organized by emperors and princes to demonstrate their harmony with and control of the natural world. Such natural combats were often linked to the feats of the Yellow Emperor, one of the most venerated Late Zhou and Early Han deities.[4]

Bear-shaped attachments were prevalent for only a relatively short period, being most widely used in the Western Han period and then gradually diminishing and disappearing. References to bears do not appear regularly in Han texts and indeed seem to diminish in frequency through the course of the period. JR

1 Excavated in 1968 (M 1:4102); reported: Zhongguo 1980b, 1:49–53.
2 See finds from Shiqiao at Xuzhou, Jiangsu province (Xuzhou 1984, 22–40, figs. 54, 56).
3 Quoted after Bodde 1975, 78.
4 Lewis 1990, 195–212.

132

Bronze *hu* vessel with bird-script design

Height 44.2 (17⅜), diam. 28 (11)
Western Han Dynasty, late second century BCE
(c. 113)
From the tomb of Liu Sheng at Lingshan,
Mancheng, Hebei Province

Hebei Provincial Museum, Shijiazhuang

Eastern Zhou and Han inlaid bronzes of this quality are exceptionally rare. Two similar wine vessels, clearly prized possessions, were found in the personal chamber of the king; the two share the form of Han wine flasks, differing from each other in the decoration of their lids and in the designs of their horizontal bands.

Set on a small sloping foot, this elegant vessel[1] has a round, bulging belly and a short, curved neck

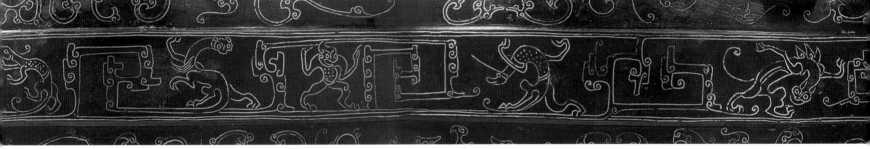

that splays outward to a domed lid with three flanges on its top; two animal-headed masks hold ring handles on the two sides. Fine curving patterns — inlaid inscriptions composed of elaborate bird-script characters — decorate the main bands of the vessel and the lid; the narrow relief borders of the body and the foot are inlaid with designs of exotic animals, which seem to emerge from the scrolls.

The inscriptions on this *hu* vessel suggest that the flask held wine for the occupant of the tomb, with the expectation that his afterlife was to be enjoyed. The inscriptions have been studied by a number of scholars,[2] and the following translation proposed:

1   Lid inscription
    We have made a cover with an inscription of gold inlay. There are three words to a sentence and it is decorated with fish patterns.

2   Neck inscription
    Ordinarily a *xizun* was used, but now we have adopted the *hu*.
    The cover is round with four bands of patterned decoration.
    When with pleasant emotions, we gather to eat and drink,
    It will be a grand occasion with abundant flavors.

3   Body inscription
    Fine food fills the gates to the bursting point.
    The more sustenance, the more we become fat and healthy.
    We desire longevity and the dispelling of disease.
    Even 10,000 years would not be too much.[3]

A similar inscription is found on the second vessel.

The decoration of the bands seems to draw on several sources: angular designs sprouting small quills appear on Eastern Zhou and Early Han objects, such as the jade in the upper part of the headrest (cat. 130), and similar designs are found on the coffin of the wife of the Marquis of Dai.[4] Exotic animals also appear in lacquer painting, particularly on pieces from Mawangdui in Hunan province

and from Yangzhou in Jiangsu province. The use
of southern Chinese object forms and decorative
motifs is likely a reflection of the political climate:
the Qin state had conquered the Chu state (the
dominant power in central southern China and the
heart of the lacquer industry) and had pushed the
king and his entourage eastward to found the Eastern Chu state. The Liu family — the founders of the
Han dynasty — came from this state, and brought
with them the practices of their own region in the
south and southeast to the seat of the court at
Chang'an (present-day Xi'an).

The placement of these vessels in the beautifully prepared back chamber implies that the pieces
were intended for the king's personal use; the
inscription itself, which makes no mention of
ancestor ceremonies but rather explains that these
sumptuous vessels, containers for wine, will bring
pleasure in a long or even eternal afterlife, suggests
considerable changes in the manner in which
offerings were presented to the ancestors. JR

1   Excavated in 1968 (M 1:5015); reported: Zhongguo 1980b,
    1:43–48.
2   See Xiao 1972, 49–52; Dien 1985, 1087–1090.
3   Translation after Dien 1985.
4   Hunan 1973, fig. 26.

133

Bronze foot in the shape of a bear standing
on top of a bird

Height 11.6 (4 ⅜)
Western Han Dynasty, late second century BCE
(c. 113)
From the tomb of Liu Sheng at Lingshan,
Mancheng, Hebei Province

Hebei Provincial Museum, Shijiazhuang

This small bronze shows a four-legged beast standing on the wings of a bird.[1] The extraordinary creature appears to be some sort of feline or bear but a
female in any event, with a large protruding (perhaps pregnant) belly and pendulous breasts. The
right arm is raised to scratch behind its right ear,
while the left arm is pushed down and braced
against the knee. The creature appears to crouch
on the back of a resting bird; one foot rests on the
joint of the bird's wing, while the other rests on the
body of the bird, which faces forward and has a
large beak, round eyes, and two earlike extensions.
The bird's long wings are drawn backward, and from
behind rises a plume or tail that seems to have eye
decoration, referring perhaps to a peacock.

The image of one creature standing on a bird
or another creature is readily linked with large
wooden lacquered sculptures from the Chu state.
In examples from late Chu tombs (third century
BCE), such as that at Yutaishan, Jiangling, Hubei
province, birds stand on crouching felines. The
birds often have wings of antlers (see cat. 118), and
appear to be guardian figures.

A variant on this Chu motif appears in an
ornament from the tomb of Dou Wan: a bird
(which would originally have held a pair of tubular
cups behind its wings) stands on a small feline.
This shape was developed directly from another
Chu type — a double cup supported by a bird, such
as that found in the Chu tomb at Baoshan.[2] It is
possible that this bronze is a variant on this theme.
Here the feline and bird have been reversed in
position, but they retain the motif of an upright
creature standing on a crouching one.

The pregnant female figure, however, may have a much more exotic origin: late versions of the Egyptian goddess Tauert, known in small figurines in the shape of an upstanding pregnant hippopotamus have come to light in parts of the Near East or Iran. (An agate carving of this pregnant figure, with a lion's head, seems to have been made in Iran.[3]) This foot or support may incorporate features borrowed from peoples along the north and western peripheries of the area; other features, in particular incense burners and bears, were adopted from the border areas and substantially modified by the Han to suit their own visual context and above all their own symbolic or iconographic significances. This medley of sources is characteristic of the richness, vitality, and originality of Han culture. JR

1   Excavated in 1968 (M 1:4146); reported: Zhongguo 1980b, 1:95–96.
2   Hubei 1991, color pl. 6:2, 3.
3   Rawson 1998b, 44–47.

134

Bronze *boshanlu* censer inlaid with gold

Height 26.0 (10 ¼), diam. 15.5 (6 ⅛)
Western Han Dynasty, late second century BCE
(c. 113)
From the tomb of Liu Sheng at Lingshan,
Mancheng, Hebei Province

Hebei Provincial Museum, Shijiazhuang

The censer[1] is exceptional both in its casting
and in its fine inlaid decoration. Swirling dragons
emerge from an openwork circular foot to support
a cup-shaped basin; the sea surges around large
rocks, which rise to form peaks around the basin's
lip. A tall rocky mountain, populated by small relief
creatures and humanlike beings, forms the lid (fig.
1), pierced by large holes between the crags.

Solid gold bands with fine incised lines form
the censer's base. Thin linear inlays and small
striations and circles indicate the texture of the
dragons' skin. The waves and their breaking crests
are imaginatively suggested by large inlaid gold
scrolls with pointed tips and small cloudlike extensions, echoed in striations on the outcrops and on
the mountain itself. While the inlay closely resembles a cloud scroll, it is plausibly a representation
of *qi* — the ultimate force or power of the universe,
embodied in clouds or moving waters, out of which
"all things condense and into which they dissolve."[2]
(The concept of *qi* was formulated gradually during
the latter part of the Eastern Zhou period and
dominated Chinese thought from the Han period
onward.)

Such *boshanlu* ("universal mountain") censers
were common during the Western Han, but do not
seem to have existed prior to that period. During
the Late Eastern Zhou period, other forms of
censers seem to have been used, including openwork bucket-shaped bronzes, which supported
burning aromatic branches or twigs. Earlier ceramic
and metalwork censers were formed by bowls on
stemmed feet, often with openwork covers composed of animal figures[3]; some of these resemble
creatures employed in decorative bronzework by
peoples on the borders of the Han empire, and it is

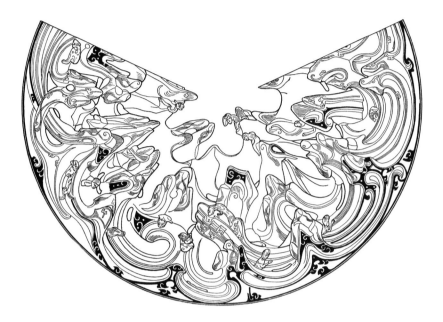

to Mount Kunlun, a peak that reached upward to the heavens, or even to a cosmic pillar joining the earth to the heavens.[6] JR

1   Excavated in 1968 (M 1:5182); reported: Zhongguo 1980b, 1:63–66.
2   For the formulation of the notion of *qi* during the period, see Graham 1989, 101–104 and references in the index.
3   Erickson 1992.
4   See Rudenko 1970, 284.
5   Watson, 1993, 49.
6   Erickson 1992; Munakata 1991, 27–34. The identification of Mount Kunlun's location changed during the Eastern Zhou and Han periods; it was first thought to be situated in the north, and later, in the west. See also Major 1993, 158–159.

FIG. 1. Cat. 134 from above. Adapted from Zhongguo 1980b, 65, fig. 45.

possible that the use of incense may have been stimulated in part by exchanges and contacts with the inhabitants of these areas; peoples on the southern borders of Siberia are known to have inhaled narcotics from basins in which hot stones were placed. This practice may have stimulated the development of incense burners in China.[4]

Over a relatively short time, the decorated, covered censer was fully integrated into a system of associations and meanings through the *boshan lu* form. The representation of a miraculous island supported by dragons may refer to the islands of Penglai, thought to be situated in the eastern sea. The First Emperor of Qin sent envoys with young boys and girls to seek out these islands in the hope of finding the drug of immortality; the islands disappeared into the sea when the voyagers glimpsed them and sought to land.[5] The Han image of mountains, however, had a broader symbolic import as well: Mount Taishan in Shandong province, in particular, was viewed as one of the main routes of access to the worlds of the immortals and to the dwelling of the Celestial Deity in the stars. Thus, the imagery of the mountain-shaped censer may embody as well the identification of tall mountains as routes to the spirit world. Indeed, it has often been suggested that such imagery refers specifically

135

Bronze ram-shaped lamp

Height 18.6 (7 ³/₈), length 23.0 (9 ¹/₈)
Western Han Dynasty, late second century BCE
(c. 113)
From the tomb of Liu Sheng at Lingshan,
Mancheng, Hebei Province

Hebei Provincial Museum, Shijiazhuang

Lamps appear relatively late in the repertoire of
Chinese bronzes, and seem to have come into use
only during the Eastern Zhou period. Fine examples
dating to the mid-fourth century have come from
the tombs of the early Zhongshan kingdom of the
Di people; these tombs contain spectacular examples, one in the shape of a tree, from which hang
various monkeys, and another in the form of an
unusual being, perhaps an immortal, holding lamp
trays supported by snakes.[1] Other pieces from the
Chu state in the south include lamps held in the

hands of servants or immortals and one in the shape of a man holding a lamp riding a camel.[2]

How interiors were illuminated prior to the appearance of lamps remains an unresolved question; wicks may have been placed in oil, within simple ceramic bowls, and torches and flares may have been used in larger buildings.

Whatever their origin, one of the extraordinary features of these lamps is the wide variety of forms and fine materials used. A simple standard form, resembling the ancient *dou* vessels, consists of a tray on a tall foot, with a spike (perhaps to hold a wick) and a tall stem.[3] A number of such lamps were found in the tombs of Liu Sheng and his consort Dou Wan. This ram-shaped lamp[4] is a relatively unassuming example of more exotic forms originating particularly in the center and north of China.[5]

Ram-shaped objects may have had specific symbolic connotations for their owners. The character for "ram" resembles *xiang*, "auspicious," and it is likely that the associations of the two would have been prized. Moreover, rams, as well as deer and camels, were popular subjects for harness and belt ornaments. These subjects may have been introduced from distant kingdoms. Artifacts, designs, and techniques borrowed from the border areas were probably not viewed as inferior and in fact may even have been cherished for their association with peoples purportedly in contact with strange deities and spirits thought to live beyond the limits of the known world. JR

1   Lee 1998, no. 54; Rawson 1996, no. 74.
2   Hubei 1996, color pl. 5.
3   For an account of Qin and Han lamps, see Ye 1983. See also Sun Ji 1991, 351–357.
4   Excavated in 1968 (M 1:5181); reported: Zhongguo 1980b, 1:66–69.
5   Capon 1992, no. 32.

136

Bronze bird-shaped lamp

Height 30 (11¾), diam. 19.0 (7½)
Western Han Dynasty, late second century BCE
(c. 113)
From the tomb of Dou Wan at Lingshan, Mancheng,
Hebei Province

Hebei Provincial Museum, Shijiazhuang

Birds are a frequent subject for lamps and appear
in several common forms. In this example,[1] found
in the tomb of Dou Wan together with cat. 137, a
bird holds a ringlike tray that contained the oil or
wax, divided into three sections, perhaps for three
different wicks. Another kind of lamp, closely related to this form, is in the shape of a bird's claw
surmounted with a tray.[2]

This finely modeled lamp shows a large three-
dimensional bird with a long neck and heavy head
and bill. The bird's wings are outstretched, and it
has a fan-shaped tail; the feathers are delineated by
grooves. It stands on the back of a coiled creature
with an animal head, suggesting that this is no
ordinary bird but rather one endowed with supernatural or special powers; viewed from above, the
bird would have appeared to hold a ring of light
in its beak (fig. 1).

Birds appeared in a number of unusual objects.
Basins supporting a flying bird on a central pillar
have been found in the fourth-century BCE tombs

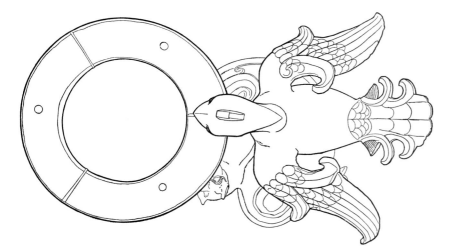

FIG. 1. Cat. 136 from above.
After Zhongguo 1980b, 236,
fig. 176.

of Zhongshan, a state ruled by the Di, who had entered Hebei province from the north. Such objects are thought to have functioned as large oil lamps.[3] The bird would thus literally have perched in a ring of fire.

The association of birds with disks or rings of light is an allusion to the bird (normally a raven) that carried the sun on its course. Best known among such stories is that of the archer Yi, who shot down nine of ten suns (or birds) to save the world from burning.[4] The myth found its way into images, such as a banner painting from Mawangdui that shows a black bird at the center of a red sun.[5] The image was refined over time, and during the Han dynasty, a bird was conventionally thought to carry the sun in its beak, as this lamp clearly illustrates.

Light, particularly the light from the sun, was much sought after in the world after death, imagined as a dark and mysterious place. Lamps held by birds would presumably have brought the sun into the tomb; mirrors (frequently metaphors for the sun, moon, and stars[6]) were preserved and buried because they too brought light. JR

1   Excavated in 1968 (M 2:3102); reported: Zhongguo 1980b: 1:261–263, fig. 176.
2   An early form of a large bird's foot mounted with a ring was found in a third-century tomb at Shangwang in Linzi, Shandong province. This tomb also produced a lamp in the form of a circular tray on a stand with the lip of the tray held in the bird's beak. See Linzi 1997, pl. 24 and color pl. 1.
3   Sun Ji 1996, 1–14. It is possible, however, that the basin held water.
4   Birrell 1993, 138–140. For the link between suns and birds see Allan 1991, 19–56.
5   Allan 1991, 36; Major 1993, 159–161.
6   Brashier 1995, 201–229.

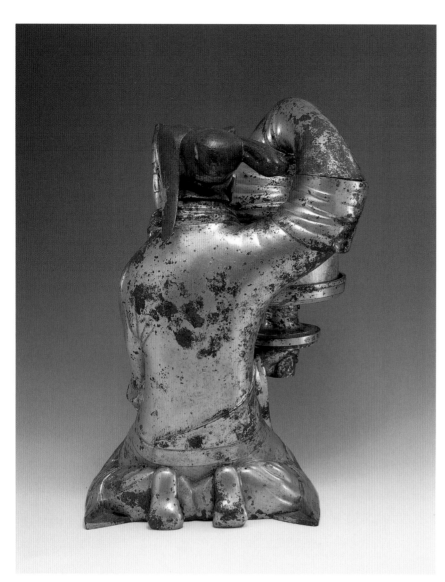

disks separated by a small stem; the upper disk has a short projecting handle and a spike in the center to hold a wick. Between this lamp tray and the chimney, two removable covers control the burning of the oil.

Six sets of inscriptions on the lamp provide some information on its history. One name mentioned repeatedly is Yang Xin Jia, thought to be the name of an imperial family member's household, granted a warrant in 179 BCE; they lost their position in 151 BCE when a member of the family was found guilty of taking part in the uprisings of 154. It is likely, therefore, that the lamp dates to the second quarter of the second century BCE, possibly to the reign of the emperor Wen Di (179–157 BCE). The inscriptions also mention the grandmother of Liu Sheng, the Empress Dowager Dou, and refer to the Changxin Palace, where the Empress Dowager lived during the mid-second century BCE. The lamp may have been given to Liu Sheng's consort, Dou Wan, who was probably a close relative of the Empress Dowager.

Among lamps made in the Warring States period and the Han dynasty, several exceptional examples in the shapes of birds, animals, and humans have been found. Each is unique and many are made of sumptuous materials, including gilded bronze, as here, or bronze inlaid with gold and silver. Such highly prized pieces would have belonged to members of the elite. The lower gentry made do with ceramic copies; examples recovered from their tombs nonetheless rival the bronze lamps in their inventiveness and exuberance. JR

1 Excavated in 1968 (M 2:4035); reported: Zhongguo 1980b, 1:255, 259–261, fig. 173. An entry on the lamp is included in Fong 1980, no. 94.

137

Gilt bronze human-shaped lamp

Height 48 (18⅞)
Western Han Dynasty, late second century BCE
(c. 113)
From the tomb of Dou Wan at Lingshan, Mancheng, Hebei Province

Hebei Provincial Museum, Shijiazhuang

This renowned lamp is remarkable for its elegance and the aura of serenity that it conveys.[1] A young woman, wearing a heavy robe and scarf, kneels, eyes open, mouth half-closed. A square cap falls in a sharp point behind her head. Her left arm is drawn across her body to support the lower part of the lamp; her right arm is raised, and the long sleeve appears to fall over the lamp, acting as the cover and the chimney. The lamp itself consists of two

THE TOMB OF

THE KING OF

NANYUE AT

XIANGGANG,

GUANGZHOU,

GUANGDONG

PROVINCE

The King of Nanyue was a member of a family that ruled a small kingdom in the area of present-day Guangzhou (Canton). Established in 203 BCE by Zhao Tuo (r. 203 – 137 BCE), who was named King of Nanyue by the Han emperor Gaozu in 196 BCE, the kingdom lay geographically outside of the traditional areas of Han power. However, archeological evidence from the tomb — identified as that of second ruler of the kingdom, Zhao Mo (r. 137 – 122 BCE), the son of Zhao Tuo — suggests that its occupant wished to be identified as a ruler equal to the imperial princes themselves; indeed, his seal (cat. 138) gives his title as "Emperor Wen."

The tomb, lined with stone slabs, was dug into a small hillside at Xianggang in Guangzhou. Its plan is similar to that of the imperial princes' tombs: a narrow access passage, entered through a storage area, leads into the front chamber, flanked to the left and right by side chambers for storage. The large rear chamber is divided into three sections: a central room (with a small annex for storage behind it), which contained the coffin, and two side rooms, which held the bodies of attendants and servants.

Remains of painted decoration in the central front chamber suggest the brilliance of the tomb's original paintwork, most of which has now disappeared. The front of the tomb held vessels and musical instruments, elephant tusks and minerals — the latter perhaps intended for alchemy. The king, encased in his jade shroud, was laid in a double coffin in the central room at the back, and fine objects, including exceptional jades and a silver box, were placed at his head and feet. The bodies of four women, all supplied with mirrors and jade pectorals, were found in the eastern chamber; the western chamber contained animal remains (possibly sacrifices), as well as the bodies of individuals who may have been the king's attendants.[1]

The discovery of the tomb brought to light an extraordinary abundance of jade objects — the king's shroud (cat. 139), numerous disks placed with the body (cats. 140 – 142), and plaques worn in groups suspended on cords to form pectorals (cat. 144). Jade vessels found in the tomb are far more numerous and sumptuous than those found in other royal burials; certainly they are of greater quality and quantity than those found in Liu Sheng's tomb. It is likely, though, that even the King of Nanyue's tomb was modest by comparison with other royal burials, such as, for example, the tombs of the Chu kings in present-day Xuzhou, which were robbed in antiquity.

The source of the king's jades remains undetermined; they may have been carved in Nanyue by artisans from other areas or imported from Chu or the northern states; in many respects the jades resemble those used by the members of the Imperial family. It is likely that Zhao Mo employed burial officials who were thoroughly familiar with burial practices at the Han metropolis. The jade shrouds, for example, imitate those of the imperial princes. The jade disks are almost identical to those known from other regions; some seem to predate Zhao Mo's reign by a century or more, suggesting access to supplies of carved jade from outside the area. The chambered design of the tomb itself mirrors that used in the eastern kingdoms.

Excavation photograph of the main chamber of the King of Nanyue's tomb.

BURIAL PRACTICES AND BELIEFS

In the years since the discovery of the tombs of Liu Sheng and of the King of Nanyue, other large and complex rock-cut tombs have been found — at Xuzhou in Jiangsu province (the capital of the Han kingdom of Chu), at Qufu in Shandong province (the kingdom of Lu), and at Yongcheng in Henan province (the kingdom of Liang) — all of them far more complex than the earlier finds.[2]

In contrast to tombs of earlier periods, which were dug vertically into soft earth, especially in the loess regions of the Yellow River, the magnificent Han tombs were laboriously tunneled into rocky hillsides along a horizontal axis. Chambers associated with specific functions branched off from the central passages. These tombs were not simple repositories; rather, they were palaces for kings and princes in the afterlife, supplied with the utensils of daily life, often in ceramic and lacquer, but also in gilded bronze, silver, and even gold. Objects that may have been used for rites connected with the spirits — incense burners, lamps, mirrors, and braziers — were also part of the tomb furnishings, but bronze ritual vessels for offerings to ancestors, so abundant in tombs predating the Western Han period, do not appear to the same extent in the rock-cut tombs.

Indeed, the contents and construction of these tombs testify to important changes in religion and ritual that occurred between the fourth and third centuries BCE.[3] Multi-chambered tombs, with specific functions assigned to each room, show the influence of the south and the Chu state — the birthplace of Liu Bang — as do the everyday utensils and forms of lacquerware. The wooden and clay guardian and servant figures similarly suggest Chu influence.

The Han use of stone, both for the tombs and for the carvings and figures contained within, derives from areas to the north and west. Ornamental work — gold belt plaques, decorative motifs, and even the forms of figures on functional objects such as lamps — reflects the style of the borderlands. It is unlikely that the Han viewed such designs simply as exotica: the periphery of the known world was thought to be inhabited by strange spirits, and it seems likely that these motifs and object forms were adapted for their magical or auspicious associations. Ferocious tigers, animals in combat, and silver boxes in Iranian taste were thus assimilated to Han functions and Han views of the universe (cats. 141–143).[4]

The east, on the other hand, may have been the source of the abundant jade objects in the inner chambers of these tombs — shrouds, sword fittings and weapons, vessels, pectorals, and other ornaments. Some of the material for objects may have originated in eastern China — in particular, the Neolithic burials of the Liangzhu culture.[5] A jade tube *(cong)* incorporated into Liu Sheng's jade shroud is one such Neolithic piece, and other ancient objects may have been recut to make the plaques of the shrouds.

The contents of the tombs suggest that the Han viewed the universe as filled with spirits of every kind — some of which could be summoned in trances induced by wine and incense, others through music and dance. Later Han tombs depict these deities and spirits, including the animals of the Four Directions, the Queen Mother of the West, Nü Wa, the creator of the world, and her companion, Fu Xi, as well as the creatures associated with the sun and the moon. The tombs thus appear to represent efforts to create microcosms of the universe for the benefit of the tomb occupants in order to ensure their prosperous afterlives. The tomb was not simply a waystation in the journey to paradise but rather an end in itself — the dwelling in the afterlife. JR

1   For the archaeological report of the tomb of the King of Nanyue, see Guangzhou 1991. See also Lam 1991 and Prüch 1998.
2   See Huang 1998, 11–34.
3   The changes described here are discussed more fully in Rawson forthcoming.

4   The spirits and monsters at the periphery of the universe are vividly described in the poem "Summons of the Soul" in the famous early anthology *Chu ci* (Songs of Chu) dating to the Late Eastern Zhou and Han periods. See Hawkes 1985, 219–231.
5   See cats. 29–36.

138

Gold seal of Emperor Wen

Height 3.1 (1 ¼), width 1.8 (¾), depth 1.8 (¾);
weight 0.15 (⅓)
Western Han Dynasty, second century BCE
From the tomb of the King of Nanyue at Xianggang,
Guangzhou, Guangdong Province

The Museum of the Western Han Tomb of the
Nanyue King, Guangzhou, Guangdong Province

Facing political difficulties in the year 134 BCE,
Zhao Mo sought the help of the Han imperial government, which dispatched an expedition to come
to his assistance (although the enemies of the
king were defeated before it reached the south).
In thanks, and as proof of his loyalty, he sent his
heir apparent, Yingqi, to serve the emperor at the
court in Xi'an. After his death in 122 BCE, Zhao Mo
was awarded the title King Wen, or Wenwang; his
successor, however, referred to him, as *Emperor* Wen,
or Wendi, the title inscribed on this seal.[1]

The right to use seals indicated that their owners had entered into (or had been accepted into),
the sphere of the court. The seal must have been
ordered and cast in the state of Nanyue, for it is
unlikely that the imperial court would have coun-
tenanced the award of the title "Emperor Wen" —
in competition with the Han emperor himself —
to the ruler of the distant small kingdom.

The tomb of the King of Nanyue has yielded
a number of seals, some in gold, others in bronze,
jade, or crystal. The fact that several of the seals
were buried with the king's attendants in the tomb
suggests that the Han afterlife included a bureaucracy that would require individuals to have seals
to authenticate their roles and to carry out official
business.

The seal has a narrow square base topped by
a scrolling dragon in relief. The seal is inscribed
Wendi, xingxi: "administrative seal of Emperor
Wen." JR

1   Excavated in 1983 (D 79); reported: Guangzhou 1991, 1:207,
    fig. 136:1.

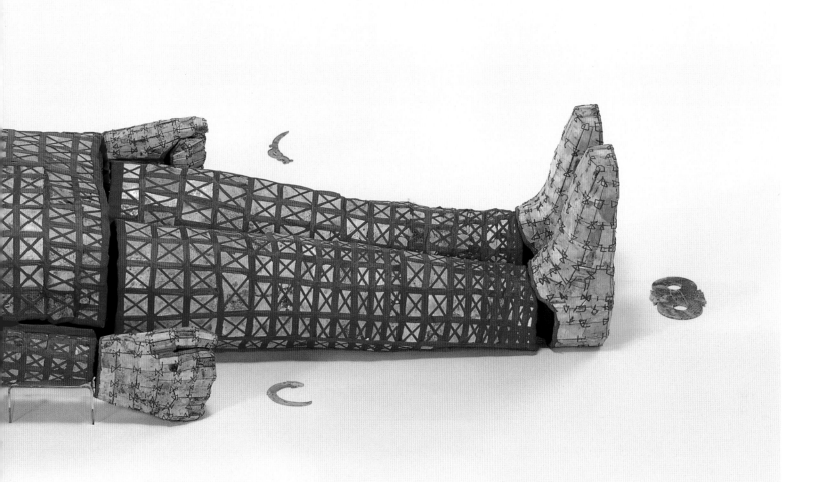

139

Jade shroud sewn with silk, and two dragon-shaped jades

Length 173 (67 ½), width 44 (17 ⅛)
Western Han Dynasty, second century BCE
From the tomb of the King of Nanyue at Xianggang, Guangzhou, Guangdong Province

The Museum of the Western Han Tomb of the Nanyue King, Guangzhou, Guangdong Province

The King of Nanyue's jade shroud reflects a burial practice copied from the kings of small states in eastern China. These kings were all members of the imperial Liu family, ruling from the time of the installation of the Han emperor in the late third century BCE. They controlled small eastern kingdoms under the supreme power of the emperor. In following so closely the practices of the imperial family, the king demonstrated his adherence to the same views and beliefs of the Han imperial house. Zhao Mo did his best to emulate the rulers of the stronger state to the north. His jade shroud,[1] however, was less complex and less carefully made than most of those that have been excavated from the tombs of the kings of Zhongshan at Mancheng, Chu at Xuzhou, Lu at Qufu, and Liang at Yongcheng.[2]

Zhao Mo's shroud consists of 2,291 jade plaques. The hands, head, and feet are constructed of plaques pierced at the four corners and sewn together, but the plaques that form the tunic, arms, and legs were simply glued to a cloth backing and decorated with silk ribbon. Whoever made and supplied the shroud to the King of Nanyue must have been familiar with the jade shrouds made for imperial family members. While it is possible that the suit was made by the imperial workshop, it could have been made in central or southern China.

Many of the jades in the tomb, like the jade shroud, resemble pieces from tombs much farther north. In particular, the carved details of the pendants, and of other decorative pieces, resemble those of jades found in the provinces of present-day Anhui, Jiangsu, and Shandong. Zhao Mo, the King of Nanyue, may have acquired his jades from the state of Chu, or he may have been in a position to entice craftsmen from the Chu state to work for him. The tomb contained many jade vessels, pendants, and fittings for the iron swords found in the tomb.[3] It is likely that both the shrouds and the jade-fitted weapons were intended to equip the king for the perils of the afterlife. Neither the shroud nor the weapons would necessarily have defeated a human enemy, but against enemies of the spirits and demons, they may have been effective as a complex protective system devised for the highest-ranking members of the elite. JR

1   Excavated in 1983 (D 50); reported: Guangzhou 1991, 1:154 – 158. The two dragon-shaped jades were originally held in the right hand of the jade shroud. Guangzhou 1991, 1: 204, 206.
2   Compare the jade shroud for Liu Sheng, cat. 129; see Zhongguo 1980b, 2: color pl. 1 – 2; 1:348, fig. 227, and Rawson 1996, no. 81.
3   For the jades, see Lam 1991.

140

Jade double-*bi* disk with spiral design

Height 7.6 (4 ⅞), width 12.4 (3), depth 0.4 (¼)
Western Han Dynasty, second century BCE
From the tomb of the King of Nanyue at Xianggang,
Guangzhou, Guangdong Province

The Museum of the Western Han Tomb of the
Nanyue King, Guangzhou, Guangdong Province

Composed of two conjoined *bi* disks, this jade is
decorated on both sides with relief spirals;[1] an
incised line borders the inner and outer edges of
these relief patterns. Complex scroll designs fill
the V-shaped interstices at the juncture of the disks
and are detailed with slight points of relief where
they curl on themselves. The jade seems originally
to have been an olive green color, now transformed
into a mottled rust-red and paler buff surface.

A more primitive form of a double disk has been
found at Zhaojiahu, Danyang,[2] but it is uncertain
whether these examples are related, and this unusual piece is otherwise unprecedented. The object
seems to have been attached to the feet of the King
of Nanyue's jade shroud (cat. 139), perhaps to hold
them together, and would thus have paralleled
the single disk that lay at the head of the shroud.
No similar conjoined disks have been found in
other tombs that contain jade shrouds; their rarity
in burial finds may be attributable to the fact that
many of these tombs have been robbed. JR

1 Excavated in 1983 (D 186); reported: Guangzhou 1991,
   1:183–184, 190, fig. 121:1.
2 See Prüch 1998, 246.

141

Jade *pei* ornament with dragon
and bird openwork

Diam. 16.1 (6 ⅜), depth 0.5 (⅛)
Western Han Dynasty, second century BCE
From the tomb of the King of Nanyue at Xianggang,
Guangzhou, Guangdong Province

The Museum of the Western Han Tomb of the
Nanyue King, Guangzhou, Guangdong Province

In a vivid picture of aggression, two creatures —
a dragon and a bird — confront each other within
a double ring.[1] This highly unusual carving derives
from the traditional jade disk with a large central
hole. In place of the normal, smooth flat surface of
the ring and the central hole, however, two narrow
rings form a double frame. At the center, a feline

dragon with a large roaring mouth, a staring eye,
and a plume behind its head pounces forward in
a double-S curve, bracing its large haunch against
the outer ring. Its striated tail twists in a double
curl between the inner and outer ring, and the foreleg reaches from within the central circle to the
outer ring. The bird turns to confront the dragon;
its beak open, it stands with one claw on the
dragon's outstretched foreleg, and a long plume
descends from its tail to form scrolls within the
two rings at the bottom; a large crest bends sharply
back from its head against the outer ring.

Found near the head of the jade shroud (cat.
139), this extraordinary ornament belongs to a rare
category of design in which jade disks of the traditional form were embellished with creatures
displayed in profile. The earliest examples of such
disks come from the tomb of Marquis Yi of Zeng[2]
with summary rendering of animals in profile
against the outer edge of the ring. Much more
elaborate examples are known from several museum
collections, including a particularly fine piece
in the Nelson-Atkins Museum in Kansas City, composed of a broad outer ring resembling a *bi* disk
and a narrow inner ring, between which a bird fills
the space with flamboyant scrolling plumes, while
two feline dragons prance along the outer edge.[3]
(This and other pieces have been attributed to finds
from Jincun and Luoyang in Henan province.
The exact provenance of these latter pieces is not
known.) These jade extravagances seem to have
been developed in the third century BCE; similar
pieces were excavated from a tomb at Yanggong,
Changfeng, in Anhui province.[4] The feline dragons
seen both on this ornament and in the Kansas
City example, were innovations of the third century
BCE. They closely resembled twisted feline creatures
(lions or tigers) embossed in gold on ornaments
excavated in Xinjiang in Chinese Central Asia,[5] and
it seems likely that such designs derive from Iranian
lion motifs. In China, this creature was transformed
into a feline dragon, where, as here, it sometimes
takes on a quite ferocious aspect.

Scenes of animals in combat, which originated
in Mesopotamia in the third millennium BCE, are

familiar in the art of the steppe area and are prevalent in the felt designs and carved woodwork of
the frozen tombs at Pazyryk in southern Siberia.[6]
The motif is also found on many items from the
Ordos and northwestern borders of the present-day
central Chinese heartland. Jenny So and Du Cheng-
sheng have noted the ways in which this subject
was introduced and assimilated in the traditional
crafts of the Yellow River, as well as areas farther
south.[7] Dragons attacked by tigers appear on the
upper surface of the interior coffin of the Marquis
of Dai's wife (fig. 1); a horselike figure appears on
the coffin's side panel in a twisted pose known both
from Mongolia and southern Siberia.

In this jade ornament, the subject of animals in
combat has received an entirely Chinese treatment.
It is contained within the *bi* disk formula, typical of
the ancient jadecarving tradition, while the swirling
lines in which the creatures are rendered have more
in common with the lacquer painted designs of the
south than with the woodcarving and goldwork of
the north. Such designs were prevalent not only in
the tomb of the King of Nanyue but also in the fittings found in the tombs built for the Liu kings of
eastern China, many of which contain gold plaques
embellished with motifs of animals in combat.[8] JR

1 Excavated in 1983 (D62); reported: Guangzhou 1991, 1:190
   –192, fig. 124.
2 See the archaeological report, Hubei 1989, 2: pl. 152:6.
3 Discussed and illustrated in Prüch 1998, 258.
4 Anhui 1982b, 47–60.
5 See Xinjiang 1981, 18–22, pl. 5:3.
6 Compare Rudenko 1970.
7 So 1980; Du 1993.
8 Rawson 1998a, 80–94, especially 88.

142

Jade monster mask with *bi* disk

Height 18.2 (7 ⅛), width 13.8 (5 ¼),
depth 0.7 (¼)
Western Han Dynasty, second century BCE
From the tomb of the King of Nanyue at Xianggang,
Guanzhou, Guangdong Province

The Museum of the Western Han Tomb of the
Nanyue King, Guangzhou, Guangdong Province

The large monster face of this jade supports a
disk to form a door handle.[1] (Such handles were
employed on furniture as well as buildings.) This
example is unusual in being made of jade, although
a similar jade monster face with a fitting for a
ring (but lacking the ring itself) was found in the
vicinity of Maoling in Xingping county, Shanxi
province.[2]

   Both jades resemble an earlier famous bronze
piece from Yi county in Hebei province on which
two felines in high relief weave in and out of the
surface of the face (similar creatures embellish the
ring). The three-dimensional effects of the bronze,
however, give way in this jade to flattened scrolling
representations of the horns or crest of the beast;
an elegant openwork feline creature flanks the right
side of the face and was, perhaps, balanced on the
left by another (now lost); a *bi* disk with a pattern
of small relief knobs substitutes for the ring of the
bronze.

   Both the bronze and the jade recall the famous
taotie faces that were common in the Shang and
Early Western Zhou periods (fifteenth to tenth
centuries BCE) but diminished in importance during the Late Western Zhou period and the Spring
and Autumn period (ninth to seventh centuries
BCE), only to reappear somewhat abruptly in the
fifth to sixth centuries BCE on numerous mold and
model fragments found at the Jin state foundry at
Houma in Shanxi province. A fragmentary model
for a bell (Beijing 1993, fig. 72) shows the design
on one of the most magnificent of the decorated
remains. This mask would appear to be a revival
of the ancient *taotie*, but details suggest otherwise:
tigerlike stripes decorate the nose of the central

creature; the two horns of the beast are gripped in the claws of large birds, and feathered wings appear at the lower extremities. The birdlike features in particular are reminiscent of griffins depicted in western Asian (especially Iranian) metalwork, and the detailed textured surfaces of the design recall the gold relief-work of Central Asia and areas further west.[3]

Clearly, given the medium, the carver of this jade could neither reproduce the intricate relief of the bronze with any ease, nor imitate the sinuous fantasy of such an earlier piece — even had it been his intention to do so. Nonetheless, features that originate in bronzework appear in the jade, in particular the incised lines that form the pupils of the creature. Other jades in the tomb of the King of Nanyue illustrate the ways in which jade carvers adapted designs from the bronzes: several of the jade sword-fittings include feline dragons similarly weaving in and out of the surface.

It is likely that the jade was part of a piece of furniture, a chest or box, that was stored in the king's tomb. The presence of the *bi* disk, however, indicates that the jade had some connection with expectations of auspicious outcomes over and above those that might be achieved by exploiting the powers of the animal face. JR

1   Excavated in 1983 (D 156); reported: Guangzhou 1991, 185–191, fig. 122:4.
2   Wang 1976, pl. 3:1.
3   For a discussion of this point see Rawson 1995, 60–75; Shanxi 1996b, figs. 25–28.

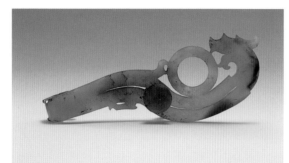

143

Jade belt hook

Height 6.2 (2 ½), width 18.8 (7 ⅜), depth 0.6 (¼)
Western Han Dynasty, second century BCE
From the tomb of the King of Nanyue at Xianggang,
Guangzhou, Guangdong Province

The Museum of the Western Han Tomb of the
Nanyue King, Guangzhou, Guangdong Province

Hooks were used to fasten the two ends of a belt:
a round stud at the back attached the object to
one end of the belt, while a loop or ring attached
to the other end of the belt slotted over the hook.
Such functional ornaments seem to have been
introduced during the sixth century BCE, possibly
from Central Asia. Among the earliest to be found
in China are some finely cast gold hooks from Yimen, near Baoji, in Shaanxi province. Gold belt
hooks seem to have been prized in areas to the west
of the Qin state; elsewhere, hooks were also made
in bronze and, less commonly, in jade; bronze
examples are sometimes decorated with gilding,
precious-metal inlays, and semiprecious stones.[1]

This example, carved from a single piece of
translucent white jade, has an unusual form, consisting of a dragon with a sinuous body in a double
band.[2] The creature's head is shown in striking
profile; its large eye is emphasized by a distinct
relief ridge, and it has small crest or horn behind
the head. In its open jaw, the dragon grasps a ring,
which is braced by one of its claws; the second claw
emerges from the underside of the body. The convex surface of the jade is exquisitely carved: sharply
cut lines delineate the head and claw, and interlink-
ing scrolls incised on the body catch the light; the
reverse of the hook is plain.

The combination of dragon and disk appears
in a painted coffin design and in a banner from
Mawangdui,[3] on which two dragons wind through
a central disk. The design may have originated in
simple pendants (produced from the fifth century
BCE onward and common in tombs of the fifth to
fourth centuries BCE) composed of carved disks
supported by dragons on either side. The painted
banner and coffin, while ostensibly simply formal
elaborations of the earlier jade pendants, in fact
constitute a more powerful rendering of the motif.
The jade belt hook seems to be a return to the
representation of these elements in ornamental
pendants. JR

1   See Rawson 1995, 303 – 307.
2   Excavated in 1983 (D 45); reported Guangzhou 1991,
    1:192 – 193, fig. 125:3.
3   For the tomb at Mawangdui, see Hunan 1973, 1: figs. 24, 38.

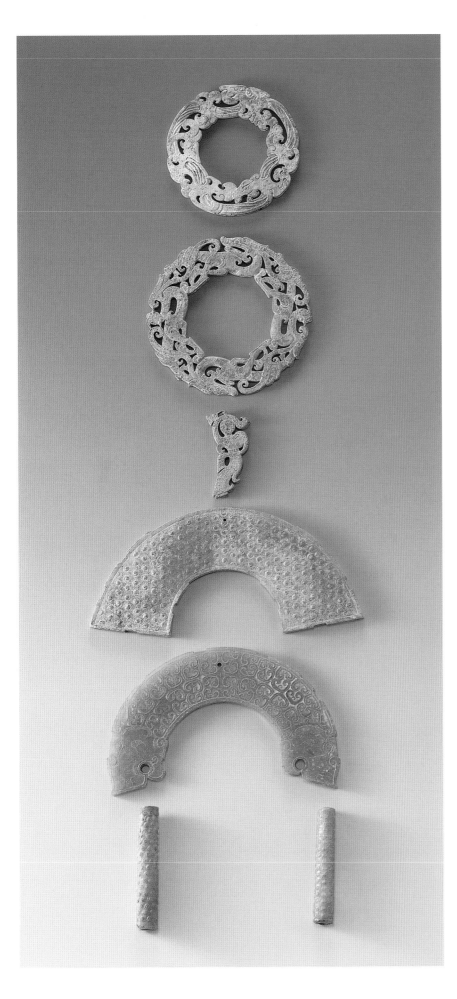

144

Jade *pei* pectoral

Length approximately 45 (17¾)
Western Han Dynasty, second century BCE
From the tomb of the King of Nanyue at Xianggang,
Guangzhou, Guangdong Province

The Museum of the Western Han Tomb of the
Nanyue King, Guangzhou, Guangdong Province

This pectoral[1] is one of twelve such sets from the
tomb of the King of Nanyue; found near the coffin
of "the Lady of the Right," it presumably belonged
to her or to another of the king's concubines. The
elite of the Late Western Zhou period used strings
of beads and jades as ornaments, suspended from
the neck as pectorals or hung from the waist as
pendants (although evidence of their continuous
use from the eighth century to the third century
BCE is lacking). A pendant consisting of a ring and
an arc-shaped pendant *(huang)* strung on a tasseled
cord hangs from the waist of the small jade figure
of a dancer that forms part of this pectoral, and
similar pendants appear on other dancing figures.
Various forms of jade ornament were current, but
each area seems to have employed its own variety.
The ornaments from the King of Nanuye's tomb,
however, are complex and individualized assemblages; it is uncertain whether ornaments such
as these would have been used in life.

The pectoral consists of two carved openwork
rings, the figure of a dancer, two *huang*, and two
tube-shaped beads. The elements would have been
strung together, probably with silken cord.

The uppermost ring is composed of three
dragonlike creatures, with bodies suggestive of
cloud shapes weaving through a ropelike strand
that recalls the tail of the dragon in cat. 141.
Their eyes are outlined with fine ridges; one of
the creatures displays his fangs in an open jaw,
while the two others clamp their jaws on part of
the jade design. The composition of the ring is
highly unusual — perhaps experimentally incorporating design elements originally developed for
other purposes. Few such pieces survive.

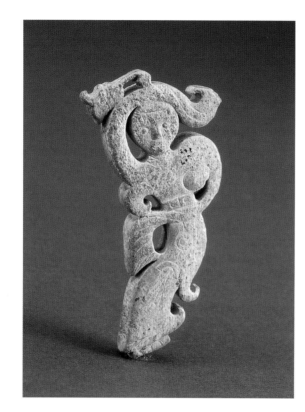

The second ring is also an unusual type, composed of an openwork design of four creatures, two of which are conventional dragons with long, pointed jaws and wings (or winglike plumes) that emerge from behind their ears. The heads of the two other (apparently winged) creatures resemble those of feline dragons, but the composition of their bodies overrides any suggestion of anatomical accuracy. It is likely that both these rings were carved in the Chu kingdom or copied from pieces from that area. A similar ring was found in Xuzhou, the capital of the Chu kingdom during the Han period.[2]

The form of the dancing figure (represented three-dimensionally in another such figure from the tomb [cat. 146]) is suggested by slight rounding of an otherwise flat surface. She has round eyes and a small nose in relief; the mouth is indicated by a slit. She holds her right arm above her head, behind which the sleeve curls upward. Her left arm is drawn across her body, which bends to the right, and the long sleeve appears to cross over an elaborate

bodice to her skirt. The small scroll above her head appears to be some sort of ornament. In contrast with the rings and the dancer, the remaining elements of the pectoral are conventional carvings. Arc-shaped pendants are familiar from many tombs of the Warring States period, and beads were commonly used as ornaments during earlier periods. JR

1 Excavated in 1983; reported: Guangzhou 1991, 1:242–245, fig. 164.
2 See Xuzhou 1984, fig. 47:2.

145

Jade *pei* ornament in the shape of a double-headed dragon

Height 6 (2 ⅜), width 10.2 (4 ⅛)
Western Han Dynasty, second century BCE
From the tomb of the King of Nanyue at Xianggang, Guangzhou, Guangdong Province

The Museum of the Western Han Tomb of the Nanyue King, Guangzhou, Guandong Province

This beautifully carved ornament[1] is a Han period transformation of a conventional type of pendant known as a *huang*. The basic form, which appears as early as the Neolithic period, is an arc-shaped section of a circle, and it occurs in many variants, especially along the east coast of China and during the Shang and Western Zhou periods. During the Early Eastern Zhou period, *huang* were decorated with animal heads at each end (several such examples have been found in the tombs of the Huang state in southern Henan province),[2] and this category of pendants appears in various Chinese states throughout the Eastern Zhou period. During the third century BCE, the heads were transformed in

a number of ingenious ways: a pendant found at Anhui Changfeng Yanggang incorporates outward-facing dragons at both ends into the design.

The carving seen here is a later form of the Anhui example. Two dragons, with broad rounded chests and feline legs, face each other aggressively, separated by a pointed projection on which is carved a rudimentary face. Each advances one paw to the center and raises the other behind its back as if poised to attack. Their jaws are open, and the creatures have small ears and crestlike extensions at the back of their heads. That the outward-facing position conventionally depicted in animal-head *huang* pendants is here reversed does not conceal the ornament's close relation to its predecessors: Like many earlier jades, it has a relief pattern on it, in this instance small raised scrolls joined by interlinked spirals, a form characteristic of the second century BCE.

Seven pendant sets were found in the eastern chamber of the king's tomb, along with the bodies of four women. This magnificent ornament seems to have been the topmost item in a complex pendant set found lying to the east of the coffin of the woman called "the Lady on the Right." Together with this piece, the assemblage comprised five other *huang*, a disk with three birds carved along the outer rim, and two rings incised with spiral grooves. The loop of this *huang* is pieced along the top with three holes, so that the assembled pendant, fixed to an attachment, could hang from the neck or from the waist. Texts such as the *Li ji* (Record of ritual) describe pendants hanging from the waist, but, given its length, it is more likely that a complex assemblage like this example would have hung from the neck over the chest. JR

1 Excavated in 1983 (E 143-9); reported: Guangzhou 1991, 1:240 – 241, fig. 163:1.
2 Rawson 1995, 259 – 266, fig. 2 and no. 17:4.

146

Jade dancing figure

Height 3.5 (1⅜), width 3.5 (1⅜), depth 1.0 (⅜)
Western Han Dynasty, second century BCE
From the tomb of the King of Nanyue at Xianggang,
Guangzhou, Guangdong Province

The Museum of the Western Han Tomb of the
Nanyue King, Guangzhou, Guandong Province

This tiny carved figure,[1] was found in the western
chamber of the tomb, together with small gaming
pieces, glass beads, and the remains of a lacquer
box. While the piercing suggests that the figure was
used as a bead pendant assemblage, it was not
located near pieces that would have composed a
pendant set and seems to have been kept inside a
box with the other trinkets. Several other dancing
figures were found in other chambers of the tomb.

Her hair coiled in a side bun, the dancer holds
one arm behind her tilted head; the long, hanging
sleeve of her robe falls behind her back. The other
arm hangs downward, and the sleeve sweeps out
in a generous hooked curve. The woman's body is
slightly twisted and sharply bent: she appears to
be rising from a kneeling position, her feet covered
by her robe. Vigorous grooving delineates the twisting flow of her long sleeves, and the woman's belt,
her crossed bodice, and her features — eyes, nose,
and mouth — are indicated by incised lines.

Jade figures of dancing women with long sleeves
seem to have been a speciality of the Western Han
period. The best known examples are a pair of
dancers and two single figures in the Freer Gallery
of Art, Smithsonian Institution, Washington. The
paired figures have been reconstructed as components of a pendant set that includes two dragon

figures, a *huang*, and some beads.[2] A more rudimentary figure was found in the tomb of Liu Sheng (cats. 129 – 137) as part of a pendant.

There is little consistency in the style or the artistic quality of these dancing figures. The present figure, carved in the round, is an elaborate, three-dimensional example; the bead in cat. 144 resembles the Freer figures, although the more stylized forms of the latter convey a more animated effect. Some dancing figures are almost flat and rectangular in form. It is unlikely, however, that stylistic differences among these figures point to differing dates of manufacture; indeed both elaborate and highly simplified dancing figures are found in the tomb of the King of Nanyue.

These figures seem to depict "jade maidens" (so named in the *Chu ci* [Songs of Chu] and in a number of Han poems of the *fu* genre) — spirit mediums whose dancing could summon up spirits. The *Shuo wen jie zi*, an early dictionary, identifies these women as "invocators *(zhu)* . . . women who can perform services to the shapeless and make the spirits come down by dancing."[3] Descriptions of these dancing jade maidens often allude to their long sleeves, whose swirling movements might have suggested the mist associated with apparitions of deities and spirits, and the image of the jade maiden was used throughout the Han period and into the early period of the division of the kingdoms. Jade maidens are also mentioned in later Tang dynasty poetry, where they are associated primarily with Daoist-types of paradise.[4] JR

1   Excavated in 1983 (C 137); reported: Guangzhou 1991, 1:120 – 121, fig. 81:1; 2:242 – 243, fig. 164:1, 3.
2   Discussed in Prüch 1998, 172, see Lawton 1982, nos. 77 – 79.
3   Quoted after Falkenhausen 1995, 279 – 300.
4   The jade carvings and their poetic context have been fully discussed in Erickson 1994, 39 – 63.

147

Jade box

Height 7.7 (3 ⅛), diam. 9.8 (3 ⅞)
Western Han Dynasty, second century BCE
From the tomb of the King of Nanyue at Xianggang,
Guangzhou, Guangdong Province

The Museum of the Western Han Tomb of the
Nanyue King, Guangzhou, Guangdong Province

This jade box,[1] consisting of a bowl-shaped base
and a shallow domed lid, is among the most exquisite jades ever excavated in China. It is of a pale
brownish green with some dark staining — the
result, in part, of use. The rim of the lid and of the
base are decorated with relief borders of interlock-
ing scrolls and a pattern of incised hooks and lines
reminiscent of the design on cat. 143. A small loop,
through which a rope-patterned ring passes to form
a handle, is carved integrally with the lid. A border
of eight petals in relief encircles the loop — an
unusual number, although designs incorporating
four elements often appear around the knobs of
mirrors. The lid's interior is decorated with birds
that arch backward over their long tails; their flowing crests resemble those of the aggressive creature
in cat. 141.

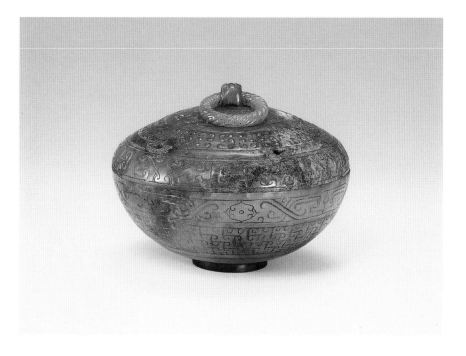

carved jade object. The silver box is decorated with low relief patterns, very similar to those in use in Iran under the Achaemenids and Parthians; a wreath pattern of V-shaped bands around the lip of the lid and the bowl indicates borrowings from a Hellenistic or Iranian source. Such a piece was clearly a rarity and a valuable one at that.[3]

Like many jade vessels of the Han period, this box resembles lacquerware of the late Warring States period and the early Han period (in particular, third-century lacquers from Yutaishan, Jiangling, Hubei province).[4] These lacquer forms were borrowed from the south and imitated in jade to provide the owner with sumptuous pieces suitable for an elegant afterlife. That jade vessels were modeled after lacquer forms, rather than after bronze ritual vessels (such as the *hu* and *ding* that survived into the Han period), suggests that lacquerware itself was prized in its users' daily lives. JR

1   Excavated in 1983 (D 46); reported: Guangzhou 1991, 1:202 – 205, fig. 133.
2   Shizishan 1998.
3   See Prüch 1998, 262 – 265.
4   See in particular the box illustrated in Hubei 1984, color pl. 2.

Jade vessels are exceptionally rare. A few have been found in the tomb of Liu Sheng (cats. 129 – 137). Others were discovered in a small storage chamber in a tomb belonging to one of the Chu kings at Shizishan (present-day Xuzhou) in Jiangsu province.[2] (The tomb was ransacked at an early date, and it is likely that the vessels recovered constitute only a portion of the tomb's original jades.) The jades of the King of Nanyue's tomb are exceptional, both in their abundance and in their quality.

Several points testify to the value of this particular vessel to its owner: it seems to have been stored in the head section of the outer coffin (perhaps for the use of the king himself), and it was found together with a number of other objects of evidently exceptional value — the beaker with the bronze basin (cat. 148), a jade rhyton, as well as the king's seal (cat. 138) and pectoral. The mending of a break in the lid — by means of bindings or rivets passed through paired holes — is additional evidence of the object's value. (The holes may have been drilled originally to attach ornaments, now lost; the drilling may in fact have caused the crack.) Finally, the presence of an unusual silver box in the main chamber indicates the value associated with the

148

Jade beaker with bronze basin stand

Height (overall) 17.0 (6 ⅝), height of basin 5.0 (1 ⅞),
diam. of basin 23.6 (9 ¼)
Western Han Dynasty, second century BCE
From the tomb of the King of Nanyue at Xianggang,
Guangzhou, Guangdong Province

The Museum of the Western Han Tomb of the
Nanyue King, Guangzhou, Guangdong Province

This complex object[1] is composed of a jade beaker
that stands within a shallow bronze basin with a
wide lip. The basin itself stands on three legs, each
consisting of a schematized face mounted on a
small animal-shaped leg; animals in relief decorate
the side of the basin between each pair of legs. An
interior flange braces the serpentine dragons that
support the beaker.

The jade object is composed of three parts that
can be disassembled: a beaker, a pedestal foot, and
a petaled flange inserted between the beaker and
its foot (fig. 1). The beaker has a narrow tapering

form, and is decorated around the lip with a ring
of scroll design, below which are tiny projections
linked by C-shaped scrolls; small pointed petals
compose the lower border, and are repeated on
the pedestal, which has narrow moldings at the top
and at the foot, and on the flange, which is formed
of three large and three small alternating petals.
Gilded dragon-heads at the ends of slender silver
bodies grip the small petals in their mouths to
support the beaker within its basin.

The complex form, materials, and workmanship
of this object indicate its value. It may have been
intended to collect the dew left by the immortals;
an Early Han period text, the *Huai nan zi*, alludes to
such "dew basins":

> When the burning-mirror sees the sun,
> It ignites tinder and produces fire,
> When the square receptacle sees the moon,
> It moistens and produces water.[2]

Square basins have not been found (although
precise matches between recovered objects and

texts are exceedingly rare events); the text's author may in any event have intended simply to contrast a dew basin's *yin* qualities with the *yang* character of a circular mirror.

The beaker form exists in a number of other examples (albeit without the flange seen here): one from the Epang palace site at Chezhangcun, at Xi'an,[3] and another from Luopowan at Guixian in Guangxi province.[4] Two very similar U-shaped beakers were found in at Shizishan at Xuzhou in Jiangsu province, the site of one of the tombs of a Han dynasty Chu king.[5] It seems likely, therefore, that this was a standard jade item made for the highest members of the elite. Lacquer versions of the U-shaped beakers have been found, and it is possible that the form originated in this more easily worked material.[6] JR

1 Excavated in 1983 (D 102); reported: Guangzhou 1991 1:202–203, fig. 132.
2 Major 1993, 65–66.
3 Wenwu jinghua 1993, no. 64.
4 Guangxi 1978, no. 89
5 Shizishan 1998, fig. 8.
6 For pottery examples, see Hubei 1993, figs. 7:2, 7:3, 8.

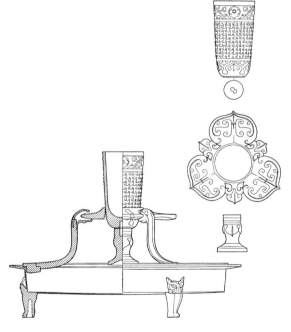

FIG. 1. Components and cross section of cat. 148. Adapted from Guangzhou 1991, 203, fig. 132.

149

Bronze mounted jade cup

Height 14.5 (5 ⅝), diam. 8.6 (3 ⅜)
Western Han Dynasty, second century BCE
From the tomb of the King of Nanyue at Xianggang,
Guangzhou, Guangdong Province

The Museum of the Western Han Tomb of the
Nanyue King, Guangzhou, Guangdong Province

The value of jade required artisans to make
economical use of the material. Carving an object
from a single piece of jade was an extravagance

that necessarily entailed much wastage. More often,
limited supplies of the precious material may
have impelled the King of Nanyue's jade carvers
to use flat jade sections — rectangular, square,
or circular — to create the large number of vessels
(whether intended for the king's life on earth or
thereafter) contained in his tomb.

The framework of this cup,[1] found in the western chamber of the King of Nanyue's tomb, consists
of two rings joined by seven vertical bronze strips.
The strips hold six rectangular jade sections, each
of which is covered with fine relief spirals linked by

incised lines. The cup sits on three molded feet that terminate in narrow points, and a handle composed of a circular ring with a flange is attached to one side. A wooden disk with three arched jade mounts and a now-missing center knob forms the vessel's lid. The jade is translucent and greenish yellow.

The form of the cup, like that of many of the jade vessels, is closely related to lacquer pieces. Lidded tubular cups were relatively common in lacquer and were often mounted in bronze fittings.[2] Since the lacquer repertoire was a major source of inspiration for jadework, it is likely that the creation of specific jade vessels was preceded by a lacquer model, and that such forms were designed to display the more precious material to maximum effect. Vessels modeled on lacquer pieces, but made entirely of jade, are also known,[3] an indication that forms based on lacquerware became a widespread design convention.

1   Excavated in 1983 (F 18); reported: Guangzhou 1991, 1:269–270, fig. 186.
2   Prüch 1997, 105–108.
3   Wenwu jinghua 1997, no. 35.

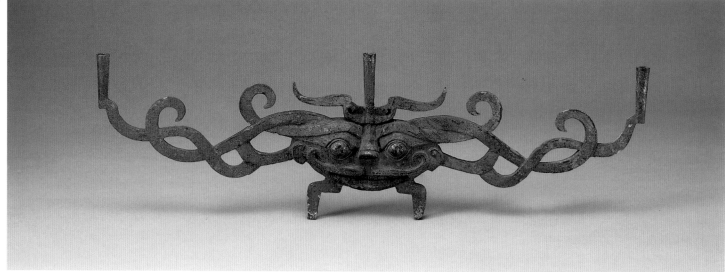

150

Three gilt bronze fittings for a screen

a. Animal mask: height 55.5 (21 ¾)
b. *Pan-long:* height 33.5 (13 ⅛), width 27.8 (10 ⅞)
c. Crouching figure: height 31.5 (12 ⅜), width 15.8 (6 ¼)
Western Han Dynasty, second century BCE
From the tomb of the King of Nanyue at Xianggang, Guangzhou, Guangdong Province

The Museum of the Western Han Tomb of the Nanyue King, Guangzhou, Guangdong Province

The remains of a lacquer screen were found against the eastern wall of the tomb's main chamber. Composed of four panels and a double-door (fig. 1), the screen was ornamented with bronze fittings,[1] three of which are exhibited here. Three pairs of fittings supported the bottom: coiled horned beasts (*pan-long*) at the edges of the outer screens, small Atlas-like crouching figures devouring snakes at the screen joints, and, on either side of the door, abstract serpentlike bronzes.

The top of the assemblage was mounted with three animal heads with scroll-like bodies, two on the outer screens and one at the center. Beneath a straight nose, gaping jaws display teeth and large fangs, and eyes bulge from a rounded face. Hornlike

plumes and two intertwined scrolls emerge from the top of the head, joining scrolls that unfurl from behind the ears. The faces recall an intricate bronze handle from the tomb of Liu Sheng, and their design may derive from a number of sources: they resemble the ancient *taotie*, while the scrolling extensions also call to mind the faces on molds from the Jin state foundry at Houma. They resemble the face patterns around the edges of *bi* disks, found in abundance in the tomb of the King of Nanyue and may also draw on designs typical of the metalwork and wood carvings from the border areas of Xinjiang and Siberia.[2]

Two birds standing upright with wings outspread and a long tails were mounted at the top screen joints. All the pieces along the top incorporate small tubular supports, which may have carried feathers, as did the paired beasts at the bottom corners. It is likely that the tails of the birds had magnificent pheasant feathers.

Remains of screens found in the tombs at Zhongshan, including a renowned fitting of a tiger grappling with a deerlike creature, are evidence of the use of screens in China back to at least the fourth century BCE. The excavators of the Zhongshan tombs have suggested that the screens may

150c

have been used in conjunction with some sort of tent or overhanging curtain; such arrangements may also have been employed in an earlier tomb at Taiyuan,[3] and a pair of canopies or tents were found in the tomb of Liu Sheng. If such was indeed the practice in China, it was perhaps stimulated by contacts to the north; ceremonies or festivities associated with the screens and tents may have been attempts to reach the spirits, perhaps by inhaling incense or making aromatic offerings. The presence of a door, however, casts an uncertainty on whether this screen was part of such an arrangement.

A much smaller lacquered screen, decorated with a *bi* disk and silk cords, and, on the reverse, the image of a dragon, was found in the tomb of the wife of the Marquis of Dai at Mawangdui.[4] The excavators of the tomb of the King of Nanyue have suggested that this screen was decorated with cloud scrolls, a pattern derived from the early Han dynasty lacquer painting designs known from sites in Yangzhou and other areas in the south.[5] JR

1   Excavated in 1983 (D 19-11, D 106, D 162); reported: Guangzhou, 1991, 1:433 – 451.
2   Discussed in Rawson 1998a, 89.
3   Tomb 251, discussed in Rawson forthcoming.
4   Hunan 1973, 1:94.
5   Prüch 1997, 134 – 189.

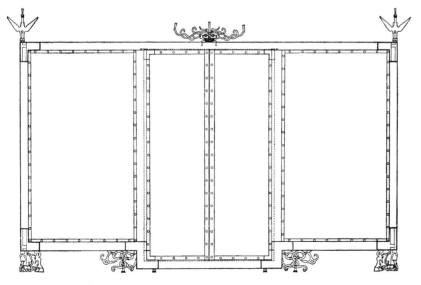

FIG. 1. Conjectural reconstruction of the screen with its fittings. After Guangzhou 1991, 449, fig. 259.

BUDDHIST

SCULPTURE FROM

MONASTERY

SITES AT

QINGZHOU,

SHANDONG

PROVINCE

In recent years a number of stunning discoveries at Qingzhou in Shandong province have made possible new advances in the study of Buddhist sculpture of the fifth to seventh centuries CE. The discovery of what may be termed "burial grounds" for Buddhist statues on the sites of former Buddhist monasteries has yielded hundreds of such pieces. The site of the Xingguo Monastery in Qingzhou yielded statuary during excavations conducted from 1979 to 1981;[1] the most recent of the Qingzhou burial-ground finds — in 1996 at the site of the Longxing Monastery — is even more impressive and is considered one of the ten great archaeological finds of that year.[2]

The large number of finds at Qingzhou reflects, at least in part, the high level of Buddhist activity in that area. The Northern Qi state (550–577 CE) alone contained forty thousand temples; when it was conquered by the northwestern state of Northern Zhou (557–581 CE), which had proscribed Buddhism, some three million clergy were defrocked,[3] an indication that as much as 10 percent of the population had been in religious orders.

Finds of groups of statues such as these are important in a number of ways. They provide a rough index of changing patterns of religious practice and belief in a specific locality. The cache at Quyang in Hebei province, for example, indicated that the worship of the Amitabha Buddha emerged during the Northern Qi period; by the Sui period (581–618 CE), statues of that deity outnumbered those of the Maitreya bodhisattva, the previously preferred focus of worship.[4]

Sculptures with at least some traces of surface paint were known from earlier finds and are in the collections of several Western museums, although their exact provenance is often unknown.[5] With the uncovering of the Qingzhou sculptures *in situ*, one can begin to study this phenomenon in a more scientific manner. The amount of surviving gilding and coloring, as well as the inlaid gold ribbons, a technique that heretofore was thought to have begun during the Tang dynasty (618–907 CE), is unprecedented and allows us to imagine what the sculpture would have looked like in its temple setting.

Finally, these finds provide a depth of material that is of much importance in the study of the artistic aspects of Buddhist iconography. Examples in museums inside and outside of China and scattered finds by archaeologists in recent years have formed the basis for an overall understanding of the development of Buddhist sculpture during the years between the Han and Tang dynasties. Buddhas of the early fourth century CE adhere to the Gandharan style — that is, exhibiting Indian and Greco-Roman characteristics — with some Chinese features. The subsequent Northern Wei (386–534 CE) style depicts the Buddha with a slender body concealed by flowing robes, almost ethereal in mood, with an Archaic smile. With the subsequent period of division between the Eastern and Western Wei (534–550 and 535–557, respectively), the figure assumes a growing naturalness, developing into the emergence of the rather plump body, with close-fitting robes, of the Northern Qi and Northern Zhou periods. Under the Sui and Tang dynasties, the style culminates in a more realistic conception, more fully rounded but stiff, with an expression of inner contemplation — even of aloofness. The many dated pieces make it possible to establish a sequence of stylistic innovations, to discern local and regional styles, to avoid generalizations based on thin evidence that may in fact reveal little more than the workmanship of one craftsmen or a particular set of circumstances (the quality of the material, the price paid by the donor, etc.), and to better gauge the overall character of a local tradition. Solid analysis awaits full publication of these remarkable finds, but already one may speak of a Qingzhou style.

Comparing the Qingzhou finds with other objects from the north, art historians initially characterized Qingzhou as a conservative, rather backwater area distant from the cultural and political centers of the state. The area was contested by the northern and southern states; it had been under the control of the south for more than half a century (409 – 469 CE) before finally being made a part of the Northern Wei state. But the new discoveries have revealed a distinctive local or regional style, in part characterized by the absence of folds (or at most by a lightly sculpted indication of drapery) on the robes of the Buddha — perhaps to provide a better surface for the paint — and a more detailed and complex ornamentation of the bodhisattvas. Elements of the southern style, perhaps harking back to the southern occupation, can be discerned in the bronze figurines of Qingzhou, and it is possible that what may be termed the Qingzhou regional style in stone sculpture is also attributed to southern influences, but that is difficult to establish because so little stone sculpture has survived in the south. The scholar Yang Hong has attributed the rich, multistyled art of the Qingzhou sculptures to a unique combination of northern patterns, southern influences, and local or regional characteristics.[6]

One of the mysteries that remains to be solved is the circumstances of the burials of these Buddhist statues. The proscription of Buddhism by the Northern Zhou state in 574 CE and the extension of that policy into the northeast after the conquest of the Northern Qi in 577 CE is often cited as the reason for specific burials. The damage wreaked on the statues before burial lends credence to that explanation. When caches include Sui pieces — that is, made after the persecution was lifted — the disturbances that attended the fall of the dynasty are cited. In other cases, such as that of the Longxing Monastery itself, Buddhist statues dating as late as the Song dynasty (960 – 1279 CE) have been found. The burials may have been carried out in succession over time, but the reports of their excavation do not make reference to stratification at the burial site. AD

1   Xia and Zhuang 1996, 59 – 67.
2   Shandongsheng 1998, 4 – 15. See also Xia 1998
3   Soper 1959, 118 – 119.
4   Yang 1960, 50.

5   See, for example, Leidy 1998, 88 – 97 and n. 2; Huang 1997, 84 – 85.
6   Yang Hong 1998, 51.

151

Painted stone standing Buddha with two bodhisattvas

Height 138 (54 ⅜), width at base 90 (35 ⅜)
Late Northern Wei Dynasty (386 – 534 CE)
From Qijisi, Qingzhou, Shandong Province

Qingzhou Municipal Museum, Shandong Province

This painted limestone sculpture, unearthed on 10 December 1994 in Qijisi, depicts a standing Buddha, flanked by two bodhisattvas against a flame-shaped nimbus with seven flying *apsaras*. The find-site corresponds to the ancient Qiji Monastery, situated (according to the *Jiajing Qingzhou Prefectural Gazeteer*, 1522 – 1566) in the northwestern corner of Dongyang city, the administrative center of Qingzhou during the Northern Wei period (386 – 534 CE). Broken prior to its burial, the sculpture was found in seven pieces.

The figures are sculpted in high relief with the head of the Buddha, his body, shoulders, hands and feet as if emerging from the stone. He stands against a magnificent aureole, elaborately carved

in low relief, with the flames reaching upward and terminating in an apex directly above the Buddha's head. Measuring eighty-three centimeters high with *uṣṇīṣa* — the cranial protuberance that is one of the thirty-two signs symbolizing his perfect wisdom and enlightenment — the Buddha's form is lean and slender, his features rendered with delicate refinement, his large eyes downcast, and a slight smile lighting his open countenance. The expression is kind and benevolent, in harmony with his gestures (*mudrās*) of "have no fear" (*abhaya*) and "gift-bestowing" (*varada*).

A halo, composed of plump lotus petals framed by multicolored concentric rings, encircles his head, terminating in an intricate rosette garland carved in low relief. These radiant emanations from the Buddha are given emphasis with gilding (the traces are visible on the face, hands, bare feet, and exposed parts of his body), and they are echoed by the large oval body halo of petals and concentric rings, all of which retain some of their original mineral colors. The Buddha's hair is dressed in tight curls with remains of sapphire blue, the traditional color of his hair, and his lips have traces of vermilion.

His monk's robe is composed of three layers: an outer shawl, draped to resemble a sleeved gown, and an inner upper and lower robe, the latter, secured with a wide chest sash. The garment is a slight modification of the more exposed Indian-style that clung to the body and, with a diagonal drape, fully revealed the right shoulder. Strongly visible on the lower half of the outer shawl is the vibrant color that covered the entire garment: a design of bright vermilion rectangles on the bias on which are painted fine lines of mineral color — malachite, ultramarine blue and ochre. On the hem of the inner garment, there is also painted a border of fine vermilion stripes. The rectangles refer to the patches or rags, which according to the *Vinaya*, the Book of Monastic Discipline, should constitute the Three Garments of a monk's robe, indicating humility and avoidance of luxury. The more Chinese appearance of the image may reflect the interest of the dowager empress Feng and the Northern Wei policy of adopting Han culture, which by the third

quarter of the fifth century had begun to influence the appearance of the originally Indian and Greco-Roman, or Gandharan, style images. From the square and powerful visages of the earlier figures at Yungang, Shanxi province, for example, the Buddhas were gradually transformed by the late fifth and early sixth centuries to slender, elongated images with a distinctly sinicized look and gentle expression.

To the left and right of the Buddha stand attendant bodhisattvas, compassionate beings that have postponed enlightenment to aid those on earth to achieve wisdom. The attendants are 53 centimeters tall, smaller than the central figure, and also stand on lotus pods, the strong stems projecting from the stone and floating above protective lions painted near the base; their slender form, delicate features, and subtle smile mirror that of the Buddha himself. With their hair combed into two buns, the attendants are depicted with bare upper torsos; their shoulders are softly draped by capelet shawls with long streamers whose flowing shapes also echo the graceful sweeps of the Buddha's robe.

Each bodhisattva holds a treasure box in his left hand which, is raised to the chest; the other hand dangles naturally. Each figure is sculpted slightly differently in the detail of their garments and gestures. The long shawls covering their shoulders fall below the waist, and the drapery ends are knotted through a pierced disk; the ribbons separate to either side of the body. The attendant on the left, who is wearing bracelets, catches the ends of the shawl in the hand, while the attendant on the right holds a peach-shaped object in the other hand, flinging the sash over the wrist. Each wears the Indian *dhoti*, which shows the same vibrant vermilion color as the Buddha's robe, but with plain borders at the hem. The garments have all been sculpted to achieve an effect of softly covering the body, with the fabric on the shoulders and trailing ribbon ends given a slightly fluttering edge.

The attendants' halos — double rows of lotus petals encircled by multicolored concentric rings — are smaller and slightly different versions of the Buddha's. Two other details differentiate these two: the bodhisattva on the left has the waist sash tied in a bow, while the figure on the right has a waist sash that hangs downward. In addition, the proportion of the features and expression of the figure on the left appear softer and more feminine, while that on the right is slightly more masculine. The colors of their long *dhoti* have been completely preserved: a bright vermilion field, on top of which are painted mineral green, sapphire blue, and ochre lines; there is also a pattern of four small rhomboid shapes forming a floral shape and inlaid with a narrow, 5-centimeter trim of gold leaf.

In the large flaming aureole, seven flying *apsaras*, or heavenly beings, are arranged with three each on the left and right, and the seventh at the apex. With one hand they hold onto the floral wreath that comprises the outermost ring of the Buddha's halo. Their colored ribbons flutter upward with a strong sense of movement, as if propelled skyward by the intensity of the Buddha's aura. Each is poised in a different aerial position and is nicely differentiated. The top five *apsaras* have refined melon-shaped faces; they are painted meticulously,

first using a white base, then flesh colors for the face, and last of all the facial features, with black eyebrows, eyes and nostrils, and red lips in careful detail. Their hair is arranged either in double or in multiple topknots, and they wear round-necked shirts. The lower two flying figures wear their hair in a single topknot, their faces are square, they wear shirts with lapels, and they sport black mustaches. Therefore, it would appear that the top five are female, while the lower two are male. The *apsaras* are painted in black, sapphire blue, malachite, and vermilion, and their ribbons are vermilion, sapphire blue, malachite and ochre. Finally, the outer edge and plain areas of the aureole have also been engraved with a fine filigree pattern of rushing flames surrounding the *apsaras*.

The decoration of the figures comprises a variety of techniques: the garland in the Buddha's body halo is defined in line-engraving; the Buddha's face, hands and feet are gilded; vivid colors cover the surface of the stone, especially the pattern of the Buddha's outer garment with its fine detail and special ornamenting with narrow inlaid gold bands.

The straight-edge manner of low-relief carving and the iconography of the triad can be seen in other dated pieces excavated in the Qingzhou area and identify the sculpture as a product of the Later Northern Dynasties period. In addition, there are a number of features that mark the rarity of this triad and that may be noted as characteristics of a Qingzhou sculptural style: the complexity of the color palette, the unusual level of detail in the carving and painting, the variety in the depictions of the attendant figures — whether their garments or their visages — and of the *apsaras* — whether their head, body or hand positions, and the detail in the painting of their features and garments. Moreover, the sense of gentle humanity in the beatific expression of the Buddha and of the attendant figures, and the majesty of the entire configuration testify to a new level of spiritual understanding of the sculptor and of the congregation and patron for which this triad was created. XM/AD

152

Painted stone standing Buddha

97 (38¼)
Northern Qi Dynasty, mid-sixth century CE
(c. 550 – 557)
From Longxingsi, Qingzhou, Shandong Province

Qingzhou Municipal Museum, Shandong Province

Unearthed on 17 November 1987 at a site approximately 100 meters east of the Qingzhou Municipal Museum, this limestone sculpture, carved in the round, depicts a gently smiling Buddha with a slender frame and delicate features standing on a lotus pod. The *Jiaqing Qingzhou Prefecture Gazeteer* (1522 – 1566) identifies the find-site as the Northern Wei period Nanyang Monastery, renamed the Longxing Monastery during the Tang dynasty.[1]

The figure's hair, sculpted in crisp curls resembling rows of snail shells, culminates in a conical

uṣṇīṣa—the seat of his transcendent knowledge. Like the Buddha figure in cat. 151, his hands are held in the have-no-fear and gift-giving *mudrās*. Clothed in a *dhoti* covered by a round-collared *kāṣāya* robe, the figure's body is suggested his clinging robes (rather than by lineation or carved detail) a representational technique typical of the Northern Qi style.

The skin of the face and visible parts of the hands and feet are gilded, while the *uṣṇīṣa*, the round collar, and the edge of the *kāṣāya* are painted sapphire blue; the lower hem of the *dhoti* is ochre. The latticelike pattern on the *kāṣāya* is a mineral green, and the fields within the latticework are painted vermilion. Threads of inlaid gold, 0.5 millimeter wide, form a border for the latticework, with a reticulated pattern of inlaid gold triangles and rhomboid shapes within those borders. The work's execution reflects remarkable skill, made all the more impressive by the remarkable preservation of the paint. XM/AD

1   The discovery of this piece and cat. 153 is reported in Xia 1997. The lotus-shaped base of the statue is not original.

153

Painted stone standing bodhisattva

95 (37⅜)
Eastern Wei Dynasty, second quarter of the
sixth century CE (c. 534–550)
From Longxingsi, Qingzhou, Shandong Province

Qingzhou Municipal Museum, Shandong Province

Unearthed with the limestone Buddha (cat. 152)
at the site of the Longxing Monastery on 17 November 1987, this carved limestone statue depicts a
smiling bodhisattva with a delicate appearance,
standing on a lotus pod.[1] The bodhisattva's hair is
combed to a high topknot, wrapped around with
strips of hair ribbon decorated with gold ornaments; small winglike ribbons hang down to the
shoulders, and a gold necklace and ornamental
chain hangs from his long neck. A broad scarf,

terminating in an elegant pattern, is draped over the figure's rounded shoulders. The left hand hangs down, holding on to one end of the scarf; the right arm is half-raised. The bodhisattva's upper torso is bare; he wears a long *dhoti,* tied at the waist with an elegantly knotted sash.

Paint was applied to the statue in three layers: first a white base, then a flesh color, and lastly, the other colors. The details of the face are particularly skillfully executed, creating a remarkably lifelike countenance: black was used to outline the upper part of the eyebrows, then the eyebrows were painted in sapphire blue. The upper parts of the eyes were drawn with ochre, fading to flesh color below the eyebrows. Sapphire blue was used to delineate the edges of the vermilion lips. The *dhoti*'s latticelike pattern of cinnabar diagonal rectangles, is framed in inlaid gold with a pattern of lines, triangles, and rhomboids. Several of the figure's characteristics — in particular, the hair ornaments and the sloping shoulders — resemble those of dated Eastern Wei bodhisattvas found in the Qingzhou area. XM/AD

1   The lotus-shaped base of the statue is not original.

Chang'an (the present-day city of Xi'an), the capital of the Tang dynasty, is situated on the Guanzhong plain of the Wei River, an important tributary of the Yellow River. During the Tang dynasty, with more than a million inhabitants, it was probably the largest and most cosmopolitan city on earth, planned according to ancient precepts on a grid system, with the palace and administrative area in the center of the northern sector of the city.[1] The city's 108 walled wards were further subdivided by main streets running north-south and east-west that intersected in the center of the wards. The names and locations of these wards can still be traced through contemporary records and archaeological excavation. One fragmentary work, written by Wei Shu in 722 CE, provides a succinct account of some forty wards in the western sector of Chang'an, naming more than forty Buddhist monasteries, fifteen Buddhist nunneries, seven Daoist temples, and three "Persian" (foreign) temples.[2] Many of these, like the plan of the city itself, had been founded under the preceding Sui dynasty, when the capital was called Daxing. In the words of a modern scholar, Wei Shu's text allows us to imagine "the beauty of the dragon and phoenix"— that is, of Chang'an in the heyday of its glory.[3]

Archaeology provides abundant confirmation of the great scale of the principal buildings of the capital and of a significant foreign presence. The concentration of great wealth around the emperor, the court, and the prominent families of Chang'an allows us a glimpse of the beliefs and fears of its inhabitants. Rare materials from throughout the known world were brought as tribute: tremendous faith was put in their intrinsic value, according to their physical properties of hardness, translucency, brilliance of color, or particular form. When fashioned into the likeness of real or imagined creatures with numinous qualities of their own, such as the gilt-bronze striding dragon (cat. 159), an image of imperial power found within the palace precincts, the resulting objects were extremely desirable and powerful.

Emperor Taizong (r. 626–649 CE) commissioned the tomb of his father (d. 635) and planned his own considerably grander tomb, Zhaoling, on commanding sites in the Beishan hills, a range running roughly east to west, north of the Guanzhong plain.[4] Altogether, eighteen of the twenty Tang emperors were buried along the same range. Each of the imperial tombs included in its precincts the tombs of other members of the imperial family and those of certain important officials. General Dou Jiao, whose splendid white jade and gold belt is shown here (cat. 157) died in 646, a mere three years before the death of Taizong. His tomb in Xianyang is much closer to the Tang capital, perhaps because he died too early to be honored in this way. The tombs of Princess Yongtai, Prince Zhanghuai, and Prince Yide, which have been excavated, all lay within the precincts of the Qianling, the tomb of Emperor Gaozong (d. 683) and Empress Wu (d. 705), but had been robbed in antiquity of their richer contents.

Other major finds in and around Chang'an have come not from tombs but from the sites of palace halls, monasteries, or private dwellings. Two very different types of finds, hoards and reliquary deposits, assume major importance. Hoards, hastily hidden in a time of crisis, are known from the end of the Western Zhou dynasty (771 CE). At that time the Zhou rulers buried their bronze vessels, abandoned Chang'an, and set up a new capital further east, in Luoyang. In the Tang dynasty, when Luoyang was again the alternative capital, the event that precipitated the burial of hoards of precious objects was the rebellion of An Lushan in 755 CE, which brought to a close the prosperous reign of Xuanzong, Emperor Ming (r. 712 – 756), who himself had to flee to Sichuan, far to the west.

The Hejiacun hoard, consisting of 270 items of gold and silver, packed into two large pottery jars and one silver jar and deposited in a pit, was found on land that in the Tang dynasty, according to Wei Shu,[5] had been the residence of Li Shouli, Prince of Bin in the Xinghua ward, just to the west of the center of Chang'an and three blocks south of the imperial city. Li Shouli was the second son of Li Xian, Prince Zhanghuai, the sixth son of Emperor Gaozong.[6] Prince Zhanghuai's own residence in the Anding ward, in the northwestern part of Chang'an, close to the palace, became the Qianfusi (Monastery of a Thousand Felicities) in 673, but it brought little good fortune to its owner who, suspected by Empress Wu of plotting to usurp the throne, was exiled to Sichuan, where he was forced to commit suicide in 684. His three sons were thrown into prison for more than ten years. Decades later, Li Shouli could forecast the weather from the aches in his back from the regular beatings he had suffered. In 706, following the death of Empress Wu, Prince Zhanghuai's remains were brought back to Chang'an by his father, and reburied in a large tomb with splendid murals of hunting and polo playing, which was excavated in 1972. Li Shouli's claims to the succession were thought to be stronger than those of the heir apparent, but he and others were appointed to "high ceremonial offices with no real power at court."[7] His household numbered more than sixty persons, none of them of any distinction; he himself was dissolute, and seemed not to be concerned about his debts, saying to his critics, "Was there ever an emperor's brother who was not given a funeral?"[8] Prophetic words perhaps, since the splendid gold and silver vessels now associated with his name come not from his tomb, which has not been found, but from a hoard. RW

1   Chen 1992, includes good maps of Tang Chang'an (152) and the Guanzhong plain (4-5).
2   Wei 1935
3   Wang Gongwu, editor's note to Wei 1935
4   Chen 1992, map at pages 4 – 5.

5   Wei 1935.
6   Liu Xu 1975, 2831-2832,
7   Twitchett 1979, 372.
8   Liu Xu 1975, 2833.

154

Parcel-gilt silver *pan* dish with mythical figure

Height 1.2 (½), diam. 15.3 (6)
Tang Dynasty, first half of the eighth century CE
(c. 713–755)
From the Hejiacun hoard, southern suburbs of
Xi'an, Shaanxi Province

Shaanxi History Museum, Xi'an

Houston and San Francisco only

This dish[1] and the next (cat. 155) are part of a set
produced by the same combination of metalworking techniques: each dish was formed of sheet silver, polished, and the design worked in repoussé
by hammering from the back; details were added
by chasing from the front, and finally the motif
was gilded, using an amalgam of gold and mercury
applied with a brush to the selected area. When the

piece is heated, the mercury rapidly evaporates in a
toxic vapor, leaving a thin coating of gold on the
surface of the piece. The effect of gilding only certain parts of the design is known as parcel-gilding.
In the Tang dynasty, this form of decoration was
particularly valued, since the process of rubbing
down and burnishing the silver surface gave the
plain areas a resplendence that, unlike that of Western silver, does not tarnish. Pieces such as this one
and those from the Famen Monastery reliquary
deposit (cats. 164–166) were still shining brilliantly
when they were discovered.

The shape of this *pan*, with its six lobes, is inspired by a mallow flower. The piece has a narrow,
flat rim and a base that is completely flat except for
the slight hollow where the decoration has been
worked. The animal in the center is a composite,
with a bovine head, a single horn, a flowing mane,
the wings of a bird in full display, cloven hoofs, and
a tail that is more frond than feather. A close parallel in both style and the treatment of the tail can be
found in the portrayal of a *kalavinka* (the human-
headed celestial bird inhabiting the Buddhist Pure
Land of the West), engraved on the edge of the stela
of the Chan Master of Great Wisdom, dated 736 CE,
in the Beilin, or Forest of Stelae, Xi'an. The date of
this dish and of the others in the set (all of which
have different shapes and motifs, but are worked in
the same fashion) may therefore be assumed to be
around the same time, reflecting the flourishing
splendor of the Tang capital during the reign of
Emperor Xuanzong (713–755). RW

1 Excavated in 1970.

155

Parcel-gilt silver *pan* dish with *sheli*

Height 1.5 (½), diam. 22.5 (8⅞)
Tang Dynasty, first half of the eight century CE
(c. 713–755)
From the Hejiacun hoard, southern suburbs of
Xi'an, Shaanxi Province

Shaanxi History Museum, Xi'an

Houston and San Francisco only

This dish,[1] like cat. 154, is one of a set of five *pan* from the Hejiacun hoard. Two of the dishes take the form of a mallow flower with six lobes; one is decorated with the image of a phoenix with its head turned back, displaying its wings and florid tail; the other shows a bear walking on all fours and looking upward. The form of this dish and the remaining *pan* are inspired by fruit, respectively, a double peach and a single peach apparently split in half. The latter features a tortoise, seen from above so that its upper carapace is completely visible, and the head, tail, and four feet project around it. In this piece, a pair of animals circle each other warily, in counterbalance, one up and one down in each half of the peach, like a pair of identical twins in the womb. As the one turns back and the other looks up, their movements and their very forms describe a figure eight. Particular care is lavished in the details of their tails, which are fringed along the edges but dotted in the center, suggesting a special kind of marking.

Conventionally identified as foxes, the animals (whose faces and snouts do not appear vulpine) may represent *sheli*, an animal implausibly identified as a cross between a fox and an ape (perhaps because of its ability to climb trees) that is said to inhabit the Wulan Mountains in present-day Mongolia, just to the north of the great bend of the Yellow River, and that was valued for its fur. Schafer, citing the *Tang shu* (Tang history), notes that animal tails of all kinds were in demand during the period—as badges of honor or to contain the essence of an animal: "[W]hite horse tails from the northwest and fox tails from the west may have been richer in holy power, but there was no question about leopard tails—they were charged with mana and apotropaic energy."[2] Brinker, describing these dishes, has pointed out how both the tortoise and the peach are Chinese symbols of longevity, and that the fox, a servant of the sun and moon, has magical powers, able to appear as a beautiful woman or a young maiden who can use the mysterious powers of Nature to heal sickness or restore the realm.[3] RW

1   Excavated in 1970.
2   Schafer 1963, 109.
3   Brinker and Goepper 1980, 343, cat. 92.

156

Parcel-gilt silver covered jar

Height 24.2 (9 ½), diam. at mouth 12.4 (4 ⅞)
From the Hejiacun hoard, southern suburbs of Xi'an, Shaanxi Province
Tang Dynasty (c. 654–755 CE)

Shaanxi History Museum, Xi'an

Houston and San Francisco only

A number of the gold and silver vessels in the Hejiacun hoard contained carefully selected, graded, and labeled minerals. An inscription written in ink inside the lid of this elaborately decorated jar[1] describes the contents as "Purple *ying*, fifty *liang;* white [transparent] *ying*, twelve *liang.*" The actual contents appear to be rose quartz (2.177 kilograms) and quartz crystal (0.505 kilograms). Such materials (there were fifteen kinds of minerals in the hoard) were intended for medicinal rather than ornamental use and were evidently precious enough in themselves to warrant being kept in containers of precious metal. Fourteen different varieties of precious stones (in small quantities) were also found in the hoard.

The jar itself has a globular body, on a flaring foot, and a handle that swings freely between two gourd-shaped pivots soldered to the body. A ring-shaped knob crowns the lid, which is decorated with a six-petaled stylized floral motif *(baoxiang)* in the center and a scrolling border with grape and pomegranate motifs. The vessel was formed by raising (hammering of sheet metal) and decorated by chasing (engraving without removing any of the metal) of the main motifs and ring-punching of the ground between them.[2] A parrot in the midst of a roundel of flowers and leaves forms the main decoration on the front and back of the jar. At the sides, just beneath the gourd-shaped pivots, the head of a duck appears in the midst of a similar roundel, and individual sprays of vegetation appear in the spaces between the roundels. The borders of florets and half-florets around the vessel's neck and foot, as well as the lozenge pattern on the handle, are typi-

cal examples of Tang decorative treatment of narrow bands.

Colorful red and green parrots often appear in Buddhist Paradise paintings of the seventh and eighth centuries, and they were evidently much sought after.[3] Flocks of parrots populated the Long Mountains on the border between the provinces of Shaanxi and Gansu provinces, defying easy capture. Others came from further afield: Qinghai and Tibet, as well as Indochina, were sources of parrots, but the most celebrated of all were the "five-colored" parrots imported from Oceania, one of which was the subject of a rhapsody composed on the order of Emperor Xuanzong (r. 712 – 756 CE). A musical instrument, decorated with parrots inlaid in amber, tortoiseshell, and mother-of-pearl, in the Shōsō-in,

was very likely a present from the Chinese court to the Japanese emperor Shōmu, who died in 756 and whose possessions were dedicated to the Tōdai-ji forty-nine days after his death.[4] RW

1 Excavated in 1970; published: Han Wei 1989.
2 Han Wei 1989, 224.
3 The examples that follow are derived from Schafer's inspiring study of Tang exotics (1963), 96 – 103.
4 Schafer 1963, 135.

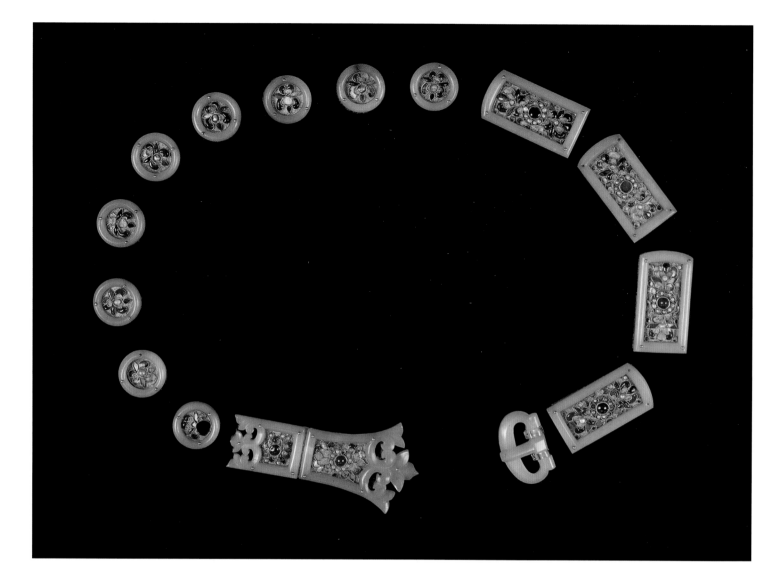

157

Jade belt inlaid with gold, pearls, and precious stones

Length approximately 150 (59)
Tang Dynasty, early seventh century CE
From the tomb of Dou Jiao, Nanliwang,
Xianyang, Shaanxi Province

Shaanxi Archaeological Institute, Xi'an

Houston and San Francisco only

This extraordinary set of belt ornaments was discovered in a tomb on the site of the new international airport at Xianyang, near Xi'an, in 1992.[1] The tomb was that of a cavalry general named Dou Jiao, an elder brother of the Tang empress Taimu. Though his name is not mentioned in Tang historical records, the epitaph tablet found in Dou Jiao's

tomb identifies him as a relative by marriage of the imperial family and records that in 618 — the year in which the Tang dynasty was founded — he and his father Dou Kang attacked and defeated Xue Ju and his son Xue Ren'gao, who had established a hegemony in the western part of the present-day province of Shaanxi. Dou Jiao was active in further campaigns in 620 and 621, and he died in 646. His tomb also yielded an iron sword 84 centimeters long, with a leather scabbard and a crystal fastening carved in the shape of a little pig; and an unusually large bronze mirror, 29 centimeters in diameter.[2]

Dou Jiao's imperial connections are a sufficient explanation of the sumptuous appearance and sophisticated workmanship of this belt. A magnificent hinged and floriated pair of jade plaques formed one end of the belt, and a jade buckle and tongue the other; four rectangular jade plaques (probably arranged two on each side) flanked these ornaments, while eight circular jade medallions were spaced at intervals around the back. A ninth medallion is pierced with a hole, shaped to allow the arched tongue of the buckle to pass through and rest over the rim of the plaque, which itself would have covered the undecorated base of the buckle. The thinness of the finished belt may be judged from the opening in the buckle, through which this last medallion would itself have to pass.

With the exception of the buckle and tongue, each of the jade fittings is inlaid with gold sheet mounted with precious stones and pearls in cabochon.[3] The remains of the belt fabric itself (reportedly hemp), backed with gilt-bronze sheet, are found at the back of the ornaments. Small gold rivets anchor the entire assembly together, three for each of the circular medallions, four or five for the larger elements. The jewels and pearls are arranged to form symmetrical floral motifs. A medallion of ten pearls in the center of each of the five largest panels, enclosing a circular dark red jewel, confirms the very early Tang date of the belt: the same motif, also with ten pearls but enclosing a blue opal, appears twice in the elaborate necklace excavated in 1957 from the tomb of the nine-year-old princess Li Jingxun, who died in 608 CE.[4] Similar medallions are commonly found in textiles and mural paintings of the Sui and early Tang dynasties, notably in the Buddhist caves at Dunhuang in Gansu province. Li Jingxun was the daughter or granddaughter of the last Northern Zhou empress: her necklace, which she was wearing in the tomb, has been described as the most sumptuous piece of personal jewelry to have been found in China, a distinction for which it must henceforth vie with Dou Jiao's gold-encrusted jade belt. The quality and workmanship of both is such that they could only have been made in the Sui and Tang palace workshops, respectively. RW

1   Excavated in 1992; reported: Yun 1993, 48–50, fig. 4.
2   Yun 1993, 49–50, fig. 4–2.
3   When previously exhibited (Tokyo 1998b, no. 89), the cabochon-mounted jewels were described as being of glass; according to the excavation report, they are of precious (or semi-precious) stones.
4   Brinker and Goepper 1981, 227–228, no. 48.

158

Two gold tree appliqués

Height 13.5 (5 ⅜) and 11.5 (4 ½),
thickness 0.4 (⅛)
Tang Dynasty, eighth century CE
From Guojiatan, near Xi'an, Shaanxi Province

Xi'an Municipal Institute of Archaeology and
Preservation of Cultural Relics, Shaanxi Province

Houston and San Francisco only

These two miniature trees worked in filigree on
gold sheet[1] form part of a set of nine pieces discovered during the building of the international
airport at Xianyang, near Xi'an, in December 1971.[2]

While they are likely to have come from a tomb,
unfortunately no report of the circumstances of
their discovery has been or is likely to be published.
The set includes the two trees exhibited here, three
phoenixes, an outstretched dragon, and three ducks
with wings displayed.[3] All the objects are on a small
scale — the dragon only 9.4 centimeters long, the
phoenixes 6.6 centimeters high, and the ducks a
mere 3.3 centimeters high. The trees are described
in considerable detail, from the roots and trunk, to
the branches and flowers or fruit with a different
configuration of the branches in each. On both,
a vine twists around the trunk. The leaves are arranged in rosettes, with a fruit or flower originally
inlaid with precious stone — one piece of green

stone survives on one of the ducks — at the center of each. The inlays would have concealed gold pins (one with a round, flat head survives in the tail of one of the phoenixes) by which the appliqués would have been attached, probably on the outer surfaces of a wooden or lacquered box.[4]

The form of the trees, especially the rosettes with their central fruit or flower, is strongly reminiscent of the *bodhi* trees seen behind the Buddha in preaching and paradise scenes, such as the silk painting (dating to the early Tang dynasty and now in the British Museum) from Dunhuang (Gansu province) that shows Buddha preaching beneath a tree.[5] A Tang dynasty densely foliaged tree, a foot or more in height, and constructed entirely of thin sheet bronze on trunks and branches of iron, with pearl-like glass flowers and fruits and tiny flying birds and *apsaras* (flying celestials), was exhibited in the 1999 Asian Arts Fair in New York, and appeared to be almost certainly Buddhist in intention. The stone reliquary of the Qingshan Monastery, dated 741 CE, is ornamented with four miniature trees on the top.[6]

Trees, and particularly flowering trees, are a constant theme in the secular and Buddhist art of the Tang dynasty. Among the Emperor Shōmu's household possessions, preserved since 756 CE in the Shōsō-in treasury in Nara, Japan, is a set of six panels that form a folding screen: each panel shows a noble lady, seated or standing, in the shade of a tree. Like the golden trees shown here, the trees depicted on the screen are carefully detailed — the roots and trunk, the twisting surface of the bark, and knots where old branches have been cut off or have died back. Pine trees represented in the hunting and polo murals in the tomb of Prince Zhang Huai (706 CE), show similar attention to a realistic configuration of living and dead branches. RW

1   Recovered in 1971; reported: Wang 1989a, 83.
2   Wang 1989, 79 – 86.
3   This duck, two of the three phoenixes, and the dragon are illustrated in Tokyo 1998b, 87, cat. 47.
4   Two of the ducks face to the right, one to the left (as do the phoenixes). In a hypothetical arrangement, the dragon would be on the top, a tree at either end, three ducks on one side, and three phoenixes on the other.
5   Whitfield 1982 – 1985, 1: pl. 7.
6   For the Qingshan Monastery, see cat. 169.

159

Gilt bronze striding dragon

Height 10.8 (4 ¼), length 18 (7)
Tang Dynasty, first half of the eighth century CE
From Xi'an, Shaanxi Province

Xi'an Municipal Institute of Archaeology and
Preservation of Cultural Relics, Shaanxi Province

Houston and San Francisco only

By the Tang dynasty (618 – 907 CE), the dragon —
long connected with immortals and Daoism — had
become a symbol of the emperor. All three associations are particularly appropriate in the case of this
gilt-bronze striding dragon, found on the site of the
Daming Palace,[1] an area of more than three square
kilometers lying just outside the north wall of the
ancient capital of Chang'an (present-day Xi'an). The
remains of more than forty buildings, as well as a

large lake, have been found within the walls of this
imperial park. Among the most important are the
Hanyuan dian (Hall of enclosing the Primal Breath),
whose pounded-earth foundations still stand to a
height of up to fifteen meters, affording a view
south over the entire city; the *Sanqing dian* (Hall of
three purities), where the court conducted Daoist
ceremonies; and the *Linde dian* (Hall of auspicious
virtue).

Built in 634, the Daming Palace assumed particular importance after 660 under Emperor Gaozong
and Empress Wu Zetian, who had it repaired in 662
and briefly called it the Penglai (Paradise) Palace.
Official events and government activities began to
take place there, rather than in the Taiji Palace —
the original seat of power, situated within the
Palace City at the northern end of the main axis of
the capital. The *Linde dian*, eleven bays wide, was
used for banquets and for receiving foreign delega-

tions. Empress Wu Zetian entertained a Japanese embassy there in 703; the largest occasion was a banquet for 3,500 guests, given by Emperor Daizong in 768.

Examples of this type of striding dragon, with a single horn, long snout, and curling tongue, have been dated as early as the Northern Wei dynasty (386–534 CE). One such example is a bronze dragon at the Fogg Art Museum, Cambridge, Massachusetts,[2] but its confident pose and the technique of its casting, which it shares with the dragon seen here, suggest a more likely dating to the Tang Dynasty. One of a pair of gilt bronze dragons excavated from the Yongle ward of the capital, some 5 kilometers to the south of Daming Palace, illustrates these features to perfection: standing on its forelegs, its body smoothly extends skyward into its hind legs, counterbalanced by the sinuous tail, as if it were performing a handstand.[3]

No particular justification seems to be needed for the portrayal of this most auspicious of mythical beasts at the Tang court, but in the context of Daoist belief it has been noted that Emperor Xuanzong (r. 712–756 CE), whose devotion to Daoism was such that his own portrait can be found alongside those of the Jade Emperor and other Daoist images,[4] introduced a cult of Five Dragons in 714. Splendid examples have been found decorating the backs of bronze mirrors; six striding dragons in pure gold, each a mere 4 centimeters long from snout to tail, were found in the Hejiacun hoard. RW

1   Recovered in 1979–1980; published: Wang 1989a, 83; Xianggang 1993, cat. 46.
2   Sullivan 1984, 110.
3   Kuhn 1993, 137–138, cat. 53; Lee 1998, cat. 59.
4   See Liu Yang, "Manifestation of the Dao: A Study in Daoist Art from the Northern Dynasties to the Tang (Fifth to Ninth Centuries)," Ph.D. dissertation, School of Oriental and African Studies, University of London, 1997 (The text is currently in preparation for publication by the University of Hawaii Press.) Chapter 13, at pages 284–285, provides a table of extant and recorded images of Emperor Xuanzong and other in Daoist halls.

DISCOVERIES

FROM THE FAMEN

MONASTERY

AT FUFENG AND

THE QINGSHAN

MONASTERY AT

LINTONG,

SHAANXI

PROVINCE

The discovery of the reliquary deposit beneath the ruins of a brick pagoda at Fufeng, about a hundred and ten kilometers west of Xi'an, is a rare instance of a perfect match between the archaeological data and historical events. The Tang scholar Han Yu's diatribe of 819 protesting the emperor's receiving the relics of the Buddha in his own palace and imploring His Majesty to cast out such filthy remains so that the people might never again be misled by them, is one of the great pieces of Chinese prose writing.[1] It was also an important milestone in the events leading to the great Buddhist persecutions of 842–845 CE, in which thousands of Buddhist monasteries were razed and hundreds of thousands of monks and nuns forced to return to lay life. The relics of which Han Yu complained came from the Chongzhensi, renamed the Famensi, or Monastery of the Gate of the Law, in 1003 under the Song dynasty (960–1279 CE).[2] Founded in 555 under the Western Wei dynasty (535–557 CE), the Famen Monastery rose to extraordinary prominence under the Tang dynasty (618–907 CE); it was closely associated with no fewer than seven Tang emperors, including the notorious Empress Wu Zetian (r. 684–705).

In August 1981, after a period of heavy rainfall, the octagonal, brick pagoda of thirteen stories, which had endured for 372 years since its construction in 1609, collapsed in ruins. After the remains had been made safe in July 1985, the provincial government decided to build a replacement, and an archaeological team from Shaanxi province, Fufeng county, and Baoji city was constituted to proceed with an excavation prior to rebuilding. The excavation proper began on 3 April 1987. Clearing of the foundations revealed not only the circular trench in which the brick pagoda had stood but also the larger, square foundations of an earlier wooden pagoda and steps leading down to a level corridor and three successive stone chambers, the innermost of which lay beneath the core of the foundations of both pagodas.

As the focus of worship in early Buddhist monasteries, every pagoda had its "foundation deposit," sealed within a stone casket or small chamber in the foundations, where it usually lay undisturbed until it became necessary to rebuild the pagoda after its destruction by fire or lightning, the ravages of war or religious persecution. Under such circumstances, the contents could be recovered and incorporated in a new deposit beneath the restored or rebuilt pagoda. In recent years, numerous foundation deposits have been recovered in the course of excavations or repairs; they constitute among the most valuable evidence for many aspects of the monasteries to which they belonged. In the present case, the relic, described by Han Yu as the Buddha's "decayed and rotten bones," was supposed to be a fingerbone. As found in the eightfold set of caskets (cat. 164), it is a hollow cylinder as thick as a finger and about an inch and a half long, with the seven principal stars of the Great Bear, or Big Dipper, engraved inside it. Three facsimiles were also discovered in the crypt, one of them contained in the jade coffin within the crystal sarcophagus (cat. 162).

The reliquary deposit appears to have been specially constructed to allow repeated access from outside. During the Tang dynasty, on no fewer than seven occasions at approximately thirty-year intervals, in 631, 660, 704, 760, 790, 819, and 873, the relics were recovered and

The Famen Monastery pagoda prior to excavation *(left)*; excavation photograph of the first chamber of the Famen Monastery crypt *(right)*.

conveyed to the Tang capital of Chang'an (or, during the reign of Empress Wu, to the city of Luoyang). In the capital, they were displayed in the imperial palace — usually in the imperial Buddhist monastery — and eventually returned to be reinterred in the crypt beneath the pagoda. An inventory stele, written in 874 by the monk Juezhi of the Xingshan Monastery, gives precise details (most of which correspond to specific items contained in the deposit) regarding the 122 gold and silver objects presented in 873 and 874 by the two emperors Yizong and Xizong.

While a full report of the excavation has yet to be published, this extraordinary array of sumptuous objects has already provided invaluable evidence regarding art at the Tang court, metalworking and textile techniques of the Late Tang dynasty, the tributary system, and diverse aspects of Buddhism (especially Esoteric Buddhism, which was then dominant in China). The order in which the exhibits are described here is designed to introduce them in a narrative fashion. First is the massive Buddhist staff (cat. 160), made in the palace workshops, which was undoubtedly carried to the pagoda in 874 at the head of the procession from the palace in Chang'an, over a hundred kilometers away. Next is the model gilt-bronze *stūpa* or pagoda (cat. 161), one of the oldest items in the entire deposit and one that affords an excellent idea of the architectural form of the original Tang pagoda standing above the crypt. It contained one of the four fingerbone relics of the Buddha and was itself packed inside a painted stone *stūpa* in the first chamber of the crypt: this *stūpa* was the first object seen when the doors were opened, and its battered edges are vivid testimony to the number of times that it had been moved back and forth.

The second chamber of the crypt contained a second stone *stūpa*, much larger than the first and dedicated by Empress Wu. Within it, covered in many layers of precious textiles, was a casket containing the second fingerbone relic. Beyond it, and close to the doors leading to the third and innermost chamber of the crypt, was a large cylindrical lacquer box containing a number of fine stoneware bowls and dishes, one of which is shown here (cat. 167).

By far the greatest number of the gold and silver items, many of which had been made for the purpose only a year or two before they were brought to the crypt in 874, were crammed into the third and innermost chamber of the crypt, beneath the very center of the pagoda. The large incense burner, together with its stand (cat. 163), was used in the ceremonies associated with the enshrinement of the relics. It was placed in the middle of the chamber, just in front of the set of eight nesting caskets that contained the third and principal fingerbone relic (the fourth was found in a crystal sarcophagus contained in a separate casket concealed beneath the rear wall of the chamber [cat. 162]). The largest of the seven surviving caskets, with images of the Guardian Kings of the four cardinal directions, is shown here (cat. 164). The remaining items probably had both secular and Buddhist uses. The spherical censer (cat. 166) could be used either to perfume clothing or to burn incense for ceremonial use. The utensils (cat. 165) used in the preparation of tea, together with a set of imported glass dishes (see cat. 168) and a glass cup found in the innermost chamber, are evidence of its widespread use at this time; tea was drunk in every Buddhist monastery and probably in most upper-class households as well. RW

1   Translated by Chen 1964, 225–226.
2   Kegasawa 1998, 61.
3   Kegasawa 1998, 59.

160

Parcel-gilt silver *khakkhara* (monk's staff)

Length 196.5 (77⅜), diam. of handle 22.5 (8⅞);
weight 2.39 (5¼)
Tang Dynasty, dated by inscription to 873 CE
From the pagoda of the Famen Monastery at Fufeng,
Shaanxi Province

Famensi Museum, Fufeng, Shaanxi Province

Washington only

This magnificent ceremonial Buddhist staff[1] was
found propped up in the rear left corner of the
innermost chamber. It is exceptional not only in
size but also in its construction and decoration.
The crowning ornament here consists of two intersecting "wheels," each of which carries six rings,
three on either side; within the wheels is a *vajra*,
or diamond club, supported on a lotus rising out
of clouds and topped by a jewel on an openwork
base; above this, the rings join and are crowned
by a lotus bud. The long shaft is engraved with
figures of twelve *pratyeka* Buddhas wearing the
kāṣāya, or outer ceremonial robe.

   Such Buddhist staffs had both practical and
symbolic functions. Usually they feature only one
wheel and six rings, symbolizing the cycle of birth
and rebirth and the six ways of existence. Carried
and shaken by a monk, the staff would announce
his presence; its noise was thought to drive away
small creatures, so that the monk might not inad-
vertently step on them and so kill living things.[2]
Such a staff also appears as an attribute of the Bodhisattva Kṣitigarbha, who is closely involved with
the Six Ways, and of Buddha Bhaiṣajyaguru — the
Medicine Buddha, whose Twelve Vows may well be
represented in this example by the twelve rings
and the twelve monks engraved on the long handle.
(Bhaiṣajyaguru is worshiped in the present life
for healing from sickness, lengthening of life, and
spiritual guidance toward rebirth in Amitābha's
Pure Land.[3]) The *vajra* so prominently displayed
in the middle of the intersecting wheels appears
on several other objects found in the crypt of the
Famen Monastery pagoda, in particular on four
*arghya*s (vessels for offerings of scented water)

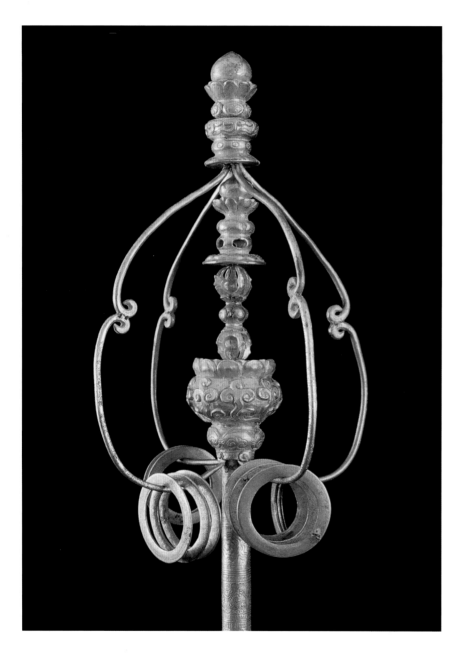

placed one in each corner of the innermost chamber, where they must have been used in an esoteric Buddhist ritual of purification before any of the other votive objects were deposited there.[4]

The inscription on the staff reads as follows: "The Wensiyuan has received the command of the twenty-third day of the third moon of the fourteenth year of Xiantong [873 CE] to make a silver staff to welcome the true body [relic] with gilded decoration and twelve rings, weighing a total of 60 liang,[5] of which 2 liang of gold and 58 liang of silver. Craftsman An Shuyun; Administrative Assistant with the rank of Purple Gold Fish Pouch Wang Quanhu; Vice-Commissioner for Court Service Qian Zhi; Commissioner of the Palace Gate Guard of the Left, General [Wu] Hongque."[6] This inscription is couched in the terms required by the regulations, probably promulgated at the beginning of the reign, under which the Wensiyuan, or Crafts Institute, operated; all of those involved had strictly defined official functions. Together with other inscriptions found on vessels and objects in the Famen Monastery deposit, the inscription is proof that during the Tang dynasty the Wensiyuan was not merely an imperial storehouse: it housed the imperial workshops, located within the palace and operated under the strictest controls.[7] RW

1 Excavated in 1987 (FD 5: 041); reported: Shaanxi 1988a, 20–22.
2 Liebert 1976, 135.
3 Yen 1998.
4 Whitfield 1990a, 252.
5 One liang during the Tang dynasty was equivalent to approximately 40 grams. François Louis (1999, 93 n. 417), provides a convenient breakdown of the weight measures and their equivalents: 4 zi = 1 qian; 10 qian = 1 liang; 16 liang = 1 jin. The approximate metric equivalents are 1 zi = 1 g; 1 qian = 4 g; 1 liang = 40 g; 1 jin = 640 g.
6 Han Wei 1995, 72. A few years before, Wu Hongque had the lower position of Administrative Assistant of High Rank (see cat. 163).
7 Han 1995, 75.

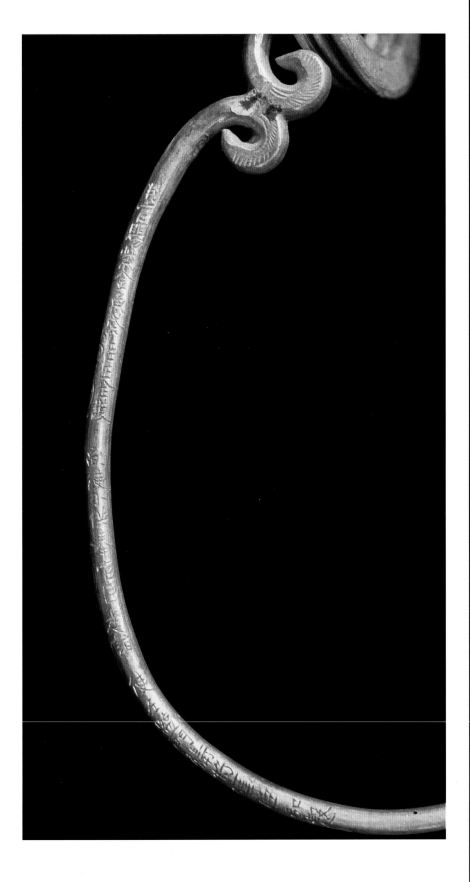

161

Gilt bronze pagoda

Height 53.5 (19 ⅞)
Tang Dynasty, seventh to eighth century CE
From the pagoda of the Famen Monastery at Fufeng,
Shaanxi Province

Famensi Museum, Fufeng, Shaanxi Province

Washington only

In India, the *stūpa*, originally a funerary monument,
was the symbol of the historical Buddha's *nīrvāṇa* —
his release from the karmic cycle of rebirth and
suffering. As the repository of his relics, it was at
the center of monastic architecture and monastic
worship. In China, its importance was reflected in
the lofty forms of multistoried pagodas, in which
only the topmost ornaments preserved the hemi-
spherical form of the Indian original. Later exam-

This pagoda was found wrapped in silks inside a larger stone *stūpa*, which was found at the far end of the first chamber,[2] flanked by two stone lions that had fallen over. The stone *stūpa* itself had tilted to one side, and extensive chips along the projecting edges suggest that it may well have been moved from its original position on one or more of the occasions when the relics were conveyed to the capital.[3] It was one of the first objects found when the doors leading from the corridor to the first chamber were opened.

Like the buildings in Tang depictions of Buddhist Pure Lands (paradises), the model rises on terraces from a lotus pool. On each of the four sides, steps and bridges, guarded by paired lions on columns, provide access across the pool to the main terrace and the four locked doors. Standing in front of the windows, two *lokapālas* (Heavenly Kings) guard the main entrance. Slender columns support the projecting eaves and tiled roof. The mast that crowns the pagoda has six canopies *(chattras)*, a seventh of distinctive, umbrella-like form, and, successively, a ring or halo, crescent moon and jewel, and a lotus bud finial. In architectural form and detail, this is a work of the early or High Tang dynasty, seventh to eighth century BCE, reflecting Pure Land Buddhism, with no hint of any Esoteric elements. The motif of a crescent moon and jewel, in particular, which ultimately derives from the crowns of Sassanian kings, appears frequently in the headdresses of Early and High Tang bodhisattvas in the cave-temples at Dunhuang. Nevertheless, the workmanship of the small parcel-gilt silver coffin contained within the pagoda, which in turn held a fingerbone relic (actually a precise replica of the principal relic found inside the set of nesting caskets, cat. 164), is similar to that of the many objects made much later, around the time of the final dedication in 874. **RW**

1 Excavated in 1987 (FD 3:002–2); reported: Shaanxi 1988a, 20.
2 Han and Zhao 1998, 351.
3 Whitfield 1990a, 253–254.

ples, such as the Famen Monastery's Ming dynasty octagonal pagoda, tended to be constructed of brick, but many early pagodas, including the earlier four-story square pagoda of the Famen Monastery, were constructed of wood, perfectly exemplified in this gilt bronze, single-story model.[1] The foundations show that the earlier Famen Monastery structure had four main supporting columns and twenty outer columns; it had five bays on each side, instead of the three that we see in this example.

162

Crystal reliquary container in the shape
of a miniature sarcophagus

Height 7 (2 7/8), length 10.5 (4 1/8)
Tang Dynasty, seventh century CE
From the pagoda of the Famen Monastery
at Fufeng, Shaanxi Province

Famensi Museum, Fufeng, Shaanxi Province

Houston and San Francisco only

In contrast to the 122 items listed in the inventory
tablet as having been offered to the true body relic
by Emperor Yizong and his son, the emperor Xizong,
only seven are noted as having been brought to the
palace in 873 from the Chongzhensi (as the Famen
Monastery was then called): "three *jiasha* (*kaṣāya*, or

monastic robes), an embroidered skirt of Empress
Wu [Zetian, d. 705], a lined jacket (*pi'ao*) embroidered in gold and silver thread, a crystal sarcophagus, and an iron casket."[1] It would appear that
these seven items had all been donated to the reliquary deposit on earlier occasions, perhaps when
Empress Wu had the relics brought to Luoyang in
704. She herself would have seen the relics once
before, in 660, when she was already becoming a
powerful figure in the court of Emperor Gaozong.
The skirt donated by the empress, a devout Buddhist, should be identified with the skirt, 16.5 by 7.2
centimeters, found with a set of miniature garments
inside a black lacquer box, in the inner chamber. It
may be that this entire set — which includes an
equally minuscule lined jacket, a tiny cushion, a
tiny *anqun*, or "altar skirt," and a *kaṣāya* measuring

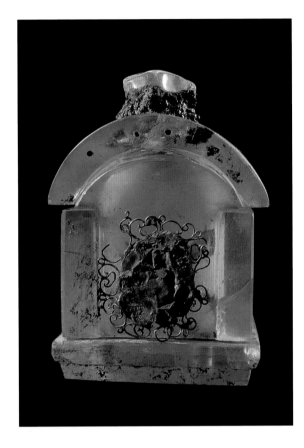

is left entirely unadorned, save for its dais, also carved from jade.

The earliest surviving Chinese reliquary deposits, dating from the Northern Wei dynasty (386–534 CE), were usually contained within a small stone chest, roughly cubical in shape. By the early Tang dynasty, however, relic containers had assumed the shape of the Chinese coffin, with a rounded lid, higher at one end than the other. The innermost coffin might be of gold, inside another of silver or silver-gilt, inside one of bronze or stone. Two such silver and silver-gilt coffins were found in the Famen Monastery deposit, one of bone within the gilt-bronze *stūpa* (cat. 161), the other made of jade in another iron casket inside the marble *lingzhang* of the middle chamber. They contained the remaining two fingerbone relics. From their style, it seems likely that these coffins were made in the eighth or the ninth century — before 874, when the deposit was opened and closed again for the last time. This cannot be the case with these made of crystal and jade, which are of truly exceptional quality and which would have been regarded in China as more precious than gold.

While we cannot reconstruct in detail what happened on each of the occasions that the relics were brought out of the crypt and transported to the palace (to be returned, normally, three days later) one must imagine that new offerings, and very possibly new containers as well, were added each time. The tiny jade coffin may have held the principal relic, and both it and the crystal sarcophagus were perhaps once enshrined within the gilt-bronze pagoda, inside the Ashoka marble *stūpa*, in the innermost chamber of the crypt. By 874, only some thirty years after the disastrous persecution of Buddhism under the Huichang reign (842–845), the time had come for the principal relic[4] to be given its own miniature pagoda of solid gold, inside a splendid new set of caskets, and accompanied by a vast array of gold and silver, glass, lacquer, and ceramic objects. The casket that held the crystal sarcophagus is adorned on its lid and four sides with forty-five images of the *Vajradhatu*, or Diamond World Mandala,[5] representing the latest Buddhist

just 11.8 by 8.4 centimeters — corresponds in number and in kind with the three *jiasha* and two women's garments mentioned in the inscription and that their slightly amateurish gold thread embroidery of clouds, lotus flowers, and *man* characters is the work of Empress Wu herself.[2]

The crystal sarcophagus exhibited here[3] was found inside a silver-gilt casket dedicated by Emperor Yizong in 871 CE to receive the Buddha relic; the silver-gilt casket was itself protected inside another of iron, and placed in a secret compartment beneath the rear wall of the innermost chamber. The crystal sarcophagus, in turn, held another, smaller coffin, made of greenish jade, which held the fingerbone relic, a hollow phalanx of soft yellow bone, slightly smaller than the white jade one found in the eight-fold set of caskets (see cat. 164). Two precious stones adorn the top of the crystal sarcophagus, and an openwork gilt bronze plaque is affixed to the higher end, but the smaller jade coffin doctrine for the most speedy attainment of enlightenment; it was safely tucked away out of sight, doubtless in a secret ceremony, before the main ceremony began. During the persecutions of 842 – 845, the Chongzhen (Famen) Monastery, as the monastery outside the capital most closely associated with the court, was allowed to survive unscathed; the fact that the four fingerbone relics are almost identical in shape and size (varying between 37 and 41 millimeters) makes it tempting to suppose that some of them had originally been enshrined elsewhere and brought to the imperial monastery for safekeeping. In 603, under the Sui dynasty, relics were sent from the capital to be enshrined in pagodas throughout the empire. Such relics, like the images that were disseminated in the same fashion by the Sui emperors, and that share a common style, must have been made to a rigorous common specification. **RW**

1   The seven objects form Kegazawa's Group A in his very thorough analysis of the relic groupings (1996).
2   These identifications are made here for the first time. Previous reports have identified the skirt with a much larger fragment of embroidery, densely embroidered with lotus flowers (Famensi 1994, 72). Wang Yarong (Wang 1988, 27) and Wang Xu (Wang and Hu 1998, 205) called the jacket a *banbi* (half-sleeve), but this term is not found anywhere in the inventory stela; the *pi'ao* of the inscription — a lined jacket — corresponds exactly to the jacket recovered from the crypt.
3   Excavated in 1987 (FD 5:044 – 7); reported: Shaanxi 1988a, 7.
4   There are different opinions regarding which was the principal relic: The yellow bone relic in its jade coffin and crystal sarcophagus; or the white jade relic, with the seven stars of the Great Bear carved inside, enshrined in the eightfold set of caskets. I-mann Lai, personal communication.
5   For a discussion of the iconography, see Han 1998. A further detailed analysis of the iconography is in preparation by I-mann Lai, doctoral candidate at the School of Oriental and African Studies, University of London.

163

Parcel-gilt silver sandalwood incense burner and stand

Censer: height 29.5 (11 ⁵/₈), diam. 24.8 (9 ³/₄), weight 6.4 (14 ¹/₈)
Stand: height 21 (8 ¹/₄), diam. 43.5 (17 ¹/₈), weight 8.9 (19 ³/₄)
Tang Dynasty, dated by inscription to 869 CE
From the pagoda of the Famen Monastery at Fufeng, Shaanxi Province

Famensi Museum, Fufeng, Shaanxi Province

Houston and San Francisco only

This impressive censer and its stand[1] were found in the center of the inner chamber. Both are described on the inventory stele among the very first of the 122 objects dedicated by Emperor Yizong in 873 CE: "an incense burner and stand together weighing 380 *liang*." An inscription incised on the underside of the censer confirms the identification: "In the tenth year of Xiantong [869 CE], the Wensiyuan made an 8-*cun* (8-inch) silver gilt decorated incense burner with stand and hanging rings, together weighing 380 *liang*. Craftsman Chen Jingquan; Administrative Assistant of High Rank Wu Hongque; Commissioner Neng Shun."[2] The numerals 1, 3, and 4 are engraved on the lid, body, and stand, respectively.

Incense and fragrances were common offerings in Buddhist worship; the smoke from the burning incense would waft through the air just as the teachings of the Buddha spread through the world. Incense burners were a common item as early as the Han dynasty (206 BCE – 220 CE). Long before that, during the Shang dynasty (c. 1600 – 1100 BCE), burnt offerings were made to the ancestral spirits and to Shangdi, the Supreme Ruler. At that time, the vessel of the greatest importance for such offerings was the *ding*, or tripod bowl. *Ding* vessels, in a variety of materials, were to become the chief altarvessel in Buddhist ceremonies as well. During the Tang dynasty, however, a five-footed form of incense burner seems to have been favored. On the evidence of Buddhist silk paintings from Dunhuang, the censer on the altar in front of the Buddha was

generally bowl-shaped, with a cover and a stand of lotus shape. Sometimes, smaller lotus blossoms on stems are shown emerging on either side of the main censer.

The present censer is of a standard Tang dynasty type but is one of the largest known[3] — almost twice the size of a similar six-legged censer, dated 741, found packed with incense in the reliquary deposit of the Qingshan Monastery at Lintong near Xi'an, excavated in 1985.[4] Its preeminent position in the innermost chamber suggests that, like the Qingshan censer, it was probably used during the ceremonies to enshrine the Buddha relic in its eight-fold set of nesting caskets. The lid is crowned by a broad lotus bud, pierced to allow the fragrant smoke to escape. On the curved shoulders of the lid are five lotus blossoms, each supporting a tortoise, from whose mouth issue two wreaths

of incense smoke. The lotuses, tortoises, and the encircling stems and foliage are all worked in repoussé, with further chasing and gilding. A broad, flat rim overhangs the sides of the vessel itself, which is supported on five sturdy legs issuing out of the mouths of dragons; these legs are fastened to the body by means of rivets around the dragons' manes. In the spaces between them hang knotted festoons, each framing what appears to be an embroidered ball. Remaining space on the vessel's sides is filled with incised wreaths of incense smoke, similar to those depicted issuing from the mouths of the tortoises on the lid. Thus, even without the actual burning of sandalwood or other incense materials, the censer continues to serve its original function.

The stand is in the form of a flat tray, to which the five legs and intermediate festoons have been

outspread wings; their sweeping tails feature engraved "eyes" and cusped outlines. Four scrolling stems issue from the central point, two of them held in the peacocks' beaks and ending in flowers, and two passing behind their tails. The remaining space between this circular design and the sides is occupied by five double-sprays with leaves and flowers. The legs, with identical animal masks, have outturned trifoliate feet instead of animal claws; the same shape, but carved in wood and elegantly painted, is to be found a century or more earlier, in an offering tray preserved in the Shōsō-in.[6] The festoons, in the form of knotted scarves with intricate parcel-gilding, have a central four-petaled flower instead of the embroidered ball used above. They hang from split pins passing through gilt floral washers inside and outside the rim of the tray. Three small rivets fasten each of the legs to the underside of the tray, carefully positioned so as to be almost hidden in the foliage. RW

1 Excavated in 1987 (FD 5:002; FD 5:075); unreported. See Shaanxi 1988a, 1–26.
2 Han 1995, 71.
3 A complete example of a five-legged censer and stand in Yue stoneware (height 66 [26]) was excavated near Hangzhou in 1980. See Wang 1996, pl. 15.
4 Tokyo 1998b, 77, no. 40.
5 Zhongguo shiku: Dunhuang Mogaoku, 3: pls. 135–136.
6 Nara 1998, no. 65.

added. The tray has five lobes and a tightly folded ribbon design inside the rim, the latter almost identical to a border pattern used at Dunhuang in the eighth century in Cave 45.[5] The center is very effectively incised and gilded (without the use of repoussé) with a pair of peacocks circling with

164

Parcel-gilt silver casket with the
Four Guardian Kings

Height 23.5 (9 ¼), width 20 (7 ⅞)
Tang Dynasty, ninth century CE
From the pagoda of the Famen Monastery at Fufeng,
Shaanxi Province

Famensi Museum, Fufeng, Shaanxi Province

Multiple containers made of valuable materials
were invariably used to hold relics (which could be
just tiny, glassy grains). In the case of the Famen
Monastery, where the relic was held to be from the
true body of Śākyamuni, the historical Buddha, the
containers had to be even more impressive. Placed
towards the rear of the innermost chamber, this is
the second of a set of eight nesting caskets.[1] Only
fragments remain of the outermost casket, which
was made of sandalwood carved with figures of
devotees and figures from the Buddhist Pure Lands,

tified by a cartouche inscribed in similar fashion to those that identify the Pure Lands on the outer sandalwood casket. These depictions closely resemble (and were likely based on) contemporary paintings on silk or paper, or murals, such as those found early this century at the Caves of the Thousand Buddhas at Dunhuang. Foremost among them, on the front of the casket, is Vaiśrāvana, Guardian King of the North, easily identified by the small *stūpa* he supports on his left hand. Behind him, one of his army of *yakṣas* takes aim at a winged demon fleeing at the top right, exactly as in a silk banner now in the British Museum.[2]

Vaiśrāvana is seated in frontal view on two dwarfish figures who crawl out to either side, his right hand grasping a *vajra*, or diamond club; the tiny figure of the earth goddess Prithvi appears beneath him, tenderly holding his right foot (a reference to the Khotanese legend with which Vaiśrāvana, as the patron saint of Khotan, is associated). The infant on the left, who offers him a jewel from a pot of treasure, may be the son granted to the childless king and nurtured by the earth goddess; other precious items are strewn about on the ground. The other three Guardian Kings, Virudhāka of the South at the back of the casket, Dhṛtarāstra and Virupākṣa of the East and West, at the left and right, respectively, are seated in similar fashion: all three, however, look to their right, as if following Vaiṣrāvana in processional order. Besides their armed followers, each of these three also has a female attendant, presenting a vase of flowers or holding an incense burner. In the case of Vaisravana, there are two male donors: a Chinese emperor, holding a lotus bud in his left hand and proferring a coin in the open palm of his right hand; and the bearded King of Khotan, offering with both hands a crystalline lump of jade from that country.

A pair of dragons amid swirling clouds circle around a single flaming pearl on the lid of the casket. The chamfered edges feature pairs of animals amid lush foliage; the vertical sides are decorated with pairs of human-headed birds, or *kalavinkas*, providers of music in the Pure Lands.

including the Pure Land of the West of Buddha Amitābha — the Buddha of Boundless Light and the focus of Pure Land worship. It was apparently surrounded by a wooden railing with carved balusters topped by gilt lotus buds, similar to the railing surrounding the gilt bronze *stūpa* (cat. 161).

The second to the seventh caskets were lowered into each other by means of lengths of silk, remnants of which remained in their original positions when the objects were discovered. Each casket was fastened by a padlock, with the appropriate key still in place. All share the same square shape with chamfered lid but are decorated in different ways. Each side of this, the second casket, shows one of the Four Guardian Kings, each of whom is iden-

Like the scenes on the side, these motifs are worked in repoussé from the inside; chased and engraved details decorate the outside. The raised motifs and chased outlines are gilded, while the silver ground behind them is stippled so that they stand out even more clearly against it. The third casket is of plain silver. Next are two caskets decorated with figural designs: the fourth with preaching scenes of four Buddhas, each associated with one of the four directions; the fifth illustrates Esoteric deities. The sixth and seventh caskets have no figural designs, but are encrusted with pearls and semiprecious stones. Finally, the eighth container, a mere two inches in height, is not a casket but a tiny single-story pagoda fashioned out of solid gold; the relic fingerbone rested on a silver post. RW

1   Excavated in 1987 (FD 5:011 – 2); reported: Shaanxi 1988a, 20 – 21.
2   Whitfield 1982 – 1985, 2: pl. 16.

165

Parcel-gilt silver tea basket

Height 17.8 (7), diam. 16.1 (6 ¼), weight 0.6 (1 ⅜)
Tang Dynasty, ninth century CE
From the pagoda of the Famen Monastery at Fufeng, Shaanxi Province

Famensi Museum, Fufeng, Shaanxi Province

This magnificent openwork lidded basket,[1] donated by Emperor Xizong in 874, exhibits a light and graceful form, from the swelling cover to the fanciful feet, which take the form of triple clusters of stamens. The swing handle describes a graceful arch, with swan-neck ends and bud finials, attached at each side by a ring passing through a loop that emerges from a four-petaled holdfast. A silver chain links the cover to the handle. Sides, lid, and even the base of the piece all feature the same openwork motif of intersecting circles, whose square holes resemble those of Chinese coins. Superimposed on the openwork are gilded flying geese (so identified in the excavation report, although their short necks suggest that they are in fact ducks), fifteen of them on the lid, and another twenty-four in pairs around the sides. A narrow gilded band of overlapping petals and another of half-florets on a stippled fish-roe ground border the lid where it meets the sides.

Unlike the gold and silver vessels made at the capital in the workshops of the Wensiyuan, this piece came to the court as tribute from southwestern China. A brief inscription is engraved around the edge of the underside: "Sent [to the court] by Li Gan, official of Gui."[2] (Gui [for Guizhou, in present-day Guangxi province] was the principal commandery on the Lingnan western circuit during the Tang dynasty.) An identically worded inscription came to light when a hoard of Tang gold and silver vessels was discovered in 1980 during field-leveling at Lantian in Shaanxi province.[3] The inscription was on the underside of a shallow dish with floral designs, pairs of mandarin ducks, and thirty-four geese or ducks flying in a narrow band around the rim. A five-lobed box, found in the same hoard, was inscribed as tribute to the inner court, with the date of the seventh year of Xiantong (866), only a few years before the openwork basket was conveyed to the Famen Monastery deposit in 874.

Another basket from the Famen Monastery deposit, listed on the inventory stele as a "knotted basket," is of lobed oval form, similar in size and incorporating the same ground-pattern of intersecting circles, but even more fanciful, being entirely constructed of silver and silver-gilt wire, including even the swing handle.[4] Remains of wood in the bottom of this second basket have suggested to some commentators that both baskets were intended to store tea, after the leaves had been steamed and then dried into bricks or flat cakes, which in more ordinary circumstances were often strung together;[5] even today, solid cakes of tea are made with a depression in the center, for ease of piercing and stringing. RW

1   Excavated in 1987 (FD 5:077), reported: Shaanxi 1988a, 16.
2   Han 1995, 71.
3   Fan 1982, figs. 2, 9.
4   Famensi 1988, 12, fig. 12, item 36; Tokyo 1998b, 172–173, no. 111.
5   Reischauer 1955, 365 n. 1395.

166

Openwork parcel-gilt silver censer

Length of chain 17.7 (9 ⅝), diam. of censer 5.8 (5)
Tang Dynasty, ninth century CE
From the pagoda of the Famen Monastery at Fufeng,
Shaanxi Province

Famensi Museum, Fufeng, Shaanxi Province

Two of the censers found in the Famen Monastery pagoda deposit are spherical in shape, each suspended from a hook by means of a chain and swivel. Both of them are recorded in the inventory stele as having been donated by Emperor Sizong in 874. They were found stored inside the parcel-gilt silver tea basket (cat. 165).[1] The larger of the two is 12.8 centimeters in diameter, not as large as the pair preserved in the Shōsō-in Treasury in Japan (each 18 centimeters in diameter), but larger than most other known examples from the Tang dynasty: two excavated from Xi'an are each only 4.8 centimeters in diameter.[2] Four have been excavated from the same area, and others are in private collections around the world.

The pattern of the smaller censer,[3] rendered in openwork with additional chasing, elegantly complements that of the larger ball-censer. The latter has six medallions on each of its two hemispheres, which are hinged together and fastened with a hook and eye. The smaller censer has three larger medallions, each with a broad gilt band with flying birds and an openwork center. Because of this censer's small size, the medallions are split between its two hemispheres, and inverted isosceles triangles are positioned between them. The surface of both censers is filled with foliage and flowers on a ring-punched ground.

The most striking feature of such globular censers is the interior gimbal mechanism, which enables the incense materials to smolder safely without any danger to the person carrying it about or keeping it within his or her clothing for warmth and perfume. In this example, the mechanism consists of two rings 4.8 and 3.8 centimeters in diameter, within which is suspended a shallow bowl, 2.8 centimeters in diameter and 1.0 centimeters deep.

The principle of its construction, similar to that of a ship's compass, was first described in the west by the Italian philosopher and mathematician Hieronymus Cardanus (1501 – 1576) in *De Subtilitate* (1550) but had been known in China since the Western Han dynasty (206 BCE – 24 CE).[4] RW

1 Famensi 1988, 13, fig. 13, item 12.
2 Lu and Han 1985, pls. 26 – 27, 28 – 29.
3 Excavated in 1987 (FD5: 081); reported: Shaanxi 1988a, 16, 17 fig. 17.
4 Brinker and Goepper 1981, 341.

167

Mi se ware *pan* dish

Height 6.1 (2 ⅜), diam. 23.8 (9 ⅜), diam. of foot
17.4 (6 ⅞)
Tang Dynasty, ninth century CE
From the pagoda of the Famen Monastery at Fufeng,
Shaanxi Province

Famensi Museum, Fufeng, Shaanxi Province

Among sixteen ceramic vessels excavated from the
middle chamber of the crypt beneath the Famen
Monastery pagoda, no fewer than thirteen were
mi se ("secret color") fine stoneware. Most of them
were contained in a lacquered wooden box, placed
beneath the large silver censer immediately in front
of the doors leading to the third and innermost
chamber.[1] They had been dedicated in 873 by Emperor Yizong, and are recorded on stone tablets as
follows: "*Mi se ci* ["porcelain"][2] bowls: seven items,
two with silver banded rims; *mi se ci pan* dishes and
diezi: six items." The ceramics actually found comprise these seven bowls and six dishes, together
with a single octagonal fluted bottle, similar to one
excavated in the 1950s from a tomb dated 871,[3] and
two pieces of white stoneware. The two bowls with
silver rims, glazed a yellowish green, are coated on
the outside with black lacquer inlaid in gold and

silver with medallions of birds, flowers, and
scrolling foliage.[4] The other bowls are plain, with
a grayish *huqing* (lake green) glaze of the finest
quality.

Celebrated in literature ever since the ninth
century as *mi se*, the ware's exact nature had long
defied precise identification; the correspondence
between the inventory stele and the ceramics recovered from the pagoda's foundation deposit has
resolved that question. The *mi se* pieces were fired
in a "dragon" kiln (a long kiln built up a slope)
in a strongly reducing atmosphere, in which the
relatively high levels of ferrous oxide and titanium
oxide, around 2.5 percent, produced both the fine
gray-green and the yellowish green glazes.[5]

The *pan* shown here,[6] with a five-lobed rim and
sides divided by five short straight lines, derives
from a silverware shape, as do the bowls, dishes,
and the octagonal bottle. (Metalworking techniques
similarly inform the inlay of the ceramic silver-
banded bowls.) The clay paste forming the body
had been refined to the point where it contained
no sand particles, and the glaze has only a very few
tiny gas bubbles. On the base, twenty-four exceedingly slender spur marks (four of them somewhat
larger than the others), form a circle on the base;
one of the other *pan* dishes shows two concentric

circles of spur marks, fourteen in the outer row and twelve in the inner row.[7] So lightly did the vessels rest on their supports during the firing that not even a hint of the spurs appears on the vessels, while the flat surface of the foot is hardly disturbed. An even, smooth gray-green glaze covers the entire vessel; the glaze on the foot has the appearance of having been partly washed off before firing, so as not to adhere too much to the spurs, which were probably flakes of quartz, set on edge in a prepared clay disk.[8] The technique of firing on spurs is seen in high-quality wares from Yaozhou and, at its most refined, on Ru wares of the Late Northern Song dynasty.

That efforts were made to ensure the highest possible quality is evident in the care taken to finish the saggers used to protect the vessels from ash and flame during the firing. These saggers are of porcelain, lidded, and lightly glazed inside and out.[9] As with some of the other bowls, traces of a buff-colored paper with a woodblock print of a woman adhered to the outside. Woodblock prints were evidently used to separate the nested bowls when they were placed in the deposit, and the ink has left an imprint on the surface of the glaze.

In literary records, the *mi se* porcelain vessels are associated with the Yue wares made in Zhejiang province. In the city of Ningbo, more than seven hundred porcelains, mostly from Yue, and including one with a molded design of a crane and the characters *Dazhong ernian* (second year of Dazhong [= Taizhong, 848]) were found in winter 1973 beneath the Tang city walls.[10] The majority were from Yue, with the characteristic fine clay body and smooth green glaze of the wares found at Famen Monastery. A reference to the "tribute kiln" inscribed on an epitaph jar dated 887, from a tomb excavated at Lake Shanglin in 1977, is evidence that

such wares were made at one or more of the 196 kilns found along the shores of the lake.[11] Fragments of an octagonal bottle very similar to the one found at Famen Monastery have also been found at one of the Shanglin kiln sites.[12] Thus the wares dedicated by Emperor Yizong in 873 were without any doubt fired as tribute ware at the Yue kilns at some time during his reign, which began in 860. The presence of such tribute wares among so many gold and silver vessels made in the imperial workshops marks an important advance in the status of ceramics, destined to be increasingly important in the Northern Song dynasty. Indeed, the control of the kilns that produced them was eventually to come directly under the administration of the court, in order to guarantee both quality and exclusivity. RW

1   Song 1992, 244. Although this is not immediately apparent from the plan in the preliminary report, some of the bowls, and the remains of the box, can be seen in the drawing of the objects in front of the doors. *Wenwu* 1988.10, 11, fig. 11.
2   In Chinese, the word *ci* ("porcelain") is used for both stoneware and porcelain. The requirement that porcelain be both white and translucent, as well as resonant, is a Western convention.
3   Feng 1988, 37.
4   Famensi 1994, 76–77.
5   Zhu Boqian 1993, 252. A reducing atmosphere is obtained by closing the kiln openings at a certain point in the firing cycle. This has the effect of starving the flames of oxygen, and some of the chemically combined oxygen in the glaze material is thereby removed or "reduced," e.g., ferric oxide (Fe_2O_3) becomes ferrous oxide (FeO).
6   Excavated in 1987 (FD 4.011); reported: Shaanxi 1988a, 24.
7   Song 1992, 248.
8   Nigel Wood, personal communication.
9   Zhu 1992, 251.
10 Lin Shimin 1976, 60–61.
11 Zhu 1992, 251.
12 Wang 1996, fig. 60.

168

Blue glass *pan* dish with engraved and
gilt designs

Height 2.2 (⅞), diam. 15.5 (6⅛)
Islamic, probably from Nishapur, ninth century CE
From the pagoda of the Famen Monastery at Fufeng,
Shaanxi Province

Famensi Museum, Fufeng, Shaanxi Province

Perhaps because of the far-reaching development
of ceramics, few glass vessels of indigenous manufacture have been discovered in China. When glass
vessels have been found, the context is very often
either Buddhist or aristocratic, or both. Ma Wenkuan, writing in 1994, notes over thirty vessels from
eleven sites, not including pieces found in Xinjiang
province at sites along the former Silk Road. Silk
paintings discovered early this century in Cave 17

at Dunhuang (Gansu province), a key point on the Silk Road, depict bodhisattvas holding transparent bowls.[1] In Buddhist reliquary deposits, it is not uncommon for the innermost container, in which the relic grains were actually held, to be a tiny glass phial. The tomb of the young princess Li Jingxun (see cat. 157) contained a transparent green glass bottle, 16.3 centimeters high, and several other small glass vessels. Such depictions and finds clearly indicate the rarity and high esteem in which glass was held, despite — or perhaps because of — the very small quantities actually produced in China.

Some vessels were imported from the west by sea. The first reference in Chinese sources to Islamic glass dates to 775 CE, when Lu Sigong, the commissioner of Lingnan, having put down a rebellion in Canton, sent a glass dish, 9 *cun* (inches) in diameter, to Emperor Daizong. The emperor's delight turned to rage when it was later discovered that Lu had given a slightly larger glass dish, 1 *chi* (10 *cun*, or inches) in diameter, to a disgraced official, and the emperor was with difficulty restrained from having Lu executed.[2]

Under such circumstances, the group of glass vessels from the Famen Monastery deposit is truly remarkable in view of the number of vessels found, their decoration, and their excellent state of preservation. Retrieved from the innermost chamber,[3] on 4 – 6 May 1987, they comprise some twenty vessels, nineteen of them intact (not all have yet been fully described[4]). Two of vessels — a plain, yellow-green teacup (height 4.9 centimeters, diam. 13 centimeters) and stand (height 3.7 centimeters, diam. 14 centimeters) — are of Chinese manufacture; the remainder are imported Mesopotamian Islamic glass, possibly made in Nishapur and brought to the Chinese court by one of the many foreign tribute missions during the Tang dynasty. One dish is luster-painted in yellow and dark brown.[5]

The dish in this exhibition[6] is one of six engraved and four plain blue dishes in a stack of ten dishes nested together, which doubtless helped to keep them intact. Convex at the center (a function of its attachment to the pontil during the blowing), the dish is decorated with gilding and engraving.

The gilding is applied in two concentric narrow bands that circumscribe the central and main fields of decoration; a third wavy band or ribbon undulates in the space between them. One other dish has both gilding and engraving, while the remaining four blue dishes are engraved but not gilt; all six, however, use similar incising techniques and in some cases the same motifs; the central motif of eight principal petals on this piece, for example, reappears on another of the engraved dishes,[7] but on a larger scale so that it fills almost the whole of the available space within the plain rim. Several of the dishes feature a five-leaflet motif; all of them use close-set hatching lines, straight or undulating (as here, within the small roundels inside and outside the gilded undulating band), with contrasting areas of plain blue reserve. The same hatching techniques and, less frequently, gilding appear on vessel fragments found in Samarra, in Nishapur, and in al-Fustāt, Egypt.[8] RW

1   Moore 1998, fig. 19.6, following a survey by An Jiayao, illustrates her line drawings of a number of examples from the mural paintings in Cave 217 and other Tang caves at Dunhuang.
2   Ma Wenkuan 1994, 233 – 234, citing the *Xin Tang shu* (New Tang history). Moore 1998, 80, gives further details from the *Zizhi tongjian* (Comprehensive mirror to aid government), with the date as 778.
3   Most of them were in the southwest corner of the chamber, close to the tea-mill and the two tea-baskets.
4   A fragment of a narrow-necked blue bottle (FD 5: 33), and a fragment of a pale yellow straight-sided cup (FD 5: 37) have been analyzed, see An 1993, 262. The analysis shows them to be common sodium glass with relatively high levels of magnesium oxide and oxide of potassium, similar to sherds from Nishapur analyzed by Brill and Fenn 1993.
5   See Kröger 1998.
6   Excavated in 1987 (FD 5:012). The dishes are not individually reported, but see generally Shaanxi 1988a, 1 – 26, and, for additional illustration, An 1990, 127, fig. 6.
7   FD 5:008. See An 1990, 126, fig. 4.
8   Some of these fragments are illustrated in Brill and Fenn 1993, 259 – 260, figs. 1 – 8.

169

Bronze ewer

Height 29.5 (11.61); diam. of mouth 4–6 (1.57–2.36),
diam. of body 13.2 (5.19), diam. of foot 8.0 (3.149)
Probably from northern India, seventh or early
eighth century CE
From the reliquary deposit at the Qingshan
Monastery, Lintong Xinfengzhen, Shaanxi Province

Lintong County Museum, Shaanxi Province

Houston and San Francisco only

The sealed and clearly labeled stone reliquary
chamber of the pagoda of the Qingshan Monastery
was discovered quite by accident at midday on 6
May 1985, at a depth of six meters, in the course of
excavating clay for brick-making. The site lies a few
hundred yards from the Han gateway, where Xiang
Yu and Liu Bang, rival contenders for the throne
of China after the fall of the Qin dynasty, famously
met to fix the border between Chu and Han in 207
BCE. The monastery itself had long since vanished
and was known only from literary records, including
one in the *Tang shu* (Tang history), recording that
the name Qingshansi — Auspicious Peak Monastery — had been conferred on it by Empress Wu
Zetian in 686 CE. More than a hundred objects,
as well as mural paintings, were found in the inner
chamber, which contained a stone shrine whose
four sides are engraved with scenes of the Buddha
preaching, his death or *nīrvāṇa*, the cremation
of his body, and the worship of his ashes. The roof
of the shrine carries four trees, perhaps in reference to the grove of sala trees where the Buddha's
nīrvāṇa took place, and a central gilded lotus bud.
Lotuses, made of pure gold with painted leaves and
paper-thin petals, stand in front of the shrine on
either side. The relics — tiny crystals — were enclosed in two small green glass bottles, inside a gold
coffin placed in turn within a silver gilt sarcophagus. Inscriptions concerning the relic deposit show
that it was sealed in 741 CE.

The bronze vase exhibited here[1] is the single
most prominent object found in the chamber, apart
from the shrine itself and its contents. It was found
just in front of the shrine, and must have been used
for the last (but not necessarily the first) time in
the consecration ceremony in 741. The six human
faces around the body, with their sharply delineated features, are distinctively Indian in character,
as is the shape of the neck, mouth, and handle of
the ewer. Fourteen years after its discovery, the
ewer's exact provenance and date remain difficult to
determine. Hildegard Scheid notes evidence that
the foot had come away and had been repaired
more than once in antiquity, before being
deposited in the relic chamber.[2] With its elegant
swan-neck handle and palmette-shaped thumb-
hold, the most likely answer is that it does indeed
come from northern India,[3] and the presumption
must be that it dates no later than the early eighth
century, and quite possibly earlier. RW

1 Excavated in 1985; published: Berger 1994, cat. 62; Kuhn
   1993, cat. 93; Tokyo 1998b, no. 42.
2 Scheid in Kuhn 1993, 253.
3 The author is indebted to Wladimir Zwalf and Mark
   Zebrowski for their observations.

During the Early Tang dynasty (seventh and eighth centuries CE), a large percentage of the Chinese hereditary aristocracy moved from its ancestral homes to the great cities of Xi'an and Luoyang. In earlier dynasties, the competition for dominance among these families was informed by the wealth from inherited lands and titles, as well as by the influence gained from generations of regional power. Because they were large landholders as well as government officials, this elite controlled not only a great deal of the political power in China but also much of the means of production, the natural resources, and the ability to trade for items. This group was powerful both in politics and, as patrons, in the arts. Their new concentration in these cities, however, both separated them from local power sources and brought them together with people of like backgrounds and interests. The accumulation of numerous wealthy, sophisticated, and worldly individuals with large amounts of leisure time in a few locations created a true metropolitan elite that demanded an abundance of exotic luxury items; their changing material demands defined aesthetic taste and fashion. Arts of all kinds flourished under their patronage, exemplified in the surviving glories of the Tang capital at Xi'an, at the time the largest and most cosmopolitan city in the world.

The major population centers of the Tang dynasty were located in the north, in what is now Hebei, Henan, and parts of Shaanxi provinces. Xi'an, located to the west of these population centers, was the logical point of entry for trade coming over the land routes that connected China to the West. Along these roads came many of the exotic foreign goods so eagerly sought by the Tang court. The seventh and eighth centuries mark the point at which the Chinese were most outward looking; this was particularly true of the hereditary aristocracy. While still confident of the superiority of Chinese culture, they were also in contact with other advanced cultures, something relatively new to China. A fascination with the material culture of peoples beyond their own immediate borders was one of the shared characteristics of the Tang nobility.

Trade over the inland routes was greatly encouraged by the large numbers of Buddhist missionaries who traveled between China and the loci of their faith in Kashmir, Afghanistan, Pakistan, and northern India. Prior to the fall of the Sassanian empire in the seventh century CE, textiles, glass, and metalwork from Persia found a ready market at the Tang court, as did music, musical instruments, and musicians from Central Asia. In addition the Chinese sought wine and exotic fruits such as peaches and grapes from oasis kingdoms in Central Asia. The major sources for jade, the most precious stone to the Chinese, were in Manasi and Hetian in modern Xinjiang. It was much sought after as a raw material for use in Chinese workshops to create a broad range of luxury goods. Exotic animals were also sought, and lions, elephants, and a whole range of other beasts found their way into the imperial zoos. The most prized animals were the great horses of Central Asia. In turn, the Chinese exported silk, ceramics, and other luxury goods.

The great cosmopolitan city of Xi'an was peopled as well by the foreign traders who sup-plied the demands of the elite, missionaries from a variety of faiths, mercenaries (who made up much of the imperial guard), those responsible for the care of the imperial stables, innumerable envoys coming to pay their respects, and vast numbers of entertainers of every imaginable type.

The contents of two tombs excavated in Xi'an reveal much about the hereditary aristocracy in this city during the late seventh and early eighth century CE. The earlier of the two was a double tomb excavated in August 1991 in Xinzhuxiang, in the eastern suburbs of Xi'an. It was built between 689 and 690 for Yu Yin, an official who served both in the Tang dynasty and during the reign of Wu Zetian. He died in 689 when he was about 49 and was interred in the tomb in 690. His wife, the princess Jinxiang, died in 722 and was interred in the tomb in 724.[1]

The tomb contains the epitaphs of both its occupants. From them we know that Yu Yin came from a line of important military figures, served in the military as a judicial adjutant and was given an honorary military title at his death. He was a resident of Luoyang, the capital during the Zhou interregnum, and the second of the great Tang cities.[2] The fact that he was buried in Xi'an reveals how powerful the attraction of that city had become to the aristocracy. Indeed, the suburbs of the Tang capital where the wealthy lived are termed the "five tomb towns" in contemporary poetry.[3]

The epitaph for Jinxiang states that she was the third daughter of Li Yuanying, who was given the title *Tengwang* (King of Teng, a largely honorary title). Her paternal grandfather was Li Yuan — Tang Gaozu, the founder of the Tang dynasty. It is noteworthy that Jinxiang was given the rank of *xianzhu*, district princess, rather than *gongzhu*, imperial princess, even though she was a direct descendent of Tang Gaozu.[4] Most excavated tombs of Tang princesses of the imperial line are single, making this double burial an anomaly that may reflect her lower rank. The interval between the death and burial of the husband and that of the wife is also unusually long.[5]

Through stylistic and typographic analysis, as well as other criteria, Chinese experts have sought to distinguish the objects placed in the tomb when it was constructed in 690 from those placed in the tomb at the time of the burial of the princess in 724. They have concluded that the basic structure of the tomb, the tomb paintings, and a small number of the objects were created in or before 690; a stone outer coffin and many of the funerary ceramics date to the time of the princess' burial. Many of the objects interred with Yu Yin were apparently re-placed during the princess' burial with others more suited for her higher status.[6] Ten of these objects — two groups of *mingqi* (funerary figurines) — are illustrated here (cats. 170 – 171).

Given the period and the princess' distinguished lineage, the fact that all but a few of the pottery funeral objects are painted, rather than glazed, is unusual. By the end of the seventh

century CE, *sancai* (three-color) glazes were becoming the preferred finish for the *mingqi* interred in the tombs of the highest-ranking Tang aristocracy. Figures found in the tomb of the
princess Jinxiang and that of the princess Yongtai suggest that the choice of paint versus glazing was a function of the decedent's status. As an imperial princess who died during the reign
of Empress Wu, Yongtai was given a high-status burial in 706 — after the Tang had been
reestablished. Her single tomb, with a large complement of paintings and superb funerary objects, contains painted pottery figures, but many of the vessels and figures are in *sancai*.[7] The
vast majority of *mingqi* in Jinxiang's tomb, by contrast, are not glazed; their surface decoration is
composed of pigments applied to a white slip over the low-fired ceramic body. The only *sancai*
pieces listed in the excavation report for the tomb are a basin and a small handleless cup — an
apparent reflection of Jinxiang's relatively low status.

    As sculptural representations of the fashions of the time, the highest-quality painted pot-
tery *mingqi* tend to be more successful than those that are glazed. While *sancai*-glazed objects
obviously required greater expenditures of materials and labor, the application of the glaze and
the nature of the glaze itself did not permit the replication of fine details in drapery or physiognomy: The colors of the glaze dominate the *mingqi*, often bearing little relation to the accurate
depiction of the figure. Because of the requirements of the glazing process, *sancai* pieces also

tend to be somewhat less freely sculpted than pieces that were meant to be painted. Such technical restrictions did not apply to painted pottery, so that it is in this material that the Tang *mingqi* artisans were best able to explore the details of facial type, fabric design and decoration, hairstyle, and the other accouterments that fascinated the Tang aristocracy.

The second tomb was discovered in 1988 during the building of a power station at Hansenzhai, in the eastern suburb of Xi'an.[8] While the tomb did not contain an epitaph with the name of the occupant or the date of burial, comparisons of its contents with those of others for which the identity of the occupant and date of burial are known have established that the occupant was not an aristocrat but rather a wealthy merchant or landowner. Stylistic analysis dates the tomb to around the second quarter of the eighth century CE — a decade or more later than the Jinxiang tomb.[9]

The Hansenzhai tomb contained a total of forty-three ceramic objects, including female and male figurines, camels (with and without riders), and a pair of spirit guardians, as well as bronze mirrors and a few wooden objects. The largest group comprised sixteen female figures, which are said to have been found near the north wall of the tomb and on top of the coffin. While these objects do not have the *sancai* glaze of those found in the highest-level Tang burials, their impressive scale and relatively high quality are an indication of the wealth attained by the affluent land-holding or merchant families of Xi'an during the seventh and eighth centuries. Six of the female figures (cat. 173) are included in this exhibition. MK

1 Xi'an 1997, 14 – 19.
2 Xi'an 1997, 14 – 19.
3 Bo, "Song of the Lute: Preface and Poem" in Watson 1984, 251.
4 Xi'an 1997, 18.
5 Xi'an 1997, 15 – 18.
6 Xi'an 1997, 15 – 18.

7 For example, see the Falconer on Horseback and Hunter with Dog on Horseback from the tomb of Princess Yongtai in Xiangang 1993, nos. 84, 85, and the Horse and Two Vessels from the same tomb reproduced in *Shaanxi sheng Bowuguan* 1990, nos. 67, 68, 70.
8 Wang 1992, 66 – 70.
9 Wang 1992, 70.

170

A group of five painted pottery hunting figures

Height 33 (13) – 35.5 (14)
Tang Dynasty, early eighth century CE
From the tomb of Yu Yin and Princess Jinxiang,
Xi'an, Shaanxi Province

Xi'an Municipal Institute of Archaeology
and Preservation of Cultural Relics,
Shaanxi Province

Washington only

A fascination with capturing or exaggerating detail
is characteristic of Tang funerary sculpture. Depictions of foreigners in particular often verge on
caricature, an approach clearly reflected in the
three foreign men in this group of hunters dressed
in exotic costumes and head gear[1]; their large
noses, bulging eyes, heavy beards, and brutish mus-
culature suggests that the Chinese found these
people somewhat inferior. The unmistakably Chinese women who complete the hunting group,
on the other hand, have regular features, and their
hunting dress suggests a more sober style.

Hunting and the hunting styles of foreign peoples (including their use of exotic animals) were of
particular interest to the leisured Tang aristocracy.

Four of the figures (the three men and one of the
women) in this group carry animals that would have
been used in the hunt. In front of his saddle, one of
the men cradles a small, wiry dog, ideal for pursuing
smaller game in the open lands west of Xi'an. The
second man holds a falcon on his arm, reflecting
a common practice of the Tang aristocracy, which
used these raptors to capture small animals and
birds. A collared, spotted cat (probably a cheetah)
sits on a thick, presumably protective pad on the
rump of the third male hunter's horse. Such felines
(not native to China) were trained as hunting animals in parts of western Asia and must have been
imported along with their foreign handlers.

Hunting was a sport of both men and women.
The two women portrayed in this set of figures are
obviously active participants in the hunt: one carries the body of a captured deer on her horse, while
an alert lynx (like the cheetah, used as a hunting
animal) accompanies the other female hunter. Their
hair arranged in tight, practical buns, both women
are dressed for the occasion in close-fitting tunics
and trousers and thickly padded belts. Their participation in the hunt and their clearly foreign
associates are an indication of the level of physical
activity and relative freedom permitted to women
during the Tang dynasty.

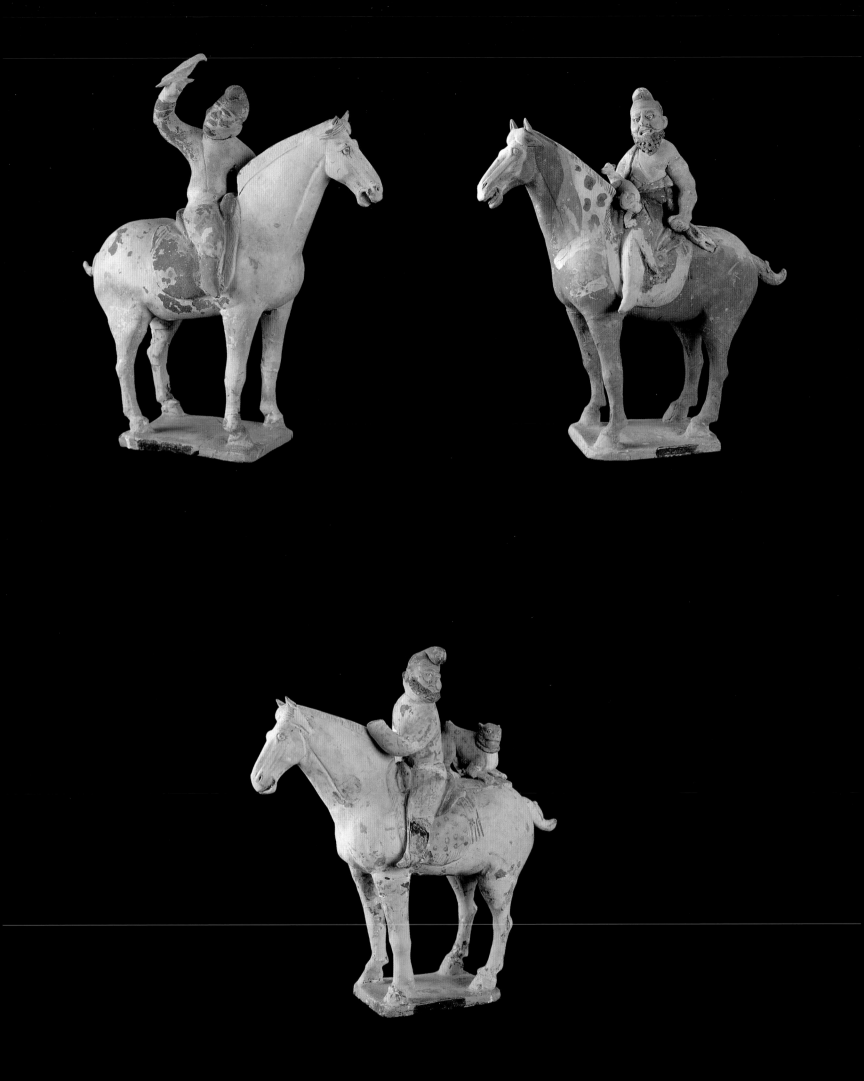

171

A group of five painted pottery female musicians

Height 30.8 (12 ⅛) – 37 (13 ½)
Tang Dynasty, early seventh century CE
From the tomb of Yu Yin and Princess Jinxiang,
Xi'an, Shaanxi Province

Xi'an Municipal Institute of Archaeology
and Preservation of Cultural Relics,
Shaanxi Province

Washington only

Among the *mingqi* found in Jinxiang's tomb was a group of five female musicians mounted on horseback.[1] While their features suggest Chinese ethnicity, there is little in the figures' dress, musical instruments, or implied approach to music that relates to native Chinese traditions; to the contrary, everything about them indicates the strong influence of Central Asia. The fascination with the music of other cultures began in the Han dynasty and continued through the Tang. Foreign music from all parts of the known world was the rage at the Tang court. Literary sources refer to performances of music originating in Japan, Korea, and many other areas; the most popular performers, however, were those from Central Asia.

In contrast to later representations of women (see cat. 173), these female figures are fairly thin, and their tight-fitting, belted tunics and trousers are appropriate for riding. Painted patterns represent different types of fabric: one woman wears a dark-colored garment (perhaps leather); another wears a thick, short-sleeved jacket with intricate designs probably intended to represent a woven fabric. Their head gear is spectacular. The most elaborate is a fantastic hat that sweeps up from one woman's head to represent a large bird. Flaps, representing the tail of the bird, cover the back of her neck and upper shoulders, and the intricately drawn patterns on the back of the hat suggest that actual feathers were used to decorate such headgear. The other women have their hair tied in

The horses depicted in this group are of a large and spirited breed much sought after by the Chinese. Originating in the grasslands of the Asian interior, such horses were much larger than the pony native to China and were valued for their speed and noble character. These qualities made the breed ideally suited for hunting as well as for battle (often against the same nomads from whom they had been obtained).

Watching the hunt was as much a spectator sport as a participatory pastime for the Tang aristocracy; the fact that the all men in this group are foreigners may indicate that hunts were staged as a form of court entertainment. MK

1 Excavated in 1991; reported: Xi'an 1997, 14 – 19.

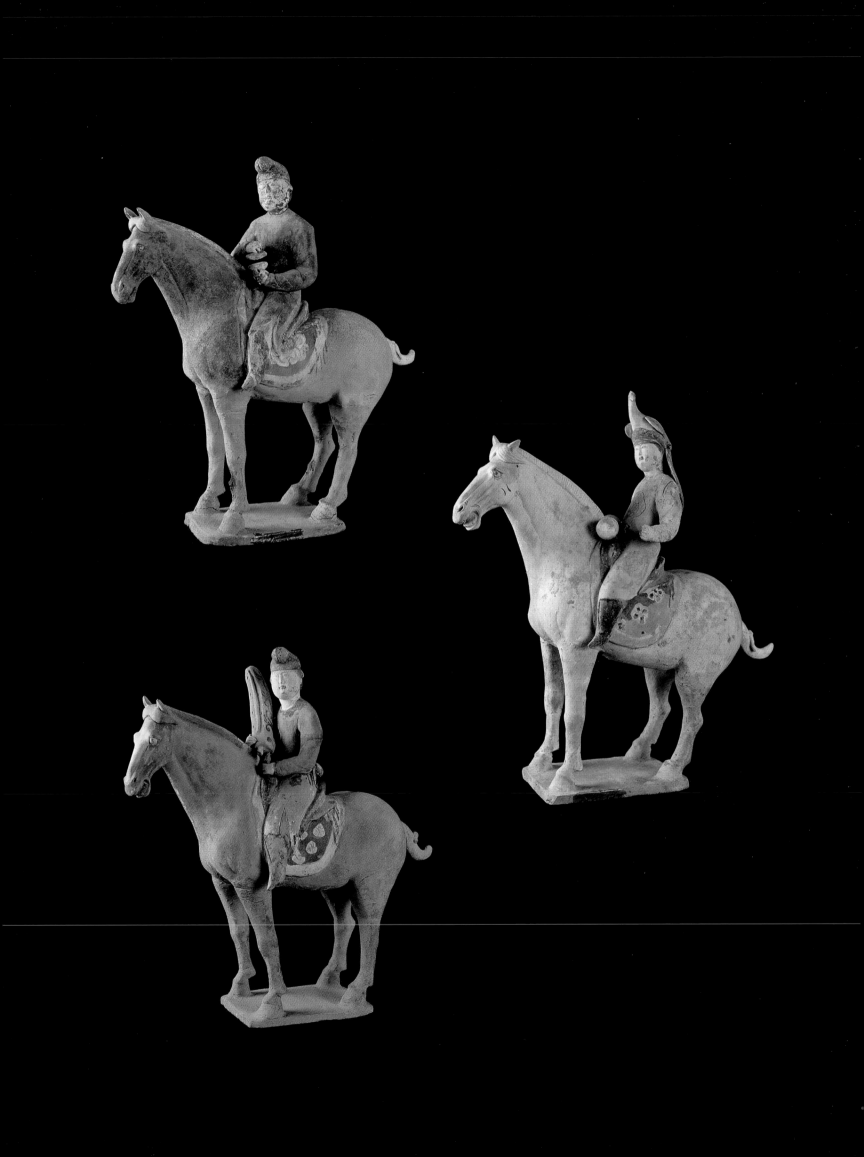

elaborate arrangements or wear the soft hats often found on figures of foreigners.

This troupe of women musicians likely represents part of the entertainment at one of the elaborate outings favored by the wealthy residents of Xi'an during the seventh and eighth centuries. In his "Song of the Beautiful Ladies," Du Fu (712–770) provides a poetic description of these entertainments.

> Third month, third day, in the air a breath
>   of newness;
> by Ch'ang-an riverbanks the beautiful ladies
>   crowd,
> warm-bodied, modest-minded, mild and
>   pure,
> with clear sleek complexions, bone and
>   flesh well matched,
> in figured-gauze robes that shine in the
>   late spring,
> worked with golden peacocks, silver
>   unicorns.
> On their heads what do they wear?
> Kingfisher glinting from hairpins that
>   dangle by sidelock borders.
> On their backs what do I see?
> Pearls that weight the waistband and subtly
>   set off the form.[2]

The first woman in the group holds a small drum in one hand and prepares to strike it with the other; another woman plays a pair of cymbals. Large stationary drums and cymbals were employed in Late Bronze Age China; these smaller, portable forms (like many Tang musical instruments, apparently of Central Asian origin) would have been far better suited to less formal performances such as that represented in this group of figures. Another musician plays the four-stringed *chuding pipa* (crook-necked lute), or *hu pipa* (barbarian lute) — the most common form of lute during the Tang dynasty. Originating in western Asia, the Tang form of the *hu pipa* reflects Central Asian influence; they were likely imported, along with the musicians who played them. Bo Zhuyi in "Song of the Lute: Preface and Poem" describes a woman playing the lute:

> She turned the pegs, brushed the strings,
>   sounding two or three notes
> before they had formed a melody, already
>   the feeling came through.
> Each string seemed tense with it, each
>   sound to hold a thought,
> as though she were protesting a lifetime of
>   wishes unfulfilled.
> . . .
> Lightly she pressed the strings, slowly
>   plucked, pulled, and snapped them,
> first performing, "Rainbow Skirts," the
>   "Waists of Green."
> The big strings plang-planged like
>   swift-falling rain;
> the little strings went buzz-buzz like secret
>   conversations;
> plang-plang, buzz-buzz mixed and mingled
>   in her playing
> like big pearls and little pearls falling on a
>   plate of jade,
> . . .
> As the piece ended, she swept the plectrum
>   in an arc before her breast,
> and all four strings made a single sound,
>   like the sound of rending silk.[3]

Two styles of harps, both known as *kanghou*, were used in Tang China. According to Tang and Song dynasty sources, the larger version of the harp originated in western Asia and reached China through Central Asia. It was often elaborately decorated with lacquer and inlaid materials. The smaller version (played by one of the musicians), was designed to be portable.[4] A Tang poem likens the sound of the *kanghou* to "10,000 real pearls cascading from a jade face."[5] Another figure plays a type of oboe, described in Tang texts as a short and thick, double-reeded instrument; it is thought to have originated in Kucha. MK

1   Excavated in 1991; reported: Xi'an 1997, 14–19.
2   Du, "Song of the Beautiful Ladies," in Watson 1984, 222.
3   Bo, "Song of the Lute: Preface and Poem" in Watson 1984, 250.
4   Zhongguo 1977, 64.
5   Zhongguo 1977, 103, Terese Bartholomew trans.

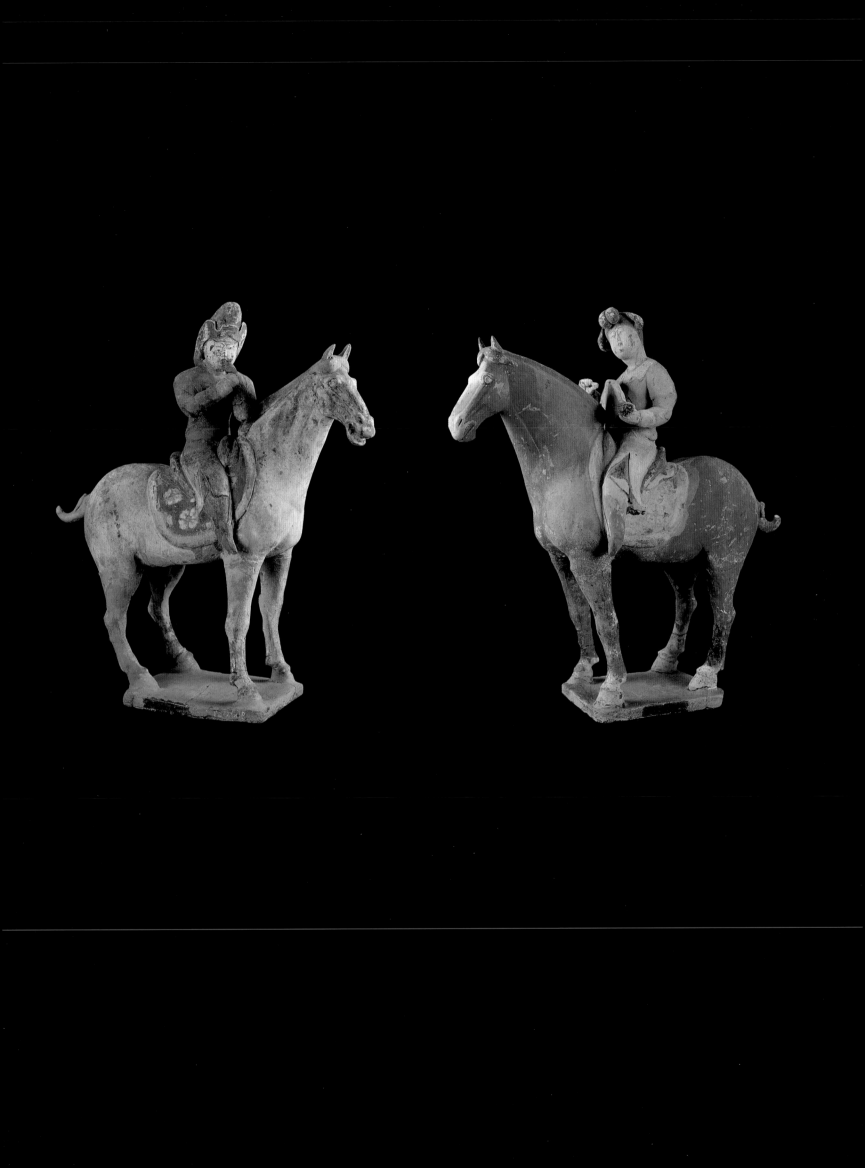

172

A group of twelve painted pottery zodiac animals

Height 38.5 (15⅛) – 41.5 (16⅜)
Tang Dynasty, eighth century CE
From an unnamed tomb in Xi'an, Shaanxi Province

Shaanxi History Museum, Xi'an

This group of figures, representing the twelve animals of the zodiac, reportedly was excavated in 1955 from a Tang dynasty site in Xi'an. Little has been published about the circumstances in which they were found, and little comparative material exists to define the nature of the tomb or the status of the individual for whom they were made. Although painted rather than glazed (glaze was the preferred finish of higher-status *sancai* pottery), the scale and quality of the objects suggests that they were made for a member of the middle ranks of the Tang aristocracy.

Numerology and astrology have been an integral to Chinese culture from at least the beginnings of its written history. Associations of animals with directions, times of the year, certain constellations, and specific qualities were central in the *yinyang wuxing* (Yin and Yang and Five Elements) beliefs of

the Han dynasty. The appearance of certain animals played an important role in Chinese beliefs regarding omens and portents and reflected a complex and evolving system of belief that spanned the Han dynasty, through the Period of Disunity, and into Tang dynasty.

The origin of the twelve animals of the Chinese zodiac, however, remains somewhat obscure. Their earliest appearance as funerary sculptures in northern Chinese tombs dates to the latter part of the Six Dynasties period (sixth century). Almost all early examples represent human bodies, in kneeling position, with animal heads; no full set has yet been found in a tomb from that period. The earliest known twelve-piece sets date from the Tang dynasty but are relatively rare; sets of zodiac animals become common only later in the Tang dynasty and during the Song period. These figures from Xi'an are unusual in their depiction of standing figures; their height as well distinguishes them from other, contemporary examples.

Some scholars have theorized that sets of zodiac animals appeared in northern China as a result of contact with western and Central Asian peoples. Certainly, the animal zodiac constituted a well-developed iconographical element in these

areas long before the earliest artistic or literary references to them in China; that these sets first appear in China during the Toba-ruled state of Northern Wei, moreover, lends additional support to the theory of the foreign origins of zodiacal sets.

This group, however, shows little evidence of foreign influence. Formed of a red clay covered with white slip, the figures retain only a few traces of their original paint. Each figure stands on a base that appears to represent stone. The heads of the individual pieces are carefully worked and elegantly capture the physical and presumed psychological characteristics of the animals they are meant to portray. Each wears a heavy robe with long full sleeves, which completely hide the figures' crossed hands; the shoes of a few of the figures peek out from beneath their robes. Such garments, typical of conservative Chinese dress, contrast markedly with the tight-fitting garments of the musicians and hunters (cats. 170, 171). MK

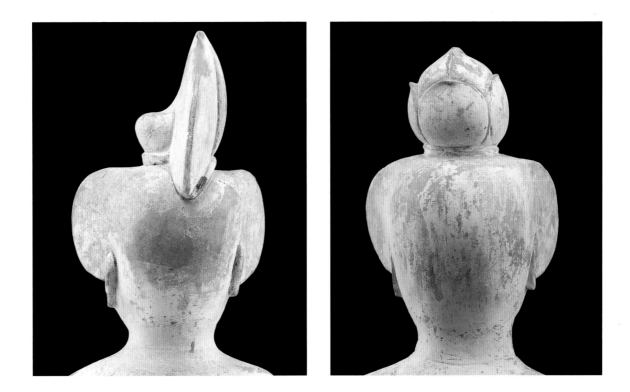

173

A group of six painted pottery female figures

Height 71–86 (28–33 ⅞)
Tang Dynasty, early to mid-eighth century CE
From the tomb at Hansenzhai, Xi'an,
Shaanxi Province

Xi'an Municipal Institute of Archaeology and
Preservation of Cultural Relics, Shaanxi Province

A large number of dated or datable tombs of the
Tang dynasty have been excavated in and around
the Tang capital near Xi'an, Shaanxi province, in
the past few decades. The funerary figurines found
in these controlled excavations have allowed for
a remarkably complete survey of the interests and
tastes of the Tang aristocracy. Among the developments that can be traced in these figures are
changes in the ideal of feminine beauty.

The ruling clan and many of the elite of the
Tang dynasty came from a group of aristocratic
families from the northwest region of China—

products of centuries of intermarriage and exchange that resulted from foreign conquest of this
region shortly after the fall of the Han dynasty in
221 CE; their links to non-Chinese people and social
customs remained strong. Nowhere was this diversity more apparent than in attitudes toward women
and the relative freedom they were allowed. Figures
from the Jinxiang tomb depict women mounted on
horseback—playing musical instruments, participating in hunts or in polo matches (see cats. 170,
171)—or performing physically demanding dances.
The women are thin and wear tight-fitting clothing
appropriate for the activities in which they are
engaged, testimony to an athletic ideal of feminine
beauty particular to the period.

By the middle of the eighth century, however,
that ideal had changed: The women depicted in
paintings and in *mingqi* are plump; they wear elaborate, loose-fitting garments and decidedly imprac-
tical shoes—dress ill-suited to a strenuous, active
life. This change is only one of many signs that

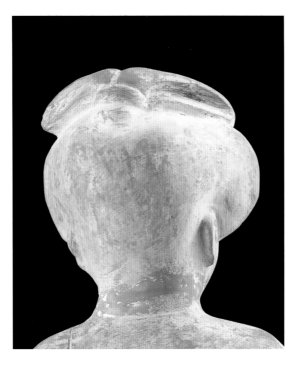

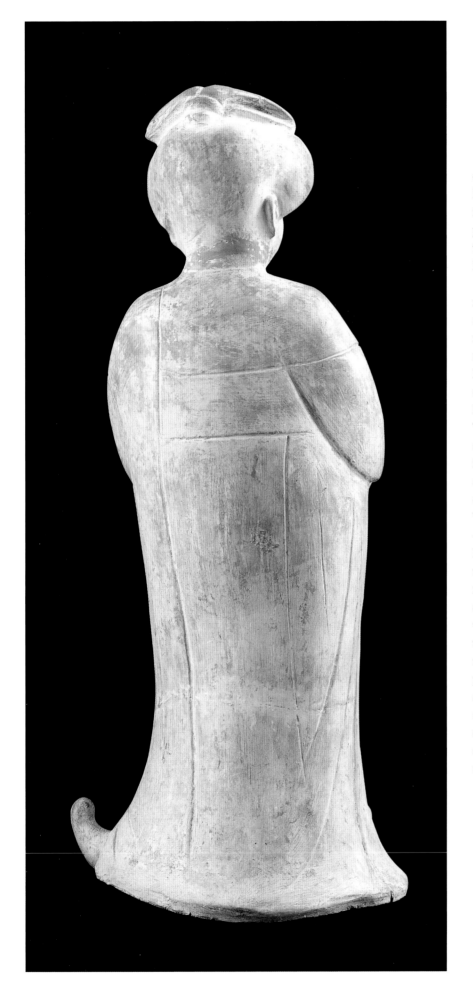

over the intervening decades the elite of China had become more sedentary and more interested in interior pursuits. They had moved far from the physically active, non-Chinese aspect of their heritage and were becoming increasingly a class of highly sophisticated dilettantes.

This group of six female figures, excavated in 1988, are of this later type. They are beautifully sculpted, and their full faces, plump bodies, elaborate coiffures, and heavy, loose-fitting gowns are sensitively depicted. Their gowns cover the entire body and sweep the ground, revealing only the tips of elaborate shoes, with upturned ends, that could have been practical only in an interior setting. The figures are given individual identities through a variety of hair styles, head positions, and subtle facial expressions. The arms of five of the figures are demurely crossed at the waist or chest; their clasped hands are covered by long, loose sleeves. While the garments are rather cursorily represented — the flow of drapery is suggested by a few incised lines — traces of brightly colored pigment indicate that the details were painted on; the actual garments they represent must have been wonderful expanses of sumptuously decorated silk. The women's soft bodies and the masses of hair piled on top of their heads suggest that they were not accustomed to physical activity. One figure — from appearances, a younger female servant or attendant — stands apart from the other five. Her hair is tied in a simple knot at the side of her head, and she wears a tunic with tight sleeves over her dress; her hands are exposed and positioned in front of her body in a gesture of offering or receipt. MK

The tomb of Wang Chuzhi, a powerful official of the Tang and the Later Liang dynasties in northern China, was excavated in 1995 near the village of Xiyanchuan in Quyang county, Hebei province.[1] The tomb's excavation, undertaken from July through November, was conducted by members of the Institute of Archaeology of Hebei province and the Cultural Relics offices of Baoding city and Quyang county. The tomb complex — constructed on a north-south axis and entered from a ramp at the south end that leads to a door inside a small outer chamber — consists of two main tomb chambers, the first and larger of which provides access to two smaller chambers that open to the east and west. From the entry door to the north wall of the rear chamber, the tomb measures about 12.5 meters. An elaborate decorative program of paintings and painted stone-carved reliefs distinguish nearly all the rooms' wall surfaces.

Just inside the tomb, a wall painting depicts two pairs of male attendants standing on either side of the entrance door. Paintings of female attendants, singly and in pairs, cover the walls of the antechamber and both side chambers. The antechamber also features a map of the stars and constellations on its ceiling, a painted frieze of colored clouds and flying cranes, a large, square landscape painting in ink on its north wall, and large screenlike panels of flowers, rocks, and birds along its main walls. The eastern side-chamber also contains an ink landscape painting in the shape of a small screen, rendered as if it were joined to a painted dressing table in front of it.[2] In the coffin chamber, two large horizontal garden panels decorate the east and west walls, and an extensive composition of a rock garden, peonies, and birds appears along the entire rear wall. In the many garden paintings, peonies — the royal flower — and red roses predominate. Painted curtains, above and sometimes beside the larger painted panels, often look as though they had just been opened for viewing.

The paintings, created on a smooth surface of white clay spread over the masonry walls, cover a total of approximately a hundred square meters. Close examination of the paintings' execution reveals that some of the larger compositions were carefully transferred from designs, or cartoons (fenben), onto the walls, while others were painted quite freely and directly.[3]

Sixteen wall niches of various sizes, each originally containing painted stone reliefs, line the small entrance hall, the large antechamber, and the coffin chamber. The tomb contained marble reliefs of the Twelve Earthly Branches, used in the traditional calendar, four of which remain in the tomb undamaged. Each is in the form of a human figure carrying or accompanied by its respective annual symbol — rat, dragon, chicken, and horse — and is set inside a painted depiction of an architectural framework, as if each figure were standing in a small pavilion amid the clouds and flying cranes on either side. The figures' long, wide, billowing sleeves, their open, frontal stance, and their careful placement within the frames convey an air of slight movement and recall many of the lively painted figures found in earlier Tang imperial tombs.[4] In fact, virtually all elements of the decor of Wang Chuzhi's tomb, from motifs to style, have their origins in the conventions established in the imperial tombs of the Tang period. Even the landscape paintings are essentially in the style of the Tang dynasty and follow Tang imperial

South wall and ceiling of the anteroom of the tomb of Wang Chuzhi. Paintings of male attendants flank the entrance; a map of the constellations decorates the ceiling. The niches contained painted figures of the Twelve Earthly Branches.

precedent, but the presence here of two landscape paintings of an independent genre undoubtedly testifies to the popularity of what was still a relatively new art — one that had already become important by the early tenth century within the context of tomb decoration.[5] The repeated effect of curtains opening around the main painted panels is an unusual feature of the decor, which seems to highlight the art of painting itself.

Most impressive and unusual of all, however, are two large, painted marble reliefs of rare artistic quality that were set into the walls of the rear chamber, which contained the body of Wang Chuzhi. The panel on the west wall, consisting of fifteen figures, depicts a complete female orchestra, together with its conductor and two dancers. The panel on the eastern wall portrays an assembly of thirteen female attendants and another person, possibly a dwarf, all carrying a variety of luxury items such as porcelain cups and cosmetic boxes. These two beautifully carved and painted relief compositions, each measuring 82 by 136 centimeters, deserve to be regarded as masterpieces of Chinese sculpture. Overall, Wang Chuzhi's tomb stands out even among the large group excavated in northern China dating from the period of the Late Tang, the Five Dynasties, Liao, Jin, and Northern Song — from roughly 900 to 1100 CE, a major era in tomb design.

Wang Chuzhi's tomb had been broken into at least twice prior to its excavation, and thieves had hacked off many of the original stone reliefs, including most of the figures representing the Twelve Earthly Branches and the large reliefs that once decorated the side walls of the entrance hallway. Thieves also removed most of the original store of grave goods, which

Southeast corner of the anteroom, showing paintings of one of the Twelve Earthly Branches and of cranes in flight.

included porcelain, gold and silver, jewelry, and bronze vessels, only bits and pieces of which remained. Three hundred coins were recovered.

A tomb epitaph carved on the same granite used throughout the tomb construction contains nearly two thousand characters recounting the official life of Wang Chuzhi. Wang's titles included Governor of Yi, Ding, and Qi Prefectures and Prince of Beiping. His biography figures prominently in the official histories of both the Tang and Later Liang dynasties. He died in the final year of the Later Liang, 923, and was buried one year later. RB

1   Excavation report in Hebei 1996a, 4 – 13. A complete report has been published as Hebei 1998.
2   The landscape paintings are discussed in a brief article by Luo Shiping in Luo 1996, 74 – 75 and are reproduced in Hebei 1998, color pls. 14 and 18 – 20. All paintings are reproduced or shown in copies in Hebei 1998.
3   This is the observation of Shi Jianwen in Hao 1996, 57.
4   Examples of Tang imperial tomb painting are reproduced in Yang 1997, 67 – 74.
5   Luo Shiping (Luo 1996) mentions Guan Tong (active c. 925) and Dong Yuan (d. 962) for comparison but generally sees their work as very early stages in the evolution of landscape painting and as products of the Tang period. Their work closely resemble many of the landscape depictions found on objects in the Shosoin and at Dunhuang, as well as the garden elements depicted in the Tang imperial tombs. For comparative materials, see Sullivan 1980. A Tang imperial tomb containing a sixfold landscape screen painted over one entire wall was recently discovered in Fuping county, Shanxi province (Jing and Wang 1997, 8 – 11 and inside back cover), providing another Tang imperial precedent for elements of the Wang Chuzhi tomb design. The Fuping county tomb may be the earliest known example of an independent landscape painting done for a burial; it appears to date from the first half of the eighth century CE.

174

Painted marble relief of attendants

Height 82 (31), width 136 (53)
Later Liang Dynasty, tenth century CE (907–923)
From the tomb of Wang Chuzhi at Xiyanchuan,
Quyang, Hebei Province

Hebei Provincial Cultural Relics Institute,
Shijiazhuang

Together with a matching scene of female musicians (cat. 175), this painted marble relief[1] framed the coffin in the rear chamber of Wang Chuzhi's tomb. Both measure 82 by 136 centimeters. The composition of this painted stone relief is similar to that of earlier depictions of attendants carrying items of daily life into the coffin chamber to ensure the well-being of the tomb's occupant. One of the best known of these earlier depictions is a procession of women in the tomb of Princess Yongtai, dated 706.[2] The women in such compositions carry feather fans, dishes, cups, cosmetic boxes, fans, and other useful domestic items. Their bodies lean forward as they walk in a slow, rhythmic procession. One of the interesting features in this composition is the tiny figure that leads the slow parade. Dressed in male clothing and carrying a small vase resting on a cloth, he is sometimes identified as a dwarf, but he could also be a child (two tiny figures in the facing relief present a similar problem of identification). The thirteen women behind him are in four rows of three abreast; one figure in the rear mirrors the small person at the front.

Despite their seeming fixed positions, the women are engaged in a subtle interplay. Turned toward the right, the nearest woman in the front group of three holds out her left hand and delicately defers to the woman in the right front corner, who has stepped out of the last rank to come forward with a tray holding a porcelain cup. As she moves forward, the women adjacent look toward her, further calling our attention to this choreographed sequence of movements. This kind of slow, deferential choreography is also evident in the painted procession in the tomb of Princess Yongtai,

indicating that such deliberate movement was a convention in Tang imperial tombs.

Another striking aspect is the large size of all thirteen of the female figures who form the composition. They are full-faced, heavy-set, substantial women, reminiscent of the image of the Tang courtesan Yang Guifei, the favorite of Emperor Xuanzong; her ample proportions changed the fashion of Tang women everywhere.[3] If it was generally assumed that the preference for ample women somehow died out toward the end of the Tang dynasty, these ample women — and others like them from the same period — make clear that for those who, like Wang Chuzhi, continued the Tang imperial traditions, the Yang Guifei ideal endured.[4] Only in the late tenth and eleventh centuries do we see the loss of this ideal in the new Song models of feminine beauty.[5] RB

1   Excavated in 1995; reported: Hebei 1996, 4–13; Hebei 1998.
2   The relevant section is reproduced in Yang 1997a, 74.
3   Kuwayama 1987, 85.
4   See, for example, a Liao tomb found at Baoshan, reproduced in Zhao 1996, 160, and in Neimenggu 1998, especially the color reproduction from Tomb 2 printed on the inside back cover. See also the Later Zhou tomb dated c. 958 mentioned in cat. 175 n. 4, where the Tang ideal still prevails.
5   In the context of tomb decoration, the slender Song ideal of feminine beauty is illustrated by the female orchestra painted on the wall of a Northern Song tomb excavated in Jiangjiagou village, Shanxi province: Shaanxi 1996, 6, fig. 4, and color frontispiece. Most secular figure paintings associated with the Five Dynasties also favor a slender female physique. See Yang 1997a, 112–113.

174

175

Painted marble relief of musicians

Height 82 (31), width 136 (53)
Later Liang Dynasty, tenth century CE (907–923)
From the Tomb of Wang Chuzhi at Xiyanchuan,
Quyang, Hebei Province

Hebei Provincial Cultural Relics Institute,
Shijiazhuang

This handsome painted marble relief was set into
the west wall of the coffin chamber, matching the
relief of attendants on the east wall. The two compositions provide two essential elements in the
appropriate decor of a royal tomb of the Tang and
Song periods — music and servants. Judging from
the prevalence of the musical performance theme
in tomb decorations, such references seem to have
been a virtual requirement. Complete orchestras

such as this one in Wang Chuzhi's tomb appear
most commonly from the Late Tang to Early Song
period and present evidence of daily life among the
aristocracy of the time. Most similar to the overall
character of the paintings and reliefs in Wang
Chuzhi's tomb is the great narrative handscroll *The
Night Revels of Han Xizai* in the Palace Museum in
Beijing,[1] which probably depicts the interior of a
princely mansion only twenty-five years or so after
the death of Wang Chuzhi in 923 CE. There, as in
Wang's tomb, bands of musicians perform, servants
attend, and pictures decorate walls and furniture.
Tombs like that of Wang Chuzhi were clearly
intended to closely emulate the palaces in which
he had once lived, and music was obviously a vital
element in the daily life of such palaces.

Wang Chuzhi's female orchestra features twelve
musicians, two tiny dancers, and what appears to

be a male conductor, or drum major. The musicians, in the midst of a vigorous performance, stand in two rows of six, forming a double arc from left to right. The tiny dancers, dressed in Central Asian costumes, assume identical positions in the lower right corner. Behind them, seen frontally, is the stolid figure of the conductor holding a tasseled baton. Since these two large painted stone reliefs are the centerpieces of the decor in the coffin chamber, it is noteworthy that in each of them, one figure — here the conductor and, in the other, the gesturing woman near the front of the group — is turned quite dramatically, as if to engage the viewer directly. This figure, in effect, directs all of the activity depicted in the two compositions toward the coffin of Wang Chuzhi, which presumably stood near the center of the room. "This music, these refreshments, are for you, Sir," these two figures seem to say.

The instrumentation in this female orchestra consists of two horizontal flutes, two vertical flutes, two drums (one large, one small), a set of chimes (fangxiang), a pipe harmonica (sheng), a harp (konghou), a zither (zheng), a lute (pipa), and a set of clappers. These are the instruments seen in one combination or another in nearly all of the many depictions of musicians from the tenth century. A much more informal band of female musicians, playing five of these same instruments while drinking wine, is seen in a painting contemporary with the tomb of Wang Chuzhi, Palace Concert, by an unknown painter of the Late Tang or early Five Dynasties period.[2] The women in the painting share the physical characteristics, hair styles, and costumes of the plump women in Wang Chuzhi's tomb. A similar group of substantial women appears in the band of musicians illustrated in a handscroll copied after the leading tenth-century master of such subjects, Zhou Wenju (fl. c. 940–975), whose activity and fame in the southern Tang kingdom at Nanjing suggests that such orchestras continued to be a form of national art even after China was divided into many small states and kingdoms.[3] Testifying to the continuing need for music in the context of

burials is the tomb of Zhang Wenzao (d. 1074), recently excavated in the Xuanhua district, Hebei province, in which a male band is depicted playing many of the same instruments.[4] Even then, 150 years later, with male musicians instead of female, a foreign ruler, and a foreign religion, the continuity of the traditions of tomb design within Hebei province is readily apparent. Another orchestra, composed of slender Song ladies, was found in a Northern Song tomb in Jiangjiagou village, Shanxi province.[5] Clearly, throughout much of northern China, the afterlife was unimaginable without music.

One of the most impressive features of the Wang Chuzhi relief is its realistic representation of musical performance. The craftsmen or artists who designed the composition must have been familiar with musical concerts to have so successfully conveyed the movements and gestures typical of performance. At top left, the two flute players lean their upper bodies forward into the flow of the music, their right elbows pulled sharply back. Below them, the drummer lifts her arm and prepares to pound the large drum she steadies in her other hand. The hands of the harpist and zither players move gracefully across their strings. The five wind players appear poised to exhale; the two vertical flute players stand very erect and straight, anchoring the swaying group with their firmly planted bodies. This representation's accuracy and sense of animation are readily obvious when compared to any of the other aforementioned concert groups, none of which convey this vivid sense of observed characteristics.

Painted pictorial reliefs of this size and quality are virtually unknown in tomb designs of the period, although other examples of painted reliefs have been found in contemporary tombs. The tradition of stone carving was, of course, long-standing, particularly in association with Buddhism.[6] The decor of Wang Chuzhi's tomb, however, makes it clear that pictorial sculpture was reaching new heights of subtlety and sophistication by the early tenth century and was comparable in every way to

the better-known developments in the art of painting during this same period. Other than Wang Chuzhi's tomb, the most dramatic demonstration of this new, high standard can be seen in the extensive program of Buddhist sculpture and painted stone reliefs created during the succeeding Song dynasty (960–1279 CE) at a cave-temple site near Chengdu in Dazu county, Sichuan province.[7]

Buddhism, with its constant need for the creation of new and more elaborate stone-carved cave-temples across China, had traditionally been the main impetus behind pictorial stone sculpture, but the national persecution of Buddhism in 845 brought an end to the great cycle of such construction and expansion. Private efforts to rebuild in the aftermath of that great tragedy began with such projects as the new temple site at Dazu in the late ninth century, but the rapid decline and end of the Tang dynasty and its breakup into numerous small states and kingdoms prevented further development until much later in the Song period, after reunification in 960.

It is possible that the marked advances in tomb design and decoration in the tenth and eleventh centuries owe something to the displacement of so many painters, sculptors, and craftsmen in the aftermath of the Buddhist persecution of 845. The Buddhist Church only began to regain some of its lost power and influence well after 960 and the establishment of the Song dynasty. The Dazu cave-temples, most of which were completed

during the Southern Song period (1127–1279 CE), testify to its recovery, but even they are not as impressive as the painted stone reliefs in the tomb of Wang Chuzhi. RB

1 Illustrated in Yang 1997a, 112–113.
2 In the National Palace Museum, Taipei; reproduced in Palace Museum 1961, no. 10.
3 The section of the scroll, now cut into four parts, that includes the musicians is reproduced in Blunden and Elvin 1988, 202–203. See also Fong 1992, 34–39.
4 Hebei 1996b, 28. Separate groups of male and female musicians depicted in multiple panels of painted, carved brick are the main feature of the tomb of Feng Hui (d. 958), Yang and Yan 1994, 48–55. Another male band found in a Liao tomb dated 1116 and a female band from a Baisha tomb dated 1099 are reproduced in Laing 1988–1989, figs. 41, 42.
5 Shaanxi 1996, 6.
6 Especially noteworthy in tomb decoration is a set of painted, carved brick reliefs found in the tomb of Feng Hui, excavated in Binxian county, Shaanxi province (cited in note 4 above). Su Bai 1957, plate 22, illustrates another painted relief panel said to be made from carved brick set into a plaster wall that was found in a Baisha tomb dated 1099. Many other examples of relief sculpture dating to the Jin dynasty are reproduced and discussed in Laing 1988–1989. A complete survey and analysis of Song tombs has been conducted by Kuhn; see, for example, Kuhn 1994, 11–159.
7 Dazu 1984.

ESSAYS

Afterword

SU BAI | Most of the treasures included in *The Golden Age of Chinese Archaeology,* which represent a six-thousand-year time span (5000 BCE to 1000 CE) and a wide geographical range — the Yellow River valley, the Yangzi region, and the Pearl River delta — were excavated by Chinese archaeologists in the last twenty-five years. Every item in this exhibition has immense artistic and historical value, and the selection presents a microcosm of Chinese archaeology's golden age.

China is a vast country comprising a rich variety of ethnicities among which the Han predominate. It stretches from the Mongolian plateau and desert in the north, to the Tibetan Mountain Plateau in the southwest. The east and southeast of China verges on the Pacific Ocean, and the west is divided by the Kunlun, Altun, Tian, and Altai mountains, and the Tarim and Junggar basins — the outlets of rivers that flow down from the mountains. These boundaries presented a considerable obstacle to the ancient Chinese as they attempted to communicate with the outside world, but once transportation and technology had improved, they were quick to enrich their civilization by interacting with an assortment of diverse cultures. The stimulation provided by this cultural interaction and intermingling contributed to the development of a distinct Chinese civilization, which would become one of the four great civilizations of the ancient world.

The domestication of the horse in approximately 3000 BCE extended the range of Chinese cultural influence, and archaeologists have found traces of imported Western culture dating as far back as the Siba Culture and the Lower Xiajiadian Culture (both contemporaneous with the Xia dynasty) in the eastern and western ends of the Great Wall. The increased contact between the West and the powerful nomadic cultures that were developing in the Great Wall region during the late Shang period accounts for the presence of western elements in the Yinxu culture of the late Shang. During the Western Han period, Zhang Qian's exploration of the western region opened up the passageway of the famous Silk Road, making way for progressive interaction and increased communication between east and west during the Han and Tang dynasties. Along with artifacts and components of culture, the Chinese imported elements of foreign philosophies and systems of belief, of which Buddhism was the most important. A long period of interaction between Confucian and Buddhist thought resulted in the birth of the Chan school of Buddhism and Neo-Confucianism, from which Chinese culture entered a new stage. An ancient Chinese saying, "tolerance creates greatness," might also be interpreted as "acceptance creates greatness," for their tolerance of other cultures and their willingness to accept new cultural elements led the Chinese to develop a rich and eclectic civilization that assimilated facets of other cultures, while retaining and enhancing a tradition of their own. Nor was the interaction one-sided, for foreign cultures as well benefited from interactions with China.

At the turning point of the twentieth century, the world continues to be internationalized. With the accelerated growth of transportation and telecommunication, world economies are becoming increasingly globalized. As the world grows smaller, the concept of a "global village" is gradually becoming a very real possibility. Increasingly we are living "in a world without the boundaries of nations." Will the cultural dichotomies between geological districts, ethnicities, and nations rapidly disappear as interaction increases? History suggests that nations tend to be more conservative about absorbing foreign culture than they are about assimilating foreign technology and economy, and it seems likely that the progression toward cultural unity will be much slower than economic globalization. But we can, perhaps, look forward to the eventual development of a unified global culture, comprising various elements from every ethnicity, without sacrificing variation in regional cultures.

For now, we sincerely hope that this cultural interaction will improve our mutual understanding. By sharing our best qualities both nations will be enriched and growth as well as unity promoted.

517

New Understandings of Chinese Prehistory

ZHANG ZHONGPEI | The last eighty years of archaeological investigation of China's prehistory have traced the habitation of the continent back some eight million years, and sketched a timeline of successive cultures in particular regions. What follows is a précis of our current understanding of China's earliest history; much of it has developed over the last twenty years.

PALAEOLITHIC ARCHAEOLOGY

Hominid remains found in China raise the likelihood that the Asian continent constitutes a locis for the origin of man. These hominid fossils include *Dryopithecus kaiyuanensis* (8 million years BP, found in Xiaolongtan, Kaiyuan county, Yunnan province); *Ramapithecus lufengsis* (6 million years BP, found in Shinuba, Lufeng county, Yunnan province); *Ramapithecus hudienensis* (4 million years BP, found in Yuanmou, Yunnan province); and *Gigantopithecus* (2 – 5 million years BP, found in the provinces of Guangxi, Sichuan, and Hubei). Fossils of *Homo erectus,* together with associated cultural remains, have also been found, including Lantian Man, Peking Man, and the oldest known traces of *Homo erectus* in China (1.7 million years BP): Yuanmou Man. Fossil remains of archaic *Homo sapiens* found in China include Dingcun Man, Jinniushan Man, Maba Man, and Chaoxian Man; remains of *Homo sapiens* (for example, Liujiang Man, Ziyang Man, and Shandingdong Man) have been found in many as forty localities. Certain inherited physical features of *Homo erectus* and *Homo sapiens* (in particular, shovel-shaped incisors, sagittal ridges, flat faces, and wide and straight noses) suggest that the Chinese of the present day are the descendants of the region's Palaeolithic inhabitants.

Stone techniques and stone tools developed uninterruptedly from the early to the late Palaeolithic period in China. While we can trace certain continuities in stoneworking, a regional diversity is also evident. Recent studies indicate the Qinling Mountains marked a dividing line between southern and northern styles of stoneworking. Toward the late Palaeolithic period, the northern style divided into three regional styles; stoneworking in the south also displays regional variation.

THE TRANSITION FROM PALAEOLITHIC THROUGH MESOLITHIC AND NEOLITHIC

Although few Mesolithic sites have been identified in China, they are widely distributed — in southern, northern, northeastern, and central China — an indication that the transition from Palaeolithic to Mesolithic cultures occurred in several areas. Though Mesolithic cultures typically relied on hunting, gathering, and fishing for subsistence, different sites indicate that specific subsistence activities were favored in particular areas. The transition to Neolithic cultures is marked by the addition of farming to the hunting-and-gathering economy of Mesolithic cultures, a development for which we have evidence in southern and northeastern China. Farming seems to have comprised two staple crops: rice was cultivated mainly in the lower and middle Yangzi regions and probably in part of the Huai River region; the cultivation of millet seems to have been concentrated in the lower and middle reaches of the Yellow River. The earliest evidence of rice agriculture, dating back approximately 12,000 years, has been located in the Yuchanyan cave in Dao county, Hunan province. The remains are admittedly sparse — two grains of wild rice and two grains of a cultivar — and it may be that the Neolithic cultures relied on wild rice in addition to the cultivated variety. Hunting, gathering, and fishing, however, continued to constitute the main sources of food: the site contained an abundance of animal and plant remains, including fifteen plant species in addition to wild and cultivated rice, twenty-eight species of animals, twenty-seven species of birds, five species of fish, thirty-three species of mollusks, as well as turtles and insects. It was not until approximately four thousand years later — with the Pengtoushan culture — that farming became the main source of food. The earliest remains of millet agriculture found thus far date back some 8,000 years to the Cishan and Peiligang cultures; we have evidence, however, that the cultivation of millet by this point was fully developed, a fact that suggests that the origins of this type of farming date back considerably further.

The types of artifacts recovered from early Neolithic sites display considerable local variation. Neither pottery nor worked stone has been found in the Emaokou and Yaozitou sites in Huairen county, Shanxi province; by contrast, pottery (but no worked stone) has been found at the Xianrendong site in Wannian county, Jiangxi province. Such variations may point to differing levels of development, or they may merely indicate that the various sites date to different periods, but the finds raise several tantalizing questions: did the inhabitants of the middle Yangzi region invent pottery first and only later take up stone working? Do the Emaokou and the Yaozitou site represent the pre-Neolithic remains of northern China, or was there also a pre-Neolithic period in the middle Yangzi region?

The earliest Neolithic sites found in southern China and in the middle Yangzi region uniformly comprise small caves. Early Neolithic sites in the Yellow River area also point to small-scale settlements, situated in this region on terraces near riverbanks. Archaeological investigations indicate that relatively large-scale, densely populated settlements developed as early as 8,000 years ago in several areas, such as the middle Yangzi region, the lower and middle reaches of the Yellow River, and the Xilamulun River areas; until that point, settlements had been composed of scattered, small groups of individuals related to one another by blood.

THE RELATIONSHIP AND CHRONOLOGY OF CHINESE NEOLITHIC CULTURES
Studies of the Neolithic period (which spans the years from 6000 to 2000 BCE) have treated a variety of topics, including astronomy, geography, agricultural techniques, science, settlements, social systems, and religion, and have considerably expanded our knowledge of the China's Neolithic peoples. What follows focuses on the relatively narrow but extremely complex topic of

the relationship and chronology of Neolithic cultures in five regions of China, which were raised by Professor Su Bingqi.

1. In the area of the Huashan Mountains and the Wei River (including regions southwest of Shanxi province and northwest of Henan province), the sequence of Neolithic cultures is as follows:

Laoguantai → Banpo → Xiyin → Phase IV of Banpo → Phase II of Quanhu →

Phase II of Miaodigou ⤢ Keshengzhuang
⤡ Sanliqiao

Objects in the exhibition from the Yangshao culture comprise pottery of the Banpo culture, the Xiyin culture, or a period of transition between the two (cats. 1–4). The Xiyin culture (c. 4000–3400 BCE), the cultural apogee of this sequence, occupied a region bounded by the present-day province of Qinghai in the west, the bend of the Yellow River in the north, Hebei province in the east, and the northwestern part of Hubei province to the south, but its influence radiated beyond these borders. The Xiyin culture comprised several regional subcultures: around 3300-3200 BCE, in its core area, it developed into what is known as Phase IV of the Banpo culture; in other areas, working from west to east, it developed into the Majiayao culture, the culture represented by the Caiyanzi site, the Miaodigou culture (cat. 5), the Yijing culture, the Qinwangzai culture, the Dasikong culture, and several other cultures. These, in turn, spun off into distinct cultures of their own: the Majiayao culture, for example, developed into the Banshan culture and then into the Manchang culture; the culture of the Caiyuanzi site developed into the Qijia culture.

2. In the areas of the lower reaches of the Yellow River and the Huang-Huai Plain, the sequence of Neolithic cultures is as follows:

Houli → Beixin → Phase I of Hougang → Dawenkou → Longshan

Several objects in this exhibition are associated with this sequence. The pottery *zun* urn (cat. 23) is representative of the Dawenkou culture; the Shandong Longshan culture is represented by a jade hair ornament from Zhufeng (cat. 24). Six artifacts from Taosi in Shanxi province (cats. 25–28) represent Phase II of the Miaodigou culture, which constitutes the earlier of two phases of the culture that inhabited Taosi; objects from the later phase are difficult to match with those of any known culture.

The Dawenkou culture falls into three phases, the Liulin phase, the Huating phase, and the Xixiahou phase, the dates of which correspond roughly to those of the Xiyin culture, Phase IV of the Banpo culture and Phase II of the Quanhu culture, and Phase II of the Miaodigou culture, respectively. Phase I of the Hougang culture grew out of the Houli-Beixin cultures and probably the Cishan culture as well, and was roughly contemporaneous with the Banpo culture. At its peak, Phase I of the Hougang culture was widely distributed in the Huabei Plain of northern China, and penetrated as far as the bend of the Yellow River and the Danjiang River area in

Henan province; it ultimately retreated under pressures from the Banpo-Xiyin cultures. Its successor, the Liulin phase of the Dawenkou culture, occupied only the central area of the Hougang culture's territory. The Dawenkou culture underwent a territorial expansion during its Xixiaohou phase, but it did not attain the scale of Phase I of the Hougang culture. The Zaolütai culture, which was distributed over northern Anhui province and eastern Henan province, was probably a collateral branch of this cultural sequence.

3. In the area of Xilamulun River, as well as the area to the immediate north and south of the southern branches of the Yanshan Mountains, the sequence of Neolithic cultures is as follows:

$$\text{Xinglongwa} \begin{cases} \nearrow \text{Hongshan, Xiaoheyan} \\ \searrow \text{Zhaobaogou} \end{cases}$$

Fifteen objects of the Hongshan culture, including nine from the Niuheliang site, are included in this exhibition (cats. 10–22). The Niuheliang site, containing the remains of altars, temples, and cairns, is the largest and most important ritual site of the Hongshan culture, and its altars and temples are the earliest known examples of such structures in China. The Xinglongwa culture dates to around 6000 BCE. The Hongshan culture spans a much longer period — the fifth and the fourth millennium BCE — and falls into early, middle, and late stages, whose dates correspond roughly with those of the Banpo culture, the Xiyin culture, and Phase IV of the Banpo culture. The dates of the Zhaobaogou culture and the Xiaoheyan culture are contemporaneous with those of the Banpo culture and the Xixiaohou Phase of the Dawenkou culture, respectively. The Zhaobaogou culture (concentrated in the south) and the Hongshan culture (concentrated in the north) were the successors of the Xinglongwa culture; there is evidence that the two intermingled over a wide area. During the period of the transition from the Xinglongwa culture to the Hongshan culture (as well as during the period of the Hongshan culture itself), this sequence was influenced by Phase I of Hougang culture, the Banpo culture, and the Xiyin culture, and it adopted certain traditions from these cultures, such as techniques of pottery making and decoration. No successor to the Zhaobaogou culture and the Xiaoheyan culture has yet been found, and it is likely that the Zhaobaogou culture was absorbed into the Hongshan culture. Some elements of the Zhaobaogou culture, however, are visible in artifacts of the Lower Xiajiadian culture (coeval with the Xia dynasty).

4. In the middle Yangzi region, the sequence of Neolithic cultures is as follows:

$$\text{Pengtoushan} \begin{cases} \text{Chengbeixi} & \to \text{Daxi} \\ \text{Lower Zaoshi} & \to \text{Tangjiagang} \end{cases} \quad\begin{matrix}\text{Youziling}\\ \\ \end{matrix} \Big\} \to \text{Qujialing} \to \text{Shijiahe} \to \text{Later Shijiahe}$$

[These are not represented in this exhibition, and the sequence is for that reason not elaborated.]

5. In the lower Yangzi region, the sequence of Neolithic cultures is as follows:

Luojiajiao → Majiabang → Songze → Liangzhu

Objects in this exhibition from the lower Yangzi region include jades associated with the Liangzhu culture excavated from the Fanshan and Yaoshan sites (cats. 29–36). These two sites were ritual and burial locations, and they belong to a group of Liangzhu sites that cover 33.4 square kilometers and comprise approximately fifty cemeteries and ritual areas, most of which remain unexcavated. (At the moment, the preservation of these sites is a more pressing priority than their excavation.)

The Luojiajiao and the Majiabang cultures developed in succession; their dates coincide roughly with those of the Banpo culture and the early phase of the Xiyin culture (that is, 5000–4000 BCE). The early phase of the Songze culture coincides with the middle phase of the Xiyin culture, and its late phase coincides with Phase IV of the Banpo culture. The early phase of the Liangzhu culture coincides with Phase IV of the Banpo culture (i.e., the Huating phase of the Dawenkou culture), and its late phase coincides with the Xixiahou phase of the Dawenkou culture, or may date somewhat later. Many other cultures occupied the lower Yangzi region, including the Hemudu culture, which was contemporaneous with the Luojiajiao culture. The Beiyinyangyin and the Xuejiagang cultures (as well as a culture represented by the Lingjiatan site at Hanshan in Anhui province), were contemporaneous with the Songze culture. What became of the cultures when their territories were occupied by the Liangzhu culture remains uncertain. The Liangzhu in any event were a highly influential culture centered around the area of Tai Lake and Hangzhou Bay and extending to the islands of Zhoushan on the eastern front, the northern part of Fujian province to the south, Poyang Lake to the west, and most of the Huai River region to the north. At its northern frontier, the Liangzhu culture had contacts with the Dawenkou culture, but its cultural influence extended even further: we have evidence that it reached as far as the northern part of Guangdong province and the Fen River area of Shanxi province.

Historic China developed principally from these five Neolithic cultural sequences, which laid the ground for the formation of civilization.

THE FORMATION OF CIVILIZATION

Su Bingqi divided China's Late Prehistory (that is, from c. 6000 BCE until the Early Bronze Age) into three periods: the Neolithic period, the Early Chalcolithic period, and the Late Chalcolithic period.[1] A copper object dating prior to Phase IV of Banpo culture has been found (notably at the Jiangzhai site), but it is only during Phase IV of the Banpo culture that copper objects, as well as the remains of copper casting, begin to appear in significant quantity. Therefore, it is appropriate to date the beginning of the Chalcolithic period to Phase IV of Banpo culture, and to associate the late Chalcolithic period with the Longshan culture.

Though China's Bronze Age is identified with the Xia dynasty, it should be noted that metallurgy did not develop uniformly throughout China. Copper objects have been found mainly in northern China, and we have evidence that copper dominated the metallurgy of cultures that were contemporaneous with the Xia dynasty. No copper object dating prior to the Xia dynasty has been found to date in the lower Yangzi region. Among the Erlitou culture — the most advanced of its contemporary cultures in metalworking — bronzes constitute 83 percent of metal objects. Bronzes similarly dominate metal objects unearthed from a burial site of the Siba culture at Huoshaoguo (71.8 percent); by contrast, copper dominates the metal objects excavated from another burial site of the Siba culture—at Donghuishan, Minghe. Cultural contacts between China and the West began during the Xia period, but copper objects were made and used in China more than 1000 years prior; the transition to the Bronze Age in China was in fact fully realized in the second millennium BCE. These data indicate that copper and bronze metallurgy in China were indigenous inventions, and there is evidence as well that many ancient cultures in China developed copper metallurgy and made the transition from copper to bronze independent of one another.

We have evidence that villages were a form of social organization as early as the Laoguantai culture (c. 6000 BCE). Data regarding social organization prior to the Laoguantai period are sparse, and we know little about the structure of small settlements or about how villages came into being. We know that around 6000 BCE, clans were the predominant form of social organization; kinship and property were transmitted matrilineally. A thousand years later (c. 5000 BCE), we find society organized in three levels: household, clan, and tribe; households were matrilineal and functioned relatively independently of the clan. By the time of the Xiyin culture (c. 4000 BCE), the matrilineal system of household organization and transmission of property had been replaced by a patrilineal system, a system that characterizes Phase IV of the Banpo culture (c. 3200 BCE) and finds its full expression around 2200 BCE with the appearance of polygamous burials.

The identification of the origins of "Chinese civilization" have been a hotly debated matter since the mid-1980s. Early China was characterized by two distinct patterns of social and economic organization, one based on agriculture and the other on herding. Herding was concentrated in the region currently defined by the Great Wall; to the west, herding developed out of agriculture, while to the east it developed out of a hunting and gathering economy. The herding civilization did not develop until the Xia period (and is thus outside the scope of this article). What follows concentrates on "agricultural civilization."

Elements of civilization necessarily predate the formation of civilization itself. Scholars generally agree on two points: that Chinese civilization can be traced back to several points of origin that followed parallel lines of development, with contacts and mutual influences; and that different cultures developed at different rates. Increasingly scholars have identified the study of the origins and formation of civilization with *guozhi dashi zai si yu rong* ("ritual and war are the most important business of the state"), rather than simply characterizing early civilization as a society founded on slavery. Though situating the formation of civilization in time remains an issue, most scholars have abandoned the identification of the Xia period as the beginning of Chinese civilization. Some place the origins of civilization in the Longshan culture period (c. 2500 – 2000 BCE); others date it nearly a thousand years earlier — to Phase IV of the Banpo culture (c. 3200 BCE). A strong argument can be made for the latter, for it represents a period during which there occurred several qualitative changes in how society was organized. These include the following:

- By the Chalcolithic period, professional craftsmen had emerged — individuals who created objects of pottery, stone, jade, and copper.
- The household, characterized by a division of labor, by now comprised the basic unit of society. Most seem to have been relatively poor, but a few amassed wealth and power and in so doing controlled organizations that had previously existed within the clan.
- Settlements and cemeteries began to assume distinctive characteristics. Settlements comprised "ordinary" and "central" settlements, the latter characterized by a large population and a large scale; some were physically organized as walled towns (often surrounded by a moat), and the power and wealth of the society were concentrated within the walls. These central settlements became the political and religious centers of specific cultures. Cemeteries as well begin to reflect social divisions, marked by the scale and the structure of the burial, as well as the quality and the quantity of burial goods. Graves of wealthy households were situated either at the center of the clan's cemetery or at some distance from the graves of their less affluent contemporaries.
- Theocracy and monarchy developed out of religion and warfare to form governing institutions. They might exist simultaneously, with equal status, or they might be embodied in an elite that held both military and theocratic power.

Though some identify Phase IV of the Banpo culture with the origins of civilization, it may be more plausibly be viewed as civilization proper — the true *guguo* (ancient state) or *fangguo* (states). The Longshan culture coincides — albeit roughly — with the legendary Yao-Shun period, during which (we are told) the powerful kings of the *fangguo* exercised the power of *Xuan xian yu neng* ("selecting people with virtue and ability"). By the Xia period — at least among the Xia culture — the power of the *fangguo* had been destroyed and a unified kingdom appeared, which by the Western Zhou period, had developed into a feudal and hereditary system.

1   Su 1994b.

The Bronze Age of China

ZOU HENG | The Bronze Age comprises three periods of Chinese history: the Xia, Shang, and Zhou dynasties. Archaeological investigation of the Bronze Age (sometimes referred to as "the Three Dynasties") began in the 1920s, but prior to 1949 no archaeological remains relating to the period associated with the Xia culture had been found. Scholars knew of its existence from references in historical texts; some identified the Xia culture with the Yangshao culture, while others identified it with the Longshan culture. The lack of physical evidence, however, rendered these identifications essentially speculative.

Archaeological investigation of the Shang dynasty began with the excavation of the site at Yinxu in Anyang, Henan province. In the course of fifteen seasons of controlled excavations, lasting from 1928 to 1937, palace foundations and imperial mausoleums from the late Shang period were discovered, along with thousands of inscribed oracle bones and a large number of bronze, jade, and ceramic objects. These discoveries indicated that the capital during the late Shang period was at the site of the present-day village of Xiaotun, Anyang, Henan province. As for Zhou dynasty archaeology, a number of burials had been discovered in Jun, Hui, and Jin counties, Henan province, and at Baoji, Shaanxi province, but no dwellings were found.

The archaeology of the Three Dynasties began in earnest only after 1949, but the last fifty years have yielded an extraordinary abundance of Xia, Shang, and Zhou sites throughout the country — and the discoveries continue. These finds have progressively resolved many scholarly issues. The last half-century of archaeological investigation in China has been an extraordinary time, and, particularly in respect to the work on China's Bronze Age, we may rightly call this period the Golden Age of Chinese archaeology.

ARCHAEOLOGY OF THE XIA DYNASTY

The earliest Chinese historical texts, such as the *Shang shu* (Book of documents) and the *Shi jing* (Classic of poetry), contain several references to the Xia dynasty. Sima Qian (145 – 86 BCE), the Western Han dynasty author, described the history of the Xia dynasty in great detail and recorded the chronology of the Xia imperial family, particularly in his *Shi ji* (Records of the historian). The existence of the Xia dynasty was undeniable — at least with respect to the written record.[1]

Archaeology has provided physical corroboration of the existence of the Xia dynasty, as it did for the Shang dynasty. Prior to the excavations at Yinxu, some scholars even doubted whether the Shang had in fact existed; the Yinxu excavations confirmed the fact that it was a thriving and distinct culture. Many Shang kings were named in the large number of inscribed oracle bones discovered at Yinxu. These records of divinations conducted by the kings and their diviners at the Shang court confirm that that the rulers named in the inscriptions by and large correspond to those named in the chronology of the Shang imperial family recorded in the chapter on the Shang *(Yin ben ji)* of the *Shi ji*. The correspondence between excavated ob-

Cat. 65, detail

jects and the written history reinforces the reliability of each. The reliability of the Shang chronology, moreover, indicates that the Xia imperial chronology in the chapter corresponding to the earlier dynasty *(Xia ben ji)* must also be correct and could not have been fabricated by Sima Qian. Archaeological finds proved the existence of the Shang dynasty; it was logical to assume that evidence for the Xia dynasty could be investigated in the same way.

The archaeology of the Xia culture can be understood by drawing on what we know of the Shang culture. The Shang kingdom was built on the ruins of a defeated Xia kingdom; therefore, Shang culture must have developed from the Xia. The discovery of early Shang sites in Zhengzhou in the 1950s paved the way for the proper investigation of the Xia. Archaeological finds demonstrated that the early Shang culture was closely related to the Erlitou culture found at Yanshi, Henan province. In other words, the Xia developed from a pre-dynastic Shang influence in northern Henan and assimilated elements of the more advanced Erlitou culture. Chinese archaeologists now recognize Phases I to IV of the Erlitou culture as the Xia culture.[2]

The Erlitou culture, or the Xia culture — names that we can now begin to use interchangeably — extended over western Henan and southwestern Shanxi provinces, a region corresponding to the heartland of the Xia kingdom and its domain as related in the ancient texts. The Shang city at Zhengzhou has been identified as the capital Bo; Erlitou cultural remains have been found beneath the Shang city, leading to the logical conclusion that the Erlitou culture predated that of the early Shang. Carbon-14 testing has dated Phases I to IV of the Erlitou culture to between 1600 and 2000 BCE, a period corresponding roughly to that described in the ancient texts.

The Erlitou culture is the earliest Bronze Age culture discovered in China. Although the excavated examples are limited, bronzes objects recovered include ritual vessels such as tripod cauldrons (ding), drinking vessels (jue) fowl-shaped wine containers (yi), and weapons such as daggers (ge), axes (yue), and arrows (zu). These bronzes were cast using relatively simple techniques with simple patterns — testimony to an early stage of bronze metallurgy. Jade ritual objects such as axes (yue), scepters (zhang), and stem-shaped ornaments have also been discovered at these sites. A considerable number of pottery vessels—a fowl-shaped wine container (yi) and a tripod drinking vessel (jue), a footed vessel (dou), a basin (pen), and a container decorated with the sculpted image of a human head (zun) — are similar to, but not identical with, early Shang examples of pottery. The most exciting find at Erlitou was the discovery of the large foundations of palaces, the largest of which extended over 10,000 square meters. The presence of these massive palace-remains suggests the existence of an established sovereign, a fact corroborated by the ancient texts.[3]

ARCHAEOLOGY OF THE SHANG DYNASTY

The Yinxu excavations of 1928–1937 confirmed the importance of the Shang dynasty. The dynasty's capital at Yinxu, relocated by King Pangeng, however, dates to the *late* period; from the standpoint of the archaeological record, what constituted the early phases of Shang culture still remained a mystery. The large number of bronzes from Yinxu, for example, provided evidence of an advanced level of bronze metallurgy, and oracle bones testified to an advanced stage in writing, but these finds also raised questions about origins of Shang material and intellectual culture. Prior to 1949, the beginnings of the late period of Shang culture, though a point of lively discussion among historians, remained a mystery.

In 1952, the site of Erligang at Zhengzhou was discovered. The site's stratigraphy and the types of artifacts recovered indicated unambiguously that the Erligang culture predated the culture at Yinxu and thus the late Shang period. In fact, the Zhengzhou site has yielded abundant Shang remains that confirm this hypothesis: architectural foundations, tomb burials, bronzes, jades, pottery, and inscribed oracle bones. The close relationship of the Zhengzhou structures and artifacts with those discovered at Yinxu — and the fact that they predate the late Shang artifacts — led archaeologists to conclude that the chief characteristics of the Yinxu culture derived from the Erligang phase at Zhengzhou. At last, one of the sources of late Shang culture at Yinxu had been found.[4]

The Shang sites at Zhengzhou cover an area as wide as that at Yinxu — a total of 25 square kilometers.[5] They contain the remains of a city with massive walls describing a circumference of 7,000 meters and covering an area of approximately 3,000,000 square meters; they represent the largest Shang urban site ever excavated. It is noteworthy that the palace foundations in the northeast of the city , which extend over more than 60,000 square meters, are significantly larger than the palace foundations at Yinxu. A city of such size would undoubtedly have been a royal capital. But to which king did it belong? After thirty years of discussion, archaeologists have finally agreed that the city was the capital Bo, established under the reign of King Tang, the founder of the Shang dynasty. The identification of the dynasty's early capital provided a basis for investigating questions posed by the history of the Xia dynasty.

Another important site in the investigation of early Shang cultures was the city of Yanshi.[6] Located near the Erlitou site, to the south of the Mang Mountain along the northern bank of the Luo River in Yanshi county, Henan province, Yanshi had developed out of an older, smaller city. The smaller city was roughly contemporaneous with the Shang city at Zhengzhou; covering an area of 810,000 square meters, it was a little more than a quarter the size of Zhengzhou. The larger city was slightly later than Zhengzhou, and it extended over an area of 1,900,000 square meters — approximately two-thirds that of Zhengzhou. Both the large and the small city were built during the reign of King Tang. Its structure indicates that the Shang city at Yanshi was important enough to have been commissioned by imperial authority, but that fact raises another question: by whose authority? Scholars are presently divided on the issue: one school of thought identifies Yanshi as the early Shang dynasty capital of Bo; another identifies it as an early Shang auxiliary capital — the Tong Palace to which the King Taijia was exiled. The early Shang capital of Bo, however, could not have been situated both at Zhengzhou and at Yanshi. Moreover, we know from written records that Yanshi was not referred to as Bo prior to the Tang dynasty (618–907 CE) and that it was much smaller than the Shang city at Zhengzhou. These facts suggest that Yanshi was the dynasty's auxiliary capital, and that Zhengzhou should be identified as the early Shang capital at Bo.

Three other early Shang cities warrant mention here. Two of them are located at the present-day city of Panlongcheng, Huangpi county, Hubei province;[7] walled remains in Yuanqu county, Shanxi province, constitute the third city.[8] All three are fairly small. Yuanqu is approximately 120,000 square meters, and the site at Panlongcheng is even smaller — only slightly more 70,000 square meters. Cities of such small scale could not have been imperial capitals, but they might have served as regional capitals of local states (fangguo).

In the years since 1949, many late Shang sites have been discovered in Henan, Hebei, Shandong, and Shanxi provinces; the Yinxu excavations constitute the most ambitious of these excavations. The site has yielded finds of great importance, such as the Great Tomb at Wuguan village, oracle bones found to the south of Xiaotun, the large-scale palace foundations along the riverbank to the east of Xiaotun, and the tomb of Fu Hao. The latter, a tomb of modest size, had not been looted, and the artifacts recovered from this one site exceed the total number of bronzes and jades found at Yinxu during the entire period of excavation: 468 bronzes (including 210 ritual vessels) and 755 jades (including 175 ritual objects) — many of them exquisite pieces.[9] The thousands of oracle bones found to the south of Xiaotun village have provided a detailed stratigraphy, which has both clarified periodization and confirmed facts described in the inscriptions themselves: the oracle bones, for example, have enabled us to date the diviner Dui (Duizu buci) securely to the era of King Wuding (the third king after Pangeng) and to determine that the oracle inscriptions of the diviner Li (Lizu buci) do not belong to this era.

ARCHAEOLOGY OF THE ZHOU DYNASTY

During the early years of the Zhou dynasty, in an effort to consolidate the regime, the rulers enfeoffed much of their territory to imperial family members and meritorious officials; in doing so, the Zhou held sway over every district of the country. The numerous vassal states in the Western Zhou realm soon established their own governing systems, as well as individual economies and cultures, and progressively became independent kingdoms. From disparate locations such as Feng and Hao (near present-day Xi'an) and the Zhouyuan, the government of the Zhou kings was centralized into one province — present-day Shaanxi — and an auxiliary capital was established at Luoyi (present-day Luoyang, in Henan province) to govern the eastern region. Excavations of Western Zhou sites at Feng-Hao and Luoyang have been underway since 1949, but looting and damage rendered the material retrieved from the excavations less than ideal.

The Zhouyuan, extending over the counties of Qishan and Fufeng in Shaanxi province, was the homeland of the Zhou people. Following the Zhou settlement of the Feng region, the area became a fiefdom of the Duke of Zhao, and it functioned as a provincial capital of the dynasty. The site has yielded several important finds. Of particular interest to scholars was the discovery of the well-preserved foundations of a palace in Fengchu, Qishan county; the remains of the structure — methodically laid out, with clearly demarcated front halls and rear bedrooms — provide a model for the structure of Western Zhou palaces.[10] A pit in the foundation yielded approximately 300 inscribed oracle bones dating from the late Shang period to the era of the early Zhou kings Cheng and Kang. The finds provide new materials for the study of the relationship between the Shang and the Zhou. Hoards of bronzes — in particular, heavy vessels associated with the Western Zhou — have periodically been uncovered in the Zhouyuan area. The hoard from Zhuangbai of Fufeng county is one of the more notable discoveries of recent years, yielding bronzes with lengthy inscriptions that have provided valuable documentation for the study of Western Zhou history.

Archaeological excavations have also provided insights into many of the individual feudal states; the large number of tombs in Sanmenxia city have told us much about the Guo state; burial finds in Pingdingshan city have shed light on the Ying state. Other finds include the ancient fiefdom of the Jin state in Yicheng and Quwo counties in Shanxi; the ancient fiefdom of the Yan state in Liulihe, Beijing; the remains of a city in the Lu state in Qufu (Confucius' home state) in Shandong; and burial sites of the Qi state in Linzi, Shandong. The Jin and Qi discoveries warrant particular attention.

The Eastern Han historians Ban Gu (32 – 92 CE) and Zheng Xuan (127 – 200 CE) both situated the ancient fiefdom of the Jin state in Jinyang (present-day Taiyuan, Shanxi province), and this identification was accepted by scholars for nearly two thousand years. During the late Ming and early Qing periods, however, the historian Gu Yanwu (1613 – 1682) disputed the so-called Taiyuan theory, believing that the Jin state was situated further south in Shanxi. His theory was not widely accepted, but in the late 1970s archaeologists conducting surveys in the Linfen area discovered the site of Tianma-Qucun on the border between Yicheng and Quwo counties. There, in the course of an excavation that lasted more than ten years, they found not only a large area of residential remains but also a vast number of Jin state tombs. Finally, in 1992, seventeen tombs of the marquises of Jin and their consorts were found, conclusively resolving the nearly two-thousand-year-old controversy regarding Jin enfoeffment.[11] This site has yielded an astonishing group of bronzes and jades; the fact that jades were found in their original positions has provided invaluable information about their function.

Archaeological investigation has similarly resolved the longstanding question of the location of the Northern Yan state. After conquering the Shang, we know that King Wu of Zhou enfoeffed the region of Northern Yan to the duke of Zhao. Some scholars had identified present-day Laishui (Ji county) and Beijing as the seat of the Northern Yan state during the Zhou period, but in the absence of physical remains, the identification was unverifiable. During the 1950s, archaeologists undertook a survey of Beijing city but were unable to find any trace of the Yan fiefdom. In the 1960s, they turned their attention to the rural area south of Beijing. At Liulidian and Dongjialin in Liulihe they found a large Western Zhou site, and excavations over the years yielded city walls dating to the early period, a wide swath of dwellings, and a number of burials, as well as a large quantity of Western Zhou bronzes, jades, laquerware, and pottery. The discovery of several bronze ritual vessels bearing inscriptions that name the marquises of Yan confirmed that this site was the ancient fiefdom of Yan. Once again, an enigma that had endured for centuries had finally been resolved.[12]

Archaeological investigation of the Eastern Zhou has encompassed an even wider area, covering nearly every province in the country. Excavations at Houma in Shanxi province, an urban site of approximately 40 square kilometers, began in the 1950s and continue to the present day. The most important find thus far is a bronzecasting foundry, a site that has yielded more than 100,000 pieces of ceramic models, molds, and earthen cores.[13] Molds were used to create a variety of objects — bells, ritual vessels, chariot fittings, weapons, tools and other implements of daily life, as well as coins shaped like cowries or spades. Some molds were used to form complex decorative patterns on bronzes — herringbone *(renziwen)*, rope, and whirlpool patterns, cloud and thunder motifs, split-bodied or coiled serpents, animal masks, dragons, tigers, oxen, fish, and birds. The casting apparatus, as well as the molds for tuyeres and remains of kilns, has provided insight into nearly every aspect of bronze metallurgy.

The recovery of approximately five thousand fragments of jade and stone from some four hundred sacrificial pits in a field southeast of the city represents another major find from the excavations at Houma. The majority of these fragments bear inscriptions in red or black ink — the briefest inscription contains ten characters, the longest more than two hundred. These documents, collectively termed the Houma Covenant Texts *(Houma mengshu)*, record covenants sworn between lords and their vassals and bear witness to the political struggles of the Jin state during the late Spring and Autumn period (770 – 475 BCE); they have provided us with a wealth of new historical information.[14] The covenant texts clearly describe the Houma region as "the location of the Jin state." At Qiaocun, another Houma site, a pottery inscription *(taowen)* bearing the phrase "Jiang Ting," identifies the site of Houma as the capital of the Jin, which in 585 BCE was relocated from the ancient city of Jiang by Duke Jing of Jin to Xintian (also known as Xinjiang).

Some of the most important burial remains have been found in the territories of the southern feudal states. Large-scale tombs of the Chu state were found in Xiasi (Xichuan county, Henan province); in Hubei province, the sites of Baoshan (Jingmen county), as well as Tianxingguan and Wangshan (Jingzhou city) yielded important tombs. The tomb of Marquis Yi of Zeng in Sui county, Hubei province, was the best preserved of these and yielded a wealth of burial goods: bronze vessels, jades, lacquered wood objects, bamboo artifacts, leather armor, and musical instruments.[15] One hundred and twenty five musical instruments were found, comprising eight types: bells *(zhong)*, chimes *(qing)*, drums *(gu)*, two types of zithers *(qin* and *se)*, reed pipes *(sheng)*, vertical flutes *(xiao)*, and bowed string instruments *(hu)*. A complete chime *(bianzhong)* comprising sixty-five bells was unearthed, together with its lacquered wood stand. The bells that compose this extraordinary set retain an excellent sound quality and are remarkably resonant.

The Xia, Shang, and Zhou dynasties held sway only within their respective territories. Beyond their borders, the "distant regions" were populated by several important cultures, in particular, the Lower Xiajiadian and the Yueshi cultures — contemporaries of the Xia — in Liaoning province and the Inner Mongolia Autonomous District.[16]

Sites of the Lower Xiajiadian culture have yielded a characteristic polychrome painted pottery, as well as several bronze objects. Contacts between the Lower Xiajiadian and the Erlitou culture are evidenced by the similarity of pottery fowl-shaped containers (yi) and tripod beakers (jue). By contrast, the Yueshi culture of Shandong and eastern Henan provinces,[17] though contemporaries of the Erlitou, produced a completely different range of artifacts — a great deal of red and brown pottery and numerous steamers (yan), but little corded ware, no tripod vessels (li), and very few bronzes.

During the Shang period, several important cultures coexisted in remote regions outside of the dynasty's borders. In the north was the Zhukaigou culture, in the west, the predynastic Zhou and Xindian cultures, and in the south the Hushou, Ba, Wucheng, and Shu cultures. The latter two are particularly significant.

The Wucheng culture in northern Jiangxi province is represented by the Great Tomb at Xin'gan, located near Chengjiacun (Dayangzhou, in Xin'gan county) approximately twenty kilometers east of Wucheng, the center of the culture.[18] The tomb chamber measures forty meters square and contained 475 bronze objects (including 50 ritual vessels and musical instruments), 100 farming and handicraft tools, 200 weapons, as well as approximately 700 jades and 100 pottery vessels. Some of these objects clearly show the influence of Shang culture from the Central Plain; others are clearly indigenous in style. In the past, it was believed that the cultures to the south were a backwater, but the objects from the Great Tomb at Xin'gan clearly militate against this view and offer proof that as early as the Shang period the cultures of the south had a material culture as advanced as those of the Central Plain.

The Shu culture was based in the Chengdu plain of Sichuan province. Sacrificial pits found at Sanxingdui, Guanghan county, are of particular interest and have yielded a wide range of exquisite objects.[19] The pits were found in the center of a site measuring approximately 12 square kilometers, enclosed by city walls with a circumference of between 1,800 and 2,000 meters. Shang influence is evident in many of the Sanxingdui objects — bronze lei and zun vessels, jade and stone daggers (ge), bi disks, and jade cong. But the artifacts also clearly display elements of an indigenous culture — in particular most of the pottery, the remarkable standing bronze figures and sculptures, the bronze animal masks, and the stone spears (mao), none of which have been found in Shang remains. Some objects seem to derive from the Shang culture but display a clearly local style—a bronze rounded vessel (lei), daggers with serrated or curved blades, and a jade scepter. The fact that indigenous features predominate in these objects has led archeologists to designate their creators as a distinct culture — Shu, the ancient name for Sichuan.

Cultures of the distant regions contemporaneous with the Zhou dynasty seem to represent continuations of the preceding Shang period cultures. The Upper Xiajiadian culture was situated in the north; in the south we find a culture designated the Earthen Tomb culture, as well as the continuation of the Ba and Shu cultures. Originating in western China, the Zhou first conquered the region, then vanquished the last Shang king. Under the command of their king, the Qin kingdom — the successor to the Zhou empire in the western part of China — unified the various warring states during the final years of the Zhou and established the First Empire.

1   Some scholars over the last century questioned whether the Xia dynasty ever in fact existed, but were unable to offer evidence to disprove the historical accounts. The historian Gu Jiegang (b. 1893) did not deny the existence of the Xia dynasty, but questioned the existence of the Great Yu, the reputed first ruler of the Xia. The modern scholar Chen Mengjia, a specialist in ancient Chinese writing, proposed that the Xia and Shang might even have been contemporaneous, but could not find any evidence to support that hypothesis.

2   See Zou 1980b.
3   Zhongguo Erlitou 1974.
4   Zou 1980a.
5   Henan 1977.
6   Zhongguo 1984.
7   Hubei 1976.
8   Zhongguo lishi 1996.
9   Zhongguo 1980a.
10 Shaanxi 1979a
11 Zou 1998.
12 Beijing 1995.
13 Shanxi 1993.
14 Shanxi 1976.
15 Hubei 1989.
16 Zhongguo 1996.
17 Shandong 1990.
18 Jiangxi 1997.
19 Sichuan 1987b.

Issues Concerning the Formation, Development, and Demise of Chu Culture

YU WEICHAO | Between 1,100 and 3,000 years ago, a culture that we now recognize as Chu made significant contributions to the cultural evolution of China as a whole and of southern China in particular. Chu culture is known to have flourished in the middle Yangzi basin as early as the second millenium BCE — during the Shang period—and from the fifth to the third century BCE, the state of Chu occupied almost the entire southern half of the Chinese landmass. By the fourth century BCE — the late Warring States period — Chu had shifted its center to the Huai River valley, where, by the second century BCE under the Han dynasty, it survived mainly in the region of the present-day city of Changsha, Hunan province.

The importance of Chu culture was recognized only relatively recently. In the 1920s the Swedish engineer Orvar Karlbeck described some Chu mirrors of the Warring States period recovered from the Huai River valley.[1] During the 1950s and after, many Chu tombs and the site of the Chu city of Ji'nancheng of the Eastern Zhou dynasty were excavated at Jiangling, Hubei province; tombs were also found at another important site — Changsha, Hunan province. Since 1980, when the second annual meeting of the Chinese Archaeological Society focused specifically on issues of Chu culture, Chu studies have become one of the most active areas in Chinese history and archaeology, with scholars both in China and abroad conducting major investigations. One of the most important of these projects seeks to establish a chronology of the Chu tombs from the Eastern Zhou period; another is investigating the origins of Chu culture.[2] While the latter remains a work in progress, much knowledge has been accumulated from the examination of recovered Chu material that spans the period of the culture's formation to its demise; this in turn has led to a better understanding of Chu history. This exhibition includes numerous Chu culture from the Eastern Zhou states in the Chu cultural sphere. What follows is a general survey of the present state of Chu studies.

DEFINING CHU CULTURE

The term "culture" has many different interpretations; here, it is used to distinguish "Chu culture" in its archaeological context — that is, the physical remains that exhibit distinctive characteristics of the life and behavior of the ancient Chu people. Archaelogy treats a culture as bounded in time and space, often with a dominant or subordinate relationship to several other communities, which, for the most part, also exhibit distinctive cultural characteristics. As long as Chu characteristics dominate a group of remains, it can be considered as part of Chu culture or relevant to it, regardless of the date, sphere, or group relationship, for such cultural characteristics could not have existed beyond the sphere of Chu's influence, nor after the demise of the culture and its constituents.[3]

However, the character and sphere of Chu culture underwent continuous change. Like many cultures, Chu was composed of various elements during its formative phase, including influences deriving from contacts with other cultures. Its borders as well were fluid, first expanding and then contracting. Because of the interactions and influences between the Chu culture and other cultures, its characteristics altered from one phase of its history to another. One constant of Chu culture, in fact, was continuous change in every phase and every geographical district.[4]

The geography of the Chu culture exemplifies its fluidity. The large distribution of archaeological remains that bear Chu traits does not completely match the area traditionally associated with Chu territory. In the beginning, the community of Chu inhabitants was presumably one of many communities that had features in common with others over a wide area. But after its indigenous growth and development, the Chu began to influence other cultures — and to a greater extent than they influenced the Chu. Therefore, the individual traditions that at one point or another likely characterized several coexisting communities or kingdoms (such as the states of Cai, Zeng, or Sui) diminished in strength to become secondary characteristics because of the dominant influence of Chu. As a result, they were incorporated into the greater cultural sphere of Chu. From this analysis, the archaeological Chu culture can be understood to encompass both a narrow and a broad definition. The narrow definition is limited to remains found only within the Chu domain, that is, the Chu culture generally known today. The broad definition encompasses the remains that exhibit significant Chu characteristics beyond political or temporal boundaries.

Prior to World War II, the properties of an archaeological culture were defined as a group of coexisting artifacts (as well as residential sites and tomb burials) exhibiting common characteristics. During the 1960s, international scholarship began to incorporate concepts of anthropology into archaeology, drawing in the material (or technological), the social, and the spiritual aspects of the culture. In China, beginning in the late 1950s, the study of social structure was added to this list. The end of the 1980s brought the notion of "cultural concept" into the study of Chu culture.[5] In that context the study of "culture " in archaeology has grown close to methods used by historians and anthropologists. In 1995, Hubei Education Publishing issued a landmark, eighteen-volume work on Chu culture, *Chuxue wenku* (The Chu study series), a publication that treats three aspects of Chu culture — material, social, and philosophical. Since many scholars have acknowledged the broad scope of Chu culture, this publication should encourage and make available more comprehensive studies.

TWO MAIN COMPONENTS IN THE FORMATION OF CHU CULTURE

Ancient texts contain abundant references to the origin and enfeoffment of Chu ancestors, as well as to the geographical location of the earliest Chu domain. Early historical texts of the Warring States period (475 – 221 BCE), identify the "first ancestor" of the Chu as a member of the Zhurong clan residing in the south.[6] Two sections of the *Classic of Poetry* contain a narrative by a Shang descendant describing a community of Chu people during the reign of King Wu Ding of the Shang.[7] The *Shi ji* (Records of the historian) by Sima Qian, reports that at the end of the Shang period the first leader of the Chu people Yuxiong was enfoeffed as "a lord of Chu" *(Chuzi)* by King Wen of the Zhou state.[8] The phrase "the Lord of Chu came to report" *(Chuzi laigao)* is found in Zhou period oracle-bone inscriptions from the Zhouyuan, Shaanxi province.[9] The texts also make reference to geographical origins. We learn that Yuxiong's son Xiongli was enfoeffed at a "place in the Sui mountains."[10] The Sui mountains may be the Jing mountains in Hubei province, from which the Sui (or Ju) River flows.[11] During the Shang and Zhou periods, the state of Chu was also referred to as "Jing-Chu," which appears to be a reference to the mountains in the same region. In the era of King Cheng of the Zhou, Xiongli's grandson Xiongyi settled in a place called Danyang.[12] A reference from the Spring and Autumn period (770 – 476 BCE) attributed to a governing official named Zige in the Chu court of King Ling confirms this: "In olden times our late King Xiongyi reigned in the Jing mountains."[13] On the basis of that reference, we can place Xiongyi's "Danyang" in the Jing mountains, not far from the settlement of his grandfather, Xiongli. What these texts tell us is that the Chu people established a state between the late Shang and early Zhou periods, when they were active in the valleys of the Ju and Zhang rivers.

The precise location of Danyang, however, remains the subject of debate; it warrants mention here because the origins of the Chu people are naturally a function of the location of their earliest settlement. Several theories, relying on references in early literary sources, propose more precise identifications for the site: (1) Zhijiang county in western Hubei province in the Yangzi valley;[14] (2) Zigui county, also in Hubei province;[15] (3) Danyangjun, in in present-day Tangtu, Anhui province;[16] and (4) north of the Dan River at the intersection of the Dan and the Xi Rivers.[17] The latter identification has been proposed by three scholars — Qian Mu, Gu Jiegang, and Tong Shuye.

The origins of the Chu people are similarly the subject of controversy. Hu Houxuan believes that they emigrated from the east, while Wang Yuzhe places their point of origin in the central area of Henan province; their move eastward to Danyang, he argues, occurred at a later date.[18] The problem with these theories is that late Shang and early Zhou cultural remains from these various areas differ greatly in character. Moreover, a site equivalent in scale and complexity to that founded by Chuzi, the earliest Chu lord, has yet to be found. Thus, in spite of the numerous historical references and the relative abundance of archaeological discoveries, the origins of the early phase of the Chu state remain uncertain.

Be that as it may, the characteristics of an archaeological culture — particularly its prototypical characteristics — may accumulate and endure over a long period. On the basis of this assumption, we may attempt to trace the early stages of Chu culture in reverse — by examining the cultural characteristics of remains from the later periods.

Since the 1980s, studies of the origins of Chu culture have been based on inferences from the cultural characteristics of Chu tombs from the later Warring States period. With respect to the broader definition of the Chu culture, sites in Hubei province can be traced to the middle and late periods of the Western Zhou (c. eleventh century – 771 BCE). Tomb burials and sites in Hubei province, such as Miaoping, Zigui,[19] the Zhenwu mountains in Xiangfan,[20] the Boyu mountains in Songzi,[21] the Mopan mountains in Dangyang,[22] and the Chu Phase I tombs in Zhaojiahu, Dangyang,[23] have yielded a great abundance of pottery vessels of the *li, yu, dou,* and *guan* types that were produced as sets, an influence that clearly reflects the Zhou culture. Burial remains roughly contemporaneous with the Erligang and Yinxu phases of the Shang dynasty have yet to be found.[24]

The forms of Chu *li, yu, dou,* and *guan* pottery vessels differ markedly from typical Zhou examples. The bottom of Chu tripod vessel *(li)* is formed as one piece; the hollow space of the legs extends from the core of the cones to the foot of each leg. Shang *li* vessels exhibit a clear division among the three legs, each of which forms a section that is integrated with the body. In Zhou-style tripods, although each leg is integrated with the body, the bottom portions of the legs are additions. The crotch of the legs is made with a curved shape, which is termed the *bie* crotch *(biedang)*. In 1980, at the second annual meeting of the Chinese Archaeological Society, Su Bingqi, after pointing out this characteristic in *li* pottery, named it "Chu-type *li*" (*ding*-type or *jia*-type li).[25] Although *li* pottery tripods were common in many cultures during the Shang and Zhou periods, the Chu-type *li* is exclusively found in Chu and Chu-influenced areas.

This type of *li* pottery was first discovered in remains dating from the Lower Erligang phase (and probably even earlier) of Panlongcheng, Huangpi. Two forms of the Chu-type *li,* large- and small-mouthed, have been found in late Western Zhou Chu tombs at Zhaojiahu, Dangyang. Because of the lack of earlier remains, we do not know when they were first intro-duced. Among the remaining artifacts of the Yinxu phase from Zhouliangyuqiao, Shashi, the *li* vessel is identified as Shang type, while the *ding* vessel that derived from the indigenous culture has two forms — large- and small-mouthed. Presumably, large- and small-mouthed *li* pottery originated in the middle Yangzi River region.

In Hubei, the presence of the Chu-type *li* dating to the Lower Erligang phase and the large numbers of *li, yu, dou,* and *guan* vessels in the Chu culture dating to the late Western Zhou pe-riod suggest that the Chu culture that developed during the late Shang and early Zhou was a combination of an indigenous culture in the middle Yangzi region with Zhou cultural elements. Burial practices and burial objects in Chu tombs dating after the Spring and Autumn period reflect regulations described in the *Zhou li* (The rites of Zhou). Thus, the Zhou culture's impact on the Chu was found not only in the function of the Zhou-type vessels, but also in the Chu's beliefs and social structure. The chapter on Chu genealogy in the *Shi ji* reports that "Yuxiong served the King Wen"; the Yi wen zhi chapter of the *Han shu,* tells us that "[Yuxiong] was the adviser to the Zhou"; and the Jin yu chapter of the *Guo yu* states that "In olden days when King Cheng of Zhou allied all the fiefs in Qiyang because the Chu were barbarians *(man)* in the Jing area….he did not treat the Chu as allies." During the early stages of the Chu establishment of a state, although they were regarded as "barbarian" by the Zhou, one generation after another traveled to the capital in the Zhouyuan. It is natural that the Chu inhabitants at this stage absorbed Zhou culture and progressed rapidly.

THE GROWTH OF THE CHU CULTURAL CHARACTER DURING THE EASTERN ZHOU PERIOD

During the early Western Zhou period, after the period of enfoeffment, the cultural characteristics of the feudal states testify to the strong influence of the dominant Zhou culture. But after King Ping moved the capital east to Luoyang, the influence of the Zhou began to wane; their hold over the individual states diminished, and the states siezed the opportunity to develop their own cultural characteristics. By the sixth century BCE — the middle Spring and Autumn period — the states of Qin, Jin, Yan, Qi, Wu, and Chu had become distinctive, individual cultures. Among them, Chu now dominated southern China and continued to do so until the late third century BCE, while the Zhou state continued to decline (it was eventually drawn into the cultural sphere of the Jin state).

The transformation of Chu culture is evident in the evolution of its pottery vessel types. The dominance of the Zhou to the north is manifested in *li, yu, dou,* and *guan* vessels that appear often among Chu remains dating to the middle and later phases of the Western Zhou period; the style and manufacture of the *li* vessels display exceptionally prominent Chu features, as do a few slender, oval-bellied jars, but indigenous Chu design is otherwise little evident. As for bronzes, the earliest Chu ritual vessels — the so-called Chu Ji Gou *pan,* Chu Yin *pan,* and Chu Yin *yi,* which date to the late Western and early Eastern Zhou periods[26] — differ little from Zhou examples. *Ding* and *gui* vessels dating to the early Spring and Autumn period from Tomb 2 in Zhaojiabang, Dangyang,[27] have no decoration on the body, few identifiable stylistic features, and lack a strongly "individual" character. By the middle Spring and Autumn period, however, Chu elements feature figure prominently in the artifacts from the Yuan Zifeng tomb in Xichuan Xiasi, Henan province,[28] and continue up to the late Warring States period tomb of Xionghan, King You of Chu, in (Lisangudui) Zhujiaji, Shou county, Anhui province,[29] as well as in thousands of excavated tombs belonging to all ranks of Chu people.

During this period, all ranks of burials of the feudal states of the Yellow River valley and the Yangzi region yield bronze and ceramic ritual vessels corresponding in type and number to the prescriptions contained in the *Zhou li.* The *Zhou li* specifies that the *ding* vessel was used as container for meat; *gui* and lidded *dou* vessels were intended for grains (including millet), *dun* and *sheng* for water; *hu, fou,* and *fang* for wine; and *pan* and *yi* for pouring water. Generally, one type of each vessel served one function, although at times two vessels might serve the same function. Vessel types changed with the passage of time; the *dun* vessel, for example, does not appear until the late Spring and Autumn period, the *fang* does not appear until the Warring States period, and the *sheng* replaced the *dun* at the end of Warring States period. While these

types of vessels are common to every feudal state, there are regional differences. States in the Central Plains generally served grains in *gui* and *dou;* water and wine were associated with *hu* vessels. By contrast, the Chu served grain in *gui, fu,* and *dun* (the latter appear more often in smaller tombs), water and wine were served in *yu-fou* and *zun-fou* vessels. Small-mouthed *ding* vessels (whose inscriptions identify them as *Tang ding* and *yugong*), used for cooking meat stews and heating water, are associated exclusively with Chu culture.

The most important ritual vessel for representing the social status of a tomb occupant was the *sheng ding,* a type of container for cooked meat and fish.[30] After the middle Spring and Autumn period, tombs of high-ranking aristocrats (such as marquises and ministers) in the Chu cultural region were provided with *ding* vessels in sets of seven or nine. *Sheng ding* with narrow waists and flat bottoms were found in the Chu tombs of Wang Ziwu, the chief minister Yuan Zifeng (the seven *ding* found in the Yuan Zifeng Tomb 2 in Xiasi once belonged to Wang Ziwu), King You of Chu, Marquis Zhao of Cao, and Marquis Yi of Zeng; examples of lidded *sheng ding* with a rounded bottom, commonly seen in the feudal states, have also been recovered from Chu tombs associated with ranks lower than the *dafu.* The narrow-waisted, flat-bottomed *ding,* which seems to have served as an auxiliary *ding* vessel,[31] is exclusively a Chu bronze type.

The Chu absorbed elements of other cultures as well from time to time. Two types of bronzes associated with Yue culture appear after the Chu vanquished the Yue state in 334 BCE: the Yue-type *ding* tripod (which has a broad belly and thin lid decorated with a cloud-and-thunder pattern in parallel lines, and three slender legs placed toward the outside of the vessel), and the Yue-type *mao* spear, with a groove at the center of the blade, a pattern decorating two sides and a pattern resembling the character for "king"on the lower part. After 278 BCE, when General Bai Qi of the Qin dynasty destroyed the Chu capital of Ying, the state moved to Chen (present-day Huaiyang, Henan province), Juyang (Taihe, Anhui province), and Shouchun (Shouxian, Anhui province), where Chu remains from the late Warring States period still retain relatively distinct cultural characteristics. Although most of the ceramic *ding* vessels from Chu tombs in Pingliangtai, Huiyang, Henan province and Yanggongxiang, Changfeng, Anhui province have Chu-type long legs, a few have Qin-type short legs. The Qin style is also evident in square bricks with petal-shaped cloud patterns and ceramic tile-ends with curved cloud pattern from the Chu city of Bojiatai in Shouchun.[32] The influence of Qin in the region of Yangzi Gorges and Hubei appears following the eastward movement of the Qin military. It may be that Qin influence had already spread to the last Chu capital before Qin vanquished the Chu state.

Nevertheless, even with the appearance of other cultural influences, the Chu culture, after the middle phase of the Spring and Autumn period, retained distinctive characteristics from its beginning to its end.

CONCEALED CHARACTERISTICS IN CHU THOUGHT AND BELIEF

On the one hand, the archaeological relics of a culture reflect its technological capabilities — a function, in part, of the material and natural environment; on the other, they reflect belief systems. The Three Dynasties (Xia, Shang, and Zhou), from the beginning of their establishment in the middle Yellow River valley, had a strong impact on the belief systems (including the rules of ritual) of the states that they subjugated. To greater or lesser degrees, their cultural characteristics penetrated the regions of the Yellow, Yangzi, and Pearl River valleys. Chu culture also exerted such an influence.

At the dawn of its civilization, China's belief system — like that of many cultures in the world — was permeated by shamanism. Shamanism endured until the late Spring and Autumn period, when it was gradually displaced by the philosophy, political thought, and ethics of hundreds of philosophical schools. However, shamanism continued in the Chu region, a legacy evidenced in a report in the Chi yue chapter of the *Lu shi chun qiu* that "the Chu's decline came from performing the music of shaman." References of similar import appear in Wang Yi's Xu (annotation) to the *Chu ci* (Songs of Chu) and the Jinge (Nine songs): "In the south, the old Chu city of Ying along the Yuan and Xiang Rivers maintained a belief in ghosts and favored sacrifice." The Di li zhi chapter of the *Han shu* also mentions that "the Chu... believed in shaman and ghosts, and favored lewd sacrifice," an indication that these customs lasted until the Han dynasty. The many imaginary figures and animal creatures made of lacquered wood from the Warring States Chu tombs are an artistic reflection of the importance of the shaman.

Scholars of philosophy have noted that Daoism, as represented by Laozi and Zhuangzi, was the mainstream in the regions of Yangzi and Huai River valleys, while the Confucianist and Mohist schools were popular in the Yellow River valley. In the winter of 1993, an ancient book of bamboo slips from Chu Tomb 1 (dated to the Warring States period) in Guodian, Jingmen, Hubei province, was unearthed; it contained fourteen fragmentary slips containing Confucian texts, three *Lao zi* fragments, and one fragment of *Tai yi sheng shui*; the latter two were popular in later religious Daoism.[33] Judging from these discoveries, while Confucianism and Daoism were practiced concurrently, Daoism received greater emphasis.

Another important document is a Warring States period Chu manuscript on silk, reportedly from Zidanku, Changsha,[34] and now in the Sackler Collection. The historian Li Ling has tentatively identified the manuscript as calendar of the four seasons *(Sishiling)* that served as a guidebook for choosing when a particular activity should take place.[35] During the Han dynasty, such texts were classified as *shushu* (mathematics and skills such as divination and astrology). Other manuscripts from the same site also belong to this category. The content of the *Sishiling* is similar to the You guan and You guan tu sections of the *Guan zi* and reflects parallels between Yin-Yang theory and Daoist thought. These manuscripts from Warring States period Chu tombs document the popularity of Daoism under the Chu. Early shamanism is manifested in Daoist thought and rhetoric, particularly in the transmitted texts of the *Lao zi* and *Zhuang zi*;[36] the *Chu ci* also reveal elements of shamanic belief.[37] Shamanism, Daoism, and *Li sao* all inform the colorful and highly imaginative thought and literature of the Chu tradition.

REMNANTS OF CHU CULTURE IN THE EARLY HAN DYNASTY

The Qin army left a trail of destruction in the course of its conquests — a practice that fundamentally altered the fabric of the six states that it subjugated. Several tombs of the Qin type have been discovered within these states, yielding objects that conform to Qin typology but contain elements of an indigenous style. Only the Changsha region seems to have retained a rich Chu culture.

Historical texts are ambiguous with regard to precise dates for the Qin occupation of the Changsha region. The chapter on the genealogy of the *Qin* and the *Bai Qi* chronicle in the *Shi ji* report that when the Qin general Bai Qi took over the Chu capital of Ying, he also dispersed other Chu regions in Qianzhong, Wujun, and Jiangnan. The Qin occupation of Changsha may have been contemporaneous with this campaign, but Changsha tombs from the period still yield ritual vessels — *sheng (he)*, *hu*, and *fang* — that are distinctly Chu in style (short-legged *ding* of the Qin type are the exception). Such burial objects endured into the early Han dynasty.

Several other discoveries testify to lasting Chu culture in the Changsha region during the early Western Han period:

- The Chu gold coin bearing the the phrase *yingcheng* continued to be minted and traded; many tombs have been found to contain clay *yingcheng* coins, placed there as burial goods, evidence that this form of money was still circulating during the period.
- The family tombs of the prince and princess of Changsha and Marquis Dai and his consort maintained features characteristic of Chu wooden coffin design — a *touxiang* (compartment at the head of the coffin), right and left *bianxiang* (compartments on the two sides), *zuxiang* (compartment at the foot), and *guanxiang* (inner coffin). As at Mawangdui Tomb 1, the corpses were wrapped in multiple layers of fabric (a Chu tradition) rather than jade shrouds (the Han practice).
- The tombs of Marquis Dai and his family at Mawangdui also sustain the practice of placing sets of seven or nine *sheng ding* vessels among the burial objects. This custom was continued in the large-scale, Qin-type tombs of aristocrats after the middle Warring States period, as well as the early Western Han tombs in the regions beyond Changsha.
- References to "Chu costume" and "Chu dance" appear in the inventory slips found in Mawangdui Tomb 3, suggesting the continuation of these Chu customs and styles.

Perhaps the most enduring legacy of Chu culture, however, was the dominance of Daoist thought. Mawangdui Tomb 3 contained a large number of manuscripts written on silk concerned with Daoism (to the notable exclusion of Confucian and Mohist philosophy). Of these, the most important are two versions of *Lao zi* and a copy of the *Huang di si jing,* which were classics of the Huanglao school popular during the early Han dynasty.[38] Other important manuscripts contained in the tomb and reflecting Daoist influence include the *Yi yin,* the *Jiu zhu,* the *Zhou yi Xi ci* ("Book of changes," an ancient text erroneously attributed to Confucius by later scholars that was the topic of commentary and interpretation by Daoist scholars), medicinal prescriptions, and divination books.[39] These manuscripts demonstrate that even during the early Western Han period, the Changsha region continued to maintain the Chu tradition with respect to Daoist thought.

CONCLUSION

The Qin dynasty guaranteed the private ownership of land — a system of ownership that permitted the establishment of large estates that endured to some extent into the era of the Emperor Wu of the Han dynasty. Under the Qin, the empire had been unified and the state strengthened. In time, a Confucian orthodoxy was proposed to meet the needs of the new society. The new school of literary thought was represented by a concept proposed by Dong Zhongshu (c. 179 – 104 BCE) known as the "intermingling of the heavenly and the human" *(Tianren heyi)* and the ethics of the "three principles and the five rules" *(sangang wuchang)*. From then on, the immovable status of Confucianism continued for two thousand years in the empire at large. The dominant Han culture developed on the basis of these circumstances, while the Chu culture in time receded into history.

For thousands of years, the Chu state flourished in the middle Yangzi region, and defined the historical development of southern China. Its cultural influence, particularly the *Lao zi* Daoist thought (informed by the Huanglao school, which developed during the early Western Han period) extended over the whole of China and has endured to the present day. Though the culture itself, as an entity, fell into demise, its contributions, particularly in the area of philosophy, have had a lasting influence. These are the most important aspects of Chu culture.

1 Karlbeck 1926.
2 Yu 1985a, 262–269.
3 Yu 1996a, 113–118.
4 Yu 1996b, 119–132.
5 Yu 1996a, 143–146.
6 See the Zheng yu chapter of the *Guo yu*, and the twenty-sixth year of the Duke of Xi in the *Zuo zhuan*.
7 See the Shang song and Yin wu chapters of the *Shi jing*.
8 See the Chu shi jia and Zhou ben ji chapters of the *Shi ji*; the phrase also appears in in the Ji jie chapter of Liu Xiang's *Bie lu*, and the Yi wen zhi chapter of the *Hanshu*.
9 Shaanxi 1979b, 38–43.
10 See the Fei gong shang chapter of the *Mo zi*.
11 See the Di xing xun chapter of the *Huai nan zi*.
12 See the Chu shi jia chapter of the *Shi ji*.
13 See twelfth year of the Duke of Zhao, in the *Zuo zhuan*
14 Xu Guang's words in the Ji jie, the Chu genealogy chapters of the *Shi ji*
15 From references quoted in the *Gua di zhi* as cited in the Shi ji zheng yi and the Jiang shui chapter of the *Shu jing zhu*.
16 As stated in the Di li zhi chapter of the *Han shu*.
17 According to Song Xiangfeng of the Qing dynasty, in chapter nine of the *Guo ting lu*, "Yuxiong of Chu resided at Danyang, and King Wu moved his capital to Ying."
18 Wang Yuzhe describes the various theories in Wang 1950.
19 Meng 1997.
20 Hubei 1995c.
21 Jingzhou 1987.
22 Yichang 1984.
23 Hubei 1992.
24 Chen 1980b. Jingzhou 1987.
25 Su 1984b.
26 Liu 1995, 1:213–218, 291–292.
27 See Hubei 1992, 114, 120, 121.
28 Henansheng 1991. Li Ling investigates the identity of the tomb's occupant in Li Ling 1981 and in 1996b.
29 Li 1936; Yin 1955a, 22; Liu 1935; Anhui 1953; Beijing 1954, 1–3; Tang 1934.
30 Yu 1985b, 67–72, 93–107.
31 See Liu 1995, chapter 4, 83–246.
32 Liu Hehui 1995 1:114–132, 180–209.
33 Jingmen 1998.
34 Li Ling 1985.
35 Li Ling 1998, 3:96–104.
36 Zhang Zhengming 1995b, 272–277, 294–299.
37 Zhao 1995, 51–99.
38 To restore the heavily damaged society and economy, the early Han promoted the Huanglao school, which advocated a "do-nothing" government. The philosphy attributed to Laozi originated in the region of the Chu state, whereas that of *Huangdi* (the Yellow Emperor), concerned primarily with immortality and divination, originated in the Qi state. Perhaps because of their resemblance, during the early Han period these two texts were intermingled and informed religious Daoism of the later periods. The popularity of the Huanglao school during the early half of the Western Han period is noted in the historical texts; the manuscripts from Mawangdui further demonstrate its prominence in the Changsha region. It is undeniable that these early philosophies had a close relationship with the local tradition of Chu thought.
39 Xiao 1974.

The Han and Tang Dynasties

XU PINGFANG | The Han and Tang cultures, which produced some of the most glorious works in the history of Chinese art, developed out of the Qin dynasty. The unification of China by the First Emperor of Qin fundamentally changed the course of Chinese history; having put an end to a patchwork of feuding states governed by lords, he established a centralized governing bureaucracy administered by local prefectures and divided into counties, standardized the written language (a particularly important determinant of national identity), as well as currency and weights and measures, and constructed roadways to link the disparate regions of his empire to one another. These measures were largely sustained by the rulers and dynasties that succeeded him.

The First Emperor's mausoleum in Lintong, Shaanxi province has been excavated and surveyed in recent years. It is constructed in the form of a large rectangle with double enclosures. The outer enclosure, entered through a gate on each of the four sides, measures 2,165 meters from north to south, and 940 meters from east to west; the inner enclosure (with single gates at the east, west, and south, and two gates at the north) measures 1,355 meters from north to south, 580 from east to west. Covering an area of approximately 250,000 square meters at the southern end of the enclosure, a flat-topped burial mound constructed of pounded earth rises to a height of 76 meters. The mound itself covers a burial palace (digong) measuring 460 by 392 meters, constructed of unfired bricks, with walls 4 meters high and 4 meters thick. The northern half of the inner enclosure is divided into two parts; to the east is a free-standing walled "city" measuring 330 meters from east to west; the western part comprises a residential hall north of the burial mound, and a side-hall north of the residential hall. To the northwest, between the inner and outer enclosures is the residence of the clerics. The area surrounding the mound contains several burial pits, including the celebrated horse-and-chariot pit inside the western gate of the inner enclosure, and a pit containing rare birds and animals outside the western gate. Auxiliary burials and horse pits were constructed outside the eastern gate of the outer enclosure and to the south; slightly to the north, 1.5 kilometers from the eastern gate, four pits of terra-cotta soldiers and horses were found in the 1970s.[1]

The construction of the mausoleum began with the First Emperor's accession to the throne in 246 BCE; by the time of his death thirty-seven years later in 210 BCE it was still not complete. Its construction required enormous expenditures, both human and material, and accounts tell us that a vast number of burial objects were entombed to supply the needs of the deceased in the afterlife. The mound remains unexcavated, but historical texts recount that the mausoleum was robbed and burned after the demise of the Qin dynasty. The excavation of the horse-and-soldier pits, however, offers some glimpses into the scale of the burial.

The rectangular Pit 1, measuring 230 by 62 meters, contained approximately 2,000 terra-cotta soldiers and horses, 20 wooden war-chariots, and 40,000 assorted bronze weapons.[2] To its northeast, the L-shaped Pit 2, measured 124 meters wide (east to west) and 98 meters long (north to south).[3] Pit 3, much smaller than the others, was dug in the shape of a Chinese char-

Cat. 161

549

acter, *ao* ("concave" or "sunken"), to resemble a squared U, and measured 17.6 meters wide (east to west) and 21.4 meters long (north to south).[4] An unfinished pit, which corresponds to accounts in the historical texts of an uncompleted mausoleum, was found between Pits 2 and 3.

The horse-and-soldier pits north of the axis formed by the mausoleum replicate the Emperor's imperial guards, arranged in inspection formation. Pit 1 was divided into eleven trenches, each of which contained 6 chariots and 18 to 20 rows of life-size warriors holding bows, crossbows, swords, and spears. The fourteen trenches of Pit 2 (the excavation of which is ongoing at this writing), were filled with chariots, cavalry, and footsoldiers.

The practice of placing pottery figurines in front of the mausoleum to represent an awesome military formation continued into the later dynasties; representations of soldiers have been discovered in the tombs of Yangling (in particular, the mausoleum of Emperor Jin Di), as well as in tombs and tomb murals of the Northern Dynasties, the Sui dynasty, and the Tang dynasty. The First Emperor's army, however, remains an extraordinary find, in particular for what it tells us about the evolution of Chinese sculpture. By the third century BCE, Chinese sculpture was capable of representing the human form with a high degree of verisimilitude; even on so massive a scale, the artists of the First Emperor's army were able to endow the figures with individuality by varying the bodies, costumes, hairstyles, and facial expressions. While the discovery of the First Emperor's mausoleum is a landmark for Chinese history and archaeology, its significance transcends the borders of China; indeed, it is one of the treasures of the world.

The continuities between the Qin and the Han dynasties, are borne out in tomb designs. The Western Han imperial mausoleums in the northern plain of the Wei River at Xi'an include features reminiscent of the design of the First Emperor's mausoleum, in particular, the shape of the enormous mounds, the rectangular tomb enclosures, and the placement of auxiliary tombs on the two sides of a road *(simadao)* that traces an east-west axis. The most important Western Han royal tombs excavated in recent years are those of Liu Sheng and his consort in Mancheng, Hebei province, and the tomb of the King of Nanyue in Guangzhou, Guangdong province.

Liu Sheng, King Jing of Zhongshan, was the son of Emperor Jin and the brother of Emperor Wu. He died in the fourth year of the Yuanding era of Emperor Wu (113 BCE); his consort Dou Wan died slightly later. They were buried side-by-side in rock-cut cliff tombs on the eastern slope of a mountain. Both tombs share an architectural plan characteristic of Western Han royal tombs: an entrance passageway, a tunnel, a front chamber flanked by two side-rooms, and a rear chamber with a circumferential corridor. The tomb of Liu Sheng measures 51.7 meters in length and 37.5 meters at its widest; that of Dou Wan is 49.7 meters long, and 65 meters wide (measured from the outer wall of each side room). Liu Sheng was buried in a coffin nested within a larger coffin *(yiguo yiguan);* Dou Wan was placed in a single coffin. In accordance with the burial practice of Han aristocrats, both were encased in "jade suits with gold threads" *(jinlü yuyi);* Liu Sheng's comprises 2,498 jade plaques; the weight of the gold used to link the plaques is estimated at 1,100 grams. While similarly shaped jade plaques had been discovered in tomb excavations prior to the Mancheng excavations, their significance as components of burial shrouds was unknown until the discovery of the tombs of Liu Shang and Dou Wan.[5]

The Western Han dynasty reached its height under the reign of Emperor Wu Di; though he reduced the power of the imperial princes and other nobles in order to enhance the sovereignty of the central government, he did not deprive them of their wealth, and the tombs of Liu Sheng and his consort, filled with exquisite and luxuriousness burial objects, reflect these circumstances.

The most important of the Han royal tombs is that of the King of Nanyue in Guangzhou. Following the demise of the Qin dynasty, a Qin military general named Zhao Tuo (from Zhending in present-day Hebei province) proclaimed himself the emperor of the Lingnan region (Guangdong province). Zhao's kingdom was subjugated by the Han in 111 BCE. On the basis of a gold seal inscribed *Wendi xingxi* and a jade seal inscribed *Zhao Mo,* the tomb at Xianggang has been identified as that of the second king of Nanyue — Zhao Mo, who died around 122 BCE)

The tomb, situated on top of a hill, is built on a north-south axis. An entrance passageway at the southern end leads into an outer storage room; behind the storage room is chamber flanked by two side rooms, a rear chamber (which contained the coffin), and another chamber behind it (which served for storage); the coffin chamber and the rear chamber were also flanked by side rooms. All were constructed with sand and stones. The tomb, which dates slightly earlier than that of Liu Sheng, measures 10.68 meters in length from the front door of the front chamber to the northern end of the rear storage chamber, and 12.24 meters in width, measured from the outer walls of the side rooms. The King of Nanyue's tomb lacks the circumferential corridors of Liu Sheng's chamber, and his jade shroud is pieced together with silk rather than gold, features that suggest that Zhao Mo was a king of lower rank than Liu Sheng (who bore the imperial surname).

The burial accouterments of the King of Nanyue's tomb comprise more 1,000 objects in a dazzling variety of materials — bronze, iron, silver and gold, pottery, jade, glass, lacquered wood, bamboo, and silk and hemp; bronzes and jades compose the vast majority of the tomb objects. The bronzes include *niu* and *yong* bells, 36 *ding* vessels, and 32 mirrors; the 280 jade objects include the jade shroud, 11 sets of pendants, and 58 sword ornaments, and Zhao Mo was buried with no fewer than 23 seals made of gold, bronze, jade, and hardstone. The tomb objects testify to a variety of artistic influences. The jade suit, jade pendants, and bronze mirrors echo the style of the Central Plains; some of the bronzes and ceramics clearly evoke the Wu, Yue, and Chu styles. Some objects display motifs often seen in cultures of the northern grasslands (such as gold apricot-leaf ornaments); a silver box decorated with petals was likely imported from Western or Central Asia, while flower ornaments (*pao*), ivory, and perfume testify to trade with lands to the south.[6]

Imperial mausoleums of the Tang dynasty were centered in the area near Xi'an, in the Guanzhong region of Shaanxi province. The princess of Jinxiang was the granddaughter of Li

Yuan (the Emperor Gaozu of the Tang dynasty), and the third daughter of Li Yuanying, the king of Teng. She married Yu Yin, the judicial adjutant (*sifa canjun*) in Shuzhou, who died in the first year of the Yongchang era (689 CE). The Princess passed away in the tenth year of the Kaiyuan era (722 CE), and was buried with her husband in the twelfth year of the era (724 CE). The couple's tomb was situated on the eastern bank of the Ba River, northeast of Xi'an.[7]

The single chamber tomb has a passageway with three ceiling funnels and a tunnel leading to the tomb chamber. A stone coffin was placed on the western side of the square tomb chamber (which measures 3.5 by 3.4 meters); burial objects were placed on the eastern half. The walls of the passageway, tunnel, and tomb chamber were originally decorated with painted murals, but these have peeled off and only traces remain. Although the tomb had been looted, several well-preserved burial figurines were recovered, the most notable of which are the figures of hunters on horseback, which exhibit a lively and realistic style.

Tang tombs dating after the Kaiyuan and Tianbao eras display simplified plans and modest burial objects, a phenomenon that likely reflects the division of the territory by the warlords and the economic decline following An Lushan's rebellion. Once the most prosperous capitals, Chang'an and Luoyang progressively fell into decline. Tombs associated with local powers, such as the Five Dynasties tomb of Wang Chuzhi in Quyang, Hebei province, by contrast, evoke the glamour of prior periods.

The mural paintings at the tomb of Wang Chuzhi retain the high Tang style. They are similar to depictions of fashionable women in the tomb of Xue Mo (dating to the sixteenth year of the Kaiyuan era, 728 CE), the tomb of Yang Xuanlue (dating to the fifth year of the Xiantong era, 864 CE), and tomb of Lady Wei, but the figures are altogether unique in their elegance and execution, likely reflecting the higher status of the tomb's occupant. Polychrome stone reliefs on the two walls of the rear chamber depict musicians and female attendants. Their floating drapery evokes a sense of rhythmic movement, as if the figures are dancing to their own music.[8]

Wang Chuzhi had been military commissioner (*jiedushi*) of Yi, Ding, and Qi prefectures. Born in Wannian county in Jingzhao during the Tang dynasty, he resided in Baoyefang at the capital Chang'an. Several generations of his family had held positions in the Army of Inspired Strategy (*shencejun*). His father, Wang Zong, was promoted from the military to Left Guard (*zuoweishi*) in Jingzhao, and served as commander supervising the remote prefecture of Xingyuan. We are told that Wang Zong "specialized in speculation, took opportunities to execute favorable trades, and as a result was as rich as a king. He amassed great wealth in the course of his employment, and thus established himself as a noble, dined on luxurious meals, and retained thousands of servants."[9] Wang Chuzhi's elder brother, Wang Chucun, held the positions of acting Minister of Justice and military commissioner of the army of Yiwu during the sixth year of the Qianfu era (879 CE); he helped to put down the rebellion of Huangchao and thus recovered imperial control of the city of Chang'an. Wang Chuzhi was military commander (*bingmashi*) in Dingzhou. He had close relationships with Li Keyong and Zhu Wen, and was granted the titles of Prince of Taiyuan and Prince of Beiping. His status as a powerful warlord in the Hebei region is reflected in the design of his tomb, which includes an antechamber, a rear chamber, and two side rooms, a design identical with the contemporaneous tomb of Zhao Dejun discovered in Beijing; such designs during the Five Dynasties were traditionally the privilege of individuals of higher rank. Wang Chuzhi died in the twentieth year of the Tianyou (923 CE). The design of the mural paintings was likely adapted from similar murals at Chang'an, a reflection of Wang Chuzhi's status as a warlord of Hebei and his social position in the capital.

Buddhist culture introduced a variety of artistic forms and influences into Han and Tang culture. Archaeological study of Chinese Buddhism has concentrated on three areas: cave temples; monastery remains, including various Buddhist images and objects unearthed from the sites; and subterranean crypts beneath Buddhist pagodas. The most important monastery remains excavated in recent years have been the Xiude Monastery in Quyang, Hebei province; the Wanfo Monastery in Chengdu, Sichuan province, and the Longxing Monastery, in Qingzhou, Shandong province. Artifacts from the pagoda crypts, such as the renowned Famen Monastery in Fufeng, Shaanxi province and the Longxing Monastery in Qingzhou, have yielded extraordinary objects that represent the artistic quintessence of Chinese Buddhist culture.

The three hundred Buddhist statues discovered in 1996 at the Longxing Monastery in Qingzhou date from the Northern Wei, Eastern Wei, Northern Qi, Sui, Tang, and the Northern Song dynasties; most of the images, however, were made during the Northern Wei and Northern Qi.[10] During the later years of the Northern Song (the early twelfth century), the creation of Buddha statues ceased altogether; existing statues were destroyed and buried. Several stylistic dominate the Longxing Buddhist images: their splendid colors and use of gold inlay and the close-fitting drapery of the figures ("as if just coming out of water"); the latter feature is characteristic of Eastern Wei and Northern Qi statues and reflects the influence of Gandharan style, contrasting with the loose gown and sash normally seen in the Northern Wei images.

The Famen Monastery was one of four Tang imperial sponsored Buddhist monasteries that enshrined relics of the Buddha. During the Zhenguan, Xianqing, Zhide, Zhenyuan, and Yuanhe eras, the imperial court ordered the skull, fingerbones and other relics to be brought from the Famen Monastery to the palace; with the persecution of Buddhism under the Huichang era (845 CE), the worship of the relics ceased, but during the fourteenth year of the Xiantong era (873 CE), the imperial court again had the relics brought to the palace and returned them to the monastery at the end of the year. One year later, the Buddha's relics were buried in the subterranean crypt beneath the pagoda and lay there undisturbed until their excavation in 1987.

The subterranean crypt of the Famen Monastery pagoda is oriented along a north-south axis, with a stairway, tunnel, antechamber, middle and rear chambers constructed of stone slabs. This remains the only known three-chambered subterranean crypt, a layout evidently derived from that of imperial mausoleums. Two stone steles were erected at the northern end of the tunnel outside the stone door of the antechamber; inscriptions on the steles record "the delivery of the True Relics from Qiyang during the Xiantong era of the Tang dynasty," and "a list of offerings, gold and silver treasures, and garments accompanying the True Relics." The stone door of the antechamber was carved with the images of the Buddha and guardians; a square pagoda made of painted white marble, guarded by a pair of stone lions, was placed in the center of the antechamber. Inside the marble pagoda, a square copper pagoda contained a gilt-silver coffin within which the Buddha's fingerbone was enshrined. The antechamber also contained stone caskets, bronze ceremonial staffs, white porcelain vases, and two packages of silk garments. The doors to the crypt's middle chamber were carved with reliefs of *lokapalas;* a white marble *lingzhang* pagoda in the center of the chamber contained an iron casket with a *luding* cover, and a gilt-silver coffin decorated with a pair of phoenixes, which contained second relic of the Buddha's fingerbone. In front of the *lingzhang* was a bronze incense burner, flanked by two polychrome stone *lokapala* figures. The middle chamber also contained a bodhisattva image which held the relic, "secret color" *(mi se)* celadon wares, lacquered boxes, and many silk textiles. The nearly square rear chamber, a carefully designed structure with an octagonal ceiling well and stone doors, contained a reliquary (comprising eight nested cases) wrapped in red brocade, with gilt bodhisattva image on its top. It was placed in the center of the chamber. The outermost case of the reliquary, made of black lacqured wood has silver fittings, and a *luding* cover; gold and polychrome carvings on the four sides depict the themes of the Buddha's preaching, Paradise, and homage to the Buddha. The other seven layers from outer to innermost are as follows: a gilt-silver case decorated with four *lokapala* figures; a plain silver case; a gilt-silver case with images of the seated Buddha; a gold case featuring a six-armed Avalokiteśvara; a gold case inlaid with precious stones and pearls; a *wufu* stone case with precious stones and pearls inlaid in gold frames; and finally a gold pagoda with single eaves, four doors, and a pearl top, which enshrines the Buddha's fingerbone. Directly in front of the reliquary was a silver incense burner resting on a stand. Four Arghya ewers with *vajra* motifs were placed in the four corners of the rear chamber. Other items, piled in two layers in the rear chamber, included objects of gold, silver, and glass, and silk garments. A pit measuring 0.65 square meters and 0.5 meters deep was dug to the north of the rear chamber; a bricked-up square niche at the northern end of the pit contained an iron case, which in turn contained a silver *luding* covered case, a sandalwood case with silver fittings, a crystal outer coffin inlaid with precious stones, and finally a jade inner coffin in which the third of the fingerbone relics was placed.[11]

The subterranean palace at the Famen Monastery has yielded 121 gold and silver objects, 8 bronzes, 16 pieces of porcelain, 20 glass dishes, 12 stone objects, and an abundance of woven silk fabric. The stele records 2,499 pieces of treasure in the crypt, although this claim is not borne out by the objects recovered. The finds from the crypt, however, are extraordinary, both in quantity and quality, and surpass all known foundation deposits. Particularly notable are the *mi se* porcelains and the gold and silver objects made in Wensi and western Zhejiang which represent the highest skill of Tang metallurgists. The crypt contained a dazzling variety of textiles, including *ling, luo, sha, juan, jin, xiu*, many of them embroidered with gold in a variety of techniques.

While they undeniably constitute artistic treasures of the highest order, the artifacts from the Famen Monastery pagoda crypt are also invaluable materials for the study of Buddhism. Many artifacts from the palace reflect elements of Esoteric Buddhism: the Five Buddhas represented on the reliquary, the Diamond World mandala; the *mojie* vajras; the *rajas* on the throne of the bodhisattva image; and the six-armed Avalokiteśvara image on the gold case of the reliquary. These elements reflect the popularity of Esoteric Buddhism among the upper class following the persecution of Buddhism during the Huichang era.[12] The treasures from the Famen Monastery are also valuable testimony to cultural interactions between China and foreign countries. The eighteen Islamic glass dishes from the crypt, whose dates are established by the stele inscriptions, may well require us to reexamine the dating of Islamic glass objects in museums throughout the world.

1 Yuan 1988, nos. 5 and 6.
2 Shaanxi 1988b.
3 Qinyong 1978
4 Qinyong 1979.
5 Zhongguo 1980b.
6 Guangzhou 1991.

7 Xi'an 1997.
8 Hebei 1998.
9 "Wang Chucun zhuan" Jiu Tangshu juan 182.
10 Shandong 1998.
11 Shaanxi 1988a.
12 Su Bai 1988.

Concordance

Fufeng 扶風
Fujian Province (Fujian Sheng)
　福建省
Fuping 富平
Fuquanshan 福泉山
Fuxin 阜新
Fuxingdi 福興地
Gan River (Gan Jiang) 贛江
Gansu Province (Gansu
　Sheng) 甘肅省
Gaochang 高昌
Gedangtou 圪墙頭
Guangdong Province (Guang-
　dong Sheng) 廣東省
Guanghan 廣漢
Guangshan 光山
Guangzhou 廣州
Guanzhong 關中
Guixian 貴縣
Guizhou Province (Guizhou
　Sheng) 貴州省
Guo (state) 虢
Guodian 郭店
Guojiatan 郭家灘
Gushi 固始
Hangtou 杭頭
Hangzhou 杭州
Hansenzhai 韓森寨
Hanshan 含山
Hao 鎬
Haojiaping 郝家坪
Hebei Province (Hebei
　Sheng) 河北省
Heicheng 黑城
Heilongjiang Province (Hei-
　longjiang Sheng) 黑龍
　江省
Hejia 賀家
Hejiacun 何家村
Hemudu 河姆渡
Henan Province (Henan
　Sheng) 河南省
Heshangling 和尚嶺
Hetaozhuang 核桃莊
Hetian 和闐

Hongshan 紅山
Hongshanhou 紅山後
Hongshanmiao 洪山廟
Hougang 後崗
Hougudui 侯古堆
Houjiazhuang 侯家莊
Houli 後李
Houloushan 後樓山
Houma 侯馬
Hua 華
Huai River (Huai He) 淮河
Huai'an 淮安
Huaiyang 淮陽
Huang (state) 黃
Huangpi 黃陂
Huashan 華山
Huayang 華陽
Huayuanzhuang 花園莊
Hubei Province (Hubei
　Sheng) 湖北省
Huixian 輝縣
Hunan Province (Hunan
　Sheng) 湖南省
Hushou 湖熟
Hutougou 胡頭溝
Hutuo River 呼沱水
Inner Mongolia Autonomous
　Region (Neimenggu Zizhi-
　qu) 內蒙古自治區
Jixian 汲縣
Ji'nan 紀南
Ji'nancheng 紀南城
Jiahu 賈湖
Jiang 絳
Jiangjiagou 姜家溝
Jiangling 江陵
Jiangnan 江南
Jiangshui 江水
Jiangsu Province (Jiangsu
　Sheng) 江蘇省
Jiangxi Province (Jiangxi
　Sheng) 江西省
Jiangzhai 姜寨
Jianping 建平
Jilin Province (Jilin Sheng)

吉林省
Jin (state) 晉
Jincun 金村
Jing 荊
Jing'an 靖安
Jingdang 京當
Jingmen 荊門
Jing Mountains (Jingshan)
　荊山
Jingzhao 京兆
Jingzhou 荊州
Jinniushan 金牛山
Jinxi 錦西
Jinyang 晉陽
Jiudian 九店
Jiulidun 九里墩
Jiuquan 酒泉
Jiuzhu 九主
Ju River (Ju Shui) 沮水
Julianghaijia 巨良海家
Jun county (Junxian) 浚縣
Juxian 莒縣
Juyang 鉅陽
Kazuo 喀左
Keshengzhuang 客省莊
Laishui 淶水
Lake Poyang 鄱陽湖
Lake Shanglin 上林湖
Lantian 藍田
Lanzhou 蘭州
Laoguantai 老官台
Laoha River (Laoha He)
　老哈河
Leigudun 擂鼓墩
Leitai 雷台
Liangchengzhen 兩城鎮
Liangzhu 良渚
Liaodong 遼東
Liaoning Province (Liaoning
　Sheng) 遼寧省
Licheng 歷城
Licun 禮村
Lijialou 李家樓
Linfen 臨汾
Lingjiatan 凌家灘

Lingnan 嶺南
Lingshan 陵山
Lingshou 靈壽
Lingyang River (Lingyang He)
　陵陽河
Lingyuan 凌源
Linjia 林家
Linqu 臨朐
Linru 臨汝
Lintong 臨潼
Linxia 臨夏
Linzi 臨淄
Liquan 澧泉
Lisangudui 李三孤堆
Lishan 驪山
Liuchengqiao 瀏城橋
Liujiang 柳江
Liulidian 劉李店
Liulihe 琉璃河
Lixian 澧縣
Liyang 歷陽
Longnan 龍南
Longshan 龍山
Longxi 隴西
Longxian 隴縣
Loulan 樓蘭
Lu 魯
Lüjiaping 呂家坪
Luojiajiao 羅家角
Luonan 洛南
Luopowan 羅泊灣
Luoyang 洛陽
Luoyi 洛邑
Machang 馬廠
Majiabang 馬家浜
Majiayao 馬家窰
Manasi 瑪納斯
Mancheng 滿城
Mang Mountain (Mangshan)
　邙山
Mashan 馬山
Mashan Zhuanchang 馬山
　磚廠
Mawangdui 馬王堆
Mengcheng 蒙城

Miaodigou 廟底溝
Miaoping 廟坪
Minhe 民和
Mogaoku 莫高窟
Mopan Mountains (Mopan-shan) 磨盤山
Mopandun 磨盤墩
Mount Kunlun (Kunlunshan) 崑崙山
Mount Taishan (Taishan) 泰山
Nanchang 南昌
Nanchengzi 南城子
Nanliwang 南里王
Nanyang 南陽
Nanyaozhuang 南窰莊
Niaodanshan 鳥旦山
Nihewan 泥河灣
Ningbo 寧波
Ningxia Hui Autonomous Region (Ningxia Huizu Zizhiqu) 寧夏回族自治區
Niuheliang 牛河梁
Ordos 鄂爾多斯
Paimashan 拍馬山
Panlongcheng 盤龍城
Peiligang 裴里崗
Pengtoushan 彭頭山
Pingdingshan 平頂山
Pingliangtai 平糧台
Pingshan 平山
Poyang (Lake) 鄱陽湖
Qi (state) 齊
Qi Prefecture 齊州
Qiangjia 強家
Qianshanyang 錢山漾
Qianzhai 前寨
Qianzhong 黔中
Qiaocun 喬村
Qin'an 秦安
Qingchuan 青川
Qinghai Province (Qinghai Sheng) 青海省
Qingzhou 青州

Qinjiagou 秦家溝
Qi Mountain (Qishan) 岐山
Qiujiahuayuan 邱家花園
Qizhen 齊鎮
Quanhu 泉護
Qucun 曲村
Qufu 曲阜
Qujialing 屈家嶺
Quwo 曲沃
Quyang 曲陽
Renjia 任家
Rizhao 日照
Rujiazhuang 茹家莊
Ruzhou 汝州
Sanguandianzi 三官甸子
Sanji 三汲
Sanliqiao 三里橋
Sanmenxia 三門峽
Sanxingdui 三星堆
Sanxingtala 三星他拉
Shaanxi Province (Shaanxi Sheng) 陝西省
Shaguotun 沙鍋屯
Shanbiaozhen 山彪鎮
Shandong Province (Shandong Sheng) 山東省
Shangguancun 上官村
Shanghai 上海
Shangsunjiazhai 上孫家寨
Shangwang 商王
Shanxi Province (Shanxi Sheng) 山西省
Shaochen 召陳
Shaoxing 紹興
Shashi 沙市
Shenyang 瀋陽
Shijiahe 石家河
Shijiayuan 史家塬
Shijiazhuang 石家莊
Shilingxia 石嶺下
Shinüba 石女壩
Shiqiao 石橋
Shixianggou 屍鄉溝
Shizhaocun 師趙村
Shizishan 獅子山

Shouchun 壽春
Shouxian 壽縣
Shouzhou 壽州
Shu 蜀
Shucheng 舒城
Shuihudi 睡虎地
Shuikou 水口
Sichuan Province (Sichuan Sheng) 四川省
Sidun 寺墩
Sihui 四會
Songhequ 宋河區
Songshan 松山
Songze 崧澤
Songzi 松滋
Sui (state) 隨
Sui Mountains (Suishan) 睢山
Suishui (Sui River) 睢水
Suixian 隨縣
Suizhou 隨州
Sujialong 蘇家壟
Sunjiagang 孫家崗
Tai Lake 太湖
Tai Mountains (Taishan) 泰山
Tai'an 泰安
Taihang Mountains (Taihangshan) 太行山
Taihe 太和
Taiyuan 太原
Tangjiagang 湯家崗
Taosi 陶寺
Tengdian 藤店
Tengzhou 滕州
Tianjin 天津
Tianma 天馬
Tianshui 天水
Tianxingguan 天星觀
Tongde 同德
Tunxi 屯溪
Wangjiayinwa 王家陰洼
Wangjiazui 汪家咀
Wangshan 望山
Wannian 萬年
Wei River (Wei He) 渭河

Wei River (Wei Shui) 渭水
Wengniuteqi 翁牛特旗
Wenxi 聞喜
Wu (state) 吳
Wuchangyidi 武昌義地
Wucheng 吳城
Wuguancun 武官村
Wuhan 武漢
Wujun 巫郡
Wulan Mountains (Wulan-shan) 烏蘭山
Wuwei 武威
Wuyang 舞陽
Xi rivers (Xi Shui) 淅水
Xi'an 西安
Xi'eshan 溪娥山
Xiajiadian 夏家店
Xiajin 下津
Xiang rivers (Xiang Jiang) 湘江
Xiangfan 襄樊
Xiangfen 襄汾
Xianggang 象崗
Xiangling 襄陵
Xianrendong 仙人洞
Xianyang 咸陽
Xiaoheyan 小河沿
Xiaolongtan 小龍潭
Xiaomeiling 小梅嶺
Xiaotun 小屯
Xiasi 下寺
Xibeigang 西北崗
Xichuan 淅川
Xilamulun River(Xilamulun He) 西拉木倫河
Xin'gan 新淦 (新贛)
Xindian 辛店
Xinfengzhen 新豐鎮
Xinglongwa 興隆窪
Xinji 新集
Xinjiang 新絳
Xinjiang 新疆
Xintian 新田
Xinyang 信陽
Xinzheng 新鄭

Xinzhuxiang　新築鄉
Xishuiquan　西水泉
Xitai　西台
Xiyanchuan　西燕川
Xiyin　西陰
Xuanhua　宣化
Xuyi　盱眙
Xuzhou　徐州
Yan (state)　燕
Yancun　閻村
Yanggongxiang　楊公鄉
Yangjiawan　楊家灣
Yangling　陽陵
Yangshao　仰韶
Yangzhou　揚州
Yangzi (Yangtze) River (Chang
　　Jiang)　長江
Yanshan (Yan mountains)
　　燕山
Yanshi　偃師
Yaoshan　瑤山
Yaozitou　窯子頭
Yellow River (Huang He)
　　黃河
Yi River (Yi Shui)　沂水
Yi Prefecture　易
Yicheng　翼城
Yidigang　義地崗
Yimen　益門
Ying　郢
Ying (state)　應
Yingkou　營口
Yiqi　奕棋
Yixian　易縣
Yongcheng　永城
Youziling　油子嶺
Yuanmou　元謀
Yuanqu　垣曲
Yuchanyan　玉蟾岩
Yuchisi　尉遲寺
Yue (state)　越
Yueshi　岳石
Yueyang　岳陽
Yuhang　餘杭
Yunmeng　雲夢

Yunnan Province (Yunnan
　　Sheng)　雲南省
Yutaishan　雨台山
Zeng (state)　曾
Zhang rivers (Zhang Shui)
　　漳水
Zhanglingshan　張陵山
Zhao (state)　趙
Zhaobaogou　趙寶溝
Zhaojiabang　趙家塝
Zhaojiahu　趙家湖
Zhaoqing　肇慶
Zhejiang Province (Zhejiang
　　Sheng)　浙江省
Zhengzhou　鄭州
Zhenwu mountains (Zhenwu-
　　shan)　真武山
Zhijiang county　枝江
Zhoukoudian　周口店
Zhouliangyuqiao　周梁玉橋
Zhoushan　舟山
Zhuangbai　莊白
Zhufeng　朱封
Zhujiaji　朱家集
Zhu Jiang　珠江
Zhukaigou　朱開溝
Zidanku　子彈庫
Zigui　秭歸
Zongri　宗日

TERMINOLOGY AND
PERSONAL NAMES

An Lushan　安祿山
An Shuyun　安淑鄖
Anding　安定
anqun　案裙
Bai Qi　白起
Bai Zhuyi (Juyi)　白居易
baihua qifang　百花齊放
baijia zhengming　百家爭鳴
Ban Gu　班固
Banpo Culture　半坡文化
Banpo Phase　半坡類型
baoxiang　寶箱
Bei Dan　北單
Beishan　北山
Beiyinyangyin Culture　北陰
　　陽營文化
bianxiang　邊箱
biedang　瘭襠
Bingmashi　兵馬使
bixie　辟邪
Bo Dong　伯戎
Bo Xianfu　伯先父
boqu wen　波曲紋
bu　卜
Cai　蔡
Changxin　長信
Chaoxian Man　巢縣人
Chen Jingfu　陳景夫
Chen Mengjia (1911–1966)
　　陳夢家
Cheng Zhou　成周
chi　螭
Chongzhensi　重真寺
Chu Culture　楚文化
Chu Shuzhisun　楚叔之孫
Chunqiu　春秋
Chuzi　楚子
Chuzi laigao　楚子來告
Cishan Culture　磁山文化
cun　寸
Cuo　譻
Da Ju　大矩

Da She　大射
Dafu　大夫
Dahecun Phase　大河村類型
Daming Gong　大明宮
dao　禱
dao jue　盜掘
Daoyintu　導引圖
Datang Xiantong Qisong Qi-
　　yang Zhenshen Zhiwen
　　大唐咸通啟送歧陽真身
　　志文
Dawenkou Culture　大汶口
　　文化
Deng Zhong　鄧仲
Di　狄
Di　帝
digong　地宮
dijing　地經
Ding　丁
Ding Wenjiang (V.K. Ting,
　　1887–1936)　丁文江
Dingcun Man　丁村人
Dong Yuan　董源
Dong Zhongshu　董仲舒
Dong Zuobin (Tung Tso-pin,
　　1895–1963)　董作賓
Dou Jiao　竇皦
Dou Kang　竇抗
Dou Wan　竇綰
Du Fu (712–770)　杜甫
Duizu buci　自組卜辭
Duke Jing of Jin　晉景公
Duke of Xi　僖公
Duke of Zhao　召公
Duke of Zhou (Zhou Gong)
　　周公
Eastern Wei　東魏
Emperor Daizong　代宗
Emperor Gaozong　高宗
Emperor Taizong　太宗
Emperor Wen Di　文帝
Emperor Xizong　熹宗
Emperor Xuanzong　玄宗
Emperor Yizong　懿宗
Empress Dowager Dou　竇太后

Empress Taimu　太穆皇后

Empress Wu　武后

Epang (Afang) Palace　阿房宮

ercengtai　二層台

Erlitou Culture　二里頭文化

Famensi (Famen Monastery)　法門寺

Fan Huozhi　軛腹志

fangguo　方國

Father Xin (Fu Xin)　父辛

Father Yi (Fu Yi)　父乙

Father Yi of the Lü (Lü Fu Yi)　旅父乙

feiyi　飛衣

fenben　粉本

Feng Hui　馮暉

Five Dynasties　五代

fu　符

fu　賦

Fu Hao　婦好

Fu Sinian (Fu Ssu-nien, 1896–1950)　傅斯年

Fu Xi　伏羲

Gao Zu　高祖

Gong Wang　共王

gongcheng　公乘

Gongsun Yang　公孫鞅

gongzhu　公主

Gu Ding　盬丁

Gu Hongzhong　顧閎中

Gu Jiegang (1893–1980)　顧頡剛

Gu Yanwu　顧炎武

guan　棺

guan　鸛

Guan Tong　關同

guanxiang　棺箱

guguo　古國

Gui　癸

guo　槨

Guo Moruo (Kuo Mo-jo, 1892–1978)　郭沫若

Guo Ying　郭痙

Guoji　虢季

guoshi　槨室

guozhi dashi zai si yu rong　國之大事在祀與戎

Hamada Kōsaku (1881–1938)　濱田耕作

Han dynasty　漢朝

Han Xizai　韓熙載

Han Yu　韓愈

hangtu　夯土

Hanyuan dian　含元殿

Henan Longshan Culture　河南龍山文化

Henan Yangshao Culture　河南仰韶文化

Hongshan Culture　紅山文化

Houma mengshu　侯馬盟書

Hu Houxuan (1911–1995)　胡厚宣

Huabei Plain　華北平原

huang zu wen kao　皇祖文考

Huangdi　黃帝

Huanglao (school)　黃老

huangwei　荒帷

Huating Phase　花廳類型

Hubei Longshan Culture　湖北龍山文化

Huichang　會昌

Hunan Longshan Culture　湖南龍山文化

huqing　湖青

Ji　姬

Jiang　姜

Jiang Ting　降 (絳) 亭

jiangjun　將軍

Jiansong Zhenshen Shisui Zhenshen Gongyang Daoju ji Jinyin Baoqi Yiwuzhang　監送真身使隨真身供養道具及金銀寶器衣物帳

jiaojing　絞經

jiasha　袈裟

jie　節

Jie　疥

jiedushi　節度使

jin　紟

Jin dynasty　金朝

jin shi xue　金石學

jin brocade　錦

Jing Shu (Xing Shu)　井叔

Jing Chu　荊楚

Jingdi　景帝

jingfang　經方

jinlü yuyi　金縷玉衣

Jinniushan Man　金牛山人

Jinxiang　金鄉

jisi keng (sacrificial pits)　祭祀坑

Jiu gao　酒高

ju　欅

Juezhi　覺智

Kang Gong　康公

Kang Gong　康宮

Ke　克

King Cheng　成王

King Cuo　䥯王

King Cuo of Zhongshan　中山䥯王

King Gong　恭王

King Huai of Chu　楚懷王

King Jing of Zhongshan　中山靖王

King Kang　康王

King Kang of Chu　楚康王

King Kaolie　考烈王

King Mu　穆王

King Tang　湯王

King Wen　(楚) 文王

King Wen (Nan Yue)　文王 (南越)

King Wu (Wu Wang)　武王

King Xiao　孝王

King Xiong Zhang of Chu (Chu Wang Xiong Zhang)　楚王酓 (熊) 章

King Yi　夷王

King Yichu of Xu　邾王義楚

King You of Chu　楚幽王

King Zhao　昭王

King Zheng of Qin　秦政王

King Zhuang of Chu　楚莊王

kui　夔

Lady Wei　衛氏

Lantian Man　藍田人

Later Liang　後梁

leiwen　雷紋

Li Ji (Li Chi, 1895–1979)　李濟

Li Jingxun　李靜訓

Li Keyong　李克用

Li Ling　李零

Li Shouli　李守禮

Li Xian　李賢

Li Yuan　李淵

Li Yuanying　李元嬰

liang　兩

Liang Qichao (1873–1929)　梁啓超

Liang Sicheng (1901–1972)　梁思城

Liang Siyong (1904–1954)　梁思永

Liangzhu Culture　良渚文化

Liao dynasty　遼朝

lingzhang　靈帳

Liu Bang　劉邦

Liu Sheng　劉勝

Liu Xiang　劉向

Liujiang Man　柳江人

Liulin Phase　劉林類型

Lizu buci　歷組卜辭

longfenghu wenxiu　龍鳳虎紋繡

Longshan Culture　龍山文化

Longxing Monastery (Longxingsi)　龍興寺

Lord of Diyang　邸昜君

Lower Erligang Phase　二里崗下層

Lower Xiajiadian Culture　夏家店下層文化

Lower Zaoshi　皂市下層

luding　盝頂

luo　羅

Luo Zhenyu (1866–1940)　羅振玉

Lü　旅

Ma Heng (1881–1955)　馬衡

Maba Man　馬壩人

Majiabang Culture　馬家浜
文化

Majiayao Culture　馬家窯
文化

Man　曼

mao　冒

Maoling　茂陵

Marquis Dai (Daihou)　軑侯

Marquis of Jin (Jinhou)　晉侯

Marquis Pi of Jin (Jinhou Pi)
晉侯邲

Marquis Su of Jin (Jinhou Su
晉侯鮇

Marquis Yi of Zeng (Zenghou
Yi)　曾侯乙

Marquis Yu of Zeng (Zenghou
Yu)　曾侯遇

Marquis Zhao of Cai (Caihou
Zhao)　蔡侯昭

Miaodigou Culture　廟底溝
文化

Miaodigou Phase　廟底溝
類型

Ming dynasty　明朝

mingmu　幎目

mingqi　明器

mi se　秘色

mojie　摩羯

Mu Xin　母辛

Nan Yue　南越

Nanyang Temple　南陽寺

Neng Shun　能順

Northern Qi dynasty　北齊

Northern Wei dynasty　北魏

Northern Zhou dynasty　北周

Nü Wa　女媧

Nüshenmiao　女神廟

Pan Cheng　番勆

Pangeng　盤庚

pao　泡

Pei Wenzhong (W.C. Pei 1904–
1982)　裴文中

Peiligang Culture　裴李崗
文化

Peking Man　北京人

Peng　倗

Penglai　蓬萊

Pengtoushan Culture　彭頭
山文化

pi'ao　皮襖

Prince of Beiping　北平王

Prince of Bin　邠王

Prince of Taiyuan　太原王

Prince Yide　懿德太子

Prince Zhanghuai　章懷太子

Princess Yongtai　永泰公主

qi　氣

qi　戚

Qi Prefecture　祁州

Qian Jia School　乾嘉學派

Qian Mu (1895–1990)　錢穆

Qian Yi　虔詣

Qianfusi　千福寺

Qianling　乾陵

Qiji Monastery (Qijisi)
七級寺

Qijia Culture　齊家文化

qin　衾

Qin dynasty　秦朝

Qin Shihuangdi　秦始皇帝

qing　卿

Qing dynasty　清朝

Qinglian'gang Culture　青蓮
崗文化

Qingshansi　慶山寺

Qu Yuan　屈原

Quanrong　犬戎

renziwen　人字紋

Ru ware　汝窯

sai dao　塞禱

San　散

sancai　三彩

sandai　三代

sangang wuchang　三綱五常

Sanqing dian　三清殿

sha　紗

Shaanxi Longshan Culture
陝西龍山文化

shan　山

Shandingdong Man　山頂
洞人

Shandong Longshan Culture
山東龍山文化

Shang dynasty　商朝

Shang Yang　商鞅

Shangdi　上帝

Shao Tuo　邵䭾

sheli　猞猁

Shen Nong　神農

shencejun　神策軍

shenyi　深衣

shi　士

shi　史

Shi Xingeng (1912–1939)
施昕更

Shu Quan　束泉

shushu　術數

Si Tu (Qiao) Mu　司兜母

Siba Culture　四壩文化

Sifa Canjun　司法參軍

sijingjiao suluo　四經絞素羅

silü yuyi　絲縷玉衣

Sima Qian (ca. 145–86 BCE)
司馬遷

simadao　司馬道

Sishiling　四時令

Song dynasty　宋朝

Song Xiangfeng　宋翔鳳

Song Yu　宋玉

Spring and Autumn Period
春秋時代

Su Bingqi (1909–1997)
蘇秉琦

Sui dynasty　隋朝

suluo　素羅

Sun Gu　孫固

Sunshu Ao　孫叔敖

Taiji　太極

Taijia　太甲

Tang dynasty　唐朝

Tang Gaozu　唐高祖

Tang Lan (1901–1979)　唐蘭

Tangshu Yu　唐叔虞

Taosi Culture　陶寺文化

Taosi Longshan Culture
陶寺龍山文化

taotie　饕餮

taowen　陶文

taxingwen　塔形紋

Tengwang　滕王

Tianren heyi　天人合一

Tianzi　天子

Tong Palace　桐宮

Tong Shuye　童書業

Torii Ryūzō (1870–1953)
鳥居龍藏

touxiang　頭箱

Ts'inghua (Qinghua)　清華

Tu Bo　土伯

Wanfo Monastery (Wanfosi)
萬佛寺

wang　王

Wang Chucun　王處存

Wang Chuzhi　王處直

Wang Guowei (1877–1927)
王國維

Wang Quanhu　王全護

Wang Yi　王逸

Wang Yuzhe　王玉哲

Wang Zong　王宗

Wangsun Gao　王孫誥

Wangzi Wu　王子午

Wangzi Yingci　王子嬰次

Warring States Period　戰國
時代

Wei　微

Wei Bo Xing　微伯瘼

Wei Hong　衛宏

Wendi xingxi　文帝行璽

Wensi Hall　文思院

Wenwang (King Wen)　文王

wo　握

Wu Ding　武丁

Wu Han (1909–1969)　吳晗

Wu Hongque　吳弘愨

Wu Jinding (1901–1948)
吳金鼎

Wu Zetian　武則天

wuren dongwu wen　舞人動
　　物紋
Wushier bingfang　五十二
　　病方
Wuxingzhan　五星占
Xi　昔
Xi　焁
Xia dynasty　夏朝
Xia Nai (1910–1985)　夏鼐
xiang　祥
Xiang Yu　項羽
Xiangmajing　相馬經
xiangtang　饗堂
xianzhu　縣主
xiao　削
Xiaoheyan Culture　小河沿
　　文化
Xin　辛
Xing　瘣
Xing Shu (Jing Shu)　井叔
Xinghua　興化
Xingshan Monastery (Xing-
　　shansi)　興善寺
Xiuide Monastery (Xiuide)
　　修德寺
Xionghan　熊悍
Xiongli　熊麗
Xiongyi　熊繹
Xiuide Monastery (Xiuide)
　　修德寺
Xixia　西夏
Xixiahou Phase　西夏侯類型
Xu　序
Xu Bingxu (Xu Xusheng, 1888–
　　1976)　徐炳旭 (徐旭生)
Xu Guang　徐廣
Xuanzong　玄宗
Xue Ju　薛舉
Xue Mo　薛莫
Xue Ren'gao　薛仁杲
Xuejiagang Culture　薛家崗
　　文化
Ya Qi　亞其
Yang Guifei　楊貴妃
Yang Xin Jia　陽信家
Yang Xuanlue　楊玄略
Yangshao Culture　仰韶文化

Yaozhou　耀州
ye shi　野史
Yi　乙
Yi (Archer)　羿
Yi Gong　乙公
yi gu pai　疑古派
Yi Zu　乙祖
yiguo yiguan　一椁一棺
Yin　殷
Yingcheng　郢稱
Yingqi　嬰齊
Yinwu　殷武
Yinxu　殷墟
yin-yang　陰陽
yinyang wuxing　陰陽五行
Yiwu Army　義武軍
Yiyin　伊尹
yong　用
Yongle　永樂
you　圅
Yu　遹
Yu　禹
Yu Xingwu (1896–1984)
　　于省吾
Yu Yin　于隱
Yuan　沅
Yuan dynasty　元朝
Yuan Fuli (1893–1987)
　　袁復禮
Yuan Kang　袁康
Yuan Zi Feng　蓮子馮
Yuanmou Man　元謀人
Yue　邙
yuexing　刖刑
yunwen　雲紋
Yuxiong　鬻熊
Zaolütai Culture　造律台
　　文化
Zazhan　雜占
Ze Ji　仄姬
Zenghou Yi (Marquis Yi of
　　Zeng)　曾侯乙
Zenghou Yi mu　曾侯乙墓
Zhang Qian　張騫
Zhang Wenzao　張文藻

Zhao Dejun　趙德均
Zhao Hu　趙胡
Zhao Mo　趙眛
Zhao Tuo　趙佗
Zhaobaogou Culture　趙寶
　　溝文化
Zhaoling　昭陵
Zhe　折
zhen mu shou　鎮墓獸
Zheng Xuan　鄭玄
Zheng Zhenduo (1898–1958)
　　鄭振鐸
zhengjing bushi　正經補史
zhong qi　重器
Zhongshan　中山
Zhou dynasty　周朝
Zhou Gong　周公
Zhou Ji　周姬
Zhou Wenju　周文矩
Zhou Xin　紂辛
Zhouyuan　周原
zhu　祝
Zhu Wen　朱溫
Zhujuntu　駐軍圖
Zhurong　祝融
zi　梓
Zige　子革
Ziyang Man　資陽人
Zu Xin　祖辛
zuo yin　左尹
Zuoce　作冊
Zuoshiku gong　左使庫工
zuoweishi　左衛使
zuxiang　足箱

ORNAMENTS, VESSELS,
WEAPONS, AND MUSICAL
INSTRUMENTS

ben　錛 (磻)
bi　匕
bi　璧
bian　籩
bianzhong　編鐘
bo　鉢
bo　鎛
boshan lu　博山爐
chan　鏟
Chu Ji Gou pan　楚季苟盤
Chu Wang Xiong Shen zhan
　　楚王酓 (熊) 審盞
Chu Wang Xiong Zhang bo
　　楚王酓 (熊) 章鎛
Chu Yin pan　楚嬴盤
Chu Yin yi　楚嬴匜
cong　琮
Da Ke ding　大克鼎
Da Yu ding　大盂鼎
Deng Zhong Xi zun　弄仲犧尊
ding　鼎
Dong fangding jia　戉方鼎甲
Dong gui　戉簋
dou　豆
dun　敦
Ejun Qi jie　鄂君啓節
erbei　耳杯
fang　鈁
fangding　方鼎
fangjia　方斝
fangxiang　方響
fangyi　方彝
fangyou　方卣
Feng you　豐卣
Feng zun　豐尊
fou　缶
fu　甫
fu　斧
fu　簠
gang　缸
ge　戈

gong (guang) 觥

gu 觚

gu 鼓

guan 罐

gui 簋

gui 簠

he 盉

he 盒

hu 壺

hu (ji blade) 胡

hu pipa 胡琵琶

huang 璜

Hui gui 誨簋

huoding 鑊鼎

ji 箕

ji 戟

jia 斝

jian 劍

jian-fou 鑒缶

jian gu 建鼓

jiao 角

jin 禁

jin shu 晉殳

jue 爵

Jue Cao ding 趠曹鼎

konghou 箜篌

lei 罍

li 鬲

Ling fangyi 令方彝

lu 爐

Lü Fu Yi gu 旅父乙觚

mao 矛

Mao Gong ding 毛公鼎

nao 鐃

niu 鈕

pan 盤

pei 佩

pen 盆

ping 瓶

pipa 琵琶

pou 瓿

pushou 鋪首

qi 戚

qibi 戚璧

qin 琴

qing 磬

Sannian Xing hu 三年瘨壺

Sanlian yan 三聯甗

se 瑟

sheng 笙

sheng 鉶

sheng 盛

Sheng ding 升鼎

shengding 生鼎

Shi Qiang pan 史墻盤

Shisannian Xing hu 十三年
瘨壺

shu 殳

Si Mu Wu fangding 司母戊
方鼎

tang 膛

Tang ding 湯鼎

Xiao Ke ding 小克鼎

Xing xu 瘨盨

xizun 犧尊

xu 須

yan (xian) 甗

yi 彝

yi 匜

yong 甬

yongzhong 甬鐘

you 卣

yu 盂

yu (lifting handles of huoding)
鋊

Yu fou 浴缶

Yu gong 浴觵

yuding 鹽鼎

yue 鉞

zeng 甑

zhan 盞

zhang 璋

Zhe fangyi 折方彝

Zhe jia 折斝

zhen 鎮

zheng 箏

zheng 鉦

zhong 鐘

zhuo 鐲

zu 鏃

zun 尊

zun fou 尊缶

zun-pan 尊盤

Bibliography

Allan 1991. Allan, Sarah. *The Shape of the Turtle: Myth, Art, and Cosmos in Early China*. Albany, 1991.

An 1988. An Zhimin. "Guanyu Liangzhu wenhua de ruogan wenti — wei jinian Liangzhu wenhua faxian wushi zhounian erzuo," *Kaogu* 1988.3, 235–245.

An 1991. An Jiayao "Dated Islamic Glass in China," *Bulletin of the Asia Institute* 5 (1991), 123–135.

An 1993. An Jiayao. "Famensi digong chutu de Yisilan boliqi." In Zhang and Han 1993, 259–265.

An 1998. An Zhimin. "Yuan Fuli zai Zhonguo shiqian kaoguxue shang de gongxian," *Kaogu* 1998.7, 86–94.

Andersson 1871. Andersson, John. *A Report on the Expedition to Western Yunnan via Bhamo.* Calcutta, 1871.

Andersson 1923. Andersson, J. Gunnar. "An Early Chinese Culture," *Bulletin of the Geological Survey of China*, no. 5, pt. 1 (1923), 1–68.

Andersson 1924. Andersson, J. Gunnar. "Arkeologiska fynd i provinsen Kansu," *Ymer* 44 (1924), 24–35.

Andersson 1934. Andersson, J. Gunnar. *Children of the Yellow Earth: Studies in Prehistoric China.* London, 1934.

Andersson 1943. Andersson, J. Gunnar. "Researches into the Prehistory of the Chinese," *Bulletin of the Museum of Far Eastern Antiquities* 15 (1943), 7–304.

Anhui 1953. Anhui sheng bowuguan choubeichu, ed. *Anhui sheng bowuguan choubeichu suo chang Chuqi tulu*, vol. 1, 1953.

Anhui 1956. Anhui sheng wenwu guanli weiyuanhui. *Shouxian Caihou mu chutu yiwu*. Beijing, 1956.

Anhui 1982a. Anhui sheng bowuguan. "Qianshan Xuejiagang xinshiqi shidai yizhi," *Kaogu xuebao* 1982.3, 283–324.

Anhui 1982b. Anhui sheng wenwu gongzuodui. "Anhui Changfeng Yanggong fajue jiu zuo Zhanguo mu," *Kaoguxue jikan* 1982.2, 47–60.

Anhui 1987. Anhui sheng bowuguan. *Anhui sheng bowuguan cang qingtongqi*. Shanghai, 1987.

Anhui 1989. Anhui sheng wenwu kaogu yanjiusuo. "Anhui Hanshan Lingjiatan xinshiqi shidai mudi fajue jianbao," *Wenwu* 1989.4, 1–30.

Asahi 1998. Asahi Xinbunsha. *Sanseitai — Chūkoku 5000 nein no nazo, kyōi no kamen ōkoku*. Tokyo, 1998.

Bagley 1977. Bagley, Robert W. "P'an-lung-ch'eng: A Shang City in Hupei," *Artibus Asiae* 39 (1977), 165–219.

Bagley 1987. Bagley, Robert W. *Shang Ritual Bronzes in the Arthur M. Sackler Collections*. New York, 1987.

Bagley 1988. Bagley, Robert W. "Sacrificial Pits of the Shang Period at Sanxingdui in Sichuan Province," *Arts Asiatiques* 43 (1988), 78–86.

Bagley 1990. Bagley, Robert W. "A Shang City in Sichuan Province," *Orientations* 21 (November, 1990), 52–67.

Bagley 1993. Bagley, Robert W. "An Early Bronze Age Tomb in Jiangxi Province." *Orientations* 24 (July, 1993), 20–36.

Baker 1998. Baker, Janet, ed. *The Flowering of a Foreign Faith: New Studies in Chinese Buddhist Art*. New Delhi, 1998.

Bao 1979. Bao Quan. "Quanguo zhongdian wenwu baohu danwei: Xi Zhou ducheng Feng Hao yizhi," *Wenwu* 1979.10, 68–70.

Behr 1996. Behr, Wolfgang. "Reimende Bronzeinschriften und die Entstehung der chinesischen Endreimdichtung." Ph.D. diss., Johann Wolfgang Goethe-Universität, 1996.

Beijing 1954. Zhongguo lishi bowuguan. *Chu wenwu zhanlan tulu*. Beijing, 1954.

Beijing 1994. Beijing daxue kaogu xuexi *et al.* "Tianma — Qucun yizhi Beizhao Jinhou mudi dier ci fajue," *Wenwu* 1994.1, 4–28.

Beijing 1995. Beijing shi wenwu yanjiusuo. *Liulihe Xizhou Yanguo mudi*. Beijing, 1995.

Berger 1994. Berger, Patricia Ann, *et al. Tomb Treasures from China: The Buried Art of Ancient Xi'an.* San Francisco, 1994.

Birrell 1993. Birrell, Anne. *Chinese Mythology: An Introduction*. Baltimore and London, 1993.

Black 1925. Black, Dividson. "The Human Skeletal Remains from Sha Kuo T'un in Comparison with Those from Yang Shao T'sun," *Palaeontologia Sinica*, ser. D, vol. 1, fasc. 3, 1925.

Black 1927. Black, Dividson. "The Lower Molar Hominid Tooth from the Chou K'ou Tien Deposit," *Palaeontologia Sinica*, ser. D, vol. 7, fasc. 1, 1927.

Black 1931. Black, Dividson. "On the Adolescent Skull of Sinanthropus Pekinensis," *Palaeontologia Sinica*, ser. D, vol. 7, fasc. 2, 1931.

Blakeley 1988. Blakeley, Barry B. "In Search of Danyang I: Historical Geography and Archaeological Sites," *Early China* 13 (1988), 116–152.

Blakeley 1990. Blakeley, Barry B. "On the Location of the Chu Capital in Early Chunqiu Times in Light of the Handong Incident of 701 BC," *Early China* 15 (1990), 49–70.

Blakeley 1992. Blakeley, Barry B. "King, Clan, and Courtier in Ancient Chu," *Asia Major*, 3d ser. 5.2 (1992), 1–40.

Blunden and Elvin 1988. Blunden, Caroline and Mark Elvin. *Cultural Atlas of China*. New York, 1988.

Bodde 1975. Bodde, Derk. *Festivals in Classical China: New Year and Other Annual Observances during the Han Dynasty (206 B.C.–A.D. 220)*. Princeton, 1975.

Bodde 1986. Bodde, Derk. "The State and Empire of Ch'in." In Twitchett and Loewe 1986, 20–98.

Boltz 1994. Boltz, William G. *The Origin and Early Development of the Chinese Writing System*. New Haven, 1994.

Boule 1928. Boule, M., H. Breuil, E. Licent, and P. Teilhard de Chardin. *Le Paléolithique de la Chine, Archives de l'Institut de Paléontologie Humaine, Mémoire* 4:1–138, Paris, 1928.

Bowie 1966. Bowie, Theodore. *Langdon Warner through His Letters*. Bloomington, 1966.

Brashier 1995. Brashier, K. E. "Longevity Like Metal and Stone: The Role of the Mirror in Han Burials," *T'oung Pao* 81 (1995), 201–229.

Breuil 1931. Breuil, Henri-Edouard-Prosper. "Le feu et l'industrie lithique et osseuse à Chou K'ou Tien," *Bulletin of the Geological Survey of China*, vol. 11, no. 2 (1931), 147–154.

Brill and Fenn 1993. Brill, Robert H., and Philip M. Fenn. "Famensi boliqi." In Zhang and Han 1993, 254–258.

Brinker and Goepper 1980. Brinker, Helmut, and Roger Goepper. *Kunstschätze aus China*. Zurich, 1980.

Bunker 1998. Bunker, Emma C. "Cultural Diversity in the Tarim Basin Vicinity and Its Impact on Ancient Chinese Culture." In Mair 1998, 2:604–618.

Cai 1986. Cai Yonghua. "Suizang mingqi guankui," *Kaogu yu Wenwu* 1986.2, 74–78.

Cao 1998. Cao Bingwu. "Quxi leixing xueshuo yu Zhongguo kaoguxue de fazhan," *Zhongyuan wenwu* 1998.1, 110–117.

Capon 1992. Capon, Edmund, *et al. Imperial China: the Living Past.* Sydney, 1992.

Ch'en 1964. Ch'en, Kenneth K. S. *Buddhism in China: A Historical Survey*. Princeton, 1964.

Chang 1969. Chang Kwang-chih, *et al. Fengpitou, Tapenkeng and the Prehistory of Taiwan*. New Haven, 1969.

Chang 1971. Chang, Hao. *Liang Ch'i-ch'ao and Intellectual Transition in China, 1890–1907*. Cambridge, 1971.

Chang 1977. Chang Kwang-chih. "Chinese Archaeology Since 1949," *Journal of Asian Studies*, vol. 36, no. 4 (1977), 623–646.

Chang 1980. Chang Kwang-chih. *Shang Civilization*. New Haven, 1980.

Chang 1983. Chang Kwang-chih. *Art, Myth and Ritual: The Path to Political Authority in Ancient China*. Cambridge, Mass., 1983.

Chang 1986a. Chang Kwang-chih. *The Archaeology of Ancient China.* 4th ed. New Haven, 1986.

Chang 1986b. Chang Kwang-chih, ed. *Studies of Shang Archaeology: Selected Papers from the International Conference on Shang Civilization.* New Haven, 1986.

Chang 1989. Chang Kwang-chih, "An Essay on Cong," *Orientations* 6 (1989), 37–43.

Chase 1991. Chase, William Thomas. *Ancient Chinese Bronze Art: Casting the Precious Sacral Vessel.* New York, 1991.

Chavannes 1913. Chavannes, Édouard. *Les Documents Chinois.* Oxford, 1913.

Chen 1936. Chen Mengjia. "Zhougong Dan fuzi kao," *Jinling xuebao* 1936.10 (1–2), 113–18.

Chen 1956. Chen Mengjia. *Yinxu buci zongshu.* Beijing, 1956.

Chen 1980a. Chen Zhenyu. "Tan huzuo niaojia gu," *Jianghan kaogu* 1980.1, 65–68.

Chen 1980b. Chen Xianyi. "Jiangling Zhangjiashan yizhi de shijue yu tansuo," *Jianghan kaogu* 1980.2, 77–86.

Chen 1986. Chen Zhida. "Yinxu yuqi de gongyi kaocha." In *Zhongguo kaoguxue yanjiu: Xia Nai xian-sheng kaogu wushi nian jinian lun-wenji.* Beijing, 1986, 210–219.

Chen 1992. Cheng Quanfang *et al. Xi'an: Legacies of Ancient Chinese Civilization.* Beijing, 1992.

Chen 1995. Chen Zhaorong. "Zhanguo zhi Qin de fujie — yi shiwu ziliao wei zhu," *Zhongyang yanjiuyuan lishi yuyan yanjiusuo jikan* 1995.66(1), 305–366.

Chen 1998. Chen Honghai, *et al.* "Shilun Zongri yizhi de wenhua xingzhi," *Kaogu* 1998.5, 15–26.

Chen and Lu 1985. Chen Mengdong and Lu Guilan. "Qinling bingy-ong jueji kao," *Wenbo* 1985.1, 14–20.

Chen and Ruan 1983. Chen Yaojun and Ruan Wenqing. "Zhen-mushou luekao," *Jianghan kaogu* 1983.3, 63–67.

Chen Wei 1983. Chen Wei. "Xichuan Xiasi erhao Chumu muzhu ji xiangguan wenti," *Jianghan kaogu* 1983.1, 32–33 and 37.

Chen Wei 1986. Chen Wei. "'Ejun Qi jie' zhi 'E' di tantao," *Jianghan kaogu* 1986.2, 88–90.

Chen Wei 1989. Chen Wei. "Ejun Qi jie yu Chuguo de mianshui wenti," *Jianghan kaogu* 1989.3, 52–58.

Chen Xingcan 1991. Chen Xingcan. "Antesheng yu Zhongguo shiqian kaoguxue de zaoqi yan-jiu," *Huaxia Kaogu* 1991.4, 39–49, (part 1); 1992.1, 83–95 (part 2).

Chen Xingcan 1997. Chen Xingcan. *Zhongguo shiqian kaoguxueshi yanjiu.* Beijing, 1997.

Chen and Zhang 1982. Chen Yaojun and Zhang Xuqiu. "Jiangling Mazhuan yihao mu chutu de Zhanguo sizhipin," *Wenwu* 1982.10, 9–11.

Cheng 1965. Cheng Te-k'un. "Archaeology in Communist China," *The China Quarterly* 23 (1965), 67–77.

Cheng and Liu 1983. Cheng Xinren and Liu Binhui. "Guzhan xiaoyi," *Jianghan kaogu* 1983.1, 74–76.

Cheung 1981. Cheung Kwong-yue. "Cong xinchutu de cailiao chongxin tantao Zhongguo wenzi qiyuan," *Xianggang zhong-wen daxue Zhongguo wenhua yan-jiusuo xuebao* 1981.12, 91–151.

Childs-Johnson 1991. Childs-Johnson, Elizabeth. "Jades of the Hongshan Culture: The Dragon and Fertility Cult Worship," *Arts Asiatiques* 56 (1991), 82–95.

China Cultural Relics Promotion Center 1992. China Cultural Relics Promotion Center, eds. *Treasures: 300 Best Excavated Antiques from China.* Beijing, 1992.

Chow 1960. Chow Tse-tsung. *The May Fourth Movement: Intellectual Revolution in Modern China.* Cambridge, 1960.

Chu 1954. Chu wenwu zhanlanhui, ed. *Chu wenwu zhanlan tulu.* Beijing, 1954.

Chunhua 1980. Chunhua xian wen-huaguan. "Shaanxi Chunhua Shijiayuan chutu Xi Zhou dad-ing," *Kaogu yu wenwu* 1980.2, 17–20.

Cotterell 1981. Cotterell, Arthur. *Der Erste Kaiser von China. Der größte archäologische Fund unserer Zeit.* Frankfurt, 1981.

Dai 1996. Dai Qing [Nancy Liu and Lawrence R. Sullivan trans.]. "Interview with Yu Weichao," *Orientations,* vol. 27, no. 7 (1996), 62–64.

Dai 1998. Dai Xiangming. *Kaogu xue-bao* 1998.4, 389–418.

Daniel 1975. Daniel, Glyn Edmund. *A Hundred and Fifty Years of Archaeology.* London, 1975.

Dazu 1984. Dazu xian wenwu baoguansuo. *Dazu shiku.* Beijing, 1984.

Deng 1992. Deng Shupin. "Long xi? Feng xi? you liang jian xin gongbu de Hongshan yuqi tanqi," *Gugong wenwu yuekan* 1992.114 (September), 4–11.

Di Cosmo 1999. Di Cosmo, Nicola. "The Northern Frontier in Pre-Imperial China." In Loewe and Shaughnessy 1999, 885-966.

Dien 1985. Dien, Albert E., Jeffrey K. Riegel, and Nancy T. Price. *Chinese Archaeological Abstracts. 3: Eastern Zhou to Han.* Los Angeles, 1985.

Dien 1999. Dien, Albert E. "Images of Dynasty: China's Golden Age of Archaeology," *Archaeology* (March/April 1999), 60–69.

Dirlik 1989. Dirlik, Arif. *Revolution and History — Origins of Marxist Historiography in China, 1919–1937.* Berkeley, 1989.

Du 1993. Du Zhengsheng. "Ouya caoyuan dongwu wenshi yu Zhongguo gudai beifang minzu zhi kaocha," *Zhongyang yanji-uyuan lishi yuyan yanjiusuo jikan* 1993.64(2), 231–408.

Du 1994. Du Jinpeng. "Lun Linqu Zhufeng Longshan wenhua yu guan shi ji xiangguan wenti," *Kaogu* 1994.1, 55–65.

Du 1998. Du Jinpeng. "Hongshan wenhua 'gouyunxing' lei yuqi tantao," *Kaogu* 1998.5, 50–64 and 81.

Dunhuang 1982. *Dunhuang yishu yan-jiusuo.* Beijing 1982.

Elisseeff 1986. Elisseeff, Danielle. *China: Treasures and Splendors.* Montreal, 1986.

Engels 1884. Engels, Friedrich. *Der Ursprung der Familie, des Privateigentums, und des Staates,* Zurich, 1884. (English trans. *The Origin of the Family, Private Property and the State,* Chicago, 1902).

Erickson 1992. Erickson, Susan N. "*Boshanlu* — Mountains Censers of the Western Han Period: A Typological and Iconological Analysis," *Archives of Asian Art* 45 (1992), 6–28.

Erickson 1994. Erickson, Susan N. "'Twirling Their Long Sleeves, They Dance Again and Again …' Jade Plaque Sleeve Dancers of the Western Han Dynasty," *Ars Orientalis* 24 (1994), 39–63.

Evans 1981. Evans, John D., Barry Cunliffe, and Colin Renfrew, eds. *Antiquity and Man: Essays in Honour of Glyn Daniel.* London, 1981.

Fairbank 1978. Fairbank, John King, ed. *The Cambridge History of China.* Vol. 10: *Late Ch'ing, 1800–1911,* part 1. New York, 1978.

Fairbank 1983. Fairbank, John King, ed. *The Cambridge History of China.* Vol. 12: *Republican China 1912–1949,* part 1. New York, 1983.

Fairbank and Feuerwerker 1986. Fairbank, John King, and Albert Feuerwerker, eds. *The Cambridge History of China.* Vol. 13: *Republican China 1912–1949,* part 2. New York, 1986.

Falkenhausen 1988. Falkenhausen, Lothar von. "Ritual Music in Bronze Age China: An Archaeological Perspective." Ph. D. diss., Harvard University, 1988.

Falkenhausen 1990. Falkenhausen, Lothar von. "Ahnenkult und Grabkult im Staat Qin: Der religiöse Hintergrund der Terrakotta-Armee." In Ledderose and Schlombs 1990, 35–48.

Falkenhausen 1992. Falkenhausen, Lothar von. "Serials on Chinese Archaeology Published in the People's Republic of China: A Bibliographic Survey," *Early China* 17 (1992), 247–295.

Falkenhausen 1993a. Falkenhausen, Lothar von. "Issues in Western

Zhou Studies, A Review Article," *Early China* 18 (1993), 139–226.

Falkenhausen 1993b. Falkenhausen, Lothar von. *Suspended Music: Chime-Bells in the Culture of Bronze Age China.* Berkeley, 1993.

Falkenhausen 1994. Falkenhausen, Lothar von. "Sources of Taoism: Reflections on Archaeological Indicators of Religious Change in Eastern Zhou China," *Taoist Resources* 5.2 (1994), 1–12.

Falkenhausen 1995a. Falkenhausen, Lothar von, and Thomas D. Rossing. "Acoustical and Musical Studies on the Sackler Bells." In So 1995, 431–484.

Falkenhausen 1995b. Falkenhausen, Lothar von. "Reflections on the Political Role of Spirit Mediums in Early China: The Wu Officials in the *Zhou Li*," *Early China* 20 (1995), 279–300.

Falkenhausen 1997. Falkenhausen, Lothar von. "Youguan Xizhou wanqi lizhi gaige ji Zhuangbai Weishi qingtongqi niandai de xin jiashe: Cong shixi mingwen shuoqi." In Tsang Cheng-hwa, ed., *Zhongguo kaoguxue yu lishixue zhi zhenghe yanjiu.* Vol. 2. Taipei, 1997, 651–676.

Famensi 1988. Famensi kaogudui. "Fufeng Famensi Tangdai digong fajue jianbao," *Kaogu yu wenwu* 1988.2, 94–106.

Famensi 1994. Famensi bowuguan. *Famensi.* Xi'an, 1994.

Fan 1982. Fan Weiyue. "Shaanxi Lantian faxian yipi Tangdai jinyinqi," *Kaogu yu wenwu* 1982.1, 46–50.

Fan 1983. Fan Yuzhou. "Linru Yancun xinshiqi shidai yizhi chutu taohua 'Guanyu shifu tu' shishi," *Zhongyuan wenwu* 1983.3, 8–10.

Fang 1978. Fang Xiaolian. "Henan Linru Zhongshanzhai xinshiqi shidai yizhi," *Kaogu* 1978.2, 138.

Fang and Liu 1984. Fang Dianchun and Liu Baohua. "Liaoning Fuxin xian Hutougou Hongshan wenhua yuqi mu de faxian," *Wenwu* 1984.6, 1–5.

Feng 1988. Feng Xianming. "Famensi chutu de miseci." In Su Bai *et al.*, "Famensita digong chutu wenwu bitan," *Wenwu* 1988.10, 36–37.

Field and Wang 1997. Field, Edward, and Wang Tao, "Xia Nai: The London Connection," *Orientations* 28. 6 (1997), 38–41.

Fitzgerald-Huber 1981. Fitzgerald-Huber, Louisa G. "The Tradition of Chinese Neolithic Pottery," *Bulletin of the Museum of Far Eastern Antiquities* 53 (1981), 1–256.

Fitzgerald-Huber 1983. Fitzgerald-Huber, Louisa G. "Some Anyang Royal Bronzes: Remarks on Shang Bronze Decor." In Kuwayama 1983, 16–43.

Fitzgerald-Huber 1995. Fitzgerald-Huber, Louisa G. "Qijia and Erlitou: The Question of Contacts with Distant Cultures," *Early China* 20 (1995), 20–21.

Fitzgerald-Huber 1999. Fitzgerald-Huber, Louisa G. "Where Have All the Documents Gone?" Delivered at the "Multiple Origins of Writing" Symposium, held at the University of Pennsylvania, 26–27 March 1999.

Fong 1980. Fong, Wen, ed. *The Great Bronze Age of China.* New York, 1980.

Fong 1992. Fong, Wen. *Beyond Representation: Chinese Painting and Calligraphy, 8ᵗʰ–14ᵗʰ Century.* New York, 1992.

Fong 1996. Fong, Wen, *et al. Possessing the Past: Treasures from the National Palace Museum, Taipei.* New York, 1996.

Freer Gallery 1946. Freer Gallery of Art. *A Descriptive and Illustrative Catalogue of Chinese Bronzes Acquired during the Administration of John Ellerton Lodge.* Washington, D.C. 1946.

Fu 1933. Fu Sinian. "Yi Xia dongxi shuo." In Zhongyang yanjiuyuan lishi yuyan yanjiusuo, ed. *Qingzhu Cai Yuanpei xiansheng liushiwu sui lunwenji.* Beijing, 1933, 2:1093–1134.

Fu 1985. Fu Xianguo. "Shilun Zhongguo xinshiqi shidai de shiyue," *Kaogu* 1985.9, 820–29.

Fu 1980. Fu Xinian. "Zhanguo Zhongshan Wang Cuomu chutu de 'zhaoyutu' ji qi lingyuan guizhi de yanjiu," *Kaogu xuebao* 1980.1, 97–118.

Funakoshi 1972. Funakoshi Akio. "Gaku Kun Kei setsu ni tsuite," *Tōhō gakuhō* 1972.43, 55–95.

Gansu 1974. Gansu sheng bowuguan, "Wuwei Leitai Hanmu," *Kaogu xuebao* 1974.2, 87–109.

Gansu 1979. Gansu sheng bowuguan. *Gansu caitao.* Beijing 1979.

Gansu 1983a. Gansu sheng bowuguan wenwu gongzuodui. "Gansu Qin'an dijiu qu fajue jianbao," *Wenwu* 1983.11, 1–14.

Gansu 1983b. Gansu sheng bowuguan wenwu gongzuodui. "Qin'an Dadiwan 405-hao xinshiqi shidai fangwu yizhi," *Wenwu* 1983.11, 15–19 and 30.

Gansu 1983c. Gansu sheng bowuguan wenwu gongzuodui. "Gansu Qin'an Dadiwan yizhi 1978 zhi 1982 nian fajue de zhuyao shouhuo," *Wenwu* 1983.11, 21–30.

Gansu 1984a. Gansu sheng bowuguan Dadiwan fajue xiaozu. "Gansu Qin'an Wangjiayinwa Yangshao wenhua yizhi de fajue," *Kaogu yu wenwu* 1984.2, 1–17 and 58.

Gansu 1984b. Gansu sheng wenwu gongzuodui. "Gansu Dongxiang Linjia yizhi fajue baogao," *Kaoguxue jikan* 1984.4, 111–161.

Gansu 1986. Gansu sheng wenwu gongzuodui. "Gansu Qin'an Dadiwan 901 hao fangzhi fajue jianbao," *Wenwu* 1986.2, 1–12.

Gao 1979. Gao Guangren. "Dawenkou wenhua de shehui xingzhi yu niandai — Jianyu Tang Lan xiansheng shangque," In Shandong daxue lishixi kaogu jiaoyanshi, ed., 1979, 110–119.

Gao 1984. Gao Ming. "Lun taofu jiantan Hanzi de qiyuan," *Beijing daxue xuebao* (Zhexue shehui kexue ban) 1984.6, 47–60.

Gao 1986. Gao Guangren. "Shandong diqu shiqian wenhua gailun." In Shandong Qilu kaogu congkan bianjibu, *Shandong shiqian wenhua lunwenji.* Jinan, 1986, 42–47.

Gao 1994. Gao Xixing. "Fufeng Juliang Haijia chutu daxing

palong deng qingtongqi," *Wenwu* 1994.2, 92–96 and 91.

Garner 1979 Garner, Sir Harry. *Chinese Lacquer.* London, 1979.

Giès and Cohen 1995. Giès, Jacques, and Monique Cohen. *Sérinde, Terre de Bouddha: Dix siècles d'art sur la Route de la Soie.* Paris, 1995.

Goepper 1996. Goepper, Roger, ed. *Das Alte China. Menschen und Götter im Reich der Mitte. 5000 v. Chr.-220 n. Chr.* Zurich, 1996.

Graham 1989. Graham, Angus Charles. *Disputers of the Tao, Philosophical Argument in Ancient China.* La Salle, 1989.

Gu 1926–1941. Gu Jiegang et al., eds. Gushi bian. 7 vols. Vols. 1–5: Beijing, 1926–1935; vols. 6–7: Shanghai, 1938–1941.

Guan 1929. Guan Baiyi. *Xinzheng guqi tulu.* Shanghai, 1929.

Guangdong 1974. Guangdong sheng bowuguan et al. "Guangdong Zhaoqing shi Beiling Songshan gu mu fajue jianbao," *Wenwu* 1974.11, 67–79.

Guangxi 1978. Guangxi zhuangzu zizhiqu wenwu guanli weiyuanhui. *Guangxi chutu wenwu.* Beijing, 1978.

Guangzhou 1991. Guangzhou shi wenwu guanli weiyuanhui et al. *Xihan Nanyuewang mu.* 2 vols. Beijing, 1991.

Guldin 1990. Guldin, Gregory Eliyu, ed. *Anthropology in China: Defining the Discipline.* Armonk, 1990.

Guldin 1994. Guldin, Gregory Eliyu, ed. *The Saga of Anthropology in China: From Malinowski to Moscow to Mao.* Armonk, 1994.

Guo 1958. Guo Deyong et al. "Gansu Lintao, Linxia laingxian kaogu diaocha jianbao," *Kaogu tongxun* 1958.9, 36–49.

Guo 1982. Guo Dewei. "Jiangling Chumu lunshu," *Kaogu xuebao* 1982.2, 155–182.

Guo 1989. Guo Dashun. "Liaoxi gu wenhua de xin renshi." In Qingzhu Su Bingqi kaogu wushiwu nian lunwen ji bianjizu, ed. *Qingzhu Su Bingqi kaogu wushiwu nian lunwen ji.* Beijing, 1989, 203–215.

Guo 1997. Guo Dashun. "Hongshan wenhua de 'wei yu wei zang' yu

Liaohe wenming qiyuan tezheng zai renshi," *Wenwu* 1997.8, 20–26.

Guo and Zhang 1984. Guo Dashun and Zhang Keju. "Liaoning sheng Kazuo xian Dongshanzui Hongshan wenhua jianzhuqun zhi fajue jianbao," *Wenwu* 1984.11, 1–11.

Guo Baojun 1951. Guo Baojun. "1950 nian chun Yinxu fajue baogao," *Kaogu xuebao* 1951.5, 1–62.

Guo Baojun 1981. Guo Baojun. *Shang Zhou tongqiqun zonghe yanjiu*. Beijing, 1981.

Guo Moruo 1930. Guo Moruo. *Zhongguo gudai shehui yanjiu*. Shanghai, 1930.

Guo Moruo 1956. Guo Moruo. "Jiaoliu jingyan, tigao kaogu gongzuo de shuiping," *Kaogu tongxun* 1956.2, 3–9.

Guo Moruo 1958. Guo Moruo."Guanyu Ejun Qi jie de yanjiu," *Wenwu cankao ziliao* 1958.4, 3–7.

Guo Moruo 1972. Guo Moruo. "Anyang xin chutu de niujiagu jiqi keci," *Kaogu*, 1972.2, 2–11.

Guo Moruo 1978–1982. Guo Moruo et al. *Jiaguwen heji*. 13 vols. 1978–82.

Gushi 1981. Gushi Hougudui yihao mu fajue xiaozu. "Henan Gushi Hougudui yihao mu fajue jianbao," *Wenwu* 1981.1, 1–8.

Hamada and Mizuno 1938. Hamada Kōsaku and Mizuno Seiichi. *Chikihō kōzankō: Manshūkoku netsuga shō Chikihō kōzankō genshi iseki*. Tokyo, 1938.

Han 1988. Han Wei. "Cong yincha fengshang kan Famensi dengdi chutu de Tangdai jinyin chaju," *Wenwu* 1988.10, 44–56.

Han 1989. Han Wei. *Haineiwai Tangdai Jingyinqi cuibian*. Xi'an, 1989.

Han 1995. Han Wei. "Famensi digong jinyinqi zanwen kaoyi," *Kaogu yu wenwu* 1995.1, 71–78.

Han and Zhao 1998. Han Jinke and Zhao Shenxiang. *Famensi*. Qishan, 1998.

Handan 1977. Handan shi wenwu baoguansuo, et al. "Hebei Cishan xinshiqi shidai yizhi shijue," *Kaogu* 1977.6, 361–372.

Hao 1984. Hao Shuping. "Xi'an Banpo bowuguan shoucang de rentou hu," *Shiqian yanjiu* 1984.4, 103.

Hao 1996. Hao Jianwen. "Qiantan Quyang Wudai mu bihua," *Wenwu* 1996.9, 78–79 and 57.

Harper 1999. Harper, Donald. "Warring States Natural Philosophy and Occult Thought." In Loewe and Shaughnessy 1999, 813–884.

Hawkes 1985. Hawkes, David, trans. *The Songs of the South, An Anthology of Ancient Chinese Poems by Qu Yuan and other Poets*. Harmondsworth, 1985.

Hayashi 1983. Hayashi Minao. "In-Shunju zenki kinbun no shoshiki to joyo goku no jidaiteki hensen," *Tōhō gakuhō* 1983.55, 1–101.

Hayashi 1984. Hayashi Minao. *In Shū jidai seidōki no kenkyū*, 2 vols. *In Shū jidai seidōki sōran*, part 1. Tokyo, 1984.

Hayashi 1986. Hayashi Minao. *In Shū jidai seidōki monyō no kenkyū. In Shū jidai seidōki sōran*, part 2. Tokyo, 1986.

Hayashi 1988a. Hayashi Minao, "Chūgoku kodai no gyokki, sō ni tsuite," *Tōhō gakuhō* 1988.60, 1–72.

Hayashi 1988b. Hayashi Minao. *Shunjū Sengoku jidai seidōki no kenkyū. In Shū jidai seidōki sōran*, part 3. Tokyo, 1988.

Hayashi 1990. Hayashi Minao. "Hongshan wenhua chutu de suowei matixing yugu," *Zhongguo wenwu bao* 1990.5, 10.

He 1985. He Jisheng."Guangdong faxian de jizuo Dongzhou muzang," *Kaogu* 1985.4, 360–364.

He 1994. He Nu. "Hubei Jiangling Beinongchang chutu Shang Zhou qingtongqi," *Wenwu* 1994.9, 86–91.

Hearn 1980. Hearn, Maxwell. "The Terracotta Army of the First Emperor of Qin (221–206 BC)." In Fong 1980, 353–373.

Hebei 1979. Hebei sheng wenwu guanlichu. "Hebei sheng Pingshan xian Zhanguo shiqi Zhongshan guo muzang fajue jianbao," *Wenwu* 1979.1, 1–31.

Hebei 1995. Hebei sheng wenwu yanjiusuo. *Cuomu: Zhanguo Zhongshuan guo guowang zhi mu*. 2 vols. Beijing, 1995.

Hebei 1996a. Hebei sheng wenwu yanjiusuo. "Hebei Quyang Wudai mu fajue jianbao," *Wenwu* 1996.9, 4–13.

Hebei 1996b. Hebei sheng wenwu yanjiusuo. "Hebei Xuanhua Liao Zhang Wenzao bihua mu fajue jianbao," *Wenwu* 1996.9, 14–46.

Hebei 1998. Hebei sheng wenwu kaogu yanjiusuo. *Wudai Wang Chuzhi mu*. Beijing, 1998.

Hedin 1943–1945. Hedin, Sven Anders, *et al. History of the Expedition in Asia (1927–1935)*, 4 vols. Stockholm, 1943–1945.

Hemudu 1980. Hemudu yizhi kaogudui. "Zhejiang Hemudu yizhi dierqi fajue de zhuyao shouhuo," *Wenwu* 1980.5, 1–15.

Henan 1958. Henan sheng wenhuaju wenwu gongzuodui diyidui. "Zhengzhou Kelawangcun yizhi fajue baogao," *Kaogu xuebao* 1958.3, 41–62.

Henan 1959. Henan sheng wenhuaju wenwu gongzuodui *Zhengzhou Erligang*. Beijing, 1959.

Henan 1977. Henan sheng bowuguan, *et al*. "Zhengzhou Shangdai chengzhi shiju jianbao," *Wenwu* 1977.1, 21–31.

Henan 1980. Henan sheng Danjiang kuqu wenwu fajuedui. "Henan sheng Xichuan xian Xiasi Chunqiu Chumu," *Wenwu* 1980.10, 13–20.

Henan 1981. Henan chutu Shang Zhou qingtongqi bianji weiyuanhui. *Henan chutu Shang Zhou qingtongqi*. Vol. 1. Beijing, 1981.

Henan 1983. Henan sheng wenwu yanjiusuo. "Dengfeng Wangchenggang yizhi de fajue," *Wenwu* 1983.3, 8–16.

Henan 1984. Henan Xinyang diqu wenguanhui and Guangshan xian wenguanhui. "Chunqiu zaoqi Huang Jun Meng fufu mu fajue baogao," *Kaogu* 1984.4, 302–332.

Henan 1986. Henan sheng wenwu yanjiu suo. *Xinyang Chumu*. Beijing, 1986.

Henan 1988. Henan sheng wenwu yanjiusuo. "Pingdingshan shi Beizhicun liang Zhou mudi yihaomu fajue jianbao,"*Huaxia kaogu* 1988.1, 30–44.

Henan 1989. Henan sheng wenwu yanjiusuo. "Henan Wuyang Jiahu xinshiqi shidai yizhi dier zhi liuci fajue jianbao," *Wenwu* 1989.1, 1–14 and 47.

Henan 1991. Henan sheng wenwu yanjiusuo et al. *Xichuan Xiasi Chunqiu Chumu*. Beijing, 1991.

Henan 1993. Henan sheng wenwu yanjiusuo. *Zhengzhou Shang cheng kaogu xinfajian, 1985–1992*. Beijing, 1993.

Henan 1995a. Henan sheng wenwu kaogu yanjiusuo. *Ruzhou Hongshanmiao*. Zhengzhou, 1995.

Henan 1995b. Henan sheng wenwu kaogu yanjiusuo. *Wenwu* 1995.1, 4–31.

Henan 1996. Henan sheng wenwu kaogu yanjiusuo. "Henan Yichuan xian Nanzhai Erlitou wenhua muzang fajue jianbao," *Kaogu* 1996.12, 36–43.

Higuchi and Enjōji 1984. Higuchi Takayasu and Enjōji Jirō, eds. *Chūgoku seidōki hyakusen*. Tokyo, 1984.

Hopkirk 1980. Hopkirk, Peter. *Foreign Devils on the Silk Road*. London, 1980.

Hou 1995. Hou Dejun. *Chu guo de kuangye, xiuqi he boli zhizao*. Wuhan, 1995.

Hu 1956. Hu Shih. *Ding Wenjiang de Zhuanji*. Taipei, 1956.

Hu 1982. Hu Qianying. "Feng Hao kaogu gongzuo sanshinian (1951–1981) de huigu," *Kaogu* 1982.10, 57–67.

Hu Lingui 1987, "Zaoqi Qin yong jianshu," *Wenbo* 1987.1, 23–35.

Hua 1952. Hua Gang. *Wusi yundong shi*. Shanghai, 1952.

Hua 1994. Hua Yubin. "Niuheliang Nüshenmiao pingtai dongpo tongxingqi qun yicun fajue jianbao," *Wenwu* 1994. 5, 54–59 and 82.

Huang 1972. Huang, Philip C. *Liang Ch'i-ch'ao and Modern Chinese Liberalism*. Seattle, 1972.

Huang 1979. Huang Jinglüe. "Shandong Juxian faxian woguo zuizao xiangxing wenzi,"

Zhongguo lishixue nianjian (1979) (1980), 126.

Huang 1981. Huang Shilin. "Xu Xusheng xiansheng zai lishixue shangde gongxian," *Kaogu* 1981.4, 383 – 384.

Huang 1982. Huang Shengzhang. *Lishi dili lunji.* Beijing, 1982.

Huang 1985. Huang Nengfu, ed. *Zhongguo meishu quanji. Gongyi meishu bian 6: Yinran zhixiu,* vol. 1.6, Beijing, 1985.

Huang 1997. Huang Yongchuan. *Fodiao zhi mei: Beichao Fojiao shidiao yishu.* Taipei, 1997.

Huang 1998. Huang Zhanyue. "Handai zhuhou wang mu lun-shu," *Kaogu xuebao* 1998.1, 11 – 34.

Hubei 1966. Hubei sheng wenhuaju wenwu gongzuodui. "Hubei Jiangling sanzuo chumu chutu dapi zhongyao wenwu," *Wenwu* 1966.5, 33 – 55.

Hubei 1972. Hubei sheng bowuguan. "Hubei Jingshan faxian Zengguo tongqi," *Wenwu* 1972.2, 47 – 53.

Hubei 1973. Hubei sheng bowuguan et al. "Hubei jiangling paima shan chumu fajue jianbao," *Kaogu* 1973.3, 151 – 161.

Hubei 1976. Hubei sheng bowuguan et al. "Panlongcheng 1974 nian-du tianyekaogu jiyao, " *Wenwu* 1976.2, 5 – 15.

Hubei 1982. Hubei sheng Jingzhou diqu bowuguan. "Jiangling Tianxingguan yihao Chumu," *Kaogu xuebao* 1982.1, 71 – 116.

Hubei 1984a. Hubei sheng Jingzhou diqu bowuguan. *Jiangling Yutaishan Chumu.* Beijing, 1984.

Hubei 1984b. Hubei sheng bowuguan Jiangling gongzuozhan. "Jiangling xie shan chumu," *Kaogu* 1984.6, 515 – 527.

Hubei 1985a. Hubei sheng Jingzhou diqu bowuguan. *Jiangling Mashan yihao chumu.* Beijing, 1985.

Hubei 1985b. Hubei sheng bowuguan. "Hubei Suizhou Leigudun erhao mu fajue jian-bao," *Wenwu* 1985.1, 16 – 36.

Hubei 1988. Hubei sheng Yichang diqu bowuguan. "Dangyag Caojiagang wuhao chumu," *Kaogu xuebao* 1988.4, 455 – 499.

Hubei 1989. Hubei sheng bowuguan. *Zenghou Yi mu.* 2 vols. Beijing, 1989.

Hubei 1991. Hubei sheng Jingsha tielu kaogudui. *Baoshan Chumu,* 2 vols. Beijing, 1991.

Hubei 1992. Hubei sheng Yichang diqu bowuguan et al. *Dangyang Zhaojiahu Chumu.* Beijing, 1992.

Hubei 1993. Hubei sheng Jingzhou diqu bowuguan. "Jiangling Gaotai 18 hao mu fajue jian-bao," *Wenwu* 1993.8,12 – 20.

Hubei 1994. Hubei sheng bowuguan et al. *Hubei chutu Zhanguo Qin Han qiqi.* Hong Kong, 1994.

Hubei 1995a. Hubei sheng wenwu kaogu yanjiusuo. *Jiangling Jiudian Dongzhou mu.* Beijing, 1995.

Hubei 1995b. Hubei sheng wenwu kaogu yanjiusuo et al. *Wangshan Chujian.* Beijing, 1995.

Hubei 1995c. Hubei sheng wenwu kaogu yanjiushuo et al. "Hubei Xiangfan Zhenwushan Zhoudai yizhi," *Kaoguxue jikan* 1995.9, 138 – 161.

Hubei 1996. Hubei sheng wenwu kaogu yanjiusuo. *Jiangling Wangshan Shazhong Chumu.* Beijing, 1996.

Hunan 1972. Hunan sheng bowuguan. "Changsha Liuchengqiao yihao mu," *Kaogu xuebao* 1972.1, 59 -72.

Hunan 1973. Hunan sheng bowuguan et al. *Changsha Mawangdui yihao Hanmu.* 2 vols. Beijing, 1973.

Hunan 1983. Hunan sheng bowuguan, ed. *Hunan sheng bowuguan.* Beijing, 1983.

Idemitsu 1995. Idemitsu Museum of Arts. *Unearthed Treasures of China from the Collection of Arthur M. Sackler Museum of Art and Archaelogy.* Tokyo 1995.

Jacobson 1988. Jacobson, Esther. "Beyond the Frontier: A Reconsideration of Cultural Interchange Between China and the Early Nomads," *Early China* 13 (1988), 201 – 240.

Jia 1950. Jia Lanpo. *Zhongguo yuan-ren.* Beijing, 1950.

Jiangling 1989. Jiangling xian wen-wuju. "Hubei Jiangling wuchang yidi chumu," *Wenwu* 1989.3, 35 – 50 and 62.

Jiangsu 1984. Jiangsu sheng wenwu guanli weiyuanhui et al. "Shaoxing 306 hao Zhanguo mu fajue jianboa," *Wenwu* 1984.1, 10 – 28.

Jiangxi 1980. Jiangxi sheng lishi bowuguan. "Jiangxi Jing'an chutu Chunqiu Xuguo qing-tongqi," *Wenwu* 1980.8, 13 – 15.

Jiangxi 1997. Jiangxi sheng wenwu kaogu yanjiusuo et al. *Xingan Shangdai damu.* Beijing, 1997.

Jiang 1995. Jiang Yuxiang, ed. *Gudai xinan sichou zhilu yanjiu.* Chengdu, 1995.

Jin 1988. Jin Weinuo, ed. *Zhongguo meishu quanji. Diaosu bian 1: Yuanshi shehui zhi Zhanguo diaosu.* Beijing, 1988.

Jin 1995. Jin Zhengyao et al. "Guanghan Sanxingdui yiwu keng qingtongqi de qian tong-weisu bizhi yanjiu," *Wenwu* 1995.2, 80 – 85.

Jing and Wang 1997. Jing Zengli and Wang Xiaomeng. "Fuping xian xin faxian de tangmu bihua," *Kaogu yu wenwu* 1997.4, 8 – 11.

Jingmen 1998. Jingmen shi bowuguan. *Guodian Chumu jian-jie.* Beijing, 1998.

Jingzhou 1973. Jingzhou diqu bowuguan. "Hubei Jiangling Tengdian yihao mu fajue jian-bao," *Wenwu* 1973.9, 7 – 17.

Jingzhou 1982. Jingzhou diqu bowuguan. "Hubei Jiangling Mashan zhuanchang yihao mu chutu dapi zhanguo shiqi sizhipin," *Wenwu* 1982.10, 1 – 8.

Jingzhou 1987. Jingzhou diqu bowuguan. "Hubei Songzi Boyushan yizhi shijue jianbao" *Wenwu ziliao congkan* 1987.10, 32 – 38.

Jingzhou 1989. Jingzhou diqu bowuguan et al. "Hubei Jiangling Jingnansi yizhi diyi, erci fajue jianbao," *Kaogu* 1989.8, 679 – 692 and 698.

Juliano 1975. Juliano, Annette L. "Three Large Ch'u Graves Recently Excavated in the Chiang-ling District of Hupei Province," *Artibus Asiae* 37, (1975), 5 – 17.

Kaifeng 1978. Kaifeng diqu wen-guanhui et al. "Henan Xinzheng Peiligang xinshiqi shidai yizhi," *Kaogu* 1978.2, 73 – 79.

Kane 1974 – 1975. Kane, Virginia C. "The Independent Bronze Industries in the South of China Contemporary with the Shang and Western Chou Dynasties," *Archives of Asian Art* 28 (1974 – 1975), 77 – 107.

Karlbeck 1926. Karlbeck, Orvar. *Notes on Some Chinese Bronze Mirrors.* Shanghai 1926.

Karlgren 1974. Karlgren, Bernhard. *The Book of Odes: Chinese Text, Transcription and Translation.* Stockholm, 1974.

Kegazawa 1996. Kegazawa Yasunori. "Shilun Famensi chutu de Tangdai wenwu yu 'Yiwuzhang,'" *Wenbo* 1996.1, 58 – 85.

Keightley 1978. Keightley, David N. *Sources of Shang History: The Oracle-Bone Inscriptions of Bronze Age China.* Berkeley, 1978.

Keightley 1983. Keightley, David N. ed. *The Origins of Chinese Civilization.* Berkeley, 1983.

Keightley 1988. Keightley, David N. "Shang Divination and Metaphysics," *Philosophy East and West* 38.4 (October 1988), 367 – 397

Keightley 1989. Keightley, David N. "The Origins of Writing in China: Scripts and Cultural Contexts," In Senner 1989, 171 – 202.

Kesner 1995. Kesner, Ladislav. "Likeness of No One: (Re)pre-senting the First Emperor's Army," *Art Bulletin* 77.1 (1995), 115 – 32.

Kesner 1996. Kesner, Ladislav. *"Real" and "Substitute" in the Early Chinese Mortuary Context: Reading the First Emperor's Necropolis,* delivered at "Mysteries of Ancient China," conference. British Museum, London 1996.

Kidder 1956. Kidder, J. Edward. *Early Chinese Bronzes in The City Art Museum of St. Louis,* St. Louis, 1956.

Klementz 1899. Klementz, D. *Turfan und sein Alterthümer.* St. Petersburg, 1899.

Kohl and Fawcett 1995. Kohl, Philip L., and Clare P. Fawcett. *Nationalism, Politics, and the Practice of Archaeology.* Cambridge, 1995.

Kuhn 1982. Kuhn, Dieter. "The Silk-Workshops of the Shang Dynasty (16th – 11th Century BC)." In Li Guohao 1982, 367 – 408.

Kuhn 1991. Kuhn, Dieter. *Status und Ritus: Das China der Aristokraten von den Anfängen bis zum 10. Jahrhundert nach Christus.* Heidelberg, 1991.

Kuhn 1992a. Kuhn, Dieter. "Zwischen dem Sarg in der Erdgrube und dem Kammergrab aus Ziegelstein." In Kuhn 1992b, 23-137.

Kuhn 1992b. Kuhn, Dieter, ed. *Arbeitsmaterialien aus chinesischen Ausgrabungsberichten (1988 – 1991) zu Gräbern aus der Han-bis Tang-Zeit.* Heidelberg, 1992.

Kuhn 1993. Kuhn, Dieter, ed. *Chinas goldenes Zeitalter: die Tang-Dynastie (618 – 907 n. Chr.) und das kulturelle Erbe der Seidenstrasse.* Heidelberg, 1993.

Kuhn 1994. Kuhn, Dieter. *Burial in Song China.* Heidelberg, 1994.

Kuhn 1995a. Kuhn, Dieter. "Silk Weaving in Ancient China: From Geometric Figures to Pattern of Pictorial Likeness," *Chinese Science* 12 (1995), 77 – 114.

Kuhn 1995b. Kuhn, Dieter. "Tod und Beerdigung im chinesischen Altertum im Spiegel von Ritualtexten und archäologischen Funden," *Tribus. Jahrbuch des Linden-Museums Stuttgart* 44 (1995), 208 – 267.

Kuhn 1996a. Kuhn, Dieter. "Totenritual und Beerdigungen im chinesischen Altertum." In Goepper 1996, 45-67.

Kuhn 1996b. Kuhn, Dieter. *A Place for the Dead. An Archaeological Documentary on Graves and Tombs of the Song Dynasty (960 – 1279).* Heidelberg, 1996.

Kuwayama 1983. Kuwayama, George, ed. *The Great Bronze Age of China: A Symposium.* Los Angeles, 1983.

Kuwayama 1987. Kuwayama, George. "The Sculptural Development of Ceramic Funerary Figures in China." In *Los Angeles County Museum* 1987, 63 – 93.

Kuwayama 1991. Kuwayama, George, ed. *Ancient Mortuary Traditions of China: Papers on Chinese Ceramic Funerary Sculptures.* Hawaii, 1991.

Kuzmina 1998. Kuzmina, Elena. "Cultural Connections of the Tarim Basin People and Pastoralists of the Asian Steppe in the Bronze Age," in Mair 1998, 1:63 – 93.

LA County Museum 1987. Los Angeles County Museum of Art, et al. *The Quest for Eternity: Chinese Ceramic Sculptures from The People's Republic of China.* Los Angeles, 1987.

Laing 1988-1989. Laing, Ellen J. "Chin 'Tartar' Dynasty (1115-1234) Material Culture," *Artibus Asiae* 49 (1988-1989), 73-126.

Lam 1991. Lam, Peter Y. K. *Jades from the Tomb of the King of Nan Yue.* Hong Kong 1991.

Lawton 1982. Lawton, Thomas. *Chinese Art of the Warring States Period, Change and Continuity, 480 – 222 BC.* Washington, D. C., 1982.

Lawton 1991. Lawton, Thomas, ed. *New Perspectives on Chu Culture During the Eastern Zhou Period.* Washington D. C., 1991.

Ledderose 1990. Ledderose, Lothar and Adele Schlombs, eds. *Jenseits der Grossen Mauer: Der Erste Kaiser von China und Seine Terrakotta-Armee.* München 1990.

Ledderose 1992. Ledderose, Lothar. "Module and Mass Production." In Palace Museum 1992, 821 – 848.

Lee 1998. Lee, Sherman, and Howard Rogers, eds. *China 5,000 Years: Innovation and Transformation in the Arts.* New York, 1998.

Leidy 1998. Leidy, Denise P. "Avalokiteshvara in Sixth-Century China." In Baker 1998, 88 – 103.

Levenson 1959. Levenson, Joseph R. *Liang Ch'i-ch'ao and the Mind of Modern China.* Cambridge, Mass. 1959.

Lewis 1990. Lewis, Mark. *Sanctioned Violence in Early China.* Albany, 1990.

Li 1936. Li Jingdan. "Shouxian Chumu diaocha baogao." In Li Ji, ed. *Tianye kaogu baogao.* 1936, 1:268 – 276.

Li 1982. Li Jixian. *Majiayao wenhua de caitao yishu.* Beijing 1982.

Li 1986a. Li Gongdu. "Liaoning Lingyuan xian Sanguandianzi Chengzishan yizhi shijue bao-gao, " *Kaogu* 1986.6, 497 – 510.

Li 1986b. Li Xiaoding. *Hanzi de qiyuan yu yanbian luncong.* Taipei, 1986.

Li 1995. Li Boqian. "Qianjin zhong de Beijing daxue kaogu xuexi," In Idemitsu 1995, 140 – 142.

Li 1998a. Li Boqian. "Shilun Wucheng wenhua." In *Zhongguo qingtong wenhua jiegou tixi yanjiu.* Beijing, 1998, 218 – 230.

Li 1998b. Li Boqian. "Chenggu tongqi qun yu zaoqi Shu wen-hua." In *Zhongguo qingtong wen-hua jiegou tixi yanjiu.* Beijing, 1998, 260 – 267.

Li Guohao 1982. Li Guohao, ed. *Explorations in the History of Science and Technology in China.* Shanghai, 1982.

Li Ji 1934. Li Ji *et al.*, eds. *Chengziya.* Nanjing, 1934.

Li Ji 1977. Li Ji. *Anyang.* Seattle, 1977.

Li Ling 1981. Li Ling. "'Chu Shuzhisun Peng' jiujing shi shui," *Zhongyuan wenwu* 1981.4, 36 – 37.

Li Ling 1983. Li Ling. "Chuguo tongqi mingwen biannian huishi," *Guwenzi yanjiu* 1983.13, 353 – 397.

Li Ling 1985. Li Ling. *Changsha Zidanku Zhanguo Chuboshu yanjiu.* Beijing, 1985.

Li Ling 1990. Li Ling. "The Formulaic Structure of Chu Divinatory Bamboo Slips," *Early China* 15 (1990), 71 – 86.

Li Ling 1995 – 1996. Li Ling. "An Archaeological Study of Taiyi (Grand One) Worship," *Early Medieval China* 2 (1995 – 1996), 1 – 39.

Li Ling 1996a. Li Ling. "Guwenzi zashi (liangpian)." In *Yu Xingwu jiaoshou bainian danchen jinian-wenji.* Changchun, 1996, 270 – 274.

Li Ling 1996b. Li Ling. "Zailun Xiasi Chumu," *Wenwu* 1996.1, 47 – 60.

Li Ling 1996c. Li Ling. "Zailun Xichuan Xiasi Chumu: du *Xichuan Xiasi Chumu*," *Wenwu* 1996.1, 47 – 60.

Li Ling 1998. Li Ling. "Du jizhong chutu faxian de xuanzhelei gushu." In *Jianbo yanjiu.* vol. 3. Nanjing, 1998, 96 – 104.

Li and Wan 1972. Li Ji and Wan Jiabao. *Yinxu chutu wushisan jian qingtong rongqi zhi yanjiu.* Taipei, 1972.

Li Xueqin 1979a. Li Xueqin. "Xizhou zhongqi qingtongqi de zhongyao biaochi — Zhou Yuan Zhuangbai Qiangjia liangchu qingtongqi jiaocang zonghe yanjiu," *Zhongguo lishi bowuguan guankan* 1979.1, 29 – 36.

Li Xueqin 1979b. Li Xueqin. *The Wonder of Chinese Bronzes.* Beijing, 1979.

Li Xueqin 1985. Li Xueqin. *Eastern Zhou and Qin Civilizations.* trans. K. C. Chang. New Haven and London, 1985.

Li Xueqin 1986. Li Xueqin, ed. *Qingtongqi,* 2 vols. Zhongguo meishu quanji: Gongyi meishu bian, vols. 4 – 5. Beijing, 1986.

Li Xueqin 1987. Li Xueqin. "Lun xinchu Dawenkou wenhua taoqi Fu Hao," *Wenwu* 1987.12, 75 – 80 and 85.

Liang 1959. Liang Qichao, "Zhongguoshi xulun." In Liang Qichao, *Yinbing shi heji,* vol. 3, no. 29, 1 – 10 (Taipei, 1959).

Liang 1995. Liang Zhonghe. "Yuchisi juluo yizhi fajue chengguo leilei," *Zhongguo wenwubao* (9 July 1995), 1.

Liang 1998. Liang Zi. "Tangdai Wensiyuan jiqi jinyinqi; jianlun Wensiyuan shezhi zhi yuanyin ji Famensi digong jinyinqi chandi zhi qubie," *Famensi wenhua yan-jiu tongxun* 1998.12, 300 – 314.

Liang and Feng 1963. Liang Xingpeng and Feng Xiaotang. "Shaanxi Chang'an, Fufeng chutu Xizhou tongqi, " *Kaogu* 1963.8, 413 – 415.

Liang and Gao 1962. Liang Siyong and Gao Quxun. *Houjiazhuang 1001 hao damu,* Taipei, 1962.

Liang and Gao 1965. Liang Siyong and Gao Quxun. *Houjiazhuang 1002 hao damu.* Taipei, 1965.

Liang and Gao 1967. Liang Siyong and Gao Quxun. *Houjiazhuang 1003 hao damu,* Taipei, 1967.

Liang and Gao 1968. Liang Siyong and Gao Quxun. *Houjiazhuang 1217 hao damu.* Taipei, 1968.

Liang and Gao 1970. Liang Siyong and Gao Quxun. *Houjiazhuang di wuben: 1004 hao damu.* Taipei, 1970.

Liang and Gao 1974. Liang Siyong and Gao Quxun. *Houjiazhuang 1500 hao damu.* Taipei, 1974.

Liang and Gao 1976. Liang Siyong and Gao Quxun. *Houjiazhuang 1550 hao damu.* Taipei, 1976.

Liang Siyong 1933. Liang Siyong. "Hougang fajue xiaoji," *Anyang fajue baogao,* no. 4, Shanghai, 1933.

Liang Siyong 1934. Liang Siyong. "Xiaotun, Longshan yu Yangshao." In Fu Sinian, ed. *Qingzhu Cai Yuanpei xiansheng liushiwu sui lunwenji.* Beijing, 1934, 2:555–568.

Liaoning 1986. Liaoning sheng wenwu kaogu yanjiusuo. "Liaoning Niuheliang Hongshan wenhua 'nüshen-miao' yu jishi zhongqun fajue jianbao," *Wenwu* 1986.8, 1–17.

Liaoning 1994. Liaoning sheng wenwu kaogu yanjiusuo, ed. *Zhongguo kaogu wenwu zhi mei: wenming shuguang qi jisi yizhen, Liaoning Hongshan wenhua tanmiao zhong.* Beijing, 1994.

Liaoning 1997a. Liaoning sheng wenwu kaogu yanjiusuo. "Liaoning Niuheliang diwu didian yihaozhong zhongxin damu (M1) fajue jianbao," *Wenwu* 1997.8, 4–8.

Liaoning 1997b. Liaoning sheng wenwu kaogu yanjiusuo. "Liaoning Niuheliang dier didian yihaozhong 21 hao mu fajue jianbao," *Wenwu* 1997.8, 9–14.

Liaoning 1997c. Liaoning sheng wenwu kaogu yanjiusuo. "Liaoning Niuheliang dier didian sihaozhong tongxingi mu de fajue," *Wenwu* 1997.8, 15–19.

Liaoning 1997d. Liaoning sheng wenwu kaogu yanjiusuo, ed. *Niuheliang Hongshan wenhua yizhi yu yuqi jingcui.* Beijing, 1997.

Licent 1932. Licent, E. *Les Collections Néolithiques du Musée Hoang-ho Pai-ho de Tien-tsin.* Tianjin, 1932.

Liebert 1976. Liebert, Gösta. *Iconographic Dictionary of the Indian Religions: Hinduism - Buddhism - Jainism.* Leiden, 1976.

Ligabue 1988. Ligabue, Giancarlo, and Sandro Salvatori, eds. *Bactria: An Ancient Oasis Civilization from the Sands of Afghanistan.* Venice, 1988.

Lin 1965. Lin Yun. "Shuo 'wang'," *Kaogu* 1965.6, 311–312.

Lin 1976. Lin Shimin. "Zhejiang Ningbo shi chutu yipi Tangdai ciqi," *Wenwu* 1976.7, 60–61.

Lin 1978. Lin, Yü-sheng. *The Crisis of Chinese Consciousness: Radical Anti-Traditionalism in the May Fourth Era.* Madison, 1978.

Lin 1983. Lin Yin, trans. *Zhou Li jin zhu jin yi.* 4th ed. Taipei, 1983.

Lin 1986. Lin, Yun. "A Reexamination of the Relationship between Bronzes of the Shang Culture and of the Northern Zone." In Chang 1986, 237–273.

Linru 1981. Linru xian wenhuaguan. "Linru Yancun xinshiqi shidai yizhi diaocha," *Zhongyuan wenwu* 1981.1, 3-5

Linzi 1997. Linzi shi bowuguan, *et al. Linzi Shangwang mudi.* Ji'nan, 1997.

Liu 1935. Liu Jie. *Chuqi tushi: Shouxian suochu Chuqi kaoshi.* Beijing, 1935.

Liu 1972. Liu Dunyuan. "Ji Liangchengzhen yizhi faxian de liang shichi," *Kaogu* 1972. 4, 56–57.

Liu 1987. Liu Xinfang. "Shi 'Xieying'," *Jianghan kaogu* 1987.1, 78–83.

Liu 1990. Liu Bin. "Liangzhu wenhua yucong chutan," *Wenwu* 1990.2, 30–37.

Liu 1995. Liu Binhui. *Chuxi qingtongqi yanjiu.* Wuhan, 1995.

Liu 1996. Liu Xiang *et al. Shang Zhou guwenzi duben.* 2nd ed. Beijing, 1996.

Liu 1998. Liu Guoxiang. "Hongshan wenhua gouyunxing yuqi yanjiu," *Kaogu* 1998.5, 65–79.

Liu Hehui 1982. Liu Hehui. "Ejun Qi jie xintan," *Kaogu yu wenwu* 1982.5, 60–65.

Liu Hehui 1995. Liu Hehui. "Chu wenhua de dongjian." In Zhang Zhengming, *Chu shi.* Wuhan, 1995, 114–132 and 180–209.

Liu Xu 1975. Liu Xu. "Wang Chucun zhuan." In *Jiu Tangshu Juan 182.* Beijing 1975, 182.

Loehr 1965. Loehr, Max. *Relics of Ancient China from the Collection of Dr. Paul Singer.* New York, 1965.

Loewe and Shaughnessy 1999. Loewe, Michael, and Edward L. Shaughnessy, eds., *The Cambridge History of Ancient China: From the Origins of Civilization to 221 B.C.* Cambridge, 1999.

Los Angeles County Museum 1987. Los Angeles County Museum of Art, *et al. The Quest for Eternity: Chinese Ceramic Sculptures from The People's Republic of China.* Los Angeles, 1987.

Louis 1999. Louis, François. *Die Goldschmiede der Tang- und Song-zeit.* Asiatische Studien monograph 32. Bern, 1999.

Lü 1958. Lü Zun'e. "Neimenggu Chifeng Hongshan kaogu diaocha baogao," *Kaogu xuebao* 1958.3, 25–40.

Lu 1993. Lu Zhaoyin. "Famensi digong jinyinqi yu Wensiyuan." In Zhang and Han 1993, 266–272.

Lu and Han 1985. Lu Jiugao and Han Wei. *Tangdai jinyinqi.* Beijing, 1985.

Lu and Han 1988. Lu Liancheng and Hu Zhisheng. *Baoji Yuguo mudi.* 2 vols. Beijing, 1988.

Luo 1910. Luo Zhenyu. *Yin Shang zhenbu wenzikao.* Shangyü, 1910.

Luo 1914. Luo Zhenyu and Wang Guowei. *Liusha zhuijian,* 3 vols. Shangyü, 1914.

Luo 1996. Luo Shiping. "Luelun Quyang Wudai mu shanshui bihua de meishu shi jiazhi," *Wenwu* 1996.9, 74–75.

Luo 1998. Luo Zhewen. *Luo Zhewen gujianzhu wenji.* Beijing, 1998.

Ma 1986. Ma Chengyuan. *Ancient Chinese Bronzes,* ed., Hsio-yen Shih. Hong Kong, 1986.

Ma 1994. Ma Chengyuan. *The Art of Bronze Unearthed at Xin'gan in Jiangxi.* Hong Kong, 1994.

Ma Wenkuan 1994. Ma Wenkuan. "Cong kaogu ziliao kan Zhongguo Tang Song shiqi yu Yisilan shijie de wenhua jiaoliu," *Han Tang yu bianjiang kaogu yanjiu* 1994.1, 231-249.

MacFarquhar 1997. MacFarquhar, Roderick. *The Cultural Revolution: A Sourcebook for Foreign Cultures* 48, Spring 1997, 2 vols. Cambridge, Mass., 1997.

MacFarquhar and Fairbank 1987. MacFarquhar, Roderick, and John King Fairbank, eds. *The Cambridge History of China.* Vol. 14: *The People's Republic, Part I: The Emergence of Revolutionary China 1949 – 1965.* New York, 1987.

MacFarquhar and Fairbank 1991. MacFarquhar, Roderick, and John King Fairbank, eds. *The Cambridge History of China.* Vol. 15: *The People's Republic, Part 2: Revolutions within the Chinese Revolution 1966 – 1982.* New York, 1991.

Mackenzie 1984 – 1986. Mackenzie, Colin. "The Evolution of Southern Bronze Styles in China during the Eastern Zhou Period," *Bulletin of the Oriental Ceramic Society of Hong Kong* 7 (1984 – 1986) (1987), 31 – 48.

Mackenzie 1991. Mackenzie, Colin. "Chu Bronze Work: A Unilinear Tradition, or A Synthesis of Diverse Sources?" In Lawton 1991, 107-157.

Mair 1998. Mair, Victor, ed. *The Bronze Age and Early Iron Age Peoples of Eastern Central Asia.* 2 vols. Philadelphia, 1998.

Major 1993. Major, John S. *Heaven and Earth in Early Han Thought, Chapters Three, Four, and Five of the Huainanzi.* Albany, 1993.

Mattos 1997. Mattos, Gilbert. "Eastern Zhou Bronze Inscriptions." In Shaughnessy 1997, 85 – 124.

Meng 1997. Meng Huaping *et al.* "Zigui Miaoping yizhi fajue de zhuyao shouhuo," *Jianghan kaogu* 1997.1, 33 – 35.

Mirsky 1977. Mirsky, Jeannette. *Sir Aurel Stein, Archaeological Explorer.* Chicago, 1977.

Mizuno 1948. Mizuno Seiichi. *Tōa Kōkogaku no hattatsu.* Kyoto, 1948.

Moore 1998. Oliver Moore. "Islamic Glass at Buddhist Sites in Medieval China." In Rachel Ward, ed. *Gilded and Enamelled Glass from the Middle East.* London, 1998, 78-84.

Morgan 1877. Morgan, Lewis H. *Ancient Society*. New York, 1877.

Mou 1989a. Mou Yongkang *et al*. *Liangzhu wenhua yuqi*. Hong Kong, 1989.

Mou 1989b. Mou Yongkang. "Liangzhu yuqi shang shen chongbai de tansuo." In Qingzhu Su Bingqi kaogu wushiwu nian lunwenji bianjizu, ed., *Qingzhu Su Bingqi kaogu wushiwu nian lunwenji*. Beijing, 1989, 184–97.

Mou 1992. Mou Lingsheng. *The Colored Figurines in Yang Ling Mausoleum of Han in China*. Xi'an, 1992.

Mou and Yun 1992. Mou Yongkang and Yun Xizheng. *Zhongguo yuqi quanji: yuanshi shehui*. Shijiazhuang, 1992.

Munakata 1991. Munakata, Kiyohiko. *Sacred Mountains in Chinese Art*. Urbana and Chicago, 1991.

Murowchick 1995. Murowchick, Robert, ed. *China: Ancient Culture, Modern Land*. Norman, 1995.

Murowchick 1997. Murowchick, Robert. "The State of Sino-Foreign Collaborative Archaeology in China," *Orientations* 28.6 (1997), 26–33.

Murphy 1994a. Murphy, J. David. "Theft and Smuggling of Cultural Relics in China and Counter-Measures Against Them." Paper presented at the meeting of INTERPOL in Illicit Traffic in Cultural Goods, Lyons, France, September 1993. In *International Journal of Cultural Property* 2.3 (1994) 312–314.

Murphy 1994b. Murphy, J. David. "The People's Republic of China and the Illicit Trade in Cultural Property: Is the Embargo Approach the Answer?" *International Journal of Cultural Property* 3.2 (1994), 227–242.

Murphy 1995. Murphy, J. David. *Plunder and Preservation: Cultural Property Law and Practice in the People's Republic of China*. Hong Kong, 1995.

Nanjing 1982. Nanjing bowuyuan. "Jiangsu Wuxian Zhanglingshan yizhi fajue jianbao," *Wenwu ziliao congkan* 1982.6, 25–35.

Nanjing 1984. Nanjing bowuyuan. "1982 nian Jiangsu Changzhou Wujin Sidun yizhi de fajue," *Kaogu* 1984.2, 109–29.

Nanjing 1985. Nanjing bowuyuan *et al*. "Jiangsu Wuxian Chenghu gujing qun de fajue," *Wenwu ziliao congkan* 1985.9, 1–22.

Nara 1992. Nara kokuritsu hakubutsukan. *Mikkyō Kōgei*. Nara, 1992.

Neimenggu 1998. Neimenggu wenwu kaogu yanjiusuo. "Neimenggu Chifeng Baoshan Liao bihua mu fajue jianbao," *Wenwu* 1998.1, 73–95.

Nelson 1995a. Nelson, Sarah Milledge, ed. *The Archaeology of Northeast China: Beyond the Great Wall*. New York, 1995.

Nelson 1995b. Nelson, Sarah Milledge. "Ritualized Pigs and the Origins of Complex Society: Hypotheses Regarding the Hongshan Culture," *Early China* 20 (1995), 1–16.

Nie 1986. Nie Xinmin. "Yetan Qin bingmayong de zhuti," *Wenbo* 1986.5, 55-61.

Nunome 1998. Nunome Shiokaze. "Famensi digong de chaqi yu Riben chadao," *Famensi wenhua yanjiu tongxun* 1998.11, 93–100.

Olsen 1987. Olsen, John W. "The Practice of Archaeology in China Today," *Antiquity* 61 (1987), 282–290.

Olsen 1992. Olsen, John W. "Archaeology in China Today," *China Exchange News* 20. 2 (1992), 3–6.

Palace Museum 1961. National Palace Museum. *Chinese Art Treasures: A Selected Group of Objects from the Chinese National Palace Museum and the Chinese National Central Museum, Taichung, Taiwan*. Geneva, 1961.

Palace Museum 1992. National Palace Museum, Taipei. *International Colloquium on Chinese Art History, 1991. Proceedings: Painting and Calligraphy, Part 2*. Taipei, 1992.

Pei 1929. Pei Wenzhong. "An Account of the Discovery of an Adult Sinanthropus Skull in the Chou K'ou Tien Deposit," *Bulletin of the Geological Survey of China* 1929, vol. 8, no. 3, 203–205.

Pei 1931. Pei Wenzhong. "Notice of the Discovery of Quartz and Other Stone Artifacts in the Lower Pleistocene Hominid-bearing Sediments of the Chou K'ou Tien Cave Deposit," *Bulletin of the Geological Survey of China* 1931, vol. 11, no. 2, 109–139.

Pei 1948. Pei Wenzhong. *Zhongguo shiqian shiqi zhi yanjiu*. Shanghai, 1948.

Pelliot 1920–1924. Pelliot, Paul. *Grottes de Touen-houang: Peintures et sculptures bouddhiques des époques Wei, T'ang, et Song*. Paris, 1920–1924.

Peng 1982. Peng Hao. "Jiangling Mazhuan yihao mu suojian zangsu lueshu," *Wenwu* 1982.10, 12–15.

Poo 1998. Poo, Mu-chou. *In Search of Personal Welfare: A View of Ancient Chinese Religion*. Albany, 1998.

Poor 1975. Poor, Robert J. *Ancient Chinese Bronzes, Ceramics and Jade in the Collection of the Honolulu Academy of Arts*. Honolulu, 1975.

Pottier 1984. Pottier, Marie-Hélène. *Matériel funéraire de la Bactriane Méridionale de l'Âge du Bronze*. Paris, 1984.

Prüch 1997. Prüch, Margarete. *Die Lacke der Westlichen Han-Zeit (206v.-6n. Chr.)*. Frankfurt, 1997.

Prüch 1998. Prüch, Margarete, with Stephan von der Schulenburg, *Schätze für König Zhao Mo, Das Grab von Nan Yue*. Frankfurt, 1998.

Prusek 1971. Prusek, Jaroslav. *Chinese Statelets and the Northern Barbarians 1400–300 B.C.* Prague, 1971.

Pumpelly 1908. Pumpelly, Raphael. *Explorations in Turkestan*. Washington D.C., 1908.

Qinghai 1979. Qinghai sheng kaogudui. "Qinghai Minhe Hetaozhuang Majiayao leixing diyi hao muzang," *Wenwu* 1979.9, 29–32.

Qinghai 1980. Qinghai sheng wenwu kaogudui. *Qinghai caitao*. Beijing, 1980.

Qinghai 1998. Qinghai sheng wenwu guanlichu, *et al*. "Qinghai Tongde xian Zongri yizhi fajue jianbao," *Kaogu* 1998.5, 1–14 and 35.

Qinyong 1978. Qinyong kaogudui. "Qinshihuang ling dongce di'erhao bingmayong keng zuantan shijue jianbao, " *Wenwu* 1978.5, 1–19.

Qinyong 1979. Qinyong kaogudui. "Qinshihuang ling dongce disanhao bingmayong keng qingli jianbao," *Wenwu* 1979.12, 1–12.

Qiu 1978. Qiu Xigui. "Hanzi xingcheng wenti de chubu tansuo," *Zhongguo yuwen* 1978.3, 162–171.

Rawson 1987a. Rawson, Jessica. *Chinese Bronzes. Art and Ritual*. London, 1987.

Rawson 1987b. Rawson, Jessica. "An Unusual Bronze You in the British Museum," *Orientations* (June 1987), 45–49.

Rawson 1989. Rawson, Jessica. "Chu Influences on the Development of Han Ritual Vessels," *Arts Asiatiques* 44 (1989), 84–89.

Rawson 1990. Rawson, Jessica. *Western Zhou Ritual Vessels from the Arthur M. Sackler Collections*. Washington D.C., 1990.

Rawson 1995. Rawson, Jessica, with Carol Michaelson. *Chinese Jade from the Neolithic to the Qing*. London, 1995.

Rawson 1996. Rawson, Jessica, ed. *Mysteries of Ancient China: New Discoveries from the Early Dynasties*. London, 1996.

Rawson 1998a. Rawson, Jessica. "Ewige Wohnstätten: Die Gräber des Königs von Nan Yue und der kaiserlichen Prinzen in Ostchina." In Prüch 1998, 80–95.

Rawson 1998b. Rawson, Jessica. "Strange Creatures," *Oriental Art* 44:2 (1998), 44–47.

Rawson 1999. Rawson, Jessica. "Western Zhou Archaeology." In Loewe and Shaughnessy 1999, 352-449.

Rawson and Bunker 1990. Rawson, Jessica, and Emma Bunker. *Ancient Chinese and Ordos Bronzes*. Hong Kong, 1990.

Rawson Forthcoming. Rawson, Jessica. "The Eternal Palaces of the Western Han: A New View of the Universe," *Artibus Asiae*. Forthcoming.

Reischauer 1955. Reischauer, Edwin O. *Ennin's Travels in Tang China.* New York, 1955.

Ren 1974. Ren Rixin. "Shandong Zhucheng xian Qianzhai yizhi diaocha," *Wenwu* 1974.1, 75.

Rietberg 1994. Museum Rietberg. *Chinesisches Gold und Silber: Die Sammlung Pierre Uldry.* Zurich, 1994.

Rudenko 1970. Rudenko, Sergei L. *Frozen Tombs of Siberia: The Pazyryk Burials of Iron-Age Horsemen.* London, 1970.

Rudolph 1963. Rudolph, Richard C. "Preliminary Notes on Sung Archaeology," *Journal of Asian Studies* 22 (1963), 169–177.

Salmony 1954. Salmony, Alfred. *Antler and Tongue: An Essay on Chinese Symbolism and Its Implications.* Ascona, 1954.

Schafer 1963. Schafer, Edward H. *The Golden Peaches of Samarkand: A Study of Tang Exotics.* Berkeley, 1963.

Schlombs 1990. Schlombs, Adele. "Die Herstellung der Terrakotta Armee." In Ledderose and Schlombs 1990, 88–97.

Scott 1997. Scott, Rosemary E., ed. *Chinese Jades.* Colloquies on Art and Archaeology in Asia 18. London, 1997.

Senner 1989. Senner, Wayne M., ed. *The Origins of Writing.* Lincoln, Nebraska, 1989.

Sensei 1981. Sensei-shō hakubusukan, ed. *Sensei-shō hakubusukan.* Tokyo, 1981.

Shaanxi 1977. Shaanxi sheng bowuguan. "Shaanxi Chang'an Fengxi chutu de Fuyu," *Kaogu* 1977.1, 71–72.

Shaanxi 1978. Shaanxi zhouyuan kaogudui. "Shaanxi Fufeng Zhuangbai yihao Xizhou qing-tongqi jiaozang fajue jianbao." *Wenwu* 1978.3, 1–18.

Shaanxi 1979a. Shaanxi zhouyuan kaogudui. "Shaanxi Qishan Fengchucun Xizhou jianju jizhi fajue jianbao," *Wenwu* 1979.10, 27–37.

Shaanxi 1979b. Shaanxi zhouyuan kaogudui. "Shaanxi Qishan Fengweicun faxian Zhouchu jiaguwen," *Wenwu* 1979.10, 38–43.

Shaanxi 1979c. Shaanxi sheng kaogu yanjiusuo. *Shaanxi chutu Shang Zhou qingtongqi.* Vol. 1. Beijing, 1979.

Shaanxi 1980. Shaanxi sheng kaogu yanjiusuo. *Shaanxi chutu Shang Zhou qingtongqi.* Vol. 2. Beijing, 1980.

Shaanxi 1986. Shaanxi sheng wen-guanhui. "Xizhou Haojing fujin bufen muzang fajue jianbao," *Wenwu* 1986.1, 1–31.

Shaanxi 1988a. Shaanxi sheng Famensi kaogudui. "Fufeng Famensi ta Tangdai digong fajue jianbao," *Wenwu* 1988.10, 1–26.

Shaanxi 1988b. Shaanxi sheng kaogu yanjiusuo et al. *Qinshihuang bingmayong keng—yihao keng fajue baogao, 1974–84, 1974–84.* 2 vols. Beijing, 1988.

Shaanxi 1990a. Shaanxi sheng kaogu yanjiusuo. *Longgangsi—Xinshiqi shidai yizhi fajue baogao.* Beijing, 1990.

Shaanxi 1990b. Shaanxi sheng bowuguan, ed. *Shaanxi sheng bowuguan.* Beijing 1990.

Shaanxi 1991. Shaanxi sheng qingyong kaogudui. "Shihuang ling yihao tongchengma qingli baogao," *Wenwu* 1991.1, 1–13.

Shaanxi 1992a. Shaanxi sheng kaogu yanjiusuo Hanling kaogu dui. "Han Jindi Yangling nanqu congzangkeng fajue diyi hao jianbao," *Wenwu* 1992.4, 1–13.

Shaanxi 1992b. Shaanxi sheng kaogu yanjiusuo Hanling kaogu dui, ed. *Zhongguo Han Yangling caiyong.* Xi'an, 1992.

Shaanxi 1995. Shaanxi sheng kaogu yanjiusuo. *Haojing Xizhou gong-shi.* Xi'an, 1995.

Shaanxi 1997. Shaanxi sheng wen-guanhui et al. "Xianyang Yangjiawan hanmu fajue jian-bao," *Wenwu* 1997.10, 10–21.

Shandong 1974. Shandong sheng wenwu guanlichu et al. *Dawenkou.* Beijing, 1974.

Shandong 1979. Shandong daxue lishixi kaogu jiaoyanshi, ed. *Dawenkou wenhua taolun wenji.* Ji'nan, 1979.

Shandong 1986. Shandong sheng Qilu kaogu congkan bianjibu, ed. *Shandong shiqian wenhua lunwenji.* Ji'nan, 1986.

Shandong 1990. Shandong daxue lishixi kaogu jiaoyanshi. *Sishui Yinjiacheng.* Beijing, 1990.

Shandong 1991a. Shandong sheng wenwu kaogu yanjiusuo et al. "Juxian Dazhujia cun Dawenkou muzang, *Kaogu xuebao* 1991.2, 167–206.

Shandong 1991b. Shandong sheng Jinning shi wenwu guanli ju. "Xue Guo gucheng kancha he muzang fajue baogao," *Kaogu Xuebao* 1991.4, 449–495.

Shandong 1998. Shandong sheng Qingzhoushi bowuguan. "Qingzhou Longxingsi Fojiao zaoxiang jiaocang qingli jian-bao," *Wenwu* 1998.2, 4–15.

Shang 1957. Shang Chengzuo. *Changsha chutu Chu qiqi tulu.* Beijing, 1957.

Shang 1963. Shang Chengzuo. "Ejun Qi jie kao," *Wenwu jinghua* 1963.2, 49–55.

Shanghai 1962. Shanghai shi wenwu baoguan weiyuanhui. "Shanghai shi Qingpu xian Songze yizhi de shijue," *Kaogu xuebao* 1962.2, 1–29.

Shanghai 1984. Shanghai shi wenwu baoguan weiyuanhui. "Shanghai Fuquanshan Liangzhu wenhua muzang," *Wenwu* 1984.2, 1–5.

Shanghai 1986. Shanghai shi wenwu baoguan weiyuanhui. "Shanghai Qingpu Fuquanshan Liangzhu wenhua mudi," *Wenwu* 1986.10, 1–25.

Shanghai and Hong Kong 1992. Shanghai Museum and Hong Kong Urban Council. *Gems of the Liangzhu Culture from the Shanghai Museum.* Hong Kong, 1992.

Shanxi 1964. Shanxi sheng wenwu guanli weiyuanhui et al. "Shanxi Changzhi Fenshuiling Zhanguo mu di'erci fajue," *Kaogu* 1964.3, 111–137.

Shanxi 1976. Shanxi sheng wenwu gongzuo weiyuanhui. *Houma mengshu.* Beijing, 1976.

Shanxi 1993. Shanxi sheng kaogu yanjiusuo. *Houma zhutong yizhi.* Beijing, 1993.

Shanxi 1994a. Shanxi sheng kaogu yanjiusou et al. "Tianma—Qucun yizhi Beizhao Jinhou mudi disan ci fajue," *Wenwu* 1994.8, 22–33 and 68.

Shanxi 1994b. Shanxi sheng kaogu yanjiusuo et al. "Tianma-Qucun yizhi beizhao Jinhou mudi disi-ci fajue," *Wenwu* 1994.8, 4–21.

Shanxi 1996a. Shanxi sheng kaogu yanjiuso et al. "Shanxi Pingding Song, Jin bihua mu jianbao," *Wenwu* 1996.5, 4–16.

Shanxi 1996b. Institute of Archaeology of Shanxi Province. *Art of the Houma Foundry.* Princeton, 1996.

Shao 1978. Shao Wangping. 1978. "Yuangu wenming de huohua—Tao *zun* shangde wenzi, " *Wenwu* 1978.9, 74–76.

Shao 1993. Shao Wangping. "Haidai xi guyu lüeshuo." In Zhongguo shehui kexueyuan kaogu yan-jiusuo, ed. *Zhongguo kaoguxue luncong.* Beijing, 1993, 131–141.

Shashi 1987. Shashi shi bowuguan. "Hubei Shashi Zhouliangyuqiao yizhi shijue jianbao," *Wenwu zil-iao congkan* 1987.10, 22–31.

Shaughnessy 1991 Shaughnessy, Edward L. *Sources of Western Zhou History: Inscribed Bronze Vessels.* Berkeley, 1991.

Shaughnessy 1997. Shaughnessy, Edward L., ed. *New Sources of Early Chinese History: An Introduction to the Reading of Inscriptions and Manuscripts.* Berkeley, 1997.

Shaughnessy 1998. "A Social Geography of the Zhouyuan," presented to the First Congress of the European Association of Asian Studies, Leiden, The Netherlands, 24 June 1998.

Shi 1938. Shi Xingeng. *Liangzhu.* Hangzhou, 1938.

Shi 1988. Shi Quan. *Gudai Jingchu dili xintan.* Wuhan, 1988.

Shi 1989. Shi Xingbang, ed. *Famensi digong zhenbao.* Xi'an, 1989.

Shi 1993. Shi Shuqing. "Guwu bao-cunfa" and "Zhongyang guwu baoguan weiyuanhui." In *Zhongguo dabaike quanshu - Wenwu bowuguan.* Beijing, 1993, 186 and 802.

Shizishan 1998. Shizishan Chuwangling kaogu fajuedui. "Xuzhou Shizishan Xihan chuwang ling fajue jianbao," *Wenwu* 1998.8, 4–33.

Sichuan 1961. Sichuan Changjiang liuyu wenwu baohu weiyuanhui wenwu kaogudui. "Sichuan Wushan Daxi xinshiqi shidai yizhi fajue jilue," *Wenwu* 1961.11, 15–21.

Sichuan 1982. Sichuan sheng bowuguan *et al.* Qingchuan xian chutu qingeng xiutian lü mudu — Sichuan Qingchuan xian Zhanguo mu fajue jianbao," *Wenwu* 1982.1, 1–21.

Sichuan 1987a. Sichuan sheng wenwu guanli weiyuanhui *et al.* "Guanghan Sanxingdui yizhi," *Kaogu yu wenwu* 1987.2, 227–254.

Sichuan 1987b. Sichuan sheng wenwu guanli weiyuanhui *et al.* "Guanghan Sanxingdui yihao jisi keng fajue jianbao," *Wenwu* 1987.10, 1–15.

Sichuan 1989. Sichuan sheng wenwu guanli weiyuanhui *et al.* "Guanghan Sanxingdui erhao jisi keng fajue jianbao," *Wenwu* 1989.5, 1–20.

Sichuan 1994. Sichuan sheng wenwu kaogu yanjiusuo. *Zhongguo kaogu wenwu zhimei — Shangdai Shuren mibao.* Beijing, 1994.

Sima 1965. Sima Qian. "Wudi benji." In *Shi Ji.* Vol. 1. Hong Kong, 1965.

Skorupski 1989. Skorupski, Tadeusz, ed. *The Buddhist Heritage: Papers Delivered at the Symposium of the Same Name Convened at the School of Oriental and African Studies, University of London, November 1985.* Buddhica Brittanica, Series Continua 1. Tring, U. K., 1989.

Skosey 1996. Skosey, Laura A. "The Legal System and Legal Tradition of the Western Zhou (ca. 1045–771 B.C.E.)." Ph. D. diss., University of Chicago, 1996.

So 1980. So, Jenny F. "The Waning of the Bronze Age. The Western Han Period (206 BC-AD 8)." In Fong 1980, 251-269.

So 1983. So, Jenny F. "Hu Vessels from Xinzheng: Towards a Definition of Chu Style." In Kuwayama 1983, 64-71.

So 1995. So, Jenny F. *Eastern Zhou Ritual Bronzes from the Arthur M. Sackler Collections.* New York, 1995.

So and Bunker 1995. So, Jenny F., and Emma C. Bunker. *Traders and Raiders on China's Northern Frontier.* Seattle and London, 1995.

Sommarstrom 1956. Sommarstrom, Bo. "The Site of Ma-kia-yao," *Bulletin of the Museum of Far Eastern Antiquities* 28 (1956), 55–158.

Song 1993. Song Boyin. "'Mise Yueqi' bianzheng." In Zhang Kaizhi and Han Jinke 1993, 241–249.

Soper 1959. Soper, Alexander C. *Literary Evidence for Early Buddhist Art in China.* Ascona, 1959.

Steele 1917 (1966). Steele, John D. *I-Li or Book of Etiquette and Ceremonial.* Taipei, 1966. (originally published in two volumes, London 1917).

Stein 1907. Stein, Aurel. *Ancient Khotan*, 2 vols. Oxford, 1907.

Stein 1912. Stein, Aurel. *Ruins of Desert Cathay*, 2 vols. London, 1912.

Stein 1921. Stein, Aurel. *Serindia*, 5 vols. Oxford, 1921.

Stein 1928. Stein, Aurel. *Innermost Asia*, 4 vols. Oxford, 1928.

Stein 1933. Stein, Aurel. *On Ancient Cental-Asian Tracks.* London, 1933.

Su 1984a. Su Bingqi. *Su Bingqi kaoguxue lunshu xuanji.* Beijing, 1984.

Su 1984b. Su Bingqi. "Chu wenhua tansuo zhong tichu de wenti - zai Zhongguo kaoguxuehui di'er ci nianhui bimushi shang de jianghua." In Su 1984a, 218–224.

Su 1986. Su Bingqi. "Liaoxi guwenhua gucheng guguo," *Wenwu* 1986.8, 41–44.

Su 1991. Su Bingqi. "Guanyu chongjian Zhongguo shiqianshi de sikao," *Kaogu* 1991.12, 1109–1118.

Su 1994a. Su Bingqi. *Huaren, long de chuanren, Zhongguo ren.* Shenyang, 1994.

Su 1994b. Su Bingqi. *Zhonnguo tongshi. 2: Yuangu shidai.* Shanghai 1994.

Su 1995. Su Bingqi. "Jianli you Zhongguo tesle de kaogu xuepai," *Kaogu* 1995.6, 561–563.

Su Bai 1957. Su Bai. *Baisha Songmu.* Beijing, 1957.

Su Bai 1988. Su Bai. "Famensi ta digong chutu wenwu fanying de yixie wenti," *Wenwu* 1988.10, 29–30.

Su Bai 1996. Su Bai. *Zhongguo shikusi yanjiu*, Beijing, 1996.

Su and Yin 1981. Su Bingqi and Yin Weiczhang. 1981. "Guanyu kaoguxue wenhua de qu xi leixing wenti," *Wenwu* 1981.5, 10–17.

Sugaya 1993. Sugaya Fuminori. *Chugoku ocho no tanjo.* Tokyo, 1993.

Suixian 1979. Suixian Leigudun yihao mu kaogu fajuedui. "Hubei Suixian Zenghou yimu fajue jianbao," *Wenwu* 1979.7,1–24.

Suizhou 1982. Suizhou shi bowuguan. "Hubei Suixian Anju chutu qingtong qi," *Wenwu* 1982.12, 51–57.

Sullivan 1980. Sullivan, Michael. *Chinese Landscape Painting. 2: The Sui and T'ang Dynasties.* Berkeley and Los Angeles, 1980.

Sullivan 1984. Sullivan, Michael. *The Arts of China.* 3rd ed. Berkeley, 1984.

Sun 1937. Sun Haibo. *Xinzheng yiqi.* Beijing, 1937.

Sun 1984. Sun Shoudao. "Sanxingtala Hongshan wenhua yulong kao," *Wenwu* 1984.6, 7–10.

Sun 1993. Sun Hua. "Sanxingdui qiwu keng de niandai ji xingzhi fenxi," *Wenwu* 1993.11, 71–78.

Sun 1996. Sun Derun. "You Xianyang qima yong tandao Zhanguo Qin qibing," *Kaogu yu Wenwu* 1996.5, 18–21.

Sun 1998. Sun Zuchu. Banpo Wenhua zai yanjui *Kaogu xuebao* 1998.4, 419–446.

Sun and Guo 1984. Sun Shoudao and Guo Dashun. "Lun Liaohe liuyu de yuanshi wenming yu long de qiyuan," *Wenwu* 1984.6, 11–17 and 20.

Sun and Guo 1986. Sun Shoudao and Guo Dashun. "Niuheliang Hongshan Wenhua nüshen touxiang de faxian yu yanjiu," *Wenwu* 1986.8, 18–24.

Sun Ji 1998. Sun Ji. "Zhoudai de zu yupei," *Wenwu*, 1998.4, 4–14.

Sun Ji 1991. Sun Ji. *Handai wuzhi wenhua ziliao tushuo.* Beijing, 1991.

Sun Ji 1996. Sun Ji. *Zhongguo shenghuo: Zhongguo guWenwu yu dongxi wenhua jiaoliu zhong de ruogan wenti.* Xianyang, 1996.

Sun Zhixin 1993. Sun, Zhixin. "The Liangzhu Culture: Its Discovery and Its Jades," *Early China* 18 (1993), 1–40.

Sun Zhixin 1996. Sun, Zhixin. "Jades of the Liangzhu Culture." Ph. D. diss., Princeton University, 1996.

Suzhou 1990. Suzhou bowuguan *et al.* "Jiangsu Wujiang Longnan xinshiqi shidai cunluo yizhi diyi, erci fajue jianbao," *Wenwu* 1990.7, 1–27.

Sylwan 1949. Sylwan, Vivi. *Investigation of Silk from Edson-Gol and Lop-nor.* Stockholm, 1949.

Tan 1962. Tan Qixiang. "Ejun Qi jie mingwen shidi." In *Zhonghua wenshi luncong.* 1962.2, 169–190.

Tan and Bai 1986. Tan Weisi and Bai Shaozhi. "Qianlun Zenghou Yimu de huangjin zhipin," *Jianghan kaogu* 1986.3, 58–62.

Tang 1934. Tang Lan. "Shouxian suochu tongqi kaolüe," *Guoxue jikan* 1934, vol. 4, no. 1, 1–10.

Tang 1962. Tang Lan. "Xizhou tongqi duandai zhong de Kanggong wenti," *Kaogu xuebao* 1962.1, 15–48.

Tang 1977. Tang Lan. "Cong Dawenkou wenhua de taoqi wenzi kan woguo zuizao wenhua de niandai," *Guangming ribao* July 14, 1977.

Tang 1978. Tang Lan. "Zailun Dawenkou wenhua de shehui xingzhi he Dawenkou taoqi wenzi," *Guangming ribao* February 23, 1978.

Tang 1979. Tang Lan. "Zhongguo nulizhi shehui de shangxian yuanzai wu liu qiannianqian." In Shandong 1979, 120–146.

Tang 1980. Tang Jinyu *et al.* "Shaanxi sheng Chenggu xian chutu Yin Shang tongqi zhengli jianbao," *Kaogu* 1980.3, 211–218.

Tang 1998. Tang Chung, ed. *East Asian Jade: Symbol of Excellence.* Hong Kong, 1998.

Teilhard de Chardin 1941. Teilhard de Chardin, Pierre. *Early Man in China.* Beijing, 1941.

Teilhard de Chardin and Young 1936. Teilhard de Chardin,

Pierre, and C.C. Young. "On the Mammalian Remains from the Archaeological Site of Anyang," *Palaeontologia Sinica*, ser. C, vol. 12, fasc. 1, 1936.

Teng 1988. Teng Shu-p'ing, "Kaogu chutu xinshiqi shidai yushicong yanjiu, "*Gugong xueshu jikan* 1988.6(1), 1–65.

Thorp 1981–1982a. Thorp, Robert L. "The Sui Xian Tomb: Re-thinking the Fifth Century," *Artibus Asiae* 43 (1981–1982), 67–110.

Thorp 1981–1982b. Thorp, Robert L. "The Date of Tomb 5 at Yinxu, Anyang," *Artibus Asiae* 43 (1981–1982), 239–246.

Thorp 1983a. Thorp, Robert L. "An Archaeological Reconstruction of the Lishan Necropolis." In Kuwayama 1983, 72–83.

Thorp 1983b. Thorp, Robert L. "Origins of Chinese Architectural Style: The Earliest Plans and Building Types," *Archives of Asian Art* 36 (1983), 22–39.

Thorp 1985. Thorp, Robert L. "The Growth of Early Shang Civilization: New Data from Ritual Vessels," *Harvard Journal of Asiatic Studies* 45 (1985), 5–75.

Thorp 1988a. Thorp, Robert L. "The Archaeology of Style at Anyang: Tomb 5 in Context," *Archives of Asian Art* 41 (1988), 47–69.

Thorp 1988b. Thorp, Robert L. *Son of Heaven: Imperial Arts of China.* Seattle, 1988.

Thorp 1991a. Thorp, Robert L. "Erlitou and the Search for the Xia," *Early China* 16 (1991), 1–38.

Thorp 1991b. Thorp, Robert L. "Mountain Tombs and Jade Burial Suits: Preparations for Eternity in the Western Han." In Kuwayama, 1991.

Thote 1987. Thote, Alain. "Une sculpture chinoise en bronze du Ve siècle avant notre ère: essai d'interprétation," *Arts Asiatiques* 42 (1987): 45–58.

Thote 1990. Thote, Alain. "Innovations techniques et diversification des commandes, l'artisanat du laque en Chine aux Ve-IVe siècles avant J.-C.," *Arts Asiatiques* 45 (1990), 76–89.

Thote 1993. Thote, Alain. "Aspects of the Serpent on Eastern Zhou Bronzes and Lacquerware." In Whitfield 1993, 150–160.

Thote 1996. Thote, Alain. "Suizhou." In *The Dictionary of Art* (vol. 29) New York, 1996.

Tokyo 1981. Tōkyō kokuritsu hakubutsukan, ed. *Chūgoku sengoku jidai no yū: Chūzan ōkoku bunbutsuten.* Tokyo, 1981.

Tokyo 1986. Tōkyō kokuritsu hakubutsukan. *Kōga bumei ten.* Tokyo, 1986.

Tokyo 1992. Tōkyō kokuritsu hakubutsukan. *Sō Kō Iotsu bō.* Tokyo, 1992.

Tokyo 1998a. Tōkyō kokuritsu hakubutsukan. *Urushi de kakareta shinpi no sekai — Chūkoku kodai shikki ten.* Tokyo 1998.

Tokyo 1998b. Tōkyō kokuritsu hakubutsukan. *Tō no Nyotei: Sokuten Bukō to sono jidai ten.* Tokyo, 1998.

Tong 1995. Tong Enzheng. "Thirty Years of Chinese Archaeology (1949–1979)." In Kohl and Fawcett 1995, 177–197.

Torii 1910. Torii Ryūzō. *Minami manshū chōsa hōkoku.* Tokyo 1910.

Torii and Torii 1914. Torii, Ryūzō. and Kimiko Torii. "Etudes Archéologiques et ethnologiques – Populations primitives de la Mongolie Orientale." Tokyo 1914. (*Journal of the College of Science, Imperial University of Tokyo.* Vol. 36, art. 4).

Twitchett 1979. Twitchett, Denis, ed. *The Cambridge History of China.* 3: *Sui and T'ang China, 589–906,* Part 1. Cambridge 1979.

Twitchett and Loewe 1986. Twitchett, Dennis and Michael Loewe, eds. *The Cambridge History of China.* 1: *The Ch'in and Han Empires (221 B.C.–A.D. 220).* Cambridge, 1986.

Wagner 1992. Wagner, Mayke. "Die Motive der bemalten neolithischen Keramik Chinas." Diss., Leipzig University, 1992.

Waley 1931. Waley, Arthor. *A Catalogue of Paintings Recovered from Tun-huang by Sir Aurel Stein.* London, 1931.

Wang 1950. Wang Yuzhe. "Chuzu gudi ji qi qianyi luxian." In *Zhou Shutao xiansheng liushi shengri jinian luwenji.* private print, 1950, 35–67.

Wang 1959. Wang Guowei. "Yin buci zhong suojian xiangong xianwang kao," and "Yin buci zhong suojian xiangong xianwang xukao." In his *Guantang jilin,* 4 vols., (original 24 vols.), Beijing, 1959 (reprint), (the original, vol. 9, pp. 1–21) Vol. 2, pp. 409–450.

Wang 1974. Wang Wenchang. "Cong Xi Zhou tong li shang yuexing shoumen nuli kan ke ji fu li de fandong benzhi," *Wenwu* 1974.4, 29.

Wang 1976. Wang Zhijie, et al. "Han Maoling ji qi peizang zhong fujin xin faxian de zhongyao Wenwu," *Wenwu* 1976.7, 51–56.

Wang 1979. Wang Ruoyu. "Cong Taixicun chutu de Shangdai zhiwu he fangzhi gongju tan dangshi de fangzhi," *Wenwu* 1979.6, 49–53.

Wang 1981. Wang Ningsheng. "Cong yuanshi jishi dao wenzi faming," *Kaogu xuebao* 1981.1, 1–44.

Wang 1984. Wang Zunguo. "Liangzhu wenhua yulianzang shulue," *Wenwu* 1984.2, 23–35.

Wang 1985. Wang Zhongshu, "Xia Nai xiansheng zhuanlüe,"*Kaogu xuebao* 1985. 4, 407–415.

Wang 1986. Wang Shimin. "Zhongguo kaoguxue jianshi." In Xia 1986, 689–695.

Wang 1987. Wang Renbo. "General Comments on Chinese Funerary Sculpture." In Los Angeles County Museum 1987, 39–61.

Wang 1988. Wang Yarong. "Famensita digong suochu fangzhipin," *Wenwu* 1988.10, 26–28.

Wang 1989a. Wang Changqi, et al. "Jieshao Xi'an shi cang zhengui *Wenwu*," *Kaogu yu wenwu* 1989.5, 79–86.

Wang 1989b. Wang Mingqin. "Hubei Jiangling Tianxingguan Chu jian de chubu yanjiu." M.A. thesis, Beijing University, 1989.

Wang 1990. Wang Jianwu et al. *Huangpu junxiaoshi lun'gao.* Zhengzhou, 1990.

Wang 1991. Wang Hengjie. "Cong minzuxue faxian de xincailiao kan Dawenkou wenhua tao *zun* de 'wenzi,'" *Kaogu* 1991.12, 1108, 1119–1120.

Wang 1992. Wang Jiuliu et al. "Xi'an dongjiao Hongqi dianji chang Tangmu," *Wenwu* 1992.9, 66–70.

Wang 1993. Wang Binghua. *Sichou zhilu kaogu yanjiu.* Wulumuqi, 1993.

Wang 1994a. Wang Xueli. *Qin yong zhuanti yanjiu.* Xi'an 1994.

Wang 1994b. Wang Xueli. *Qin Shihuanling yanjiu.* Shanghai 1994.

Wang 1995. Wang Jihuai. "Zhuanjia zuotan Anhui Mengcheng Yuchisi yizhi fajue de shouhuo," *Kaogu* 1995.4, 338–345.

Wang 1996. Wang Qingzheng, ed. *Yue yao, mi se yao.* Shanghai, 1996.

Wang 1997a. Wang Jihuai. "Yuanshi diyicun — Yuchisi yizhi jixing," *Wenwu tiandi* 1997.2, 36–39.

Wang 1997b. Wang Tao. "Establishing the Chinese Archaeological School: Su Bingqi and Contemporary Chinese Archaeology," *Antiquity* 71 (1997), 31–36.

Wang and Hu 1998. Wang Xu and Hu Lyiaoyun. "Famensi zhiwu jiekai hou de baocun zhuangkuang he yi jiezhan bufen de chubu yanjiu," *Famensi wenhua yanjiu tongxun* 1998.13, 203–205.

Wang Shuming 1986. Wang Shuming. "Tan Lingyanghe yu Dazhucun chutu de tao *zun* wenzi'." In Shandong sheng, ed. *Qilu kaogu congkan bianjibu,* 1986, 249–308.

Wang Shuming 1987. Wang Shuming. "Shandong Juxian Lingyanghe Dawenkou wenhua muzang fajue jianbao," *Shiqian yanjiu* 1987.3, 62–82.

Wang Shuming 1989. Wang Shuming. "Kaogu faxian zhong de tao *gang* yu woguo gudai de niangjiu," *Haidai kaogu* 1989.1, 370–389.

Wang Shuming 1991. Wang Shuming. "Dawenkou wenhua faxian tao *zun* yu tao *zun* wenzi zongshu," *Gugong wenwu yuekan* 1991.10, 58–73.

Wang and Wang 1993. Wang Xu and Wang Yarong. "Guanghan chutu qingtong li ren xiang fushi guanjian," *Wenwu* 1993.9, 60–68.

Wang and Xiong 1989. Wang Zhaolin and Xiong Lei. "Report from China: Discovery of Rare Buddhist Relics." *Oriental Art*, n.s., 31.1 (1989), 61–65.

Watson 1961. Watson, Burton. *Records of the Grand Historian of China, Translated from the Shih chi of Ssu-ma Ch'ien.* New York and London, 1961.

Watson 1984. Watson, Burton, ed. and trans. *Columbia Book of Chinese Poetry.* New York, 1984.

Watson 1993. Watson, Burton. *Records of the Grand Historian, Qin Dynasty.* Hong Kong and New York, 1993.

Watson, W. 1981. Watson, William. "The Progress of Archaeology in China." In Evans *et al.* 1981, 65–71.

Weber 1973. Weber, Charles D. *Chinese Pictorial Vessels of the Late Chou Period.* Ascona, 1973.

Wei 1935. Wei Shu. *Lingjing xinji.* Shanghai, 1935.

Wei 1935–1936. Wei Hong. *Han juiyi buyi.* Shanghai, 1935–36.

Wei 1937. Wei Juxian. *Zhongguo kaoguxue shi.* Shanghai, 1937.

Wei 1994. Wei Fan. "Niuheliang Hongshan wenhua disan didian jishi zhong shiguan mu," *Liaohai wenwu xuekan* 1994.1, 9–13 and 101.

Weidenreich 1936. Weidenreich, Franz. "The Mandibles of Sinanthropus pekinensis: A Comparative Study," *Palaeontologia Sinica*, new ser. D, vol. 7, fasc. 3 (1936), 1–162.

Weidenreich 1937. Weidenreich, Franz. "The Dentition of Sinanthropus pekinensis: A Comparative Odontography of the Hominids," *Palaeontologia Sinica*, new ser. D, vol. 1 (1937), 1–180.

Weidenreich 1939. Weidenreich, Franz. "Six Lectures on Sinanthropus pekinensis and Related Problems," *Bulletin of the Geological Survey of China* 19.1 (1939), 1–110.

Weidenreich 1943. Weidenreich, Franz. "The Skull of Sinanthropus pekinensis: A Comparative Study on a Primitive Hominid Skull," *Palaeontologia Sinica*, new ser. D, vol. 10, (1943), 1–484.

Wen 1990. Wen Guang. "Dui 'Jiangsu sheng Liyang xian toushanshiyan yanjiu' yiwen de buchong," *Yanshi kuangwuxue zazhi* 1990.9(2), 136.

Wen and Jing 1992. Wen, Guang and Jing Zhichun, "Chinese Neolithic Jade: A Preliminary Geoarchaeological Study," *Geoarchaeology: An International Journal* 7: 3 (1992), 251–275.

Wen and Jing 1997. Wen, Guang and Jing Zhichun. "A Geoarchaeological Study of Chinese Archaic Jade." In Scott 1997, 105–122.

Weng and Yang 1982. Weng, Wan-go, and Yang Boda. *The Palace Museum, Peking: Treasures of the Forbidden City.* New York, 1982.

Wengniute 1984. Wengniute qi wenhuaguan. "Neimenggu Wengniute qi Sanxingtala cun faxian yulong," *Wenwu* 1984.6, 6 and 10.

Wenwu 1990. Wenwu bianji weiyuanhui, ed. *Wenwu kaogu gongzuo shinian 1979–1989.* Beijing, 1990.

Wenwu Jinghua 1990. Zhongguo wenwu jinghua bianji weiyuanhui, ed. *Zhongguo wenwu jinghua.* Beijing, 1990.

Wenwu Jinghua 1992. Zhongguo wenwu jinghua bianji weiyuanhui, ed. *Zhongguo Wenwu jinghua,* Beijing, 1992.

Wenwu Jinghua 1993. Zhongguo wenwu jinghua bianji weiyuanhui, ed. *Zhongguo Wenwu jinghua,* Beijing, 1993.

Wenwu Jinghua 1997. Zhongguo wenwu jinghua bianji weiyuanhui, ed. *Zhongguo Wenwu jinghua,* Beijing, 1997.

Wenwuju 1999. Guojia wenwuju, "Kaogu fajue guanli banfa," *Zhongguo wenwubao,* January 13, 1999.

Whitfield 1982–1985. Whitfield, Roderick. *The Art of Central Asia: The Stein Collection at the British Museum.* 3 vols. Tokyo, 1982–1985.

Whitfield 1985. Whitfield, Roderick. "Buddhist Monuments in China and Some Recent Finds." In Skorupski 1989, 129–142.

Whitfield 1990a. Whitfield, Roderick. "Esoteric Buddhist Elements in the Famensi Deposit," *Asiatische Studien* 44 (1990), 247–266.

Whitfield 1990b. Whitfield, Roderick. "The Significance of the Famensi Deposit," *Orientations* 5 (1990), 84–85.

Whitfield 1993. Whitfield, Roderick, ed. *The Problem of Meaning in Early Chinese Ritual Bronzes.* London, 1993.

Wu 1930. Wu Jinding. "Pingling fanggu," *Zhongyang yanjiuyuan lishi yuyan yanjiusuo jikan* 1930.1, 471–486.

Wu 1992. Wu Min. *Zhixiu.* Taipei, 1992

Wu 1996. Wu Shichi. *Zhongguo yuanshi yishu.* Beijing, 1996.

Wu Hung 1985. Wu Hung. "Bird Motifs in Eastern Yi Art," *Orientations* 16, no. 10 (October 1985), 30–41.

Wu Hung 1988. Wu Hung. "From Temple to Tomb: Ancient Chinese Religion and Art in Transition," *Early China* 13 (1988), 78–104.

Wu Hung 1995. Wu Hung. *Monumentality in Early Chinese Art and Architecture.* Stanford, 1995.

Wu Hung 1997a Wu Hung. "All About Eyes: Two Groups of Sculptures from the Sanxingdui Culture," *Orientations* 28 (September, 1997), 58–66.

Wu Hung 1997b. Wu Hung. "The Princes of Jade Revisited: The Material Symbolism of Jade as Observed in Mancheng Tomb." In Scott 1997, 147–169.

Wu Hung 1998. Wu Hung. "Realities of Life After Death: Constructing a Posthumous World in Funerary Art." In Lee 1998, 103–113.

Wu and Olsen 1985. Wu Rukang and John W. Olsen, eds. *Palaeoanthropology and Palaeolithic Archaeology in the People's Republic of China.* Orlando, 1985.

Wu Sheng 1958. Wu sheng chutu zhongyao wenwu zhanlan choubei weiyuanhui. *Wu Sheng chutu zhongyao Wenwu zhanlan tulu.* Beijing, 1958.

Xi'an 1988. Xi'an Banpo bowuguan. *Jiangzhai – Xinshiqi shidai yizhi fajue baogao.* 2 vols. Beijing 1988.

Xi'an 1997. Xi'an shi wenwu guanli weiyuanhui. "Xi'an Tang Jinxiang xianzhu mu qingli jianbao," *Wenwu* 1997.1, 4–19.

Xia 1948. Xia Nai. "Qijiaqi muzang de faxian jiqi niandai zhi gaiding," *Zhongguo kaogu xuebao* 1948.3, 101–117.

Xia 1955. Xia Nai. "Fangshexing tongweisu zai kaoguxue shangde yingyong," *Kaogu tongxun* 1955.4, 73–78.

Xia 1977. Xia Nai. "Tan-14 ceding niandai he Zhongguo shiqian kaoguxue," *Kaogu* 1977.4, 217–232.

Xia 1978. Xia Nai. "Guo Moruo tongzhi duiyu Zhongguo kaoguxue de zhuoyue gongxian," *Kaogu* 1978. 4, 217–222.

Xia 1979. Xia Nai. "Wusi yundong he Zhongguo jindai kaoguxue de xingqi," *Kaogu* 1979.3, 193–196.

Xia 1982. Xia Nai. "Guo Moruo tongzhi he tianye kaoguxue," *Kaogu* 1982.5, 452–455.

Xia 1985. Xia Nai. *Zhongguo wenming de qiyuan.* Beijing, 1985.

Xia 1986. Xia Nai *et al.*, eds. *Zhongguo dabaike quanshu: Kaogu xue.* Beijing and Shanghai, 1986.

Xia 1990. Xia Nai. "What Is Archaeology?" In Guldin 1990, 57–67.

Xia 1996. Xia Mingcai and Zhuang Mingjun. "Shandong Qingzhou Xingguosi guzhi chutu shizaoxiang," *Wenwu* 1996.5, 59–67.

Xia 1997. Xia Mingcai *et al.* "Shandong Qingzhou chutu liangjian beichao caihui shi zaoxiang," *Wenwu* 1997.2, 80–81.

Xia 1998. Xia Mingcai. "The Discovery of a Large Cache of Buddhist Images at the Site of Longxing Si," *Orientations* (June 1998), 41–49.

Xia and Wang 1986. Xia Nai and Wang Zhongshu. "Kaogu xue." In Xia 1986, 1–21.

Xia and Zhuang 1996. Xia Mingcai and Zhuang Mingjun. "Shandong Qingzhou Xingguosi guzhi chutu shi ziaoxiang." Wenwu 1996.5, 59–67.

Xianggang 1993. Xianggang yishuguan et al. Silu zhi du: Chang'an guibao. Hong Kong, 1993.

Xiao 1972. Xiao Yun. "Mancheng Hanmu chutu de cuojinyin niaochongshu tonghu," Kaogu 1972.5, 49–52.

Xiao 1974. Xiao Han. "Changsha Mawangdui Hanmu boshu gaishu," Wenwu 1974.9, 40–44.

Xiao 1992. Xiao Bing. "Liangzhu yuqi shenren shoumian wen xinjie," Dongnan wenhua 1992.3/4, 50–65.

Xie 1991. Xie Yuanzhen. "Ejun Qi jie mingwen bushi," Zhongguo lishi bowuguan guankan 1991.15–16, 152–153.

Xie 1993. Xie Chensheng. "Zheng Zhenduo," In Zhongguo dabaike quanshu – Wenwu bowuguan. Beijing, 1993, 738–739.

Xie 1994. Xie Zhongli. "'Yuqi shidai' — yige xin gainian de fenxi," Kaogu 1994.9, 832–836.

Xinjiang 1981. Xinjiang shehui kex-ueyuan kaogu yanjiusuo. "Xinjiang Alagou shuxue muguomu fajue jianb," Wenwu 1981.1, 18–22.

Xinyang 1989a. Xinyang diqu wen-guanhui. "Henan Xinyang Shi Pingxi wuhao Chunqiu mu fajue jianbao," Kaogu 1989.1, 20–25.

Xinyang 1989b. Xinyang diqu wen-guanhui. "Henan Guangshan Chunqiu Huang Jituofu mu fajue jianbao," Kaogu 1989.1, 26–32.

Xu 1931. Xu Xusheng. Xiyou riji. Beijing, 1931.

Xu 1996a. Xu Lianggao. "Cong Shang Zhou renxiang yishu kan Zhongguo gudai wu ouxiang chongbai chuantong," In Kaogu qiu zhi ji. Beijing, 1996, 334–352.

Xu 1996b. Xu, Jay. "The Cemetery of the Western Zhou Lords of Jin," Artibus Asiae 56 (1996), 193–231.

Xuzhou 1984. Xuzhou bowuguan. "Xuzhou Shiqiao Hanmu qingli baogao," Wenwu 1984.11, 22–40.

Xuzhou 1993. Xuzhou bowuguan. "Xuzhou Houlou Shanxi Xihan mu fajue baogao," Wenwu 1993.4, 29–45.

Yan 1989. Yan Wenming. Yanshao wenhua yanjiu. Beijing, 1989.

Yan and Linduff 1990. Yan Ge and Katheryn M. Linduff. "Sanxingdui: A New Bronze Age Site in Southwest China," Antiquity 64 (1990), 505–513.

Yang 1960. Yang Boda. "Quyang Xiudesi chutu jinian zaoxiang de yishu fengge yu tezheng, " Gugong bowuyuan yuankan 1960.2, 43–60.

Yang 1982. Yang Jialuo, ed. Yi Li zhu shu ji buzheng. Taipei, 1982.

Yang 1985. Yang Kuan. Zhongguo gudai lingqin zhidu yanjiu. Shanghai 1985.

Yang 1987. Yang Hongxun. Jianzhu kaogu xue lunwen ji. Beijing, 1987.

Yang 1991. Yang Keyang, ed. Zhongguo meishu quanji. Gongyi meishu bian 1: Taoci (vol. 1). Shanghai, 1991.

Yang 1993a. Yang Meili. "Juanyun shan jiji cuishi shui linlin: Xinshiqi shidai beifang xi huanxing yuqi xilie zhiyi — gouyunxing qi," Gugong Wenwu yuekan 1993.126, 82–91.

Yang 1993b. Yang Meili. "Suhe qian-gui fangchuan jingzuo: Xinshiqi shidai beifang xi huanxing yuqi xilie zhisi: yuanjiao fangbi yu mati tongxing qi," Gugong wenwu yuekan 1993.129, 46–55.

Yang 1997a. Yang Xin et al. Three Thousand Years of Chinese Painting. New Haven, 1997.

Yang 1997b. Yang Mulin et al. "Houma liangda wenwu fanzui jituan fumieji," Zhongguo wen-wubao June 25, 1997.

Yang Hong 1980. Yang Hong. Zhongguo gudai bingqi luncong. Beijing, 1980.

Yang Hong 1998. Yang Hong. "Guanyu Nanbeichao shi Qingzhou kaogu de sikao," Wenwu 1998.2, 46–53.

Yang Hu 1989. Yang Hu. "Guanyu Hongshan wenhua de jige wenti." In Qingzhu Su Bingqi kaogu wushiwu nian lunwen ji.

ed. Qingzhu Su Bingqi kaogu wushiwu nian lunwen ji bianjizu. Beijing, 1989, 216–226.

Yang Hu 1994. Yang Hu. "Liaoxi diqu xinshiqi, tongshi bingyong shidai kaogu wenhua xulie yu fenqi," Wenwu 1994.5, 37–52.

Yang Xiaoneng 1988. Yang Xiaoneng. Sculpture of Prehistoric China. Hong Kong, 1988.

Yang Xiaoneng 1989. Yang Xiaoneng. "Zhongguo yuanshi shehui diaosu yishu gaishu," Wenwu 1989.3, 63–70 and 93.

Yang Xiaoneng 1999. Yang Xiaoneng. Reflections of Early China: Decor, Pictographs, and Pictorial Inscriptions. Seattle and London, 1999.

Yang and Yan 1994. Yang Zhongmin and Yan Kexing. "Shaanxi Binxian Wudai Fenghui mu cai-hui zhuandiao," Wenwu 1994.11, 48–55 and 90.

Yang and Yang 1986. Yang Xizhang and Yang Baocheng. "Shangdai de qingtong yue." In Zhongguo kaoguxue yanjiu. Beijing, 1986, 128–138.

Ye 1983. Ye Xiaoyan. "Zhanguo Qinhan de deng ji youguan wenti," Wenwu 1983.7, 78–86.

Yen 1998. Yen, Chi-hung. "Bhaisajyaguru at Gunhuang" Ph. D. diss., University of London, 1998.

Yichang 1984. Yichang diqu bowuguan. "Dangyang Mopanshan Xizhou yizhi shijue jianbao," Jianghan kaogu 1984.2, 7–12 and 28.

Yin 1955. Yin Difei. "Guanyu Shouxian Chuqi, " Kaogu tongx-un 1955.2, 21–31.

Yin Da 1955. Yin Da. "Guanyu Chifeng Hongshanhou de xin shiqi shidai yizhi." In Zhongguo xin shiqi shidai. Beijing, 1955.

Yin and Luo 1958. Yin Difei and Luo Changming. "Shouxian chutu de 'Ejun qi jinjie'," Wenwu cankao ziliao 1958.4, 8–11.

Yu 1963. Yu Xingwu. " 'Ejun Qi jie' kaoshi," Kaogu 1963.8, 442–447.

Yu 1973. Yu Xingwu. "Guanyu guwenzi yanjiu de ruogan wenti," Wenwu 1973.2, 32–35.

Yu 1983. Yu Danchu. "Ershi shijichu xifang jindai kaoguxue sixiang

zai Zhongguo de jieshao he yingxiang," Kaogu yu wenwu 1983. 4, 107–111.

Yu 1984. Yu Weichao et al. "Zuotan Dongshanzui yizhi," Wenwu 1984.11, 12–21.

Yu 1985a. Yu Weichao and Gao Ming. "Chu wenhua de faxian yu yanjiu." In Yu Weichao, Xianqin lianghan kaoguxue lunji. Beijing, 1985, 262–269.

Yu 1985b. Yu Weichao. "Zhoudai yongding zhidu yanjiu." In Yu Weichao, Xianqin lianghan kaoguxue lunji. Beijing, 1985, 62–114.

Yu 1995. Yu Weichao. "Menschen und Götter in der Kultur von Chu." In Goepper 1996, 130–135.

Yu 1996a. Yu Weichao. "Guanyu Chu wenhua de gainian wenti." In Wang Ran, ed., Kaoguxue shi shemo: Yu Weichao kaoguxue lilun wenxuan. Beijing, 1996, 113–118.

Yu 1996b. Yu Weichao. "Chu wenhua de yanjiu yu wenhua yinsu de fenxi." In Wang Ran, ed., Kaoguxue shi shemo: Yu Weichao kaoguxue lilun wenxuan. Beijing, 1996, 119–132.

Yu 1996c. Yu Weichao. "Guanyu kaoguxue wenhua de fanchou wenti." In Wang Ran, ed., Kaoguxue shi shemo: Yu Weichao kaoguxue lilun wenxuan. Beijing, 1996, 143–146.

Yu 1999. Yu Weichao. "Huaihe de guangmang: Huanghe yu Changjiang de lianjie," Dongnan wenhua 1999.1, 28–29.

Yu and Gao 1978–79. Yu Weichao and Gao Ming. "Zhoudai yongding zhidu yanjiu," Beijing daxue xuebao 1978.1, 84–89 (part 1); 1978. 2, 84–97 (part 2); 1979.1, 83–96 (part 3).

Yu and Zhang 1992. Yu Weichao and Zhang Aibing. "Kaoguxue xinli-jie lungang," Zhongguo shehui kexue 1992, no. 6, 147–166.

Yuan 1983–1984. Yuan Fuli. "Sanshi niandai Zhong Rui hezuo de Xibei kexue kaochatuan. " In Zhongguo keji shiliao, vol. 4 (1983), no. 3, 12–25; no. 4, 53–61; vol. 5 (1984), no. 1, 67–72, no. 2, 54–58, no. 3, 64–69.

Yuan 1987. Yuan Kang. "Waizhuan ji baojian," Yue jue shu in Siku

Quanshu. Vol. 463. Shanghai, 1987.

Yuan 1988. Yuan Zhongyi. "Qinshihuangling kaogu jiyao, " *Kaogu yu wenwu* 1988.5/6, 133–146.

Yuan 1990. Yuan Zhongyi, ed. *Qin Shihuangling bingma yong yanjiu.* Beijing 1990.

Yun 1993. Yun Anzhi. "Shanxi Changan xian Liwang cun yu Xianyang feijichang cutu daliang Sui Tang zhengui wenwu," *Kaogu yu wenwu* 1993.6, 45–52 and 24.

Yunmeng 1981. Yunmeng shuihudi qinmu bianxiezu. *Yunmeng Shuihudi Qinmu.* Beijing, 1981.

Yunnan 1959. Yunnan sheng bowuguan. *Yunnan Jinning Shizhaishan gumuqun fajue baogao.* Beijing, 1959.

Zhang 1981. Zhang Shaowen. "Yuanshi yishu de guibao — Ji Yangshao wenhua caitao shang de 'Guanyu shifu tu," *Zhongyuan wenwu* 1981.1, 21–24.

Zhang 1983. Zhang Guangli et al. "Huanghe zhongshang you diqu chutu de shiqian renxing caihui yu taosu chushi," *Kaogu yu wenwu* 1983.3, 49.

Zhang 1985. Zhang Yachu. "Xichuan Xiasi erhaomu de muzhu, niandai yu yihaomu bianzhong de mingcheng wenti," *Wenwu* 1985.4, 54–58.

Zhang 1988. Zhang Xiangwen, ed. *Zhonghua wuqiannian wenhua jikan — Zhixiu pian.* Taipei, 1988.

Zhang 1990a. Zhang Aibing. "Kaoguxue shi shenmo? — Yu Weichao xiansheng fangtan lu," *Dongnan wenhua* 1990. 3, 67–73.

Zhang 1990b. Zhang Pengchuan. *Zhongguo caitao tupu.* Beijing, 1990.

Zhang 1993. Zhang Xiaopo. "Linxia faxian caitao rentou xiang," *Wenwu* 1993.5, 39.

Zhang 1998. Zhang Jinghe. "Antesheng zai huabei de kaogu huodong," *Shijie hanxue* 1998.1, 162–176.

Zhang Changshou 1990. Zhang Changshou. "Lun Jingshu tongqi (1983–1986 nian Fengxi fajue ziliao zhier," *Wenwu* 1990.7, 32–35.

Zhang Changshou 1991. Zhang Changshou. "Shuo 'Wangjunxue'—1983–1986 nian Fengxi fajue ziliao zhi si," *Wenwu* 1991.12, 87–89 and 75.

Zhang Changshou 1992. Zhang Changshou. "Qiangliu yu huangwei –1983–1986 Fengxi fajue ziliao zhi wu," *Wenwu* 1992.4, 49–52.

Zhang Changshou 1993. Zhang Changshou. "Xi Zhou de zangyu — 1983–1986 nian Fengxi fajue ziliao zhi ba," *Wenwu* 1993.9, 55–59.

Zhang Changshou 1994. Zhang Changshou. "Xizhou de yubing xingqi — 1983–86 nian Fengxi fajue ziliao zhi jiu,"*Kaogu* 1994.6, 551–555.

Zhang and Han 1993. Zhang Kaizhi and Han Jinke. *Shoujie guoji Famensi lishi wenhua xueshu taolunhui lunwenji.* Xi'an, 1993.

Zhang and Zhang 1992. Zhang Changshou and Zhang Xiaoguang. "Xizhou shiqi de tong qi mu qiju (1983–1986 nian Fengxi fajue ziliao zhi liu," *Kaogu* 1992.6, 550–558.

Zhang and Zhang 1994. Zhang Changshou and Zhang Xiaoguang. "Jingshu mudi suojian Xizhou lunyu," *Kaogu xuebao* 1994.2, 155–172.

Zhang Zhengming 1991. Zhang Zhengming. *Chu wenhua shi.* 2nd ed. Shanghai, 1991.

Zhang Zhengming 1995a. Zhang Zhengming, ed. *Chuxue Wenku.* 18 vols. Wuhan, 1995.

Zhang Zhengming 1995b. Zhang Zhengming. *Chushi.* Wuhan, 1995.

Zhao 1984. Zhao Yongfu. "1961–62 nian Fengxi fajue jianbao," *Kaogu* 1984.9: 784–789.

Zhao 1986. Zhao Shigang. "Xichuan Xiasi Chumu Wangsun Gaozhong de fenxi," *Jianghan kaogu* 1986.3, 45–57.

Zhao 1992. Zhao Feng. *Sichou yishu shi.* Hangzhou, 1992.

Zhao 1994. Zhao Dianzeng, ed. *Zhongguo qingtongqi quanji 13: Ba Shu.* Beijing, 1994.

Zhao 1995. Zhao Hui. *Chuci wenhua beijing yanjiu.* Wuhan, 1995.

Zhao 1996. Zhao Fangzhi, ed. *Caoyuan wenhua: Youmu minzu de guangkuo wutai.* Xianggang, 1996.

Zhejiang 1960. Zhejiang sheng wenwu guanli weiyuanhui. "Wuxing Qianshanyang yizhi diyi, erci fajue baogao," *Kaogu xuebao* 1960.2, 73–91.

Zhejiang 1978. Zhejiang sheng wenwu guanli weiyuanhui. "Hemudu yizhi diyiqi fajie baogao," 1978.1, 39–94.

Zhejiang 1984. Zhejiang sheng wenwu guanli weiyuanhui et al. 1984. "Shaoxing 306 hao Zhanguo mu fajue jianbao," *Wenwu* 1984.1, 10–28.

Zhejiang 1988a. Zhejiang sheng wenwu kaogu yanjiusuo Fanshan kaogudui. "Zhejiang Yuhang Fanshan Liangzhu mudi fajue jianbao," *Wenwu* 1988.1, 1–31.

Zhejiang 1988b. Zhejiang sheng wenwu kaogu yanjiusuo. "Yuhang Yaoshan Liangzhu wenhua jitan fajue baogao," *Wenwu* 1988.1, 32–51.

Zhejiang 1989. Zhejiang sheng wenwu kaogu yanjiusuo et al. *Liangzhu Wenwu yuqi.* Hong Kong, 1989.

Zheng 1934. Zheng Xuan. "Qiuguan sikao diwu. Zhanglu pian." In *Zhou li Zheng zhu.* Beijing, 1934.

Zheng 1956. Zheng Zhenduo. "Kaogu shiye de chengjiu he jinhou nuli de fangxiang," *Kaogu tongxun* 1956, 2, 9–16.

Zheng 1982. Zheng Jiexiang. "'Buanyu shifu tu' xinlun," *Zhongyuan Wenwu* 1982.2, 48–51.

Zheng 1989. Zheng Zhenxiang. "Yinxu yuqi tanyuan." In Qingzhu Su Bingqi kaogu wushiwu nian lunwenji bianjizu, *Qingzhu Su Bingqi kaogu wushiwu nian lunwenji.* Beijing, 1989, 315–325.

Zheng 1998. Zheng Tong. "Shanxi Linfen Xiajin mudi fajue jianbao," *Wenwu* 1998.12, 4–13.

Zhengzhou 1979. Zhengzhou shi bowuguan. "Zhengzhou Dahecun yizhi fajue baogao," *Kaogu xuebao* 1979.3, 301–375.

Zhongguo 1959. Zhongguo kexueyuan kaogu yanjiusuo. *Miaodigou yu Sanliqiao.* Beijing, 1959.

Zhongguo 1961. Zhongguo kexueyuan kaogu yanjiusuo, ed. *Xin Zhongguo de kaogu shouhuo.* Beijing, 1961.

Zhongguo 1962. Zhongguo kexueyuan kaogu yanjiusuo. *Fengxi fajue baogao: 1955–1957 nian Shaanxi Chang'an xian Fengxi xiang kaogu fajue ziliao.* Beijing, 1962.

Zhongguo 1963. Zhongguo kexueyuan kaogu yanjiusuo et al. *Xi'an Banpo.* Beijing, 1963.

Zhongguo 1965a. Zhongguo kexueyuan kaogu yanjiusuo. *Chang'an Zhangjiapo Xizhou tongqiqun.* Beijing, 1965.

Zhongguo 1965b. Zhongguo kexueyuan kaogu yanjiusuo. *Jingshan Qujialing.* Beijing, 1965.

Zhongguo 1977. Zhongguo wudao yishu yanjiuhui wudaoshi yanjiuzu. *Chuan Tang shi zhong de yuewu ziliao.* Mingguwu, 1977.

Zhongguo 1980a. Zhongguo shehui kexueyuan kaogu yanjiusuo. *Yinxu Fu Hao mu.* Beijing, 1980.

Zhongguo 1980b. Zhongguo shehui kexueyuan kaogu yanjiusuo et al. *Mancheng Hanmu fajue baogao,* 2 vols., Beijing, 1980.

Zhongguo 1980c. Zhongguo shehui kexueyuan kaogu yanjiusuo. *Xiaotun nandi jiagu.* Vol. 1. Shanghai, 1980.

Zhongguo 1982. Zhongguo shehui kexueyuan kaogu yanjiusuo. *Yinxu yuqi.* Beijing, 1982.

Zhongguo 1983a. Zhongguo shehui kexueyuan kaogu yanjiusuo. *Xiaotun nandi jiagu.* Vol. 2. Shanghai, 1983.

Zhongguo 1983b. Zhongguo shehui kexueyuan kaogu yanjiusuo. *Baoji Beishouling.* Beijing, 1983.

Zhongguo 1984a. Zhongguo shehui kexueyuan kaogu yanjiusuo, ed. *Xin Zhongguo de kaogu faxian he yanjiu.* Beijing, 1984.

Zhongguo 1984b. Zhongguo shehui kexueyuan kaogu yanjiusuo. "Zhongguo Kaoguxue de Huangjin shidai," *Kaogu* 1984.10, 865–871.

Zhongguo 1985. Zhongguo shehui kexueyuan kaogu yanjiusuo. *Yinxu qingtongqi.* Beijing, 1985.

Zhongguo 1992. Zhongguo shehui kexueyuan kaogu yanjiuso. *Zhongguo kaoguxue zhong tan shisi niandai shujuji 1965 – 1991.* Beijing, 1992.

Zhongguo 1993. Zhongguo shehui kexueyuan kaogu yanjiuso. *Kaogu jinghua.* Beijing,1993.

Zhongguo 1994. Zhongguo shehui kexueyuan kaogu yanjiusuo. *Yinxu de fajue yu yanjiu.* Beijing, 1994.

Zhongguo 1996. Zhongguo shehui kexueyuan kaogu yanjiusuo. *Dadianzi: Xiajiadian xiaceng wenhua yizhi yu mudi fajue baogao.* Beijing, 1996.

Zhongguo 1998a. Zhongguo shehui kexueyuan kaogu yanjiusuo. *Anyang Yinxu Guojiazhuang Shangdai muzang.* Beijing, 1998.

Zhongguo 1998b. Zhongguo shehui kexueyuan kaogu yanjiusuo kaogu ziliao xinxi zhongxin. "1991 nian yilai Zhongguo wenming qiyuan yanjiu shuping," *Kaogu* 1998.6, 90 – 95.

Zhongguo Anhui 1994. Zhongguo shehui kexueyuan kaogu yanjiusuo Anhui gongzuodui. "Anhui Mengcheng Yuchisi yizhi fajue jianbao," *Kaogu* 1994.1, 1 – 13.

Zhongguo Anyang 1976. Zhongguo kexueyuan kaogu yanjiusuo Anyang gongzuodui. "1975 nian Anyang Yinxu de xin faxian." *Kaogu* 1976.4, 264 – 272.

Zhongguo Anyang 1993. Zhongguo kexueyuan kaogu yanjiusuo Anyang gongzuodui. "1991 nian Anyang Huayuanzhuang dongdi, nandi fajue jianbao 1991," *Kaogu* 1993.6, 488 – 499.

Zhongguo Erlitou 1974. Zhongguo kexueyuan kaogu yanjiusuo Erlitou gongzuodui. "Henan Yanshi Erlitou zao Shang gongdian yizhi fajue jianbao," *Kaogu* 1974.4, 234 – 248.

Zhongguo Erlitou 1983. Zhongguo shehui kexueyuan kaogu yanjiusuo Erlitou gongzuodui. "1980 nian qiu Henan Yanshi Erlitou yizhi fajue jianbao," *Kaogu* 1983.3, 199 – 205.

Zhongguo Erlitou 1984. Zhongguo shehui kexueyuan kaogu yanjiusuo Erlitou gongzuodui. "1981 nian Henan Yanshi Erlitou muzang fajue jianbao," *Kaogu* 1984.1, 37 – 40.

Zhongguo Erlitou 1986. Zhongguo shehui kexueyuan kaogu yanjiusuo Erlitou gongzuodui. "1984 nian qiu Henan Yanshi Erlitou yizhi faxian de jizuo muzang," *Kaogu* 1986.4, 318 – 323.

Zhongguo Erlitou 1991. Zhongguo shehui kexueyuan kaogu yanjiusuo Erlitou gongzuodui. "Henan Yanshi Erlitou yizhi faxian xin de tongqi," *Kaogu* 1991.12, 1138 – 1139.

Zhongguo Erlitou 1992. Zhongguo shehui kexueyuan kaogu yanjiusuo Erlitou gongzuodui. "1987 nian Yanshi Erlitou yizhi muzang fajue jianbao," *Kaogu* 1992.4, 294 – 303.

Zhongguo Feng Hao 1984. Zhongguo shehui kexueyuan kaogu yanjiusuo Feng Hao fajuedui. "Chang'an Fengxi zao Zhou muzang fajue jilüe," *Kaogu* 1984.9, 779 – 783.

Zhongguo Fengxi 1962. Zhongguo kexueyuan kaogu yanjiusuo Fengxi fajuedui. "1960 nian qiu Shaanxi Chang'an Zhangjiapo fajue jianbao," *Kaogu* 1962.1, 20 – 22.

Zhongguo Fengxi 1963. Zhongguo kexueyuan kaogu yanjiusuo Fengxi fajuedui. "1961 – 62 nian Shaanxi Chang'an Fengdong shijue jianbao," *Kaogu* 1963.8, 403 – 412.

Zhongguo Fengxi 1965. Zhongguo kexueyuan kaogu yanjiusuo Fengxi fajuedui. "Shaanxi Chang'an Zhangjiapo Xizhou mu qingli jianbao," *Kaogu* 1965.9, 447 – 450.

Zhongguo Fengxi 1980. Zhongguo shehui kexueyuan kaogu yanjiusuo Fengxi fajuedui. "1967 nian Chang'an Zhangjiapo Xizhou muzang de fajue," *Kaogu xuebao* 1980.4, 457 – 502.

Zhongguo Fengxi 1981. Zhongguo shehui kexueyuan kaogu yanjiusuo Fengxi fajuedui. "1976 – 1978 nian Chang'an Fengxi fajue jianbao," *Kaogu* 1981.1, 13 – 18.

Zhongguo Fengxi 1983. Zhongguo shehui kexueyuan kaogu yanjiusuo Fengxi fajuedui. "Shaanxi Chang'an xian Xinwangcun xinchu Xizhou tongding," *Kaogu* 1983.3, 217 – 219.

Zhongguo Fengxi 1984. Zhongguo shehui kexueyuan kaogu yanjiusuo Fengxi fajuedui. "Chang'an Fengxi zao Zhou muzang fajue jilue," *Kaogu* 1984.9, 779 – 783.

Zhongguo Fengxi 1986. Zhongguo shehui kexueyuan kaogu yanjiusuo Fengxi fajuedui. "Chang'an Zhangjiapo Xizhou Jingshu mu fajue jianbao," *Kaogu* 1986.1, 22 – 27 and 11.

Zhongguo Fengxi 1989. Zhongguo shehui kexueyuan kaogu yanjiusuo Fengxi fajuedui. "Chang'an Zhangjiapo M183 Xizhou dongshimu fajue jianbao," *Kaogu* 1989.6, 524 – 529.

Zhongguo Fengxi 1990. Zhongguo shehui kexueyuan kaogu yanjiusuo Fengxi fajuedui. "Shaanxi Chang'an Zhangjiapo M 170 hao Jingshu mu fajue jianbao," *Kaogu* 1990.6, 504 – 510.

Zhongguo Ganqing 1990. Zhongguo shehui kexueyuan kaogu yanjiusuo Ganqing gongzuodui. "Gansu Tianshui Shizhaocun shiqian wenhua yizhi fajue," *Kaogu* 1990.7, 577 – 586.

Zhongguo Hancheng 1994. Zhongguo shehui kexueyuan kaogu yanjiusuo Hancheng dui. "Han Chang'an cheng yaozhi fajue baogao," *Kaogu xuebao,* 1994.1, 99 – 129.

Zhongguo Lishi 1984. Zhongguo lishi bowuguan. *Zhongguo Lishi Bowuguan.* Beijing, 1984.

Zhongguo Lishi 1986. Zhongguo lishi bowuguan kaogubu *et al.* "1982 – 1984 nian Shanxi Yuanqu gucheng Dongyuan yizhi fajue jianbao," *Wenwu* 1986.6, 27 – 40, and 75

Zhongguo Lishi 1996. Zhongguo lishi bowuguan kaogubu *et al. Yuanqu Shangcheng (I) 1985 – 1986 niandu kancha baogao.* Beijing, 1996.

Zhongguo Luoyang 1965. Zhongguo kexueyuan kaogu yanjiusuo Luoyang fajuedui. "Henan Yanshi Erlitou yizhi fajue jianbao," *Kaogu* 1965.5, 215 – 224.

Zhongguo Luoyang 1984. Zhongguo shehui kexueyuan kaogu yanjiusuo Luoyang Han Wei gucheng gongzuodui. "Yanshi Shangcheng de chubu kantan he fajue," *Kaogu* 1984.6, 488 – 504.

Zhongguo Neimenggu 1982. Zhongguo shehui kexueyuan kaogu yanjiusuo Neimenggu gongzuodui. "Chifeng Xishuiquan Hongshan wenhua yizhi," *Kaogu xuebao* 1982.2, 183 – 198.

Zhongguo Neimenggu 1987. Zhongguo shehui kexueyuan kaogu yanjiusuo Neimenggu gongzuodui. "Neimenggu Aohan qi Xiaoshan yizhi," *Kaogu* 1987.6, 481 – 506.

Zhongguo Shaanxi 1984. Zhongguo shehui kexueyuan kaogu yanjiusuo Shaanxi gongzuodui. "Shaanxi Huayang Nanchengzi yizhi de fajue," *Kaogu* 1984.6, 481 – 487.

Zhongguo Shandong 1979. Zhongguo shehui kexueyuan kaogu yanjiusuo Shandong gongzuodui *et al.* "Shandong Yanzhou Wangyin xinshiqi shidai yizhi fajue jianbao," *Kaogu* 1979.1, 5 – 14.

Zhongguo Shandong 1984. Zhongguo shehui kexueyuan kaogu yanjiusuo Shandong dui *et al.,* "Shandong Tengxian Beixin yizhi fajue baogao," *Kaogu xuebao* 1984.2, 159 – 191.

Zhongguo Shandong 1990. Zhongguo shehui kexueyuan kaogu yanjiusuo Shandong gongzuodui. "Shandong Linqu Zhufeng Longshan wenhua muzang," *Kaogu* 1990.7, 587 – 594.

Zhongguo Shanxi 1980. Zhongguo shehui kexueyuan kaogu yanjiusuo Shanxi gongzuodui *et al.* "Shanxi Xiangfen xian Taosi yishi fajue jianbao," *Kaogu* 1980, 18 – 31.

Zhongguo Shanxi 1983. Zhongguo shehui kexueyuan kaogu yanjiusuo Shanxi gongzuodui *et al.* "1978 – 1980 nian Shanxi Xiangfen Taosi mudi fajue jianbao," *Kaogu* 1983.1, 30 – 42.

Zhongguo Shanxi 1984. Zhongguo shehui kexueyuan kaogu yanjiusuo Shanxi gongzuodui. "Shanxi Xiangfen Taosi yizhi shouci faxian tongqi," *Kaogu* 1984, 1069–1071.

Zhongguo Ziran 1985. Zhongguo kexueyuan ziran kexueshi yanjiusuo, ed., *Zhongguo gudai jianzhu jishushi*, Beijing, 1985.

Zhou and Zhang 1984. Zhou Xiaolu and Zhang Min. "Zhiyu shuo — Changjiang xiayou xinshiqi shidai sanjian yuzhipin feiqiwu de yanjiu," *Nanjing bowuyuan jikan* 1984.7, 46–50.

Zhu 1984. Zhu Feisu. "Shixia wenhua muzang suo fanying de ruogan wenti." In Zhongguo kaogu xuehui, ed. *Zhongguo kaogu xuehui disanci nianhui lunwenji*. Beijing, 1984, 90–95.

Zhu 1990. Zhu Qixin. "Buddhist Treasures from Famensi: The Recent Excavation of a Tang Crypt," *Orientations* 5 (1990), 77–83.

Zhu 1993. Zhu Boqian. "Guci zhongde guibao – miseci." In Zhang and Han, 1993, 250–253.

Zhu and Li 1995. Zhu Dexi and Li Jiahao. "Ejun Qi jie kaoshi (bapian)." In *Zhu Dexi guwenzi lunji*. Beijing, 1995, 189–202.

Zou 1980a. Zou Heng. "Shilun Zhengzhou xinfaxian de Yinshang wenhua yizhi." In Zou Heng, *Xia Shang Zhou kaoguxue lunwen ji*. Beijing, 1980, 3–29,

Zou 1980b. Zou Heng. "Shilun Xia wenhua. " In Zou Heng, *Xia Shang Zhou kaoguxue lunwenji*. Beijing, 1980, 95–182.

Zou 1998. Zou Heng. "Jishi fengdi kaolue." In Zou Heng, *Xia Shang Zhou kaoguxue lunwenji xuji*. Beijing, 1998, 308–312.

Index